Understanding Machine Learning

Machine learning is one of the fastest growing areas of computer science, with far-reaching applications. The aim of this textbook is to introduce machine learning, and the algorithmic paradigms it offers, in a principled way. The book provides an extensive theoretical account of the fundamental ideas underlying machine learning and the mathematical derivations that transform these principles into practical algorithms. Following a presentation of the basics of the field, the book covers a wide array of central topics that have not been addressed by previous textbooks. These include a discussion of the computational complexity of learning and the concepts of convexity and stability; important algorithmic paradigms including stochastic gradient descent, neural networks, and structured output learning; and emerging theoretical concepts such as the PAC-Bayes approach and compression-based bounds. Designed for an advanced undergraduate or beginning graduate course, the text makes the fundamentals and algorithms of machine learning accessible to students and nonexpert readers in statistics, computer science, mathematics, and engineering.

Shai Shalev-Shwartz is an Associate Professor in the School of Computer Science and Engineering at The Hebrew University, Israel.

Shai Ben-David is a Professor in the School of Computer Science at the University of Waterloo, Canada.

UNDERSTANDING MACHINE LEARNING

From Theory to Algorithms

Shai Shalev-Shwartz
The Hebrew University, Jerusalem

Shai Ben-David
University of Waterloo, Canada

CAMBRIDGE
UNIVERSITY PRESS

CAMBRIDGE
UNIVERSITY PRESS

314 to 321, 3rd Floor, Plot No. 3, Splendor Forum, Jasola District Centre, New Delhi 110025, India

Cambridge University Press is part of the University of Cambridge.

It furthers the University's mission by disseminating knowledge in the pursuit of education, learning and research at the highest international levels of excellence.

www.cambridge.org
Information on this title: www.cambridge.org/9781107057135

First published 2014
First South Asia edition 2015
Reprinted 2015, 2017, 2018

This South Asia edition is based on Shai Shalev-Shwartz and Shai Ben-David / Understanding Machine Learning: From Theory to Algorithms / 9781107057135 / 2014

Printed in India by Rajkamal Electric Press

A catalogue record for this publication is available from the British Library

ISBN 978-1-107-51282-5 Paperback

Triple-S dedicates the book to triple-M

Contents

Preface

The term *machine learning* refers to the automated detection of meaningful patterns in data. In the past couple of decades it has become a common tool in almost any task that requires information extraction from large data sets. We are surrounded by a machine learning–based technology: Search engines learn how to bring us the best results (while placing profitable ads), antispam software learns to filter our e-mail messages, and credit card transactions are secured by a software that learns how to detect frauds. Digital cameras learn to detect faces and intelligent personal assistance applications on smart-phones learn to recognize voice commands. Cars are equipped with accident-prevention systems that are built using machine learning algorithms. Machine learning is also widely used in scientific applications such as bioinformatics, medicine, and astronomy.

One common feature of all of these applications is that, in contrast to more traditional uses of computers, in these cases, due to the complexity of the patterns that need to be detected, a human programmer cannot provide an explicit, fine-detailed specification of how such tasks should be executed. Taking examples from intelligent beings, many of our skills are acquired or refined through *learning* from our experience (rather than following explicit instructions given to us). Machine learning tools are concerned with endowing programs with the ability to "learn" and adapt.

The first goal of this book is to provide a rigorous, yet easy-to-follow, introduction to the main concepts underlying machine learning: What is learning? How can a machine learn? How do we quantify the resources needed to learn a given concept? Is learning always possible? Can we know whether the learning process succeeded or failed?

The second goal of this book is to present several key machine learning algorithms. We chose to present algorithms that on one hand are successfully used in practice and on the other hand give a wide spectrum of different learning techniques. Additionally, we pay specific attention to algorithms appropriate for large-scale learning (a.k.a. "Big Data"), since in recent years, our world has become increasingly "digitized" and the amount of data available for learning is dramatically increasing. As a result, in many applications data is plentiful and computation time is the main bottleneck. We therefore explicitly quantify both the amount of data and the amount of computation time needed to learn a given concept.

The book is divided into four parts. The first part aims at giving an initial rigorous answer to the fundamental questions of learning. We describe a generalization of Valiant's Probably Approximately Correct (PAC) learning model, which is a first solid answer to the question "What is learning?" We describe the Empirical Risk Minimization (ERM), Structural Risk Minimization (SRM), and Minimum Description Length (MDL) learning rules, which show "how a machine can learn." We quantify the amount of data needed for learning using the ERM, SRM, and MDL rules and show how learning might fail by deriving a "no-free-lunch" theorem. We also discuss how much computation time is required for learning. In the second part of the book we describe various learning algorithms. For some of the algorithms, we first present a more general learning principle and then show how the algorithm follows the principle. While the first two parts of the book focus on the PAC model, the third part extends the scope by presenting a wider variety of learning models. Finally, the last part of the book is devoted to advanced theory.

We made an attempt to keep the book as self-contained as possible. However, the reader is assumed to be comfortable with basic notions of probability, linear algebra, analysis, and algorithms. The first three parts of the book are intended for first-year graduate students in computer science, engineering, mathematics, or statistics. It can also be accessible to undergraduate students with the adequate background. The more advanced chapters can be used by researchers intending to gather a deeper theoretical understanding.

ACKNOWLEDGMENTS

The book is based on Introduction to Machine Learning courses taught by Shai Shalev-Shwartz at Hebrew University and by Shai Ben-David at the University of Waterloo. The first draft of the book grew out of the lecture notes for the course that was taught at Hebrew University by Shai Shalev-Shwartz during 2010–2013. We greatly appreciate the help of Ohad Shamir, who served as a teaching assistant for the course in 2010, and of Alon Gonen, who served as TA for the course in 2011–2013. Ohad and Alon prepared a few lecture notes and many of the exercises. Alon, to whom we are indebted for his help throughout the entire making of the book, has also prepared a solution manual.

We are deeply grateful for the most valuable work of Dana Rubinstein. Dana has scientifically proofread and edited the manuscript, transforming it from lecture-based chapters into fluent and coherent text.

Special thanks to Amit Daniely, who helped us with a careful read of the advanced part of the book and wrote the advanced chapter on multiclass learnability. We are also grateful for the members of a book reading club in Jerusalem who have carefully read and constructively criticized every line of the manuscript. The members of the reading club are Maya Alroy, Yossi Arjevani, Aharon Birnbaum, Alon Cohen, Alon Gonen, Roi Livni, Ofer Meshi, Dan Rosenbaum, Dana Rubinstein, Shahar Somin, Alon Vinnikov, and Yoav Wald. We would also like to thank Gal Elidan, Amir Globerson, Nika Haghtalab, Shie Mannor, Amnon Shashua, Nati Srebro, and Ruth Urner for helpful discussions.

1

Introduction

The subject of this book is automated learning, or, as we will more often call it, Machine Learning (ML). That is, we wish to program computers so that they can "learn" from input available to them. Roughly speaking, learning is the process of converting experience into expertise or knowledge. The input to a learning algorithm is training data, representing experience, and the output is some expertise, which usually takes the form of another computer program that can perform some task. Seeking a formal-mathematical understanding of this concept, we'll have to be more explicit about what we mean by each of the involved terms: What is the training data our programs will access? How can the process of learning be automated? How can we evaluate the success of such a process (namely, the quality of the output of a learning program)?

1.1 WHAT IS LEARNING?

Let us begin by considering a couple of examples from naturally occurring animal learning. Some of the most fundamental issues in ML arise already in that context, which we are all familiar with.

Bait Shyness – Rats Learning to Avoid Poisonous Baits: When rats encounter food items with novel look or smell, they will first eat very small amounts, and subsequent feeding will depend on the flavor of the food and its physiological effect. If the food produces an ill effect, the novel food will often be associated with the illness, and subsequently, the rats will not eat it. Clearly, there is a learning mechanism in play here – the animal used past experience with some food to acquire expertise in detecting the safety of this food. If past experience with the food was negatively labeled, the animal predicts that it will also have a negative effect when encountered in the future.

Inspired by the preceding example of successful learning, let us demonstrate a typical machine learning task. Suppose we would like to program a machine that learns how to filter spam e-mails. A naive solution would be seemingly similar to the way rats learn how to avoid poisonous baits. The machine will simply *memorize* all previous e-mails that had been labeled as spam e-mails by the human user. When a new e-mail arrives, the machine will search for it in the set of previous spam e-mails. If it matches one of them, it will be trashed. Otherwise, it will be moved to the user's inbox folder.

While the preceding "learning by memorization" approach is sometimes useful, it lacks an important aspect of learning systems – the ability to label unseen e-mail messages. A successful learner should be able to progress from individual examples to broader *generalization*. This is also referred to as *inductive reasoning* or *inductive inference*. In the bait shyness example presented previously, after the rats encounter an example of a certain type of food, they apply their attitude toward it on new, unseen examples of food of similar smell and taste. To achieve generalization in the spam filtering task, the learner can scan the previously seen e-mails, and extract a set of words whose appearance in an e-mail message is indicative of spam. Then, when a new e-mail arrives, the machine can check whether one of the suspicious words appears in it, and predict its label accordingly. Such a system would potentially be able correctly to predict the label of unseen e-mails.

However, inductive reasoning might lead us to false conclusions. To illustrate this, let us consider again an example from animal learning.

Pigeon Superstition: In an experiment performed by the psychologist B. F. Skinner, he placed a bunch of hungry pigeons in a cage. An automatic mechanism had been attached to the cage, delivering food to the pigeons at regular intervals with no reference whatsoever to the birds' behavior. The hungry pigeons went around the cage, and when food was first delivered, it found each pigeon engaged in some activity (pecking, turning the head, etc.). The arrival of food reinforced each bird's specific action, and consequently, each bird tended to spend some more time doing that very same action. That, in turn, increased the chance that the next random food delivery would find each bird engaged in that activity again. What results is a chain of events that reinforces the pigeons' association of the delivery of the food with whatever chance actions they had been performing when it was first delivered. They subsequently continue to perform these same actions diligently.[1]

What distinguishes learning mechanisms that result in superstition from useful learning? This question is crucial to the development of automated learners. While human learners can rely on common sense to filter out random meaningless learning conclusions, once we export the task of learning to a machine, we must provide well defined crisp principles that will protect the program from reaching senseless or useless conclusions. The development of such principles is a central goal of the theory of machine learning.

What, then, made the rats' learning more successful than that of the pigeons? As a first step toward answering this question, let us have a closer look at the bait shyness phenomenon in rats.

Bait Shyness revisited – rats fail to acquire conditioning between food and electric shock or between sound and nausea: The bait shyness mechanism in rats turns out to be more complex than what one may expect. In experiments carried out by Garcia (Garcia & Koelling 1996), it was demonstrated that if the unpleasant stimulus that follows food consumption is replaced by, say, electrical shock (rather than nausea), then no conditioning occurs. Even after repeated trials in which the consumption

[1] See: http://psychclassics.yorku.ca/Skinner/Pigeon

of some food is followed by the administration of unpleasant electrical shock, the rats do not tend to avoid that food. Similar failure of conditioning occurs when the characteristic of the food that implies nausea (such as taste or smell) is replaced by a vocal signal. The rats seem to have some "built in" prior knowledge telling them that, while temporal correlation between food and nausea can be causal, it is unlikely that there would be a causal relationship between food consumption and electrical shocks or between sounds and nausea.

We conclude that one distinguishing feature between the bait shyness learning and the pigeon superstition is the incorporation of *prior knowledge* that biases the learning mechanism. This is also referred to as *inductive bias*. The pigeons in the experiment are willing to adopt *any* explanation for the occurrence of food. However, the rats "know" that food cannot cause an electric shock and that the co-occurrence of noise with some food is not likely to affect the nutritional value of that food. The rats' learning process is biased toward detecting some kind of patterns while ignoring other temporal correlations between events.

It turns out that the incorporation of prior knowledge, biasing the learning process, is inevitable for the success of learning algorithms (this is formally stated and proved as the "No-Free-Lunch theorem" in Chapter 5). The development of tools for expressing domain expertise, translating it into a learning bias, and quantifying the effect of such a bias on the success of learning is a central theme of the theory of machine learning. Roughly speaking, the stronger the prior knowledge (or prior assumptions) that one starts the learning process with, the easier it is to learn from further examples. However, the stronger these prior assumptions are, the less flexible the learning is – it is bound, a priori, by the commitment to these assumptions. We shall discuss these issues explicitly in Chapter 5.

1.2 WHEN DO WE NEED MACHINE LEARNING?

When do we need machine learning rather than directly program our computers to carry out the task at hand? Two aspects of a given problem may call for the use of programs that learn and improve on the basis of their "experience": the problem's complexity and the need for adaptivity.

Tasks That Are Too Complex to Program.

- *Tasks Performed by Animals/Humans:* There are numerous tasks that we human beings perform routinely, yet our introspection concerning how we do them is not sufficiently elaborate to extract a well defined program. Examples of such tasks include driving, speech recognition, and image understanding. In all of these tasks, state of the art machine learning programs, programs that "learn from their experience," achieve quite satisfactory results, once exposed to sufficiently many training examples.
- *Tasks beyond Human Capabilities:* Another wide family of tasks that benefit from machine learning techniques are related to the analysis of very large and complex data sets: astronomical data, turning medical archives into medical knowledge, weather prediction, analysis of genomic data, Web search engines, and electronic commerce. With more and more available

digitally recorded data, it becomes obvious that there are treasures of meaningful information buried in data archives that are way too large and too complex for humans to make sense of. Learning to detect meaningful patterns in large and complex data sets is a promising domain in which the combination of programs that learn with the almost unlimited memory capacity and ever increasing processing speed of computers opens up new horizons.

Adaptivity. One limiting feature of programmed tools is their rigidity – once the program has been written down and installed, it stays unchanged. However, many tasks change over time or from one user to another. Machine learning tools – programs whose behavior adapts to their input data – offer a solution to such issues; they are, by nature, adaptive to changes in the environment they interact with. Typical successful applications of machine learning to such problems include programs that decode handwritten text, where a fixed program can adapt to variations between the handwriting of different users; spam detection programs, adapting automatically to changes in the nature of spam e-mails; and speech recognition programs.

1.3 TYPES OF LEARNING

Learning is, of course, a very wide domain. Consequently, the field of machine learning has branched into several subfields dealing with different types of learning tasks. We give a rough taxonomy of learning paradigms, aiming to provide some perspective of where the content of this book sits within the wide field of machine learning.

We describe four parameters along which learning paradigms can be classified.

Supervised versus Unsupervised Since learning involves an interaction between the learner and the environment, one can divide learning tasks according to the nature of that interaction. The first distinction to note is the difference between supervised and unsupervised learning. As an illustrative example, consider the task of learning to detect spam e-mail versus the task of anomaly detection. For the spam detection task, we consider a setting in which the learner receives training e-mails for which the label spam/not-spam is provided. On the basis of such training the learner should figure out a rule for labeling a newly arriving e-mail message. In contrast, for the task of anomaly detection, all the learner gets as training is a large body of e-mail messages (with no labels) and the learner's task is to detect "unusual" messages.

More abstractly, viewing learning as a process of "using experience to gain expertise," supervised learning describes a scenario in which the "experience," a training example, contains significant information (say, the spam/not-spam labels) that is missing in the unseen "test examples" to which the learned expertise is to be applied. In this setting, the acquired expertise is aimed to predict that missing information for the test data. In such cases, we can think of the environment as a teacher that "supervises" the learner by providing the extra information (labels). In unsupervised learning, however, there is no distinction between training and test data. The learner processes input data with the goal of coming up with some summary, or compressed version of that data. Clustering a data set into subsets of similar objets is a typical example of such a task.

There is also an intermediate learning setting in which, while the training examples contain more information than the test examples, the learner is required to predict even more information for the test examples. For example, one may try to learn a value function that describes for each setting of a chess board the degree by which White's position is better than the Black's. Yet, the only information available to the learner at training time is positions that occurred throughout actual chess games, labeled by who eventually won that game. Such learning frameworks are mainly investigated under the title of *reinforcement learning*.

Active versus Passive Learners Learning paradigms can vary by the role played by the learner. We distinguish between "active" and "passive" learners. An active learner interacts with the environment at training time, say, by posing queries or performing experiments, while a passive learner only observes the information provided by the environment (or the teacher) without influencing or directing it. Note that the learner of a spam filter is usually passive – waiting for users to mark the e-mails coming to them. In an active setting, one could imagine asking users to label specific e-mails chosen by the learner, or even composed by the learner, to enhance its understanding of what spam is.

Helpfulness of the Teacher When one thinks about human learning, of a baby at home or a student at school, the process often involves a helpful teacher, who is trying to feed the learner with the information most useful for achieving the learning goal. In contrast, when a scientist learns about nature, the environment, playing the role of the teacher, can be best thought of as passive – apples drop, stars shine, and the rain falls without regard to the needs of the learner. We model such learning scenarios by postulating that the training data (or the learner's experience) is generated by some random process. This is the basic building block in the branch of "statistical learning." Finally, learning also occurs when the learner's input is generated by an adversarial "teacher." This may be the case in the spam filtering example (if the spammer makes an effort to mislead the spam filtering designer) or in learning to detect fraud. One also uses an adversarial teacher model as a worst-case scenario, when no milder setup can be safely assumed. If you can learn against an adversarial teacher, you are guaranteed to succeed interacting any odd teacher.

Online versus Batch Learning Protocol The last parameter we mention is the distinction between situations in which the learner has to respond online, throughout the learning process, and settings in which the learner has to engage the acquired expertise only after having a chance to process large amounts of data. For example, a stockbroker has to make daily decisions, based on the experience collected so far. He may become an expert over time, but might have made costly mistakes in the process. In contrast, in many data mining settings, the learner – the data miner – has large amounts of training data to play with before having to output conclusions.

In this book we shall discuss only a subset of the possible learning paradigms. Our main focus is on supervised statistical batch learning with a passive learner (for example, trying to learn how to generate patients' prognoses, based on large archives of records of patients that were independently collected and are already labeled by the fate of the recorded patients). We shall also briefly discuss online learning and batch unsupervised learning (in particular, clustering).

1.4 RELATIONS TO OTHER FIELDS

As an interdisciplinary field, machine learning shares common threads with the mathematical fields of statistics, information theory, game theory, and optimization. It is naturally a subfield of computer science, as our goal is to program machines so that they will learn. In a sense, machine learning can be viewed as a branch of AI (Artificial Intelligence), since, after all, the ability to turn experience into expertise or to detect meaningful patterns in complex sensory data is a cornerstone of human (and animal) intelligence. However, one should note that, in contrast with traditional AI, machine learning is not trying to build automated imitation of intelligent behavior, but rather to use the strengths and special abilities of computers to complement human intelligence, often performing tasks that fall way beyond human capabilities. For example, the ability to scan and process huge databases allows machine learning programs to detect patterns that are outside the scope of human perception.

The component of experience, or training, in machine learning often refers to data that is randomly generated. The task of the learner is to process such randomly generated examples toward drawing conclusions that hold for the environment from which these examples are picked. This description of machine learning highlights its close relationship with statistics. Indeed there is a lot in common between the two disciplines, in terms of both the goals and techniques used. There are, however, a few significant differences of emphasis; if a doctor comes up with the hypothesis that there is a correlation between smoking and heart disease, it is the statistician's role to view samples of patients and check the validity of that hypothesis (this is the common statistical task of hypothesis testing). In contrast, machine learning aims to use the data gathered from samples of patients to come up with a description of the causes of heart disease. The hope is that automated techniques may be able to figure out meaningful patterns (or hypotheses) that may have been missed by the human observer.

In contrast with traditional statistics, in machine learning in general, and in this book in particular, algorithmic considerations play a major role. Machine learning is about the execution of learning by computers; hence algorithmic issues are pivotal. We develop algorithms to perform the learning tasks and are concerned with their computational efficiency. Another difference is that while statistics is often interested in asymptotic behavior (like the convergence of sample-based statistical estimates as the sample sizes grow to infinity), the theory of machine learning focuses on finite sample bounds. Namely, given the size of available samples, machine learning theory aims to figure out the degree of accuracy that a learner can expect on the basis of such samples.

There are further differences between these two disciplines, of which we shall mention only one more here. While in statistics it is common to work under the assumption of certain presubscribed data models (such as assuming the normality of data-generating distributions, or the linearity of functional dependencies), in machine learning the emphasis is on working under a "distribution-free" setting, where the learner assumes as little as possible about the nature of the data distribution and allows the learning algorithm to figure out which models best approximate the data-generating process. A precise discussion of this issue requires some technical preliminaries, and we will come back to it later in the book, and in particular in Chapter 5.

1.5 HOW TO READ THIS BOOK

The first part of the book provides the basic theoretical principles that underlie machine learning (ML). In a sense, this is the foundation upon which the rest of the book is built. This part could serve as a basis for a minicourse on the theoretical foundations of ML.

The second part of the book introduces the most commonly used algorithmic approaches to supervised machine learning. A subset of these chapters may also be used for introducing machine learning in a general AI course to computer science, Math, or engineering students.

The third part of the book extends the scope of discussion from statistical classification to other learning models. It covers online learning, unsupervised learning, dimensionality reduction, generative models, and feature learning.

The fourth part of the book, Advanced Theory, is geared toward readers who have interest in research and provides the more technical mathematical techniques that serve to analyze and drive forward the field of theoretical machine learning.

The Appendixes provide some technical tools used in the book. In particular, we list basic results from measure concentration and linear algebra.

A few sections are marked by an asterisk, which means they are addressed to more advanced students. Each chapter is concluded with a list of exercises. A solution manual is provided in the course Web site.

1.5.1 Possible Course Plans Based on This Book

A 14 Week Introduction Course for Graduate Students:

1. Chapters 2–4.
2. Chapter 9 (without the VC calculation).
3. Chapters 5–6 (without proofs).
4. Chapter 10.
5. Chapters 7, 11 (without proofs).
6. Chapters 12, 13 (with some of the easier proofs).
7. Chapter 14 (with some of the easier proofs).
8. Chapter 15.
9. Chapter 16.
10. Chapter 18.

11. Chapter 22.
12. Chapter 23 (without proofs for compressed sensing).
13. Chapter 24.
14. Chapter 25.

A 14 Week Advanced Course for Graduate Students:

1. Chapters 26, 27.
2. (continued)
3. Chapters 6, 28.
4. Chapter 7.
5. Chapter 31.
6. Chapter 30.
7. Chapters 12, 13.
8. Chapter 14.
9. Chapter 8.
10. Chapter 17.
11. Chapter 29.
12. Chapter 19.
13. Chapter 20.
14. Chapter 21.

1.6 NOTATION

Most of the notation we use throughout the book is either standard or defined on the spot. In this section we describe our main conventions and provide a table summarizing our notation (Table 1.1). The reader is encouraged to skip this section and return to it if during the reading of the book some notation is unclear.

We denote scalars and abstract objects with lowercase letters (e.g. x and λ). Often, we would like to emphasize that some object is a vector and then we use boldface letters (e.g. $\mathbf{x}$ and $\boldsymbol{\lambda}$). The ith element of a vector $\mathbf{x}$ is denoted by x_i. We use uppercase letters to denote matrices, sets, and sequences. The meaning should be clear from the context. As we will see momentarily, the input of a learning algorithm is a sequence of training examples. We denote by z an abstract example and by $S = z_1, \ldots, z_m$ a sequence of m examples. Historically, S is often referred to as a training *set*; however, we will always assume that S is a *sequence* rather than a set. A sequence of m vectors is denoted by $\mathbf{x}_1, \ldots, \mathbf{x}_m$. The ith element of $\mathbf{x}_t$ is denoted by $x_{t,i}$.

Throughout the book, we make use of basic notions from probability. We denote by $\mathcal{D}$ a distribution over some set,[2] for example, Z. We use the notation $z \sim \mathcal{D}$ to denote that z is sampled according to $\mathcal{D}$. Given a random variable $f : Z \to \mathbb{R}$, its expected value is denoted by $\mathbb{E}_{z\sim\mathcal{D}}[f(z)]$. We sometimes use the shorthand $\mathbb{E}[f]$ when the dependence on z is clear from the context. For $f : Z \to \{\text{true}, \text{false}\}$ we also use $\mathbb{P}_{z\sim\mathcal{D}}[f(z)]$ to denote $\mathcal{D}(\{z : f(z) = \text{true}\})$. In the next chapter we will also

[2] To be mathematically precise, $\mathcal{D}$ should be defined over some σ-algebra of subsets of Z. The user who is not familiar with measure theory can skip the few footnotes and remarks regarding more formal measurability definitions and assumptions.

Table 1.1. Summary of notation

symbol	meaning
$\mathbb{R}$	the set of real numbers
$\mathbb{R}^d$	the set of d-dimensional vectors over $\mathbb{R}$
$\mathbb{R}_+$	the set of non-negative real numbers
$\mathbb{N}$	the set of natural numbers
$O, o, \Theta, \omega, \Omega, \tilde{O}$	asymptotic notation (see text)
$\mathbb{1}_{[\text{Boolean expression}]}$	indicator function (equals 1 if expression is true and 0 o.w.)
$[a]_+$	$= \max\{0, a\}$
$[n]$	the set $\{1, \ldots, n\}$ (for $n \in \mathbb{N}$)
$\mathbf{x}, \mathbf{v}, \mathbf{w}$	(column) vectors
x_i, v_i, w_i	the ith element of a vector
$\langle \mathbf{x}, \mathbf{v} \rangle$	$= \sum_{i=1}^d x_i v_i$ (inner product)
$\|\mathbf{x}\|_2$ or $\|\mathbf{x}\|$	$= \sqrt{\langle \mathbf{x}, \mathbf{x} \rangle}$ (the ℓ_2 norm of $\mathbf{x}$)
$\|\mathbf{x}\|_1$	$= \sum_{i=1}^d \lvert x_i \rvert$ (the ℓ_1 norm of $\mathbf{x}$)
$\|\mathbf{x}\|_\infty$	$= \max_i \lvert x_i \rvert$ (the ℓ_∞ norm of $\mathbf{x}$)
$\|\mathbf{x}\|_0$	the number of nonzero elements of $\mathbf{x}$
$A \in \mathbb{R}^{d,k}$	a $d \times k$ matrix over $\mathbb{R}$
$A^\top$	the transpose of A
$A_{i,j}$	the (i, j) element of A
$\mathbf{x}\mathbf{x}^\top$	the $d \times d$ matrix A s.t. $A_{i,j} = x_i x_j$ (where $\mathbf{x} \in \mathbb{R}^d$)
$\mathbf{x}_1, \ldots, \mathbf{x}_m$	a sequence of m vectors
$x_{i,j}$	the jth element of the ith vector in the sequence
$\mathbf{w}^{(1)}, \ldots, \mathbf{w}^{(T)}$	the values of a vector $\mathbf{w}$ during an iterative algorithm
$w_i^{(t)}$	the ith element of the vector $\mathbf{w}^{(t)}$
$\mathcal{X}$	instances domain (a set)
$\mathcal{Y}$	labels domain (a set)
Z	examples domain (a set)
$\mathcal{H}$	hypothesis class (a set)
$\ell : \mathcal{H} \times Z \to \mathbb{R}_+$	loss function
$\mathcal{D}$	a distribution over some set (usually over Z or over $\mathcal{X}$)
$\mathcal{D}(A)$	the probability of a set $A \subseteq Z$ according to $\mathcal{D}$
$z \sim \mathcal{D}$	sampling z according to $\mathcal{D}$
$S = z_1, \ldots, z_m$	a sequence of m examples
$S \sim \mathcal{D}^m$	sampling $S = z_1, \ldots, z_m$ i.i.d. according to $\mathcal{D}$
$\mathbb{P}, \mathbb{E}$	probability and expectation of a random variable
$\mathbb{P}_{z \sim \mathcal{D}}[f(z)]$	$= \mathcal{D}(\{z : f(z) = \text{true}\})$ for $f : Z \to \{\text{true}, \text{false}\}$
$\mathbb{E}_{z \sim \mathcal{D}}[f(z)]$	expectation of the random variable $f : Z \to \mathbb{R}$
$N(\boldsymbol{\mu}, C)$	Gaussian distribution with expectation $\boldsymbol{\mu}$ and covariance C
$f'(x)$	the derivative of a function $f : \mathbb{R} \to \mathbb{R}$ at x
$f''(x)$	the second derivative of a function $f : \mathbb{R} \to \mathbb{R}$ at x
$\frac{\partial f(\mathbf{w})}{\partial w_i}$	the partial derivative of a function $f : \mathbb{R}^d \to \mathbb{R}$ at $\mathbf{w}$ w.r.t. w_i
$\nabla f(\mathbf{w})$	the gradient of a function $f : \mathbb{R}^d \to \mathbb{R}$ at $\mathbf{w}$
$\partial f(\mathbf{w})$	the differential set of a function $f : \mathbb{R}^d \to \mathbb{R}$ at $\mathbf{w}$
$\min_{x \in C} f(x)$	$= \min\{f(x) : x \in C\}$ (minimal value of f over C)
$\max_{x \in C} f(x)$	$= \max\{f(x) : x \in C\}$ (maximal value of f over C)
$\operatorname{argmin}_{x \in C} f(x)$	the set $\{x \in C : f(x) = \min_{z \in C} f(z)\}$
$\operatorname{argmax}_{x \in C} f(x)$	the set $\{x \in C : f(x) = \max_{z \in C} f(z)\}$
$\log$	the natural logarithm

introduce the notation $\mathcal{D}^m$ to denote the probability over Z^m induced by sampling $(z_1,\ldots,z_m)$ where each point z_i is sampled from $\mathcal{D}$ independently of the other points.

In general, we have made an effort to avoid asymptotic notation. However, we occasionally use it to clarify the main results. In particular, given $f:\mathbb{R}\to\mathbb{R}_+$ and $g:\mathbb{R}\to\mathbb{R}_+$ we write $f=O(g)$ if there exist $x_0,\alpha\in\mathbb{R}_+$ such that for all $x>x_0$ we have $f(x)\le\alpha g(x)$. We write $f=o(g)$ if for every $\alpha>0$ there exists x_0 such that for all $x>x_0$ we have $f(x)\le\alpha g(x)$. We write $f=\Omega(g)$ if there exist $x_0,\alpha\in\mathbb{R}_+$ such that for all $x>x_0$ we have $f(x)\ge\alpha g(x)$. The notation $f=\omega(g)$ is defined analogously. The notation $f=\Theta(g)$ means that $f=O(g)$ and $g=O(f)$. Finally, the notation $f=\tilde{O}(g)$ means that there exists $k\in\mathbb{N}$ such that $f(x)=O(g(x)\log^k(g(x)))$.

The inner product between vectors $\mathbf{x}$ and $\mathbf{w}$ is denoted by $\langle\mathbf{x},\mathbf{w}\rangle$. Whenever we do not specify the vector space we assume that it is the d-dimensional Euclidean space and then $\langle\mathbf{x},\mathbf{w}\rangle=\sum_{i=1}^d x_i w_i$. The Euclidean (or ℓ_2) norm of a vector $\mathbf{w}$ is $\|\mathbf{w}\|_2=\sqrt{\langle\mathbf{w},\mathbf{w}\rangle}$. We omit the subscript from the ℓ_2 norm when it is clear from the context. We also use other ℓ_p norms, $\|\mathbf{w}\|_p=\left(\sum_i|w_i|^p\right)^{1/p}$, and in particular $\|\mathbf{w}\|_1=\sum_i|w_i|$ and $\|\mathbf{w}\|_\infty=\max_i|w_i|$.

We use the notation $\min_{x\in C}f(x)$ to denote the minimum value of the set $\{f(x):x\in C\}$. To be mathematically more precise, we should use $\inf_{x\in C}f(x)$ whenever the minimum is not achievable. However, in the context of this book the distinction between infimum and minimum is often of little interest. Hence, to simplify the presentation, we sometimes use the min notation even when inf is more adequate. An analogous remark applies to max versus sup.

PART 1

Foundations

2

A Gentle Start

Let us begin our mathematical analysis by showing how successful learning can be achieved in a relatively simplified setting. Imagine you have just arrived in some small Pacific island. You soon find out that papayas are a significant ingredient in the local diet. However, you have never before tasted papayas. You have to learn how to predict whether a papaya you see in the market is tasty or not. First, you need to decide which features of a papaya your prediction should be based on. On the basis of your previous experience with other fruits, you decide to use two features: the papaya's color, ranging from dark green, through orange and red to dark brown, and the papaya's softness, ranging from rock hard to mushy. Your input for figuring out your prediction rule is a sample of papayas that you have examined for color and softness and then tasted and found out whether they were tasty or not. Let us analyze this task as a demonstration of the considerations involved in learning problems.

Our first step is to describe a formal model aimed to capture such learning tasks.

2.1 A FORMAL MODEL – THE STATISTICAL LEARNING FRAMEWORK

The learner's input: In the basic statistical learning setting, the learner has access to the following:

Domain set: An arbitrary set, $\mathcal{X}$. This is the set of objects that we may wish to label. For example, in the papaya learning problem mentioned before, the domain set will be the set of all papayas. Usually, these domain points will be represented by a vector of *features* (like the papaya's color and softness). We also refer to domain points as *instances* and to $\mathcal{X}$ as instance space.

Label set: For our current discussion, we will restrict the label set to be a two-element set, usually $\{0,1\}$ or $\{-1,+1\}$. Let $\mathcal{Y}$ denote our set of possible labels. For our papayas example, let $\mathcal{Y}$ be $\{0,1\}$, where 1 represents being tasty and 0 stands for being not-tasty.

Training data: $S = ((x_1, y_1)\dots(x_m, y_m))$ is a finite sequence of pairs in $\mathcal{X}\times\mathcal{Y}$: that is, a sequence of labeled domain points. This is the input that the learner has access to (like a set of papayas that have been tasted and their color, softness, and tastiness). Such labeled examples are often called *training examples*. We sometimes also refer to S as a *training set*.[1]

The learner's output: The learner is requested to output a *prediction rule*, $h : \mathcal{X} \to \mathcal{Y}$. This function is also called a *predictor*, a *hypothesis*, or a *classifier*. The predictor can be used to predict the label of new domain points. In our papayas example, it is a rule that our learner will employ to predict whether future papayas he examines in the farmers' market are going to be tasty or not. We use the notation $A(S)$ to denote the hypothesis that a learning algorithm, A, returns upon receiving the training sequence S.

A simple data-generation model We now explain how the training data is generated. First, we assume that the instances (the papayas we encounter) are generated by some probability distribution (in this case, representing the environment). Let us denote that probability distribution over $\mathcal{X}$ by $\mathcal{D}$. It is important to note that we do not assume that the learner knows anything about this distribution. For the type of learning tasks we discuss, this could be any arbitrary probability distribution. As to the labels, in the current discussion we assume that there is some "correct" labeling function, $f : \mathcal{X} \to \mathcal{Y}$, and that $y_i = f(x_i)$ for all i. This assumption will be relaxed in the next chapter. The labeling function is unknown to the learner. In fact, this is just what the learner is trying to figure out. In summary, each pair in the training data S is generated by first sampling a point x_i according to $\mathcal{D}$ and then labeling it by f.

Measures of success: We define the *error of a classifier* to be the probability that it does not predict the correct label on a random data point generated by the aforementioned underlying distribution. That is, the error of h is the probability to draw a random instance x, according to the distribution $\mathcal{D}$, such that $h(x)$ does not equal $f(x)$.

Formally, given a domain subset,[2] $A \subset \mathcal{X}$, the probability distribution, $\mathcal{D}$, assigns a number, $\mathcal{D}(A)$, which determines how likely it is to observe a point $x \in A$. In many cases, we refer to A as an event and express it using a function $\pi : \mathcal{X} \to \{0,1\}$, namely, $A = \{x \in \mathcal{X} : \pi(x) = 1\}$. In that case, we also use the notation $\mathbb{P}_{x\sim\mathcal{D}}[\pi(x)]$ to express $\mathcal{D}(A)$.

We define the error of a prediction rule, $h : \mathcal{X} \to \mathcal{Y}$, to be

$$L_{\mathcal{D},f}(h) \stackrel{\text{def}}{=} \mathop{\mathbb{P}}_{x\sim\mathcal{D}}[h(x) \neq f(x)] \stackrel{\text{def}}{=} \mathcal{D}(\{x : h(x) \neq f(x)\}). \tag{2.1}$$

That is, the error of such h is the probability of randomly choosing an example x for which $h(x) \neq f(x)$. The subscript $(\mathcal{D}, f)$ indicates that the error is measured with respect to the probability distribution $\mathcal{D}$ and the correct labeling function f. We omit this subscript when it is clear from the context. $L_{(\mathcal{D},f)}(h)$ has several synonymous names such as the *generalization error*, the *risk*, or the *true error* of h, and we will use these names interchangeably throughout

[1] Despite the "set" notation, S is a sequence. In particular, the same example may appear twice in S and some algorithms can take into account the order of examples in S.

[2] Strictly speaking, we should be more careful and require that A is a member of some σ-algebra of subsets of $\mathcal{X}$, over which $\mathcal{D}$ is defined. We will formally define our measurability assumptions in the next chapter.

the book. We use the letter L for the error, since we view this error as the *loss* of the learner. We will later also discuss other possible formulations of such loss.

A note about the information available to the learner The learner is blind to the underlying distribution $\mathcal{D}$ over the world and to the labeling function f. In our papayas example, we have just arrived in a new island and we have no clue as to how papayas are distributed and how to predict their tastiness. The only way the learner can interact with the environment is through observing the training set.

In the next section we describe a simple learning paradigm for the preceding setup and analyze its performance.

2.2 EMPIRICAL RISK MINIMIZATION

As mentioned earlier, a learning algorithm receives as input a training set S, sampled from an unknown distribution $\mathcal{D}$ and labeled by some target function f, and should output a predictor $h_S : \mathcal{X} \to \mathcal{Y}$ (the subscript S emphasizes the fact that the output predictor depends on S). The goal of the algorithm is to find h_S that minimizes the error with respect to the unknown $\mathcal{D}$ and f.

Since the learner does not know what $\mathcal{D}$ and f are, the true error is not directly available to the learner. A useful notion of error that can be calculated by the learner is the *training error* – the error the classifier incurs over the training sample:

$$L_S(h) \stackrel{\text{def}}{=} \frac{|\{i \in [m] : h(x_i) \neq y_i\}|}{m}, \tag{2.2}$$

where $[m] = \{1, \ldots, m\}$.

The terms *empirical error* and *empirical risk* are often used interchangeably for this error.

Since the training sample is the snapshot of the world that is available to the learner, it makes sense to search for a solution that works well on that data. This learning paradigm – coming up with a predictor h that minimizes $L_S(h)$ – is called *Empirical Risk Minimization* or ERM for short.

2.2.1 Something May Go Wrong – Overfitting

Although the ERM rule seems very natural, without being careful, this approach may fail miserably.

To demonstrate such a failure, let us go back to the problem of learning to predict the taste of a papaya on the basis of its softness and color. Consider a sample as depicted in the following:

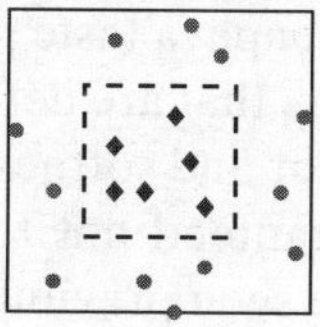

Assume that the probability distribution $\mathcal{D}$ is such that instances are distributed uniformly within the larger square and the labeling function, f, determines the label to be 1 if the instance is within the inner square, and 0 otherwise. The area of the larger square in the picture is 2 and the area of the inner square is 1. Consider the following predictor:

$$h_S(x) = \begin{cases} y_i & \text{if } \exists i \in [m] \text{ s.t. } x_i = x \\ 0 & \text{otherwise.} \end{cases} \tag{2.3}$$

While this predictor might seem rather artificial, in Exercise 2.1 we show a natural representation of it using polynomials. Clearly, no matter what the sample is, $L_S(h_S) = 0$, and therefore this predictor may be chosen by an ERM algorithm (it is one of the empirical-minimum-cost hypotheses; no classifier can have smaller error). On the other hand, the true error of any classifier that predicts the label 1 only on a finite number of instances is, in this case, 1/2. Thus, $L_{\mathcal{D}}(h_S) = 1/2$. We have found a predictor whose performance on the training set is excellent, yet its performance on the true "world" is very poor. This phenomenon is called *overfitting*. Intuitively, overfitting occurs when our hypothesis fits the training data "too well" (perhaps like the everyday experience that a person who provides a perfect detailed explanation for each of his single actions may raise suspicion).

2.3 EMPIRICAL RISK MINIMIZATION WITH INDUCTIVE BIAS

We have just demonstrated that the ERM rule might lead to overfitting. Rather than giving up on the ERM paradigm, we will look for ways to rectify it. We will search for conditions under which there is a guarantee that ERM does not overfit, namely, conditions under which when the ERM predictor has good performance with respect to the training data, it is also highly likely to perform well over the underlying data distribution.

A common solution is to apply the ERM learning rule over a restricted search space. Formally, the learner should choose in advance (before seeing the data) a set of predictors. This set is called a *hypothesis class* and is denoted by $\mathcal{H}$. Each $h \in \mathcal{H}$ is a function mapping from $\mathcal{X}$ to $\mathcal{Y}$. For a given class $\mathcal{H}$, and a training sample, S, the $\mathrm{ERM}_{\mathcal{H}}$ learner uses the ERM rule to choose a predictor $h \in \mathcal{H}$, with the lowest possible error over S. Formally,

$$\mathrm{ERM}_{\mathcal{H}}(S) \in \underset{h \in \mathcal{H}}{\operatorname{argmin}}\, L_S(h),$$

where argmin stands for the set of hypotheses in $\mathcal{H}$ that achieve the minimum value of $L_S(h)$ over $\mathcal{H}$. By restricting the learner to choosing a predictor from $\mathcal{H}$, we *bias* it toward a particular set of predictors. Such restrictions are often called an *inductive bias*. Since the choice of such a restriction is determined before the learner sees the training data, it should ideally be based on some prior knowledge about the problem to be learned. For example, for the papaya taste prediction problem we may choose the class $\mathcal{H}$ to be the set of predictors that are determined by axis aligned rectangles (in the space determined by the color and softness coordinates). We will later show that $\mathrm{ERM}_{\mathcal{H}}$ over this class is guaranteed not to overfit. On the other hand, the example of overfitting that we have seen previously, demonstrates that choosing $\mathcal{H}$

to be a class of predictors that includes all functions that assign the value 1 to a finite set of domain points does not suffice to guarantee that $\mathrm{ERM}_{\mathcal{H}}$ will not overfit.

A fundamental question in learning theory is, over which hypothesis classes $\mathrm{ERM}_{\mathcal{H}}$ learning will not result in overfitting. We will study this question later in the book.

Intuitively, choosing a more restricted hypothesis class better protects us against overfitting but at the same time might cause us a stronger inductive bias. We will get back to this fundamental tradeoff later.

2.3.1 Finite Hypothesis Classes

The simplest type of restriction on a class is imposing an upper bound on its size (that is, the number of predictors h in $\mathcal{H}$). In this section, we show that if $\mathcal{H}$ is a finite class then $\mathrm{ERM}_{\mathcal{H}}$ will not overfit, provided it is based on a sufficiently large training sample (this size requirement will depend on the size of $\mathcal{H}$).

Limiting the learner to prediction rules within some finite hypothesis class may be considered as a reasonably mild restriction. For example, $\mathcal{H}$ can be the set of all predictors that can be implemented by a C++ program written in at most 10^9 bits of code. In our papayas example, we mentioned previously the class of axis aligned rectangles. While this is an infinite class, if we discretize the representation of real numbers, say, by using a 64 bits floating-point representation, the hypothesis class becomes a finite class.

Let us now analyze the performance of the $\mathrm{ERM}_{\mathcal{H}}$ learning rule assuming that $\mathcal{H}$ is a finite class. For a training sample, S, labeled according to some $f : \mathcal{X} \to \mathcal{Y}$, let h_S denote a result of applying ERM_H to S, namely,

$$h_S \in \operatorname*{argmin}_{h \in \mathcal{H}} L_S(h). \tag{2.4}$$

In this chapter, we make the following simplifying assumption (which will be relaxed in the next chapter).

Definition 2.1 (The Realizability Assumption). There exists $h^\star \in \mathcal{H}$ s.t. $L_{(\mathcal{D},f)}(h^\star) = 0$. Note that this assumption implies that with probability 1 over random samples, S, where the instances of S are sampled according to $\mathcal{D}$ and are labeled by f, we have $L_S(h^\star) = 0$.

The realizability assumption implies that for every ERM hypothesis we have that[3] $L_S(h_S) = 0$. However, we are interested in the *true* risk of h_S, $L_{(\mathcal{D},f)}(h_S)$, rather than its empirical risk.

Clearly, any guarantee on the error with respect to the underlying distribution, $\mathcal{D}$, for an algorithm that has access only to a sample S should depend on the relationship between $\mathcal{D}$ and S. The common assumption in statistical machine learning is that the training sample S is generated by sampling points from the distribution $\mathcal{D}$ independently of each other. Formally,

[3] Mathematically speaking, this holds with probability 1. To simplify the presentation, we sometimes omit the "with probability 1" specifier.

The i.i.d. assumption: The examples in the training set are independently and identically distributed (i.i.d.) according to the distribution $\mathcal{D}$. That is, every x_i in S is freshly sampled according to $\mathcal{D}$ and then labeled according to the labeling function, f. We denote this assumption by $S \sim \mathcal{D}^m$ where m is the size of S, and $\mathcal{D}^m$ denotes the probability over m-tuples induced by applying $\mathcal{D}$ to pick each element of the tuple independently of the other members of the tuple.

Intuitively, the training set S is a window through which the learner gets partial information about the distribution $\mathcal{D}$ over the world and the labeling function, f. The larger the sample gets, the more likely it is to reflect more accurately the distribution and labeling used to generate it.

Since $L_{(\mathcal{D},f)}(h_S)$ depends on the training set, S, and that training set is picked by a random process, there is randomness in the choice of the predictor h_S and, consequently, in the risk $L_{(\mathcal{D},f)}(h_S)$. Formally, we say that it is a random variable. It is not realistic to expect that with full certainty S will suffice to direct the learner toward a good classifier (from the point of view of $\mathcal{D}$), as there is always some probability that the sampled training data happens to be very nonrepresentative of the underlying $\mathcal{D}$. If we go back to the papaya tasting example, there is always some (small) chance that all the papayas we have happened to taste were not tasty, in spite of the fact that, say, 70% of the papayas in our island are tasty. In such a case, $\mathrm{ERM}_{\mathcal{H}}(S)$ may be the constant function that labels every papaya as "not tasty" (and has 70% error on the true distribution of papapyas in the island). We will therefore address the *probability* to sample a training set for which $L_{(\mathcal{D},f)}(h_S)$ is not too large. Usually, we denote the probability of getting a nonrepresentative sample by δ, and call $(1-\delta)$ the *confidence parameter* of our prediction.

On top of that, since we cannot guarantee perfect label prediction, we introduce another parameter for the quality of prediction, the *accuracy parameter*, commonly denoted by ϵ. We interpret the event $L_{(\mathcal{D},f)}(h_S) > \epsilon$ as a failure of the learner, while if $L_{(\mathcal{D},f)}(h_S) \leq \epsilon$ we view the output of the algorithm as an approximately correct predictor. Therefore (fixing some labeling function $f : \mathcal{X} \rightarrow \mathcal{Y}$), we are interested in upper bounding the probability to sample m-tuple of instances that will lead to failure of the learner. Formally, let $S|_x = (x_1, \ldots, x_m)$ be the instances of the training set. We would like to upper bound

$$\mathcal{D}^m(\{S|_x : L_{(\mathcal{D},f)}(h_S) > \epsilon\}).$$

Let $\mathcal{H}_B$ be the set of "bad" hypotheses, that is,

$$\mathcal{H}_B = \{h \in \mathcal{H} : L_{(\mathcal{D},f)}(h) > \epsilon\}.$$

In addition, let

$$M = \{S|_x : \exists h \in \mathcal{H}_B, L_S(h) = 0\}$$

be the set of misleading samples: Namely, for every $S|_x \in M$, there is a "bad" hypothesis, $h \in \mathcal{H}_B$, that looks like a "good" hypothesis on $S|_x$. Now, recall that we would like to bound the probability of the event $L_{(\mathcal{D},f)}(h_S) > \epsilon$. But, since the realizability assumption implies that $L_S(h_S) = 0$, it follows that the event $L_{(\mathcal{D},f)}(h_S) > \epsilon$ can only happen if for some $h \in \mathcal{H}_B$ we have $L_S(h) = 0$. In other words, this event will only happen if our sample is in the set of misleading samples, M. Formally, we have shown that

$$\{S|_x : L_{(\mathcal{D},f)}(h_S) > \epsilon\} \subseteq M.$$

Note that we can rewrite M as

$$M = \bigcup_{h \in \mathcal{H}_B} \{S|_x : L_S(h) = 0\}. \tag{2.5}$$

Hence,

$$\mathcal{D}^m(\{S|_x : L_{(\mathcal{D},f)}(h_S) > \epsilon\}) \leq \mathcal{D}^m(M) = \mathcal{D}^m(\cup_{h \in \mathcal{H}_B} \{S|_x : L_S(h) = 0\}). \tag{2.6}$$

Next, we upper bound the right-hand side of the preceding equation using the *union bound* – a basic property of probabilities.

Lemma 2.2 (Union Bound). *For any two sets A, B and a distribution $\mathcal{D}$ we have*

$$\mathcal{D}(A \cup B) \leq \mathcal{D}(A) + \mathcal{D}(B).$$

Applying the union bound to the right-hand side of Equation (2.6) yields

$$\mathcal{D}^m(\{S|_x : L_{(\mathcal{D},f)}(h_S) > \epsilon\}) \leq \sum_{h \in \mathcal{H}_B} \mathcal{D}^m(\{S|_x : L_S(h) = 0\}). \tag{2.7}$$

Next, let us bound each summand of the right-hand side of the preceding inequality. Fix some "bad" hypothesis $h \in \mathcal{H}_B$. The event $L_S(h) = 0$ is equivalent to the event $\forall i, h(x_i) = f(x_i)$. Since the examples in the training set are sampled i.i.d. we get that

$$\begin{aligned}\mathcal{D}^m(\{S|_x : L_S(h) = 0\}) &= \mathcal{D}^m(\{S|_x : \forall i, h(x_i) = f(x_i)\}) \\ &= \prod_{i=1}^{m} \mathcal{D}(\{x_i : h(x_i) = f(x_i)\}).\end{aligned} \tag{2.8}$$

For each individual sampling of an element of the training set we have

$$\mathcal{D}(\{x_i : h(x_i) = y_i\}) = 1 - L_{(\mathcal{D},f)}(h) \leq 1 - \epsilon,$$

where the last inequality follows from the fact that $h \in \mathcal{H}_B$. Combining the previous equation with Equation (2.8) and using the inequality $1 - \epsilon \leq e^{-\epsilon}$ we obtain that for every $h \in \mathcal{H}_B$,

$$\mathcal{D}^m(\{S|_x : L_S(h) = 0\}) \leq (1 - \epsilon)^m \leq e^{-\epsilon m}. \tag{2.9}$$

Combining this equation with Equation (2.7) we conclude that

$$\mathcal{D}^m(\{S|_x : L_{(\mathcal{D},f)}(h_S) > \epsilon\}) \leq |\mathcal{H}_B| \, e^{-\epsilon m} \leq |\mathcal{H}| \, e^{-\epsilon m}.$$

A graphical illustration which explains how we used the union bound is given in Figure 2.1.

Corollary 2.3. *Let $\mathcal{H}$ be a finite hypothesis class. Let $\delta \in (0,1)$ and $\epsilon > 0$ and let m be an integer that satisfies*

$$m \geq \frac{\log(|\mathcal{H}|/\delta)}{\epsilon}.$$

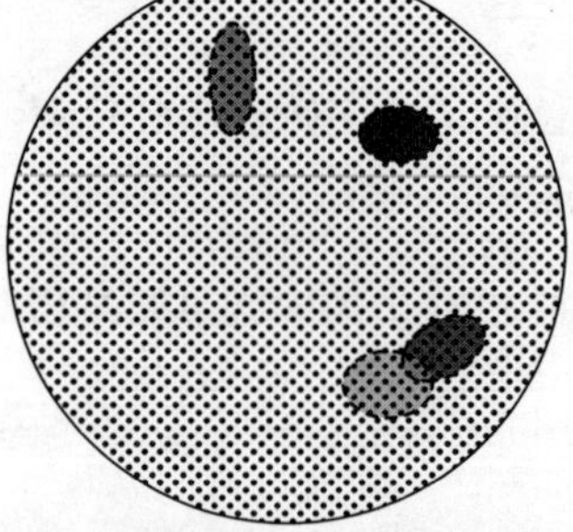

Figure 2.1. Each point in the large circle represents a possible m-tuple of instances. Each colored oval represents the set of "misleading" m-tuple of instances for some "bad" predictor $h \in \mathcal{H}_B$. The ERM can potentially overfit whenever it gets a misleading training set S. That is, for some $h \in \mathcal{H}_B$ we have $L_S(h) = 0$. Equation (2.9) guarantees that for each individual bad hypothesis, $h \in \mathcal{H}_B$, at most $(1-\epsilon)^m$-fraction of the training sets would be misleading. In particular, the larger m is, the smaller each of these colored ovals becomes. The union bound formalizes the fact that the area representing the training sets that are misleading with respect to some $h \in \mathcal{H}_B$ (that is, the training sets in M) is at most the sum of the areas of the colored ovals. Therefore, it is bounded by $|\mathcal{H}_B|$ times the maximum size of a colored oval. Any sample S outside the colored ovals cannot cause the ERM rule to overfit.

Then, for any labeling function, f, and for any distribution, $\mathcal{D}$, for which the realizability assumption holds (that is, for some $h \in \mathcal{H}$, $L_{(\mathcal{D},f)}(h) = 0$), with probability of at least $1-\delta$ over the choice of an i.i.d. sample S of size m, we have that for every ERM hypothesis, h_S, it holds that

$$L_{(\mathcal{D},f)}(h_S) \leq \epsilon.$$

The preceeding corollary tells us that for a sufficiently large m, the $\text{ERM}_{\mathcal{H}}$ rule over a finite hypothesis class will be *probably* (with confidence $1-\delta$) *approximately* (up to an error of ϵ) correct. In the next chapter we formally define the model of Probably Approximately Correct (PAC) learning.

2.4 EXERCISES

2.1 **Overfitting of polynomial matching:** We have shown that the predictor defined in Equation (2.3) leads to overfitting. While this predictor seems to be very unnatural, the goal of this exercise is to show that it can be described as a thresholded polynomial. That is, show that given a training set $S = \{(\mathbf{x}_i, f(\mathbf{x}_i))\}_{i=1}^m \subseteq (\mathbb{R}^d \times \{0,1\})^m$, there exists a polynomial p_S such that $h_S(\mathbf{x}) = 1$ if and only if $p_S(\mathbf{x}) \geq 0$, where h_S is as defined in Equation (2.3). It follows that learning the class of all thresholded polynomials using the ERM rule may lead to overfitting.

2.2 Let $\mathcal{H}$ be a class of binary classifiers over a domain $\mathcal{X}$. Let $\mathcal{D}$ be an unknown distribution over $\mathcal{X}$, and let f be the target hypothesis in $\mathcal{H}$. Fix some $h \in \mathcal{H}$. Show that the expected value of $L_S(h)$ over the choice of $S|_x$ equals $L_{(\mathcal{D},f)}(h)$, namely,

$$\mathop{\mathbb{E}}_{S|_x \sim \mathcal{D}^m} [L_S(h)] = L_{(\mathcal{D},f)}(h).$$

2.3 **Axis aligned rectangles:** An axis aligned rectangle classifier in the plane is a classifier that assigns the value 1 to a point if and only if it is inside a certain rectangle.

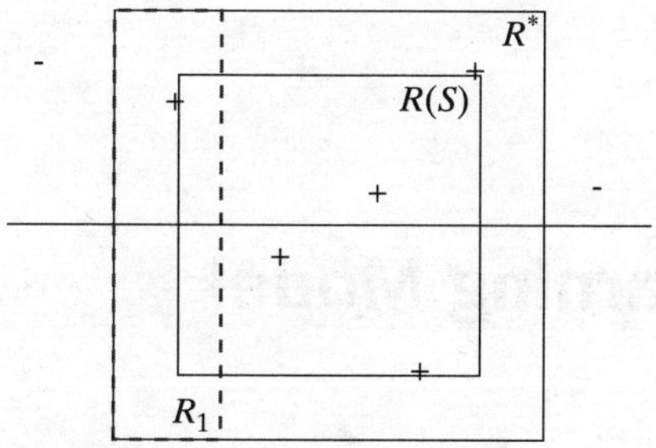

Figure 2.2. Axis aligned rectangles.

Formally, given real numbers $a_1 \leq b_1, a_2 \leq b_2$, define the classifier $h_{(a_1,b_1,a_2,b_2)}$ by

$$h_{(a_1,b_1,a_2,b_2)}(x_1,x_2) = \begin{cases} 1 & \text{if } a_1 \leq x_1 \leq b_1 \text{ and } a_2 \leq x_2 \leq b_2 \\ 0 & \text{otherwise} \end{cases}. \quad (2.10)$$

The class of all axis aligned rectangles in the plane is defined as

$$\mathcal{H}^2_{\text{rec}} = \{h_{(a_1,b_1,a_2,b_2)} : a_1 \leq b_1, \text{ and } a_2 \leq b_2\}.$$

Note that this is an infinite size hypothesis class. Throughout this exercise we rely on the realizability assumption.

1. Let A be the algorithm that returns the smallest rectangle enclosing all positive examples in the training set. Show that A is an ERM.
2. Show that if A receives a training set of size $\geq \frac{4\log(4/\delta)}{\epsilon}$ then, with probability of at least $1-\delta$ it returns a hypothesis with error of at most ϵ.
   Hint: Fix some distribution $\mathcal{D}$ over $\mathcal{X}$, let $R^* = R(a_1^*, b_1^*, a_2^*, b_2^*)$ be the rectangle that generates the labels, and let f be the corresponding hypothesis. Let $a_1 \geq a_1^*$ be a number such that the probability mass (with respect to $\mathcal{D}$) of the rectangle $R_1 = R(a_1^*, a_1, a_2^*, b_2^*)$ is exactly $\epsilon/4$. Similarly, let b_1, a_2, b_2 be numbers such that the probability masses of the rectangles $R_2 = R(b_1, b_1^*, a_2^*, b_2^*)$, $R_3 = R(a_1^*, b_1^*, a_2^*, a_2)$, $R_4 = R(a_1^*, b_1^*, b_2, b_2^*)$ are all exactly $\epsilon/4$. Let $R(S)$ be the rectangle returned by A. See illustration in Figure 2.2.
   - Show that $R(S) \subseteq R^*$.
   - Show that if S contains (positive) examples in all of the rectangles R_1, R_2, R_3, R_4, then the hypothesis returned by A has error of at most ϵ.
   - For each $i \in \{1, \ldots, 4\}$, upper bound the probability that S does not contain an example from R_i.
   - Use the union bound to conclude the argument.
3. Repeat the previous question for the class of axis aligned rectangles in $\mathbb{R}^d$.
4. Show that the runtime of applying the algorithm A mentioned earlier is polynomial in $d, 1/\epsilon$, and in $\log(1/\delta)$.

3

A Formal Learning Model

In this chapter we define our main formal learning model – the PAC learning model and its extensions. We will consider other notions of learnability in Chapter 7.

3.1 PAC LEARNING

In the previous chapter we have shown that for a finite hypothesis class, if the ERM rule with respect to that class is applied on a sufficiently large training sample (whose size is independent of the underlying distribution or labeling function) then the output hypothesis will be probably approximately correct. More generally, we now define*Probably Approximately Correct* (PAC) learning.

Definition 3.1 (PAC Learnability). A hypothesis class $\mathcal{H}$ is PAC learnable if there exist a function $m_{\mathcal{H}} : (0,1)^2 \to \mathbb{N}$ and a learning algorithm with the following property: For every $\epsilon, \delta \in (0,1)$, for every distribution $\mathcal{D}$ over $\mathcal{X}$, and for every labeling function $f : \mathcal{X} \to \{0,1\}$, if the realizable assumption holds with respect to $\mathcal{H}, \mathcal{D}, f$, then when running the learning algorithm on $m \geq m_{\mathcal{H}}(\epsilon, \delta)$ i.i.d. examples generated by $\mathcal{D}$ and labeled by f, the algorithm returns a hypothesis h such that, with probability of at least $1 - \delta$ (over the choice of the examples), $L_{(\mathcal{D},f)}(h) \leq \epsilon$.

The definition of Probably Approximately Correct learnability contains two approximation parameters. The accuracy parameter ϵ determines how far the output classifier can be from the optimal one (this corresponds to the "approximately correct"), and a confidence parameter δ indicating how likely the classifier is to meet that accuracy requirement (corresponds to the "probably" part of "PAC"). Under the data access model that we are investigating, these approximations are inevitable. Since the training set is randomly generated, there may always be a small chance that it will happen to be noninformative (for example, there is always some chance that the training set will contain only one domain point, sampled over and over again). Furthermore, even when we are lucky enough to get a training sample that does faithfully represent $\mathcal{D}$, because it is just a finite sample, there may always be some fine details of $\mathcal{D}$ that it fails to reflect. Our accuracy parameter, ϵ, allows "forgiving" the learner's classifier for making minor errors.

Sample Complexity

The function $m_{\mathcal{H}} : (0,1)^2 \rightarrow \mathbb{N}$ determines the *sample complexity* of learning $\mathcal{H}$: that is, how many examples are required to guarantee a probably approximately correct solution. The sample complexity is a function of the accuracy (ϵ) and confidence (δ) parameters. It also depends on properties of the hypothesis class $\mathcal{H}$ – for example, for a finite class we showed that the sample complexity depends on log the size of $\mathcal{H}$.

Note that if $\mathcal{H}$ is PAC learnable, there are many functions $m_{\mathcal{H}}$ that satisfy the requirements given in the definition of PAC learnability. Therefore, to be precise, we will define the sample complexity of learning $\mathcal{H}$ to be the "minimal function," in the sense that for any ϵ, δ, $m_{\mathcal{H}}(\epsilon, \delta)$ is the minimal integer that satisfies the requirements of PAC learning with accuracy ϵ and confidence δ.

Let us now recall the conclusion of the analysis of finite hypothesis classes from the previous chapter. It can be rephrased as stating:

Corollary 3.2. *Every finite hypothesis class is PAC learnable with sample complexity*

$$m_{\mathcal{H}}(\epsilon, \delta) \leq \left\lceil \frac{\log(|\mathcal{H}|/\delta)}{\epsilon} \right\rceil.$$

There are infinite classes that are learnable as well (see, for example, Exercise 3.3). Later on we will show that what determines the PAC learnability of a class is not its finiteness but rather a combinatorial measure called the *VC dimension*.

3.2 A MORE GENERAL LEARNING MODEL

The model we have just described can be readily generalized, so that it can be made relevant to a wider scope of learning tasks. We consider generalizations in two aspects:

Removing the Realizability Assumption

We have required that the learning algorithm succeeds on a pair of data distribution $\mathcal{D}$ and labeling function f provided that the realizability assumption is met. For practical learning tasks, this assumption may be too strong (can we really guarantee that there is a rectangle in the color-hardness space that *fully determines* which papayas are tasty?). In the next subsection, we will describe the *agnostic PAC* model in which this realizability assumption is waived.

Learning Problems beyond Binary Classification

The learning task that we have been discussing so far has to do with predicting a binary label to a given example (like being tasty or not). However, many learning tasks take a different form. For example, one may wish to predict a real valued number (say, the temperature at 9:00 p.m. tomorrow) or a label picked from a finite set of labels (like the topic of the main story in tomorrow's paper). It turns out that our analysis of learning can be readily extended to such and many other scenarios by allowing a variety of loss functions. We shall discuss that in Section 3.2.2 later.

3.2.1 Releasing the Realizability Assumption – Agnostic PAC Learning

A More Realistic Model for the Data-Generating Distribution

Recall that the realizability assumption requires that there exists $h^\star \in \mathcal{H}$ such that $\mathbb{P}_{x\sim\mathcal{D}}[h^\star(x) = f(x)] = 1$. In many practical problems this assumption does not hold. Furthermore, it is maybe more realistic not to assume that the labels are fully determined by the features we measure on input elements (in the case of the papayas, it is plausible that two papayas of the same color and softness will have different taste). In the following, we relax the realizability assumption by replacing the "target labeling function" with a more flexible notion, a data-labels generating distribution.

Formally, from now on, let $\mathcal{D}$ be a probability distribution over $\mathcal{X} \times \mathcal{Y}$, where, as before, $\mathcal{X}$ is our domain set and $\mathcal{Y}$ is a set of labels (usually we will consider $\mathcal{Y} = \{0,1\}$). That is, $\mathcal{D}$ is a *joint distribution* over domain points and labels. One can view such a distribution as being composed of two parts: a distribution $\mathcal{D}_x$ over unlabeled domain points (sometimes called the *marginal distribution*) and a *conditional* probability over labels for each domain point, $\mathcal{D}((x,y)|x)$. In the papaya example, $\mathcal{D}_x$ determines the probability of encountering a papaya whose color and hardness fall in some color-hardness values domain, and the conditional probability is the probability that a papaya with color and hardness represented by x is tasty. Indeed, such modeling allows for two papayas that share the same color and hardness to belong to different taste categories.

The empirical and the True Error Revised

For a probability distribution, $\mathcal{D}$, over $\mathcal{X} \times \mathcal{Y}$, one can measure how likely h is to make an error when labeled points are randomly drawn according to $\mathcal{D}$. We redefine the true error (or risk) of a prediction rule h to be

$$L_{\mathcal{D}}(h) \stackrel{\text{def}}{=} \mathbb{P}_{(x,y)\sim\mathcal{D}}[h(x) \neq y] \stackrel{\text{def}}{=} \mathcal{D}(\{(x,y) : h(x) \neq y\}). \tag{3.1}$$

We would like to find a predictor, h, for which that error will be minimized. However, the learner does not know the data generating $\mathcal{D}$. What the learner does have access to is the training data, S. The definition of the empirical risk remains the same as before, namely,

$$L_S(h) \stackrel{\text{def}}{=} \frac{|\{i \in [m] : h(x_i) \neq y_i\}|}{m}.$$

Given S, a learner can compute $L_S(h)$ for any function $h : X \to \{0,1\}$. Note that $L_S(h) = L_{D(\text{uniform over } S)}(h)$.

The Goal

We wish to find some hypothesis, $h : \mathcal{X} \to \mathcal{Y}$, that (probably approximately) minimizes the true risk, $L_{\mathcal{D}}(h)$.

The Bayes Optimal Predictor.
Given any probability distribution $\mathcal{D}$ over $\mathcal{X} \times \{0,1\}$, the best label predicting function from $\mathcal{X}$ to $\{0,1\}$ will be

$$f_{\mathcal{D}}(x) = \begin{cases} 1 & \text{if } \mathbb{P}[y=1|x] \geq 1/2 \\ 0 & \text{otherwise} \end{cases}$$

It is easy to verify (see Exercise 3.7) that for every probability distribution $\mathcal{D}$, the Bayes optimal predictor $f_{\mathcal{D}}$ is optimal, in the sense that no other classifier, $g : \mathcal{X} \to \{0,1\}$, has a lower error. That is, for every classifier g, $L_{\mathcal{D}}(f_{\mathcal{D}}) \leq L_{\mathcal{D}}(g)$.

Unfortunately, since we do not know $\mathcal{D}$, we cannot utilize this optimal predictor $f_{\mathcal{D}}$. What the learner does have access to is the training sample. We can now present the formal definition of agnostic PAC learnability, which is a natural extension of the definition of PAC learnability to the more realistic, nonrealizable, learning setup we have just discussed.

Clearly, we cannot hope that the learning algorithm will find a hypothesis whose error is smaller than the minimal possible error, that of the Bayes predictor. Furthermore, as we shall prove later, once we make no prior assumptions about the data-generating distribution, no algorithm can be guaranteed to find a predictor that is as good as the Bayes optimal one. Instead, we require that the learning algorithm will find a predictor whose error is not much larger than the best possible error of a predictor in some given benchmark hypothesis class. Of course, the strength of such a requirement depends on the choice of that hypothesis class.

Definition 3.3 (Agnostic PAC Learnability). A hypothesis class $\mathcal{H}$ is agnostic PAC learnable if there exist a function $m_{\mathcal{H}} : (0,1)^2 \to \mathbb{N}$ and a learning algorithm with the following property: For every $\epsilon, \delta \in (0,1)$ and for every distribution $\mathcal{D}$ over $\mathcal{X} \times \mathcal{Y}$, when running the learning algorithm on $m \geq m_{\mathcal{H}}(\epsilon, \delta)$ i.i.d. examples generated by $\mathcal{D}$, the algorithm returns a hypothesis h such that, with probability of at least $1-\delta$ (over the choice of the m training examples),

$$L_{\mathcal{D}}(h) \leq \min_{h' \in \mathcal{H}} L_{\mathcal{D}}(h') + \epsilon.$$

Clearly, if the realizability assumption holds, agnostic PAC learning provides the same guarantee as PAC learning. In that sense, agnostic PAC learning generalizes the definition of PAC learning. When the realizability assumption does not hold, no learner can guarantee an arbitrarily small error. Nevertheless, under the definition of agnostic PAC learning, a learner can still declare success if its error is not much larger than the best error achievable by a predictor from the class $\mathcal{H}$. This is in contrast to PAC learning, in which the learner is required to achieve a small error in absolute terms and not relative to the best error achievable by the hypothesis class.

3.2.2 The Scope of Learning Problems Modeled

We next extend our model so that it can be applied to a wide variety of learning tasks. Let us consider some examples of different learning tasks.

- **Multiclass Classification** Our classification does not have to be binary. Take, for example, the task of document classification: We wish to design a program that will be able to classify given documents according to topics (e.g., news, sports, biology, medicine). A learning algorithm for such a task will have access to examples of correctly classified documents and, on the basis of these examples, should output a program that can take as input a new document and output a topic classification for that document. Here, the *domain set* is the set of all potential documents. Once again, we would usually represent documents by a set of *features* that could include counts of different key words in the document, as well as other possibly relevant features like the size of the document or its origin. The *label set* in this task will be the set of possible document topics (so $\mathcal{Y}$ will be some large finite set). Once we determine our domain and label sets, the other components of our framework look exactly the same as in the papaya tasting example; Our *training sample* will be a finite sequence of (feature vector, label) pairs, the learner's output will be a function from the domain set to the label set, and, finally, for our measure of success, we can use the probability, over (document, topic) pairs, of the event that our predictor suggests a wrong label.

- **Regression** In this task, one wishes to find some simple *pattern* in the data – a functional relationship between the $\mathcal{X}$ and $\mathcal{Y}$ components of the data. For example, one wishes to find a linear function that best predicts a baby's birth weight on the basis of ultrasound measures of his head circumference, abdominal circumference, and femur length. Here, our domain set $\mathcal{X}$ is some subset of $\mathbb{R}^3$ (the three ultrasound measurements), and the set of "labels," $\mathcal{Y}$, is the the set of real numbers (the weight in grams). In this context, it is more adequate to call $\mathcal{Y}$ the *target* set. Our training data as well as the learner's output are as before (a finite sequence of (x, y) pairs, and a function from $\mathcal{X}$ to $\mathcal{Y}$ respectively). However, our measure of success is different. We may evaluate the quality of a hypothesis function, $h : \mathcal{X} \to \mathcal{Y}$, by the *expected square difference* between the true labels and their predicted values, namely,

$$L_{\mathcal{D}}(h) \stackrel{\text{def}}{=} \mathop{\mathbb{E}}_{(x,y)\sim\mathcal{D}} (h(x) - y)^2. \tag{3.2}$$

To accommodate a wide range of learning tasks we generalize our formalism of the measure of success as follows:

Generalized Loss Functions

Given any set $\mathcal{H}$ (that plays the role of our hypotheses, or models) and some domain Z let ℓ be any function from $\mathcal{H} \times Z$ to the set of nonnegative real numbers, $\ell : \mathcal{H} \times Z \to \mathbb{R}_+$. We call such functions *loss functions*.

Note that for prediction problems, we have that $Z = \mathcal{X} \times \mathcal{Y}$. However, our notion of the loss function is generalized beyond prediction tasks, and therefore it allows Z to be any domain of examples (for instance, in unsupervised learning tasks such as the one described in Chapter 22, Z is not a product of an instance domain and a label domain).

We now define the *risk function* to be the expected loss of a classifier, $h \in \mathcal{H}$, with respect to a probability distribution D over Z, namely,

$$L_{\mathcal{D}}(h) \stackrel{\text{def}}{=} \mathop{\mathbb{E}}_{z\sim\mathcal{D}} [\ell(h, z)]. \tag{3.3}$$

That is, we consider the expectation of the loss of h over objects z picked randomly according to $\mathcal{D}$. Similarly, we define the *empirical risk* to be the expected loss over a given sample $S = (z_1, \ldots, z_m) \in Z^m$, namely,

$$L_S(h) \stackrel{\text{def}}{=} \frac{1}{m} \sum_{i=1}^{m} \ell(h, z_i). \tag{3.4}$$

The loss functions used in the preceding examples of classification and regression tasks are as follows:

- **0–1 loss:** Here, our random variable z ranges over the set of pairs $\mathcal{X} \times \mathcal{Y}$ and the loss function is

$$\ell_{0-1}(h, (x, y)) \stackrel{\text{def}}{=} \begin{cases} 0 & \text{if } h(x) = y \\ 1 & \text{if } h(x) \neq y \end{cases}$$

  This loss function is used in binary or multiclass classification problems.
  One should note that, for a random variable, α, taking the values $\{0, 1\}$, $\mathbb{E}_{\alpha \sim D}[\alpha] = \mathbb{P}_{\alpha \sim D}[\alpha = 1]$. Consequently, for this loss function, the definitions of $L_{\mathcal{D}}(h)$ given in Equation (3.3) and Equation (3.1) coincide.
- **Square Loss:** Here, our random variable z ranges over the set of pairs $\mathcal{X} \times \mathcal{Y}$ and the loss function is

$$\ell_{sq}(h, (x, y)) \stackrel{\text{def}}{=} (h(x) - y)^2.$$

  This loss function is used in regression problems.

We will later see more examples of useful instantiations of loss functions.

To summarize, we formally define agnostic PAC learnability for general loss functions.

Definition 3.4 (Agnostic PAC Learnability for General Loss Functions). A hypothesis class $\mathcal{H}$ is agnostic PAC learnable with respect to a set Z and a loss function $\ell : \mathcal{H} \times Z \to \mathbb{R}_+$, if there exist a function $m_{\mathcal{H}} : (0, 1)^2 \to \mathbb{N}$ and a learning algorithm with the following property: For every $\epsilon, \delta \in (0, 1)$ and for every distribution $\mathcal{D}$ over Z, when running the learning algorithm on $m \geq m_{\mathcal{H}}(\epsilon, \delta)$ i.i.d. examples generated by $\mathcal{D}$, the algorithm returns $h \in \mathcal{H}$ such that, with probability of at least $1 - \delta$ (over the choice of the m training examples),

$$L_{\mathcal{D}}(h) \leq \min_{h' \in \mathcal{H}} L_{\mathcal{D}}(h') + \epsilon,$$

where $L_{\mathcal{D}}(h) = \mathbb{E}_{z \sim \mathcal{D}}[\ell(h, z)]$.

Remark 3.1 (A Note About Measurability*). In the aforementioned definition, for every $h \in \mathcal{H}$, we view the function $\ell(h, \cdot) : Z \to \mathbb{R}_+$ as a random variable and define $L_{\mathcal{D}}(h)$ to be the expected value of this random variable. For that, we need to require that the function $\ell(h, \cdot)$ is measurable. Formally, we assume that there is a σ-algebra of subsets of Z, over which the probability $\mathcal{D}$ is defined, and that the preimage of every initial segment in $\mathbb{R}_+$ is in this σ-algebra. In the specific case of binary classification with the 0–1 loss, the σ-algebra is over $\mathcal{X} \times \{0, 1\}$ and our assumption on ℓ is equivalent to the assumption that for every h, the set $\{(x, h(x)) : x \in \mathcal{X}\}$ is in the σ-algebra.

Remark 3.2 (Proper versus Representation-Independent Learning*). In the preceding definition, we required that the algorithm will return a hypothesis from $\mathcal{H}$. In some situations, $\mathcal{H}$ is a subset of a set $\mathcal{H}'$, and the loss function can be naturally extended to be a function from $\mathcal{H}' \times Z$ to the reals. In this case, we may allow the algorithm to return a hypothesis $h' \in \mathcal{H}'$, as long as it satisfies the requirement $L_{\mathcal{D}}(h') \leq \min_{h \in \mathcal{H}} L_{\mathcal{D}}(h) + \epsilon$. Allowing the algorithm to output a hypothesis from $\mathcal{H}'$ is called *representation independent* learning, while proper learning occurs when the algorithm must output a hypothesis from $\mathcal{H}$. Representation independent learning is sometimes called "improper learning," although there is nothing improper in representation independent learning.

3.3 SUMMARY

In this chapter we defined our main formal learning model – PAC learning. The basic model relies on the realizability assumption, while the agnostic variant does not impose any restrictions on the underlying distribution over the examples. We also generalized the PAC model to arbitrary loss functions. We will sometimes refer to the most general model simply as PAC learning, omitting the "agnostic" prefix and letting the reader infer what the underlying loss function is from the context. When we would like to emphasize that we are dealing with the original PAC setting we mention that the realizability assumption holds. In Chapter 7 we will discuss other notions of learnability.

3.4 BIBLIOGRAPHIC REMARKS

Our most general definition of agnostic PAC learning with general loss functions follows the works of Vladimir Vapnik and Alexey Chervonenkis (Vapnik and Chervonenkis 1971). In particular, we follow Vapnik's general setting of learning (Vapnik 1982, Vapnik 1992, Vapnik 1995, Vapnik 1998).

PAC learning was introduced by Valiant (1984). Valiant was named the winner of the 2010 Turing Award for the introduction of the PAC model. Valiant's definition requires that the sample complexity will be polynomial in $1/\epsilon$ and in $1/\delta$, as well as in the representation size of hypotheses in the class (see also Kearns and Vazirani (1994)). As we will see in Chapter 6, if a problem is at all PAC learnable then the sample complexity depends polynomially on $1/\epsilon$ and $\log(1/\delta)$. Valiant's definition also requires that the *runtime* of the learning algorithm will be polynomial in these quantities. In contrast, we chose to distinguish between the statistical aspect of learning and the computational aspect of learning. We will elaborate on the computational aspect later on in Chapter 8, where we introduce the full PAC learning model of Valiant. For expository reasons, we use the term PAC learning even when we ignore the runtime aspect of learning. Finally, the formalization of agnostic PAC learning is due to Haussler (1992).

3.5 EXERCISES

3.1 **Monotonicity of Sample Complexity:** Let $\mathcal{H}$ be a hypothesis class for a binary classification task. Suppose that $\mathcal{H}$ is PAC learnable and its sample complexity is given by $m_{\mathcal{H}}(\cdot,\cdot)$. Show that $m_{\mathcal{H}}$ is monotonically nonincreasing in each of its parameters. That is, show that given $\delta \in (0,1)$, and given $0 < \epsilon_1 \leq \epsilon_2 < 1$, we have that $m_{\mathcal{H}}(\epsilon_1,\delta) \geq m_{\mathcal{H}}(\epsilon_2,\delta)$. Similarly, show that given $\epsilon \in (0,1)$, and given $0 < \delta_1 \leq \delta_2 < 1$, we have that $m_{\mathcal{H}}(\epsilon,\delta_1) \geq m_{\mathcal{H}}(\epsilon,\delta_2)$.

3.2 Let $\mathcal{X}$ be a discrete domain, and let $\mathcal{H}_{\text{Singleton}} = \{h_z : z \in \mathcal{X}\} \cup \{h^-\}$, where for each $z \in \mathcal{X}$, h_z is the function defined by $h_z(x) = 1$ if $x = z$ and $h_z(x) = 0$ if $x \neq z$. h^- is simply the all-negative hypothesis, namely, $\forall x \in X$, $h^-(x) = 0$. The realizability assumption here implies that the true hypothesis f labels negatively all examples in the domain, perhaps except one.
   1. Describe an algorithm that implements the ERM rule for learning $\mathcal{H}_{\text{Singleton}}$ in the realizable setup.
   2. Show that $\mathcal{H}_{\text{Singleton}}$ is PAC learnable. Provide an upper bound on the sample complexity.

3.3 Let $\mathcal{X} = \mathbb{R}^2$, $\mathcal{Y} = \{0,1\}$, and let $\mathcal{H}$ be the class of concentric circles in the plane, that is, $\mathcal{H} = \{h_r : r \in \mathbb{R}_+\}$, where $h_r(x) = \mathbb{1}_{[\|x\| \leq r]}$. Prove that $\mathcal{H}$ is PAC learnable (assume realizability), and its sample complexity is bounded by

$$m_{\mathcal{H}}(\epsilon,\delta) \leq \left\lceil \frac{\log(1/\delta)}{\epsilon} \right\rceil.$$

3.4 In this question, we study the hypothesis class of *Boolean conjunctions* defined as follows. The instance space is $\mathcal{X} = \{0,1\}^d$ and the label set is $\mathcal{Y} = \{0,1\}$. A literal over the variables $x_1,\ldots,x_d$ is a simple Boolean function that takes the form $f(\mathbf{x}) = x_i$, for some $i \in [d]$, or $f(\mathbf{x}) = 1 - x_i$ for some $i \in [d]$. We use the notation $\bar{x}_i$ as a shorthand for $1 - x_i$. A conjunction is any product of literals. In Boolean logic, the product is denoted using the $\wedge$ sign. For example, the function $h(\mathbf{x}) = x_1 \cdot (1 - x_2)$ is written as $x_1 \wedge \bar{x}_2$.

We consider the hypothesis class of all conjunctions of literals over the d variables. The empty conjunction is interpreted as the all-positive hypothesis (namely, the function that returns $h(\mathbf{x}) = 1$ for all $\mathbf{x}$). The conjunction $x_1 \wedge \bar{x}_1$ (and similarly any conjunction involving a literal and its negation) is allowed and interpreted as the all-negative hypothesis (namely, the conjunction that returns $h(\mathbf{x}) = 0$ for all $\mathbf{x}$). We assume realizability: Namely, we assume that there exists a Boolean conjunction that generates the labels. Thus, each example $(\mathbf{x}, y) \in \mathcal{X} \times \mathcal{Y}$ consists of an assignment to the d Boolean variables $x_1,\ldots,x_d$, and its truth value (0 for false and 1 for true).

For instance, let $d = 3$ and suppose that the true conjunction is $x_1 \wedge \bar{x}_2$. Then, the training set S might contain the following instances:

$$((1,1,1),0), ((1,0,1),1), ((0,1,0),0)((1,0,0),1).$$

Prove that the hypothesis class of all conjunctions over d variables is PAC learnable and bound its sample complexity. Propose an algorithm that implements the ERM rule, whose runtime is polynomial in $d \cdot m$.

3.5 Let $\mathcal{X}$ be a domain and let $\mathcal{D}_1, \mathcal{D}_2, \ldots, \mathcal{D}_m$ be a sequence of distributions over $\mathcal{X}$. Let $\mathcal{H}$ be a finite class of binary classifiers over $\mathcal{X}$ and let $f \in \mathcal{H}$. Suppose we are getting a sample S of m examples, such that the instances are independent but are not identically distributed; the ith instance is sampled from $\mathcal{D}_i$ and then y_i is set to be $f(\mathbf{x}_i)$. Let $\bar{\mathcal{D}}_m$ denote the average, that is, $\bar{\mathcal{D}}_m = (\mathcal{D}_1 + \cdots + \mathcal{D}_m)/m$.

Fix an accuracy parameter $\epsilon \in (0,1)$. Show that

$$\mathbb{P}\left[\exists h \in \mathcal{H} \text{ s.t. } L_{(\bar{\mathcal{D}}_m, f)}(h) > \epsilon \text{ and } L_{(S,f)}(h) = 0\right] \le |\mathcal{H}| e^{-\epsilon m}.$$

Hint: Use the geometric-arithmetic mean inequality.

3.6 Let $\mathcal{H}$ be a hypothesis class of binary classifiers. Show that if $\mathcal{H}$ is agnostic PAC learnable, then $\mathcal{H}$ is PAC learnable as well. Furthermore, if A is a successful agnostic PAC learner for $\mathcal{H}$, then A is also a successful PAC learner for $\mathcal{H}$.

3.7 (*) **The Bayes optimal predictor:** Show that for every probability distribution $\mathcal{D}$, the Bayes optimal predictor $f_{\mathcal{D}}$ is optimal, in the sense that for every classifier g from $\mathcal{X}$ to $\{0,1\}$, $L_{\mathcal{D}}(f_{\mathcal{D}}) \le L_{\mathcal{D}}(g)$.

3.8 (*) We say that a learning algorithm A *is better than* B *with respect to* some probability distribution, $\mathcal{D}$, if

$$L_{\mathcal{D}}(A(S)) \le L_{\mathcal{D}}(B(S))$$

for all samples $S \in (\mathcal{X} \times \{0,1\})^m$. We say that a learning algorithm A *is better than* B, if it is better than B with respect to all probability distributions $\mathcal{D}$ over $\mathcal{X} \times \{0,1\}$.

1. A probabilistic label predictor is a function that assigns to every domain point x a probability value, $h(x) \in [0,1]$, that determines the probability of predicting the label 1. That is, given such an h and an input, x, the label for x is predicted by tossing a coin with bias $h(x)$ toward Heads and predicting 1 iff the coin comes up Heads. Formally, we define a probabilistic label predictor as a function, $h : \mathcal{X} \to [0,1]$. The loss of such h on an example (x,y) is defined to be $|h(x) - y|$, which is exactly the probability that the prediction of h will not be equal to y. Note that if h is deterministic, that is, returns values in $\{0,1\}$, then $|h(x) - y| = \mathbb{1}_{[h(x) \neq y]}$.
Prove that for every data-generating distribution $\mathcal{D}$ over $\mathcal{X} \times \{0,1\}$, the Bayes optimal predictor has the smallest risk (w.r.t. the loss function $\ell(h,(x,y)) = |h(x) - y|$, among all possible label predictors, including probabilistic ones).
2. Let $\mathcal{X}$ be a domain and $\{0,1\}$ be a set of labels. Prove that for every distribution $\mathcal{D}$ over $\mathcal{X} \times \{0,1\}$, there exist a learning algorithm $A_{\mathcal{D}}$ that is better than any other learning algorithm with respect to $\mathcal{D}$.
3. Prove that for every learning algorithm A there exist a probability distribution, $\mathcal{D}$, and a learning algorithm B such that A is not better than B w.r.t. $\mathcal{D}$.

3.9 Consider a variant of the PAC model in which there are two example oracles: one that generates positive examples and one that generates negative examples, both according to the underlying distribution $\mathcal{D}$ on $\mathcal{X}$. Formally, given a target function $f : \mathcal{X} \to \{0,1\}$, let $\mathcal{D}^+$ be the distribution over $\mathcal{X}^+ = \{x \in \mathcal{X} : f(x) = 1\}$ defined by $\mathcal{D}^+(A) = \mathcal{D}(A)/\mathcal{D}(\mathcal{X}^+)$, for every $A \subset \mathcal{X}^+$. Similarly, $\mathcal{D}^-$ is the distribution over $\mathcal{X}^-$ induced by $\mathcal{D}$.

The definition of PAC learnability in the two-oracle model is the same as the standard definition of PAC learnability except that here the learner has access to $m^+_{\mathcal{H}}(\epsilon,\delta)$ i.i.d. examples from $\mathcal{D}^+$ and $m^-(\epsilon,\delta)$ i.i.d. examples from $\mathcal{D}^-$. The learner's goal is to output h s.t. with probability at least $1-\delta$ (over the choice of the two training sets, and possibly over the nondeterministic decisions made by the learning algorithm), both $L_{(\mathcal{D}^+,f)}(h) \le \epsilon$ and $L_{(\mathcal{D}^-,f)}(h) \le \epsilon$.

1. (*) Show that if $\mathcal{H}$ is PAC learnable (in the standard one-oracle model), then $\mathcal{H}$ is PAC learnable in the two-oracle model.
2. (**) Define h^+ to be the always-plus hypothesis and h^- to be the always-minus hypothesis. Assume that $h^+, h^- \in \mathcal{H}$. Show that if $\mathcal{H}$ is PAC learnable in the two-oracle model, then $\mathcal{H}$ is PAC learnable in the standard one-oracle model.

4

Learning via Uniform Convergence

The first formal learning model that we have discussed was the PAC model. In Chapter 2 we have shown that under the realizability assumption, any finite hypothesis class is PAC learnable. In this chapter we will develop a general tool, *uniform convergence*, and apply it to show that any finite class is learnable in the agnostic PAC model with general loss functions, as long as the range loss function is bounded.

4.1 UNIFORM CONVERGENCE IS SUFFICIENT FOR LEARNABILITY

The idea behind the learning condition discussed in this chapter is very simple. Recall that, given a hypothesis class, $\mathcal{H}$, the ERM learning paradigm works as follows: Upon receiving a training sample, S, the learner evaluates the risk (or error) of each h in $\mathcal{H}$ on the given sample and outputs a member of $\mathcal{H}$ that minimizes this empirical risk. The hope is that an h that minimizes the empirical risk with respect to S is a risk minimizer (or has risk close to the minimum) with respect to the true data probability distribution as well. For that, it suffices to ensure that the empirical risks of all members of $\mathcal{H}$ are good approximations of their true risk. Put another way, we need that uniformly over all hypotheses in the hypothesis class, the empirical risk will be close to the true risk, as formalized in the following.

Definition 4.1 (ϵ-representative sample). A training set S is called ϵ-representative (w.r.t. domain Z, hypothesis class $\mathcal{H}$, loss function ℓ, and distribution $\mathcal{D}$) if

$$\forall h \in \mathcal{H}, \ |L_S(h) - L_{\mathcal{D}}(h)| \leq \epsilon.$$

The next simple lemma states that whenever the sample is $(\epsilon/2)$-representative, the ERM learning rule is guaranteed to return a good hypothesis.

Lemma 4.2. *Assume that a training set S is $\frac{\epsilon}{2}$-representative (w.r.t. domain Z, hypothesis class $\mathcal{H}$, loss function ℓ, and distribution $\mathcal{D}$). Then, any output of* $\mathrm{ERM}_{\mathcal{H}}(S)$*, namely, any* $h_S \in \operatorname{argmin}_{h\in\mathcal{H}} L_S(h)$*, satisfies*

$$L_{\mathcal{D}}(h_S) \leq \min_{h\in\mathcal{H}} L_{\mathcal{D}}(h) + \epsilon.$$

Proof. For every $h \in \mathcal{H}$,

$$L_{\mathcal{D}}(h_S) \le L_S(h_S) + \tfrac{\epsilon}{2} \le L_S(h) + \tfrac{\epsilon}{2} \le L_{\mathcal{D}}(h) + \tfrac{\epsilon}{2} + \tfrac{\epsilon}{2} = L_{\mathcal{D}}(h) + \epsilon,$$

where the first and third inequalities are due to the assumption that S is $\frac{\epsilon}{2}$-representative (Definition 4.1) and the second inequality holds since h_S is an ERM predictor. □

The preceding lemma implies that to ensure that the ERM rule is an agnostic PAC learner, it suffices to show that with probability of at least $1-\delta$ over the random choice of a training set, it will be an ϵ-representative training set. The uniform convergence condition formalizes this requirement.

Definition 4.3 (Uniform Convergence). We say that a hypothesis class $\mathcal{H}$ has the *uniform convergence property* (w.r.t. a domain Z and a loss function ℓ) if there exists a function $m_{\mathcal{H}}^{\text{UC}} : (0,1)^2 \to \mathbb{N}$ such that for every $\epsilon, \delta \in (0,1)$ and for every probability distribution $\mathcal{D}$ over Z, if S is a sample of $m \ge m_{\mathcal{H}}^{\text{UC}}(\epsilon,\delta)$ examples drawn i.i.d. according to $\mathcal{D}$, then, with probability of at least $1-\delta$, S is ϵ-representative.

Similar to the definition of sample complexity for PAC learning, the function $m_{\mathcal{H}}^{\text{UC}}$ measures the (minimal) sample complexity of obtaining the uniform convergence property, namely, how many examples we need to ensure that with probability of at least $1-\delta$ the sample would be ϵ-representative.
The term *uniform* here refers to having a fixed sample size that works for all members of $\mathcal{H}$ and over all possible probability distributions over the domain.

The following corollary follows directly from Lemma 4.2 and the definition of uniform convergence.

Corollary 4.4. *If a class $\mathcal{H}$ has the uniform convergence property with a function $m_{\mathcal{H}}^{UC}$ then the class is agnostically PAC learnable with the sample complexity $m_{\mathcal{H}}(\epsilon,\delta) \le m_{\mathcal{H}}^{UC}(\epsilon/2,\delta)$. Furthermore, in that case, the* $\text{ERM}_{\mathcal{H}}$ *paradigm is a successful agnostic PAC learner for $\mathcal{H}$.*

4.2 FINITE CLASSES ARE AGNOSTIC PAC LEARNABLE

In view of Corollary 4.4, the claim that every finite hypothesis class is agnostic PAC learnable will follow once we establish that uniform convergence holds for a finite hypothesis class.

To show that uniform convergence holds we follow a two step argument, similar to the derivation in Chapter 2. The first step applies the union bound while the second step employs a measure concentration inequality. We now explain these two steps in detail.

Fix some ϵ, δ. We need to find a sample size m that guarantees that for any $\mathcal{D}$, with probability of at least $1-\delta$ of the choice of $S = (z_1,\ldots,z_m)$ sampled i.i.d. from $\mathcal{D}$ we have that for all $h \in \mathcal{H}$, $|L_S(h) - L_{\mathcal{D}}(h)| \le \epsilon$. That is,

$$\mathcal{D}^m(\{S : \forall h \in \mathcal{H}, |L_S(h) - L_{\mathcal{D}}(h)| \le \epsilon\}) \ge 1-\delta.$$

Equivalently, we need to show that

$$\mathcal{D}^m(\{S : \exists h \in \mathcal{H}, |L_S(h) - L_{\mathcal{D}}(h)| > \epsilon\}) < \delta.$$

Writing

$$\{S : \exists h \in \mathcal{H}, |L_S(h) - L_{\mathcal{D}}(h)| > \epsilon\} = \cup_{h\in\mathcal{H}}\{S : |L_S(h) - L_{\mathcal{D}}(h)| > \epsilon\},$$

and applying the union bound (Lemma 2.2) we obtain

$$\mathcal{D}^m(\{S : \exists h \in \mathcal{H}, |L_S(h) - L_{\mathcal{D}}(h)| > \epsilon\}) \le \sum_{h\in\mathcal{H}} \mathcal{D}^m(\{S : |L_S(h) - L_{\mathcal{D}}(h)| > \epsilon\}). \quad (4.1)$$

Our second step will be to argue that each summand of the right-hand side of this inequality is small enough (for a sufficiently large m). That is, we will show that for any fixed hypothesis, h, (which is chosen in advance prior to the sampling of the training set), the gap between the true and empirical risks, $|L_S(h) - L_{\mathcal{D}}(h)|$, is likely to be small.

Recall that $L_{\mathcal{D}}(h) = \mathbb{E}_{z\sim\mathcal{D}}[\ell(h,z)]$ and that $L_S(h) = \frac{1}{m}\sum_{i=1}^{m}\ell(h,z_i)$. Since each z_i is sampled i.i.d. from $\mathcal{D}$, the expected value of the random variable $\ell(h,z_i)$ is $L_{\mathcal{D}}(h)$. By the linearity of expectation, it follows that $L_{\mathcal{D}}(h)$ is also the expected value of $L_S(h)$. Hence, the quantity $|L_{\mathcal{D}}(h) - L_S(h)|$ is the deviation of the random variable $L_S(h)$ from its expectation. We therefore need to show that the measure of $L_S(h)$ is *concentrated* around its expected value.

A basic statistical fact, the *law of large numbers*, states that when m goes to infinity, empirical averages converge to their true expectation. This is true for $L_S(h)$, since it is the empirical average of m i.i.d random variables. However, since the law of large numbers is only an asymptotic result, it provides no information about the gap between the empirically estimated error and its true value for any given, finite, sample size.

Instead, we will use a measure concentration inequality due to Hoeffding, which quantifies the gap between empirical averages and their expected value.

Lemma 4.5 (Hoeffding's Inequality). *Let $\theta_1,\ldots,\theta_m$ be a sequence of i.i.d. random variables and assume that for all i, $\mathbb{E}[\theta_i] = \mu$ and $\mathbb{P}[a \le \theta_i \le b] = 1$. Then, for any $\epsilon > 0$*

$$\mathbb{P}\left[\left|\frac{1}{m}\sum_{i=1}^{m}\theta_i - \mu\right| > \epsilon\right] \le 2\exp\left(-2m\epsilon^2/(b-a)^2\right).$$

The proof can be found in Appendix B.

Getting back to our problem, let θ_i be the random variable $\ell(h,z_i)$. Since h is fixed and $z_1,\ldots,z_m$ are sampled i.i.d., it follows that $\theta_1,\ldots,\theta_m$ are also i.i.d. random variables. Furthermore, $L_S(h) = \frac{1}{m}\sum_{i=1}^{m}\theta_i$ and $L_{\mathcal{D}}(h) = \mu$. Let us further assume that the range of ℓ is $[0,1]$ and therefore $\theta_i \in [0,1]$. We therefore obtain that

$$\mathcal{D}^m(\{S : |L_S(h) - L_{\mathcal{D}}(h)| > \epsilon\}) = \mathbb{P}\left[\left|\frac{1}{m}\sum_{i=1}^{m}\theta_i - \mu\right| > \epsilon\right] \le 2\exp\left(-2m\epsilon^2\right). \quad (4.2)$$

Combining this with Equation (4.1) yields

$$\begin{aligned}\mathcal{D}^m(\{S : \exists h \in \mathcal{H}, |L_S(h) - L_{\mathcal{D}}(h)| > \epsilon\}) &\le \sum_{h\in\mathcal{H}} 2\exp\left(-2m\epsilon^2\right) \\ &= 2|\mathcal{H}|\exp\left(-2m\epsilon^2\right).\end{aligned}$$

Finally, if we choose

$$m \geq \frac{\log(2|\mathcal{H}|/\delta)}{2\epsilon^2}$$

then

$$\mathcal{D}^m(\{S : \exists h \in \mathcal{H}, |L_S(h) - L_{\mathcal{D}}(h)| > \epsilon\}) \leq \delta.$$

Corollary 4.6. *Let $\mathcal{H}$ be a finite hypothesis class, let Z be a domain, and let $\ell : \mathcal{H} \times Z \to [0,1]$ be a loss function. Then, $\mathcal{H}$ enjoys the uniform convergence property with sample complexity*

$$m_{\mathcal{H}}^{UC}(\epsilon, \delta) \leq \left\lceil \frac{\log(2|\mathcal{H}|/\delta)}{2\epsilon^2} \right\rceil.$$

Furthermore, the class is agnostically PAC learnable using the ERM algorithm with sample complexity

$$m_{\mathcal{H}}(\epsilon, \delta) \leq m_{\mathcal{H}}^{UC}(\epsilon/2, \delta) \leq \left\lceil \frac{2\log(2|\mathcal{H}|/\delta)}{\epsilon^2} \right\rceil.$$

Remark 4.1 (The "Discretization Trick"). While the preceding corollary only applies to finite hypothesis classes, there is a simple trick that allows us to get a very good estimate of the practical sample complexity of infinite hypothesis classes. Consider a hypothesis class that is parameterized by d parameters. For example, let $\mathcal{X} = \mathbb{R}$, $\mathcal{Y} = \{\pm 1\}$, and the hypothesis class, $\mathcal{H}$, be all functions of the form $h_\theta(x) = \text{sign}(x - \theta)$. That is, each hypothesis is parameterized by one parameter, $\theta \in \mathbb{R}$, and the hypothesis outputs 1 for all instances larger than θ and outputs -1 for instances smaller than θ. This is a hypothesis class of an infinite size. However, if we are going to learn this hypothesis class in practice, using a computer, we will probably maintain real numbers using floating point representation, say, of 64 bits. It follows that in practice, our hypothesis class is parameterized by the set of scalars that can be represented using a 64 bits floating point number. There are at most 2^{64} such numbers; hence the actual size of our hypothesis class is at most 2^{64}. More generally, if our hypothesis class is parameterized by d numbers, in practice we learn a hypothesis class of size at most 2^{64d}. Applying Corollary 4.6 we obtain that the sample complexity of such classes is bounded by $\frac{128d + 2\log(2/\delta)}{\epsilon^2}$. This upper bound on the sample complexity has the deficiency of being dependent on the specific representation of real numbers used by our machine. In Chapter 6 we will introduce a rigorous way to analyze the sample complexity of infinite size hypothesis classes. Nevertheless, the discretization trick can be used to get a rough estimate of the sample complexity in many practical situations.

4.3 SUMMARY

If the uniform convergence property holds for a hypothesis class $\mathcal{H}$ then in most cases the empirical risks of hypotheses in $\mathcal{H}$ will faithfully represent their true risks. Uniform convergence suffices for agnostic PAC learnability using the ERM rule. We have shown that finite hypothesis classes enjoy the uniform convergence property and are hence agnostic PAC learnable.

4.4 BIBLIOGRAPHIC REMARKS

Classes of functions for which the uniform convergence property holds are also called Glivenko-Cantelli classes, named after Valery Ivanovich Glivenko and Francesco Paolo Cantelli, who proved the first uniform convergence result in the 1930s. See (Dudley, Gine & Zinn 1991). The relation between uniform convergence and learnability was thoroughly studied by Vapnik – see (Vapnik 1992, Vapnik 1995, Vapnik 1998). In fact, as we will see later in Chapter 6, the fundamental theorem of learning theory states that in binary classification problems, uniform convergence is not only a sufficient condition for learnability but is also a necessary condition. This is not the case for more general learning problems (see (Shalev-Shwartz, Shamir, Srebro & Sridharan 2010)).

4.5 EXERCISES

4.1 In this exercise, we show that the (ϵ, δ) requirement on the convergence of errors in our definitions of PAC learning, is, in fact, quite close to a simpler looking requirement about averages (or expectations). Prove that the following two statements are equivalent (for any learning algorithm A, any probability distribution $\mathcal{D}$, and any loss function whose range is $[0,1]$):

1. For every $\epsilon, \delta > 0$, there exists $m(\epsilon, \delta)$ such that $\forall m \geq m(\epsilon, \delta)$

$$\underset{S \sim \mathcal{D}^m}{\mathbb{P}} [L_{\mathcal{D}}(A(S)) > \epsilon] < \delta$$

2.

$$\lim_{m \to \infty} \underset{S \sim \mathcal{D}^m}{\mathbb{E}} [L_{\mathcal{D}}(A(S))] = 0$$

(where $\mathbb{E}_{S \sim \mathcal{D}^m}$ denotes the expectation over samples S of size m).

4.2 **Bounded loss functions:** In Corollary 4.6 we assumed that the range of the loss function is $[0,1]$. Prove that if the range of the loss function is $[a,b]$ then the sample complexity satisfies

$$m_{\mathcal{H}}(\epsilon, \delta) \leq m_{\mathcal{H}}^{\mathrm{UC}}(\epsilon/2, \delta) \leq \left\lceil \frac{2\log(2|\mathcal{H}|/\delta)(b-a)^2}{\epsilon^2} \right\rceil.$$

5

The Bias-Complexity Trade-off

In Chapter 2 we saw that unless one is careful, the training data can mislead the learner, and result in overfitting. To overcome this problem, we restricted the search space to some hypothesis class $\mathcal{H}$. Such a hypothesis class can be viewed as reflecting some prior knowledge that the learner has about the task – a belief that one of the members of the class $\mathcal{H}$ is a low-error model for the task. For example, in our papayas taste problem, on the basis of our previous experience with other fruits, we may assume that some rectangle in the color-hardness plane predicts (at least approximately) the papaya's tastiness.

Is such prior knowledge really necessary for the success of learning? Maybe there exists some kind of universal learner, that is, a learner who has no prior knowledge about a certain task and is ready to be challenged by any task? Let us elaborate on this point. A specific learning task is defined by an unknown distribution $\mathcal{D}$ over $\mathcal{X} \times \mathcal{Y}$, where the goal of the learner is to find a predictor $h : \mathcal{X} \to \mathcal{Y}$, whose risk, $L_{\mathcal{D}}(h)$, is small enough. The question is therefore whether there exist a learning algorithm A and a training set size m, such that for every distribution $\mathcal{D}$, if A receives m i.i.d. examples from $\mathcal{D}$, there is a high chance it outputs a predictor h that has a low risk.

The first part of this chapter addresses this question formally. The No-Free-Lunch theorem states that no such universal learner exists. To be more precise, the theorem states that for binary classification prediction tasks, for every learner there exists a distribution on which it fails. We say that the learner fails if, upon receiving i.i.d. examples from that distribution, its output hypothesis is likely to have a large risk, say, ≥ 0.3, whereas for the same distribution, there exists another learner that will output a hypothesis with a small risk. In other words, the theorem states that no learner can succeed on all learnable tasks – every learner has tasks on which it fails while other learners succeed.

Therefore, when approaching a particular learning problem, defined by some distribution $\mathcal{D}$, we should have some prior knowledge on $\mathcal{D}$. One type of such prior knowledge is that $\mathcal{D}$ comes from some specific parametric family of distributions. We will study learning under such assumptions later on in Chapter 24. Another type of prior knowledge on $\mathcal{D}$, which we assumed when defining the PAC learning model, is that there exists h in some predefined hypothesis class $\mathcal{H}$, such that $L_{\mathcal{D}}(h) = 0$. A softer type of prior knowledge on $\mathcal{D}$ is assuming that $\min_{h\in\mathcal{H}} L_{\mathcal{D}}(h)$ is small. In a sense, this weaker assumption on $\mathcal{D}$ is a prerequisite for using the agnostic PAC model, in which we require that the risk of the output hypothesis will not be much larger than $\min_{h\in\mathcal{H}} L_{\mathcal{D}}(h)$.

In the second part of this chapter we study the benefits and pitfalls of using a hypothesis class as a means of formalizing prior knowledge. We decompose the error of an ERM algorithm over a class $\mathcal{H}$ into two components. The first component reflects the quality of our prior knowledge, measured by the minimal risk of a hypothesis in our hypothesis class, $\min_{h\in\mathcal{H}} L_{\mathcal{D}}(h)$. This component is also called the *approximation error*, or the *bias* of the algorithm toward choosing a hypothesis from $\mathcal{H}$. The second component is the error due to overfitting, which depends on the size or the complexity of the class $\mathcal{H}$ and is called the *estimation error*. These two terms imply a tradeoff between choosing a more complex $\mathcal{H}$ (which can decrease the bias but increases the risk of overfitting) or a less complex $\mathcal{H}$ (which might increase the bias but decreases the potential overfitting).

5.1 THE NO-FREE-LUNCH THEOREM

In this part we prove that there is no universal learner. We do this by showing that no learner can succeed on all learning tasks, as formalized in the following theorem:

Theorem 5.1. (No-Free-Lunch) *Let A be any learning algorithm for the task of binary classification with respect to the* $0-1$ *loss over a domain $\mathcal{X}$. Let m be any number smaller than $|\mathcal{X}|/2$, representing a training set size. Then, there exists a distribution $\mathcal{D}$ over $\mathcal{X} \times \{0,1\}$ such that:*

1. *There exists a function $f : \mathcal{X} \to \{0,1\}$ with $L_{\mathcal{D}}(f) = 0$.*
2. *With probability of at least $1/7$ over the choice of $S \sim \mathcal{D}^m$ we have that $L_{\mathcal{D}}(A(S)) \geq 1/8$.*

This theorem states that for every learner, there exists a task on which it fails, even though that task can be successfully learned by another learner. Indeed, a trivial successful learner in this case would be an ERM learner with the hypothesis class $\mathcal{H} = \{f\}$, or more generally, ERM with respect to any finite hypothesis class that contains f and whose size satisfies the equation $m \geq 8\log(7|\mathcal{H}|/6)$ (see Corollary 2.3).

Proof. Let C be a subset of $\mathcal{X}$ of size $2m$. The intuition of the proof is that any learning algorithm that observes only half of the instances in C has no information on what should be the labels of the rest of the instances in C. Therefore, there exists a "reality," that is, some target function f, that would contradict the labels that $A(S)$ predicts on the unobserved instances in C.

Note that there are $T = 2^{2m}$ possible functions from C to $\{0,1\}$. Denote these functions by $f_1,\ldots,f_T$. For each such function, let $\mathcal{D}_i$ be a distribution over $C \times \{0,1\}$ defined by

$$\mathcal{D}_i(\{(x,y)\}) = \begin{cases} 1/|C| & \text{if } y = f_i(x) \\ 0 & \text{otherwise.} \end{cases}$$

That is, the probability to choose a pair (x, y) is $1/|C|$ if the label y is indeed the true label according to f_i, and the probability is 0 if $y \neq f_i(x)$. Clearly, $L_{\mathcal{D}_i}(f_i) = 0$.

We will show that for every algorithm, A, that receives a training set of m examples from $C \times \{0,1\}$ and returns a function $A(S) : C \to \{0,1\}$, it holds that

$$\max_{i \in [T]} \mathop{\mathbb{E}}_{S \sim \mathcal{D}_i^m} [L_{\mathcal{D}_i}(A(S))] \geq 1/4. \tag{5.1}$$

Clearly, this means that for every algorithm, A', that receives a training set of m examples from $\mathcal{X} \times \{0,1\}$ there exist a function $f : \mathcal{X} \to \{0,1\}$ and a distribution $\mathcal{D}$ over $\mathcal{X} \times \{0,1\}$, such that $L_{\mathcal{D}}(f) = 0$ and

$$\mathop{\mathbb{E}}_{S \sim \mathcal{D}^m} [L_{\mathcal{D}}(A'(S))] \geq 1/4. \tag{5.2}$$

It is easy to verify that the preceding suffices for showing that $\mathbb{P}[L_{\mathcal{D}}(A'(S)) \geq 1/8] \geq 1/7$, which is what we need to prove (see Exercise 5.1).

We now turn to proving that Equation (5.1) holds. There are $k = (2m)^m$ possible sequences of m examples from C. Denote these sequences by $S_1, \ldots, S_k$. Also, if $S_j = (x_1, \ldots, x_m)$ we denote by S_j^i the sequence containing the instances in S_j labeled by the function f_i, namely, $S_j^i = ((x_1, f_i(x_1)), \ldots, (x_m, f_i(x_m)))$. If the distribution is $\mathcal{D}_i$ then the possible training sets A can receive are $S_1^i, \ldots, S_k^i$, and all these training sets have the same probability of being sampled. Therefore,

$$\mathop{\mathbb{E}}_{S \sim \mathcal{D}_i^m} [L_{\mathcal{D}_i}(A(S))] = \frac{1}{k} \sum_{j=1}^{k} L_{\mathcal{D}_i}(A(S_j^i)). \tag{5.3}$$

Using the facts that "maximum" is larger than "average" and that "average" is larger than "minimum," we have

$$\begin{aligned}
\max_{i \in [T]} \frac{1}{k} \sum_{j=1}^{k} L_{\mathcal{D}_i}(A(S_j^i)) &\geq \frac{1}{T} \sum_{i=1}^{T} \frac{1}{k} \sum_{j=1}^{k} L_{\mathcal{D}_i}(A(S_j^i)) \\
&= \frac{1}{k} \sum_{j=1}^{k} \frac{1}{T} \sum_{i=1}^{T} L_{\mathcal{D}_i}(A(S_j^i)) \\
&\geq \min_{j \in [k]} \frac{1}{T} \sum_{i=1}^{T} L_{\mathcal{D}_i}(A(S_j^i)).
\end{aligned} \tag{5.4}$$

Next, fix some $j \in [k]$. Denote $S_j = (x_1, \ldots, x_m)$ and let $v_1, \ldots, v_p$ be the examples in C that do not appear in S_j. Clearly, $p \geq m$. Therefore, for every function $h : C \to$

$\{0,1\}$ and every i we have

$$\begin{aligned}L_{\mathcal{D}_i}(h) &= \frac{1}{2m}\sum_{x\in C}\mathbb{1}_{[h(x)\neq f_i(x)]}\\ &\geq \frac{1}{2m}\sum_{r=1}^{p}\mathbb{1}_{[h(v_r)\neq f_i(v_r)]}\\ &\geq \frac{1}{2p}\sum_{r=1}^{p}\mathbb{1}_{[h(v_r)\neq f_i(v_r)]}.\end{aligned} \tag{5.5}$$

Hence,

$$\begin{aligned}\frac{1}{T}\sum_{i=1}^{T} L_{\mathcal{D}_i}(A(S_j^i)) &\geq \frac{1}{T}\sum_{i=1}^{T}\frac{1}{2p}\sum_{r=1}^{p}\mathbb{1}_{[A(S_j^i)(v_r)\neq f_i(v_r)]}\\ &= \frac{1}{2p}\sum_{r=1}^{p}\frac{1}{T}\sum_{i=1}^{T}\mathbb{1}_{[A(S_j^i)(v_r)\neq f_i(v_r)]}\\ &\geq \frac{1}{2}\cdot\min_{r\in[p]}\frac{1}{T}\sum_{i=1}^{T}\mathbb{1}_{[A(S_j^i)(v_r)\neq f_i(v_r)]}.\end{aligned} \tag{5.6}$$

Next, fix some $r\in[p]$. We can partition all the functions in $f_1,\ldots,f_T$ into $T/2$ disjoint pairs, where for a pair $(f_i,f_{i'})$ we have that for every $c\in C$, $f_i(c)\neq f_{i'}(c)$ if and only if $c=v_r$. Since for such a pair we must have $S_j^i = S_j^{i'}$, it follows that

$$\mathbb{1}_{[A(S_j^i)(v_r)\neq f_i(v_r)]} + \mathbb{1}_{[A(S_j^{i'})(v_r)\neq f_{i'}(v_r)]} = 1,$$

which yields

$$\frac{1}{T}\sum_{i=1}^{T}\mathbb{1}_{[A(S_j^i)(v_r)\neq f_i(v_r)]} = \frac{1}{2}.$$

Combining this with Equation (5.6), Equation (5.4), and Equation (5.3), we obtain that Equation (5.1) holds, which concludes our proof. □

5.1.1 No-Free-Lunch and Prior Knowledge

How does the No-Free-Lunch result relate to the need for prior knowledge? Let us consider an ERM predictor over the hypothesis class $\mathcal{H}$ of all the functions f from X to $\{0,1\}$. This class represents lack of prior knowledge: Every possible function from the domain to the label set is considered a good candidate. According to the No-Free-Lunch theorem, any algorithm that chooses its output from hypotheses in $\mathcal{H}$, and in particular the ERM predictor, will fail on some learning task. Therefore, this class is not PAC learnable, as formalized in the following corollary:

Corollary 5.2. *Let $\mathcal{X}$ be an infinite domain set and let $\mathcal{H}$ be the set of all functions from $\mathcal{X}$ to $\{0,1\}$. Then, $\mathcal{H}$ is not PAC learnable.*

Proof. Assume, by way of contradiction, that the class is learnable. Choose some $\epsilon < 1/8$ and $\delta < 1/7$. By the definition of PAC learnability, there must be some learning algorithm A and an integer $m = m(\epsilon, \delta)$, such that for any data-generating distribution over $\mathcal{X} \times \{0,1\}$, if for some function $f : \mathcal{X} \to \{0,1\}$, $L_{\mathcal{D}}(f) = 0$, then with probability greater than $1 - \delta$ when A is applied to samples S of size m, generated i.i.d. by $\mathcal{D}$, $L_{\mathcal{D}}(A(S)) \leq \epsilon$. However, applying the No-Free-Lunch theorem, since $|\mathcal{X}| > 2m$, for every learning algorithm (and in particular for the algorithm A), there exists a distribution $\mathcal{D}$ such that with probability greater than $1/7 > \delta$, $L_{\mathcal{D}}(A(S)) > 1/8 > \epsilon$, which leads to the desired contradiction. □

How can we prevent such failures? We can escape the hazards foreseen by the No-Free-Lunch theorem by using our prior knowledge about a specific learning task, to avoid the distributions that will cause us to fail when learning that task. Such prior knowledge can be expressed by restricting our hypothesis class.

But how should we choose a good hypothesis class? On the one hand, we want to believe that this class includes the hypothesis that has no error at all (in the PAC setting), or at least that the smallest error achievable by a hypothesis from this class is indeed rather small (in the agnostic setting). On the other hand, we have just seen that we cannot simply choose the richest class – the class of all functions over the given domain. This tradeoff is discussed in the following section.

5.2 ERROR DECOMPOSITION

To answer this question we decompose the error of an $\mathrm{ERM}_{\mathcal{H}}$ predictor into two components as follows. Let h_S be an $\mathrm{ERM}_{\mathcal{H}}$ hypothesis. Then, we can write

$$L_{\mathcal{D}}(h_S) = \epsilon_{\mathrm{app}} + \epsilon_{\mathrm{est}} \quad \text{where}: \; \epsilon_{\mathrm{app}} = \min_{h \in \mathcal{H}} L_{\mathcal{D}}(h), \quad \epsilon_{\mathrm{est}} = L_{\mathcal{D}}(h_S) - \epsilon_{\mathrm{app}}. \tag{5.7}$$

- **The Approximation Error** – the minimum risk achievable by a predictor in the hypothesis class. This term measures how much risk we have because we restrict ourselves to a specific class, namely, how much *inductive bias* we have. The approximation error does not depend on the sample size and is determined by the hypothesis class chosen. Enlarging the hypothesis class can decrease the approximation error.

  Under the realizability assumption, the approximation error is zero. In the agnostic case, however, the approximation error can be large.[1]
- **The Estimation Error** – the difference between the approximation error and the error achieved by the ERM predictor. The estimation error results because the empirical risk (i.e., training error) is only an estimate of the true risk, and so the predictor minimizing the empirical risk is only an estimate of the predictor minimizing the true risk.

  The quality of this estimation depends on the training set size and on the size, or complexity, of the hypothesis class. As we have shown, for a finite hypothesis class, ϵ_{est} increases (logarithmically) with $|\mathcal{H}|$ and decreases with m. We can

[1] In fact, it always includes the error of the Bayes optimal predictor (see Chapter 3), the minimal yet inevitable error, because of the possible nondeterminism of the world in this model. Sometimes in the literature the term *approximation error* refers not to $\min_{h \in \mathcal{H}} L_{\mathcal{D}}(h)$, but rather to the excess error over that of the Bayes optimal predictor, namely, $\min_{h \in \mathcal{H}} L_{\mathcal{D}}(h) - \epsilon_{\mathrm{Bayes}}$.

think of the size of $\mathcal{H}$ as a measure of its complexity. In future chapters we will define other complexity measures of hypothesis classes.

Since our goal is to minimize the total risk, we face a tradeoff, called the *bias-complexity tradeoff*. On one hand, choosing $\mathcal{H}$ to be a very rich class decreases the approximation error but at the same time might increase the estimation error, as a rich $\mathcal{H}$ might lead to *overfitting*. On the other hand, choosing $\mathcal{H}$ to be a very small set reduces the estimation error but might increase the approximation error or, in other words, might lead to *underfitting*. Of course, a great choice for $\mathcal{H}$ is the class that contains only one classifier – the Bayes optimal classifier. But the Bayes optimal classifier depends on the underlying distribution $\mathcal{D}$, which we do not know (indeed, learning would have been unnecessary had we known $\mathcal{D}$).

Learning theory studies how rich we can make $\mathcal{H}$ while still maintaining reasonable estimation error. In many cases, empirical research focuses on designing good hypothesis classes for a certain domain. Here, "good" means classes for which the approximation error would not be excessively high. The idea is that although we are not experts and do not know how to construct the optimal classifier, we still have some prior knowledge of the specific problem at hand, which enables us to design hypothesis classes for which both the approximation error and the estimation error are not too large. Getting back to our papayas example, we do not know how exactly the color and hardness of a papaya predict its taste, but we do know that papaya is a fruit and on the basis of previous experience with other fruit we conjecture that a rectangle in the color-hardness space may be a good predictor.

5.3 SUMMARY

The No-Free-Lunch theorem states that there is no universal learner. Every learner has to be specified to some task, and use some prior knowledge about that task, in order to succeed. So far we have modeled our prior knowledge by restricting our output hypothesis to be a member of a chosen hypothesis class. When choosing this hypothesis class, we face a tradeoff, between a larger, or more complex, class that is more likely to have a small approximation error, and a more restricted class that would guarantee that the estimation error will be small. In the next chapter we will study in more detail the behavior of the estimation error. In Chapter 7 we will discuss alternative ways to express prior knowledge.

5.4 BIBLIOGRAPHIC REMARKS

(Wolpert & Macready 1997) proved several no-free-lunch theorems for optimization, but these are rather different from the theorem we prove here. The theorem we prove here is closely related to lower bounds in VC theory, as we will study in the next chapter.

5.5 EXERCISES

5.1 Prove that Equation (5.2) suffices for showing that $\mathbb{P}[L_{\mathcal{D}}(A(S)) \geq 1/8] \geq 1/7$.
Hint: Let θ be a random variable that receives values in $[0, 1]$ and whose expectation satisfies $\mathbb{E}[\theta] \geq 1/4$. Use Lemma B.1 to show that $\mathbb{P}[\theta \geq 1/8] \geq 1/7$.

5.2 Assume you are asked to design a learning algorithm to predict whether patients are going to suffer a heart attack. Relevant patient features the algorithm may have access to include blood pressure (BP), body-mass index (BMI), age (A), level of physical activity (P), and income (I).

You have to choose between two algorithms; the first picks an axis aligned rectangle in the two dimensional space spanned by the features BP and BMI and the other picks an axis aligned rectangle in the five dimensional space spanned by all the preceding features.

1. Explain the pros and cons of each choice.
2. Explain how the number of available labeled training samples will affect your choice.

5.3 Prove that if $|\mathcal{X}| \geq km$ for a positive integer $k \geq 2$, then we can replace the lower bound of 1/4 in the No-Free-Lunch theorem with $\frac{k-1}{2k} = \frac{1}{2} - \frac{1}{2k}$. Namely, let A be a learning algorithm for the task of binary classification. Let m be any number smaller than $|\mathcal{X}|/k$, representing a training set size. Then, there exists a distribution $\mathcal{D}$ over $\mathcal{X} \times \{0, 1\}$ such that:

- There exists a function $f : \mathcal{X} \to \{0, 1\}$ with $L_{\mathcal{D}}(f) = 0$.
- $\mathbb{E}_{S \sim \mathcal{D}^m}[L_{\mathcal{D}}(A(S))] \geq \frac{1}{2} - \frac{1}{2k}$.

6

The VC-Dimension

In the previous chapter, we decomposed the error of the $\mathrm{ERM}_{\mathcal{H}}$ rule into approximation error and estimation error. The approximation error depends on the fit of our prior knowledge (as reflected by the choice of the hypothesis class $\mathcal{H}$) to the underlying unknown distribution. In contrast, the definition of PAC learnability requires that the estimation error would be bounded uniformly over all distributions.

Our current goal is to figure out which classes $\mathcal{H}$ are PAC learnable, and to characterize exactly the sample complexity of learning a given hypothesis class. So far we have seen that finite classes are learnable, but that the class of all functions (over an infinite size domain) is not. What makes one class learnable and the other unlearnable? Can infinite-size classes be learnable, and, if so, what determines their sample complexity?

We begin the chapter by showing that infinite classes can indeed be learnable, and thus, finiteness of the hypothesis class is not a necessary condition for learnability. We then present a remarkably crisp characterization of the family of learnable classes in the setup of binary valued classification with the zero-one loss. This characterization was first discovered by Vladimir Vapnik and Alexey Chervonenkis in 1970 and relies on a combinatorial notion called the Vapnik-Chervonenkis dimension (VC-dimension). We formally define the VC-dimension, provide several examples, and then state the fundamental theorem of statistical learning theory, which integrates the concepts of learnability, VC-dimension, the ERM rule, and uniform convergence.

6.1 INFINITE-SIZE CLASSES CAN BE LEARNABLE

In Chapter 4 we saw that finite classes are learnable, and in fact the sample complexity of a hypothesis class is upper bounded by the log of its size. To show that the size of the hypothesis class is not the right characterization of its sample complexity, we first present a simple example of an infinite-size hypothesis class that is learnable.

Example 6.1. Let $\mathcal{H}$ be the set of threshold functions over the real line, namely, $\mathcal{H} = \{h_a : a \in \mathbb{R}\}$, where $h_a : \mathbb{R} \to \{0,1\}$ is a function such that $h_a(x) = \mathbb{1}_{[x<a]}$. To remind the reader, $\mathbb{1}_{[x<a]}$ is 1 if $x < a$ and 0 otherwise. Clearly, $\mathcal{H}$ is of infinite size. Nevertheless, the following lemma shows that $\mathcal{H}$ is learnable in the PAC model using the ERM algorithm.

Lemma 6.1. *Let $\mathcal{H}$ be the class of thresholds as defined earlier. Then, $\mathcal{H}$ is PAC learnable, using the ERM rule, with sample complexity of $m_{\mathcal{H}}(\epsilon,\delta) \le \lceil \log(2/\delta)/\epsilon \rceil$.*

Proof. Let $a^\star$ be a threshold such that the hypothesis $h^\star(x) = \mathbb{1}_{[x<a^\star]}$ achieves $L_{\mathcal{D}}(h^\star) = 0$. Let $\mathcal{D}_x$ be the marginal distribution over the domain $\mathcal{X}$ and let $a_0 < a^\star < a_1$ be such that

$$\mathop{\mathbb{P}}_{x\sim\mathcal{D}_x}[x \in (a_0, a^\star)] = \mathop{\mathbb{P}}_{x\sim\mathcal{D}_x}[x \in (a^\star, a_1)] = \epsilon.$$

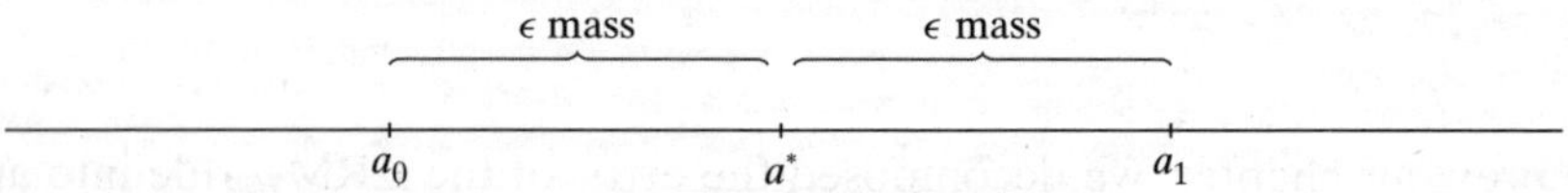

(If $\mathcal{D}_x(-\infty, a^\star) \le \epsilon$ we set $a_0 = -\infty$ and similarly for a_1). Given a training set S, let $b_0 = \max\{x : (x,1) \in S\}$ and $b_1 = \min\{x : (x,0) \in S\}$ (if no example in S is positive we set $b_0 = -\infty$ and if no example in S is negative we set $b_1 = \infty$). Let b_S be a threshold corresponding to an ERM hypothesis, h_S, which implies that $b_S \in (b_0, b_1)$. Therefore, a sufficient condition for $L_{\mathcal{D}}(h_S) \le \epsilon$ is that both $b_0 \ge a_0$ and $b_1 \le a_1$. In other words,

$$\mathop{\mathbb{P}}_{S\sim\mathcal{D}^m}[L_{\mathcal{D}}(h_S) > \epsilon] \le \mathop{\mathbb{P}}_{S\sim\mathcal{D}^m}[b_0 < a_0 \vee b_1 > a_1],$$

and using the union bound we can bound the preceding by

$$\mathop{\mathbb{P}}_{S\sim\mathcal{D}^m}[L_{\mathcal{D}}(h_S) > \epsilon] \le \mathop{\mathbb{P}}_{S\sim\mathcal{D}^m}[b_0 < a_0] + \mathop{\mathbb{P}}_{S\sim\mathcal{D}^m}[b_1 > a_1]. \tag{6.1}$$

The event $b_0 < a_0$ happens if and only if all examples in S are not in the interval (a_0, a^*), whose probability mass is defined to be ϵ, namely,

$$\mathop{\mathbb{P}}_{S\sim\mathcal{D}^m}[b_0 < a_0] = \mathop{\mathbb{P}}_{S\sim\mathcal{D}^m}[\forall (x,y) \in S,\ x \notin (a_0, a^\star)] = (1-\epsilon)^m \le e^{-\epsilon m}.$$

Since we assume $m > \log(2/\delta)/\epsilon$ it follows that the equation is at most $\delta/2$. In the same way it is easy to see that $\mathbb{P}_{S\sim\mathcal{D}^m}[b_1 > a_1] \le \delta/2$. Combining with Equation (6.1) we conclude our proof. □

6.2 THE VC-DIMENSION

We see, therefore, that while finiteness of $\mathcal{H}$ is a sufficient condition for learnability, it is not a necessary condition. As we will show, a property called the VC-dimension of a hypothesis class gives the correct characterization of its learnability. To motivate the definition of the VC-dimension, let us recall the No-Free-Lunch theorem (Theorem 5.1) and its proof. There, we have shown that without restricting the hypothesis class, for any learning algorithm, an adversary can construct a distribution for which the learning algorithm will perform poorly, while there is another learning algorithm that will succeed on the same distribution. To do so, the adversary used a finite set $C \subset \mathcal{X}$ and considered a family of distributions that are concentrated on elements of C. Each distribution was derived from a "true" target function from C to $\{0,1\}$. To make any algorithm fail, the adversary used the power of choosing a target function from the set of *all* possible functions from C to $\{0,1\}$.

When considering PAC learnability of a hypothesis class $\mathcal{H}$, the adversary is restricted to constructing distributions for which some hypothesis $h \in \mathcal{H}$ achieves a zero risk. Since we are considering distributions that are concentrated on elements of C, we should study how $\mathcal{H}$ behaves on C, which leads to the following definition.

Definition 6.2 (Restriction of $\mathcal{H}$ to C). Let $\mathcal{H}$ be a class of functions from $\mathcal{X}$ to $\{0,1\}$ and let $C = \{c_1, \ldots, c_m\} \subset \mathcal{X}$. The restriction of $\mathcal{H}$ to C is the set of functions from C to $\{0,1\}$ that can be derived from $\mathcal{H}$. That is,

$$\mathcal{H}_C = \{(h(c_1), \ldots, h(c_m)) : h \in \mathcal{H}\},$$

where we represent each function from C to $\{0,1\}$ as a vector in $\{0,1\}^{|C|}$.

If the restriction of $\mathcal{H}$ to C is the set of all functions from C to $\{0,1\}$, then we say that $\mathcal{H}$ *shatters* the set C. Formally:

Definition 6.3 (Shattering). A hypothesis class $\mathcal{H}$ shatters a finite set $C \subset \mathcal{X}$ if the restriction of $\mathcal{H}$ to C is the set of all functions from C to $\{0,1\}$. That is, $|\mathcal{H}_C| = 2^{|C|}$.

Example 6.2. Let $\mathcal{H}$ be the class of threshold functions over $\mathbb{R}$. Take a set $C = \{c_1\}$. Now, if we take $a = c_1 + 1$, then we have $h_a(c_1) = 1$, and if we take $a = c_1 - 1$, then we have $h_a(c_1) = 0$. Therefore, $\mathcal{H}_C$ is the set of all functions from C to $\{0,1\}$, and $\mathcal{H}$ shatters C. Now take a set $C = \{c_1, c_2\}$, where $c_1 \le c_2$. No $h \in \mathcal{H}$ can account for the labeling $(0,1)$, because any threshold that assigns the label 0 to c_1 must assign the label 0 to c_2 as well. Therefore not all functions from C to $\{0,1\}$ are included in $\mathcal{H}_C$; hence C is not shattered by $\mathcal{H}$.

Getting back to the construction of an adversarial distribution as in the proof of the No-Free-Lunch theorem (Theorem 5.1), we see that whenever some set C is shattered by $\mathcal{H}$, the adversary is not restricted by $\mathcal{H}$, as they can construct a distribution over C based on *any* target function from C to $\{0,1\}$, while still maintaining the realizability assumption. This immediately yields:

Corollary 6.4. *Let $\mathcal{H}$ be a hypothesis class of functions from $\mathcal{X}$ to $\{0,1\}$. Let m be a training set size. Assume that there exists a set $C \subset \mathcal{X}$ of size $2m$ that is shattered by $\mathcal{H}$. Then, for any learning algorithm, A, there exist a distribution $\mathcal{D}$ over $\mathcal{X} \times \{0,1\}$ and a predictor $h \in \mathcal{H}$ such that $L_{\mathcal{D}}(h) = 0$ but with probability of at least $1/7$ over the choice of $S \sim \mathcal{D}^m$ we have that $L_{\mathcal{D}}(A(S)) \ge 1/8$.*

Corollary 6.4 tells us that if $\mathcal{H}$ shatters some set C of size $2m$ then we cannot learn $\mathcal{H}$ using m examples. Intuitively, if a set C is shattered by $\mathcal{H}$, and we receive a sample containing half the instances of C, the labels of these instances give us no information about the labels of the rest of the instances in C – every possible labeling of the rest of the instances can be explained by some hypothesis in $\mathcal{H}$. Philosophically,

If someone can explain every phenomenon, his explanations are worthless.

This leads us directly to the definition of the VC dimension.

Definition 6.5 (VC-dimension). The VC-dimension of a hypothesis class $\mathcal{H}$, denoted VCdim($\mathcal{H}$), is the maximal size of a set $C \subset \mathcal{X}$ that can be shattered by $\mathcal{H}$. If $\mathcal{H}$ can shatter sets of arbitrarily large size we say that $\mathcal{H}$ has infinite VC-dimension.

A direct consequence of Corollary 6.4 is therefore:

Theorem 6.6. *Let $\mathcal{H}$ be a class of infinite VC-dimension. Then, $\mathcal{H}$ is not PAC learnable.*

Proof. Since $\mathcal{H}$ has an infinite VC-dimension, for any training set size m, there exists a shattered set of size $2m$, and the claim follows by Corollary 6.4. □

We shall see later in this chapter that the converse is also true: A finite VC-dimension guarantees learnability. Hence, the VC-dimension characterizes PAC learnability. But before delving into more theory, we first show several examples.

6.3 EXAMPLES

In this section we calculate the VC-dimension of several hypothesis classes. To show that $\text{VCdim}(\mathcal{H}) = d$ we need to show that

1. There exists a set C of size d that is shattered by $\mathcal{H}$.
2. Every set C of size $d+1$ is not shattered by $\mathcal{H}$.

6.3.1 Threshold Functions

Let $\mathcal{H}$ be the class of threshold functions over $\mathbb{R}$. Recall Example 6.2, where we have shown that for an arbitrary set $C = \{c_1\}$, $\mathcal{H}$ shatters C; therefore $\text{VCdim}(\mathcal{H}) \geq 1$. We have also shown that for an arbitrary set $C = \{c_1, c_2\}$ where $c_1 \leq c_2$, $\mathcal{H}$ does not shatter C. We therefore conclude that $\text{VCdim}(\mathcal{H}) = 1$.

6.3.2 Intervals

Let $\mathcal{H}$ be the class of intervals over $\mathbb{R}$, namely, $\mathcal{H} = \{h_{a,b} : a, b \in \mathbb{R}, a < b\}$, where $h_{a,b} : \mathbb{R} \to \{0,1\}$ is a function such that $h_{a,b}(x) = \mathbb{1}_{[x \in (a,b)]}$. Take the set $C = \{1,2\}$. Then, $\mathcal{H}$ shatters C (make sure you understand why) and therefore $\text{VCdim}(\mathcal{H}) \geq 2$. Now take an arbitrary set $C = \{c_1, c_2, c_3\}$ and assume without loss of generality that $c_1 \leq c_2 \leq c_3$. Then, the labeling $(1,0,1)$ cannot be obtained by an interval and therefore $\mathcal{H}$ does not shatter C. We therefore conclude that $\text{VCdim}(\mathcal{H}) = 2$.

6.3.3 Axis Aligned Rectangles

Let $\mathcal{H}$ be the class of axis aligned rectangles, formally:

$$\mathcal{H} = \{h_{(a_1,a_2,b_1,b_2)} : a_1 \leq a_2 \text{ and } b_1 \leq b_2\}$$

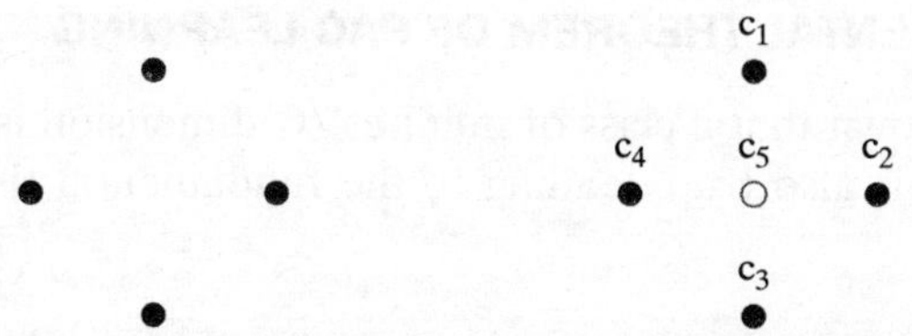

Figure 6.1. Left: 4 points that are shattered by axis aligned rectangles. Right: Any axis aligned rectangle cannot label c_5 by 0 and the rest of the points by 1.

where

$$h_{(a_1,a_2,b_1,b_2)}(x_1,x_2) = \begin{cases} 1 & \text{if } a_1 \le x_1 \le a_2 \quad \text{and} \quad b_1 \le x_2 \le b_2 \\ 0 & \text{otherwise} \end{cases} \tag{6.2}$$

We shall show in the following that $\text{VCdim}(\mathcal{H}) = 4$. To prove this we need to find a set of 4 points that are shattered by $\mathcal{H}$, and show that no set of 5 points can be shattered by $\mathcal{H}$. Finding a set of 4 points that are shattered is easy (see Figure 6.1). Now, consider any set $C \subset \mathbb{R}^2$ of 5 points. In C, take a leftmost point (whose first coordinate is the smallest in C), a rightmost point (first coordinate is the largest), a lowest point (second coordinate is the smallest), and a highest point (second coordinate is the largest). Without loss of generality, denote $C = \{c_1,\ldots,c_5\}$ and let c_5 be the point that was not selected. Now, define the labeling $(1,1,1,1,0)$. It is impossible to obtain this labeling by an axis aligned rectangle. Indeed, such a rectangle must contain $c_1,\ldots,c_4$; but in this case the rectangle contains c_5 as well, because its coordinates are within the intervals defined by the selected points. So, C is not shattered by H, and therefore $\text{VCdim}(H) = 4$.

6.3.4 Finite Classes

Let $\mathcal{H}$ be a finite class. Then, clearly, for any set C we have $|\mathcal{H}_C| \le |\mathcal{H}|$ and thus C cannot be shattered if $|\mathcal{H}| < 2^{|C|}$. This implies that $\text{VCdim}(\mathcal{H}) \le \log_2(|\mathcal{H}|)$. This shows that the PAC learnability of finite classes follows from the more general statement of PAC learnability of classes with finite VC-dimension, which we shall see in the next section. Note, however, that the VC-dimension of a finite class $\mathcal{H}$ can be significantly smaller than $\log_2(|\mathcal{H}|)$. For example, let $\mathcal{X} = \{1,\ldots,k\}$, for some integer k, and consider the class of threshold functions (as defined in Example 6.2). Then, $|\mathcal{H}| = k$ but $\text{VCdim}(\mathcal{H}) = 1$. Since k can be arbitrarily large, the gap between $\log_2(|\mathcal{H}|)$ and $\text{VCdim}(\mathcal{H})$ can be arbitrarily large.

6.3.5 VC-Dimension and the Number of Parameters

In the previous examples, the VC-dimension happened to equal the number of parameters defining the hypothesis class. While this is often the case, it is not always true. Consider, for example, the domain $\mathcal{X} = \mathbb{R}$, and the hypothesis class $\mathcal{H} = \{h_\theta : \theta \in \mathbb{R}\}$ where $h_\theta : \mathcal{X} \to \{0,1\}$ is defined by $h_\theta(x) = \lceil 0.5 \sin(\theta x) \rceil$. It is possible to prove that $\text{VCdim}(\mathcal{H}) = \infty$, namely, for *every* d, one can find d points that are shattered by $\mathcal{H}$ (see Exercise 6.8).

6.4 THE FUNDAMENTAL THEOREM OF PAC LEARNING

We have already shown that a class of infinite VC-dimension is not learnable. The converse statement is also true, leading to the fundamental theorem of statistical learning theory:

Theorem 6.7 (The Fundamental Theorem of Statistical Learning). *Let $\mathcal{H}$ be a hypothesis class of functions from a domain $\mathcal{X}$ to $\{0,1\}$ and let the loss function be the* $0-1$ *loss. Then, the following are equivalent:*

1. *$\mathcal{H}$ has the uniform convergence property.*
2. *Any ERM rule is a successful agnostic PAC learner for $\mathcal{H}$.*
3. *$\mathcal{H}$ is agnostic PAC learnable.*
4. *$\mathcal{H}$ is PAC learnable.*
5. *Any ERM rule is a successful PAC learner for $\mathcal{H}$.*
6. *$\mathcal{H}$ has a finite VC-dimension.*

The proof of the theorem is given in the next section.

Not only does the VC-dimension characterize PAC learnability; it even determines the sample complexity.

Theorem 6.8 (The Fundamental Theorem of Statistical Learning – Quantitative Version). *Let $\mathcal{H}$ be a hypothesis class of functions from a domain $\mathcal{X}$ to $\{0,1\}$ and let the loss function be the* $0-1$ *loss. Assume that* $\mathrm{VCdim}(\mathcal{H}) = d < \infty$. *Then, there are absolute constants C_1, C_2 such that*

1. *$\mathcal{H}$ has the uniform convergence property with sample complexity*
$$C_1 \frac{d + \log(1/\delta)}{\epsilon^2} \leq m_{\mathcal{H}}^{UC}(\epsilon, \delta) \leq C_2 \frac{d + \log(1/\delta)}{\epsilon^2}$$
2. *$\mathcal{H}$ is agnostic PAC learnable with sample complexity*
$$C_1 \frac{d + \log(1/\delta)}{\epsilon^2} \leq m_{\mathcal{H}}(\epsilon, \delta) \leq C_2 \frac{d + \log(1/\delta)}{\epsilon^2}$$
3. *$\mathcal{H}$ is PAC learnable with sample complexity*
$$C_1 \frac{d + \log(1/\delta)}{\epsilon} \leq m_{\mathcal{H}}(\epsilon, \delta) \leq C_2 \frac{d \log(1/\epsilon) + \log(1/\delta)}{\epsilon}$$

The proof of this theorem is given in Chapter 28.

Remark 6.3. We stated the fundamental theorem for binary classification tasks. A similar result holds for some other learning problems such as regression with the absolute loss or the squared loss. However, the theorem does not hold for all learning tasks. In particular, learnability is sometimes possible even though the uniform convergence property does not hold (we will see an example in Chapter 13, Exercise 6.2). Furthermore, in some situations, the ERM rule fails but learnability is possible with other learning rules.

6.5 PROOF OF THEOREM 6.7

We have already seen that $1 \to 2$ in Chapter 4. The implications $2 \to 3$ and $3 \to 4$ are trivial and so is $2 \to 5$. The implications $4 \to 6$ and $5 \to 6$ follow from the No-Free-Lunch theorem. The difficult part is to show that $6 \to 1$. The proof is based on two main claims:

- If $\text{VCdim}(\mathcal{H}) = d$, then even though $\mathcal{H}$ might be infinite, when restricting it to a finite set $C \subset \mathcal{X}$, its "effective" size, $|\mathcal{H}_C|$, is only $O(|C|^d)$. That is, the size of $\mathcal{H}_C$ grows polynomially rather than exponentially with $|C|$. This claim is often referred to as *Sauer's lemma*, but it has also been stated and proved independently by Shelah and by Perles. The formal statement is given in Section 6.5.1 later.
- In Section 4 we have shown that finite hypothesis classes enjoy the uniform convergence property. In Section 6.5.2 later we generalize this result and show that uniform convergence holds whenever the hypothesis class has a "small effective size." By "small effective size" we mean classes for which $|\mathcal{H}_C|$ grows polynomially with $|C|$.

6.5.1 Sauer's Lemma and the Growth Function

We defined the notion of *shattering*, by considering the restriction of $\mathcal{H}$ to a finite set of instances. The growth function measures the maximal "effective" size of $\mathcal{H}$ on a set of m examples. Formally:

Definition 6.9 (Growth Function). Let $\mathcal{H}$ be a hypothesis class. Then the *growth function* of $\mathcal{H}$, denoted $\tau_{\mathcal{H}} : \mathbb{N} \to \mathbb{N}$, is defined as

$$\tau_{\mathcal{H}}(m) = \max_{C \subset \mathcal{X}: |C| = m} |\mathcal{H}_C|.$$

In words, $\tau_H(m)$ is the number of different functions from a set C of size m to $\{0,1\}$ that can be obtained by restricting $\mathcal{H}$ to C.

Obviously, if $\text{VCdim}(\mathcal{H}) = d$ then for any $m \le d$ we have $\tau_{\mathcal{H}}(m) = 2^m$. In such cases, $\mathcal{H}$ induces all possible functions from C to $\{0,1\}$. The following beautiful lemma, proposed independently by Sauer, Shelah, and Perles, shows that when m becomes larger than the VC-dimension, the growth function increases polynomially rather than exponentially with m.

Lemma 6.10 (Sauer-Shelah-Perles). *Let $\mathcal{H}$ be a hypothesis class with* $\text{VCdim}(\mathcal{H}) \le d < \infty$. *Then, for all m, $\tau_{\mathcal{H}}(m) \le \sum_{i=0}^{d} \binom{m}{i}$. In particular, if $m > d+1$ then $\tau_{\mathcal{H}}(m) \le (em/d)^d$.*

Proof of Sauer's Lemma*

To prove the lemma it suffices to prove the following stronger claim: For any $C = \{c_1, \ldots, c_m\}$ we have

$$\forall \mathcal{H}, \quad |\mathcal{H}_C| \le |\{B \subseteq C : \mathcal{H} \text{ shatters } B\}|. \tag{6.3}$$

The reason why Equation (6.3) is sufficient to prove the lemma is that if $\mathrm{VCdim}(\mathcal{H}) \leq d$ then no set whose size is larger than d is shattered by $\mathcal{H}$ and therefore

$$|\{B \subseteq C : \mathcal{H} \text{ shatters } B\}| \leq \sum_{i=0}^{d} \binom{m}{i}.$$

When $m > d+1$ the right-hand side of the preceding is at most $(em/d)^d$ (see Lemma A.5 in Appendix A).

We are left with proving Equation (6.3) and we do it using an inductive argument. For $m = 1$, no matter what $\mathcal{H}$ is, either both sides of Equation (6.3) equal 1 or both sides equal 2 (the empty set is always considered to be shattered by $\mathcal{H}$). Assume Equation (6.3) holds for sets of size $k < m$ and let us prove it for sets of size m. Fix $\mathcal{H}$ and $C = \{c_1, \ldots, c_m\}$. Denote $C' = \{c_2, \ldots, c_m\}$ and in addition, define the following two sets:

$$Y_0 = \{(y_2, \ldots, y_m) : (0, y_2, \ldots, y_m) \in \mathcal{H}_C \vee (1, y_2, \ldots, y_m) \in \mathcal{H}_C\},$$

and

$$Y_1 = \{(y_2, \ldots, y_m) : (0, y_2, \ldots, y_m) \in \mathcal{H}_C \wedge (1, y_2, \ldots, y_m) \in \mathcal{H}_C\}.$$

It is easy to verify that $|\mathcal{H}_C| = |Y_0| + |Y_1|$. Additionally, since $Y_0 = \mathcal{H}_{C'}$, using the induction assumption (applied on $\mathcal{H}$ and C') we have that

$$|Y_0| = |\mathcal{H}_{C'}| \leq |\{B \subseteq C' : \mathcal{H} \text{ shatters } B\}| = |\{B \subseteq C : c_1 \notin B \wedge \mathcal{H} \text{ shatters } B\}|.$$

Next, define $\mathcal{H}' \subseteq \mathcal{H}$ to be

$$\begin{aligned}\mathcal{H}' = \{h \in \mathcal{H} : \exists h' \in \mathcal{H} \text{ s.t. } & (1 - h'(c_1), h'(c_2), \ldots, h'(c_m)) \\ & = (h(c_1), h(c_2), \ldots, h(c_m))\},\end{aligned}$$

namely, $\mathcal{H}'$ contains pairs of hypotheses that agree on C' and differ on c_1. Using this definition, it is clear that if $\mathcal{H}'$ shatters a set $B \subseteq C'$ then it also shatters the set $B \cup \{c_1\}$ and vice versa. Combining this with the fact that $Y_1 = \mathcal{H}'_{C'}$ and using the inductive assumption (now applied on $\mathcal{H}'$ and C') we obtain that

$$\begin{aligned}|Y_1| = |\mathcal{H}'_{C'}| &\leq |\{B \subseteq C' : \mathcal{H}' \text{ shatters } B\}| = |\{B \subseteq C' : \mathcal{H}' \text{ shatters } B \cup \{c_1\}\}| \\ &= |\{B \subseteq C : c_1 \in B \wedge \mathcal{H}' \text{ shatters } B\}| \leq |\{B \subseteq C : c_1 \in B \wedge \mathcal{H} \text{ shatters } B\}|.\end{aligned}$$

Overall, we have shown that

$$\begin{aligned}|\mathcal{H}_C| &= |Y_0| + |Y_1| \\ &\leq |\{B \subseteq C : c_1 \notin B \wedge \mathcal{H} \text{ shatters } B\}| + |\{B \subseteq C : c_1 \in B \wedge \mathcal{H} \text{ shatters } B\}| \\ &= |\{B \subseteq C : \mathcal{H} \text{ shatters } B\}|,\end{aligned}$$

which concludes our proof.

6.5.2 Uniform Convergence for Classes of Small Effective Size

In this section we prove that if $\mathcal{H}$ has small effective size then it enjoys the uniform convergence property. Formally,

Theorem 6.11. *Let $\mathcal{H}$ be a class and let $\tau_{\mathcal{H}}$ be its growth function. Then, for every $\mathcal{D}$ and every $\delta \in (0,1)$, with probability of at least $1-\delta$ over the choice of $S \sim \mathcal{D}^m$ we have*

$$|L_{\mathcal{D}}(h) - L_S(h)| \leq \frac{4 + \sqrt{\log(\tau_{\mathcal{H}}(2m))}}{\delta\sqrt{2m}}.$$

Before proving the theorem, let us first conclude the proof of Theorem 6.7.

Proof of Theorem 6.7. It suffices to prove that if the VC-dimension is finite then the uniform convergence property holds. We will prove that

$$m_{\mathcal{H}}^{\mathrm{UC}}(\epsilon,\delta) \leq 4\frac{16d}{(\delta\epsilon)^2}\log\left(\frac{16d}{(\delta\epsilon)^2}\right) + \frac{16d\log(2e/d)}{(\delta\epsilon)^2}.$$

From Sauer's lemma we have that for $m > d$, $\tau_{\mathcal{H}}(2m) \leq (2em/d)^d$. Combining this with Theorem 6.11 we obtain that with probability of at least $1-\delta$,

$$|L_S(h) - L_{\mathcal{D}}(h)| \leq \frac{4 + \sqrt{d\log(2em/d)}}{\delta\sqrt{2m}}.$$

For simplicity assume that $\sqrt{d\log(2em/d)} \geq 4$; hence,

$$|L_S(h) - L_{\mathcal{D}}(h)| \leq \frac{1}{\delta}\sqrt{\frac{2d\log(2em/d)}{m}}.$$

To ensure that the preceding is at most ϵ we need that

$$m \geq \frac{2d\log(m)}{(\delta\epsilon)^2} + \frac{2d\log(2e/d)}{(\delta\epsilon)^2}.$$

Standard algebraic manipulations (see Lemma A.2 in Appendix A) show that a sufficient condition for the preceding to hold is that

$$m \geq 4\frac{2d}{(\delta\epsilon)^2}\log\left(\frac{2d}{(\delta\epsilon)^2}\right) + \frac{4d\log(2e/d)}{(\delta\epsilon)^2}.$$

□

Remark 6.4. The upper bound on $m_{\mathcal{H}}^{\mathrm{UC}}$ we derived in the proof Theorem 6.7 is not the tightest possible. A tighter analysis that yields the bounds given in Theorem 6.8 can be found in Chapter 28.

Proof of Theorem 6.11*

We will start by showing that

$$\mathop{\mathbb{E}}_{S\sim\mathcal{D}^m}\left[\sup_{h\in\mathcal{H}}|L_{\mathcal{D}}(h) - L_S(h)|\right] \leq \frac{4 + \sqrt{\log(\tau_{\mathcal{H}}(2m))}}{\sqrt{2m}}. \tag{6.4}$$

Since the random variable $\sup_{h\in\mathcal{H}}|L_{\mathcal{D}}(h) - L_S(h)|$ is nonnegative, the proof of the theorem follows directly from the preceding using Markov's inequality (see Section B.1).

To bound the left-hand side of Equation (6.4) we first note that for every $h \in \mathcal{H}$, we can rewrite $L_{\mathcal{D}}(h) = \mathbb{E}_{S' \sim \mathcal{D}^m}[L_{S'}(h)]$, where $S' = z'_1, \ldots, z'_m$ is an additional i.i.d. sample. Therefore,

$$\mathop{\mathbb{E}}_{S \sim \mathcal{D}^m}\left[\sup_{h \in \mathcal{H}} |L_{\mathcal{D}}(h) - L_S(h)|\right] = \mathop{\mathbb{E}}_{S \sim \mathcal{D}^m}\left[\sup_{h \in \mathcal{H}} \left| \mathop{\mathbb{E}}_{S' \sim \mathcal{D}^m} L_{S'}(h) - L_S(h)\right|\right].$$

A generalization of the triangle inequality yields

$$\left| \mathop{\mathbb{E}}_{S' \sim \mathcal{D}^m}[L_{S'}(h) - L_S(h)]\right| \leq \mathop{\mathbb{E}}_{S' \sim \mathcal{D}^m} |L_{S'}(h) - L_S(h)|,$$

and the fact that supermum of expectation is smaller than expectation of supremum yields

$$\sup_{h \in \mathcal{H}} \mathop{\mathbb{E}}_{S' \sim \mathcal{D}^m} |L_{S'}(h) - L_S(h)| \leq \mathop{\mathbb{E}}_{S' \sim \mathcal{D}^m} \sup_{h \in \mathcal{H}} |L_{S'}(h) - L_S(h)|.$$

Formally, the previous two inequalities follow from Jensen's inequality. Combining all we obtain

$$\begin{aligned}\mathop{\mathbb{E}}_{S \sim \mathcal{D}^m}\left[\sup_{h \in \mathcal{H}} |L_{\mathcal{D}}(h) - L_S(h)|\right] &\leq \mathop{\mathbb{E}}_{S, S' \sim \mathcal{D}^m}\left[\sup_{h \in \mathcal{H}} |L_{S'}(h) - L_S(h)|\right] \\ &= \mathop{\mathbb{E}}_{S, S' \sim \mathcal{D}^m}\left[\sup_{h \in \mathcal{H}} \frac{1}{m}\left|\sum_{i=1}^{m} (\ell(h, z'_i) - \ell(h, z_i))\right|\right]. \qquad (6.5)\end{aligned}$$

The expectation on the right-hand side is over a choice of two i.i.d. samples $S = z_1, \ldots, z_m$ and $S' = z'_1, \ldots, z'_m$. Since all of these $2m$ vectors are chosen i.i.d., nothing will change if we replace the name of the random vector z_i with the name of the random vector z'_i. If we do it, instead of the term $(\ell(h, z'_i) - \ell(h, z_i))$ in Equation (6.5) we will have the term $-(\ell(h, z'_i) - \ell(h, z_i))$. It follows that for every $\boldsymbol{\sigma} \in \{\pm 1\}^m$ we have that Equation (6.5) equals

$$\mathop{\mathbb{E}}_{S, S' \sim \mathcal{D}^m}\left[\sup_{h \in \mathcal{H}} \frac{1}{m}\left|\sum_{i=1}^{m} \sigma_i(\ell(h, z'_i) - \ell(h, z_i))\right|\right]$$

Since this holds for every $\boldsymbol{\sigma} \in \{\pm 1\}^m$, it also holds if we sample each component of $\boldsymbol{\sigma}$ uniformly at random from the uniform distribution over $\{\pm 1\}$, denoted $U_{\pm}$. Hence, Equation (6.5) also equals

$$\mathop{\mathbb{E}}_{\boldsymbol{\sigma} \sim U_{\pm}^m} \mathop{\mathbb{E}}_{S, S' \sim \mathcal{D}^m}\left[\sup_{h \in \mathcal{H}} \frac{1}{m}\left|\sum_{i=1}^{m} \sigma_i(\ell(h, z'_i) - \ell(h, z_i))\right|\right],$$

and by the linearity of expectation it also equals

$$\mathop{\mathbb{E}}_{S, S' \sim \mathcal{D}^m} \mathop{\mathbb{E}}_{\boldsymbol{\sigma} \sim U_{\pm}^m}\left[\sup_{h \in \mathcal{H}} \frac{1}{m}\left|\sum_{i=1}^{m} \sigma_i(\ell(h, z'_i) - \ell(h, z_i))\right|\right].$$

Next, fix S and S', and let C be the instances appearing in S and S'. Then, we can take the supremum only over $h \in \mathcal{H}_C$. Therefore,

$$\underset{\sigma \sim U_\pm^m}{\mathbb{E}} \left[\sup_{h \in \mathcal{H}} \frac{1}{m} \left| \sum_{i=1}^{m} \sigma_i (\ell(h, z_i') - \ell(h, z_i)) \right| \right]$$

$$= \underset{\sigma \sim U_\pm^m}{\mathbb{E}} \left[\max_{h \in \mathcal{H}_C} \frac{1}{m} \left| \sum_{i=1}^{m} \sigma_i (\ell(h, z_i') - \ell(h, z_i)) \right| \right].$$

Fix some $h \in \mathcal{H}_C$ and denote $\theta_h = \frac{1}{m} \sum_{i=1}^{m} \sigma_i (\ell(h, z_i') - \ell(h, z_i))$. Since $\mathbb{E}[\theta_h] = 0$ and θ_h is an average of independent variables, each of which takes values in $[-1, 1]$, we have by Hoeffding's inequality that for every $\rho > 0$,

$$\mathbb{P}[|\theta_h| > \rho] \leq 2 \exp\left(-2m\rho^2\right).$$

Applying the union bound over $h \in \mathcal{H}_C$, we obtain that for any $\rho > 0$,

$$\mathbb{P}\left[\max_{h \in \mathcal{H}_C} |\theta_h| > \rho\right] \leq 2|\mathcal{H}_C| \exp\left(-2m\rho^2\right).$$

Finally, Lemma A.4 in Appendix A tells us that the preceding implies

$$\mathbb{E}\left[\max_{h \in \mathcal{H}_C} |\theta_h|\right] \leq \frac{4 + \sqrt{\log(|\mathcal{H}_C|)}}{\sqrt{2m}}.$$

Combining all with the definition of $\tau_{\mathcal{H}}$, we have shown that

$$\underset{S \sim \mathcal{D}^m}{\mathbb{E}} \left[\sup_{h \in \mathcal{H}} |L_{\mathcal{D}}(h) - L_S(h)|\right] \leq \frac{4 + \sqrt{\log(\tau_{\mathcal{H}}(2m))}}{\sqrt{2m}}.$$

6.6 SUMMARY

The fundamental theorem of learning theory characterizes PAC learnability of classes of binary classifiers using VC-dimension. The VC-dimension of a class is a combinatorial property that denotes the maximal sample size that can be shattered by the class. The fundamental theorem states that a class is PAC learnable if and only if its VC-dimension is finite and specifies the sample complexity required for PAC learning. The theorem also shows that if a problem is at all learnable, then uniform convergence holds and therefore the problem is learnable using the ERM rule.

6.7 BIBLIOGRAPHIC REMARKS

The definition of VC-dimension and its relation to learnability and to uniform convergence is due to the seminal work of Vapnik and Chervonenkis (1971). The relation to the definition of PAC learnability is due to Blumer, Ehrenfeucht, Haussler, and Warmuth (1989).

Several generalizations of the VC-dimension have been proposed. For example, the fat-shattering dimension characterizes learnability of some regression problems (Kearns, Schapire & Sellie 1994; Alon, Ben-David, Cesa-Bianchi & Haussler

1997; Bartlett, Long & Williamson 1994; Anthony & Bartlet 1999), and the Natarajan dimension characterizes learnability of some multiclass learning problems (Natarajan 1989). However, in general, there is no equivalence between learnability and uniform convergence. See (Shalev-Shwartz, Shamir, Srebro & Sridharan 2010; Daniely, Sabato, Ben-David & Shalev-Shwartz 2011).

Sauer's lemma has been proved by Sauer in response to a problem of Erdos (Sauer 1972). Shelah (with Perles) proved it as a useful lemma for Shelah's theory of stable models (Shelah 1972). Gil Kalai tells[1] us that at some later time, Benjy Weiss asked Perles about such a result in the context of ergodic theory, and Perles, who forgot that he had proved it once, proved it again. Vapnik and Chervonenkis proved the lemma in the context of statistical learning theory.

6.8 EXERCISES

6.1 Show the following monotonicity property of VC-dimension: For every two hypothesis classes if $\mathcal{H}' \subseteq \mathcal{H}$ then $\text{VCdim}(\mathcal{H}') \leq \text{VCdim}(\mathcal{H})$.

6.2 Given some finite domain set, $\mathcal{X}$, and a number $k \leq |\mathcal{X}|$, figure out the VC-dimension of each of the following classes (and prove your claims):
1. $\mathcal{H}^{\mathcal{X}}_{=k} = \{h \in \{0,1\}^{\mathcal{X}} : |\{x : h(x) = 1\}| = k\}$: that is, the set of all functions that assign the value 1 to exactly k elements of $\mathcal{X}$.
2. $\mathcal{H}_{at-most-k} = \{h \in \{0,1\}^{\mathcal{X}} : |\{x : h(x) = 1\}| \leq k \text{ or } |\{x : h(x) = 0\}| \leq k\}$.

6.3 Let $\mathcal{X}$ be the Boolean hypercube $\{0,1\}^n$. For a set $I \subseteq \{1, 2, \ldots, n\}$ we define a *parity function* h_I as follows. On a binary vector $\mathbf{x} = (x_1, x_2, \ldots, x_n) \in \{0,1\}^n$,

$$h_I(\mathbf{x}) = \left(\sum_{i \in I} x_i\right) \bmod 2\,.$$

(That is, h_I computes parity of bits in I.) What is the VC-dimension of the class of all such parity functions, $\mathcal{H}_{n\text{-parity}} = \{h_I : I \subseteq \{1, 2, \ldots, n\}\}$?

6.4 We proved Sauer's lemma by proving that for every class $\mathcal{H}$ of finite VC-dimension d, and every subset A of the domain,

$$|\mathcal{H}_A| \leq |\{B \subseteq A : \mathcal{H} \text{ shatters } B\}| \leq \sum_{i=0}^{d} \binom{|A|}{i}\,.$$

Show that there are cases in which the previous two inequalities are strict (namely, the $\leq$ can be replaced by $<$) and cases in which they can be replaced by equalities. Demonstrate all four combinations of $=$ and $<$.

6.5 **VC-dimension of axis aligned rectangles in $\mathbb{R}^d$:** Let $\mathcal{H}^d_{\text{rec}}$ be the class of axis aligned rectangles in $\mathbb{R}^d$. We have already seen that $\text{VCdim}(\mathcal{H}^2_{\text{rec}}) = 4$. Prove that in general, $\text{VCdim}(\mathcal{H}^d_{\text{rec}}) = 2d$.

6.6 **VC-dimension of Boolean conjunctions:** Let $\mathcal{H}^d_{con}$ be the class of Boolean conjunctions over the variables $x_1, \ldots, x_d$ ($d \geq 2$). We already know that this class is finite and thus (agnostic) PAC learnable. In this question we calculate $\text{VCdim}(\mathcal{H}^d_{con})$.
1. Show that $|\mathcal{H}^d_{con}| \leq 3^d + 1$.
2. Conclude that $\text{VCdim}(\mathcal{H}) \leq d \log 3$.
3. Show that $\mathcal{H}^d_{con}$ shatters the set of unit vectors $\{\mathbf{e}_i : i \leq d\}$.

[1] http://gilkalai.wordpress.com/2008/09/28/extremal-combinatorics-iii-some-basic-theorems

4. (**) Show that $\text{VCdim}(\mathcal{H}^d_{con}) \leq d$.
Hint: Assume by contradiction that there exists a set $C = \{c_1, \ldots, c_{d+1}\}$ that is shattered by $\mathcal{H}^d_{con}$. Let $h_1, \ldots, h_{d+1}$ be hypotheses in $\mathcal{H}^d_{con}$ that satisfy

$$\forall i, j \in [d+1],\ h_i(c_j) = \begin{cases} 0 & i = j \\ 1 & \text{otherwise} \end{cases}$$

For each $i \in [d+1]$, h_i (or more accurately, the conjunction that corresponds to h_i) contains some literal ℓ_i which is false on c_i and true on c_j for each $j \neq i$. Use the Pigeonhole principle to show that there must be a pair $i < j \leq d+1$ such that ℓ_i and ℓ_j use the same x_k and use that fact to derive a contradiction to the requirements from the conjunctions h_i, h_j.
5. Consider the class $\mathcal{H}^d_{mcon}$ of monotone Boolean conjunctions over $\{0,1\}^d$. Monotonicity here means that the conjunctions do not contain negations. As in $\mathcal{H}^d_{con}$, the empty conjunction is interpreted as the all-positive hypothesis. We augment $\mathcal{H}^d_{mcon}$ with the all-negative hypothesis h^-. Show that $\text{VCdim}(\mathcal{H}^d_{mcon}) = d$.

6.7 We have shown that for a finite hypothesis class $\mathcal{H}$, $\text{VCdim}(\mathcal{H}) \leq \lfloor \log(|\mathcal{H}|) \rfloor$. However, this is just an upper bound. The VC-dimension of a class can be much lower than that:
1. Find an example of a class $\mathcal{H}$ of functions over the real interval $\mathcal{X} = [0,1]$ such that $\mathcal{H}$ is infinite while $\text{VCdim}(\mathcal{H}) = 1$.
2. Give an example of a finite hypothesis class $\mathcal{H}$ over the domain $\mathcal{X} = [0,1]$, where $\text{VCdim}(\mathcal{H}) = \lfloor \log_2(|\mathcal{H}|) \rfloor$.

6.8 (*) It is often the case that the VC-dimension of a hypothesis class equals (or can be bounded above by) the number of parameters one needs to set in order to define each hypothesis in the class. For instance, if $\mathcal{H}$ is the class of axis aligned rectangles in $\mathbb{R}^d$, then $\text{VCdim}(\mathcal{H}) = 2d$, which is equal to the number of parameters used to define a rectangle in $\mathbb{R}^d$. Here is an example that shows that this is not always the case. We will see that a hypothesis class might be very complex and even not learnable, although it has a small number of parameters.

Consider the domain $\mathcal{X} = \mathbb{R}$, and the hypothesis class

$$\mathcal{H} = \{x \mapsto \lceil \sin(\theta x) \rceil : \theta \in \mathbb{R}\}$$

(here, we take $\lceil -1 \rceil = 0$). Prove that $\text{VCdim}(\mathcal{H}) = \infty$.
Hint: There is more than one way to prove the required result. One option is by applying the following lemma: If $0.x_1x_2x_3\ldots$, is the binary expansion of $x \in (0,1)$, then for any natural number m, $\lceil \sin(2^m \pi x) \rceil = (1 - x_m)$, provided that $\exists k \geq m$ s.t. $x_k = 1$.

6.9 Let $\mathcal{H}$ be the class of signed intervals, that is,
$\mathcal{H} = \{h_{a,b,s} : a \leq b, s \in \{-1, 1\}\}$ where

$$h_{a,b,s}(x) = \begin{cases} s & \text{if } x \in [a,b] \\ -s & \text{if } x \notin [a,b] \end{cases}$$

Calculate $\text{VCdim}(\mathcal{H})$.

6.10 Let $\mathcal{H}$ be a class of functions from $\mathcal{X}$ to $\{0,1\}$.
1. Prove that if $\text{VCdim}(\mathcal{H}) \geq d$, for any d, then for some probability distribution $\mathcal{D}$ over $\mathcal{X} \times \{0,1\}$, for every sample size, m,

$$\mathop{\mathbb{E}}_{S \sim \mathcal{D}^m}[L_{\mathcal{D}}(A(S))] \geq \min_{h \in \mathcal{H}} L_{\mathcal{D}}(h) + \frac{d-m}{2d}$$

Hint: Use Exercise 6.3 in Chapter 5.

2. Prove that for every $\mathcal{H}$ that is PAC learnable, $\text{VCdim}(\mathcal{H}) < \infty$. (Note that this is the implication $3 \rightarrow 6$ in Theorem 6.7.)

6.11 **VC of union:** Let $\mathcal{H}_1, \ldots, \mathcal{H}_r$ be hypothesis classes over some fixed domain set $\mathcal{X}$. Let $d = \max_i \text{VCdim}(\mathcal{H}_i)$ and assume for simplicity that $d \geq 3$.

1. Prove that

$$\text{VCdim}\left(\cup_{i=1}^{r} \mathcal{H}_i\right) \leq 4d\log(2d) + 2\log(r).$$

Hint: Take a set of k examples and assume that they are shattered by the union class. Therefore, the union class can produce all 2^k possible labelings on these examples. Use Sauer's lemma to show that the union class cannot produce more than rk^d labelings. Therefore, $2^k < rk^d$. Now use Lemma A.2.

2. (*) Prove that for $r = 2$ it holds that

$$\text{VCdim}(\mathcal{H}_1 \cup \mathcal{H}_2) \leq 2d + 1.$$

6.12 **Dudley classes:** In this question we discuss an algebraic framework for defining concept classes over $\mathbb{R}^n$ and show a connection between the VC dimension of such classes and their algebraic properties. Given a function $f : \mathbb{R}^n \rightarrow \mathbb{R}$ we define the corresponding function, $POS(f)(x) = \mathbb{1}_{[f(x)>0]}$. For a class $\mathcal{F}$ of real valued functions we define a corresponding class of functions $POS(\mathcal{F}) = \{POS(f) : f \in \mathcal{F}\}$. We say that a family, $\mathcal{F}$, of real valued functions is *linearly closed* if for all $f, g \in \mathcal{F}$ and $r \in \mathbb{R}$, $(f + rg) \in \mathcal{F}$ (where addition and scalar multiplication of functions are defined point wise, namely, for all $x \in \mathbb{R}^n$, $(f + rg)(x) = f(x) + rg(x)$). Note that if a family of functions is linearly closed then we can view it as a vector space over the reals. For a function $g : \mathbb{R}^n \rightarrow \mathbb{R}$ and a family of functions $\mathcal{F}$, let $\mathcal{F} + g \stackrel{\text{def}}{=} \{f + g : f \in \mathcal{F}\}$. Hypothesis classes that have a representation as $POS(\mathcal{F} + g)$ for some vector space of functions $\mathcal{F}$ and some function g are called *Dudley classes*.

1. Show that for every $g : \mathbb{R}^n \rightarrow \mathbb{R}$ and every vector space of functions $\mathcal{F}$ as defined earlier, $\text{VCdim}(POS(\mathcal{F} + g)) = \text{VCdim}(POS(\mathcal{F}))$.
2. (**) For every linearly closed family of real valued functions $\mathcal{F}$, the VC-dimension of the corresponding class $POS(\mathcal{F})$ equals the linear dimension of $\mathcal{F}$ (as a vector space). *Hint:* Let $f_1, \ldots, f_d$ be a basis for the vector space $\mathcal{F}$. Consider the mapping $x \mapsto (f_1(x), \ldots, f_d(x))$ (from $\mathbb{R}^n$ to $\mathbb{R}^d$). Note that this mapping induces a matching between functions over $\mathbb{R}^n$ of the form $POS(f)$ and homogeneous linear halfspaces in $\mathbb{R}^d$ (the VC-dimension of the class of homogeneous linear halfspaces is analyzed in Chapter 9).
3. Show that each of the following classes can be represented as a Dudley class:
   1. The class HS_n of halfspaces over $\mathbb{R}^n$ (see Chapter 9).
   2. The class HHS_n of all homogeneous halfspaces over $\mathbb{R}^n$ (see Chapter 9).
   3. The class B_d of all functions defined by (open) balls in $\mathbb{R}^d$. Use the Dudley representation to figure out the VC-dimension of this class.
   4. Let P_n^d denote the class of functions defined by polynomial inequalities of degree $\leq d$, namely,

$$P_n^d = \{h_p : p \text{ is a polynomial of degree } \leq d \text{ in the variables } x_1, \ldots, x_n\},$$

where for $\mathbf{x} = (x_1 \ldots, x_n)$, $h_p(\mathbf{x}) = \mathbb{1}_{[p(\mathbf{x}) \geq 0]}$ (the degree of a multivariable polynomial is the maximal sum of variable exponents over all of its terms. For example, the degree of $p(\mathbf{x}) = 3x_1^3x_2^2 + 4x_3x_7^2$ is 5).

1. Use the Dudley representation to figure out the VC-dimension of the class P_1^d – the class of all d-degree polynomials over $\mathbb{R}$.
2. Prove that the class of all polynomial classifiers over $\mathbb{R}$ has infinite VC-dimension.
3. Use the Dudley representation to figure out the VC-dimension of the class P_n^d (as a function of d and n).

7

Nonuniform Learnability

The notions of PAC learnability discussed so far in the book allow the sample sizes to depend on the accuracy and confidence parameters, but they are uniform with respect to the labeling rule and the underlying data distribution. Consequently, classes that are learnable in that respect are limited (they must have a finite VC-dimension, as stated by Theorem 6.7). In this chapter we consider more relaxed, weaker notions of learnability. We discuss the usefulness of such notions and provide characterization of the concept classes that are learnable using these definitions.

We begin this discussion by defining a notion of "nonuniform learnability" that allows the sample size to depend on the hypothesis to which the learner is compared. We then provide a characterization of nonuniform learnability and show that nonuniform learnability is a strict relaxation of agnostic PAC learnability. We also show that a sufficient condition for nonuniform learnability is that $\mathcal{H}$ is a countable union of hypothesis classes, each of which enjoys the uniform convergence property. These results will be proved in Section 7.2 by introducing a new learning paradigm, which is called Structural Risk Minimization (SRM). In Section 7.3 we specify the SRM paradigm for countable hypothesis classes, which yields the Minimum Description Length (MDL) paradigm. The MDL paradigm gives a formal justification to a philosophical principle of induction called Occam's razor. Next, in Section 7.4 we introduce *consistency* as an even weaker notion of learnability. Finally, we discuss the significance and usefulness of the different notions of learnability.

7.1 NONUNIFORM LEARNABILITY

"Nonuniform learnability" allows the sample size to be nonuniform with respect to the different hypotheses with which the learner is competing. We say that a hypothesis h is (ϵ, δ)-competitive with another hypothesis h' if, with probability higher than $(1-\delta)$,

$$L_{\mathcal{D}}(h) \leq L_{\mathcal{D}}(h') + \epsilon.$$

In PAC learnability, this notion of "competitiveness" is not very useful, as we are looking for a hypothesis with an absolute low risk (in the realizable case) or with a low risk compared to the minimal risk achieved by hypotheses in our class (in the agnostic case). Therefore, the sample size depends only on the accuracy and confidence parameters. In nonuniform learnability, however, we allow the sample size to be of the form $m_{\mathcal{H}}(\epsilon,\delta,h)$; namely, it depends also on the h with which we are competing. Formally,

Definition 7.1. A hypothesis class $\mathcal{H}$ is *nonuniformly learnable* if there exist a learning algorithm, A, and a function $m_{\mathcal{H}}^{\mathrm{NUL}} : (0,1)^2 \times \mathcal{H} \to \mathbb{N}$ such that, for every $\epsilon,\delta \in (0,1)$ and for every $h \in \mathcal{H}$, if $m \geq m_{\mathcal{H}}^{\mathrm{NUL}}(\epsilon,\delta,h)$ then for every distribution $\mathcal{D}$, with probability of at least $1-\delta$ over the choice of $S \sim \mathcal{D}^m$, it holds that

$$L_{\mathcal{D}}(A(S)) \leq L_{\mathcal{D}}(h) + \epsilon.$$

At this point it might be useful to recall the definition of agnostic PAC learnability (Definition 3.3):
A hypothesis class $\mathcal{H}$ is agnostically PAC learnable if there exist a learning algorithm, A, and a function $m_{\mathcal{H}} : (0,1)^2 \to \mathbb{N}$ such that, for every $\epsilon,\delta \in (0,1)$ and for every distribution $\mathcal{D}$, if $m \geq m_{\mathcal{H}}(\epsilon,\delta)$, then with probability of at least $1-\delta$ over the choice of $S \sim \mathcal{D}^m$ it holds that

$$L_{\mathcal{D}}(A(S)) \leq \min_{h' \in \mathcal{H}} L_{\mathcal{D}}(h') + \epsilon.$$

Note that this implies that for every $h \in \mathcal{H}$

$$L_{\mathcal{D}}(A(S)) \leq L_{\mathcal{D}}(h) + \epsilon.$$

In both types of learnability, we require that the output hypothesis will be (ϵ,δ)-competitive with every other hypothesis in the class. But the difference between these two notions of learnability is the question of whether the sample size m may depend on the hypothesis h to which the error of $A(S)$ is compared. Note that that nonuniform learnability is a relaxation of agnostic PAC learnability. That is, if a class is agnostic PAC learnable then it is also nonuniformly learnable.

7.1.1 Characterizing Nonuniform Learnability

Our goal now is to characterize nonuniform learnability. In the previous chapter we have found a crisp characterization of PAC learnable classes, by showing that a class of binary classifiers is agnostic PAC learnable if and only if its VC-dimension is finite. In the following theorem we find a different characterization for nonuniform learnable classes for the task of binary classification.

Theorem 7.2. *A hypothesis class $\mathcal{H}$ of binary classifiers is nonuniformly learnable if and only if it is a countable union of agnostic PAC learnable hypothesis classes.*

The proof of Theorem 7.2 relies on the following result of independent interest:

Theorem 7.3. *Let $\mathcal{H}$ be a hypothesis class that can be written as a countable union of hypothesis classes, $\mathcal{H} = \bigcup_{n\in\mathbb{N}} \mathcal{H}_n$, where each $\mathcal{H}_n$ enjoys the uniform convergence property. Then, $\mathcal{H}$ is nonuniformly learnable.*

Recall that in Chapter 4 we have shown that uniform convergence is sufficient for agnostic PAC learnability. Theorem 7.3 generalizes this result to nonuniform learnability. The proof of this theorem will be given in the next section by introducing a new learning paradigm. We now turn to proving Theorem 7.2.

Proof of Theorem 7.2. First assume that $\mathcal{H} = \bigcup_{n\in\mathbb{N}} \mathcal{H}_n$ where each $\mathcal{H}_n$ is agnostic PAC learnable. Using the fundamental theorem of statistical learning, it follows that each $\mathcal{H}_n$ has the uniform convergence property. Therefore, using Theorem 7.3 we obtain that $\mathcal{H}$ is nonuniform learnable.

For the other direction, assume that $\mathcal{H}$ is nonuniform learnable using some algorithm A. For every $n \in \mathbb{N}$, let $\mathcal{H}_n = \{h \in \mathcal{H} : m_{\mathcal{H}}^{\mathrm{NUL}}(1/8, 1/7, h) \leq n\}$. Clearly, $\mathcal{H} = \cup_{n\in\mathbb{N}}\mathcal{H}_n$. In addition, using the definition of $m_{\mathcal{H}}^{\mathrm{NUL}}$ we know that for any distribution $\mathcal{D}$ that satisfies the realizability assumption with respect to $\mathcal{H}_n$, with probability of at least $6/7$ over $S \sim \mathcal{D}^n$ we have that $L_{\mathcal{D}}(A(S)) \leq 1/8$. Using the fundamental theorem of statistical learning, this implies that the VC-dimension of $\mathcal{H}_n$ must be finite, and therefore $\mathcal{H}_n$ is agnostic PAC learnable. □

The following example shows that nonuniform learnability is a strict relaxation of agnostic PAC learnability; namely, there are hypothesis classes that are nonuniform learnable but are not agnostic PAC learnable.

Example 7.1. Consider a binary classification problem with the instance domain being $\mathcal{X} = \mathbb{R}$. For every $n \in \mathbb{N}$ let $\mathcal{H}_n$ be the class of polynomial classifiers of degree n; namely, $\mathcal{H}_n$ is the set of all classifiers of the form $h(x) = \mathrm{sign}(p(x))$ where $p : \mathbb{R} \to \mathbb{R}$ is a polynomial of degree n. Let $\mathcal{H} = \bigcup_{n\in\mathbb{N}} \mathcal{H}_n$. Therefore, $\mathcal{H}$ is the class of all polynomial classifiers over $\mathbb{R}$. It is easy to verify that $\mathrm{VCdim}(\mathcal{H}) = \infty$ while $\mathrm{VCdim}(\mathcal{H}_n) = n+1$ (see Exercise 7.12). Hence, $\mathcal{H}$ is not PAC learnable, while on the basis of Theorem 7.3, $\mathcal{H}$ is nonuniformly learnable.

7.2 STRUCTURAL RISK MINIMIZATION

So far, we have encoded our prior knowledge by specifying a hypothesis class $\mathcal{H}$, which we believe includes a good predictor for the learning task at hand. Yet another way to express our prior knowledge is by specifying preferences over hypotheses within $\mathcal{H}$. In the Structural Risk Minimization (SRM) paradigm, we do so by first assuming that $\mathcal{H}$ can be written as $\mathcal{H} = \bigcup_{n\in\mathbb{N}} \mathcal{H}_n$ and then specifying a weight function, $w : \mathbb{N} \to [0,1]$, which assigns a weight to each hypothesis class, $\mathcal{H}_n$, such that a higher weight reflects a stronger preference for the hypothesis class. In this section we discuss how to learn with such prior knowledge. In the next section we describe a couple of important weighting schemes, including Minimum Description Length.

Concretely, let $\mathcal{H}$ be a hypothesis class that can be written as $\mathcal{H} = \bigcup_{n\in\mathbb{N}} \mathcal{H}_n$. For example, $\mathcal{H}$ may be the class of all polynomial classifiers where each $\mathcal{H}_n$ is the class of polynomial classifiers of degree n (see Example 7.1). Assume that for each n, the class $\mathcal{H}_n$ enjoys the uniform convergence property (see Definition 4.3 in Chapter 4) with a sample complexity function $m_{\mathcal{H}_n}^{\mathrm{UC}}(\epsilon, \delta)$. Let us also define the function $\epsilon_n : \mathbb{N} \times (0,1) \to (0,1)$ by

$$\epsilon_n(m, \delta) = \min\{\epsilon \in (0,1) : m_{\mathcal{H}_n}^{\mathrm{UC}}(\epsilon, \delta) \leq m\}. \tag{7.1}$$

In words, we have a fixed sample size m, and we are interested in the lowest possible upper bound on the gap between empirical and true risks achievable by using a sample of m examples.

From the definitions of uniform convergence and ϵ_n, it follows that for every m and δ, with probability of at least $1-\delta$ over the choice of $S \sim \mathcal{D}^m$ we have that

$$\forall h \in \mathcal{H}_n, \ |L_{\mathcal{D}}(h) - L_S(h)| \le \epsilon_n(m, \delta). \qquad (7.2)$$

Let $w : \mathbb{N} \to [0,1]$ be a function such that $\sum_{n=1}^{\infty} w(n) \le 1$. We refer to w as a *weight function* over the hypothesis classes $\mathcal{H}_1, \mathcal{H}_2, \ldots$. Such a weight function can reflect the importance that the learner attributes to each hypothesis class, or some measure of the complexity of different hypothesis classes. If $\mathcal{H}$ is a finite union of N hypothesis classes, one can simply assign the same weight of $1/N$ to all hypothesis classes. This equal weighting corresponds to no a priori preference to any hypothesis class. Of course, if one believes (as prior knowledge) that a certain hypothesis class is more likely to contain the correct target function, then it should be assigned a larger weight, reflecting this prior knowledge. When $\mathcal{H}$ is a (countable) infinite union of hypothesis classes, a uniform weighting is not possible but many other weighting schemes may work. For example, one can choose $w(n) = \frac{6}{\pi^2 n^2}$ or $w(n) = 2^{-n}$. Later in this chapter we will provide another convenient way to define weighting functions using description languages.

The SRM rule follows a "bound minimization" approach. This means that the goal of the paradigm is to find a hypothesis that minimizes a certain upper bound on the true risk. The bound that the SRM rule wishes to minimize is given in the following theorem.

Theorem 7.4. *Let $w : \mathbb{N} \to [0,1]$ be a function such that $\sum_{n=1}^{\infty} w(n) \le 1$. Let $\mathcal{H}$ be a hypothesis class that can be written as $\mathcal{H} = \bigcup_{n \in \mathbb{N}} \mathcal{H}_n$, where for each n, $\mathcal{H}_n$ satisfies the uniform convergence property with a sample complexity function $m^{UC}_{\mathcal{H}_n}$. Let ϵ_n be as defined in Equation (7.1). Then, for every $\delta \in (0,1)$ and distribution $\mathcal{D}$, with probability of at least $1-\delta$ over the choice of $S \sim \mathcal{D}^m$, the following bound holds (simultaneously) for every $n \in \mathbb{N}$ and $h \in \mathcal{H}_n$.*

$$|L_{\mathcal{D}}(h) - L_S(h)| \le \epsilon_n(m, w(n) \cdot \delta).$$

Therefore, for every $\delta \in (0,1)$ and distribution $\mathcal{D}$, with probability of at least $1-\delta$ it holds that

$$\forall h \in \mathcal{H}, \ L_{\mathcal{D}}(h) \le L_S(h) + \min_{n: h \in \mathcal{H}_n} \epsilon_n(m, w(n) \cdot \delta). \qquad (7.3)$$

Proof. For each n define $\delta_n = w(n)\delta$. Applying the assumption that uniform convergence holds for all n with the rate given in Equation (7.2), we obtain that if we fix n in advance, then with probability of at least $1-\delta_n$ over the choice of $S \sim \mathcal{D}^m$,

$$\forall h \in \mathcal{H}_n, \ |L_{\mathcal{D}}(h) - L_S(h)| \le \epsilon_n(m, \delta_n).$$

Applying the union bound over $n = 1, 2, \ldots$, we obtain that with probability of at least $1 - \sum_n \delta_n = 1 - \delta \sum_n w(n) \ge 1 - \delta$, the preceding holds for all n, which concludes our proof. □

Denote

$$n(h) = \min\{n : h \in \mathcal{H}_n\}, \qquad (7.4)$$

and then Equation (7.3) implies that

$$L_{\mathcal{D}}(h) \le L_S(h) + \epsilon_{n(h)}(m, w(n(h)) \cdot \delta).$$

The SRM paradigm searches for h that minimizes this bound, as formalized in the following pseudocode:

Structural Risk Minimization (SRM)

prior knowledge:
$\mathcal{H} = \bigcup_n \mathcal{H}_n$ where $\mathcal{H}_n$ has uniform convergence with $m^{\mathrm{UC}}_{\mathcal{H}_n}$
$w : \mathbb{N} \to [0,1]$ where $\sum_n w(n) \le 1$
define: ϵ_n as in Equation (7.1); $n(h)$ as in Equation (7.4)
input: training set $S \sim \mathcal{D}^m$, confidence δ
output: $h \in \mathrm{argmin}_{h \in \mathcal{H}} \left[L_S(h) + \epsilon_{n(h)}(m, w(n(h)) \cdot \delta) \right]$

Unlike the ERM paradigm discussed in previous chapters, we no longer just care about the empirical risk, $L_S(h)$, but we are willing to trade some of our bias toward low empirical risk with a bias toward classes for which $\epsilon_{n(h)}(m, w(n(h)) \cdot \delta)$ is smaller, for the sake of a smaller estimation error.

Next we show that the SRM paradigm can be used for nonuniform learning of every class, which is a countable union of uniformly converging hypothesis classes.

Theorem 7.5. *Let $\mathcal{H}$ be a hypothesis class such that $\mathcal{H} = \bigcup_{n \in \mathbb{N}} \mathcal{H}_n$, where each $\mathcal{H}_n$ has the uniform convergence property with sample complexity $m^{UC}_{\mathcal{H}_n}$. Let $w : \mathbb{N} \to [0,1]$ be such that $w(n) = \frac{6}{n^2 \pi^2}$. Then, $\mathcal{H}$ is nonuniformly learnable using the SRM rule with rate*

$$m^{NUL}_{\mathcal{H}}(\epsilon, \delta, h) \le m^{UC}_{\mathcal{H}_{n(h)}}\left(\epsilon/2, \frac{6\delta}{(\pi n(h))^2}\right).$$

Proof. Let A be the SRM algorithm with respect to the weighting function w. For every $h \in \mathcal{H}$, ϵ, and δ, let $m \ge m^{\mathrm{UC}}_{\mathcal{H}_{n(h)}}(\epsilon, w(n(h))\delta)$. Using the fact that $\sum_n w(n) = 1$, we can apply Theorem 7.4 to get that, with probability of at least $1 - \delta$ over the choice of $S \sim \mathcal{D}^m$, we have that for every $h' \in \mathcal{H}$,

$$L_{\mathcal{D}}(h') \le L_S(h') + \epsilon_{n(h')}(m, w(n(h'))\delta).$$

The preceding holds in particular for the hypothesis $A(S)$ returned by the SRM rule. By the definition of SRM we obtain that

$$L_{\mathcal{D}}(A(S)) \le \min_{h'} \left[L_S(h') + \epsilon_{n(h')}(m, w(n(h'))\delta) \right] \le L_S(h) + \epsilon_{n(h)}(m, w(n(h))\delta).$$

Finally, if $m \ge m^{\mathrm{UC}}_{\mathcal{H}_{n(h)}}(\epsilon/2, w(n(h))\delta)$ then clearly $\epsilon_{n(h)}(m, w(n(h))\delta) \le \epsilon/2$. In addition, from the uniform convergence property of each $\mathcal{H}_n$ we have that with probability of more than $1 - \delta$,

$$L_S(h) \le L_{\mathcal{D}}(h) + \epsilon/2.$$

Combining all the preceding we obtain that $L_{\mathcal{D}}(A(S)) \le L_{\mathcal{D}}(h) + \epsilon$, which concludes our proof. □

Note that the previous theorem also proves Theorem 7.3.

Remark 7.2 (No-Free-Lunch for Nonuniform Learnability). We have shown that any countable union of classes of finite VC-dimension is nonuniformly learnable. It turns out that, for any infinite domain set, $\mathcal{X}$, the class of all binary valued functions over $\mathcal{X}$ is not a countable union of classes of finite VC-dimension. We leave the proof of this claim as a (nontrivial) exercise (see Exercise 7.5). It follows that, in some sense, the No-Free-Lunch theorem holds for nonuniform learning as well: namely, whenever the domain is not finite, there exists no nonuniform learner with respect to the class of all deterministic binary classifiers (although for each such classifier there exists a trivial algorithm that learns it – ERM with respect to the hypothesis class that contains only this classifier).

It is interesting to compare the nonuniform learnability result given in Theorem 7.5 to the task of agnostic PAC learning any specific $\mathcal{H}_n$ separately. The prior knowledge, or bias, of a nonuniform learner for $\mathcal{H}$ is weaker – it is searching for a model throughout the entire class $\mathcal{H}$, rather than being focused on one specific $\mathcal{H}_n$. The cost of this weakening of prior knowledge is the increase in sample complexity needed to compete with any specific $h \in \mathcal{H}_n$. For a concrete evaluation of this gap, consider the task of binary classification with the zero-one loss. Assume that for all n, $\mathrm{VCdim}(\mathcal{H}_n) = n$. Since $m^{\mathrm{UC}}_{\mathcal{H}_n}(\epsilon,\delta) = C\,\frac{n+\log(1/\delta)}{\epsilon^2}$ (where C is the contant appearing in Theorem 6.8), a straightforward calculation shows that

$$m^{\mathrm{NUL}}_{\mathcal{H}}(\epsilon,\delta,h) - m^{\mathrm{UC}}_{\mathcal{H}_n}(\epsilon/2,\delta) \le 4C\,\frac{2\log(2n)}{\epsilon^2}.$$

That is, the cost of relaxing the learner's prior knowledge from a specific $\mathcal{H}_n$ that contains the target h to a countable union of classes depends on the log of the index of the first class in which h resides. That cost increases with the index of the class, which can be interpreted as reflecting the value of knowing a good priority order on the hypotheses in $\mathcal{H}$.

7.3 MINIMUM DESCRIPTION LENGTH AND OCCAM'S RAZOR

Let $\mathcal{H}$ be a countable hypothesis class. Then, we can write $\mathcal{H}$ as a countable union of singleton classes, namely, $\mathcal{H} = \bigcup_{n\in\mathbb{N}}\{h_n\}$. By Hoeffding's inequality (Lemma 4.5), each singleton class has the uniform convergence property with rate $m^{\mathrm{UC}}(\epsilon,\delta) = \frac{\log(2/\delta)}{2\epsilon^2}$. Therefore, the function ϵ_n given in Equation (7.1) becomes $\epsilon_n(m,\delta) = \sqrt{\frac{\log(2/\delta)}{2m}}$ and the SRM rule becomes

$$\underset{h_n\in\mathcal{H}}{\operatorname{argmin}}\left[L_S(h) + \sqrt{\frac{-\log(w(n)) + \log(2/\delta)}{2m}}\right].$$

Equivalently, we can think of w as a function from $\mathcal{H}$ to $[0,1]$, and then the SRM rule becomes

$$\underset{h\in\mathcal{H}}{\operatorname{argmin}}\left[L_S(h) + \sqrt{\frac{-\log(w(h)) + \log(2/\delta)}{2m}}\right].$$

It follows that in this case, the prior knowledge is solely determined by the weight we assign to each hypothesis. We assign higher weights to hypotheses that we believe are more likely to be the correct one, and in the learning algorithm we prefer hypotheses that have higher weights.

In this section we discuss a particular convenient way to define a weight function over $\mathcal{H}$, which is derived from the length of descriptions given to hypotheses. Having a hypothesis class, one can wonder about how we describe, or represent, each hypothesis in the class. We naturally fix some description language. This can be English, or a programming language, or some set of mathematical formulas. In any of these languages, a description consists of finite strings of symbols (or characters) drawn from some fixed alphabet. We shall now formalize these notions.

Let $\mathcal{H}$ be the hypothesis class we wish to describe. Fix some finite set Σ of symbols (or "characters"), which we call the alphabet. For concreteness, we let $\Sigma = \{0,1\}$. A string is a finite sequence of symbols from Σ; for example, $\sigma = (0,1,1,1,0)$ is a string of length 5. We denote by $|\sigma|$ the length of a string. The set of all finite length strings is denoted Σ^*. A description language for $\mathcal{H}$ is a function $d : \mathcal{H} \to \Sigma^*$, mapping each member h of $\mathcal{H}$ to a string $d(h)$. $d(h)$ is called "the description of h," and its length is denoted by $|h|$.

We shall require that description languages be *prefix-free*; namely, for every distinct h, h', $d(h)$ is not a prefix of $d(h')$. That is, we do not allow that any string $d(h)$ is exactly the first $|h|$ symbols of any longer string $d(h')$. Prefix-free collections of strings enjoy the following combinatorial property:

Lemma 7.6 (Kraft Inequality). *If $\mathcal{S} \subseteq \{0,1\}^*$ is a prefix-free set of strings, then*

$$\sum_{\sigma \in \mathcal{S}} \frac{1}{2^{|\sigma|}} \leq 1.$$

Proof. Define a probability distribution over the members of $\mathcal{S}$ as follows: Repeatedly toss an unbiased coin, with faces labeled 0 and 1, until the sequence of outcomes is a member of $\mathcal{S}$; at that point, stop. For each $\sigma \in \mathcal{S}$, let $P(\sigma)$ be the probability that this process generates the string σ. Note that since $\mathcal{S}$ is prefix-free, for every $\sigma \in \mathcal{S}$, if the coin toss outcomes follow the bits of σ then we will stop only once the sequence of outcomes equals σ. We therefore get that, for every $\sigma \in \mathcal{S}$, $P(\sigma) = \frac{1}{2^{|\sigma|}}$. Since probabilities add up to at most 1, our proof is concluded. □

In light of Kraft's inequality, any prefix-free description language of a hypothesis class, $\mathcal{H}$, gives rise to a weighting function w over that hypothesis class – we will simply set $w(h) = \frac{1}{2^{|h|}}$. This observation immediately yields the following:

Theorem 7.7. *Let $\mathcal{H}$ be a hypothesis class and let $d : \mathcal{H} \to \{0,1\}^*$ be a prefix-free description language for $\mathcal{H}$. Then, for every sample size, m, every confidence parameter, $\delta > 0$, and every probability distribution, $\mathcal{D}$, with probability greater than $1 - \delta$ over the choice of $S \sim \mathcal{D}^m$ we have that,*

$$\forall h \in \mathcal{H}, \;\; L_{\mathcal{D}}(h) \leq L_S(h) + \sqrt{\frac{|h| + \ln(2/\delta)}{2m}},$$

where $|h|$ is the length of $d(h)$.

Proof. Choose $w(h) = 1/2^{|h|}$, apply Theorem 7.4 with $\epsilon_n(m,\delta) = \sqrt{\frac{\ln(2/\delta)}{2m}}$, and note that $\ln(2^{|h|}) = |h| \ln(2) < |h|$. □

As was the case with Theorem 7.4, this result suggests a learning paradigm for $\mathcal{H}$ – given a training set, S, search for a hypothesis $h \in \mathcal{H}$ that minimizes the bound, $L_S(h) + \sqrt{\frac{|h|+\ln(2/\delta)}{2m}}$. In particular, it suggests trading off empirical risk for saving description length. This yields the Minimum Description Length learning paradigm.

Minimum Description Length (MDL)

prior knowledge:
$\mathcal{H}$ is a countable hypothesis class
$\mathcal{H}$ is described by a prefix-free language over $\{0,1\}$
For every $h \in \mathcal{H}$, $|h|$ is the length of the representation of h
input: A training set $S \sim \mathcal{D}^m$, confidence δ
output: $h \in \text{argmin}_{h\in\mathcal{H}} \left[L_S(h) + \sqrt{\frac{|h|+\ln(2/\delta)}{2m}} \right]$

Example 7.3. Let $\mathcal{H}$ be the class of all predictors that can be implemented using some programming language, say, C++. Let us represent each program using the binary string obtained by running the gzip command on the program (this yields a prefix-free description language over the alphabet $\{0,1\}$). Then, $|h|$ is simply the length (in bits) of the output of gzip when running on the C++ program corresponding to h.

7.3.1 Occam's Razor

Theorem 7.7 suggests that, having two hypotheses sharing the same empirical risk, the true risk of the one that has shorter description can be bounded by a lower value. Thus, this result can be viewed as conveying a philosophical message:

A short explanation (that is, a hypothesis that has a short length) tends to be more valid than a long explanation.

This is a well known principle, called Occam's razor, after William of Ockham, a 14th-century English logician, who is believed to have been the first to phrase it explicitly. Here, we provide one possible justification to this principle. The inequality of Theorem 7.7 shows that the more complex a hypothesis h is (in the sense of having a longer description), the larger the sample size it has to fit to guarantee that it has a small true risk, $L_{\mathcal{D}}(h)$.

At a second glance, our Occam razor claim might seem somewhat problematic. In the context in which the Occam razor principle is usually invoked in science, the language according to which complexity is measured is a natural language, whereas here we may consider any arbitrary abstract description language. Assume that we have two hypotheses such that $|h'|$ is much smaller than $|h|$. By the preceding result, if both have the same error on a given training set, S, then the true error of h may be much higher than the true error of h', so one should prefer h' over h. However, we could have chosen a different description language, say, one that assigns a string of length 3 to h and a string of length 100000 to h'. Suddenly it looks as if one should prefer h over h'. But these are the same h and h' for which we argued two sentences ago that h' should be preferable. Where is the catch here?

Indeed, there is no inherent generalizability difference between hypotheses. The crucial aspect here is the dependency order between the initial choice of language (or, preference over hypotheses) and the training set. As we know from the basic Hoeffding's bound (Equation (4.2)), if we commit to any hypothesis *before* seeing the data, then we are guaranteed a rather small estimation error term $L_{\mathcal{D}}(h) \leq L_S(h) + \sqrt{\frac{\ln(2/\delta)}{2m}}$. Choosing a description language (or, equivalently, some weighting of hypotheses) is a weak form of committing to a hypothesis. Rather than committing to a single hypothesis, we spread out our commitment among many. As long as it is done independently of the training sample, our generalization bound holds. Just as the choice of a single hypothesis to be evaluated by a sample can be arbitrary, so is the choice of description language.

7.4 OTHER NOTIONS OF LEARNABILITY – CONSISTENCY

The notion of learnability can be further relaxed by allowing the needed sample sizes to depend not only on ϵ, δ, and h but also on the underlying data-generating probability distribution $\mathcal{D}$ (that is used to generate the training sample and to determine the risk). This type of performance guarantee is captured by the notion of *consistency*[1] of a learning rule.

Definition 7.8 (Consistency). Let Z be a domain set, let $\mathcal{P}$ be a set of probability distributions over Z, and let $\mathcal{H}$ be a hypothesis class. A learning rule A is *consistent* with respect to $\mathcal{H}$ and $\mathcal{P}$ if there exists a function $m_{\mathcal{H}}^{\mathrm{CON}} : (0,1)^2 \times \mathcal{H} \times \mathcal{P} \to \mathbb{N}$ such that, for every $\epsilon, \delta \in (0,1)$, every $h \in \mathcal{H}$, and every $\mathcal{D} \in \mathcal{P}$, if $m \geq m_{\mathcal{H}}^{\mathrm{NUL}}(\epsilon, \delta, h, \mathcal{D})$ then with probability of at least $1-\delta$ over the choice of $S \sim \mathcal{D}^m$ it holds that

$$L_{\mathcal{D}}(A(S)) \leq L_{\mathcal{D}}(h) + \epsilon.$$

If $\mathcal{P}$ is the set of all distributions,[2] we say that A is *universally consistent* with respect to $\mathcal{H}$.

The notion of consistency is, of course, a relaxation of our previous notion of nonuniform learnability. Clearly if an algorithm nonuniformly learns a class $\mathcal{H}$ it is also universally consistent for that class. The relaxation is strict in the sense that there are consistent learning rules that are not successful nonuniform learners. For example, the algorithm Memorize defined in Example 7.4 later is universally consistent for the class of all binary classifiers over $\mathbb{N}$. However, as we have argued before, this class is not nonuniformly learnable.

Example 7.4. Consider the classification prediction algorithm Memorize defined as follows. The algorithm memorizes the training examples, and, given a test point x, it

[1] In the literature, consistency is often defined using the notion of either convergence in probability (corresponding to weak consistency) or almost sure convergence (corresponding to strong consistency).

[2] Formally, we assume that Z is endowed with some sigma algebra of subsets Ω, and by "all distributions" we mean all probability distributions that have Ω contained in their associated family of measurable subsets.

predicts the majority label among all labeled instances of x that exist in the training sample (and some fixed default label if no instance of x appears in the training set). It is possible to show (see Exercise 7.6) that the Memorize algorithm is universally consistent for every countable domain $\mathcal{X}$ and a finite label set $\mathcal{Y}$ (w.r.t. the zero-one loss).

Intuitively, it is not obvious that the Memorize algorithm should be viewed as a *learner*, since it lacks the aspect of generalization, namely, of using observed data to predict the labels of unseen examples. The fact that Memorize is a consistent algorithm for the class of all functions over any countable domain set therefore raises doubt about the usefulness of consistency guarantees. Furthermore, the sharp-eyed reader may notice that the "bad learner" we introduced in Chapter 2, which led to overfitting, is in fact the Memorize algorithm. In the next section we discuss the significance of the different notions of learnability and revisit the No-Free-Lunch theorem in light of the different definitions of learnability.

7.5 DISCUSSING THE DIFFERENT NOTIONS OF LEARNABILITY

We have given three definitions of learnability and we now discuss their usefulness. As is usually the case, the usefulness of a mathematical definition depends on what we need it for. We therefore list several possible goals that we aim to achieve by defining learnability and discuss the usefulness of the different definitions in light of these goals.

What Is the Risk of the Learned Hypothesis?

The first possible goal of deriving performance guarantees on a learning algorithm is bounding the risk of the output predictor. Here, both PAC learning and nonuniform learning give us an upper bound on the true risk of the learned hypothesis based on its empirical risk. Consistency guarantees do not provide such a bound. However, it is always possible to estimate the risk of the output predictor using a validation set (as will be described in Chapter 11).

How Many Examples Are Required to Be as Good as the Best Hypothesis in $\mathcal{H}$?

When approaching a learning problem, a natural question is how many examples we need to collect in order to learn it. Here, PAC learning gives a crisp answer. However, for both nonuniform learning and consistency, we do not know in advance how many examples are required to learn $\mathcal{H}$. In nonuniform learning this number depends on the best hypothesis in $\mathcal{H}$, and in consistency it also depends on the underlying distribution. In this sense, PAC learning is the only useful definition of learnability. On the flip side, one should keep in mind that even if the estimation error of the predictor we learn is small, its risk may still be large if $\mathcal{H}$ has a large approximation error. So, for the question "How many examples are required to be as good as the Bayes optimal predictor?" even PAC guarantees do not provide us with a crisp answer. This reflects the fact that the usefulness of PAC learning relies on the quality of our prior knowledge.

PAC guarantees also help us to understand what we should do next if our learning algorithm returns a hypothesis with a large risk, since we can bound the part of the error that stems from estimation error and therefore know how much of the error is attributed to approximation error. If the approximation error is large, we know that we should use a different hypothesis class. Similarly, if a nonuniform algorithm fails, we can consider a different weighting function over (subsets of) hypotheses. However, when a consistent algorithm fails, we have no idea whether this is because of the estimation error or the approximation error. Furthermore, even if we are sure we have a problem with the estimation error term, we do not know how many more examples are needed to make the estimation error small.

How to Learn? How to Express Prior Knowledge?

Maybe the most useful aspect of the theory of learning is in providing an answer to the question of "how to learn." The definition of PAC learning yields the limitation of learning (via the No-Free-Lunch theorem) and the necessity of prior knowledge. It gives us a crisp way to encode prior knowledge by choosing a hypothesis class, and once this choice is made, we have a generic learning rule – ERM. The definition of nonuniform learnability also yields a crisp way to encode prior knowledge by specifying weights over (subsets of) hypotheses of $\mathcal{H}$. Once this choice is made, we again have a generic learning rule – SRM. The SRM rule is also advantageous in model selection tasks, where prior knowledge is partial. We elaborate on model selection in Chapter 11 and here we give a brief example.

Consider the problem of fitting a one dimensional polynomial to data; namely, our goal is to learn a function, $h : \mathbb{R} \to \mathbb{R}$, and as prior knowledge we consider the hypothesis class of polynomials. However, we might be uncertain regarding which degree d would give the best results for our data set: A small degree might not fit the data well (i.e., it will have a large approximation error), whereas a high degree might lead to overfitting (i.e., it will have a large estimation error). In the following we depict the result of fitting a polynomial of degrees 2, 3, and 10 to the same training set.

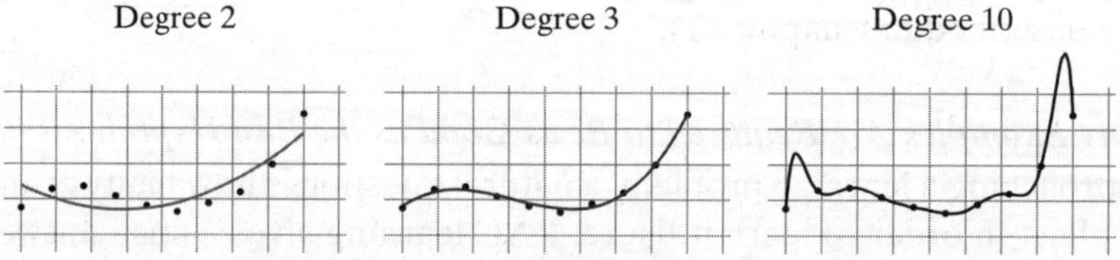

It is easy to see that the empirical risk decreases as we enlarge the degree. Therefore, if we choose $\mathcal{H}$ to be the class of all polynomials up to degree 10 then the ERM rule with respect to this class would output a 10 degree polynomial and would overfit. On the other hand, if we choose too small a hypothesis class, say, polynomials up to degree 2, then the ERM would suffer from underfitting (i.e., a large approximation error). In contrast, we can use the SRM rule on the set of all polynomials, while ordering subsets of $\mathcal{H}$ according to their degree, and this will yield a 3rd degree polynomial since the combination of its empirical risk and the bound on its estimation error is the smallest. In other words, the SRM rule enables us to select the right model on the basis of the data itself. The price we pay for this flexibility (besides a slight increase of the estimation error relative to PAC learning w.r.t. the optimal degree) is that we do not know in advance how many examples are needed to compete with the best hypothesis in $\mathcal{H}$.

Unlike the notions of PAC learnability and nonuniform learnability, the definition of consistency does not yield a natural learning paradigm or a way to encode prior knowledge. In fact, in many cases there is no need for prior knowledge at all. For example, we saw that even the Memorize algorithm, which intuitively should not be called a learning algorithm, is a consistent algorithm for any class defined over a countable domain and a finite label set. This hints that consistency is a very weak requirement.

Which Learning Algorithm Should We Prefer?
One may argue that even though consistency is a weak requirement, it is desirable that a learning algorithm will be consistent with respect to the set of all functions from $\mathcal{X}$ to $\mathcal{Y}$, which gives us a guarantee that for enough training examples, we will always be as good as the Bayes optimal predictor. Therefore, if we have two algorithms, where one is consistent and the other one is not consistent, we should prefer the consistent algorithm. However, this argument is problematic for two reasons. First, maybe it is the case that for most "natural" distributions we will observe in practice that the sample complexity of the consistent algorithm will be so large so that in every practical situation we will not obtain enough examples to enjoy this guarantee. Second, it is not very hard to make any PAC or nonuniform learner consistent with respect to the class of all functions from $\mathcal{X}$ to $\mathcal{Y}$. Concretely, consider a countable domain, $\mathcal{X}$, a finite label set $\mathcal{Y}$, and a hypothesis class, $\mathcal{H}$, of functions from $\mathcal{X}$ to $\mathcal{Y}$. We can make any nonuniform learner for $\mathcal{H}$ be consistent with respect to the class of *all* classifiers from $\mathcal{X}$ to $\mathcal{Y}$ using the following simple trick: Upon receiving a training set, we will first run the nonuniform learner over the training set, and then we will obtain a bound on the true risk of the learned predictor. If this bound is small enough we are done. Otherwise, we revert to the Memorize algorithm. This simple modification makes the algorithm consistent with respect to all functions from $\mathcal{X}$ to $\mathcal{Y}$. Since it is easy to make any algorithm consistent, it may not be wise to prefer one algorithm over the other just because of consistency considerations.

7.5.1 The No-Free-Lunch Theorem Revisited

Recall that the No-Free-Lunch theorem (Theorem 5.1 from Chapter 5) implies that no algorithm can learn the class of all classifiers over an infinite domain. In contrast, in this chapter we saw that the Memorize algorithm is consistent with respect to the class of all classifiers over a countable infinite domain. To understand why these two statements do not contradict each other, let us first recall the formal statement of the No-Free-Lunch theorem.

Let $\mathcal{X}$ be a countable infinite domain and let $\mathcal{Y} = \{\pm 1\}$. The No-Free-Lunch theorem implies the following: For any algorithm, A, and a training set size, m, there exist a distribution over $\mathcal{X}$ and a function $h^\star : \mathcal{X} \to \mathcal{Y}$, such that if A will get a sample of m i.i.d. training examples, labeled by $h^\star$, then A is likely to return a classifier with a larger error.

The consistency of Memorize implies the following: For every distribution over $\mathcal{X}$ and a labeling function $h^\star : \mathcal{X} \to \mathcal{Y}$, there exists a training set size m (that depends on the distribution and on $h^\star$) such that if Memorize receives at least m examples it is likely to return a classifier with a small error.

We see that in the No-Free-Lunch theorem, we first fix the training set size, and then find a distribution and a labeling function that are bad for this training set size. In contrast, in consistency guarantees, we first fix the distribution and the labeling function, and only then do we find a training set size that suffices for learning this particular distribution and labeling function.

7.6 SUMMARY

We introduced nonuniform learnability as a relaxation of PAC learnability and consistency as a relaxation of nonuniform learnability. This means that even classes of infinite VC-dimension can be learnable, in some weaker sense of learnability. We discussed the usefulness of the different definitions of learnability.

For hypothesis classes that are countable, we can apply the Minimum Description Length scheme, where hypotheses with shorter descriptions are preferred, following the principle of Occam's razor. An interesting example is the hypothesis class of all predictors we can implement in C++ (or any other programming language), which we can learn (nonuniformly) using the MDL scheme.

Arguably, the class of all predictors we can implement in C++ is a powerful class of functions and probably contains all that we can hope to learn in practice. The ability to learn this class is impressive, and, seemingly, this chapter should have been the last chapter of this book. This is not the case, because of the computational aspect of learning: that is, the runtime needed to apply the learning rule. For example, to implement the MDL paradigm with respect to all C++ programs, we need to perform an exhaustive search over all C++ programs, which will take forever. Even the implementation of the ERM paradigm with respect to all C++ programs of description length at most 1000 bits requires an exhaustive search over 2^{1000} hypotheses. While the sample complexity of learning this class is just $\frac{1000+\log(2/\delta)}{\epsilon^2}$, the runtime is $\geq 2^{1000}$. This is a huge number – much larger than the number of atoms in the visible universe. In the next chapter we formally define the computational complexity of learning. In the second part of this book we will study hypothesis classes for which the ERM or SRM schemes can be implemented efficiently.

7.7 BIBLIOGRAPHIC REMARKS

Our definition of nonuniform learnability is related to the definition of an Occam-algorithm in Blumer, Ehrenfeucht, Haussler and Warmuth (1987). The concept of SRM is due to (Vapnik & Chervonenkis 1974, Vapnik 1995). The concept of MDL is due to (Rissanen 1978, Rissanen 1983). The relation between SRM and MDL is discussed in Vapnik (1995). These notions are also closely related to the notion of *regularization* (e.g., Tikhonov 1943). We will elaborate on regularization in the second part of this book.

The notion of consistency of estimators dates back to Fisher (1922). Our presentation of consistency follows Steinwart and Christmann (2008), who also derived several no-free-lunch theorems.

7.8 EXERCISES

7.1 Prove that for any finite class $\mathcal{H}$, and any description language $d : \mathcal{H} \to \{0,1\}^*$, the VC-dimension of $\mathcal{H}$ is at most $2\sup\{|d(h)| : h \in \mathcal{H}\}$ – the maximum description length of a predictor in $\mathcal{H}$. Furthermore, if d is a prefix-free description then $\text{VCdim}(H) \le \sup\{|d(h)| : h \in \mathcal{H}\}$.

7.2 Let $\mathcal{H} = \{h_n : n \in \mathbb{N}\}$ be an infinite countable hypothesis class for binary classification. Show that it is impossible to assign weights to the hypotheses in $\mathcal{H}$ such that
- $\mathcal{H}$ could be learned nonuniformly using these weights. That is, the weighting function $w : \mathcal{H} \to [0,1]$ should satisfy the condition $\sum_{h\in\mathcal{H}} w(h) \le 1$.
- The weights would be monotonically nondecreasing. That is, if $i < j$, then $w(h_i) \le w(h_j)$.

7.3
- Consider a hypothesis class $\mathcal{H} = \bigcup_{n=1}^{\infty} \mathcal{H}_n$, where for every $n \in \mathbb{N}$, $\mathcal{H}_n$ is finite. Find a weighting function $w : \mathcal{H} \to [0,1]$ such that $\sum_{h\in\mathcal{H}} w(h) \le 1$ and so that for all $h \in \mathcal{H}$, $w(h)$ is determined by $n(h) = \min\{n : h \in \mathcal{H}_n\}$ and by $|\mathcal{H}_{n(h)}|$.
- **(*)** Define such a function w when for all n $\mathcal{H}_n$ is countable (possibly infinite).

7.4 Let $\mathcal{H}$ be some hypothesis class. For any $h \in \mathcal{H}$, let $|h|$ denote the description length of h, according to some fixed description language. Consider the MDL learning paradigm in which the algorithm returns:

$$h_S \in \arg\min_{h\in\mathcal{H}} \left[L_S(h) + \sqrt{\frac{|h| + \ln(2/\delta)}{2m}} \right],$$

where S is a sample of size m. For any $B > 0$, let $\mathcal{H}_B = \{h \in \mathcal{H} : |h| \le B\}$, and define

$$h_B^* = \arg\min_{h\in\mathcal{H}_B} L_{\mathcal{D}}(h).$$

Prove a bound on $L_{\mathcal{D}}(h_S) - L_{\mathcal{D}}(h_B^*)$ in terms of B, the confidence parameter δ, and the size of the training set m.
- Note: Such bounds are known as *oracle inequalities* in the literature: We wish to estimate how good we are compared to a reference classifier (or "oracle") h_B^*.

7.5 In this question we wish to show a No-Free-Lunch result for nonuniform learnability: namely, that, over any infinite domain, the class of *all* functions is not learnable even under the relaxed nonuniform variation of learning.

Recall that an algorithm, A, *nonuniformly learns* a hypothesis class $\mathcal{H}$ if there exists a function $m_{\mathcal{H}}^{\text{NUL}} : (0,1)^2 \times \mathcal{H} \to \mathbb{N}$ such that, for every $\epsilon, \delta \in (0,1)$ and for every $h \in \mathcal{H}$, if $m \ge m_{\mathcal{H}}^{\text{NUL}}(\epsilon, \delta, h)$ then for every distribution $\mathcal{D}$, with probability of at least $1-\delta$ over the choice of $S \sim \mathcal{D}^m$, it holds that

$$L_{\mathcal{D}}(A(S)) \le L_{\mathcal{D}}(h) + \epsilon.$$

If such an algorithm exists then we say that $\mathcal{H}$ is *nonuniformly learnable*.

1. Let A be a nonuniform learner for a class $\mathcal{H}$. For each $n \in \mathbb{N}$ define $\mathcal{H}_n^A = \{h \in \mathcal{H} : m^{\text{NUL}}(0.1, 0.1, h) \le n\}$. Prove that each such class $\mathcal{H}_n$ has a finite VC-dimension.
2. Prove that if a class $\mathcal{H}$ is nonuniformly learnable then there are classes $\mathcal{H}_n$ so that $\mathcal{H} = \bigcup_{n\in\mathbb{N}} \mathcal{H}_n$ and, for every $n \in \mathbb{N}$, $\text{VCdim}(\mathcal{H}_n)$ is finite.
3. Let $\mathcal{H}$ be a class that shatters an infinite set. Then, for every sequence of classes $(\mathcal{H}_n : n \in \mathbb{N})$ such that $\mathcal{H} = \bigcup_{n\in\mathbb{N}} \mathcal{H}_n$, there exists some n for which $\text{VCdim}(\mathcal{H}_n) = \infty$.

   Hint: Given a class $\mathcal{H}$ that shatters some infinite set K, and a sequence of classes $(\mathcal{H}_n : n \in \mathbb{N})$, each having a finite VC-dimension, start by defining subsets $K_n \subseteq K$ such that, for all n, $|K_n| >$ VCdim$(\mathcal{H}_n)$ and for any $n \ne m$, $K_n \cap K_m = \emptyset$. Now, pick *for each such K_n a function $f_n : K_n \rightarrow \{0,1\}$ so that no $h \in \mathcal{H}_n$ agrees with f_n on the domain K_n. Finally, define $f : X \rightarrow \{0,1\}$ by combining these f_n's and prove that $f \in \left(\mathcal{H} \setminus \bigcup_{n\in\mathbb{N}} \mathcal{H}_n\right)$.*

5. Construct a class $\mathcal{H}_1$ of functions from the unit interval $[0,1]$ to $\{0,1\}$ that is nonuniformly learnable but not PAC learnable.
6. Construct a class $\mathcal{H}_2$ of functions from the unit interval $[0,1]$ to $\{0,1\}$ that is not nonuniformly learnable.

7.6 In this question we wish to show that the algorithm Memorize is a consistent learner for every class of (binary-valued) functions over any countable domain. Let $\mathcal{X}$ be a countable domain and let $\mathcal{D}$ be a probability distribution over $\mathcal{X}$.

1. Let $\{x_i : i \in \mathbb{N}\}$ be an enumeration of the elements of $\mathcal{X}$ so that for all $i \leq j$, $\mathcal{D}(\{x_i\}) \leq \mathcal{D}(\{x_j\})$. Prove that
$$\lim_{n\to\infty} \sum_{i\geq n} \mathcal{D}(\{x_i\}) = 0.$$
2. Given any $\epsilon > 0$ prove that there exists $\epsilon_D > 0$ such that
$$\mathcal{D}(\{x \in \mathcal{X} : \mathcal{D}(\{x\}) < \epsilon_D\}) < \epsilon.$$
3. Prove that for every $\eta > 0$, if n is such that $\mathcal{D}(\{x_i\}) < \eta$ for all $i > n$, then for every $m \in \mathbb{N}$,
$$\mathop{\mathbb{P}}_{S\sim\mathcal{D}^m}[\exists x_i : (\mathcal{D}(\{x_i\}) > \eta \text{ and } x_i \notin S)] \leq ne^{-\eta m}.$$
4. Conclude that if $\mathcal{X}$ is countable then for every probability distribution $\mathcal{D}$ over $\mathcal{X}$ there exists a function $m_{\mathcal{D}} : (0,1) \times (0,1) \rightarrow \mathbb{N}$ such that for every $\epsilon, \delta > 0$ if $m > m_{\mathcal{D}}(\epsilon, \delta)$ then
$$\mathop{\mathbb{P}}_{S\sim\mathcal{D}^m}[\mathcal{D}(\{x : x \notin S\}) > \epsilon] < \delta.$$
5. Prove that Memorize is a consistent learner for every class of (binary-valued) functions over any countable domain.

8 The Runtime of Learning

So far in the book we have studied the statistical perspective of learning, namely, how many samples are needed for learning. In other words, we focused on the amount of information learning requires. However, when considering automated learning, computational resources also play a major role in determining the complexity of a task: that is, how much *computation* is involved in carrying out a learning task. Once a sufficient training sample is available to the learner, there is some computation to be done to extract a hypothesis or figure out the label of a given test instance. These computational resources are crucial in any practical application of machine learning. We refer to these two types of resources as the *sample complexity* and the *computational complexity*. In this chapter, we turn our attention to the computational complexity of learning.

The computational complexity of learning should be viewed in the wider context of the computational complexity of general algorithmic tasks. This area has been extensively investigated; see, for example, (Sipser 2006). The introductory comments that follow summarize the basic ideas of that general theory that are most relevant to our discussion.

The actual runtime (in seconds) of an algorithm depends on the specific machine the algorithm is being implemented on (e.g., what the clock rate of the machine's CPU is). To avoid dependence on the specific machine, it is common to analyze the runtime of algorithms in an asymptotic sense. For example, we say that the computational complexity of the merge-sort algorithm, which sorts a list of n items, is $O(n \log(n))$. This implies that we can implement the algorithm on any machine that satisfies the requirements of some accepted abstract model of computation, and the actual runtime in seconds will satisfy the following: there exist constants c and n_0, which can depend on the actual machine, such that, for any value of $n > n_0$, the runtime in seconds of sorting any n items will be at most $c\, n \log(n)$. It is common to use the term *feasible* or *efficiently computable* for tasks that can be performed by an algorithm whose running time is $O(p(n))$ for some polynomial function p. One should note that this type of analysis depends on defining what is the input size n of any instance to which the algorithm is expected to be applied. For "purely algorithmic" tasks, as discussed in the common computational complexity literature, this input size is clearly defined; the algorithm gets an input instance, say, a list to be sorted, or an arithmetic operation to be calculated, which has a well defined size (say, the number of bits in its representation). For machine learning tasks, the notion of an input size is not so clear. An algorithm aims to detect some pattern in a data set and can only access random samples of that data.

We start the chapter by discussing this issue and define the computational complexity of learning. For advanced students, we also provide a detailed formal definition. We then move on to consider the computational complexity of implementing the ERM rule. We first give several examples of hypothesis classes where the ERM rule can be efficiently implemented, and then consider some cases where, although the class is indeed efficiently learnable, ERM implementation is computationally hard. It follows that hardness of implementing ERM does not imply hardness of learning. Finally, we briefly discuss how one can show hardness of a given learning task, namely, that no learning algorithm can solve it efficiently.

8.1 COMPUTATIONAL COMPLEXITY OF LEARNING

Recall that a learning algorithm has access to a domain of examples, Z, a hypothesis class, $\mathcal{H}$, a loss function, ℓ, and a training set of examples from Z that are sampled i.i.d. according to an unknown distribution $\mathcal{D}$. Given parameters ϵ, δ, the algorithm should output a hypothesis h such that with probability of at least $1-\delta$,

$$L_{\mathcal{D}}(h) \leq \min_{h' \in \mathcal{H}} L_{\mathcal{D}}(h') + \epsilon.$$

As mentioned before, the actual runtime of an algorithm in seconds depends on the specific machine. To allow machine independent analysis, we use the standard approach in computational complexity theory. First, we rely on a notion of an abstract machine, such as a Turing machine (or a Turing machine over the reals [Blum, Shub & Smale 1989]). Second, we analyze the runtime in an asymptotic sense, while ignoring constant factors; thus the specific machine is not important as long as it implements the abstract machine. Usually, the asymptote is with respect to the size of the input to the algorithm. For example, for the merge-sort algorithm mentioned before, we analyze the runtime as a function of the number of items that need to be sorted.

In the context of learning algorithms, there is no clear notion of "input size." One might define the input size to be the size of the training set the algorithm receives, but that would be rather pointless. If we give the algorithm a very large number of examples, much larger than the sample complexity of the learning problem, the algorithm can simply ignore the extra examples. Therefore, a larger training set does not make the learning problem more difficult, and, consequently, the runtime available for a learning algorithm should not increase as we increase the size of the training set. Just the same, we can still analyze the runtime as a function of natural parameters of the problem such as the target accuracy, the confidence of achieving that accuracy, the dimensionality of the domain set, or some measures of the complexity of the hypothesis class with which the algorithm's output is compared.

To illustrate this, consider a learning algorithm for the task of learning axis aligned rectangles. A specific problem of learning axis aligned rectangles is derived by specifying ϵ, δ, and the dimension of the instance space. We can define a sequence of problems of the type "rectangles learning" by fixing ϵ, δ and varying the dimension to be $d = 2, 3, 4, \ldots$. We can also define another sequence of "rectangles learning" problems by fixing d, δ and varying the target accuracy to be $\epsilon = \frac{1}{2}, \frac{1}{3}, \ldots$. One can of course choose other sequences of such problems. Once a sequence of the problems is fixed, one can analyze the asymptotic runtime as a function of variables of that sequence.

Before we introduce the formal definition, there is one more subtlety we need to tackle. On the basis of the preceding, a learning algorithm can "cheat," by transferring the computational burden to the output hypothesis. For example, the algorithm can simply define the output hypothesis to be the function that stores the training set in its memory, and whenever it gets a test example x it calculates the ERM hypothesis on the training set and applies it on x. Note that in this case, our algorithm has a fixed output (namely, the function that we have just described) and can run in constant time. However, learning is still hard – the hardness is now in implementing the output classifier to obtain a label prediction. To prevent this "cheating," we shall require that the output of a learning algorithm must be applied to predict the label of a new example in time that does not exceed the runtime of training (that is, computing the output classifier from the input training sample). In the next subsection the advanced reader may find a formal definition of the computational complexity of learning.

8.1.1 Formal Definition*

The definition that follows relies on a notion of an underlying abstract machine, which is usually either a Turing machine or a Turing machine over the reals. We will measure the computational complexity of an algorithm using the number of "operations" it needs to perform, where we assume that for any machine that implements the underlying abstract machine there exists a constant c such that any such "operation" can be performed on the machine using c seconds.

Definition 8.1 (The Computational Complexity of a Learning Algorithm). We define the complexity of learning in two steps. First we consider the computational complexity of a fixed learning problem (determined by a triplet $(Z, \mathcal{H}, \ell)$ – a domain set, a benchmark hypothesis class, and a loss function). Then, in the second step we consider the rate of change of that complexity along a sequence of such tasks.

1. Given a function $f : (0,1)^2 \to \mathbb{N}$, a learning task $(Z, \mathcal{H}, \ell)$, and a learning algorithm, $\mathcal{A}$, we say that $\mathcal{A}$ solves the learning task in time $O(f)$ if there exists some constant number c, such that for every probability distribution $\mathcal{D}$ over Z, and input ϵ, $\delta \in (0,1)$, when $\mathcal{A}$ has access to samples generated i.i.d. by $\mathcal{D}$,
   - $\mathcal{A}$ terminates after performing at most $cf(\epsilon, \delta)$ operations
   - The output of $\mathcal{A}$, denoted $h_{\mathcal{A}}$, can be applied to predict the label of a new example while performing at most $cf(\epsilon, \delta)$ operations

- The output of $\mathcal{A}$ is probably approximately correct; namely, with probability of at least $1-\delta$ (over the random samples $\mathcal{A}$ receives), $L_{\mathcal{D}}(h_{\mathcal{A}}) \leq \min_{h' \in \mathcal{H}} L_{\mathcal{D}}(h') + \epsilon$

2. Consider a sequence of learning problems, $(Z_n, \mathcal{H}_n, \ell_n)_{n=1}^{\infty}$, where problem n is defined by a domain Z_n, a hypothesis class $\mathcal{H}_n$, and a loss function ℓ_n. Let $\mathcal{A}$ be a learning algorithm designed for solving learning problems of this form. Given a function $g : \mathbb{N} \times (0,1)^2 \to \mathbb{N}$, we say that the runtime of $\mathcal{A}$ with respect to the preceding sequence is $O(g)$, if for all n, $\mathcal{A}$ solves the problem $(Z_n, \mathcal{H}_n, \ell_n)$ in time $O(f_n)$, where $f_n : (0,1)^2 \to \mathbb{N}$ is defined by $f_n(\epsilon, \delta) = g(n, \epsilon, \delta)$.

We say that $\mathcal{A}$ is an *efficient* algorithm with respect to a sequence $(Z_n, \mathcal{H}_n, \ell_n)$ if its runtime is $O(p(n, 1/\epsilon, 1/\delta))$ for some polynomial p.

From this definition we see that the question whether a general learning problem can be solved efficiently depends on how it can be broken into a sequence of specific learning problems. For example, consider the problem of learning a finite hypothesis class. As we showed in previous chapters, the ERM rule over $\mathcal{H}$ is guaranteed to (ϵ, δ)-learn $\mathcal{H}$ if the number of training examples is order of $m_{\mathcal{H}}(\epsilon, \delta) = \log(|\mathcal{H}|/\delta)/\epsilon^2$. Assuming that the evaluation of a hypothesis on an example takes a constant time, it is possible to implement the ERM rule in time $O(|\mathcal{H}| m_{\mathcal{H}}(\epsilon, \delta))$ by performing an exhaustive search over $\mathcal{H}$ with a training set of size $m_{\mathcal{H}}(\epsilon, \delta)$. For any fixed finite $\mathcal{H}$, the exhaustive search algorithm runs in polynomial time. Furthermore, if we define a sequence of problems in which $|\mathcal{H}_n| = n$, then the exhaustive search is still considered to be efficient. However, if we define a sequence of problems for which $|\mathcal{H}_n| = 2^n$, then the sample complexity is still polynomial in n but the computational complexity of the exhaustive search algorithm grows exponentially with n (thus, rendered inefficient).

8.2 IMPLEMENTING THE ERM RULE

Given a hypothesis class $\mathcal{H}$, the $\text{ERM}_{\mathcal{H}}$ rule is maybe the most natural learning paradigm. Furthermore, for binary classification problems we saw that if learning is at all possible, it is possible with the ERM rule. In this section we discuss the computational complexity of implementing the ERM rule for several hypothesis classes.

Given a hypothesis class, $\mathcal{H}$, a domain set Z, and a loss function ℓ, the corresponding $\text{ERM}_{\mathcal{H}}$ rule can be defined as follows:

On a finite input sample $S \in Z^m$ output some $h \in \mathcal{H}$ that minimizes the empirical loss, $L_S(h) = \frac{1}{|S|} \sum_{z \in S} \ell(h, z)$.

This section studies the runtime of implementing the ERM rule for several examples of learning tasks.

8.2.1 Finite Classes

Limiting the hypothesis class to be a finite class may be considered as a reasonably mild restriction. For example, $\mathcal{H}$ can be the set of all predictors that can be implemented by a C++ program written in at most 10000 bits of code. Other examples of useful finite classes are any hypothesis class that can be parameterized by a finite number of parameters, where we are satisfied with a representation of each of the parameters using a finite number of bits, for example, the class of axis aligned rectangles in the Euclidean space, $\mathbb{R}^d$, when the parameters defining any given rectangle are specified up to some limited precision.

As we have shown in previous chapters, the sample complexity of learning a finite class is upper bounded by $m_{\mathcal{H}}(\epsilon,\delta) = c\log(c|\mathcal{H}|/\delta)/\epsilon^c$, where $c = 1$ in the realizable case and $c = 2$ in the nonrealizable case. Therefore, the sample complexity has a mild dependence on the size of $\mathcal{H}$. In the example of C++ programs mentioned before, the number of hypotheses is $2^{10,000}$ but the sample complexity is only $c(10,000 + \log(c/\delta))/\epsilon^c$.

A straightforward approach for implementing the ERM rule over a finite hypothesis class is to perform an exhaustive search. That is, for each $h \in \mathcal{H}$ we calculate the empirical risk, $L_S(h)$, and return a hypothesis that minimizes the empirical risk. Assuming that the evaluation of $\ell(h,z)$ on a single example takes a constant amount of time, k, the runtime of this exhaustive search becomes $k|\mathcal{H}|m$, where m is the size of the training set. If we let m to be the upper bound on the sample complexity mentioned, then the runtime becomes $k|\mathcal{H}|c\log(c|\mathcal{H}|/\delta)/\epsilon^c$.

The linear dependence of the runtime on the size of $\mathcal{H}$ makes this approach inefficient (and unrealistic) for large classes. Formally, if we define a sequence of problems $(Z_n, \mathcal{H}_n, \ell_n)_{n=1}^{\infty}$ such that $\log(|\mathcal{H}_n|) = n$, then the exhaustive search approach yields an exponential runtime. In the example of C++ programs, if $\mathcal{H}_n$ is the set of functions that can be implemented by a C++ program written in at most n bits of code, then the runtime grows exponentially with n, implying that the exhaustive search approach is unrealistic for practical use. In fact, this problem is one of the reasons we are dealing with other hypothesis classes, like classes of linear predictors, which we will encounter in the next chapter, and not just focusing on finite classes.

It is important to realize that the inefficiency of one algorithmic approach (such as the exhaustive search) does not yet imply that no efficient ERM implementation exists. Indeed, we will show examples in which the ERM rule can be implemented efficiently.

8.2.2 Axis Aligned Rectangles

Let $\mathcal{H}_n$ be the class of axis aligned rectangles in $\mathbb{R}^n$, namely,

$$\mathcal{H}_n = \{h_{(a_1,\ldots,a_n,b_1,\ldots,b_n)} : \forall i, a_i \le b_i\}$$

where

$$h_{(a_1,\ldots,a_n,b_1,\ldots,b_n)}(\mathbf{x}, y) = \begin{cases} 1 & \text{if } \forall i,\ x_i \in [a_i, b_i] \\ 0 & \text{otherwise} \end{cases} \tag{8.1}$$

Efficiently Learnable in the Realizable Case

Consider implementing the ERM rule in the realizable case. That is, we are given a training set $S = (\mathbf{x}_1, y_1), \ldots, (\mathbf{x}_m, y_m)$ of examples, such that there exists an axis aligned rectangle, $h \in \mathcal{H}_n$, for which $h(\mathbf{x}_i) = y_i$ for all i. Our goal is to find such an axis aligned rectangle with a zero training error, namely, a rectangle that is consistent with all the labels in S.

We show later that this can be done in time $O(nm)$. Indeed, for each $i \in [n]$, set $a_i = \min\{x_i : (\mathbf{x}, 1) \in S\}$ and $b_i = \max\{x_i : (\mathbf{x}, 1) \in S\}$. In words, we take a_i to be the minimal value of the i'th coordinate of a positive example in S and b_i to be the maximal value of the i'th coordinate of a positive example in S. It is easy to verify that the resulting rectangle has zero training error and that the runtime of finding each a_i and b_i is $O(m)$. Hence, the total runtime of this procedure is $O(nm)$.

Not Efficiently Learnable in the Agnostic Case

In the agnostic case, we do not assume that some hypothesis h perfectly predicts the labels of all the examples in the training set. Our goal is therefore to find h that minimizes the number of examples for which $y_i \neq h(\mathbf{x}_i)$. It turns out that for many common hypothesis classes, including the classes of axis aligned rectangles we consider here, solving the ERM problem in the agnostic setting is NP-hard (and, in most cases, it is even NP-hard to find some $h \in \mathcal{H}$ whose error is no more than some constant $c > 1$ times that of the empirical risk minimizer in $\mathcal{H}$). That is, unless P = NP, there is no algorithm whose running time is polynomial in m and n that is guaranteed to find an ERM hypothesis for these problems (Ben-David, Eiron & Long 2003).

On the other hand, it is worthwhile noticing that, if we fix one specific hypothesis class, say, axis aligned rectangles in some fixed dimension, n, then there exist efficient learning algorithms for this class. In other words, there are successful agnostic PAC learners that run in time polynomial in $1/\epsilon$ and $1/\delta$ (but their dependence on the dimension n is not polynomial).

To see this, recall the implementation of the ERM rule we presented for the realizable case, from which it follows that an axis aligned rectangle is determined by at most $2n$ examples. Therefore, given a training set of size m, we can perform an exhaustive search over all subsets of the training set of size at most $2n$ examples and construct a rectangle from each such subset. Then, we can pick the rectangle with the minimal training error. This procedure is guaranteed to find an ERM hypothesis, and the runtime of the procedure is $m^{O(n)}$. It follows that if n is fixed, the runtime is polynomial in the sample size. This does not contradict the aforementioned hardness result, since there we argued that unless P=NP one cannot have an algorithm whose dependence on the dimension n is polynomial as well.

8.2.3 Boolean Conjunctions

A Boolean conjunction is a mapping from $\mathcal{X} = \{0,1\}^n$ to $\mathcal{Y} = \{0,1\}$ that can be expressed as a proposition formula of the form $x_{i_1} \wedge \ldots \wedge x_{i_k} \wedge \neg x_{j_1} \wedge \ldots \wedge \neg x_{j_r}$, for some indices $i_1, \ldots, i_k, j_1, \ldots, j_r \in [n]$. The function that such a proposition formula defines is

$$h(\mathbf{x}) = \begin{cases} 1 & \text{if } x_{i_1} = \cdots = x_{i_k} = 1 \text{ and } x_{j_1} = \cdots = x_{j_r} = 0 \\ 0 & \text{otherwise} \end{cases}$$

Let $\mathcal{H}_C^n$ be the class of all Boolean conjunctions over $\{0,1\}^n$. The size of $\mathcal{H}_C^n$ is at most $3^n + 1$ (since in a conjunction formula, each element of $\mathbf{x}$ either appears, or appears with a negation sign, or does not appear at all, and we also have the all negative formula). Hence, the sample complexity of learning $\mathcal{H}_C^n$ using the ERM rule is at most $d \log(3/\delta)/\epsilon$.

Efficiently Learnable in the Realizable Case

Next, we show that it is possible to solve the ERM problem for $\mathcal{H}_C^n$ in time polynomial in n and m. The idea is to define an ERM conjunction by including in the hypothesis conjunction all the literals that do not contradict any positively labeled example. Let $\mathbf{v}_1, \ldots, \mathbf{v}_{m^+}$ be all the positively labeled instances in the input sample S. We define, by induction on $i \le m^+$, a sequence of hypotheses (or conjunctions). Let h_0 be the conjunction of all possible literals. That is, $h_0 = x_1 \wedge \neg x_1 \wedge x_2 \wedge \ldots \wedge x_n \wedge \neg x_n$. Note that h_0 assigns the label 0 to all the elements of $\mathcal{X}$. We obtain h_{i+1} by deleting from the conjunction h_i all the literals that are not satisfied by $\mathbf{v}_{i+1}$. The algorithm outputs the hypothesis h_{m^+}. Note that h_{m^+} labels positively all the positively labeled examples in S. Furthermore, for every $i \le m^+$, h_i is the most restrictive conjunction that labels $\mathbf{v}_1, \ldots, \mathbf{v}_i$ positively. Now, since we consider learning in the realizable setup, there exists a conjunction hypothesis, $f \in \mathcal{H}_C^n$, that is consistent with all the examples in S. Since h_{m^+} is the most restrictive conjunction that labels positively all the positively labeled members of S, any instance labeled 0 by f is also labeled 0 by h_{m^+}. It follows that h_{m^+} has zero training error (w.r.t. S) and is therefore a legal ERM hypothesis. Note that the running time of this algorithm is $O(mn)$.

Not Efficiently Learnable in the Agnostic Case

As in the case of axis aligned rectangles, unless P = NP, there is no algorithm whose running time is polynomial in m and n that guaranteed to find an ERM hypothesis for the class of Boolean conjunctions in the unrealizable case.

8.2.4 Learning 3-Term DNF

We next show that a slight generalization of the class of Boolean conjunctions leads to intractability of solving the ERM problem even in the realizable case. Consider the class of 3-term disjunctive normal form formulae (3-term DNF). The instance space is $\mathcal{X} = \{0,1\}^n$ and each hypothesis is represented by the Boolean formula of the form $h(\mathbf{x}) = A_1(\mathbf{x}) \vee A_2(\mathbf{x}) \vee A_3(\mathbf{x})$, where each $A_i(\mathbf{x})$ is a Boolean conjunction (as defined in the previous section). The output of $h(\mathbf{x})$ is 1 if either $A_1(\mathbf{x})$ or $A_2(\mathbf{x})$ or $A_3(\mathbf{x})$ outputs the label 1. If all three conjunctions output the label 0 then $h(\mathbf{x}) = 0$.

Let $\mathcal{H}_{3DNF}^n$ be the hypothesis class of all such 3-term DNF formulae. The size of $\mathcal{H}_{3DNF}^n$ is at most 3^{3n}. Hence, the sample complexity of learning $\mathcal{H}_{3DNF}^n$ using the ERM rule is at most $3n \log(3/\delta)/\epsilon$.

However, from the computational perspective, this learning problem is hard. It has been shown (see (Pitt & Valiant 1988, Kearns, Schapire & Sellie 1994)) that unless RP = NP, there is no polynomial time algorithm that *properly* learns a sequence of 3-term DNF learning problems in which the dimension of the n'th problem is n. By "properly" we mean that the algorithm should output a hypothesis that is a 3-term DNF formula. In particular, since $\mathrm{ERM}_{\mathcal{H}^n_{3DNF}}$ outputs a 3-term DNF formula it is a proper learner and therefore it is hard to implement it. The proof uses a reduction of the graph 3-coloring problem to the problem of PAC learning 3-term DNF. The detailed technique is given in Exercise 8.4. See also (Kearns and Vazirani 1994, section 1.4).

8.3 EFFICIENTLY LEARNABLE, BUT NOT BY A PROPER ERM

In the previous section we saw that it is impossible to implement the ERM rule efficiently for the class $\mathcal{H}^n_{3DNF}$ of 3-DNF formulae. In this section we show that it is possible to learn this class efficiently, but using ERM with respect to a larger class.

Representation Independent Learning Is Not Hard

Next we show that it is possible to learn 3-term DNF formulae efficiently. There is no contradiction to the hardness result mentioned in the previous section as we now allow "representation independent" learning. That is, we allow the learning algorithm to output a hypothesis that is not a 3-term DNF formula. The basic idea is to replace the original hypothesis class of 3-term DNF formula with a larger hypothesis class so that the new class is easily learnable. The learning algorithm might return a hypothesis that does not belong to the original hypothesis class; hence the name "representation independent" learning. We emphasize that in most situations, returning a hypothesis with good predictive ability is what we are really interested in doing.

We start by noting that because $\vee$ distributes over $\wedge$, each 3-term DNF formula can be rewritten as

$$A_1 \vee A_2 \vee A_3 = \bigwedge_{u \in A_1, v \in A_2, w \in A_3} (u \vee v \vee w)$$

Next, let us define: $\psi : \{0,1\}^n \to \{0,1\}^{(2n)^3}$ such that for each triplet of literals u, v, w there is a variable in the range of ψ indicating if $u \vee v \vee w$ is true or false. So, for each 3-DNF formula over $\{0,1\}^n$ there is a conjunction over $\{0,1\}^{(2n)^3}$, with the same truth table. Since we assume that the data is realizable, we can solve the ERM problem with respect to the class of conjunctions over $\{0,1\}^{(2n)^3}$. Furthermore, the sample complexity of learning the class of conjunctions in the higher dimensional space is at most $n^3 \log(1/\delta)/\epsilon$. Thus, the overall runtime of this approach is polynomial in n.

Intuitively, the idea is as follows. We started with a hypothesis class for which learning is hard. We switched to another representation where the hypothesis class is larger than the original class but has more structure, which allows for a more efficient ERM search. In the new representation, solving the ERM problem is easy.

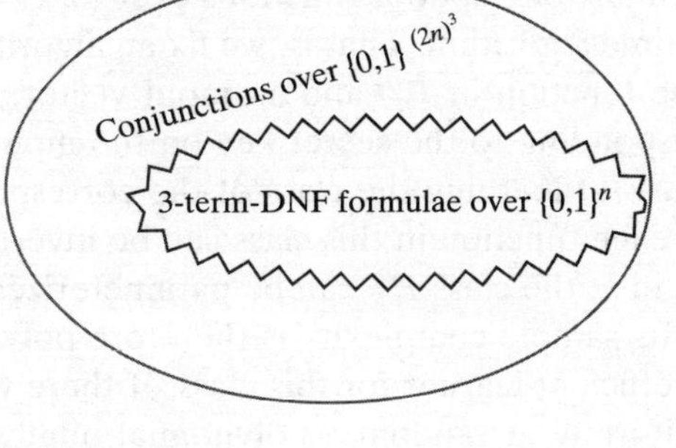

8.4 HARDNESS OF LEARNING*

We have just demonstrated that the computational hardness of implementing $\text{ERM}_{\mathcal{H}}$ does not imply that such a class $\mathcal{H}$ is not learnable. How can we prove that a learning problem is computationally hard?

One approach is to rely on cryptographic assumptions. In some sense, cryptography is the opposite of learning. In learning we try to uncover some rule underlying the examples we see, whereas in cryptography, the goal is to make sure that nobody will be able to discover some secret, in spite of having access to some partial information about it. On that high level intuitive sense, results about the cryptographic security of some system translate into results about the unlearnability of some corresponding task. Regrettably, currently one has no way of proving that a cryptographic protocol is not breakable. Even the common assumption of $\text{P} \neq \text{NP}$ does not suffice for that (although it can be shown to be necessary for most common cryptographic scenarios). The common approach for proving that cryptographic protocols are secure is to start with some *cryptographic assumptions*. The more these are used as a basis for cryptography, the stronger is our belief that they really hold (or, at least, that algorithms that will refute them are hard to come by).

We now briefly describe the basic idea of how to deduce hardness of learnability from cryptographic assumptions. Many cryptographic systems rely on the assumption that there exists a one way function. Roughly speaking, a one way function is a function $f : \{0,1\}^n \to \{0,1\}^n$ (more formally, it is a sequence of functions, one for each dimension n) that is easy to compute but is hard to invert. More formally, f can be computed in time $\text{poly}(n)$ but for any randomized polynomial time algorithm A, and for every polynomial $p(\cdot)$,

$$\mathbb{P}[f(A(f(\mathbf{x}))) = f(\mathbf{x})] < \frac{1}{p(n)},$$

where the probability is taken over a random choice of $\mathbf{x}$ according to the uniform distribution over $\{0,1\}^n$ and the randomness of A.

A one way function, f, is called trapdoor one way function if, for some polynomial function p, for every n there exists a bit-string s_n (called a secret key) of length $\leq p(n)$, such that there is a polynomial time algorithm that, for every n and every $\mathbf{x} \in \{0,1\}^n$, on input $(f(\mathbf{x}), s_n)$ outputs $\mathbf{x}$. In other words, although f is hard to invert, once one has access to its secret key, inverting f becomes feasible. Such functions are parameterized by their secret key.

Now, let F_n be a family of trapdoor functions over $\{0,1\}^n$ that can be calculated by some polynomial time algorithm. That is, we fix an algorithm that given a secret key (representing one function in F_n) and an input vector, it calculates the value of the function corresponding to the secret key on the input vector in polynomial time. Consider the task of learning the class of the corresponding inverses, $H_F^n = \{f^{-1} : f \in F_n\}$. Since each function in this class can be inverted by some secret key s_n of size polynomial in n, the class H_F^n can be parameterized by these keys and its size is at most $2^{p(n)}$. Its sample complexity is therefore polynomial in n. We claim that there can be no efficient learner for this class. If there were such a learner, L, then by sampling uniformly at random a polynomial number of strings in $\{0,1\}^n$, and computing f over them, we could generate a labeled training sample of pairs $(f(\mathbf{x}), \mathbf{x})$, which should suffice for our learner to figure out an (ϵ, δ) approximation of f^{-1} (w.r.t. the uniform distribution over the range of f), which would violate the one way property of f.

A more detailed treatment, as well as a concrete example, can be found in (Kearns and Vazirani 1994, chapter 6). Using reductions, they also show that the class of functions that can be calculated by small Boolean circuits is not efficiently learnable, even in the realizable case.

8.5 SUMMARY

The runtime of learning algorithms is asymptotically analyzed as a function of different parameters of the learning problem, such as the size of the hypothesis class, our measure of accuracy, our measure of confidence, or the size of the domain set. We have demonstrated cases in which the ERM rule can be implemented efficiently. For example, we derived efficient algorithms for solving the ERM problem for the class of Boolean conjunctions and the class of axis aligned rectangles, under the realizability assumption. However, implementing ERM for these classes in the agnostic case is NP-hard. Recall that from the statistical perspective, there is no difference between the realizable and agnostic cases (i.e., a class is learnable in both cases if and only if it has a finite VC-dimension). In contrast, as we saw, from the computational perspective the difference is immense. We have also shown another example, the class of 3-term DNF, where implementing ERM is hard even in the realizable case, yet the class is efficiently learnable by another algorithm.

Hardness of implementing the ERM rule for several natural hypothesis classes has motivated the development of alternative learning methods, which we will discuss in the next part of this book.

8.6 BIBLIOGRAPHIC REMARKS

Valiant (1984) introduced the efficient PAC learning model in which the runtime of the algorithm is required to be polynomial in $1/\epsilon$, $1/\delta$, and the representation size of hypotheses in the class. A detailed discussion and thorough bibliographic notes are given in Kearns and Vazirani (1994).

8.7 EXERCISES

8.1 Let $\mathcal{H}$ be the class of intervals on the line (formally equivalent to axis aligned rectangles in dimension $n=1$). Propose an implementation of the $\text{ERM}_{\mathcal{H}}$ learning rule (in the agnostic case) that given a training set of size m, runs in time $O(m^2)$.
Hint: Use dynamic programming.

8.2 Let $\mathcal{H}_1, \mathcal{H}_2, \ldots$ be a sequence of hypothesis classes for binary classification. Assume that there is a learning algorithm that implements the ERM rule in the realizable case such that the output hypothesis of the algorithm for each class $\mathcal{H}_n$ only depends on $O(n)$ examples out of the training set. Furthermore, assume that such a hypothesis can be calculated given these $O(n)$ examples in time $O(n)$, and that the empirical risk of each such hypothesis can be evaluated in time $O(mn)$. For example, if $\mathcal{H}_n$ is the class of axis aligned rectangles in $\mathbb{R}^n$, we saw that it is possible to find an ERM hypothesis in the realizable case that is defined by at most $2n$ examples. Prove that in such cases, it is possible to find an ERM hypothesis for $\mathcal{H}_n$ in the unrealizable case in time $O(mn\, m^{O(n)})$.

8.3 In this exercise, we present several classes for which finding an ERM classifier is computationally hard. First, we introduce the class of n-dimensional halfspaces, HS_n, for a domain $\mathcal{X}=\mathbb{R}^n$. This is the class of all functions of the form $h_{\mathbf{w},b}(\mathbf{x}) = \text{sign}(\langle \mathbf{w},\mathbf{x}\rangle + b)$ where $\mathbf{w},\mathbf{x}\in\mathbb{R}^n$, $\langle \mathbf{w},\mathbf{x}\rangle$ is their inner product, and $b\in\mathbb{R}$. See a detailed description in Chapter 9.

1. Show that $\text{ERM}_{\mathcal{H}}$ over the class $\mathcal{H}=HS_n$ of linear predictors is computationally hard. More precisely, we consider the sequence of problems in which the dimension n grows linearly and the number of examples m is set to be some constant times n.
Hint: You can prove the hardness by a reduction from the following problem:

   Max FS: Given a system of linear inequalities, $A\mathbf{x} > \mathbf{b}$ with $A \in R^{m\times n}$ and $\mathbf{b}\in\mathbb{R}^m$ (that is, a system of m linear inequalities in n variables, $\mathbf{x}=(x_1,\ldots,x_n)$), find a subsystem containing as many inequalities as possible that has a solution (such a subsystem is called *feasible*).

   It has been shown (Sankaran 1993) that the problem Max FS is NP-hard.
   Show that any algorithm that finds an ERM_{HS_n} hypothesis for any training sample $S\in(\mathbb{R}^n\times\{+1,-1\})^m$ can be used to solve the Max FS problem of size m,n.
   Hint: Define a mapping that transforms linear inequalities in n variables into labeled points in $\mathbb{R}^n$, and a mapping that transforms vectors in $\mathbb{R}^n$ to halfspaces, such that a vector $\mathbf{w}$ satisfies an inequality q if and only if the labeled point that corresponds to q is classified correctly by the halfspace corresponding to $\mathbf{w}$. Conclude that the problem of empirical risk minimization for halfspaces in also NP-hard (that is, if it can be solved in time polynomial in the sample size, m, and the Euclidean dimension, n, then every problem in the class NP can be solved in polynomial time).
2. Let $\mathcal{X}=\mathbb{R}^n$ and let $\mathcal{H}_k^n$ be the class of all intersections of k-many linear halfspaces in $\mathbb{R}^n$. In this exercise, we wish to show that $\text{ERM}_{\mathcal{H}_k^n}$ is computationally hard for every $k\geq 3$. Precisely, we consider a sequence of problems where $k\geq 3$ is a constant and n grows linearly. The training set size, m, also grows linearly with n.
Toward this goal, consider the k-coloring problem for graphs, defined as follows:

   Given a graph $G=(V,E)$, and a number k, determine whether there exists a function $f: V\to\{1\ldots k\}$ so that for every $(u,v)\in E$, $f(u)\neq f(v)$.

The k-coloring problem is known to be NP-hard for every $k \geq 3$ (Karp 1972).
We wish to reduce the k-coloring problem to $ERM_{\mathcal{H}_k^n}$: that is, to prove that if there is an algorithm that solves the $ERM_{\mathcal{H}_k^n}$ problem in time polynomial in k, n, and the sample size m, then there is a polynomial time algorithm for the graph k-coloring problem.
Given a graph $G = (V, E)$, let $\{v_1 \dots v_n\}$ be the vertices in V. Construct a sample $S(G) \in (\mathbb{R}^n \times \{\pm 1\})^m$, where $m = |V| + |E|$, as follows:

- For every $v_i \in V$, construct an instance $\mathbf{e}_i$ with a negative label.
- For every edge $(v_i, v_j) \in E$, construct an instance $(\mathbf{e}_i + \mathbf{e}_j)/2$ with a positive label.

1. Prove that if there exists some $h \in \mathcal{H}_k^n$ that has zero error over $S(G)$ then G is k-colorable.
   Hint: Let $h = \bigcap_{j=1}^k h_j$ be an ERM classifier in $\mathcal{H}_k^n$ over S. Define a coloring of V by setting $f(v_i)$ to be the minimal j such that $h_j(\mathbf{e}_i) = -1$. Use the fact that halfspaces are convex sets to show that it cannot be true that two vertices that are connected by an edge have the same color.
2. Prove that if G is k-colorable then there exists some $h \in H_k^n$ that has zero error over $S(G)$.
   Hint: Given a coloring f of the vertices of G, we should come up with k hyperplanes, $h_1 \dots h_k$ whose intersection is a perfect classifier for $S(G)$. Let $b = 0.6$ for all of these hyperplanes and, for $t \leq k$ let the i'th weight of the t'th hyperplane, $w_{t,i}$, be -1 if $f(v_i) = t$ and 0 otherwise.
3. On the basis of the preceding, prove that for any $k \geq 3$, the $\text{ERM}_{\mathcal{H}_k^n}$ problem is NP-hard.

8.4 In this exercise we show that hardness of solving the ERM problem is equivalent to hardness of proper PAC learning. Recall that by "properness" of the algorithm we mean that it must output a hypothesis from the hypothesis class. To formalize this statement, we first need the following definition.

Definition 8.2. The complexity class Randomized Polynomial (RP) time is the class of all decision problems (that is, problems in which on any instance one has to find out whether the answer is YES or NO) for which there exists a probabilistic algorithm (namely, the algorithm is allowed to flip random coins while it is running) with these properties:

- On any input instance the algorithm runs in polynomial time in the input size.
- If the correct answer is NO, the algorithm must return NO.
- If the correct answer is YES, the algorithm returns YES with probability $a \geq 1/2$ and returns NO with probability $1 - a$.[1]

Clearly the class RP contains the class P. It is also known that RP is contained in the class NP. It is not known whether any equality holds among these three complexity classes, but it is widely believed that NP is strictly larger than RP. In particular, it is believed that NP-hard problems cannot be solved by a randomized polynomial time algorithm.

- Show that if a class $\mathcal{H}$ is *properly* PAC learnable by a polynomial time algorithm, then the $\text{ERM}_{\mathcal{H}}$ problem is in the class RP. In particular, this implies that whenever the $\text{ERM}_{\mathcal{H}}$ problem is NP-hard (for example, the class of intersections of

[1] The constant 1/2 in the definition can be replaced by any constant in $(0, 1)$.

halfspaces discussed in the previous exercise), then, unless NP = RP, there exists no polynomial time proper PAC learning algorithm for $\mathcal{H}$.

Hint: Assume you have an algorithm A that properly PAC learns a class $\mathcal{H}$ in time polynomial in some class parameter n as well as in $1/\epsilon$ and $1/\delta$. Your goal is to use that algorithm as a subroutine to contract an algorithm B for solving the ERM$_{\mathcal{H}}$ problem in random polynomial time. Given a training set, $S \in (\mathcal{X} \times \{\pm 1\}^m)$, and some $h \in \mathcal{H}$ whose error on S is zero, apply the PAC learning algorithm to the uniform distribution over S and run it so that with probability ≥ 0.3 it finds a function $h \in \mathcal{H}$ that has error less than $\epsilon = 1/|S|$ (with respect to that uniform distribution). Show that the algorithm just described satisfies the requirements for being a RP solver for ERM$_{\mathcal{H}}$.

PART 2

From Theory to Algorithms

9 Linear Predictors

In this chapter we will study the family of linear predictors, one of the most useful families of hypothesis classes. Many learning algorithms that are being widely used in practice rely on linear predictors, first and foremost because of the ability to learn them efficiently in many cases. In addition, linear predictors are intuitive, are easy to interpret, and fit the data reasonably well in many natural learning problems.

We will introduce several hypothesis classes belonging to this family – halfspaces, linear regression predictors, and logistic regression predictors – and present relevant learning algorithms: linear programming and the Perceptron algorithm for the class of halfspaces and the Least Squares algorithm for linear regression. This chapter is focused on learning linear predictors using the ERM approach; however, in later chapters we will see alternative paradigms for learning these hypothesis classes.

First, we define the class of affine functions as

$$L_d = \{h_{\mathbf{w},b} : \mathbf{w} \in \mathbb{R}^d, b \in \mathbb{R}\},$$

where

$$h_{\mathbf{w},b}(\mathbf{x}) = \langle \mathbf{w}, \mathbf{x} \rangle + b = \left(\sum_{i=1}^{d} w_i x_i \right) + b.$$

It will be convenient also to use the notation

$$L_d = \{\mathbf{x} \mapsto \langle \mathbf{w}, \mathbf{x} \rangle + b : \mathbf{w} \in \mathbb{R}^d, b \in \mathbb{R}\},$$

which reads as follows: L_d is a set of functions, where each function is parameterized by $\mathbf{w} \in \mathbb{R}^d$ and $b \in \mathbb{R}$, and each such function takes as input a vector x and returns as output the scalar $\langle \mathbf{w}, \mathbf{x} \rangle + b$.

The different hypothesis classes of linear predictors are compositions of a function $\phi : \mathbb{R} \to \mathcal{Y}$ on L_d. For example, in binary classification, we can choose ϕ to be the sign function, and for regression problems, where $\mathcal{Y} = \mathbb{R}$, ϕ is simply the identity function.

It may be more convenient to incorporate b, called the *bias*, into $\mathbf{w}$ as an extra coordinate and add an extra coordinate with a value of 1 to all $\mathbf{x} \in \mathcal{X}$; namely, let $\mathbf{w}' = (b, w_1, w_2, \ldots w_d) \in \mathbb{R}^{d+1}$ and let $\mathbf{x}' = (1, x_1, x_2, \ldots, x_d) \in \mathbb{R}^{d+1}$. Therefore,

$$h_{\mathbf{w},b}(\mathbf{x}) = \langle \mathbf{w}, \mathbf{x} \rangle + b = \langle \mathbf{w}', \mathbf{x}' \rangle.$$

It follows that each affine function in $\mathbb{R}^d$ can be rewritten as a homogenous linear function in $\mathbb{R}^{d+1}$ applied over the transformation that appends the constant 1 to each input vector. Therefore, whenever it simplifies the presentation, we will omit the bias term and refer to L_d as the class of homogenous linear functions of the form $h_{\mathbf{w}}(\mathbf{x}) = \langle \mathbf{w}, \mathbf{x} \rangle$.

Throughout the book we often use the general term "linear functions" for both affine functions and (homogenous) linear functions.

9.1 HALFSPACES

The first hypothesis class we consider is the class of halfspaces, designed for binary classification problems, namely, $\mathcal{X} = \mathbb{R}^d$ and $\mathcal{Y} = \{-1, +1\}$. The class of halfspaces is defined as follows:

$$HS_d = \text{sign} \circ L_d = \{\mathbf{x} \mapsto \text{sign}(h_{\mathbf{w},b}(\mathbf{x})) : h_{\mathbf{w},b} \in L_d\}.$$

In other words, each halfspace hypothesis in HS_d is parameterized by $\mathbf{w} \in \mathbb{R}^d$ and $b \in \mathbb{R}$ and upon receiving a vector $\mathbf{x}$ the hypothesis returns the label $\text{sign}(\langle \mathbf{w}, \mathbf{x} \rangle + b)$.

To illustrate this hypothesis class geometrically, it is instructive to consider the case $d = 2$. Each hypothesis forms a hyperplane that is perpendicular to the vector $\mathbf{w}$ and intersects the vertical axis at the point $(0, -b/w_2)$. The instances that are "above" the hyperplane, that is, share an acute angle with $\mathbf{w}$, are labeled positively. Instances that are "below" the hyperplane, that is, share an obtuse angle with $\mathbf{w}$, are labeled negatively.

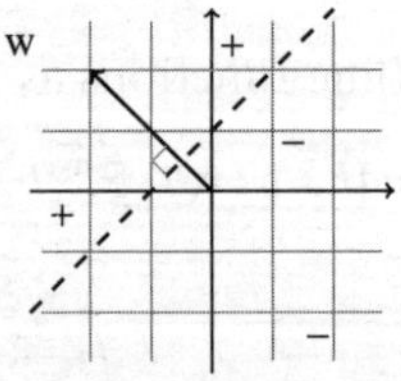

In Section 9.1.3 we will show that $\text{VCdim}(HS_d) = d + 1$. It follows that we can learn halfspaces using the ERM paradigm, as long as the sample size is $\Omega\left(\frac{d+\log(1/\delta)}{\epsilon}\right)$. Therefore, we now discuss how to implement an ERM procedure for halfspaces.

We introduce in the following two solutions to finding an ERM halfspace in the realizable case. In the context of halfspaces, the realizable case is often referred to as the "separable" case, since it is possible to separate with a hyperplane all the positive examples from all the negative examples. Implementing the ERM rule in the nonseparable case (i.e., the agnostic case) is known to be computationally hard (Ben-David and Simon, 2001). There are several approaches to learning nonseparable data. The most popular one is to use *surrogate loss functions*, namely, to learn a halfspace that does not necessarily minimize the empirical risk with the 0–1 loss, but rather with respect to a diffferent loss function. For example, in Section 9.3 we will describe the logistic regression approach, which can be implemented efficiently even in the nonseparable case. We will study surrogate loss functions in more detail later on in Chapter 12.

9.1.1 Linear Programming for the Class of Halfspaces

Linear programs (LP) are problems that can be expressed as maximizing a linear function subject to linear inequalities. That is,

$$\max_{\mathbf{w}\in\mathbb{R}^d} \quad \langle \mathbf{u}, \mathbf{w}\rangle$$
$$\text{subject to} \quad A\mathbf{w} \geq \mathbf{v}$$

where $\mathbf{w} \in \mathbb{R}^d$ is the vector of variables we wish to determine, A is an $m \times d$ matrix, and $\mathbf{v} \in \mathbb{R}^m, \mathbf{u} \in \mathbb{R}^d$ are vectors. Linear programs can be solved efficiently,[1] and furthermore, there are publicly available implementations of LP solvers.

We will show that the ERM problem for halfspaces in the realizable case can be expressed as a linear program. For simplicity, we assume the homogenous case. Let $S = \{(\mathbf{x}_i, y_i)\}_{i=1}^m$ be a training set of size m. Since we assume the realizable case, an ERM predictor should have zero errors on the training set. That is, we are looking for some vector $\mathbf{w} \in \mathbb{R}^d$ for which

$$\text{sign}(\langle \mathbf{w}, \mathbf{x}_i\rangle) = y_i, \qquad \forall i = 1, \ldots, m.$$

Equivalently, we are looking for some vector $\mathbf{w}$ for which

$$y_i \langle \mathbf{w}, \mathbf{x}_i\rangle > 0, \qquad \forall i = 1, \ldots, m.$$

Let $\mathbf{w}^*$ be a vector that satisfies this condition (it must exist since we assume realizability). Define $\gamma = \min_i (y_i \langle \mathbf{w}^*, \mathbf{x}_i\rangle)$ and let $\bar{\mathbf{w}} = \frac{\mathbf{w}^*}{\gamma}$. Therefore, for all i we have

$$y_i \langle \bar{\mathbf{w}}, x_i\rangle = \frac{1}{\gamma} y_i \langle \mathbf{w}^*, \mathbf{x}_i\rangle \geq 1.$$

We have thus shown that there exists a vector that satisfies

$$y_i \langle \mathbf{w}, \mathbf{x}_i\rangle \geq 1, \qquad \forall i = 1, \ldots, m. \tag{9.1}$$

And clearly, such a vector is an ERM predictor.

To find a vector that satisfies Equation (9.1) we can rely on an LP solver as follows. Set A to be the $m \times d$ matrix whose rows are the instances multiplied by y_i. That is, $A_{i,j} = y_i\, x_{i,j}$, where $x_{i,j}$ is the j'th element of the vector $\mathbf{x}_i$. Let $\mathbf{v}$ be the vector $(1, \ldots, 1) \in \mathbb{R}^m$. Then, Equation (9.1) can be rewritten as

$$A\mathbf{w} \geq \mathbf{v}.$$

The LP form requires a maximization objective, yet all the $\mathbf{w}$ that satisfy the constraints are equal candidates as output hypotheses. Thus, we set a "dummy" objective, $\mathbf{u} = (0, \ldots, 0) \in \mathbb{R}^d$.

[1] Namely, in time polynomial in m, d, and in the representation size of real numbers.

9.1.2 Perceptron for Halfspaces

A different implementation of the ERM rule is the Perceptron algorithm of Rosenblatt (Rosenblatt 1958). The Perceptron is an iterative algorithm that constructs a sequence of vectors $\mathbf{w}^{(1)}, \mathbf{w}^{(2)}, \ldots$. Initially, $\mathbf{w}^{(1)}$ is set to be the all-zeros vector. At iteration t, the Perceptron finds an example i that is mislabeled by $\mathbf{w}^{(t)}$, namely, an example for which $\text{sign}(\langle \mathbf{w}^{(t)}, \mathbf{x}_i \rangle) \neq y_i$. Then, the Perceptron updates $\mathbf{w}^{(t)}$ by adding to it the instance $\mathbf{x}_i$ scaled by the label y_i. That is, $\mathbf{w}^{(t+1)} = \mathbf{w}^{(t)} + y_i \mathbf{x}_i$. Recall that our goal is to have $y_i \langle \mathbf{w}, \mathbf{x}_i \rangle > 0$ for all i and note that

$$y_i \langle \mathbf{w}^{(t+1)}, \mathbf{x}_i \rangle = y_i \langle \mathbf{w}^{(t)} + y_i \mathbf{x}_i, \mathbf{x}_i \rangle = y_i \langle \mathbf{w}^{(t)}, \mathbf{x}_i \rangle + \|\mathbf{x}_i\|^2.$$

Hence, the update of the Perceptron guides the solution to be "more correct" on the i'th example.

Batch Perceptron

input: A training set $(\mathbf{x}_1, y_1), \ldots, (\mathbf{x}_m, y_m)$
initialize: $\mathbf{w}^{(1)} = (0, \ldots, 0)$
for $t = 1, 2, \ldots$
  if $(\exists\, i \text{ s.t. } y_i \langle \mathbf{w}^{(t)}, \mathbf{x}_i \rangle \leq 0)$ then
    $\mathbf{w}^{(t+1)} = \mathbf{w}^{(t)} + y_i \mathbf{x}_i$
  else
    output $\mathbf{w}^{(t)}$

The following theorem guarantees that in the realizable case, the algorithm stops with all sample points correctly classified.

Theorem 9.1. *Assume that* $(\mathbf{x}_1, y_1), \ldots, (\mathbf{x}_m, y_m)$ *is separable, let* $B = \min\{\|\mathbf{w}\| : \forall i \in [m],\ y_i \langle \mathbf{w}, \mathbf{x}_i \rangle \geq 1\}$, *and let* $R = \max_i \|\mathbf{x}_i\|$. *Then, the Perceptron algorithm stops after at most* $(RB)^2$ *iterations, and when it stops it holds that* $\forall i \in [m],\ y_i \langle \mathbf{w}^{(t)}, \mathbf{x}_i \rangle > 0$.

Proof. By the definition of the stopping condition, if the Perceptron stops it must have separated all the examples. We will show that if the Perceptron runs for T iterations, then we must have $T \leq (RB)^2$, which implies the Perceptron must stop after at most $(RB)^2$ iterations.

Let $\mathbf{w}^\star$ be a vector that achieves the minimum in the definition of B. That is, $y_i \langle \mathbf{w}^\star, x_i \rangle \geq 1$ for all i, and among all vectors that satisfy these constraints, $\mathbf{w}^\star$ is of minimal norm.

The idea of the proof is to show that after performing T iterations, the cosine of the angle between $\mathbf{w}^\star$ and $\mathbf{w}^{(T+1)}$ is at least $\frac{\sqrt{T}}{RB}$. That is, we will show that

$$\frac{\langle \mathbf{w}^\star, \mathbf{w}^{(T+1)} \rangle}{\|\mathbf{w}^\star\| \, \|\mathbf{w}^{(T+1)}\|} \geq \frac{\sqrt{T}}{RB}. \tag{9.2}$$

By the Cauchy-Schwartz inequality, the left-hand side of Equation (9.2) is at most 1. Therefore, Equation (9.2) would imply that

$$1 \geq \frac{\sqrt{T}}{RB} \quad \Rightarrow \quad T \leq (RB)^2,$$

which will conclude our proof.

To show that Equation (9.2) holds, we first show that $\langle \mathbf{w}^\star, \mathbf{w}^{(T+1)} \rangle \geq T$. Indeed, at the first iteration, $\mathbf{w}^{(1)} = (0,\ldots,0)$ and therefore $\langle \mathbf{w}^\star, \mathbf{w}^{(1)} \rangle = 0$, while on iteration t, if we update using example $(\mathbf{x}_i, y_i)$ we have that

$$\begin{aligned}\langle \mathbf{w}^\star, \mathbf{w}^{(t+1)} \rangle - \langle \mathbf{w}^\star, \mathbf{w}^{(t)} \rangle &= \langle \mathbf{w}^\star, \mathbf{w}^{(t+1)} - \mathbf{w}^{(t)} \rangle \\ &= \langle \mathbf{w}^\star, y_i \mathbf{x}_i \rangle = y_i \langle \mathbf{w}^\star, \mathbf{x}_i \rangle \\ &\geq 1.\end{aligned}$$

Therefore, after performing T iterations, we get

$$\langle \mathbf{w}^\star, \mathbf{w}^{(T+1)} \rangle = \sum_{t=1}^{T} \left(\langle \mathbf{w}^\star, \mathbf{w}^{(t+1)} \rangle - \langle \mathbf{w}^\star, \mathbf{w}^{(t)} \rangle \right) \geq T, \tag{9.3}$$

as required.

Next, we upper bound $\|\mathbf{w}^{(T+1)}\|$. For each iteration t we have that

$$\begin{aligned}\|\mathbf{w}^{(t+1)}\|^2 &= \|\mathbf{w}^{(t)} + y_i \mathbf{x}_i\|^2 \\ &= \|\mathbf{w}^{(t)}\|^2 + 2y_i \langle \mathbf{w}^{(t)}, \mathbf{x}_i \rangle + y_i^2 \|\mathbf{x}_i\|^2 \\ &\leq \|\mathbf{w}^{(t)}\|^2 + R^2 \end{aligned} \tag{9.4}$$

where the last inequality is due to the fact that example i is necessarily such that $y_i \langle \mathbf{w}^{(t)}, \mathbf{x}_i \rangle \leq 0$, and the norm of $\mathbf{x}_i$ is at most R. Now, since $\|\mathbf{w}^{(1)}\|^2 = 0$, if we use Equation (9.4) recursively for T iterations, we obtain that

$$\|\mathbf{w}^{(T+1)}\|^2 \leq TR^2 \;\Rightarrow\; \|\mathbf{w}^{(T+1)}\| \leq \sqrt{T}R. \tag{9.5}$$

Combining Equation (9.3) with Equation (9.5), and using the fact that $\|\mathbf{w}^\star\| = B$, we obtain that

$$\frac{\langle \mathbf{w}^{(T+1)}, \mathbf{w}^\star \rangle}{\|\mathbf{w}^\star\| \, \|\mathbf{w}^{(T+1)}\|} \geq \frac{T}{B\sqrt{T}R} = \frac{\sqrt{T}}{BR}.$$

We have thus shown that Equation (9.2) holds, and this concludes our proof. □

Remark 9.1. The Perceptron is simple to implement and is guaranteed to converge. However, the convergence rate depends on the parameter B, which in some situations might be exponentially large in d. In such cases, it would be better to implement the ERM problem by solving a linear program, as described in the previous section. Nevertheless, for many natural data sets, the size of B is not too large, and the Perceptron converges quite fast.

9.1.3 The VC Dimension of Halfspaces

To compute the VC dimension of halfspaces, we start with the homogenous case.

Theorem 9.2. *The VC dimension of the class of homogenous halfspaces in $\mathbb{R}^d$ is d.*

Proof. First, consider the set of vectors $\mathbf{e}_1,\ldots,\mathbf{e}_d$, where for every i the vector $\mathbf{e}_i$ is the all zeros vector except 1 in the i'th coordinate. This set is shattered by the class of homogenous halfspaces. Indeed, for every labeling $y_1, \ldots, y_d$, set $\mathbf{w} = (y_1, \ldots, y_d)$, and then $\langle \mathbf{w}, \mathbf{e}_i \rangle = y_i$ for all i.

Next, let $\mathbf{x}_1, \ldots, \mathbf{x}_{d+1}$ be a set of $d+1$ vectors in $\mathbb{R}^d$. Then, there must exist real numbers $a_1, \ldots, a_{d+1}$, not all of them are zero, such that $\sum_{i=1}^{d+1} a_i \mathbf{x}_i = \mathbf{0}$. Let $I = \{i : a_i > 0\}$ and $J = \{j : a_j < 0\}$. Either I or J is nonempty. Let us first assume that both of them are nonempty. Then,

$$\sum_{i \in I} a_i \mathbf{x}_i = \sum_{j \in J} |a_j| \mathbf{x}_j.$$

Now, suppose that $\mathbf{x}_1, \ldots, \mathbf{x}_{d+1}$ are shattered by the class of homogenous classes. Then, there must exist a vector $\mathbf{w}$ such that $\langle \mathbf{w}, \mathbf{x}_i \rangle > 0$ for all $i \in I$ while $\langle \mathbf{w}, \mathbf{x}_j \rangle < 0$ for every $j \in J$. It follows that

$$0 < \sum_{i \in I} a_i \langle \mathbf{x}_i, \mathbf{w} \rangle = \left\langle \sum_{i \in I} a_i \mathbf{x}_i, \mathbf{w} \right\rangle = \left\langle \sum_{j \in J} |a_j| \mathbf{x}_j, \mathbf{w} \right\rangle = \sum_{j \in J} |a_j| \langle \mathbf{x}_j, \mathbf{w} \rangle < 0,$$

which leads to a contradiction. Finally, if J (respectively, I) is empty then the right-most (respectively, left-most) inequality should be replaced by an equality, which still leads to a contradiction. □

Theorem 9.3. *The VC dimension of the class of nonhomogenous halfspaces in $\mathbb{R}^d$ is $d+1$.*

Proof. First, as in the proof of Theorem 9.2, it is easy to verify that the set of vectors $\mathbf{0}, \mathbf{e}_1, \ldots, \mathbf{e}_d$ is shattered by the class of nonhomogenous halfspaces. Second, suppose that the vectors $\mathbf{x}_1, \ldots, \mathbf{x}_{d+2}$ are shattered by the class of nonhomogenous halfspaces. But, using the reduction we have shown in the beginning of this chapter, it follows that there are $d+2$ vectors in $\mathbb{R}^{d+1}$ that are shattered by the class of homogenous halfspaces. But this contradicts Theorem 9.2. □

9.2 LINEAR REGRESSION

Linear regression is a common statistical tool for modeling the relationship between some "explanatory" variables and some real valued outcome. Cast as a learning problem, the domain set $\mathcal{X}$ is a subset of $\mathbb{R}^d$, for some d, and the label set $\mathcal{Y}$ is the set of real numbers. We would like to learn a linear function $h : \mathbb{R}^d \to \mathbb{R}$ that best approximates the relationship between our variables (say, for example, predicting the weight of a baby as a function of her age and weight at birth). Figure 9.1 shows an example of a linear regression predictor for $d = 1$.

The hypothesis class of linear regression predictors is simply the set of linear functions,

$$\mathcal{H}_{reg} = L_d = \{\mathbf{x} \mapsto \langle \mathbf{w}, \mathbf{x} \rangle + b : \mathbf{w} \in \mathbb{R}^d, \ b \in \mathbb{R}\}.$$

Next we need to define a loss function for regression. While in classification the definition of the loss is straightforward, as $\ell(h, (\mathbf{x}, y))$ simply indicates whether $h(\mathbf{x})$ correctly predicts y or not, in regression, if the baby's weight is 3 kg, both the predictions 3.00001 kg and 4 kg are "wrong," but we would clearly prefer the former over the latter. We therefore need to define how much we shall be "penalized" for

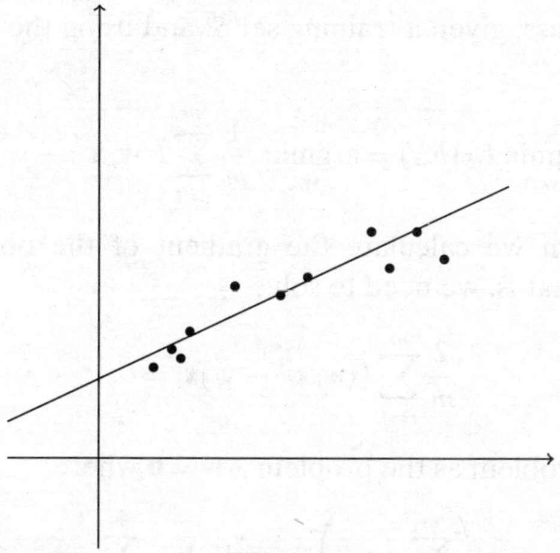

Figure 9.1. Linear regression for $d = 1$. For instance, the x-axis may denote the age of the baby, and the y-axis her weight.

the discrepancy between $h(\mathbf{x})$ and y. One common way is to use the squared-loss function, namely,

$$\ell(h, (\mathbf{x}, y)) = (h(\mathbf{x}) - y)^2.$$

For this loss function, the empirical risk function is called the Mean Squared Error, namely,

$$L_S(h) = \frac{1}{m} \sum_{i=1}^{m} (h(\mathbf{x}_i) - y_i)^2.$$

In the next subsection, we will see how to implement the ERM rule for linear regression with respect to the squared loss. Of course, there are a variety of other loss functions that one can use, for example, the absolute value loss function, $\ell(h, (\mathbf{x}, y)) = |h(\mathbf{x}) - y|$. The ERM rule for the absolute value loss function can be implemented using linear programming (see Exercise 9.1).

Note that since linear regression is not a binary prediction task, we cannot analyze its sample complexity using the VC-dimension. One possible analysis of the sample complexity of linear regression is by relying on the "discretization trick" (see Remark 4.1 in Chapter 4); namely, if we are happy with a representation of each element of the vector $\mathbf{w}$ and the bias b using a finite number of bits (say a 64 bits floating point representation), then the hypothesis class becomes finite and its size is at most $2^{64(d+1)}$. We can now rely on sample complexity bounds for finite hypothesis classes as described in Chapter 4. Note, however, that to apply the sample complexity bounds from Chapter 4 we also need that the loss function will be bounded. Later in the book we will describe more rigorous means to analyze the sample complexity of regression problems.

9.2.1 Least Squares

Least squares is the algorithm that solves the ERM problem for the hypothesis class of linear regression predictors with respect to the squared loss. The ERM problem with respect to this class, given a training set S, and using the homogenous version of L_d, is to find

$$\operatorname*{argmin}_{\mathbf{w}} L_S(h_{\mathbf{w}}) = \operatorname*{argmin}_{\mathbf{w}} \frac{1}{m}\sum_{i=1}^{m}(\langle \mathbf{w}, \mathbf{x}_i\rangle - y_i)^2.$$

To solve the problem we calculate the gradient of the objective function and compare it to zero. That is, we need to solve

$$\frac{2}{m}\sum_{i=1}^{m}(\langle \mathbf{w}, \mathbf{x}_i\rangle - y_i)\mathbf{x}_i = 0.$$

We can rewrite the problem as the problem $A\mathbf{w} = \mathbf{b}$ where

$$A = \left(\sum_{i=1}^{m} \mathbf{x}_i\, \mathbf{x}_i^\top\right) \quad \text{and} \quad \mathbf{b} = \sum_{i=1}^{m} y_i \mathbf{x}_i. \tag{9.6}$$

Or, in matrix form:

$$A = \begin{pmatrix} \vdots & & \vdots \\ \mathbf{x}_1 & \cdots & \mathbf{x}_m \\ \vdots & & \vdots \end{pmatrix} \begin{pmatrix} \vdots & & \vdots \\ \mathbf{x}_1 & \cdots & \mathbf{x}_m \\ \vdots & & \vdots \end{pmatrix}^\top, \tag{9.7}$$

$$\mathbf{b} = \begin{pmatrix} \vdots & & \vdots \\ \mathbf{x}_1 & \cdots & \mathbf{x}_m \\ \vdots & & \vdots \end{pmatrix} \begin{pmatrix} y_1 \\ \vdots \\ y_m \end{pmatrix}. \tag{9.8}$$

If A is invertible then the solution to the ERM problem is

$$\mathbf{w} = A^{-1}\mathbf{b}.$$

The case in which A is not invertible requires a few standard tools from linear algebra, which are available in Appendix C. It can be easily shown that if the training instances do not span the entire space of $\mathbb{R}^d$ then A is not invertible. Nevertheless, we can always find a solution to the system $A\mathbf{w} = \mathbf{b}$ because $\mathbf{b}$ is in the range of A. Indeed, since A is symmetric we can write it using its eigenvalue decomposition as $A = VDV^\top$, where D is a diagonal matrix and V is an orthonormal matrix (that is, $V^\top V$ is the identity $d \times d$ matrix). Define D^+ to be the diagonal matrix such that $D^+_{i,i} = 0$ if $D_{i,i} = 0$ and otherwise $D^+_{i,i} = 1/D_{i,i}$. Now, define

$$A^+ = VD^+V^\top \quad \text{and} \quad \hat{\mathbf{w}} = A^+\mathbf{b}.$$

Let $\mathbf{v}_i$ denote the i'th column of V. Then, we have

$$A\hat{\mathbf{w}} = AA^+\mathbf{b} = VDV^\top VD^+V^\top\mathbf{b} = VDD^+V^\top\mathbf{b} = \sum_{i:D_{i,i}\neq 0} \mathbf{v}_i\mathbf{v}_i^\top \mathbf{b}.$$

That is, $A\hat{\mathbf{w}}$ is the projection of $\mathbf{b}$ onto the span of those vectors $\mathbf{v}_i$ for which $D_{i,i} \neq 0$. Since the linear span of $\mathbf{x}_1, \ldots, \mathbf{x}_m$ is the same as the linear span of those $\mathbf{v}_i$, and $\mathbf{b}$ is in the linear span of the $\mathbf{x}_i$, we obtain that $A\hat{\mathbf{w}} = \mathbf{b}$, which concludes our argument.

9.2.2 Linear Regression for Polynomial Regression Tasks

Some learning tasks call for nonlinear predictors, such as polynomial predictors. Take, for instance, a one dimensional polynomial function of degree n, that is,

$$p(x) = a_0 + a_1 x + a_2 x^2 + \cdots + a_n x^n$$

where $(a_0, \ldots, a_n)$ is a vector of coefficients of size $n+1$. In the following we depict a training set that is better fitted using a 3rd degree polynomial predictor than using a linear predictor.

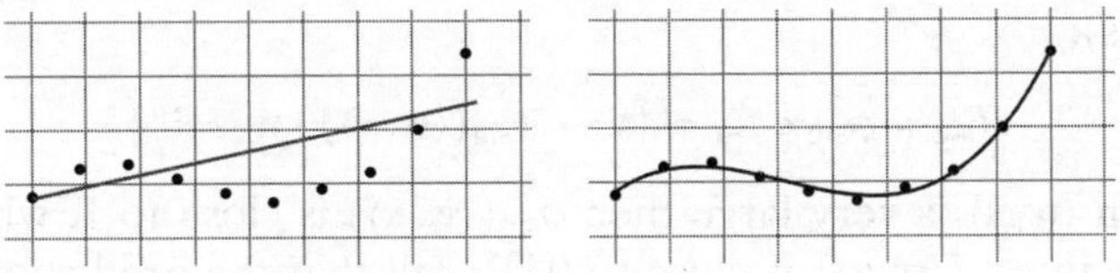

We will focus here on the class of one dimensional, n-degree, polynomial regression predictors, namely,

$$\mathcal{H}^n_{poly} = \{x \mapsto p(x)\},$$

where p is a one dimensional polynomial of degree n, parameterized by a vector of coefficients $(a_0, \ldots, a_n)$. Note that $\mathcal{X} = \mathbb{R}$, since this is a one dimensional polynomial, and $\mathcal{Y} = \mathbb{R}$, as this is a regression problem.

One way to learn this class is by reduction to the problem of linear regression, which we have already shown how to solve. To translate a polynomial regression problem to a linear regression problem, we define the mapping $\psi : \mathbb{R} \to \mathbb{R}^{n+1}$ such that $\psi(x) = (1, x, x^2, \ldots, x^n)$. Then we have that

$$p(\psi(x)) = a_0 + a_1 x + a_2 x^2 + \cdots + a_n x^n = \langle \mathbf{a}, \psi(x) \rangle$$

and we can find the optimal vector of coefficients $\mathbf{a}$ by using the Least Squares algorithm as shown earlier.

9.3 LOGISTIC REGRESSION

In logistic regression we learn a family of functions h from $\mathbb{R}^d$ to the interval $[0,1]$. However, logistic regression is used for classification tasks: We can interpret $h(\mathbf{x})$ as the *probability* that the label of $\mathbf{x}$ is 1. The hypothesis class associated with logistic regression is the composition of a sigmoid function $\phi_{\text{sig}} : \mathbb{R} \to [0,1]$ over the class of linear functions L_d. In particular, the sigmoid function used in logistic regression is the *logistic function*, defined as

$$\phi_{\text{sig}}(z) = \frac{1}{1 + \exp(-z)}. \qquad (9.9)$$

The name "sigmoid" means "S-shaped," referring to the plot of this function, shown in the figure:

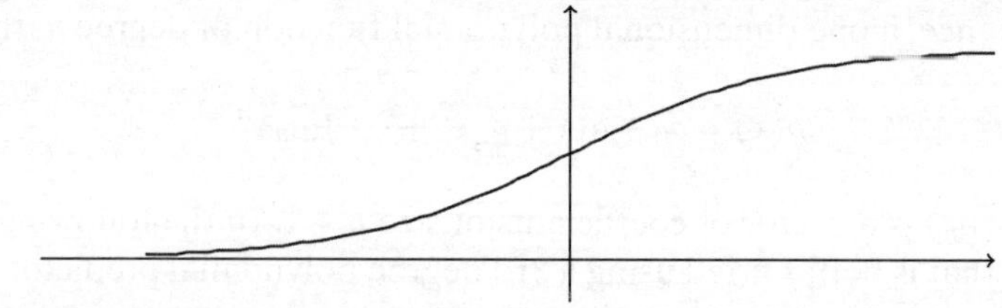

The hypothesis class is therefore (where for simplicity we are using homogenous linear functions):

$$H_{\text{sig}} = \phi_{\text{sig}} \circ L_d = \{\mathbf{x} \mapsto \phi_{\text{sig}}(\langle \mathbf{w}, \mathbf{x} \rangle) : \mathbf{w} \in \mathbb{R}^d\}.$$

Note that when $\langle \mathbf{w}, \mathbf{x} \rangle$ is very large then $\phi_{\text{sig}}(\langle \mathbf{w}, \mathbf{x} \rangle)$ is close to 1, whereas if $\langle \mathbf{w}, \mathbf{x} \rangle$ is very small then $\phi_{\text{sig}}(\langle \mathbf{w}, \mathbf{x} \rangle)$ is close to 0. Recall that the prediction of the halfspace corresponding to a vector $\mathbf{w}$ is $\text{sign}(\langle \mathbf{w}, \mathbf{x} \rangle)$. Therefore, the predictions of the halfspace hypothesis and the logistic hypothesis are very similar whenever $|\langle \mathbf{w}, \mathbf{x} \rangle|$ is large. However, when $|\langle \mathbf{w}, \mathbf{x} \rangle|$ is close to 0 we have that $\phi_{\text{sig}}(\langle \mathbf{w}, \mathbf{x} \rangle) \approx \frac{1}{2}$. Intuitively, the logistic hypothesis is not sure about the value of the label so it guesses that the label is $\text{sign}(\langle \mathbf{w}, \mathbf{x} \rangle)$ with probability slightly larger than 50%. In contrast, the halfspace hypothesis always outputs a deterministic prediction of either 1 or −1, even if $|\langle \mathbf{w}, \mathbf{x} \rangle|$ is very close to 0.

Next, we need to specify a loss function. That is, we should define how bad it is to predict some $h_{\mathbf{w}}(\mathbf{x}) \in [0,1]$ given that the true label is $y \in \{\pm 1\}$. Clearly, we would like that $h_{\mathbf{w}}(\mathbf{x})$ would be large if $y = 1$ and that $1 - h_{\mathbf{w}}(\mathbf{x})$ (i.e., the probability of predicting −1) would be large if $y = -1$. Note that

$$1 - h_{\mathbf{w}}(\mathbf{x}) = 1 - \frac{1}{1 + \exp(-\langle \mathbf{w}, \mathbf{x} \rangle)} = \frac{\exp(-\langle \mathbf{w}, \mathbf{x} \rangle)}{1 + \exp(-\langle \mathbf{w}, \mathbf{x} \rangle)} = \frac{1}{1 + \exp(\langle \mathbf{w}, \mathbf{x} \rangle)}.$$

Therefore, any reasonable loss function would increase monotonically with $\frac{1}{1+\exp(y\langle \mathbf{w}, \mathbf{x} \rangle)}$, or equivalently, would increase monotonically with $1 + \exp(-y\langle \mathbf{w}, \mathbf{x} \rangle)$. The logistic loss function used in logistic regression penalizes $h_{\mathbf{w}}$ based on the log of $1 + \exp(-y\langle \mathbf{w}, \mathbf{x} \rangle)$ (recall that log is a monotonic function). That is,

$$\ell(h_{\mathbf{w}}, (\mathbf{x}, y)) = \log\left(1 + \exp(-y\langle \mathbf{w}, \mathbf{x} \rangle)\right).$$

Therefore, given a training set $S = (\mathbf{x}_1, y_1), \ldots, (\mathbf{x}_m, y_m)$, the ERM problem associated with logistic regression is

$$\underset{\mathbf{w} \in \mathbb{R}^d}{\text{argmin}} \frac{1}{m} \sum_{i=1}^{m} \log\left(1 + \exp(-y_i\langle \mathbf{w}, \mathbf{x}_i \rangle)\right). \tag{9.10}$$

The advantage of the logistic loss function is that it is a *convex* function with respect to $\mathbf{w}$; hence the ERM problem can be solved efficiently using standard methods. We will study how to learn with convex functions, and in particular specify a simple algorithm for minimizing convex functions, in later chapters.

The ERM problem associated with logistic regression (Equation (9.10)) is identical to the problem of finding a Maximum Likelihood Estimator, a well-known statistical approach for finding the parameters that maximize the joint probability of a given data set assuming a specific parametric probability function. We will study the Maximum Likelihood approach in Chapter 24.

9.4 SUMMARY

The family of linear predictors is one of the most useful families of hypothesis classes, and many learning algorithms that are being widely used in practice rely on linear predictors. We have shown efficient algorithms for learning linear predictors with respect to the zero-one loss in the separable case and with respect to the squared and logistic losses in the unrealizable case. In later chapters we will present the properties of the loss function that enable efficient learning.

Naturally, linear predictors are effective whenever we assume, as prior knowledge, that some linear predictor attains low risk with respect to the underlying distribution. In the next chapter we show how to construct nonlinear predictors by composing linear predictors on top of simple classes. This will enable us to employ linear predictors for a variety of prior knowledge assumptions.

9.5 BIBLIOGRAPHIC REMARKS

The Perceptron algorithm dates back to Rosenblatt (1958). The proof of its convergence rate is due to (Agmon 1954, Novikoff 1962). Least Squares regression goes back to Gauss (1795), Legendre (1805), and Adrain (1808).

9.6 EXERCISES

9.1 Show how to cast the ERM problem of linear regression with respect to the absolute value loss function, $\ell(h,(\mathbf{x},y)) = |h(\mathbf{x}) - y|$, as a linear program; namely, show how to write the problem

$$\min_{\mathbf{w}} \sum_{i=1}^{m} |\langle \mathbf{w}, \mathbf{x}_i \rangle - y_i|$$

as a linear program.
Hint: Start with proving that for any $c \in \mathbb{R}$,

$$|c| = \min_{a \geq 0} a \text{ s.t. } c \leq a \text{ and } c \geq -a.$$

9.2 Show that the matrix A defined in Equation (9.6) is invertible if and only if $\mathbf{x}_1, \ldots, \mathbf{x}_m$ span $\mathbb{R}^d$.

9.3 Show that Theorem 9.1 is tight in the following sense: For any positive integer m, there exist a vector $\mathbf{w}^* \in \mathbb{R}^d$ (for some appropriate d) and a sequence of examples $\{(\mathbf{x}_1, y_1), \ldots, (\mathbf{x}_m, y_m)\}$ such that the following hold:
- $R = \max_i \|\mathbf{x}_i\| \leq 1$.
- $\|\mathbf{w}^*\|^2 = m$, and for all $i \leq m$, $y_i\langle \mathbf{x}_i, \mathbf{w}^* \rangle \geq 1$. Note that, using the notation in Theorem 9.1, we therefore get

$$B = \min\{\|\mathbf{w}\| : \forall i \in [m],\ \ y_i\langle \mathbf{w}, x_i \rangle \geq 1\} \leq \sqrt{m}.$$

Thus, $(BR)^2 \leq m$.

- When running the Perceptron on this sequence of examples it makes m updates before converging.

Hint: Choose $d = m$ and for every i choose $\mathbf{x}_i = \mathbf{e}_i$.

9.4 **(*)** Given any number m, find an example of a sequence of labeled examples $((\mathbf{x}_1, y_1), \ldots, (\mathbf{x}_m, y_m)) \in (\mathbb{R}^3 \times \{-1, +1\})^m$ on which the upper bound of Theorem 9.1 equals m and the perceptron algorithm is bound to make m mistakes.
Hint: Set each $\mathbf{x}_i$ to be a third dimensional vector of the form (a, b, y_i), where $a^2 + b^2 = R^2 - 1$. Let $\mathbf{w}^*$ be the vector $(0, 0, 1)$. Now, go over the proof of the Perceptron's upper bound (Theorem 9.1), see where we used inequalities ($\leq$) rather than equalities ($=$), and figure out scenarios where the inequality actually holds with equality.

9.5 Suppose we modify the Perceptron algorithm as follows: In the update step, instead of performing $\mathbf{w}^{(t+1)} = \mathbf{w}^{(t)} + y_i \mathbf{x}_i$ whenever we make a mistake, we perform $\mathbf{w}^{(t+1)} = \mathbf{w}^{(t)} + \eta y_i \mathbf{x}_i$ for some $\eta > 0$. Prove that the modified Perceptron will perform the same number of iterations as the vanilla Perceptron and will converge to a vector that points to the same direction as the output of the vanilla Perceptron.

9.6 In this problem, we will get bounds on the VC-dimension of the class of (closed) balls in $\mathbb{R}^d$, that is,

$$\mathcal{B}_d = \{B_{\mathbf{v},r} : \mathbf{v} \in \mathbb{R}^d, r > 0\},$$

where

$$B_{\mathbf{v},r}(\mathbf{x}) = \begin{cases} 1 & \text{if } \|\mathbf{x} - \mathbf{v}\| \leq r \\ 0 & \text{otherwise} \end{cases}.$$

1. Consider the mapping $\phi : \mathbb{R}^d \to \mathbb{R}^{d+1}$ defined by $\phi(\mathbf{x}) = (\mathbf{x}, \|\mathbf{x}\|^2)$. Show that if $\mathbf{x}_1, \ldots, \mathbf{x}_m$ are shattered by $\mathcal{B}_d$ then $\phi(\mathbf{x}_1), \ldots, \phi(\mathbf{x}_m)$ are shattered by the class of halfspaces in $\mathbb{R}^{d+1}$ (in this question we assume that $\text{sign}(0) = 1$). What does this tell us about $\text{VCdim}(\mathcal{B}_d)$?
2. **(*)** Find a set of $d+1$ points in $\mathbb{R}^d$ that is shattered by $\mathcal{B}_d$. Conclude that

$$d + 1 \leq \text{VCdim}(\mathcal{B}_d) \leq d + 2.$$

10 Boosting

Boosting is an algorithmic paradigm that grew out of a theoretical question and became a very practical machine learning tool. The boosting approach uses a generalization of linear predictors to address two major issues that have been raised earlier in the book. The first is the bias-complexity tradeoff. We have seen (in Chapter 5) that the error of an ERM learner can be decomposed into a sum of *approximation error* and *estimation error*. The more expressive the hypothesis class the learner is searching over, the smaller the approximation error is, but the larger the estimation error becomes. A learner is thus faced with the problem of picking a good tradeoff between these two considerations. The boosting paradigm allows the learner to have smooth control over this tradeoff. The learning starts with a basic class (that might have a large approximation error), and as it progresses the class that the predictor may belong to grows richer.

The second issue that boosting addresses is the computational complexity of learning. As seen in Chapter 8, for many interesting concept classes the task of finding an ERM hypothesis may be computationally infeasible. A boosting algorithm amplifies the accuracy of *weak learners*. Intuitively, one can think of a weak learner as an algorithm that uses a simple "rule of thumb" to output a hypothesis that comes from an easy-to-learn hypothesis class and performs just slightly better than a random guess. When a weak learner can be implemented efficiently, boosting provides a tool for aggregating such weak hypotheses to approximate gradually good predictors for larger, and harder to learn, classes.

In this chapter we will describe and analyze a practically useful boosting algorithm, AdaBoost (a shorthand for Adaptive Boosting). The AdaBoost algorithm outputs a hypothesis that is a linear combination of simple hypotheses. In other words, AdaBoost relies on the family of hypothesis classes obtained by composing a linear predictor on top of simple classes. We will show that AdaBoost enables us to control the tradeoff between the approximation and estimation errors by varying a single parameter.

AdaBoost demonstrates a general theme, that will recur later in the book, of expanding the expressiveness of linear predictors by composing them on top of other functions. This will be elaborated in Section 10.3.

AdaBoost stemmed from the theoretical question of whether an efficient weak learner can be "boosted" into an efficient strong learner. This question was raised by Kearns and Valiant in 1988 and solved in 1990 by Robert Schapire, then a graduate student at MIT. However, the proposed mechanism was not very practical. In 1995, Robert Schapire and Yoav Freund proposed the AdaBoost algorithm, which was the first truly practical implementation of boosting. This simple and elegant algorithm became hugely popular, and Freund and Schapire's work has been recognized by numerous awards.

Furthermore, boosting is a great example for the practical impact of learning theory. While boosting originated as a purely theoretical problem, it has led to popular and widely used algorithms. Indeed, as we shall demonstrate later in this chapter, AdaBoost has been successfully used for learning to detect faces in images.

10.1 WEAK LEARNABILITY

Recall the definition of PAC learning given in Chapter 3: A hypothesis class, $\mathcal{H}$, is PAC learnable if there exist $m_{\mathcal{H}} : (0,1)^2 \to \mathbb{N}$ and a learning algorithm with the following property: For every $\epsilon, \delta \in (0,1)$, for every distribution $\mathcal{D}$ over $\mathcal{X}$, and for every labeling function $f : \mathcal{X} \to \{\pm 1\}$, if the realizable assumption holds with respect to $\mathcal{H}, \mathcal{D}, f$, then when running the learning algorithm on $m \geq m_{\mathcal{H}}(\epsilon, \delta)$ i.i.d. examples generated by $\mathcal{D}$ and labeled by f, the algorithm returns a hypothesis h such that, with probability of at least $1 - \delta$, $L_{(\mathcal{D}, f)}(h) \leq \epsilon$.

Furthermore, the fundamental theorem of learning theory (Theorem 6.8 in Chapter 6) characterizes the family of learnable classes and states that every PAC learnable class can be learned using any ERM algorithm. However, the definition of PAC learning and the fundamental theorem of learning theory ignores the computational aspect of learning. Indeed, as we have shown in Chapter 8, there are cases in which implementing the ERM rule is computationally hard (even in the realizable case).

However, perhaps we can trade computational hardness with the requirement for accuracy. Given a distribution $\mathcal{D}$ and a target labeling function f, maybe there exists an efficiently computable learning algorithm whose error is just slightly better than a random guess? This motivates the following definition.

Definition 10.1 (γ-Weak-Learnability).

- A learning algorithm, A, is a γ-weak-learner for a class $\mathcal{H}$ if there exists a function $m_{\mathcal{H}} : (0,1) \to \mathbb{N}$ such that for every $\delta \in (0,1)$, for every distribution $\mathcal{D}$ over $\mathcal{X}$, and for every labeling function $f : \mathcal{X} \to \{\pm 1\}$, if the realizable assumption holds with respect to $\mathcal{H}, \mathcal{D}, f$, then when running the learning algorithm on $m \geq m_{\mathcal{H}}(\delta)$ i.i.d. examples generated by $\mathcal{D}$ and labeled by f, the algorithm returns a hypothesis h such that, with probability of at least $1 - \delta$, $L_{(\mathcal{D}, f)}(h) \leq 1/2 - \gamma$.
- A hypothesis class $\mathcal{H}$ is γ-weak-learnable if there exists a γ-weak-learner for that class.

This definition is almost identical to the definition of PAC learning, which here we will call *strong learning*, with one crucial difference: Strong learnability implies the ability to find an arbitrarily good classifier (with error rate at most ϵ for an arbitrarily small $\epsilon > 0$). In weak learnability, however, we only need to output a hypothesis whose error rate is at most $1/2 - \gamma$, namely, whose error rate is slightly better than what a random labeling would give us. The hope is that it may be easier to come up with efficient weak learners than with efficient (full) PAC learners.

The fundamental theorem of learning (Theorem 6.8) states that if a hypothesis class $\mathcal{H}$ has a VC dimension d, then the sample complexity of PAC learning $\mathcal{H}$ satisfies $m_{\mathcal{H}}(\epsilon, \delta) \geq C_1 \frac{d+\log(1/\delta)}{\epsilon}$, where C_1 is a constant. Applying this with $\epsilon = 1/2 - \gamma$ we immediately obtain that if $d = \infty$ then $\mathcal{H}$ is not γ-weak-learnable. This implies that from the statistical perspective (i.e., if we ignore computational complexity), weak learnability is also characterized by the VC dimension of $\mathcal{H}$ and therefore is just as hard as PAC (strong) learning. However, when we do consider computational complexity, the potential advantage of weak learning is that maybe there is an algorithm that satisfies the requirements of weak learning and can be implemented efficiently.

One possible approach is to take a "simple" hypothesis class, denoted B, and to apply ERM with respect to B as the weak learning algorithm. For this to work, we need that B will satisfy two requirements:

- ERM_B is efficiently implementable.
- For every sample that is labeled by some hypothesis from $\mathcal{H}$, any ERM_B hypothesis will have an error of at most $1/2 - \gamma$.

Then, the immediate question is whether we can boost an *efficient* weak learner into an *efficient* strong learner. In the next section we will show that this is indeed possible, but before that, let us show an example in which efficient weak learnability of a class $\mathcal{H}$ is possible using a base hypothesis class B.

Example 10.1 (Weak Learning of 3-Piece Classifiers Using Decision Stumps). Let $\mathcal{X} = \mathbb{R}$ and let $\mathcal{H}$ be the class of 3-piece classifiers, namely, $\mathcal{H} = \{h_{\theta_1,\theta_2,b} : \theta_1, \theta_2 \in \mathbb{R}, \theta_1 < \theta_2, b \in \{\pm 1\}\}$, where for every x,

$$h_{\theta_1,\theta_2,b}(x) = \begin{cases} +b & \text{if } x < \theta_1 \text{ or } x > \theta_2 \\ -b & \text{if } \theta_1 \leq x \leq \theta_2 \end{cases}$$

An example hypothesis (for $b = 1$) is illustrated as follows:

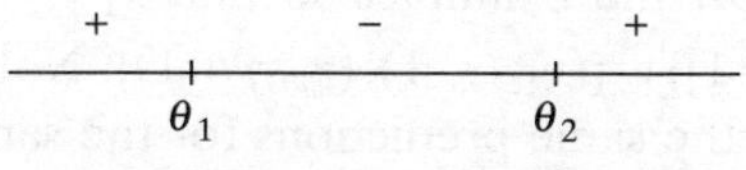

Let B be the class of Decision Stumps, that is, $B = \{x \mapsto \text{sign}(x - \theta) \cdot b : \theta \in \mathbb{R}, b \in \{\pm 1\}\}$. In the following we show that ERM_B is a γ-weak learner for $\mathcal{H}$, for $\gamma = 1/12$.

To see that, we first show that for every distribution that is consistent with $\mathcal{H}$, there exists a decision stump with $L_{\mathcal{D}}(h) \leq 1/3$. Indeed, just note that every classifier in $\mathcal{H}$ consists of three regions (two unbounded rays and a center interval) with alternate labels. For any pair of such regions, there exists a decision stump that agrees with the labeling of these two components. Note that for every distribution $\mathcal{D}$ over $\mathbb{R}$ and every partitioning of the line into three such regions, one of these regions must have $\mathcal{D}$-weight of at most $1/3$. Let $h \in \mathcal{H}$ be a zero error hypothesis. A decision stump that disagrees with h only on such a region has an error of at most $1/3$.

Finally, since the VC-dimension of decision stumps is 2, if the sample size is greater than $\Omega(\log(1/\delta)/\epsilon^2)$, then with probability of at least $1-\delta$, the ERM_B rule returns a hypothesis with an error of at most $1/3+\epsilon$. Setting $\epsilon = 1/12$ we obtain that thc crror of ERM_B is at most $1/3 + 1/12 = 1/2 - 1/12$.

We see that ERM_B is a γ-weak learner for $\mathcal{H}$. We next show how to implement the ERM rule efficiently for decision stumps.

10.1.1 Efficient Implementation of ERM for Decision Stumps

Let $\mathcal{X} = \mathbb{R}^d$ and consider the base hypothesis class of decision stumps over $\mathbb{R}^d$, namely,

$$\mathcal{H}_{\text{DS}} = \{\mathbf{x} \mapsto \text{sign}(\theta - x_i) \cdot b : \theta \in \mathbb{R}, i \in [d], b \in \{\pm 1\}\}.$$

For simplicity, assume that $b = 1$; that is, we focus on all the hypotheses in $\mathcal{H}_{\text{DS}}$ of the form $\text{sign}(\theta - x_i)$. Let $S = ((\mathbf{x}_1, y_1), \ldots, (\mathbf{x}_m, y_m))$ be a training set. We will show how to implement an ERM rule, namely, how to find a decision stump that minimizes $L_S(h)$. Furthermore, since in the next section we will show that AdaBoost requires finding a hypothesis with a small risk relative to some distribution over S, we will show here how to minimize such risk functions. Concretely, let $\mathbf{D}$ be a probability vector in $\mathbb{R}^m$ (that is, all elements of $\mathbf{D}$ are nonnegative and $\sum_i D_i = 1$). The weak learner we describe later receives $\mathbf{D}$ and S and outputs a decision stump $h : \mathcal{X} \to \mathcal{Y}$ that minimizes the risk w.r.t. $\mathbf{D}$,

$$L_{\mathbf{D}}(h) = \sum_{i=1}^{m} D_i \mathbb{1}_{[h(\mathbf{x}_i) \neq y_i]}.$$

Note that if $\mathbf{D} = (1/m, \ldots, 1/m)$ then $L_{\mathbf{D}}(h) = L_S(h)$.

Recall that each decision stump is parameterized by an index $j \in [d]$ and a threshold θ. Therefore, minimizing $L_{\mathbf{D}}(h)$ amounts to solving the problem

$$\min_{j \in [d]} \min_{\theta \in \mathbb{R}} \left(\sum_{i:y_i=1} D_i \mathbb{1}_{[x_{i,j} > \theta]} + \sum_{i:y_i=-1} D_i \mathbb{1}_{[x_{i,j} \leq \theta]} \right). \tag{10.1}$$

Fix $j \in [d]$ and let us sort the examples so that $x_{1,j} \leq x_{2,j} \leq \ldots \leq x_{m,j}$. Define $\Theta_j = \{\frac{x_{i,j}+x_{i+1,j}}{2} : i \in [m-1]\} \cup \{(x_{1,j} - 1), (x_{m,j} + 1)\}$. Note that for any $\theta \in \mathbb{R}$ there exists $\theta' \in \Theta_j$ that yields the same predictions for the sample S as the threshold θ. Therefore, instead of minimizing over $\theta \in \mathbb{R}$ we can minimize over $\theta \in \Theta_j$.

This already gives us an efficient procedure: Choose $j \in [d]$ and $\theta \in \Theta_j$ that minimize the objective value of Equation (10.1). For every j and $\theta \in \Theta_j$ we have to calculate a sum over m examples; therefore the runtime of this approach would be $O(dm^2)$. We next show a simple trick that enables us to minimize the objective in time $O(dm)$.

The observation is as follows. Suppose we have calculated the objective for $\theta \in (x_{i-1,j}, x_{i,j})$. Let $F(\theta)$ be the value of the objective. Then, when we consider $\theta' \in (x_{i,j}, x_{i+1,j})$ we have that

$$F(\theta') = F(\theta) - D_i \mathbb{1}_{[y_i=1]} + D_i \mathbb{1}_{[y_i=-1]} = F(\theta) - y_i D_i.$$

Therefore, we can calculate the objective at θ' in a constant time, given the objective at the previous threshold, θ. It follows that after a preprocessing step in which we sort the examples with respect to each coordinate, the minimization problem can be performed in time $O(dm)$. This yields the following pseudocode.

ERM for Decision Stumps

input:
  training set $S = (\mathbf{x}_1, y_1), \ldots, (\mathbf{x}_m, y_m)$
  distribution vector $\mathbf{D}$
goal: Find $j^\star, \theta^\star$ that solve Equation (10.1)
initialize: $F^\star = \infty$
for $j = 1, \ldots, d$
  sort S using the j'th coordinate, and denote
   $x_{1,j} \le x_{2,j} \le \cdots \le x_{m,j} \le x_{m+1,j} \stackrel{\text{def}}{=} x_{m,j} + 1$
  $F = \sum_{i:y_i=1} D_i$
  if $F < F^\star$
   $F^\star = F, \theta^\star = x_{1,j} - 1, j^\star = j$
  for $i = 1, \ldots, m$
   $F = F - y_i D_i$
   if $F < F^\star$ and $x_{i,j} \ne x_{i+1,j}$
    $F^\star = F, \theta^\star = \frac{1}{2}(x_{i,j} + x_{i+1,j}), j^\star = j$
output $j^\star, \theta^\star$

10.2 ADABOOST

AdaBoost (short for Adaptive Boosting) is an algorithm that has access to a weak learner and finds a hypothesis with a low empirical risk. The AdaBoost algorithm receives as input a training set of examples $S = (\mathbf{x}_1, y_1), \ldots, (\mathbf{x}_m, y_m)$, where for each i, $y_i = f(\mathbf{x}_i)$ for some labeling function f. The boosting process proceeds in a sequence of consecutive rounds. At round t, the booster first defines a distribution over the examples in S, denoted $\mathbf{D}^{(t)}$. That is, $\mathbf{D}^{(t)} \in \mathbb{R}_+^m$ and $\sum_{i=1}^m D_i^{(t)} = 1$. Then, the booster passes the distribution $\mathbf{D}^{(t)}$ and the sample S to the weak learner. (That way, the weak learner can construct i.i.d. examples according to $\mathbf{D}^{(t)}$ and f.) The weak learner is assumed to return a "weak" hypothesis, h_t, whose error,

$$\epsilon_t \stackrel{\text{def}}{=} L_{\mathbf{D}^{(t)}}(h_t) \stackrel{\text{def}}{=} \sum_{i=1}^m D_i^{(t)} \mathbb{1}_{[h_t(\mathbf{x}_i) \ne y_i]},$$

is at most $\frac{1}{2} - \gamma$ (of course, there is a probability of at most δ that the weak learner fails). Then, AdaBoost assigns a weight for h_t as follows: $w_t = \frac{1}{2}\log\left(\frac{1}{\epsilon_t} - 1\right)$. That is, the weight of h_t is inversely proportional to the error of h_t. At the end of the round, AdaBoost updates the distribution so that examples on which h_t errs will get a higher probability mass while examples on which h_t is correct will get a lower probability mass. Intuitively, this will force the weak learner to focus on the problematic examples in the next round. The output of the AdaBoost algorithm is a "strong" classifier that is based on a weighted sum of all the weak hypotheses. The pseudocode of AdaBoost is presented in the following.

AdaBoost

input:
  training set $S = (\mathbf{x}_1, y_1), \ldots, (\mathbf{x}_m, y_m)$
  weak learner WL
  number of rounds T
initialize $\mathbf{D}^{(1)} = (\frac{1}{m}, \ldots, \frac{1}{m})$.
for $t = 1, \ldots, T$:
  invoke weak learner $h_t = \mathrm{WL}(\mathbf{D}^{(t)}, S)$
  compute $\epsilon_t = \sum_{i=1}^m D_i^{(t)} \mathbb{1}_{[y_i \neq h_t(\mathbf{x}_i)]}$
  let $w_t = \frac{1}{2} \log\left(\frac{1}{\epsilon_t} - 1\right)$
  update $D_i^{(t+1)} = \frac{D_i^{(t)} \exp(-w_t y_i h_t(\mathbf{x}_i))}{\sum_{j=1}^m D_j^{(t)} \exp(-w_t y_j h_t(\mathbf{x}_j))}$ for all $i = 1, \ldots, m$
output the hypothesis $h_s(\mathbf{x}) = \mathrm{sign}\left(\sum_{t=1}^T w_t h_t(\mathbf{x})\right)$.

The following theorem shows that the training error of the output hypothesis decreases exponentially fast with the number of boosting rounds.

Theorem 10.2. *Let S be a training set and assume that at each iteration of AdaBoost, the weak learner returns a hypothesis for which $\epsilon_t \leq 1/2 - \gamma$. Then, the training error of the output hypothesis of AdaBoost is at most*

$$L_S(h_s) = \frac{1}{m} \sum_{i=1}^m \mathbb{1}_{[h_s(\mathbf{x}_i) \neq y_i]} \leq \exp(-2\gamma^2 T).$$

Proof. For each t, denote $f_t = \sum_{p \leq t} w_p h_p$. Therefore, the output of AdaBoost is f_T. In addition, denote

$$Z_t = \frac{1}{m} \sum_{i=1}^m e^{-y_i f_t(x_i)}.$$

Note that for any hypothesis we have that $\mathbb{1}_{[h(x) \neq y]} \leq e^{-yh(x)}$. Therefore, $L_S(f_T) \leq Z_T$, so it suffices to show that $Z_T \leq e^{-2\gamma^2 T}$. To upper bound Z_T we rewrite it as

$$Z_T = \frac{Z_T}{Z_0} = \frac{Z_T}{Z_{T-1}} \cdot \frac{Z_{T-1}}{Z_{T-2}} \cdots \frac{Z_2}{Z_1} \cdot \frac{Z_1}{Z_0}, \tag{10.2}$$

where we used the fact that $Z_0 = 1$ because $f_0 \equiv 0$. Therefore, it suffices to show that for every round t,

$$\frac{Z_{t+1}}{Z_t} \leq e^{-2\gamma^2}. \tag{10.3}$$

To do so, we first note that using a simple inductive argument, for all t and i,

$$D_i^{(t+1)} = \frac{e^{-y_i f_t(x_i)}}{\sum_{j=1}^m e^{-y_j f_t(x_j)}}.$$

Hence,

$$\frac{Z_{t+1}}{Z_t} = \frac{\sum_{i=1}^m e^{-y_i f_{t+1}(x_i)}}{\sum_{j=1}^m e^{-y_j f_t(x_j)}}$$

$$= \frac{\sum_{i=1}^m e^{-y_i f_t(x_i)} e^{-y_i w_{t+1} h_{t+1}(x_i)}}{\sum_{j=1}^m e^{-y_j f_t(x_j)}}$$

$$= \sum_{i=1}^m D_i^{(t+1)} e^{-y_i w_{t+1} h_{t+1}(x_i)}$$

$$= e^{-w_{t+1}} \sum_{i:y_i h_{t+1}(x_i)=1} D_i^{(t+1)} + e^{w_{t+1}} \sum_{i:y_i h_{t+1}(x_i)=-1} D_i^{(t+1)}$$

$$= e^{-w_{t+1}}(1-\epsilon_{t+1}) + e^{w_{t+1}}\epsilon_{t+1}$$

$$= \frac{1}{\sqrt{1/\epsilon_{t+1}-1}}(1-\epsilon_{t+1}) + \sqrt{1/\epsilon_{t+1}-1}\,\epsilon_{t+1}$$

$$= \sqrt{\frac{\epsilon_{t+1}}{1-\epsilon_{t+1}}}(1-\epsilon_{t+1}) + \sqrt{\frac{1-\epsilon_{t+1}}{\epsilon_{t+1}}}\epsilon_{t+1}$$

$$= 2\sqrt{\epsilon_{t+1}(1-\epsilon_{t+1})}.$$

By our assumption, $\epsilon_{t+1} \le \frac{1}{2} - \gamma$. Since the function $g(a) = a(1-a)$ is monotonically increasing in $[0, 1/2]$, we obtain that

$$2\sqrt{\epsilon_{t+1}(1-\epsilon_{t+1})} \le 2\sqrt{\left(\frac{1}{2}-\gamma\right)\left(\frac{1}{2}+\gamma\right)} = \sqrt{1-4\gamma^2}.$$

Finally, using the inequality $1 - a \le e^{-a}$ we have that $\sqrt{1-4\gamma^2} \le e^{-4\gamma^2/2} = e^{-2\gamma^2}$. This shows that Equation (10.3) holds and thus concludes our proof. □

Each iteration of AdaBoost involves $O(m)$ operations as well as a single call to the weak learner. Therefore, if the weak learner can be implemented efficiently (as happens in the case of ERM with respect to decision stumps) then the total training process will be efficient.

Remark 10.2. Theorem 10.2 assumes that at each iteration of AdaBoost, the weak learner returns a hypothesis with weighted sample error of at most $1/2 - \gamma$. According to the definition of a weak learner, it can fail with probability δ. Using the union bound, the probability that the weak learner will not fail at all of the iterations is at least $1 - \delta T$. As we show in Exercise 10.1, the dependence of the sample complexity on δ can always be logarithmic in $1/\delta$, and therefore invoking the weak learner with a very small δ is not problematic. We can therefore assume that δT is also small. Furthermore, since the weak learner is only applied with distributions over the training set, in many cases we can implement the weak learner so that it will have a zero probability of failure (i.e., $\delta = 0$). This is the case, for example, in the weak learner that finds the minimum value of $L_{\mathbf{D}}(h)$ for decision stumps, as described in the previous section.

Theorem 10.2 tells us that the empirical risk of the hypothesis constructed by AdaBoost goes to zero as T grows. However, what we really care about is the true risk of the output hypothesis. To argue about the true risk, we note that the output of AdaBoost is in fact a composition of a halfspace over the predictions of the T weak hypotheses constructed by the weak learner. In the next section we show that if the weak hypotheses come from a base hypothesis class of low VC-dimension, then the estimation error of AdaBoost will be small; namely, the true risk of the output of AdaBoost would not be very far from its empirical risk.

10.3 LINEAR COMBINATIONS OF BASE HYPOTHESES

As mentioned previously, a popular approach for constructing a weak learner is to apply the ERM rule with respect to a base hypothesis class (e.g., ERM over decision stumps). We have also seen that boosting outputs a composition of a halfspace over the predictions of the weak hypotheses. Therefore, given a base hypothesis class B (e.g., decision stumps), the output of AdaBoost will be a member of the following class:

$$L(B,T) = \left\{ x \mapsto \mathrm{sign}\left(\sum_{t=1}^{T} w_t h_t(x) \right) : \mathbf{w} \in \mathbb{R}^T, \ \forall t, \quad h_t \in B \right\}. \tag{10.4}$$

That is, each $h \in L(B,T)$ is parameterized by T base hypotheses from B and by a vector $w \in \mathbb{R}^T$. The prediction of such an h on an instance x is obtained by first applying the T base hypotheses to construct the vector $\psi(x) = (h_1(x), \ldots, h_T(x)) \in \mathbb{R}^T$, and then applying the (homogenous) halfspace defined by $\mathbf{w}$ on $\psi(x)$.

In this section we analyze the estimation error of $L(B,T)$ by bounding the VC-dimension of $L(B,T)$ in terms of the VC-dimension of B and T. We will show that, up to logarithmic factors, the VC-dimension of $L(B,T)$ is bounded by T times the VC-dimension of B. It follows that the estimation error of AdaBoost grows linearly with T. On the other hand, the empirical risk of AdaBoost decreases with T. In fact, as we demonstrate later, T can be used to decrease the approximation error of $L(B,T)$. Therefore, the parameter T of AdaBoost enables us to control the bias-complexity tradeoff.

To demonstrate how the expressive power of $L(B,T)$ increases with T, consider the simple example, in which $\mathcal{X} = \mathbb{R}$ and the base class is Decision Stumps,

$$\mathcal{H}_{\mathrm{DS1}} = \{x \mapsto \mathrm{sign}(x - \theta) \cdot b : \ \theta \in \mathbb{R}, b \in \{\pm 1\}\}.$$

Note that in this one dimensional case, $\mathcal{H}_{\mathrm{DS1}}$ is in fact equivalent to (nonhomogenous) halfspaces on $\mathbb{R}$.

Now, let $\mathcal{H}$ be the rather complex class (compared to halfspaces on the line) of piece-wise constant functions. Let g_r be a piece-wise constant function with at most r pieces; that is, there exist thresholds $-\infty = \theta_0 < \theta_1 < \theta_2 < \cdots < \theta_r = \infty$ such that

$$g_r(x) = \sum_{i=1}^{r} \alpha_i \mathbb{1}_{[x \in (\theta_{i-1}, \theta_i]]} \quad \forall i, \ \ \alpha_i \in \{\pm 1\}.$$

Denote by $\mathcal{G}_r$ the class of all such piece-wise constant classifiers with at most r pieces.

In the following we show that $\mathcal{G}_T \subseteq L(\mathcal{H}_{\text{DS1}}, T)$; namely, the class of halfspaces over T decision stumps yields all the piece-wise constant classifiers with at most T pieces.

Indeed, without loss of generality consider any $g \in \mathcal{G}_T$ with $\alpha_t = (-1)^t$. This implies that if x is in the interval $(\theta_{t-1}, \theta_t]$, then $g(x) = (-1)^t$. For example:

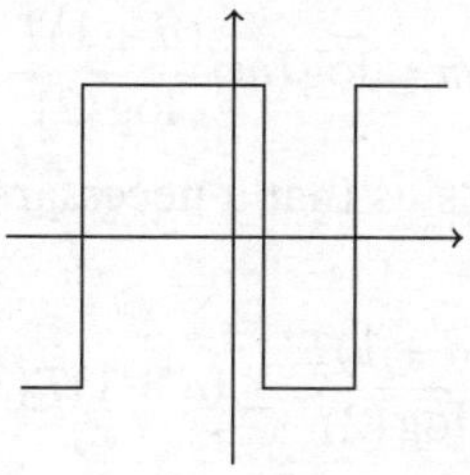

Now, the function

$$h(x) = \text{sign}\left(\sum_{t=1}^{T} w_t \, \text{sign}(x - \theta_{t-1})\right), \tag{10.5}$$

where $w_1 = 0.5$ and for $t > 1$, $w_t = (-1)^t$, is in $L(\mathcal{H}_{\text{DS1}}, T)$ and is equal to g (see Exercise 10.2).

From this example we obtain that $L(\mathcal{H}_{\text{DS1}}, T)$ can shatter any set of $T+1$ instances in $\mathbb{R}$; hence the VC-dimension of $L(\mathcal{H}_{\text{DS1}}, T)$ is at least $T+1$. Therefore, T is a parameter that can control the bias-complexity tradeoff: Enlarging T yields a more expressive hypothesis class but on the other hand might increase the estimation error. In the next subsection we formally upper bound the VC-dimension of $L(B, T)$ for any base class B.

10.3.1 The VC-Dimension of $L(B, T)$

The following lemma tells us that the VC-dimension of $L(B, T)$ is upper bounded by $\tilde{O}(\text{VCdim}(B)T)$ (the $\tilde{O}$ notation ignores constants and logarithmic factors).

Lemma 10.3. *Let B be a base class and let $L(B, T)$ be as defined in Equation (10.4). Assume that both T and* VCdim(B) *are at least* 3. *Then,*

$$\text{VCdim}(L(B,T)) \le T\,(\text{VCdim}(B)+1)(3\log(T\,(\text{VCdim}(B)+1))+2).$$

Proof. Denote $d = \text{VCdim}(B)$. Let $C = \{x_1, \ldots, x_m\}$ be a set that is shattered by $L(B, T)$. Each labeling of C by $h \in L(B, T)$ is obtained by first choosing $h_1, \ldots, h_T \in B$ and then applying a halfspace hypothesis over the vector $(h_1(x), \ldots, h_T(x))$. By Sauer's lemma, there are at most $(em/d)^d$ different dichotomies (i.e., labelings) induced by B over C. Therefore, we need to choose T hypotheses, out of at most $(em/d)^d$ different hypotheses. There are at most $(em/d)^{dT}$ ways to do it. Next, for each such choice, we apply a linear predictor, which yields at most $(em/T)^T$ dichotomies. Therefore, the overall number of dichotomies we can construct is upper bounded by

$$(em/d)^{dT}\,(em/T)^T \le m^{(d+1)T},$$

where we used the assumption that both d and T are at least 3. Since we assume that C is shattered, we must have that the preceding is at least 2^m, which yields

$$2^m \le m^{(d+1)T}.$$

Therefore,

$$m \le \log(m)\frac{(d+1)T}{\log(2)}.$$

Lemma A.1 in Appendix A tells us that a necessary condition for the preceding to hold is that

$$m \le 2\frac{(d+1)T}{\log(2)}\log\frac{(d+1)T}{\log(2)} \le (d+1)T(3\log((d+1)T)+2),$$

which concludes our proof. □

In Exercise 10.4 we show that for some base classes, B, it also holds that $\mathrm{VCdim}(L(B,T)) \ge \Omega(\mathrm{VCdim}(B)\,T)$.

10.4 ADABOOST FOR FACE RECOGNITION

We now turn to a base hypothesis that has been proposed by Viola and Jones for the task of face recognition. In this task, the instance space is images, represented as matrices of gray level values of pixels. To be concrete, let us take images of size 24×24 pixels, and therefore our instance space is the set of real valued matrices of size 24×24. The goal is to learn a classifier, $h : \mathcal{X} \to \{\pm 1\}$, that given an image as input, should output whether the image is of a human face or not.

Each hypothesis in the base class is of the form $h(x) = f(g(x))$, where f is a decision stump hypothesis and $g : \mathbb{R}^{24,24} \to \mathbb{R}$ is a function that maps an image to a scalar. Each function g is parameterized by

- An axis aligned rectangle R. Since each image is of size 24×24, there are at most 24^4 axis aligned rectangles.
- A type, $t \in \{A, B, C, D\}$. Each type corresponds to a mask, as depicted in Figure 10.1.

To calculate g we stretch the mask t to fit the rectangle R and then calculate the sum of the pixels (that is, sum of their gray level values) that lie within the outer rectangles and subtract it from the sum of pixels in the inner rectangles.

Since the number of such functions g is at most $24^4 \cdot 4$, we can implement a weak learner for the base hypothesis class by first calculating all the possible outputs of g on each image, and then apply the weak learner of decision stumps described in the previous subsection. It is possible to perform the first step very efficiently by a preprocessing step in which we calculate the integral image of each image in the training set. See Exercise 10.5 for details.

In Figure 10.2 we depict the first two features selected by AdaBoost when running it with the base features proposed by Viola and Jones.

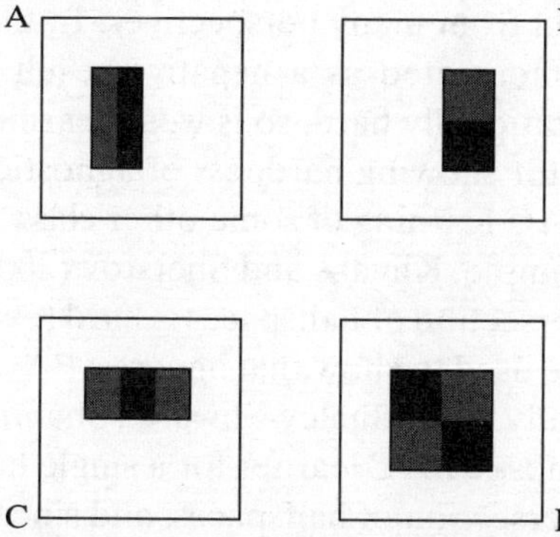

Figure 10.1. The four types of functions, g, used by the base hypotheses for face recognition. The value of g for type A or B is the difference between the sum of the pixels within two rectangular regions. These regions have the same size and shape and are horizontally or vertically adjacent. For type C, the value of g is the sum within two outside rectangles subtracted from the sum in a center rectangle. For type D, we compute the difference between diagonal pairs of rectangles.

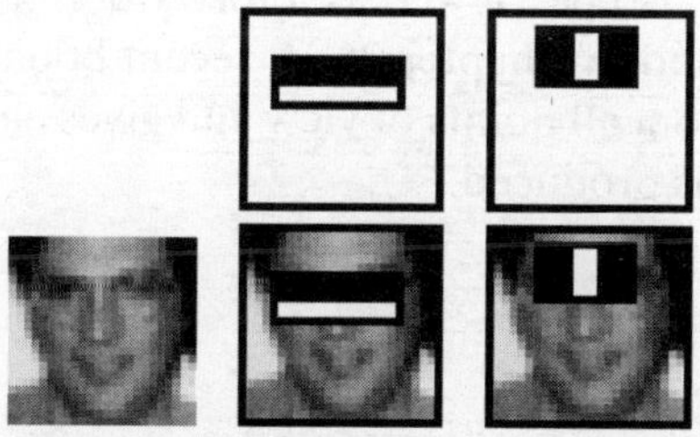

Figure 10.2. The first and second features selected by AdaBoost, as implemented by Viola and Jones. The two features are shown in the top row and then overlaid on a typical training face in the bottom row. The first feature measures the difference in intensity between the region of the eyes and a region across the upper cheeks. The feature capitalizes on the observation that the eye region is often darker than the cheeks. The second feature compares the intensities in the eye regions to the intensity across the bridge of the nose.

10.5 SUMMARY

Boosting is a method for amplifying the accuracy of weak learners. In this chapter we described the AdaBoost algorithm. We have shown that after T iterations of AdaBoost, it returns a hypothesis from the class $L(B,T)$, obtained by composing a linear classifier on T hypotheses from a base class B. We have demonstrated how the parameter T controls the tradeoff between approximation and estimation errors. In the next chapter we will study how to tune parameters such as T, on the basis of the data.

10.6 BIBLIOGRAPHIC REMARKS

As mentioned before, boosting stemmed from the theoretical question of whether an efficient weak learner can be "boosted" into an efficient strong learner (Kearns & Valiant 1988) and solved by Schapire (1990). The AdaBoost algorithm has been proposed in Freund and Schapire (1995).

Boosting can be viewed from many perspectives. In the purely theoretical context, AdaBoost can be interpreted as a negative result: If strong learning of a hypothesis class is computationally hard, so is weak learning of this class. This negative result can be useful for showing hardness of agnostic PAC learning of a class B based on hardness of PAC learning of some other class $\mathcal{H}$, as long as $\mathcal{H}$ is weakly learnable using B. For example, Klivans and Sherstov (2006) have shown that PAC learning of the class of intersection of halfspaces is hard (even in the realizable case). This hardness result can be used to show that agnostic PAC learning of a single halfspace is also computationally hard (Shalev-Shwartz, Shamir & Sridharan 2010). The idea is to show that an agnostic PAC learner for a single halfspace can yield a weak learner for the class of intersection of halfspaces, and since such a weak learner can be boosted, we will obtain a strong learner for the class of intersection of halfspaces.

AdaBoost also shows an equivalence between the existence of a weak learner and separability of the data using a linear classifier over the predictions of base hypotheses. This result is closely related to von Neumann's minimax theorem (von Neumann 1928), a fundamental result in game theory.

AdaBoost is also related to the concept of margin, which we will study later on in Chapter 15. It can also be viewed as a forward greedy selection algorithm, a topic that will be presented in Chapter 25. A recent book by Schapire and Freund (2012) covers boosting from all points of view and gives easy access to the wealth of research that this field has produced.

10.7 EXERCISES

10.1 **Boosting the Confidence:** Let A be an algorithm that guarantees the following: There exist some constant $\delta_0 \in (0,1)$ and a function $m_{\mathcal{H}} : (0,1) \to \mathbb{N}$ such that for every $\epsilon \in (0,1)$, if $m \geq m_{\mathcal{H}}(\epsilon)$ then for every distribution $\mathcal{D}$ it holds that with probability of at least $1-\delta_0$, $L_{\mathcal{D}}(A(S)) \leq \min_{h\in\mathcal{H}} L_{\mathcal{D}}(h) + \epsilon$.

Suggest a procedure that relies on A and learns $\mathcal{H}$ in the usual agnostic PAC learning model and has a sample complexity of

$$m_{\mathcal{H}}(\epsilon,\delta) \leq k\, m_{\mathcal{H}}(\epsilon) + \left\lceil \frac{2\log(4k/\delta)}{\epsilon^2} \right\rceil,$$

where

$$k = \lceil \log(\delta)/\log(\delta_0) \rceil.$$

Hint: Divide the data into $k+1$ chunks, where each of the first k chunks is of size $m_{\mathcal{H}}(\epsilon)$ examples. Train the first k chunks using A. Argue that the probability that for all of these chunks we have $L_{\mathcal{D}}(A(S)) > \min_{h\in\mathcal{H}} L_{\mathcal{D}}(h) + \epsilon$ is at most $\delta_0^k \leq \delta/2$. Finally, use the last chunk to choose from the k hypotheses that A generated from the k chunks (by relying on Corollary 4.6).

10.2 Prove that the function h given in Equation (10.5) equals the piece-wise constant function defined according to the same thresholds as h.

10.3 We have informally argued that the AdaBoost algorithm uses the weighting mechanism to "force" the weak learner to focus on the problematic examples in the next iteration. In this question we will find some rigorous justification for this argument.

Show that the error of h_t w.r.t. the distribution $\mathbf{D}^{(t+1)}$ is exactly 1/2. That is, show that for every $t \in [T]$

$$\sum_{i=1}^{m} D_i^{(t+1)} \mathbb{1}_{[y_i \neq h_t(\mathbf{x}_i)]} = 1/2.$$

10.4 In this exercise we discuss the VC-dimension of classes of the form $L(B,T)$. We proved an upper bound of $O(dT\log(dT))$, where $d = \mathrm{VCdim}(B)$. Here we wish to prove an almost matching lower bound. However, that will not be the case for all classes B.

1. Note that for every class B and every number $T \geq 1$, $\mathrm{VCdim}(B) \leq \mathrm{VCdim}(L(B,T))$. Find a class B for which $\mathrm{VCdim}(B) = \mathrm{VCdim}(L(B,T))$ for every $T \geq 1$.
   Hint: Take $\mathcal{X}$ to be a finite set.
2. Let B_d be the class of decision stumps over $\mathbb{R}^d$. Prove that $\log(d) \leq \mathrm{VCdim}(B_d) \leq 5 + 2\log(d)$.
   Hints:
   - For the upper bound, rely on Exercise 10.11.
   - For the lower bound, assume $d = 2^k$. Let A be a $k \times d$ matrix whose columns are all the d binary vectors in $\{\pm 1\}^k$. The rows of A form a set of k vectors in R^d. Show that this set is shattered by decision stumps over $\mathbb{R}^d$.
3. Let $T \geq 1$ be any integer. Prove that $\mathrm{VCdim}(L(B_d,T)) \geq 0.5T\log(d)$.
   Hint: Construct a set of $\frac{T}{2}k$ instances by taking the rows of the matrix A from the previous question, and the rows of the matrices $2A, 3A, 4A, \ldots, \frac{T}{2}A$. Show that the resulting set is shattered by $L(B_d,T)$.

10.5 **Efficiently Calculating the Viola and Jones Features Using an Integral Image:** Let A be a 24×24 matrix representing an image. The integral image of A, denoted by $I(A)$, is the matrix B such that $B_{i,j} = \sum_{i' \leq i, j' \leq j} A_{i,j}$.

- Show that $I(A)$ can be calculated from A in time linear in the size of A.
- Show how every Viola and Jones feature can be calculated from $I(A)$ in a constant amount of time (that is, the runtime does not depend on the size of the rectangle defining the feature).

11

Model Selection and Validation

In the previous chapter we have described the AdaBoost algorithm and have shown how the parameter T of AdaBoost controls the bias-complexity tradeoff. But how do we set T in practice? More generally, when approaching some practical problem, we usually can think of several algorithms that may yield a good solution, each of which might have several parameters. How can we choose the best algorithm for the particular problem at hand? And how do we set the algorithm's parameters? This task is often called *model selection*.

To illustrate the model selection task, consider the problem of learning a one dimensional regression function, $h : \mathbb{R} \to \mathbb{R}$. Suppose that we obtain a training set as depicted in the figure.

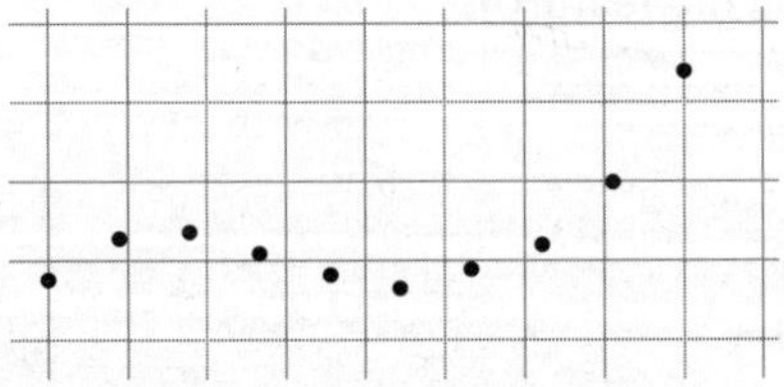

We can consider fitting a polynomial to the data, as described in Chapter 9. However, we might be uncertain regarding which degree d would give the best results for our data set: A small degree may not fit the data well (i.e., it will have a large approximation error), whereas a high degree may lead to overfitting (i.e., it will have a large estimation error). In the following we depict the result of fitting a polynomial of degrees 2, 3, and 10. It is easy to see that the empirical risk decreases as we enlarge the degree. However, looking at the graphs, our intuition tells us that setting the degree to 3 may be better than setting it to 10. It follows that the empirical risk alone is not enough for model selection.

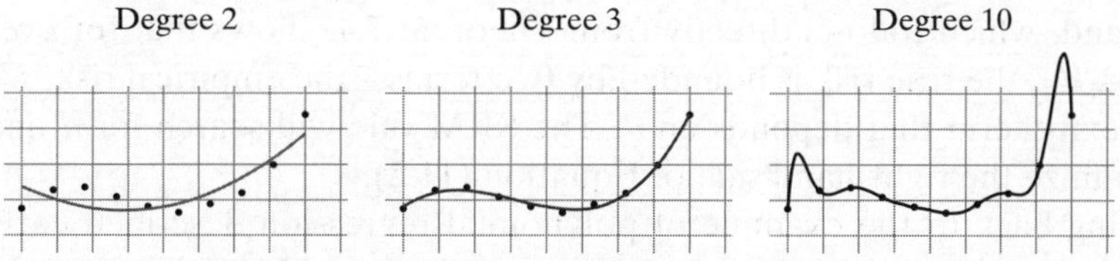

In this chapter we will present two approaches for model selection. The first approach is based on the Structural Risk Minimization (SRM) paradigm we have described and analyzed in Chapter 7.2. SRM is particularly useful when a learning algorithm depends on a parameter that controls the bias-complexity tradeoff (such as the degree of the fitted polynomial in the preceding example or the parameter T in AdaBoost). The second approach relies on the concept of *validation*. The basic idea is to partition the training set into two sets. One is used for training each of the candidate models, and the second is used for deciding which of them yields the best results.

In model selection tasks, we try to find the right balance between approximation and estimation errors. More generally, if our learning algorithm fails to find a predictor with a small risk, it is important to understand whether we suffer from overfitting or underfitting. In Section 11.3 we discuss how this can be achieved.

11.1 MODEL SELECTION USING SRM

The SRM paradigm has been described and analyzed in Section 7.2. Here we show how SRM can be used for tuning the tradeoff between bias and complexity without deciding on a specific hypothesis class in advance. Consider a countable sequence of hypothesis classes $\mathcal{H}_1, \mathcal{H}_2, \mathcal{H}_3, \ldots$. For example, in the problem of polynomial regression mentioned, we can take $\mathcal{H}_d$ to be the set of polynomials of degree at most d. Another example is taking $\mathcal{H}_d$ to be the class $L(B,d)$ used by AdaBoost, as described in the previous chapter.

We assume that for every d, the class $\mathcal{H}_d$ enjoys the uniform convergence property (see Definition 4.3 in Chapter 4) with a sample complexity function of the form

$$m^{\text{UC}}_{\mathcal{H}_d}(\epsilon, \delta) \le \frac{g(d)\log(1/\delta)}{\epsilon^2}, \tag{11.1}$$

where $g : \mathbb{N} \to \mathbb{R}$ is some monotonically increasing function. For example, in the case of binary classification problems, we can take $g(d)$ to be the VC-dimension of the class $\mathcal{H}_d$ multiplied by a universal constant (the one appearing in the fundamental theorem of learning; see Theorem 6.8). For the classes $L(B,d)$ used by AdaBoost, the function g will simply grow with d.

Recall that the SRM rule follows a "bound minimization" approach, where in our case the bound is as follows: With probability of at least $1-\delta$, for every $d \in \mathbb{N}$ and $h \in \mathcal{H}_d$,

$$L_{\mathcal{D}}(h) \le L_S(h) + \sqrt{\frac{g(d)(\log(1/\delta) + 2\log(d) + \log(\pi^2/6))}{m}}. \tag{11.2}$$

This bound, which follows directly from Theorem 7.4, shows that for every d and every $h \in \mathcal{H}_d$, the true risk is bounded by two terms – the empirical risk, $L_S(h)$, and a complexity term that depends on d. The SRM rule will search for d and $h \in \mathcal{H}_d$ that minimize the right-hand side of Equation (11.2).

Getting back to the example of polynomial regression described earlier, even though the empirical risk of the 10th degree polynomial is smaller than that of the 3rd degree polynomial, we would still prefer the 3rd degree polynomial since its complexity (as reflected by the value of the function $g(d)$) is much smaller.

While the SRM approach can be useful in some situations, in many practical cases the upper bound given in Equation (11.2) is pessimistic. In the next section we present a more practical approach.

11.2 VALIDATION

We would often like to get a better estimation of the true risk of the output predictor of a learning algorithm. So far we have derived bounds on the estimation error of a hypothesis class, which tell us that for *all* hypotheses in the class, the true risk is not very far from the empirical risk. However, these bounds might be loose and pessimistic, as they hold for all hypotheses and all possible data distributions. A more accurate estimation of the true risk can be obtained by using some of the training data as a validation set, over which one can evalutate the success of the algorithm's output predictor. This procedure is called *validation*.

Naturally, a better estimation of the true risk is useful for model selection, as we will describe in Section 11.2.2.

11.2.1 Hold Out Set

The simplest way to estimate the true error of a predictor h is by sampling an additional set of examples, independent of the training set, and using the empirical error on this validation set as our estimator. Formally, let $V = (\mathbf{x}_1, y_1), \ldots, (\mathbf{x}_{m_v}, y_{m_v})$ be a set of fresh m_v examples that are sampled according to $\mathcal{D}$ (independently of the m examples of the training set S). Using Hoeffding's inequality (Lemma 4.5) we have the following:

Theorem 11.1. *Let h be some predictor and assume that the loss function is in* $[0,1]$. *Then, for every $\delta \in (0,1)$, with probability of at least $1-\delta$ over the choice of a validation set V of size m_v we have*

$$\left|L_V(h) - L_{\mathcal{D}}(h)\right| \le \sqrt{\frac{\log(2/\delta)}{2m_v}}.$$

The bound in Theorem 11.1 does not depend on the algorithm or the training set used to construct h and is tighter than the usual bounds that we have seen so far. The reason for the tightness of this bound is that it is in terms of an estimate on a fresh validation set that is independent of the way h was generated. To illustrate this point, suppose that h was obtained by applying an ERM predictor with respect to a hypothesis class of VC-dimension d, over a training set of m examples. Then, from the fundamental theorem of learning (Theorem 6.8) we obtain the bound

$$L_{\mathcal{D}}(h) \le L_S(h) + \sqrt{C \frac{d + \log(1/\delta)}{m}},$$

where C is the constant appearing in Theorem 6.8. In contrast, from Theorem 11.1 we obtain the bound

$$L_{\mathcal{D}}(h) \le L_V(h) + \sqrt{\frac{\log(2/\delta)}{2m_v}}.$$

Therefore, taking m_v to be order of m, we obtain an estimate that is more accurate by a factor that depends on the VC-dimension. On the other hand, the price we pay for using such an estimate is that it requires an additional sample on top of the sample used for training the learner.

Sampling a training set and then sampling an independent validation set is equivalent to randomly partitioning our random set of examples into two parts, using one part for training and the other one for validation. For this reason, the validation set is often referred to as a *hold out* set.

11.2.2 Validation for Model Selection

Validation can be naturally used for model selection as follows. We first train different algorithms (or the same algorithm with different parameters) on the given training set. Let $\mathcal{H} = \{h_1, \ldots, h_r\}$ be the set of all output predictors of the different algorithms. For example, in the case of training polynomial regressors, we would have each h_r be the output of polynomial regression of degree r. Now, to choose a single predictor from $\mathcal{H}$ we sample a fresh validation set and choose the predictor that minimizes the error over the validation set. In other words, we apply $\mathrm{ERM}_{\mathcal{H}}$ over the validation set.

This process is very similar to learning a finite hypothesis class. The only difference is that $\mathcal{H}$ is not fixed ahead of time but rather depends on the training set. However, since the validation set is independent of the training set we get that it is also independent of $\mathcal{H}$ and therefore the same technique we used to derive bounds for finite hypothesis classes holds here as well. In particular, combining Theorem 11.1 with the union bound we obtain:

Theorem 11.2. *Let $\mathcal{H} = \{h_1, \ldots, h_r\}$ be an arbitrary set of predictors and assume that the loss function is in $[0,1]$. Assume that a validation set V of size m_v is sampled independent of $\mathcal{H}$. Then, with probability of at least $1-\delta$ over the choice of V we have*

$$\forall h \in \mathcal{H},\ \left|L_{\mathcal{D}}(h) - L_V(h)\right| \le \sqrt{\frac{\log(2|\mathcal{H}|/\delta)}{2m_v}}.$$

This theorem tells us that the error on the validation set approximates the true error as long as $\mathcal{H}$ is not too large. However, if we try too many methods (resulting in $|\mathcal{H}|$ that is large relative to the size of the validation set) then we're in danger of overfitting.

To illustrate how validation is useful for model selection, consider again the example of fitting a one dimensional polynomial as described in the beginning of this chapter. In the following we depict the same training set, with ERM polynomials of degree 2, 3, and 10, but this time we also depict an additional validation set (marked as unfilled circles). The polynomial of degree 10 has minimal training error, yet the polynomial of degree 3 has the minimal validation error, and hence it will be chosen as the best model.

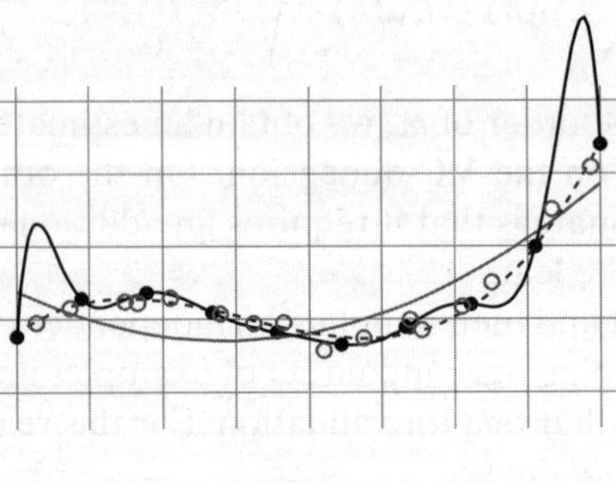

11.2.3 The Model-Selection Curve

The model selection curve shows the training error and validation error as a function of the complexity of the model considered. For example, for the polynomial fitting problem mentioned previously, the curve will look like:

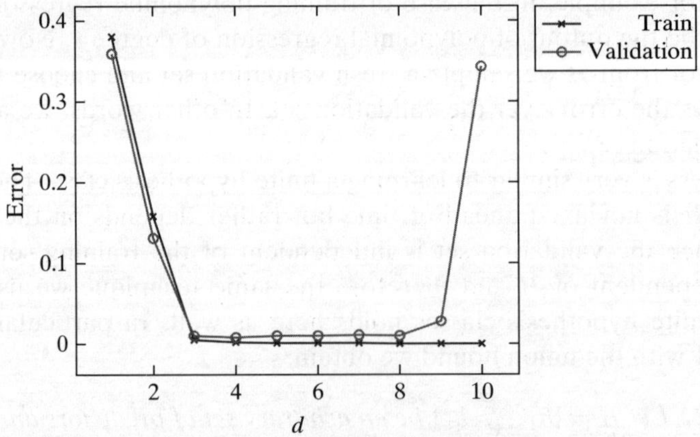

As can be shown, the training error is monotonically decreasing as we increase the polynomial degree (which is the complexity of the model in our case). On the other hand, the validation error first decreases but then starts to increase, which indicates that we are starting to suffer from overfitting.

Plotting such curves can help us understand whether we are searching the correct regime of our parameter space. Often, there may be more than a single parameter to tune, and the possible number of values each parameter can take might be quite large. For example, in Chapter 13 we describe the concept of *regularization*, in which the parameter of the learning algorithm is a real number. In such cases, we start with a rough grid of values for the parameter(s) and plot the corresponding model-selection curve. On the basis of the curve we will zoom in to the correct regime and employ a finer grid to search over. It is important to verify that we are in the relevant regime. For example, in the polynomial fitting problem described, if we start searching degrees from the set of values $\{1, 10, 20\}$ and do not employ a finer grid based on the resulting curve, we will end up with a rather poor model.

11.2.4 *k*-Fold Cross Validation

The validation procedure described so far assumes that data is plentiful and that we have the ability to sample a fresh validation set. But in some applications, data is scarce and we do not want to "waste" data on validation. The k-fold cross validation technique is designed to give an accurate estimate of the true error without wasting too much data.

In k-fold cross validation the original training set is partitioned into k subsets (folds) of size m/k (for simplicity, assume that m/k is an integer). For each fold, the algorithm is trained on the union of the other folds and then the error of its output is estimated using the fold. Finally, the average of all these errors is the estimate of the true error. The special case $k = m$, where m is the number of examples, is called *leave-one-out* (LOO).

k-Fold cross validation is often used for model selection (or parameter tuning), and once the best parameter is chosen, the algorithm is retrained using this parameter on the entire training set. A pseudocode of k-fold cross validation for model selection is given in the following. The procedure receives as input a training set, S, a set of possible parameter values, Θ, an integer, k, representing the number of folds, and a learning algorithm, A, which receives as input a training set as well as a parameter $\theta \in \Theta$. It outputs the best parameter as well as the hypothesis trained by this parameter on the entire training set.

k-Fold Cross Validation for Model Selection

input:
  training set $S = (\mathbf{x}_1, y_1), \ldots, (\mathbf{x}_m, y_m)$
  set of parameter values Θ
  learning algorithm A
  integer k
partition S into $S_1, S_2, \ldots, S_k$
foreach $\theta \in \Theta$
  for $i = 1 \ldots k$
    $h_{i,\theta} = A(S \setminus S_i; \theta)$
  $\text{error}(\theta) = \frac{1}{k}\sum_{i=1}^{k} L_{S_i}(h_{i,\theta})$
output
  $\theta^\star = \text{argmin}_\theta\,[\text{error}(\theta)]$
  $h_{\theta^\star} = A(S; \theta^\star)$

The cross validation method often works very well in practice. However, it might sometime fail, as the artificial example given in Exercise 11.1 shows. Rigorously understanding the exact behavior of cross validation is still an open problem. Rogers and Wagner (Rogers & Wagner 1978) have shown that for k local rules (e.g., k Nearest Neighbor; see Chapter 19) the cross validation procedure gives a very good estimate of the true error. Other papers show that cross validation works for stable algorithms (we will study stability and its relation to learnability in Chapter 13).

11.2.5 Train-Validation-Test Split

In most practical applications, we split the available examples into three sets. The first set is used for training our algorithm and the second is used as a validation set for model selection. After we select the best model, we test the performance of the output predictor on the third set, which is often called the "test set." The number obtained is used as an estimator of the true error of the learned predictor.

11.3 WHAT TO DO IF LEARNING FAILS

Consider the following scenario: You were given a learning task and have approached it with a choice of a hypothesis class, a learning algorithm, and parameters. You used a validation set to tune the parameters and tested the learned predictor on a test set. The test results, unfortunately, turn out to be unsatisfactory. What went wrong then, and what should you do next?

There are many elements that can be "fixed." The main approaches are listed in the following:

- Get a larger sample
- Change the hypothesis class by
  - Enlarging it
  - Reducing it
  - Completely changing it
  - Changing the parameters you consider
- Change the feature representation of the data
- Change the optimization algorithm used to apply your learning rule

In order to find the best remedy, it is essential first to understand the cause of the bad performance. Recall that in Chapter 5 we decomposed the true error of the learned predictor into approximation error and estimation error. The approximation error is defined to be $L_{\mathcal{D}}(h^\star)$ for some $h^\star \in \operatorname{argmin}_{h\in\mathcal{H}} L_{\mathcal{D}}(h)$, while the estimation error is defined to be $L_{\mathcal{D}}(h_S) - L_{\mathcal{D}}(h^\star)$, where h_S is the learned predictor (which is based on the training set S).

The approximation error of the class does not depend on the sample size or on the algorithm being used. It only depends on the distribution $\mathcal{D}$ and on the hypothesis class $\mathcal{H}$. Therefore, if the approximation error is large, it will not help us to enlarge the training set size, and it also does not make sense to reduce the hypothesis class. What can be beneficial in this case is to enlarge the hypothesis class or completely change it (if we have some alternative prior knowledge in the form of a different hypothesis class). We can also consider applying the same hypothesis class but on a different feature representation of the data (see Chapter 25).

The estimation error of the class does depend on the sample size. Therefore, if we have a large estimation error we can make an effort to obtain more training examples. We can also consider reducing the hypothesis class. However, it doesn't make sense to enlarge the hypothesis class in that case.

Error Decomposition Using Validation

We see that understanding whether our problem is due to approximation error or estimation error is very useful for finding the best remedy. In the previous section we saw how to estimate $L_{\mathcal{D}}(h_S)$ using the empirical risk on a validation set. However, it is more difficult to estimate the approximation error of the class. Instead, we give a different error decomposition, one that can be estimated from the train and validation sets.

$$L_{\mathcal{D}}(h_S) = (L_{\mathcal{D}}(h_S) - L_V(h_S)) + (L_V(h_S) - L_S(h_S)) + L_S(h_S).$$

The first term, $(L_{\mathcal{D}}(h_S) - L_V(h_S))$, can be bounded quite tightly using Theorem 11.1. Intuitively, when the second term, $(L_V(h_S) - L_S(h_S))$, is large we say that our algorithm suffers from "overfitting" while when the empirical risk term, $L_S(h_S)$, is large we say that our algorithm suffers from "underfitting." Note that these two terms are not necessarily good estimates of the estimation and approximation errors. To illustrate this, consider the case in which $\mathcal{H}$ is a class of VC-dimension d, and $\mathcal{D}$ is a distribution such that the approximation error of $\mathcal{H}$ with respect to $\mathcal{D}$ is 1/4. As long as the size of our training set is smaller than d we will have $L_S(h_S) = 0$ for every ERM hypothesis. Therefore, the training risk, $L_S(h_S)$, and the approximation error, $L_{\mathcal{D}}(h^\star)$, can be significantly different. Nevertheless, as we show later, the values of $L_S(h_S)$ and $(L_V(h_S) - L_S(h_S))$ still provide us useful information.

Consider first the case in which $L_S(h_S)$ is large. We can write

$$L_S(h_S) = (L_S(h_S) - L_S(h^\star)) + (L_S(h^\star) - L_{\mathcal{D}}(h^\star)) + L_{\mathcal{D}}(h^\star).$$

When h_S is an $\text{ERM}_{\mathcal{H}}$ hypothesis we have that $L_S(h_S) - L_S(h^\star) \le 0$. In addition, since $h^\star$ does not depend on S, the term $(L_S(h^\star) - L_{\mathcal{D}}(h^\star))$ can be bounded quite tightly (as in Theorem 11.1). The last term is the approximation error. It follows that if $L_S(h_S)$ is large then so is the approximation error, and the remedy to the failure of our algorithm should be tailored accordingly (as discussed previously).

Remark 11.1. It is possible that the approximation error of our class is small, yet the value of $L_S(h_S)$ is large. For example, maybe we had a bug in our ERM implementation, and the algorithm returns a hypothesis h_S that is not an ERM. It may also be the case that finding an ERM hypothesis is computationally hard, and our algorithm applies some heuristic trying to find an approximate ERM. In some cases, it is hard to know how good h_S is relative to an ERM hypothesis. But, sometimes it is possible at least to know whether there are better hypotheses. For example, in the next chapter we will study convex learning problems in which there are optimality conditions that can be checked to verify whether our optimization algorithm converged to an ERM solution. In other cases, the solution may depend on randomness in initializing the algorithm, so we can try different randomly selected initial points to see whether better solutions pop out.

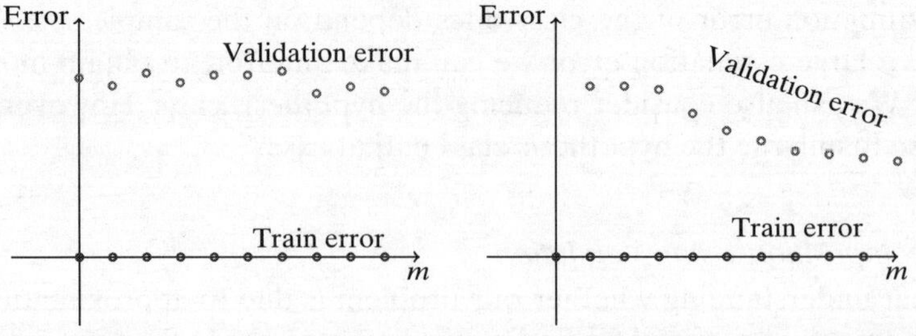

Figure 11.1. Examples of learning curves. Left: This learning curve corresponds to the scenario in which the number of examples is always smaller than the VC dimension of the class. Right: This learning curve corresponds to the scenario in which the approximation error is zero and the number of examples is larger than the VC dimension of the class.

Next consider the case in which $L_S(h_S)$ is small. As we argued before, this does not necessarily imply that the approximation error is small. Indeed, consider two scenarios, in both of which we are trying to learn a hypothesis class of VC-dimension d using the ERM learning rule. In the first scenario, we have a training set of $m < d$ examples and the approximation error of the class is high. In the second scenario, we have a training set of $m > 2d$ examples and the approximation error of the class is zero. In both cases $L_S(h_S) = 0$. How can we distinguish between the two cases?

Learning Curves

One possible way to distinguish between the two cases is by plotting *learning curves*. To produce a learning curve we train the algorithm on prefixes of the data of increasing sizes. For example, we can first train the algorithm on the first 10% of the examples, then on 20% of them, and so on. For each prefix we calculate the training error (on the prefix the algorithm is being trained on) and the validation error (on a predefined validation set). Such learning curves can help us distinguish between the two aforementioned scenarios. In the first scenario we expect the validation error to be approximately 1/2 for all prefixes, as we didn't really learn anything. In the second scenario the validation error will start as a constant but then should start decreasing (it must start decreasing once the training set size is larger than the VC-dimension). An illustration of the two cases is given in Figure 11.1.

In general, as long as the approximation error is greater than zero we expect the training error to grow with the sample size, as a larger amount of data points makes it harder to provide an explanation for all of them. On the other hand, the validation error tends to decrease with the increase in sample size. If the VC-dimension is finite, when the sample size goes to infinity, the validation and train errors converge to the approximation error. Therefore, by extrapolating the training and validation curves we can try to guess the value of the approximation error, or at least to get a rough estimate on an interval in which the approximation error resides.

Getting back to the problem of finding the best remedy for the failure of our algorithm, if we observe that $L_S(h_S)$ is small while the validation error is large, then in any case we know that the size of our training set is not sufficient for learning the class $\mathcal{H}$. We can then plot a learning curve. If we see that the validation error is starting to decrease then the best solution is to increase the number of examples (if we can afford to enlarge the data). Another reasonable solution is to decrease the complexity of the hypothesis class. On the other hand, if we see that the validation error is kept around 1/2 then we have no evidence that the approximation error of $\mathcal{H}$ is good. It may be the case that increasing the training set size will not help us at all. Obtaining more data can still help us, as at some point we can see whether the validation error starts to decrease or whether the training error starts to increase. But, if more data is expensive, it may be better first to try to reduce the complexity of the hypothesis class.

To summarize the discussion, the following steps should be applied:

1. If learning involves parameter tuning, plot the model-selection curve to make sure that you tuned the parameters appropriately (see Section 11.2.3).
2. If the training error is excessively large consider enlarging the hypothesis class, completely change it, or change the feature representation of the data.
3. If the training error is small, plot learning curves and try to deduce from them whether the problem is estimation error or approximation error.
4. If the approximation error seems to be small enough, try to obtain more data. If this is not possible, consider reducing the complexity of the hypothesis class.
5. If the approximation error seems to be large as well, try to change the hypothesis class or the feature representation of the data completely.

11.4 SUMMARY

Model selection is the task of selecting an appropriate model for the learning task based on the data itself. We have shown how this can be done using the SRM learning paradigm or using the more practical approach of validation. If our learning algorithm fails, a decomposition of the algorithm's error should be performed using learning curves, so as to find the best remedy.

11.5 EXERCISES

11.1 **Failure of k-fold cross validation** Consider a case in that the label is chosen at random according to $\mathbb{P}[y=1]=\mathbb{P}[y=0]=1/2$. Consider a learning algorithm that outputs the constant predictor $h(\mathbf{x})=1$ if the parity of the labels on the training set is 1 and otherwise the algorithm outputs the constant predictor $h(\mathbf{x})=0$. Prove that the difference between the leave-one-out estimate and the true error in such a case is always 1/2.

11.2 Let $\mathcal{H}_1,\ldots,\mathcal{H}_k$ be k hypothesis classes. Suppose you are given m i.i.d. training examples and you would like to learn the class $\mathcal{H}=\cup_{i=1}^k \mathcal{H}_i$. Consider two alternative approaches:

- Learn $\mathcal{H}$ on the m examples using the ERM rule
- Divide the m examples into a training set of size $(1-\alpha)m$ and a validation set of size αm, for some $\alpha \in (0,1)$. Then, apply the approach of model selection using validation. That is, first train each class $\mathcal{H}_i$ on the $(1-\alpha)m$ training examples using the ERM rule with respect to $\mathcal{H}_i$, and let $\hat{h}_1,\ldots,\hat{h}_k$ be the resulting hypotheses. Second, apply the ERM rule with respect to the finite class $\{\hat{h}_1,\ldots,\hat{h}_k\}$ on the αm validation examples.

Describe scenarios in which the first method is better than the second and vice versa.

12

Convex Learning Problems

In this chapter we introduce *convex learning problems*. Convex learning comprises an important family of learning problems, mainly because most of what we can learn efficiently falls into it. We have already encountered linear regression with the squared loss and logistic regression, which are convex problems, and indeed they can be learned efficiently. We have also seen nonconvex problems, such as halfspaces with the 0-1 loss, which is known to be computationally hard to learn in the unrealizable case.

In general, a convex learning problem is a problem whose hypothesis class is a convex set, and whose loss function is a convex function for each example. We begin the chapter with some required definitions of convexity. Besides convexity, we will define Lipschitzness and smoothness, which are additional properties of the loss function that facilitate successful learning. We next turn to defining convex learning problems and demonstrate the necessity for further constraints such as Boundedness and Lipschitzness or Smoothness. We define these more restricted families of learning problems and claim that Convex-Smooth/Lipschitz-Bounded problems are learnable. These claims will be proven in the next two chapters, in which we will present two learning paradigms that successfully learn all problems that are either convex-Lipschitz-bounded or convex-smooth-bounded.

Finally, in Section 12.3, we show how one can handle some nonconvex problems by minimizing "surrogate" loss functions that are convex (instead of the original nonconvex loss function). Surrogate convex loss functions give rise to efficient solutions but might increase the risk of the learned predictor.

12.1 CONVEXITY, LIPSCHITZNESS, AND SMOOTHNESS

12.1.1 Convexity

Definition 12.1 (Convex Set). A set C in a vector space is convex if for any two vectors $\mathbf{u}, \mathbf{v}$ in C, the line segment between $\mathbf{u}$ and $\mathbf{v}$ is contained in C. That is, for any $\alpha \in [0,1]$ we have that $\alpha\mathbf{u} + (1-\alpha)\mathbf{v} \in C$.

Examples of convex and nonconvex sets in $\mathbb{R}^2$ are given in the following. For the nonconvex sets, we depict two points in the set such that the line between the two points is not contained in the set.

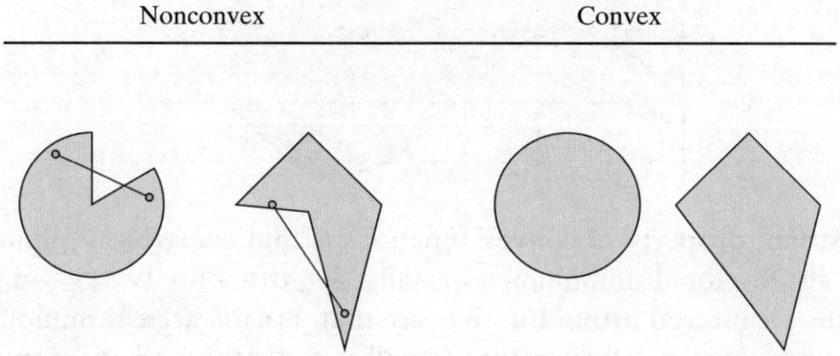

Given $\alpha \in [0,1]$, the combination, $\alpha\mathbf{u} + (1-\alpha)\mathbf{v}$ of the points $\mathbf{u}, \mathbf{v}$ is called a *convex combination.*

Definition 12.2 (Convex Function). Let C be a convex set. A function $f : C \to \mathbb{R}$ is convex if for every $\mathbf{u}, \mathbf{v} \in C$ and $\alpha \in [0,1]$,

$$f(\alpha\mathbf{u} + (1-\alpha)\mathbf{v}) \leq \alpha f(\mathbf{u}) + (1-\alpha) f(\mathbf{v}).$$

In words, f is convex if for any $\mathbf{u}, \mathbf{v}$, the graph of f between $\mathbf{u}$ and $\mathbf{v}$ lies below the line segment joining $f(\mathbf{u})$ and $f(\mathbf{v})$. An illustration of a convex function, $f : \mathbb{R} \to \mathbb{R}$, is depicted in the following.

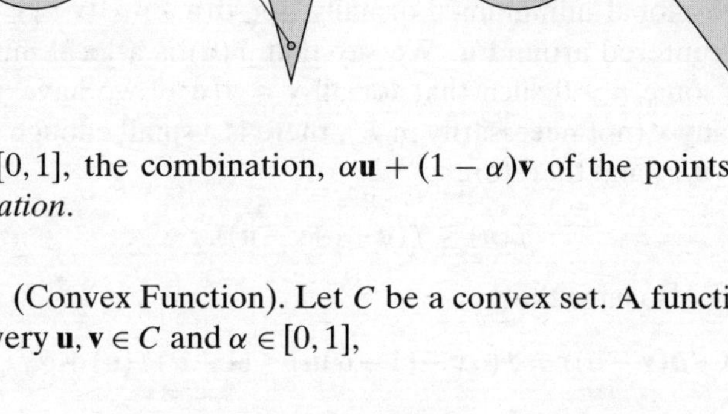

The *epigraph* of a function f is the set

$$\text{epigraph(f)} = \{(\mathbf{x}, \beta) : f(\mathbf{x}) \leq \beta\}. \tag{12.1}$$

It is easy to verify that a function f is convex if and only if its epigraph is a convex set. An illustration of a nonconvex function $f : \mathbb{R} \to \mathbb{R}$, along with its epigraph, is given in the following.

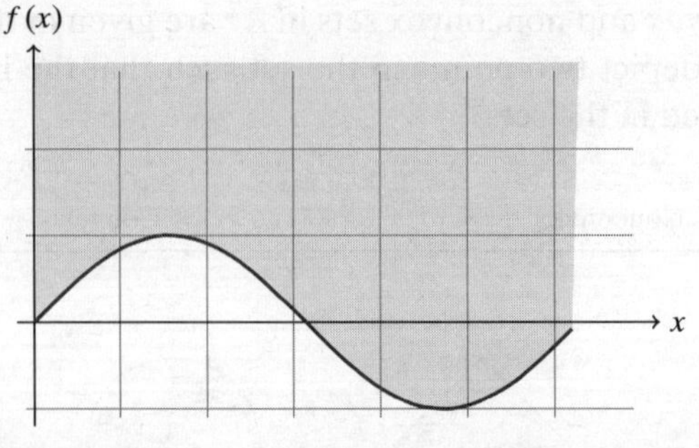

An important property of convex functions is that every local minimum of the function is also a global minimum. Formally, let $B(\mathbf{u}, r) = \{\mathbf{v} : \|\mathbf{v} - \mathbf{u}\| \leq r\}$ be a ball of radius r centered around $\mathbf{u}$. We say that $f(\mathbf{u})$ is a local minimum of f at $\mathbf{u}$ if there exists some $r > 0$ such that for all $\mathbf{v} \in B(\mathbf{u}, r)$ we have $f(\mathbf{v}) \geq f(\mathbf{u})$. It follows that for any $\mathbf{v}$ (not necessarily in B), there is a small enough $\alpha > 0$ such that $\mathbf{u} + \alpha(\mathbf{v} - \mathbf{u}) \in B(\mathbf{u}, r)$ and therefore

$$f(\mathbf{u}) \leq f(\mathbf{u} + \alpha(\mathbf{v} - \mathbf{u})). \tag{12.2}$$

If f is convex, we also have that

$$f(\mathbf{u} + \alpha(\mathbf{v} - \mathbf{u})) = f(\alpha\mathbf{v} + (1-\alpha)\mathbf{u}) \leq (1-\alpha) f(\mathbf{u}) + \alpha f(\mathbf{v}). \tag{12.3}$$

Combining these two equations and rearranging terms, we conclude that $f(\mathbf{u}) \leq f(\mathbf{v})$. Since this holds for every $\mathbf{v}$, it follows that $f(\mathbf{u})$ is also a global minimum of f.

Another important property of convex functions is that for every $\mathbf{w}$ we can construct a tangent to f at $\mathbf{w}$ that lies below f everywhere. If f is differentiable, this tangent is the linear function $l(\mathbf{u}) = f(\mathbf{w}) + \langle \nabla f(\mathbf{w}), \mathbf{u} - \mathbf{w} \rangle$, where $\nabla f(\mathbf{w})$ is the gradient of f at $\mathbf{w}$, namely, the vector of partial derivatives of f, $\nabla f(\mathbf{w}) = \left(\frac{\partial f(\mathbf{w})}{\partial w_1}, \ldots, \frac{\partial f(\mathbf{w})}{\partial w_d}\right)$. That is, for convex differentiable functions,

$$\forall \mathbf{u}, \;\; f(\mathbf{u}) \geq f(\mathbf{w}) + \langle \nabla f(\mathbf{w}), \mathbf{u} - \mathbf{w} \rangle. \tag{12.4}$$

In Chapter 14 we will generalize this inequality to nondifferentiable functions. An illustration of Equation (12.4) is given in the following.

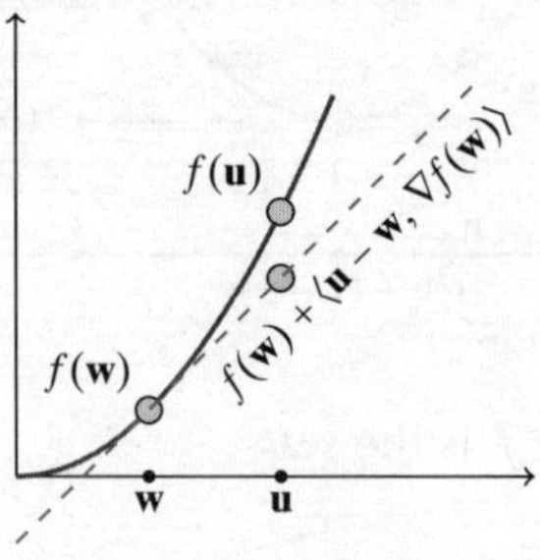

If f is a scalar differentiable function, there is an easy way to check whether it is convex.

Lemma 12.3. *Let $f : \mathbb{R} \to \mathbb{R}$ be a scalar twice differential function, and let f', f'' be its first and second derivatives, respectively. Then, the following are equivalent:*

1. *f is convex*
2. *f' is monotonically nondecreasing*
3. *f'' is nonnegative*

Example 12.1.

- The scalar function $f(x) = x^2$ is convex. To see this, note that $f'(x) = 2x$ and $f''(x) = 2 > 0$.
- The scalar function $f(x) = \log(1 + \exp(x))$ is convex. To see this, observe that $f'(x) = \frac{\exp(x)}{1+\exp(x)} = \frac{1}{\exp(-x)+1}$. This is a monotonically increasing function since the exponent function is a monotonically increasing function.

The following claim shows that the composition of a convex scalar function with a linear function yields a convex vector-valued function.

Claim 12.4. *Assume that $f : \mathbb{R}^d \to \mathbb{R}$ can be written as $f(\mathbf{w}) = g(\langle \mathbf{w}, \mathbf{x} \rangle + y)$, for some $\mathbf{x} \in \mathbb{R}^d$, $y \in \mathbb{R}$, and $g : \mathbb{R} \to \mathbb{R}$. Then, convexity of g implies the convexity of f.*

Proof. Let $\mathbf{w}_1, \mathbf{w}_2 \in \mathbb{R}^d$ and $\alpha \in [0,1]$. We have

$$\begin{aligned} f(\alpha \mathbf{w}_1 + (1-\alpha)\mathbf{w}_2) &= g(\langle \alpha \mathbf{w}_1 + (1-\alpha)\mathbf{w}_2, \mathbf{x} \rangle + y) \\ &= g(\alpha \langle \mathbf{w}_1, \mathbf{x} \rangle + (1-\alpha)\langle \mathbf{w}_2, \mathbf{x} \rangle + y) \\ &= g(\alpha(\langle \mathbf{w}_1, \mathbf{x} \rangle + y) + (1-\alpha)(\langle \mathbf{w}_2, \mathbf{x} \rangle + y)) \\ &\le \alpha g(\langle \mathbf{w}_1, \mathbf{x} \rangle + y) + (1-\alpha) g(\langle \mathbf{w}_2, \mathbf{x} \rangle + y), \end{aligned}$$

where the last inequality follows from the convexity of g. □

Example 12.2.

- Given some $\mathbf{x} \in \mathbb{R}^d$ and $y \in \mathbb{R}$, let $f : \mathbb{R}^d \to \mathbb{R}$ be defined as $f(\mathbf{w}) = (\langle \mathbf{w}, \mathbf{x} \rangle - y)^2$. Then, f is a composition of the function $g(a) = a^2$ onto a linear function, and hence f is a convex function.
- Given some $\mathbf{x} \in \mathbb{R}^d$ and $y \in \{\pm 1\}$, let $f : \mathbb{R}^d \to \mathbb{R}$ be defined as $f(\mathbf{w}) = \log(1 + \exp(-y\langle \mathbf{w}, \mathbf{x} \rangle))$. Then, f is a composition of the function $g(a) = \log(1 + \exp(a))$ onto a linear function, and hence f is a convex function.

Finally, the following lemma shows that the maximum of convex functions is convex and that a weighted sum of convex functions, with nonnegative weights, is also convex.

Claim 12.5. *For $i = 1, \ldots, r$, let $f_i : \mathbb{R}^d \to \mathbb{R}$ be a convex function. The following functions from $\mathbb{R}^d$ to $\mathbb{R}$ are also convex.*

- $g(x) = \max_{i \in [r]} f_i(x)$
- $g(x) = \sum_{i=1}^{r} w_i f_i(x)$, *where for all i, $w_i \ge 0$.*

Proof. The first claim follows by

$$\begin{aligned}
g(\alpha u+(1-\alpha)v) &= \max_i f_i(\alpha u+(1-\alpha)v) \\
&\le \max_i [\alpha f_i(u)+(1-\alpha)f_i(v)] \\
&\le \alpha \max_i f_i(u)+(1-\alpha)\max_i f_i(v) \\
&= \alpha g(u)+(1-\alpha)g(v).
\end{aligned}$$

For the second claim

$$\begin{aligned}
g(\alpha u+(1-\alpha)v) &= \sum_i w_i f_i(\alpha u+(1-\alpha)v) \\
&\le \sum_i w_i [\alpha f_i(u)+(1-\alpha)f_i(v)] \\
&= \alpha \sum_i w_i f_i(u)+(1-\alpha)\sum_i w_i f_i(v) \\
&= \alpha g(u)+(1-\alpha)g(v).
\end{aligned}$$

□

Example 12.3. The function $g(x) = |x|$ is convex. To see this, note that $g(x) = \max\{x, -x\}$ and that both the function $f_1(x) = x$ and $f_2(x) = -x$ are convex.

12.1.2 Lipschitzness

The definition of Lipschitzness that follows is with respect to the Euclidean norm over $\mathbb{R}^d$. However, it is possible to define Lipschitzness with respect to any norm.

Definition 12.6 (Lipschitzness). Let $C \subset \mathbb{R}^d$. A function $f : \mathbb{R}^d \to \mathbb{R}^k$ is ρ-Lipschitz over C if for every $\mathbf{w}_1, \mathbf{w}_2 \in C$ we have that $\|f(\mathbf{w}_1) - f(\mathbf{w}_2)\| \le \rho\, \|\mathbf{w}_1 - \mathbf{w}_2\|$.

Intuitively, a Lipschitz function cannot change too fast. Note that if $f : \mathbb{R} \to \mathbb{R}$ is differentiable, then by the mean value theorem we have

$$f(w_1) - f(w_2) = f'(u)(w_1 - w_2),$$

where u is some point between w_1 and w_2. It follows that if the derivative of f is everywhere bounded (in absolute value) by ρ, then the function is ρ-Lipschitz.

Example 12.4.

- The function $f(x) = |x|$ is 1-Lipschitz over $\mathbb{R}$. This follows from the triangle inequality: For every x_1, x_2,

$$|x_1| - |x_2| = |x_1 - x_2 + x_2| - |x_2| \le |x_1 - x_2| + |x_2| - |x_2| = |x_1 - x_2|.$$

  Since this holds for both x_1, x_2 and x_2, x_1, we obtain that $||x_1| - |x_2|| \le |x_1 - x_2|$.
- The function $f(x) = \log(1+\exp(x))$ is 1-Lipschitz over $\mathbb{R}$. To see this, observe that

$$|f'(x)| = \left|\frac{\exp(x)}{1+\exp(x)}\right| = \left|\frac{1}{\exp(-x)+1}\right| \le 1.$$

- The function $f(x) = x^2$ is not ρ-Lipschitz over $\mathbb{R}$ for any ρ. To see this, take $x_1 = 0$ and $x_2 = 1 + \rho$, then

$$f(x_2) - f(x_1) = (1+\rho)^2 > \rho(1+\rho) = \rho|x_2 - x_1|.$$

However, this function is ρ-Lipschitz over the set $C = \{x : |x| \le \rho/2\}$. Indeed, for any $x_1, x_2 \in C$ we have

$$|x_1^2 - x_2^2| = |x_1 + x_2|\,|x_1 - x_2| \le 2(\rho/2)\,|x_1 - x_2| = \rho|x_1 - x_2|.$$

- The linear function $f : \mathbb{R}^d \to \mathbb{R}$ defined by $f(\mathbf{w}) = \langle \mathbf{v}, \mathbf{w} \rangle + b$ where $\mathbf{v} \in \mathbb{R}^d$ is $\|\mathbf{v}\|$-Lipschitz. Indeed, using Cauchy-Schwartz inequality,

$$|f(\mathbf{w}_1) - f(\mathbf{w}_2)| = |\langle \mathbf{v}, \mathbf{w}_1 - \mathbf{w}_2 \rangle| \le \|\mathbf{v}\|\,\|\mathbf{w}_1 - \mathbf{w}_2\|.$$

The following claim shows that composition of Lipschitz functions preserves Lipschitzness.

Claim 12.7. *Let $f(\mathbf{x}) = g_1(g_2(\mathbf{x}))$, where g_1 is ρ_1-Lipschitz and g_2 is ρ_2-Lipschitz. Then, f is $(\rho_1\rho_2)$-Lipschitz. In particular, if g_2 is the linear function, $g_2(\mathbf{x}) = \langle \mathbf{v}, \mathbf{x} \rangle + b$, for some $\mathbf{v} \in \mathbb{R}^d, b \in \mathbb{R}$, then f is $(\rho_1\,\|\mathbf{v}\|)$-Lipschitz.*

Proof.

$$\begin{aligned}|f(\mathbf{w}_1) - f(\mathbf{w}_2)| &= |g_1(g_2(\mathbf{w}_1)) - g_1(g_2(\mathbf{w}_2))| \\ &\le \rho_1 \|g_2(\mathbf{w}_1) - g_2(\mathbf{w}_2)\| \\ &\le \rho_1\,\rho_2\,\|\mathbf{w}_1 - \mathbf{w}_2\|.\end{aligned}$$

□

12.1.3 Smoothness

The definition of a smooth function relies on the notion of *gradient*. Recall that the gradient of a differentiable function $f : \mathbb{R}^d \to \mathbb{R}$ at $\mathbf{w}$, denoted $\nabla f(\mathbf{w})$, is the vector of partial derivatives of f, namely, $\nabla f(\mathbf{w}) = \left(\frac{\partial f(\mathbf{w})}{\partial w_1}, \ldots, \frac{\partial f(\mathbf{w})}{\partial w_d}\right)$.

Definition 12.8 (Smoothness). A differentiable function $f : \mathbb{R}^d \to \mathbb{R}$ is β-smooth if its gradient is β-Lipschitz; namely, for all $\mathbf{v}, \mathbf{w}$ we have $\|\nabla f(\mathbf{v}) - \nabla f(\mathbf{w})\| \le \beta\|\mathbf{v} - \mathbf{w}\|$.

It is possible to show that smoothness implies that for all $\mathbf{v}, \mathbf{w}$ we have

$$f(\mathbf{v}) \le f(\mathbf{w}) + \langle \nabla f(\mathbf{w}), \mathbf{v} - \mathbf{w} \rangle + \frac{\beta}{2}\|\mathbf{v} - \mathbf{w}\|^2. \tag{12.5}$$

Recall that convexity of f implies that $f(\mathbf{v}) \ge f(\mathbf{w}) + \langle \nabla f(\mathbf{w}), \mathbf{v} - \mathbf{w} \rangle$. Therefore, when a function is both convex and smooth, we have both upper and lower bounds on the difference between the function and its first order approximation.

Setting $\mathbf{v} = \mathbf{w} - \frac{1}{\beta}\nabla f(\mathbf{w})$ in the right-hand side of Equation (12.5) and rearranging terms, we obtain

$$\frac{1}{2\beta}\|\nabla f(\mathbf{w})\|^2 \le f(\mathbf{w}) - f(\mathbf{v}).$$

If we further assume that $f(\mathbf{v}) \geq 0$ for all $\mathbf{v}$ we conclude that smoothness implies the following:

$$\|\nabla f(\mathbf{w})\|^2 \leq 2\beta f(\mathbf{w}). \tag{12.6}$$

A function that satisfies this property is also called a *self-bounded* function.

Example 12.5.

- The function $f(x) = x^2$ is 2-smooth. This follows directly from the fact that $f'(x) = 2x$. Note that for this particular function Equation (12.5) and Equation (12.6) hold with equality.
- The function $f(x) = \log(1 + \exp(x))$ is (1/4)-smooth. Indeed, since $f'(x) = \frac{1}{1+\exp(-x)}$ we have that

$$|f''(x)| = \frac{\exp(-x)}{(1+\exp(-x))^2} = \frac{1}{(1+\exp(-x))(1+\exp(x))} \leq 1/4.$$

Hence, f' is (1/4)-Lipschitz. Since this function is nonnegative, Equation (12.6) holds as well.

The following claim shows that a composition of a smooth scalar function over a linear function preserves smoothness.

Claim 12.9. *Let $f(\mathbf{w}) = g(\langle \mathbf{w}, \mathbf{x}\rangle + b)$, where $g : \mathbb{R} \to \mathbb{R}$ is a β-smooth function, $\mathbf{x} \in \mathbb{R}^d$, and $b \in \mathbb{R}$. Then, f is $(\beta\,\|\mathbf{x}\|^2)$-smooth.*

Proof. By the chain rule we have that $\nabla f(\mathbf{w}) = g'(\langle \mathbf{w}, \mathbf{x}\rangle + b)\mathbf{x}$, where g' is the derivative of g. Using the smoothness of g and the Cauchy-Schwartz inequality we therefore obtain

$$\begin{aligned}
f(\mathbf{v}) &= g(\langle \mathbf{v}, \mathbf{x}\rangle + b) \\
&\leq g(\langle \mathbf{w}, \mathbf{x}\rangle + b) + g'(\langle \mathbf{w}, \mathbf{x}\rangle + b)\langle \mathbf{v} - \mathbf{w}, \mathbf{x}\rangle + \frac{\beta}{2}(\langle \mathbf{v} - \mathbf{w}, \mathbf{x}\rangle)^2 \\
&\leq g(\langle \mathbf{w}, \mathbf{x}\rangle + b) + g'(\langle \mathbf{w}, \mathbf{x}\rangle + b)\langle \mathbf{v} - \mathbf{w}, \mathbf{x}\rangle + \frac{\beta}{2}(\|\mathbf{v} - \mathbf{w}\|\,\|\mathbf{x}\|)^2 \\
&= f(\mathbf{w}) + \langle \nabla f(\mathbf{w}), \mathbf{v} - \mathbf{w}\rangle + \frac{\beta\|\mathbf{x}\|^2}{2}\|\mathbf{v} - \mathbf{w}\|^2.
\end{aligned}$$

□

Example 12.6.

- For any $\mathbf{x} \in \mathbb{R}^d$ and $y \in \mathbb{R}$, let $f(\mathbf{w}) = (\langle \mathbf{w}, \mathbf{x}\rangle - y)^2$. Then, f is $(2\|\mathbf{x}\|^2)$-smooth.
- For any $\mathbf{x} \in \mathbb{R}^d$ and $y \in \{\pm 1\}$, let $f(\mathbf{w}) = \log(1 + \exp(-y\langle \mathbf{w}, \mathbf{x}\rangle))$. Then, f is $(\|\mathbf{x}\|^2/4)$-smooth.

12.2 CONVEX LEARNING PROBLEMS

Recall that in our general definition of learning (Definition 3.4 in Chapter 3), we have a hypothesis class $\mathcal{H}$, a set of examples Z, and a loss function $\ell : \mathcal{H} \times Z \to \mathbb{R}_+$. So far in the book we have mainly thought of Z as being the product of an instance space and a target space, $Z = \mathcal{X} \times \mathcal{Y}$, and $\mathcal{H}$ being a set of functions from $\mathcal{X}$ to $\mathcal{Y}$. However, $\mathcal{H}$ can be an arbitrary set. Indeed, throughout this chapter, we consider hypothesis classes $\mathcal{H}$ that are subsets of the Euclidean space $\mathbb{R}^d$. That is, every hypothesis is some real-valued vector. We shall, therefore, denote a hypothesis in $\mathcal{H}$ by $\mathbf{w}$. Now we can finally define convex learning problems:

Definition 12.10 (Convex Learning Problem). A learning problem, $(\mathcal{H}, Z, \ell)$, is called convex if the hypothesis class $\mathcal{H}$ is a convex set and for all $z \in Z$, the loss function, $\ell(\cdot, z)$, is a convex function (where, for any z, $\ell(\cdot, z)$ denotes the function $f : \mathcal{H} \to \mathbb{R}$ defined by $f(\mathbf{w}) = \ell(\mathbf{w}, z)$).

Example 12.7 (Linear Regression with the Squared Loss). Recall that linear regression is a tool for modeling the relationship between some "explanatory" variables and some real valued outcome (see Chapter 9). The domain set $\mathcal{X}$ is a subset of $\mathbb{R}^d$, for some d, and the label set $\mathcal{Y}$ is the set of real numbers. We would like to learn a linear function $h : \mathbb{R}^d \to \mathbb{R}$ that best approximates the relationship between our variables. In Chapter 9 we defined the hypothesis class as the set of homogenous linear functions, $\mathcal{H} = \{\mathbf{x} \mapsto \langle \mathbf{w}, \mathbf{x} \rangle : \mathbf{w} \in \mathbb{R}^d\}$, and used the squared loss function, $\ell(h, (\mathbf{x}, y)) = (h(\mathbf{x}) - y)^2$. However, we can equivalently model the learning problem as a convex learning problem as follows. Each linear function is parameterized by a vector $\mathbf{w} \in \mathbb{R}^d$. Hence, we can define $\mathcal{H}$ to be the set of all such parameters, namely, $\mathcal{H} = \mathbb{R}^d$. The set of examples is $Z = \mathcal{X} \times \mathcal{Y} = \mathbb{R}^d \times \mathbb{R} = \mathbb{R}^{d+1}$, and the loss function is $\ell(\mathbf{w}, (\mathbf{x}, y)) = (\langle \mathbf{w}, \mathbf{x} \rangle - y)^2$. Clearly, the set $\mathcal{H}$ is a convex set. The loss function is also convex with respect to its first argument (see Example 12.2).

Lemma 12.11. *If ℓ is a convex loss function and the class $\mathcal{H}$ is convex, then the* $\mathrm{ERM}_{\mathcal{H}}$ *problem, of minimizing the empirical loss over $\mathcal{H}$, is a convex optimization problem (that is, a problem of minimizing a convex function over a convex set).*

Proof. Recall that the $\mathrm{ERM}_{\mathcal{H}}$ problem is defined by

$$\mathrm{ERM}_{\mathcal{H}}(S) = \underset{\mathbf{w} \in \mathcal{H}}{\operatorname{argmin}}\, L_S(\mathbf{w}).$$

Since, for a sample $S = z_1, \ldots, z_m$, for every $\mathbf{w}$, $L_S(\mathbf{w}) = \frac{1}{m}\sum_{i=1}^{m} \ell(\mathbf{w}, z_i)$, Claim 12.5 implies that $L_S(\mathbf{w})$ is a convex function. Therefore, the ERM rule is a problem of minimizing a convex function subject to the constraint that the solution should be in a convex set. □

Under mild conditions, such problems can be solved efficiently using generic optimization algorithms. In particular, in Chapter 14 we will present a very simple algorithm for minimizing convex functions.

12.2.1 Learnability of Convex Learning Problems

We have argued that for many cases, implementing the ERM rule for convex learning problems can be done efficiently. But is convexity a sufficient condition for the learnability of a problem?

To make the quesion more specific: In VC theory, we saw that halfspaces in d-dimension are learnable (perhaps inefficiently). We also argued in Chapter 9 using the "discretization trick" that if the problem is of d parameters, it is learnable with a sample complexity being a function of d. That is, for a constant d, the problem should be learnable. So, maybe all convex learning problems over $\mathbb{R}^d$, are learnable?

Example 12.8 later shows that the answer is negative, even when d is low. Not all convex learning problems over $\mathbb{R}^d$ are learnable. There is no contradiction to VC theory since VC theory only deals with binary classification while here we consider a wide family of problems. There is also no contradiction to the "discretization trick" as there we assumed that the loss function is bounded and also assumed that a representation of each parameter using a finite number of bits suffices. As we will show later, under some additional restricting conditions that hold in many practical scenarios, convex problems are learnable.

Example 12.8 (Nonlearnability of Linear Regression Even If $d = 1$). Let $\mathcal{H} = \mathbb{R}$, and the loss be the squared loss: $\ell(w,(x,y)) = (wx - y)^2$ (we're referring to the homogenous case). Let A be any deterministic algorithm.[1] Assume, by way of contradiction, that A is a successful PAC learner for this problem. That is, there exists a function $m(\cdot,\cdot)$, such that for every distribution $\mathcal{D}$ and for every ϵ, δ if A receives a training set of size $m \geq m(\epsilon,\delta)$, it should output, with probability of at least $1-\delta$, a hypothesis $\hat{w} = A(S)$, such that $L_{\mathcal{D}}(\hat{w}) - \min_w L_{\mathcal{D}}(w) \leq \epsilon$.

Choose $\epsilon = 1/100, \delta = 1/2$, let $m \geq m(\epsilon,\delta)$, and set $\mu = \frac{\log(100/99)}{2m}$. We will define two distributions, and will show that A is likely to fail on at least one of them. The first distribution, $\mathcal{D}_1$, is supported on two examples, $z_1 = (1,0)$ and $z_2 = (\mu,-1)$, where the probability mass of the first example is μ while the probability mass of the second example is $1-\mu$. The second distribution, $\mathcal{D}_2$, is supported entirely on z_2.

Observe that for both distributions, the probability that all examples of the training set will be of the second type is at least 99%. This is trivially true for $\mathcal{D}_2$, whereas for $\mathcal{D}_1$, the probability of this event is

$$(1-\mu)^m \geq e^{-2\mu m} = 0.99.$$

Since we assume that A is a deterministic algorithm, upon receiving a training set of m examples, each of which is $(\mu,-1)$, the algorithm will output some $\hat{w}$. Now, if $\hat{w} < -1/(2\mu)$, we will set the distribution to be $\mathcal{D}_1$. Hence,

$$L_{\mathcal{D}_1}(\hat{w}) \geq \mu(\hat{w})^2 \geq 1/(4\mu).$$

However,

$$\min_w L_{\mathcal{D}_1}(w) \leq L_{\mathcal{D}_1}(0) = (1-\mu).$$

It follows that

$$L_{\mathcal{D}_1}(\hat{w}) - \min_w L_{\mathcal{D}_1}(w) \geq \frac{1}{4\mu} - (1-\mu) > \epsilon.$$

Therefore, such algorithm A fails on $\mathcal{D}_1$. On the other hand, if $\hat{w} \geq -1/(2\mu)$ then we'll set the distribution to be $\mathcal{D}_2$. Then we have that $L_{\mathcal{D}_2}(\hat{w}) \geq 1/4$ while $\min_w L_{\mathcal{D}_2}(w) = 0$, so A fails on $\mathcal{D}_2$. In summary, we have shown that for every A there exists a distribution on which A fails, which implies that the problem is not PAC learnable.

[1] Namely, given S the output of A is determined. This requirement is for the sake of simplicity. A slightly more involved argument will show that nondeterministic algorithms will also fail to learn the problem.

A possible solution to this problem is to add another constraint on the hypothesis class. In addition to the convexity requirement, we require that $\mathcal{H}$ will be *bounded*; namely, we assume that for some predefined scalar B, every hypothesis $\mathbf{w} \in \mathcal{H}$ satisfies $\|\mathbf{w}\| \leq B$.

Boundedness and convexity alone are still not sufficient for ensuring that the problem is learnable, as the following example demonstrates.

Example 12.9. As in Example 12.8, consider a regression problem with the squared loss. However, this time let $\mathcal{H} = \{w : |w| \leq 1\} \subset \mathbb{R}$ be a bounded hypothesis class. It is easy to verify that $\mathcal{H}$ is convex. The argument will be the same as in Example 12.8, except that now the two distributions, $\mathcal{D}_1, \mathcal{D}_2$ will be supported on $z_1 = (1/\mu, 0)$ and $z_2 = (1, -1)$. If the algorithm A returns $\hat{w} < -1/2$ upon receiving m examples of the second type, then we will set the distribution to be $\mathcal{D}_1$ and have that

$$L_{\mathcal{D}_1}(\hat{w}) - \min_w L_{\mathcal{D}_1}(w) \geq \mu(\hat{w}/\mu)^2 - L_{\mathcal{D}_1}(0) \geq 1/(4\mu) - (1-\mu) > \epsilon.$$

Similarly, if $\hat{w} \geq -1/2$ we will set the distribution to be $\mathcal{D}_2$ and have that

$$L_{\mathcal{D}_2}(\hat{w}) - \min_w L_{\mathcal{D}_2}(w) \geq (-1/2+1)^2 - 0 > \epsilon.$$

This example shows that we need additional assumptions on the learning problem, and this time the solution is in Lipschitzness or smoothness of the loss function. This motivates a definition of two families of learning problems, convex-Lipschitz-bounded and convex-smooth-bounded, which are defined later.

12.2.2 Convex-Lipschitz/Smooth-Bounded Learning Problems

Definition 12.12 (Convex-Lipschitz-Bounded Learning Problem). A learning problem, $(\mathcal{H}, Z, \ell)$, is called Convex-Lipschitz-Bounded, with parameters ρ, B if the following holds:

- The hypothesis class $\mathcal{H}$ is a convex set and for all $\mathbf{w} \in \mathcal{H}$ we have $\|\mathbf{w}\| \leq B$.
- For all $z \in Z$, the loss function, $\ell(\cdot, z)$, is a convex and ρ-Lipschitz function.

Example 12.10. Let $\mathcal{X} = \{\mathbf{x} \in \mathbb{R}^d : \|\mathbf{x}\| \leq \rho\}$ and $\mathcal{Y} = \mathbb{R}$. Let $\mathcal{H} = \{\mathbf{w} \in \mathbb{R}^d : \|\mathbf{w}\| \leq B\}$ and let the loss function be $\ell(\mathbf{w}, (\mathbf{x}, y)) = |\langle \mathbf{w}, \mathbf{x} \rangle - y|$. This corresponds to a regression problem with the absolute-value loss, where we assume that the instances are in a ball of radius ρ and we restrict the hypotheses to be homogenous linear functions defined by a vector $\mathbf{w}$ whose norm is bounded by B. Then, the resulting problem is Convex-Lipschitz-Bounded with parameters ρ, B.

Definition 12.13 (Convex-Smooth-Bounded Learning Problem). A learning problem, $(\mathcal{H}, Z, \ell)$, is called Convex-Smooth-Bounded, with parameters β, B if the following holds:

- The hypothesis class $\mathcal{H}$ is a convex set and for all $\mathbf{w} \in \mathcal{H}$ we have $\|\mathbf{w}\| \leq B$.
- For all $z \in Z$, the loss function, $\ell(\cdot, z)$, is a convex, nonnegative, and β-smooth function.

Note that we also required that the loss function is nonnegative. This is needed to ensure that the loss function is self-bounded, as described in the previous section.

Example 12.11. Let $\mathcal{X} = \{\mathbf{x} \in \mathbb{R}^d : \|\mathbf{x}\| \leq \beta/2\}$ and $\mathcal{Y} = \mathbb{R}$. Let $\mathcal{H} = \{\mathbf{w} \in \mathbb{R}^d : \|\mathbf{w}\| \leq B\}$ and let the loss function be $\ell(\mathbf{w}, (\mathbf{x}, y)) = (\langle \mathbf{w}, \mathbf{x} \rangle - y)^2$. This corresponds to a regression problem with the squared loss, where we assume that the instances are in a ball of radius $\beta/2$ and we restrict the hypotheses to be homogenous linear functions defined by a vector $\mathbf{w}$ whose norm is bounded by B. Then, the resulting problem is Convex-Smooth-Bounded with parameters β, B.

We claim that these two families of learning problems are learnable. That is, the properties of convexity, boundedness, and Lipschitzness or smoothness of the loss function are sufficient for learnability. We will prove this claim in the next chapters by introducing algorithms that learn these problems successfully.

12.3 SURROGATE LOSS FUNCTIONS

As mentioned, and as we will see in the next chapters, convex problems can be learned efficiently. However, in many cases, the natural loss function is not convex and, in particular, implementing the ERM rule is hard.

As an example, consider the problem of learning the hypothesis class of halfspaces with respect to the 0−1 loss. That is,

$$\ell^{0-1}(\mathbf{w}, (\mathbf{x}, y)) = \mathbb{1}_{[y \neq \text{sign}(\langle \mathbf{w}, \mathbf{x} \rangle)]} = \mathbb{1}_{[y\langle \mathbf{w}, \mathbf{x} \rangle \leq 0]}.$$

This loss function is not convex with respect to $\mathbf{w}$ and indeed, when trying to minimize the empirical risk with respect to this loss function we might encounter local minima (see Exercise 12.1). Furthermore, as discussed in Chapter 8, solving the ERM problem with respect to the 0−1 loss in the unrealizable case is known to be NP-hard.

To circumvent the hardness result, one popular approach is to upper bound the nonconvex loss function by a convex surrogate loss function. As its name indicates, the requirements from a convex surrogate loss are as follows:

1. It should be convex.
2. It should upper bound the original loss.

For example, in the context of learning halfspaces, we can define the so-called hinge loss as a convex surrogate for the 0−1 loss, as follows:

$$\ell^{\text{hinge}}(\mathbf{w}, (\mathbf{x}, y)) \stackrel{\text{def}}{=} \max\{0, 1 - y\langle \mathbf{w}, \mathbf{x} \rangle\}.$$

Clearly, for all $\mathbf{w}$ and all $(\mathbf{x}, y)$, $\ell^{0-1}(\mathbf{w}, (\mathbf{x}, y)) \leq \ell^{\text{hinge}}(\mathbf{w}, (\mathbf{x}, y))$. In addition, the convexity of the hinge loss follows directly from Claim 12.5. Hence, the hinge loss satisfies the requirements of a convex surrogate loss function for the zero-one loss. An illustration of the functions ℓ^{0-1} and ℓ^{hinge} is given in the following.

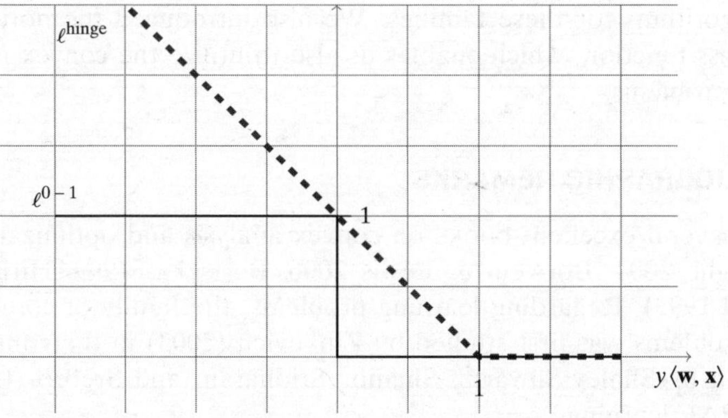

Once we have defined the surrogate convex loss, we can learn the problem with respect to it. The generalization requirement from a hinge loss learner will have the form

$$L_{\mathcal{D}}^{\text{hinge}}(A(S)) \le \min_{\mathbf{w}\in\mathcal{H}} L_{\mathcal{D}}^{\text{hinge}}(\mathbf{w}) + \epsilon,$$

where $L_{\mathcal{D}}^{\text{hinge}}(\mathbf{w}) = \mathbb{E}_{(\mathbf{x},y)\sim\mathcal{D}}[\ell^{\text{hinge}}(\mathbf{w},(\mathbf{x},y))]$. Using the surrogate property, we can lower bound the left-hand side by $L_{\mathcal{D}}^{0-1}(A(S))$, which yields

$$L_{\mathcal{D}}^{0-1}(A(S)) \le \min_{\mathbf{w}\in\mathcal{H}} L_{\mathcal{D}}^{\text{hinge}}(\mathbf{w}) + \epsilon.$$

We can further rewrite the upper bound as follows:

$$L_{\mathcal{D}}^{0-1}(A(S)) \le \min_{\mathbf{w}\in\mathcal{H}} L_{\mathcal{D}}^{0-1}(\mathbf{w}) + \left(\min_{\mathbf{w}\in\mathcal{H}} L_{\mathcal{D}}^{\text{hinge}}(\mathbf{w}) - \min_{\mathbf{w}\in\mathcal{H}} L_{\mathcal{D}}^{0-1}(\mathbf{w})\right) + \epsilon.$$

That is, the 0–1 error of the learned predictor is upper bounded by three terms:

- *Approximation error*: This is the term $\min_{\mathbf{w}\in\mathcal{H}} L_{\mathcal{D}}^{0-1}(\mathbf{w})$, which measures how well the hypothesis class performs on the distribution. We already elaborated on this error term in Chapter 5.
- *Estimation error*: This is the error that results from the fact that we only receive a training set and do not observe the distribution $\mathcal{D}$. We already elaborated on this error term in Chapter 5.
- *Optimization error*: This is the term $\left(\min_{\mathbf{w}\in\mathcal{H}} L_{\mathcal{D}}^{\text{hinge}}(\mathbf{w}) - \min_{\mathbf{w}\in\mathcal{H}} L_{\mathcal{D}}^{0-1}(\mathbf{w})\right)$ that measures the difference between the approximation error with respect to the surrogate loss and the approximation error with respect to the original loss. The optimization error is a result of our inability to minimize the training loss with respect to the original loss. The size of this error depends on the specific distribution of the data and on the specific surrogate loss we are using.

12.4 SUMMARY

We introduced two families of learning problems: convex-Lipschitz-bounded and convex-smooth-bounded. In the next two chapters we will describe two generic learning algorithms for these families. We also introduced the notion of convex surrogate loss function, which enables us also to utilize the convex machinery for nonconvex problems.

12.5 BIBLIOGRAPHIC REMARKS

There are several excellent books on convex analysis and optimization (Boyd & Vandenberghe 2004, Borwein & Lewis 2006, Bertsekas 1999, Hiriart-Urruty & Lemaréchal 1993). Regarding learning problems, the family of convex-Lipschitz-bounded problems was first studied by Zinkevich (2003) in the context of online learning and by Shalev-Shwartz, Shamir, Sridharan, and Srebro ((2009)) in the context of PAC learning.

12.6 EXERCISES

12.1 Construct an example showing that the 0–1 loss function may suffer from local minima; namely, construct a training sample $S \in (X \times \{\pm 1\})^m$ (say, for $X = \mathbb{R}^2$), for which there exist a vector $\mathbf{w}$ and some $\epsilon > 0$ such that
   1. For any $\mathbf{w}'$ such that $\|w - w'\| \leq \epsilon$ we have $L_S(\mathbf{w}) \leq L_S(\mathbf{w}')$ (where the loss here is the 0–1 loss). This means that $\mathbf{w}$ is a local minimum of L_S.
   2. There exists some $\mathbf{w}^*$ such that $L_S(\mathbf{w}^*) < L_S(\mathbf{w})$. This means that $\mathbf{w}$ is not a global minimum of L_S.

12.2 Consider the learning problem of logistic regression: Let $\mathcal{H} = \mathcal{X} = \{\mathbf{x} \in \mathbb{R}^d : \|\mathbf{x}\| \leq B\}$, for some scalar $B > 0$, let $\mathcal{Y} = \{\pm 1\}$, and let the loss function ℓ be defined as $\ell(\mathbf{w}, (\mathbf{x}, y)) = \log(1 + \exp(-y\langle \mathbf{w}, \mathbf{x}\rangle))$. Show that the resulting learning problem is both convex-Lipschitz-bounded and convex-smooth-bounded. Specify the parameters of Lipschitzness and smoothness.

12.3 Consider the problem of learning halfspaces with the hinge loss. We limit our domain to the Euclidean ball with radius R. That is, $\mathcal{X} = \{\mathbf{x} : \|\mathbf{x}\|_2 \leq R\}$. The label set is $\mathcal{Y} = \{\pm 1\}$ and the loss function ℓ is defined by $\ell(\mathbf{w}, (\mathbf{x}, y)) = \max\{0, 1 - y\langle \mathbf{w}, \mathbf{x}\rangle\}$. We already know that the loss function is convex. Show that it is R-Lipschitz.

12.4 **(*) Convex-Lipschitz-Boundedness Is Not Sufficient for Computational Efficiency:** In the next chapter we show that from the statistical perspective, all convex-Lipschitz-bounded problems are learnable (in the agnostic PAC model). However, our main motivation to learn such problems resulted from the computational perspective – convex optimization is often efficiently solvable. Yet the goal of this exercise is to show that convexity alone is not sufficient for efficiency. We show that even for the case $d = 1$, there is a convex-Lipschitz-bounded problem which cannot be learned by any computable learner.

   Let the hypothesis class be $\mathcal{H} = [0, 1]$ and let the example domain, Z, be the set of all Turing machines. Define the loss function as follows. For every Turing machine $T \in Z$, let $\ell(0, T) = 1$ if T halts on the input 0 and $\ell(0, T) = 0$ if T doesn't halt on the input 0. Similarly, let $\ell(1, T) = 0$ if T halts on the input 0 and $\ell(1, T) = 1$ if T doesn't halt on the input 0. Finally, for $h \in (0, 1)$, let $\ell(h, T) = h\ell(0, T) + (1 - h)\ell(1, T)$.
   1. Show that the resulting learning problem is convex-Lipschitz-bounded.
   2. Show that no computable algorithm can learn the problem.

13

Regularization and Stability

In the previous chapter we introduced the families of convex-Lipschitz-bounded and convex-smooth-bounded learning problems. In this section we show that all learning problems in these two families are learnable. For some learning problems of this type it is possible to show that uniform convergence holds; hence they are learnable using the ERM rule. However, this is not true for all learning problems of this type. Yet, we will introduce another learning rule and will show that it learns all convex-Lipschitz-bounded and convex-smooth-bounded learning problems.

The new learning paradigm we introduce in this chapter is called *Regularized Loss Minimization*, or RLM for short. In RLM we minimize the sum of the empirical risk and a regularization function. Intuitively, the regularization function measures the complexity of hypotheses. Indeed, one interpretation of the regularization function is the structural risk minimization paradigm we discussed in Chapter 7. Another view of regularization is as a *stabilizer* of the learning algorithm. An algorithm is considered stable if a slight change of its input does not change its output much. We will formally define the notion of stability (what we mean by "slight change of input" and by "does not change much the output") and prove its close relation to learnability. Finally, we will show that using the squared ℓ_2 norm as a regularization function stabilizes all convex-Lipschitz or convex-smooth learning problems. Hence, RLM can be used as a general learning rule for these families of learning problems.

13.1 REGULARIZED LOSS MINIMIZATION

Regularized Loss Minimization (RLM) is a learning rule in which we jointly minimize the empirical risk and a regularization function. Formally, a regularization function is a mapping $R : \mathbb{R}^d \to \mathbb{R}$, and the regularized loss minimization rule outputs a hypothesis in

$$\underset{\mathbf{w}}{\operatorname{argmin}} \left(L_S(\mathbf{w}) + R(\mathbf{w}) \right). \tag{13.1}$$

Regularized loss minimization shares similarities with minimum description length algorithms and structural risk minimization (see Chapter 7). Intuitively, the "complexity" of hypotheses is measured by the value of the regularization function, and the algorithm balances between low empirical risk and "simpler," or "less complex," hypotheses.

There are many possible regularization functions one can use, reflecting some prior belief about the problem (similarly to the description language in Minimum Description Length). Throughout this section we will focus on one of the most simple regularization functions: $R(\mathbf{w}) = \lambda\|\mathbf{w}\|^2$, where $\lambda > 0$ is a scalar and the norm is the ℓ_2 norm, $\|\mathbf{w}\| = \sqrt{\sum_{i=1}^{d} w_i^2}$. This yields the learning rule:

$$A(S) = \underset{\mathbf{w}}{\operatorname{argmin}} \left(L_S(\mathbf{w}) + \lambda\|\mathbf{w}\|^2 \right). \tag{13.2}$$

This type of regularization function is often called Tikhonov regularization.

As mentioned before, one interpretation of Equation (13.2) is using structural risk minimization, where the norm of $\mathbf{w}$ is a measure of its "complexity." Recall that in the previous chapter we introduced the notion of bounded hypothesis classes. Therefore, we can define a sequence of hypothesis classes, $\mathcal{H}_1 \subset \mathcal{H}_2 \subset \mathcal{H}_3 \ldots$, where $\mathcal{H}_i = \{\mathbf{w} : \|\mathbf{w}\|_2 \le i\}$. If the sample complexity of each $\mathcal{H}_i$ depends on i then the RLM rule is similar to the SRM rule for this sequence of nested classes.

A different interpretation of regularization is as a stabilizer. In the next section we define the notion of stability and prove that stable learning rules do not overfit. But first, let us demonstrate the RLM rule for linear regression with the squared loss.

13.1.1 Ridge Regression

Applying the RLM rule with Tikhonov regularization to linear regression with the squared loss, we obtain the following learning rule:

$$\underset{\mathbf{w}\in\mathbb{R}^d}{\operatorname{argmin}} \left(\lambda\|\mathbf{w}\|_2^2 + \frac{1}{m}\sum_{i=1}^{m} \frac{1}{2}(\langle \mathbf{w}, \mathbf{x}_i\rangle - y_i)^2 \right). \tag{13.3}$$

Performing linear regression using Equation (13.3) is called *ridge regression*.

To solve Equation (13.3) we compare the gradient of the objective to zero and obtain the set of linear equations

$$(2\lambda m I + A)\mathbf{w} = \mathbf{b},$$

where I is the identity matrix and $A, \mathbf{b}$ are as defined in Equation (9.6), namely,

$$A = \left(\sum_{i=1}^{m} \mathbf{x}_i \mathbf{x}_i^\top \right) \quad \text{and} \quad \mathbf{b} = \sum_{i=1}^{m} y_i \mathbf{x}_i\,. \tag{13.4}$$

Since A is a positive semidefinite matrix, the matrix $2\lambda m I + A$ has all its eigenvalues bounded below by $2\lambda m$. Hence, this matrix is invertible and the solution to ridge regression becomes

$$\mathbf{w} = (2\lambda m I + A)^{-1}\mathbf{b}. \tag{13.5}$$

In the next section we formally show how regularization stabilizes the algorithm and prevents overfitting. In particular, the analysis presented in the next sections (particularly, Corollary 13.11) will yield:

Theorem 13.1. *Let $\mathcal{D}$ be a distribution over $\mathcal{X} \times [-1,1]$, where $\mathcal{X} = \{\mathbf{x} \in \mathbb{R}^d : \|\mathbf{x}\| \le 1\}$. Let $\mathcal{H} = \{\mathbf{w} \in \mathbb{R}^d : \|\mathbf{w}\| \le B\}$. For any $\epsilon \in (0,1)$, let $m \ge 150\, B^2/\epsilon^2$. Then, applying the ridge regression algorithm with parameter $\lambda = \epsilon/(3B^2)$ satisfies*

$$\mathop{\mathbb{E}}_{S\sim\mathcal{D}^m}[L_{\mathcal{D}}(A(S))] \le \min_{\mathbf{w}\in\mathcal{H}} L_{\mathcal{D}}(\mathbf{w}) + \epsilon.$$

Remark 13.1. The preceding theorem tells us how many examples are needed to guarantee that the *expected value* of the risk of the learned predictor will be bounded by the approximation error of the class plus ϵ. In the usual definition of agnostic PAC learning we require that the risk of the learned predictor will be bounded with probability of at least $1-\delta$. In Exercise 13.1 we show how an algorithm with a bounded expected risk can be used to construct an agnostic PAC learner.

13.2 STABLE RULES DO NOT OVERFIT

Intuitively, a learning algorithm is stable if a small change of the input to the algorithm does not change the output of the algorithm much. Of course, there are many ways to define what we mean by "a small change of the input" and what we mean by "does not change the output much". In this section we define a specific notion of stability and prove that under this definition, stable rules do not overfit.

Let A be a learning algorithm, let $S = (z_1,\ldots,z_m)$ be a training set of m examples, and let $A(S)$ denote the output of A. The algorithm A suffers from overfitting if the difference between the true risk of its output, $L_{\mathcal{D}}(A(S))$, and the empirical risk of its output, $L_S(A(S))$, is large. As mentioned in Remark 13.1, throughout this chapter we focus on the expectation (with respect to the choice of S) of this quantity, namely, $\mathbb{E}_S[L_{\mathcal{D}}(A(S)) - L_S(A(S))]$.

We next define the notion of stability. Given the training set S and an additional example z', let $S^{(i)}$ be the training set obtained by replacing the i'th example of S with z'; namely, $S^{(i)} = (z_1,\ldots,z_{i-1}, z', z_{i+1},\ldots,z_m)$. In our definition of stability, "a small change of the input" means that we feed A with $S^{(i)}$ instead of with S. That is, we only replace one training example. We measure the effect of this small change of the input on the output of A, by comparing the loss of the hypothesis $A(S)$ on z_i to the loss of the hypothesis $A(S^{(i)})$ on z_i. Intuitively, a good learning algorithm will have $\ell(A(S^{(i)}), z_i) - \ell(A(S), z_i) \ge 0$, since in the first term the learning algorithm does not observe the example z_i while in the second term z_i is indeed observed. If the preceding difference is very large we suspect that the learning algorithm might overfit. This is because the learning algorithm drastically changes its prediction on z_i if it observes it in the training set. This is formalized in the following theorem.

Theorem 13.2. *Let $\mathcal{D}$ be a distribution. Let $S = (z_1,\ldots,z_m)$ be an i.i.d. sequence of examples and let z' be another i.i.d. example. Let $U(m)$ be the uniform distribution over $[m]$. Then, for any learning algorithm,*

$$\mathop{\mathbb{E}}_{S\sim\mathcal{D}^m}[L_{\mathcal{D}}(A(S)) - L_S(A(S))] = \mathop{\mathbb{E}}_{(S,z')\sim\mathcal{D}^{m+1}, i\sim U(m)}[\ell(A(S^{(i)}, z_i)) - \ell(A(S), z_i)]. \quad (13.6)$$

Proof. Since S and z' are both drawn i.i.d. from $\mathcal{D}$, we have that for every i,

$$\mathop{\mathbb{E}}_S[L_{\mathcal{D}}(A(S))] = \mathop{\mathbb{E}}_{S,z'}[\ell(A(S), z')] = \mathop{\mathbb{E}}_{S,z'}[\ell(A(S^{(i)}), z_i)].$$

On the other hand, we can write

$$\mathbb{E}_S[L_S(A(S))] = \mathbb{E}_{S,i}[\ell(A(S), z_i)].$$

Combining the two equations we conclude our proof. □

When the right-hand side of Equation (13.6) is small, we say that A is a *stable* algorithm – changing a single example in the training set does not lead to a significant change. Formally,

Definition 13.3 (On-Average-Replace-One-Stable). Let $\epsilon : \mathbb{N} \to \mathbb{R}$ be a monotonically decreasing function. We say that a learning algorithm A is on-average-replace-one-stable with rate $\epsilon(m)$ if for every distribution $\mathcal{D}$

$$\mathop{\mathbb{E}}_{(S,z')\sim\mathcal{D}^{m+1}, i\sim U(m)}[\ell(A(S^{(i)}, z_i)) - \ell(A(S), z_i)] \leq \epsilon(m).$$

Theorem 13.2 tells us that a learning algorithm does not overfit if and only if it is on-average-replace-one-stable. Of course, a learning algorithm that does not overfit is not necessarily a good learning algorithm – take, for example, an algorithm A that always outputs the same hypothesis. A useful algorithm should find a hypothesis that on one hand fits the training set (i.e., has a low empirical risk) and on the other hand does not overfit. Or, in light of Theorem 13.2, the algorithm should both fit the training set and at the same time be stable. As we shall see, the parameter λ of the RLM rule balances between fitting the training set and being stable.

13.3 TIKHONOV REGULARIZATION AS A STABILIZER

In the previous section we saw that stable rules do not overfit. In this section we show that applying the RLM rule with Tikhonov regularization, $\lambda\|\mathbf{w}\|^2$, leads to a stable algorithm. We will assume that the loss function is convex and that it is either Lipschitz or smooth.

The main property of the Tikhonov regularization that we rely on is that it makes the objective of RLM *strongly convex*, as defined in the following.

Definition 13.4 (Strongly Convex Functions). A function f is λ-strongly convex if for all $\mathbf{w}$, $\mathbf{u}$, and $\alpha \in (0, 1)$ we have

$$f(\alpha\mathbf{w} + (1-\alpha)\mathbf{u}) \leq \alpha f(\mathbf{w}) + (1-\alpha)f(\mathbf{u}) - \frac{\lambda}{2}\alpha(1-\alpha)\|\mathbf{w}-\mathbf{u}\|^2.$$

Clearly, every convex function is 0-strongly convex. An illustration of strong convexity is given in the following figure.

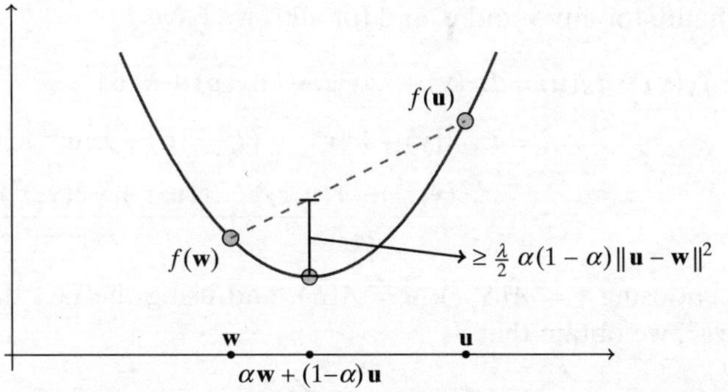

The following lemma implies that the objective of RLM is (2λ)-strongly convex. In addition, it underscores an important property of strong convexity.

Lemma 13.5.

1. *The function $f(\mathbf{w}) = \lambda\|\mathbf{w}\|^2$ is 2λ-strongly convex.*
2. *If f is λ-strongly convex and g is convex, then $f+g$ is λ-strongly convex.*
3. *If f is λ-strongly convex and $\mathbf{u}$ is a minimizer of f, then, for any $\mathbf{w}$,*

$$f(\mathbf{w}) - f(\mathbf{u}) \ge \frac{\lambda}{2}\|\mathbf{w}-\mathbf{u}\|^2.$$

Proof. The first two points follow directly from the definition. To prove the last point, we divide the definition of strong convexity by α and rearrange terms to get that

$$\frac{f(\mathbf{u}+\alpha(\mathbf{w}-\mathbf{u})) - f(\mathbf{u})}{\alpha} \le f(\mathbf{w}) - f(\mathbf{u}) - \frac{\lambda}{2}(1-\alpha)\|\mathbf{w}-\mathbf{u}\|^2.$$

Taking the limit $\alpha \to 0$ we obtain that the right-hand side converges to $f(\mathbf{w}) - f(\mathbf{u}) - \frac{\lambda}{2}\|\mathbf{w}-\mathbf{u}\|^2$. On the other hand, the left-hand side becomes the derivative of the function $g(\alpha) = f(\mathbf{u}+\alpha(\mathbf{w}-\mathbf{u}))$ at $\alpha = 0$. Since $\mathbf{u}$ is a minimizer of f, it follows that $\alpha = 0$ is a minimizer of g, and therefore the left-hand side of the preceding goes to zero in the limit $\alpha \to 0$, which concludes our proof. □

We now turn to prove that RLM is stable. Let $S = (z_1, \ldots, z_m)$ be a training set, let z' be an additional example, and let $S^{(i)} = (z_1, \ldots, z_{i-1}, z', z_{i+1}, \ldots, z_m)$. Let A be the RLM rule, namely,

$$A(S) = \underset{\mathbf{w}}{\operatorname{argmin}} \left(L_S(\mathbf{w}) + \lambda\|\mathbf{w}\|^2 \right).$$

Denote $f_S(\mathbf{w}) = L_S(\mathbf{w}) + \lambda\|\mathbf{w}\|^2$, and on the basis of Lemma 13.5 we know that f_S is (2λ)-strongly convex. Relying on part 3 of the lemma, it follows that for any $\mathbf{v}$,

$$f_S(\mathbf{v}) - f_S(A(S)) \ge \lambda\|\mathbf{v} - A(S)\|^2. \tag{13.7}$$

On the other hand, for any $\mathbf{v}$ and $\mathbf{u}$, and for all i, we have

$$\begin{aligned} f_S(\mathbf{v}) - f_S(\mathbf{u}) &= L_S(\mathbf{v}) + \lambda\|\mathbf{v}\|^2 - (L_S(\mathbf{u}) + \lambda\|\mathbf{u}\|^2) \\ &= L_{S^{(i)}}(\mathbf{v}) + \lambda\|\mathbf{v}\|^2 - (L_{S^{(i)}}(\mathbf{u}) + \lambda\|\mathbf{u}\|^2) \\ &\quad + \frac{\ell(\mathbf{v}, z_i) - \ell(\mathbf{u}, z_i)}{m} + \frac{\ell(\mathbf{u}, z') - \ell(\mathbf{v}, z')}{m}. \end{aligned} \tag{13.8}$$

In particular, choosing $\mathbf{v} = A(S^{(i)})$, $\mathbf{u} = A(S)$, and using the fact that $\mathbf{v}$ minimizes $L_{S^{(i)}}(\mathbf{w}) + \lambda\|\mathbf{w}\|^2$, we obtain that

$$f_S(A(S^{(i)})) - f_S(A(S)) \le \frac{\ell(A(S^{(i)}), z_i) - \ell(A(S), z_i)}{m} + \frac{\ell(A(S), z') - \ell(A(S^{(i)}), z')}{m}. \tag{13.9}$$

Combining this with Equation (13.7) we obtain that

$$\lambda\|A(S^{(i)}) - A(S)\|^2 \le \frac{\ell(A(S^{(i)}), z_i) - \ell(A(S), z_i)}{m} + \frac{\ell(A(S), z') - \ell(A(S^{(i)}), z')}{m}. \tag{13.10}$$

The two subsections that follow continue the stability analysis for either Lipschitz or smooth loss functions. For both families of loss functions we show that RLM is stable and therefore it does not overfit.

13.3.1 Lipschitz Loss

If the loss function, $\ell(\cdot, z_i)$, is ρ-Lipschitz, then by the definition of Lipschitzness,

$$\ell(A(S^{(i)}), z_i) - \ell(A(S), z_i) \le \rho\,\|A(S^{(i)}) - A(S)\|. \tag{13.11}$$

Similarly,

$$\ell(A(S), z') - \ell(A(S^{(i)}), z') \le \rho\,\|A(S^{(i)}) - A(S)\|.$$

Plugging these inequalities into Equation (13.10) we obtain

$$\lambda\|A(S^{(i)}) - A(S)\|^2 \le \frac{2\,\rho\,\|A(S^{(i)}) - A(S)\|}{m},$$

which yields

$$\|A(S^{(i)}) - A(S)\| \le \frac{2\,\rho}{\lambda\, m}.$$

Plugging the preceding back into Equation (13.11) we conclude that

$$\ell(A(S^{(i)}), z_i) - \ell(A(S), z_i) \le \frac{2\,\rho^2}{\lambda\, m}.$$

Since this holds for any S, z', i we immediately obtain:

Corollary 13.6. *Assume that the loss function is convex and ρ-Lipschitz. Then, the RLM rule with the regularizer $\lambda\|\mathbf{w}\|^2$ is on-average-replace-one-stable with rate $\frac{2\rho^2}{\lambda m}$.*

It follows (using Theorem 13.2) that

$$\mathop{\mathbb{E}}_{S\sim\mathcal{D}^m}[L_{\mathcal{D}}(A(S)) - L_S(A(S))] \le \frac{2\rho^2}{\lambda m}.$$

13.3.2 Smooth and Nonnegative Loss

If the loss is β-smooth and nonnegative then it is also self-bounded (see Section 12.1):

$$\|\nabla f(\mathbf{w})\|^2 \le 2\beta f(\mathbf{w}). \tag{13.12}$$

We further assume that $\lambda \ge \frac{2\beta}{m}$, or, in other words, that $\beta \le \lambda m/2$. By the smoothness assumption we have that

$$\ell(A(S^{(i)}), z_i) - \ell(A(S), z_i) \le \langle \nabla \ell(A(S), z_i), A(S^{(i)}) - A(S)\rangle + \frac{\beta}{2}\|A(S^{(i)}) - A(S)\|^2. \tag{13.13}$$

Using the Cauchy-Schwartz inequality and Equation (12.6) we further obtain that

$$\begin{aligned}
&\ell(A(S^{(i)}), z_i) - \ell(A(S), z_i) \\
&\quad\le \|\nabla \ell(A(S), z_i)\|\,\|A(S^{(i)}) - A(S)\| + \frac{\beta}{2}\|A(S^{(i)}) - A(S)\|^2 \\
&\quad\le \sqrt{2\beta \ell(A(S), z_i)}\,\|A(S^{(i)}) - A(S)\| + \frac{\beta}{2}\|A(S^{(i)}) - A(S)\|^2. \qquad (13.14)
\end{aligned}$$

By a symmetric argument it holds that

$$\begin{aligned}
&\ell(A(S), z') - \ell(A(S^{(i)}), z') \\
&\quad\le \sqrt{2\beta \ell(A(S^{(i)}), z')}\,\|A(S^{(i)}) - A(S)\| + \frac{\beta}{2}\|A(S^{(i)}) - A(S)\|^2.
\end{aligned}$$

Plugging these inequalities into Equation (13.10) and rearranging terms we obtain that

$$\|A(S^{(i)}) - A(S)\| \le \frac{\sqrt{2\beta}}{(\lambda m - \beta)}\left(\sqrt{\ell(A(S), z_i)} + \sqrt{\ell(A(S^{(i)}), z')}\right).$$

Combining the preceding with the assumption $\beta \le \lambda m/2$ yields

$$\|A(S^{(i)}) - A(S)\| \le \frac{\sqrt{8\beta}}{\lambda m}\left(\sqrt{\ell(A(S), z_i)} + \sqrt{\ell(A(S^{(i)}), z')}\right).$$

Combining the preceding with Equation (13.14) and again using the assumption $\beta \le \lambda m/2$ yield

$$\begin{aligned}
&\ell(A(S^{(i)}), z_i) - \ell(A(S), z_i) \\
&\quad \le \sqrt{2\beta \ell(A(S), z_i)}\, \|A(S^{(i)}) - A(S)\| + \frac{\beta}{2}\|A(S^{(i)}) - A(S)\|^2 \\
&\quad \le \left(\frac{4\beta}{\lambda m} + \frac{8\beta^2}{(\lambda m)^2}\right)\left(\sqrt{\ell(A(S), z_i)} + \sqrt{\ell(A(S^{(i)}), z')}\right)^2 \\
&\quad \le \frac{8\beta}{\lambda m}\left(\sqrt{\ell(A(S), z_i)} + \sqrt{\ell(A(S^{(i)}), z')}\right)^2 \\
&\quad \le \frac{24\beta}{\lambda m}\left(\ell(A(S), z_i) + \ell(A(S^{(i)}), z')\right),
\end{aligned}$$

where in the last step we used the inequality $(a+b)^2 \le 3(a^2+b^2)$. Taking expectation with respect to S, z', i and noting that $\mathbb{E}[\ell(A(S), z_i)] = \mathbb{E}[\ell(A(S^{(i)}),\ z')] = \mathbb{E}[L_S(A(S))]$, we conclude that:

Corollary 13.7. *Assume that the loss function is β-smooth and nonnegative. Then, the RLM rule with the regularizer $\lambda\|\mathbf{w}\|^2$, where $\lambda \ge \frac{2\beta}{m}$, satisfies*

$$\mathbb{E}\left[\ell(A(S^{(i)}), z_i) - \ell(A(S), z_i)\right] \le \frac{48\beta}{\lambda m}\mathbb{E}[L_S(A(S))].$$

Note that if for all z we have $\ell(\mathbf{0},\ z) \le C$, for some scalar $C > 0$, then for every S,

$$L_S(A(S)) \le L_S(A(S)) + \lambda\|A(S)\|^2 \le L_S(\mathbf{0}) + \lambda\|\mathbf{0}\|^2 = L_S(\mathbf{0}) \le C.$$

Hence, Corollary 13.7 also implies that

$$\mathbb{E}\left[\ell(A(S^{(i)}), z_i) - \ell(A(S), z_i)\right] \le \frac{48\,\beta\, C}{\lambda m}.$$

13.4 CONTROLLING THE FITTING-STABILITY TRADE-OFF

We can rewrite the expected risk of a learning algorithm as

$$\mathbb{E}_S[L_{\mathcal{D}}(A(S))] = \mathbb{E}_S[L_S(A(S))] + \mathbb{E}_S[L_{\mathcal{D}}(A(S)) - L_S(A(S))]. \tag{13.15}$$

The first term reflects how well $A(S)$ fits the training set while the second term reflects the difference between the true and empirical risks of $A(S)$. As we have shown in Theorem 13.2, the second term is equivalent to the stability of A. Since our goal is to minimize the risk of the algorithm, we need that the sum of both terms will be small.

In the previous section we have bounded the stability term. We have shown that the stability term decreases as the regularization parameter, λ, increases. On the other hand, the empirical risk increases with λ. We therefore face a tradeoff between fitting and overfitting. This tradeoff is quite similar to the bias-complexity tradeoff we discussed previously in the book.

We now derive bounds on the empirical risk term for the RLM rule. Recall that the RLM rule is defined as $A(S) = \text{argmin}_{\mathbf{w}} \left(L_S(\mathbf{w}) + \lambda\|\mathbf{w}\|^2\right)$. Fix some arbitrary vector $\mathbf{w}^*$. We have

$$L_S(A(S)) \le L_S(A(S)) + \lambda\|A(S)\|^2 \le L_S(\mathbf{w}^*) + \lambda\|\mathbf{w}^*\|^2.$$

Taking expectation of both sides with respect to S and noting that $\mathbb{E}_S[L_S(\mathbf{w}^*)] = L_{\mathcal{D}}(\mathbf{w}^*)$, we obtain that

$$\mathop{\mathbb{E}}_S[L_S(A(S))] \le L_{\mathcal{D}}(\mathbf{w}^*) + \lambda\|\mathbf{w}^*\|^2. \tag{13.16}$$

Plugging this into Equation (13.15) we obtain

$$\mathop{\mathbb{E}}_S[L_{\mathcal{D}}(A(S))] \le L_{\mathcal{D}}(\mathbf{w}^*) + \lambda\|\mathbf{w}^*\|^2 + \mathop{\mathbb{E}}_S[L_{\mathcal{D}}(A(S)) - L_S(A(S))].$$

Combining the preceding with Corollary 13.6 we conclude:

Corollary 13.8. *Assume that the loss function is convex and ρ-Lipschitz. Then, the RLM rule with the regularization function $\lambda\|\mathbf{w}\|^2$ satisfies*

$$\forall \mathbf{w}^*,\ \mathop{\mathbb{E}}_S[L_{\mathcal{D}}(A(S))] \le L_{\mathcal{D}}(\mathbf{w}^*) + \lambda\|\mathbf{w}^*\|^2 + \frac{2\rho^2}{\lambda m}.$$

This bound is often called an *oracle inequality* – if we think of $\mathbf{w}^*$ as a hypothesis with low risk, the bound tells us how many examples are needed so that $A(S)$ will be almost as good as $\mathbf{w}^*$, had we known the norm of $\mathbf{w}^*$. In practice, however, we usually do not know the norm of $\mathbf{w}^*$. We therefore usually tune λ on the basis of a validation set, as described in Chapter 11.

We can also easily derive a PAC-like guarantee[1] from Corollary 13.8 for convex-Lipschitz-bounded learning problems:

Corollary 13.9. *Let $(\mathcal{H}, Z, \ell)$ be a convex-Lipschitz-bounded learning problem with parameters ρ, B. For any training set size m, let $\lambda = \sqrt{\frac{2\rho^2}{B^2 m}}$. Then, the RLM rule with the regularization function $\lambda\|\mathbf{w}\|^2$ satisfies*

$$\mathop{\mathbb{E}}_S[L_{\mathcal{D}}(A(S))] \le \min_{\mathbf{w}\in\mathcal{H}} L_{\mathcal{D}}(\mathbf{w}) + \rho\, B\sqrt{\frac{8}{m}}.$$

In particular, for every $\epsilon > 0$, if $m \ge \frac{8\rho^2 B^2}{\epsilon^2}$ then for every distribution $\mathcal{D}$, $\mathbb{E}_S[L_{\mathcal{D}}(A(S))] \le \min_{\mathbf{w}\in\mathcal{H}} L_{\mathcal{D}}(\mathbf{w}) + \epsilon$.

The preceding corollary holds for Lipschitz loss functions. If instead the loss function is smooth and nonnegative, then we can combine Equation (13.16) with Corollary 13.7 to get:

Corollary 13.10. *Assume that the loss function is convex, β-smooth, and nonnegative. Then, the RLM rule with the regularization function $\lambda\|\mathbf{w}\|^2$, for $\lambda \ge \frac{2\beta}{m}$, satisfies the*

[1] Again, the bound below is on the expected risk, but using Exercise 13.1 it can be used to derive an agnostic PAC learning guarantee.

following for all $\mathbf{w}^*$*:*

$$\mathop{\mathbb{E}}_S[L_{\mathcal{D}}(A(S))] \le \left(1+\frac{48\beta}{\lambda m}\right)\mathop{\mathbb{E}}_S[L_S(A(S))] \le \left(1+\frac{48\beta}{\lambda m}\right)\left(L_{\mathcal{D}}(\mathbf{w}^*)+\lambda\|\mathbf{w}^*\|^2\right).$$

For example, if we choose $\lambda = \frac{48\beta}{m}$ we obtain from the preceding that the expected true risk of $A(S)$ is at most twice the expected empirical risk of $A(S)$. Furthermore, for this value of λ, the expected empirical risk of $A(S)$ is at most $L_{\mathcal{D}}(\mathbf{w}^*) + \frac{48\beta}{m}\|\mathbf{w}^*\|^2$.

We can also derive a learnability guarantee for convex-smooth-bounded learning problems based on Corollary 13.10.

Corollary 13.11. *Let $(\mathcal{H}, Z, \ell)$ be a convex-smooth-bounded learning problem with parameters β, B. Assume in addition that $\ell(\mathbf{0}, z) \le 1$ for all $z \in Z$. For any $\epsilon \in (0,1)$ let $m \ge \frac{150\beta B^2}{\epsilon^2}$ and set $\lambda = \epsilon/(3B^2)$. Then, for every distribution $\mathcal{D}$,*

$$\mathop{\mathbb{E}}_S[L_{\mathcal{D}}(A(S))] \le \min_{\mathbf{w}\in\mathcal{H}} L_{\mathcal{D}}(\mathbf{w}) + \epsilon.$$

13.5 SUMMARY

We introduced stability and showed that if an algorithm is stable then it does not overfit. Furthermore, for convex-Lipschitz-bounded or convex-smooth-bounded problems, the RLM rule with Tikhonov regularization leads to a stable learning algorithm. We discussed how the regularization parameter, λ, controls the tradeoff between fitting and overfitting. Finally, we have shown that all learning problems that are from the families of convex-Lipschitz-bounded and convex-smooth-bounded problems are learnable using the RLM rule. The RLM paradigm is the basis for many popular learning algorithms, including ridge regression (which we discussed in this chapter) and support vector machines (which will be discussed in Chapter 15).

In the next chapter we will present Stochastic Gradient Descent, which gives us a very practical alternative way to learn convex-Lipschitz-bounded and convex-smooth-bounded problems and can also be used for efficiently implementing the RLM rule.

13.6 BIBLIOGRAPHIC REMARKS

Stability is widely used in many mathematical contexts. For example, the necessity of stability for so-called inverse problems to be well posed was first recognized by Hadamard (1902). The idea of regularization and its relation to stability became widely known through the works of Tikhonov (1943) and Phillips (1962). In the context of modern learning theory, the use of stability can be traced back at least to the work of Rogers and Wager (1978), which noted that the sensitivity of a learning algorithm with regard to small changes in the sample controls the variance of the leave-one-out estimate. The authors used this observation to obtain generalization bounds for the k-nearest neighbor algorithm (see Chapter 19). These results were later extended to other "local" learning algorithms (see Devroye, Györfi & Lugosi (1996) and references therein). In addition, practical methods have been developed to introduce stability into learning algorithms, in particular the Bagging technique introduced by (Breiman 1996).

Over the last decade, stability was studied as a generic condition for learnability. See (Kearns & Ron 1999, Bousquet & Elisseeff 2002, Kutin & Niyogi 2002, Rakhlin, Mukherjee & Poggio 2005, Mukherjee, Niyogi, Poggio & Rifkin 2006). Our presentation follows the work of Shalev-Shwartz, Shamir, Srebro, and Sridharan (2010), who showed that stability is sufficient and necessary for learning. They have also shown that all convex-Lipschitz-bounded learning problems are learnable using RLM, even though for some convex-Lipschitz-bounded learning problems uniform convergence does not hold in a strong sense.

13.7 EXERCISES

13.1 **From Bounded Expected Risk to Agnostic PAC Learning:** Let A be an algorithm that guarantees the following: If $m \geq m_{\mathcal{H}}(\epsilon)$ then for every distribution $\mathcal{D}$ it holds that

$$\mathop{\mathbb{E}}_{S\sim\mathcal{D}^m}[L_{\mathcal{D}}(A(S))] \leq \min_{h\in\mathcal{H}} L_{\mathcal{D}}(h) + \epsilon.$$

- Show that for every $\delta \in (0,1)$, if $m \geq m_{\mathcal{H}}(\epsilon\,\delta)$ then with probability of at least $1-\delta$ it holds that $L_{\mathcal{D}}(A(S)) \leq \min_{h\in\mathcal{H}} L_{\mathcal{D}}(h) + \epsilon$.
  Hint: Observe that the random variable $L_{\mathcal{D}}(A(S)) - \min_{h\in\mathcal{H}} L_{\mathcal{D}}(h)$ is nonnegative and rely on Markov's inequality.
- For every $\delta \in (0,1)$ let

$$m_{\mathcal{H}}(\epsilon,\,\delta) = m_{\mathcal{H}}(\epsilon/2)\lceil\log_2(1/\delta)\rceil + \left\lceil \frac{\log(4/\delta) + \log(\lceil\log_2(1/\delta)\rceil)}{\epsilon^2}\right\rceil.$$

  Suggest a procedure that agnostic PAC learns the problem with sample complexity of $m_{\mathcal{H}}(\epsilon,\delta)$, assuming that the loss function is bounded by 1.
  Hint: Let $k = \lceil\log_2(1/\delta)\rceil$. Divide the data into $k+1$ chunks, where each of the first k chunks is of size $m_{\mathcal{H}}(\epsilon/2)$ examples. Train the first k chunks using A. On the basis of the previous question argue that the probability that for all of these chunks we have $L_{\mathcal{D}}(A(S)) > \min_{h\in\mathcal{H}} L_{\mathcal{D}}(h) + \epsilon$ is at most $2^{-k} \leq \delta/2$. Finally, use the last chunk as a validation set.

13.2 **Learnability without Uniform Convergence:** Let $\mathcal{B}$ be the unit ball of $\mathbb{R}^d$, let $\mathcal{H} = \mathcal{B}$, let $Z = \mathcal{B} \times \{0,1\}^d$, and let $\ell : Z \times \mathcal{H} \to \mathbb{R}$ be defined as follows:

$$\ell(\mathbf{w}, (\mathbf{x}, \boldsymbol{\alpha})) = \sum_{i=1}^{d} \alpha_i (x_i - w_i)^2.$$

This problem corresponds to an *unsupervised* learning task, meaning that we do not try to predict the label of $\mathbf{x}$. Instead, what we try to do is to find the "center of mass" of the distribution over $\mathcal{B}$. However, there is a twist, modeled by the vectors $\boldsymbol{\alpha}$. Each example is a pair $(\mathbf{x}, \boldsymbol{\alpha})$, where $\mathbf{x}$ is the instance $\mathbf{x}$ and $\boldsymbol{\alpha}$ indicates which features of $\mathbf{x}$ are "active" and which are "turned off." A hypothesis is a vector $\mathbf{w}$ representing the center of mass of the distribution, and the loss function is the squared Euclidean distance between $\mathbf{x}$ and $\mathbf{w}$, but only with respect to the "active" elements of $\mathbf{x}$.

- Show that this problem is learnable using the RLM rule with a sample complexity that does not depend on d.

- Consider a distribution $\mathcal{D}$ over Z as follows: $\mathbf{x}$ is fixed to be some $\mathbf{x}_0$, and each element of $\boldsymbol{\alpha}$ is sampled to be either 1 or 0 with equal probability. Show that the rate of uniform convergence of this problem grows with d.
  Hint: Let m be a training set size. Show that if $d \gg 2^m$, then there is a high probability of sampling a set of examples such that there exists some $j \in [d]$ for which $\alpha_j = 1$ for all the examples in the training set. Show that such a sample cannot be ϵ-representative. Conclude that the sample complexity of uniform convergence must grow with $\log(d)$.
- Conclude that if we take d to infinity we obtain a problem that is learnable but for which the uniform convergence property does not hold. Compare to the fundamental theorem of statistical learning.

13.3 **Stability and Asymptotic ERM Are Sufficient for Learnability:**
We say that a learning rule A is an *AERM (Asymptotic Empirical Risk Minimizer)* with rate $\epsilon(m)$ if for every distribution $\mathcal{D}$ it holds that

$$\mathop{\mathbb{E}}_{S\sim\mathcal{D}^m}\left[L_S(A(S)) - \min_{h\in\mathcal{H}} L_S(h)\right] \leq \epsilon(m).$$

We say that a learning rule A learns a class $\mathcal{H}$ with rate $\epsilon(m)$ if for every distribution $\mathcal{D}$ it holds that

$$\mathop{\mathbb{E}}_{S\sim\mathcal{D}^m}\left[L_{\mathcal{D}}(A(S)) - \min_{h\in\mathcal{H}} L_{\mathcal{D}}(h)\right] \leq \epsilon(m).$$

Prove the following:

Theorem 13.12. *If a learning algorithm A is on-average-replace-one-stable with rate $\epsilon_1(m)$ and is an AERM with rate $\epsilon_2(m)$, then it learns $\mathcal{H}$ with rate $\epsilon_1(m) + \epsilon_2(m)$.*

13.4 **Strong Convexity with Respect to General Norms:**
Throughout the section we used the ℓ_2 norm. In this exercise we generalize some of the results to general norms. Let $\|\cdot\|$ be some arbitrary norm, and let f be a strongly convex function with respect to this norm (see Definition 13.4).

1. Show that items 2–3 of Lemma 13.5 hold for every norm.
2. **(*)** Give an example of a norm for which item 1 of Lemma 13.5 does not hold.
3. Let $R(\mathbf{w})$ be a function that is (2λ)-strongly convex with respect to some norm $\|\cdot\|$. Let A be an RLM rule with respect to R, namely,

$$A(S) = \operatorname*{argmin}_{\mathbf{w}} \left(L_S(\mathbf{w}) + R(\mathbf{w})\right).$$

   Assume that for every z, the loss function $\ell(\cdot, z)$ is ρ-Lipschitz with respect to the same norm, namely,

$$\forall z,\ \forall \mathbf{w},\ \mathbf{v},\quad \ell(\mathbf{w}, z) - \ell(\mathbf{v}, z) \leq \rho\,\|\mathbf{w} - \mathbf{v}\|.$$

   Prove that A is on-average-replace-one-stable with rate $\frac{2\rho^2}{\lambda m}$.
4. **(*)** Let $q \in (1, 2)$ and consider the ℓ_q-norm

$$\|\mathbf{w}\|_q = \left(\sum_{i=1}^{d} |w_i|^q\right)^{1/q}.$$

It can be shown (see, for example, Shalev-Shwartz (2007)) that the function

$$R(\mathbf{w}) = \frac{1}{2(q-1)} \|\mathbf{w}\|_q^2$$

is 1-strongly convex with respect to $\|\mathbf{w}\|_q$. Show that if $q = \frac{\log(d)}{\log(d)-1}$ then $R(\mathbf{w})$ is $\left(\frac{1}{3\log(d)}\right)$-strongly convex with respect to the ℓ_1 norm over $\mathbb{R}^d$.

14

Stochastic Gradient Descent

Recall that the goal of learning is to minimize the risk function, $L_{\mathcal{D}}(h) = \mathbb{E}_{z\sim\mathcal{D}}[\ell(h,z)]$. We cannot directly minimize the risk function since it depends on the unknown distribution $\mathcal{D}$. So far in the book, we have discussed learning methods that depend on the empirical risk. That is, we first sample a training set S and define the empirical risk function $L_S(h)$. Then, the learner picks a hypothesis based on the value of $L_S(h)$. For example, the ERM rule tells us to pick the hypothesis that minimizes $L_S(h)$ over the hypothesis class, $\mathcal{H}$. Or, in the previous chapter, we discussed regularized risk minimization, in which we pick a hypothesis that jointly minimizes $L_S(h)$ and a regularization function over h.

In this chapter we describe and analyze a rather different learning approach, which is called *Stochastic Gradient Descent* (SGD). As in Chapter 12 we will focus on the important family of convex learning problems, and following the notation in that chapter, we will refer to hypotheses as vectors $\mathbf{w}$ that come from a convex hypothesis class, $\mathcal{H}$. In SGD, we try to minimize the risk function $L_{\mathcal{D}}(\mathbf{w})$ directly using a gradient descent procedure. Gradient descent is an iterative optimization procedure in which at each step we improve the solution by taking a step along the negative of the gradient of the function to be minimized at the current point. Of course, in our case, we are minimizing the risk function, and since we do not know $\mathcal{D}$ we also do not know the gradient of $L_{\mathcal{D}}(\mathbf{w})$. SGD circumvents this problem by allowing the optimization procedure to take a step along a random direction, as long as the expected value of the direction is the negative of the gradient. And, as we shall see, finding a random direction whose expected value corresponds to the gradient is rather simple even though we do not know the underlying distribution $\mathcal{D}$.

The advantage of SGD, in the context of convex learning problems, over the regularized risk minimization learning rule is that SGD is an efficient algorithm that can be implemented in a few lines of code, yet still enjoys the same sample complexity as the regularized risk minimization rule. The simplicity of SGD also allows us to use it in situations when it is not possible to apply methods that are based on the empirical risk, but this is beyond the scope of this book.

We start this chapter with the basic gradient descent algorithm and analyze its convergence rate for convex-Lipschitz functions. Next, we introduce the notion of subgradient and show that gradient descent can be applied for nondifferentiable functions as well. The core of this chapter is Section 14.3, in which we describe the Stochastic Gradient Descent algorithm, along with several useful variants. We show that SGD enjoys an expected convergence rate similar to the rate of gradient descent. Finally, we turn to the applicability of SGD to learning problems.

14.1 GRADIENT DESCENT

Before we describe the stochastic gradient descent method, we would like to describe the standard gradient descent approach for minimizing a differentiable convex function $f(\mathbf{w})$.

The gradient of a differentiable function $f : \mathbb{R}^d \to \mathbb{R}$ at $\mathbf{w}$, denoted $\nabla f(\mathbf{w})$, is the vector of partial derivatives of f, namely, $\nabla f(\mathbf{w}) = \left(\frac{\partial f(\mathbf{w})}{\partial w[1]}, \ldots, \frac{\partial f(\mathbf{w})}{\partial w[d]}\right)$. Gradient descent is an iterative algorithm. We start with an initial value of $\mathbf{w}$ (say, $\mathbf{w}^{(1)} = \mathbf{0}$). Then, at each iteration, we take a step in the direction of the negative of the gradient at the current point. That is, the update step is

$$\mathbf{w}^{(t+1)} = \mathbf{w}^{(t)} - \eta \nabla f(\mathbf{w}^{(t)}), \tag{14.1}$$

where $\eta > 0$ is a parameter to be discussed later. Intuitively, since the gradient points in the direction of the greatest rate of increase of f around $\mathbf{w}^{(t)}$, the algorithm makes a small step in the opposite direction, thus decreasing the value of the function. Eventually, after T iterations, the algorithm outputs the averaged vector, $\bar{\mathbf{w}} = \frac{1}{T}\sum_{t=1}^{T} \mathbf{w}^{(t)}$. The output could also be the last vector, $\mathbf{w}^{(T)}$, or the best performing vector, $\operatorname{argmin}_{t\in[T]} f(\mathbf{w}^{(t)})$, but taking the average turns out to be rather useful, especially when we generalize gradient descent to nondifferentiable functions and to the stochastic case.

Another way to motivate gradient descent is by relying on Taylor approximation. The gradient of f at $\mathbf{w}$ yields the first order Taylor approximation of f around $\mathbf{w}$ by $f(\mathbf{u}) \approx f(\mathbf{w}) + \langle \mathbf{u} - \mathbf{w}, \nabla f(\mathbf{w})\rangle$. When f is convex, this approximation lower bounds f, that is,

$$f(\mathbf{u}) \geq f(\mathbf{w}) + \langle \mathbf{u} - \mathbf{w}, \nabla f(\mathbf{w})\rangle.$$

Therefore, for $\mathbf{w}$ close to $\mathbf{w}^{(t)}$ we have that $f(\mathbf{w}) \approx f(\mathbf{w}^{(t)}) + \langle \mathbf{w} - \mathbf{w}^{(t)}, \nabla f(\mathbf{w}^{(t)})\rangle$. Hence we can minimize the approximation of $f(\mathbf{w})$. However, the approximation might become loose for $\mathbf{w}$, which is far away from $\mathbf{w}^{(t)}$. Therefore, we would like to minimize jointly the distance between $\mathbf{w}$ and $\mathbf{w}^{(t)}$ and the approximation of f around $\mathbf{w}^{(t)}$. If the parameter η controls the tradeoff between the two terms, we obtain the update rule

$$\mathbf{w}^{(t+1)} = \operatorname*{argmin}_{\mathbf{w}} \frac{1}{2}\|\mathbf{w} - \mathbf{w}^{(t)}\|^2 + \eta\left(f(\mathbf{w}^{(t)}) + \langle \mathbf{w} - \mathbf{w}^{(t)}, \nabla f(\mathbf{w}^{(t)})\rangle\right).$$

Solving the preceding by taking the derivative with respect to $\mathbf{w}$ and comparing it to zero yields the same update rule as in Equation (14.1).

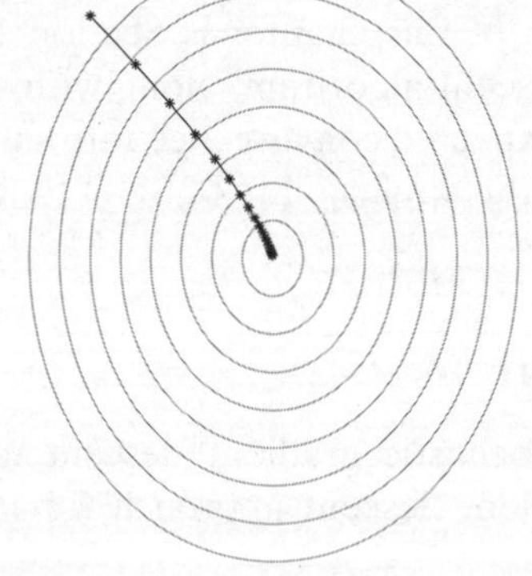

Figure 14.1. An illustration of the gradient descent algorithm. The function to be minimized is $1.25(x_1+6)^2+(x_2-8)^2$.

14.1.1 Analysis of GD for Convex-Lipschitz Functions

To analyze the convergence rate of the GD algorithm, we limit ourselves to the case of convex-Lipschitz functions (as we have seen, many problems lend themselves easily to this setting). Let $\mathbf{w}^\star$ be any vector and let B be an upper bound on $\|\mathbf{w}^\star\|$. It is convenient to think of $\mathbf{w}^\star$ as the minimizer of $f(\mathbf{w})$, but the analysis that follows holds for every $\mathbf{w}^\star$.

We would like to obtain an upper bound on the suboptimality of our solution with respect to $\mathbf{w}^\star$, namely, $f(\bar{\mathbf{w}})-f(\mathbf{w}^\star)$, where $\bar{\mathbf{w}}=\frac{1}{T}\sum_{t=1}^T \mathbf{w}^{(t)}$. From the definition of $\bar{\mathbf{w}}$, and using Jensen's inequality, we have that

$$\begin{aligned} f(\bar{\mathbf{w}})-f(\mathbf{w}^\star) &= f\left(\frac{1}{T}\sum_{t=1}^T \mathbf{w}^{(t)}\right)-f(\mathbf{w}^\star) \\ &\le \frac{1}{T}\sum_{t=1}^T \left(f(\mathbf{w}^{(t)})\right)-f(\mathbf{w}^\star) \\ &= \frac{1}{T}\sum_{t=1}^T \left(f(\mathbf{w}^{(t)})-f(\mathbf{w}^\star)\right). \end{aligned} \tag{14.2}$$

For every t, because of the convexity of f, we have that

$$f(\mathbf{w}^{(t)})-f(\mathbf{w}^\star) \le \langle \mathbf{w}^{(t)}-\mathbf{w}^\star, \nabla f(\mathbf{w}^{(t)})\rangle. \tag{14.3}$$

Combining the preceding we obtain

$$f(\bar{\mathbf{w}})-f(\mathbf{w}^\star) \le \frac{1}{T}\sum_{t=1}^T \langle \mathbf{w}^{(t)}-\mathbf{w}^\star, \nabla f(\mathbf{w}^{(t)})\rangle.$$

To bound the right-hand side we rely on the following lemma:

Lemma 14.1. *Let $\mathbf{v}_1,\ldots,\mathbf{v}_T$ be an arbitrary sequence of vectors. Any algorithm with an initialization $\mathbf{w}^{(1)}=0$ and an update rule of the form*

$$\mathbf{w}^{(t+1)}=\mathbf{w}^{(t)}-\eta\mathbf{v}_t \tag{14.4}$$

satisfies

$$\sum_{t=1}^{T}\langle \mathbf{w}^{(t)} - \mathbf{w}^{\star}, \mathbf{v}_t\rangle \le \frac{\|\mathbf{w}^{\star}\|^2}{2\eta} + \frac{\eta}{2}\sum_{t=1}^{T}\|\mathbf{v}_t\|^2. \tag{14.5}$$

In particular, for every $B, \rho > 0$, if for all t we have that $\|\mathbf{v}_t\| \le \rho$ and if we set $\eta = \sqrt{\frac{B^2}{\rho^2 T}}$, then for every $\mathbf{w}^{\star}$ with $\|\mathbf{w}^{\star}\| \le B$ we have

$$\frac{1}{T}\sum_{t=1}^{T}\langle \mathbf{w}^{(t)} - \mathbf{w}^{\star}, \mathbf{v}_t\rangle \le \frac{B\,\rho}{\sqrt{T}}.$$

Proof. Using algebraic manipulations (completing the square), we obtain:

$$\begin{aligned}\langle \mathbf{w}^{(t)} - \mathbf{w}^{\star}, \mathbf{v}_t\rangle &= \frac{1}{\eta}\langle \mathbf{w}^{(t)} - \mathbf{w}^{\star}, \eta\mathbf{v}_t\rangle\\ &= \frac{1}{2\eta}(-\|\mathbf{w}^{(t)} - \mathbf{w}^{\star} - \eta\mathbf{v}_t\|^2 + \|\mathbf{w}^{(t)} - \mathbf{w}^{\star}\|^2 + \eta^2\|\mathbf{v}_t\|^2)\\ &= \frac{1}{2\eta}(-\|\mathbf{w}^{(t+1)} - \mathbf{w}^{\star}\|^2 + \|\mathbf{w}^{(t)} - \mathbf{w}^{\star}\|^2) + \frac{\eta}{2}\|\mathbf{v}_t\|^2,\end{aligned}$$

where the last equality follows from the definition of the update rule. Summing the equality over t, we have

$$\sum_{t=1}^{T}\langle \mathbf{w}^{(t)} - \mathbf{w}^{\star}, \mathbf{v}_t\rangle = \frac{1}{2\eta}\sum_{t=1}^{T}\left(-\|\mathbf{w}^{(t+1)} - \mathbf{w}^{\star}\|^2 + \|\mathbf{w}^{(t)} - \mathbf{w}^{\star}\|^2\right) + \frac{\eta}{2}\sum_{t=1}^{T}\|\mathbf{v}_t\|^2. \tag{14.6}$$

The first sum on the right-hand side is a telescopic sum that collapses to

$$\|\mathbf{w}^{(1)} - \mathbf{w}^{\star}\|^2 - \|\mathbf{w}^{(T+1)} - \mathbf{w}^{\star}\|^2.$$

Plugging this in Equation (14.6), we have

$$\begin{aligned}\sum_{t=1}^{T}\langle \mathbf{w}^{(t)} - \mathbf{w}^{\star}, \mathbf{v}_t\rangle &= \frac{1}{2\eta}(\|\mathbf{w}^{(1)} - \mathbf{w}^{\star}\|^2 - \|\mathbf{w}^{(T+1)} - \mathbf{w}^{\star}\|^2) + \frac{\eta}{2}\sum_{t=1}^{T}\|\mathbf{v}_t\|^2\\ &\le \frac{1}{2\eta}\|\mathbf{w}^{(1)} - \mathbf{w}^{\star}\|^2 + \frac{\eta}{2}\sum_{t=1}^{T}\|\mathbf{v}_t\|^2\\ &= \frac{1}{2\eta}\|\mathbf{w}^{\star}\|^2 + \frac{\eta}{2}\sum_{t=1}^{T}\|\mathbf{v}_t\|^2,\end{aligned}$$

where the last equality is due to the definition $\mathbf{w}^{(1)} = 0$. This proves the first part of the lemma (Equation (14.5)). The second part follows by upper bounding $\|\mathbf{w}^{\star}\|$ by B, $\|\mathbf{v}_t\|$ by ρ, dividing by T, and plugging in the value of η. □

Lemma 14.1 applies to the GD algorithm with $\mathbf{v}_t = \nabla f(\mathbf{w}^{(t)})$. As we will show later in Lemma 14.7, if f is ρ-Lipschitz, then $\|\nabla f(\mathbf{w}^{(t)})\| \le \rho$. We therefore satisfy the lemma's conditions and achieve the following corollary:

Corollary 14.2. *Let f be a convex, ρ-Lipschitz function, and let $\mathbf{w}^\star \in \operatorname{argmin}_{\{\mathbf{w}:\|\mathbf{w}\|\le B\}} f(\mathbf{w})$. If we run the GD algorithm on f for T steps with $\eta = \sqrt{\frac{B^2}{\rho^2 T}}$, then the output vector $\bar{\mathbf{w}}$ satisfies*

$$f(\bar{\mathbf{w}}) - f(\mathbf{w}^\star) \le \frac{B\,\rho}{\sqrt{T}}.$$

Furthermore, for every $\epsilon > 0$, to achieve $f(\bar{\mathbf{w}}) - f(\mathbf{w}^\star) \le \epsilon$, it suffices to run the GD algorithm for a number of iterations that satisfies

$$T \ge \frac{B^2\rho^2}{\epsilon^2}.$$

14.2 SUBGRADIENTS

The GD algorithm requires that the function f be differentiable. We now generalize the discussion beyond differentiable functions. We will show that the GD algorithm can be applied to nondifferentiable functions by using a so-called subgradient of $f(\mathbf{w})$ at $\mathbf{w}^{(t)}$, instead of the gradient.

To motivate the definition of subgradients, recall that for a convex function f, the gradient at $\mathbf{w}$ defines the slope of a tangent that lies below f, that is,

$$\forall \mathbf{u}, \quad f(\mathbf{u}) \ge f(\mathbf{w}) + \langle \mathbf{u} - \mathbf{w}, \nabla f(\mathbf{w}) \rangle. \tag{14.7}$$

An illustration is given on the left-hand side of Figure 14.2.

The existence of a tangent that lies below f is an important property of convex functions, which is in fact an alternative characterization of convexity.

Lemma 14.3. *Let S be an open convex set. A function $f : S \to \mathbb{R}$ is convex iff for every $\mathbf{w} \in S$ there exists $\mathbf{v}$ such that*

$$\forall \mathbf{u} \in S, \quad f(\mathbf{u}) \ge f(\mathbf{w}) + \langle \mathbf{u} - \mathbf{w}, \mathbf{v} \rangle. \tag{14.8}$$

The proof of this lemma can be found in many convex analysis textbooks (e.g., (Borwein & Lewis 2006)). The preceding inequality leads us to the definition of subgradients.

Definition 14.4. (Subgradients). A vector $\mathbf{v}$ that satisfies Equation (14.8) is called a *subgradient* of f at $\mathbf{w}$. The set of subgradients of f at $\mathbf{w}$ is called the *differential set* and denoted $\partial f(\mathbf{w})$.

An illustration of subgradients is given on the right-hand side of Figure 14.2. For scalar functions, a subgradient of a convex function f at w is a slope of a line that touches f at w and is not above f elsewhere.

14.2.1 Calculating Subgradients

How do we construct subgradients of a given convex function? If a function is differentiable at a point $\mathbf{w}$, then the differential set is trivial, as the following claim shows.

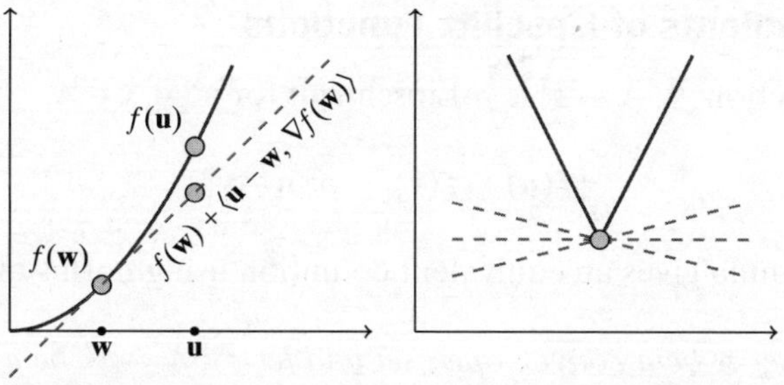

Figure 14.2. Left: The right-hand side of Equation (14.7) is the tangent of f at $\mathbf{w}$. For a convex function, the tangent lower bounds f. Right: Illustration of several subgradients of a nondifferentiable convex function.

Claim 14.5. *If f is differentiable at $\mathbf{w}$ then $\partial f(\mathbf{w})$ contains a single element – the gradient of f at $\mathbf{w}$, $\nabla f(\mathbf{w})$.*

Example 14.1 (The Differential Set of the Absolute Function). Consider the absolute value function $f(x) = |x|$. Using Claim 14.5, we can easily construct the differential set for the differentiable parts of f, and the only point that requires special attention is $x_0 = 0$. At that point, it is easy to verify that the subdifferential is the set of all numbers between -1 and 1. Hence:

$$\partial f(x) = \begin{cases} \{1\} & \text{if } x > 0 \\ \{-1\} & \text{if } x < 0 \\ [-1,1] & \text{if } x = 0 \end{cases}$$

For many practical uses, we do not need to calculate the whole set of subgradients at a given point, as one member of this set would suffice. The following claim shows how to construct a sub-gradient for pointwise maximum functions.

Claim 14.6. *Let $g(\mathbf{w}) = \max_{i\in[r]} g_i(\mathbf{w})$ for r convex differentiable functions $g_1, \ldots, g_r$. Given some $\mathbf{w}$, let $j \in \operatorname{argmax}_i g_i(\mathbf{w})$. Then $\nabla g_j(\mathbf{w}) \in \partial g(\mathbf{w})$.*

Proof. Since g_j is convex we have that for all $\mathbf{u}$

$$g_j(\mathbf{u}) \geq g_j(\mathbf{w}) + \langle \mathbf{u} - \mathbf{w}, \nabla g_j(\mathbf{w}) \rangle.$$

Since $g(\mathbf{w}) = g_j(\mathbf{w})$ and $g(\mathbf{u}) \geq g_j(\mathbf{u})$ we obtain that

$$g(\mathbf{u}) \geq g(\mathbf{w}) + \langle \mathbf{u} - \mathbf{w}, \nabla g_j(\mathbf{w}) \rangle,$$

which concludes our proof. □

Example 14.2 (A Subgradient of the Hinge Loss). Recall the hinge loss function from Section 12.3, $f(\mathbf{w}) = \max\{0, 1 - y\langle \mathbf{w}, \mathbf{x} \rangle\}$ for some vector $\mathbf{x}$ and scalar y. To calculate a subgradient of the hinge loss at some $\mathbf{w}$ we rely on the preceding claim and obtain that the vector $\mathbf{v}$ defined in the following is a subgradient of the hinge loss at $\mathbf{w}$:

$$\mathbf{v} = \begin{cases} \mathbf{0} & \text{if } 1 - y\langle \mathbf{w}, \mathbf{x} \rangle \leq 0 \\ -y\mathbf{x} & \text{if } 1 - y\langle \mathbf{w}, \mathbf{x} \rangle > 0 \end{cases}$$

14.2.2 Subgradients of Lipschitz Functions

Recall that a function $f : A \to \mathbb{R}$ is ρ-Lipschitz if for all $\mathbf{u}, \mathbf{v} \in A$

$$|f(\mathbf{u}) - f(\mathbf{v})| \leq \rho\, \|\mathbf{u} - \mathbf{v}\|.$$

The following lemma gives an equivalent definition using norms of subgradients.

Lemma 14.7. *Let A be a convex open set and let $f : A \to \mathbb{R}$ be a convex function. Then, f is ρ-Lipschitz over A iff for all $\mathbf{w} \in A$ and $\mathbf{v} \in \partial f(\mathbf{w})$ we have that $\|\mathbf{v}\| \leq \rho$.*

Proof. Assume that for all $\mathbf{v} \in \partial f(\mathbf{w})$ we have that $\|\mathbf{v}\| \leq \rho$. Since $\mathbf{v} \in \partial f(\mathbf{w})$ we have

$$f(\mathbf{w}) - f(\mathbf{u}) \leq \langle \mathbf{v}, \mathbf{w} - \mathbf{u} \rangle.$$

Bounding the right-hand side using Cauchy-Schwartz inequality we obtain

$$f(\mathbf{w}) - f(\mathbf{u}) \leq \langle \mathbf{v}, \mathbf{w} - \mathbf{u} \rangle \leq \|\mathbf{v}\|\, \|\mathbf{w} - \mathbf{u}\| \leq \rho\, \|\mathbf{w} - \mathbf{u}\|.$$

An analogous argument can show that $f(\mathbf{u}) - f(\mathbf{w}) \leq \rho\, \|\mathbf{w} - \mathbf{u}\|$. Hence f is ρ-Lipschitz.

Now assume that f is ρ-Lipschitz. Choose some $\mathbf{w} \in A, \mathbf{v} \in \partial f(\mathbf{w})$. Since A is open, there exists $\epsilon > 0$ such that $\mathbf{u} = \mathbf{w} + \epsilon \mathbf{v}/\|\mathbf{v}\|$ belongs to A. Therefore, $\langle \mathbf{u} - \mathbf{w}, \mathbf{v} \rangle = \epsilon \|\mathbf{v}\|$ and $\|\mathbf{u} - \mathbf{w}\| = \epsilon$. From the definition of the subgradient,

$$f(\mathbf{u}) - f(\mathbf{w}) \geq \langle \mathbf{v}, \mathbf{u} - \mathbf{w} \rangle = \epsilon \|\mathbf{v}\|.$$

On the other hand, from the Lipschitzness of f we have

$$\rho\epsilon = \rho\, \|\mathbf{u} - \mathbf{w}\| \geq f(\mathbf{u}) - f(\mathbf{w}).$$

Combining the two inequalities we conclude that $\|\mathbf{v}\| \leq \rho$. □

14.2.3 Subgradient Descent

The gradient descent algorithm can be generalized to nondifferentiable functions by using a subgradient of $f(\mathbf{w})$ at $\mathbf{w}^{(t)}$, instead of the gradient. The analysis of the convergence rate remains unchanged: Simply note that Equation (14.3) is true for subgradients as well.

14.3 STOCHASTIC GRADIENT DESCENT (SGD)

In stochastic gradient descent we do not require the update direction to be based exactly on the gradient. Instead, we allow the direction to be a random vector and only require that its *expected value* at each iteration will equal the gradient direction. Or, more generally, we require that the expected value of the random vector will be a subgradient of the function at the current vector.

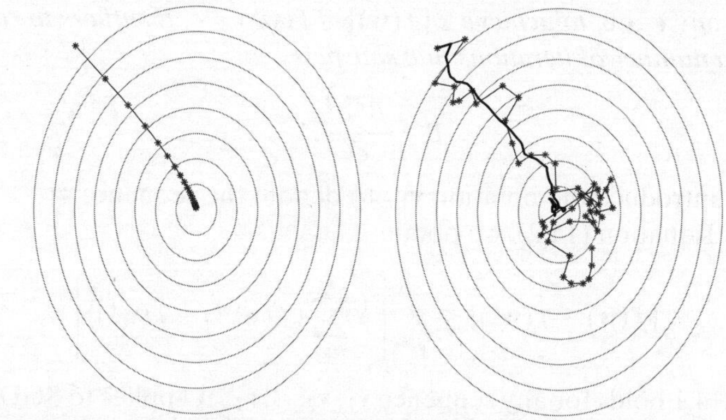

Figure 14.3. An illustration of the gradient descent algorithm (left) and the stochastic gradient descent algorithm (right). The function to be minimized is $1.25(x+6)^2+(y-8)^2$. For the stochastic case, the solid line depicts the averaged value of $\mathbf{w}$.

Stochastic Gradient Descent (SGD) for minimizing $f(\mathbf{w})$

parameters: Scalar $\eta > 0$, integer $T > 0$
initialize: $\mathbf{w}^{(1)} = \mathbf{0}$
for $t = 1, 2, \ldots, T$
  choose $\mathbf{v}_t$ at random from a distribution such that $\mathbb{E}[\mathbf{v}_t \,|\, \mathbf{w}^{(t)}] \in \partial f(\mathbf{w}^{(t)})$
  update $\mathbf{w}^{(t+1)} = \mathbf{w}^{(t)} - \eta \mathbf{v}_t$
output $\bar{\mathbf{w}} = \frac{1}{T}\sum_{t=1}^{T} \mathbf{w}^{(t)}$

An illustration of stochastic gradient descent versus gradient descent is given in Figure 14.3. As we will see in Section 14.5, in the context of learning problems, it is easy to find a random vector whose expectation is a subgradient of the risk function.

14.3.1 Analysis of SGD for Convex-Lipschitz-Bounded Functions

Recall the bound we achieved for the GD algorithm in Corollary 14.2. For the stochastic case, in which only the expectation of $\mathbf{v}_t$ is in $\partial f(\mathbf{w}^{(t)})$, we cannot directly apply Equation (14.3). However, since the expected value of $\mathbf{v}_t$ is a subgradient of f at $\mathbf{w}^{(t)}$, we can still derive a similar bound on the *expected* output of stochastic gradient descent. This is formalized in the following theorem.

Theorem 14.8. *Let $B, \rho > 0$. Let f be a convex function and let $\mathbf{w}^\star \in \operatorname{argmin}_{\mathbf{w}:\|\mathbf{w}\|\le B} f(\mathbf{w})$. Assume that SGD is run for T iterations with $\eta = \sqrt{\frac{B^2}{\rho^2 T}}$. Assume also that for all t, $\|\mathbf{v}_t\| \le \rho$ with probability 1. Then,*

$$\mathbb{E}[f(\bar{\mathbf{w}})] - f(\mathbf{w}^\star) \le \frac{B\rho}{\sqrt{T}}.$$

Therefore, for any $\epsilon > 0$, to achieve $\mathbb{E}[f(\bar{\mathbf{w}})] - f(\mathbf{w}^\star) \le \epsilon$, it suffices to run the SGD algorithm for a number of iterations that satisfies

$$T \ge \frac{B^2 \rho^2}{\epsilon^2}.$$

Proof. Let us introduce the notation $\mathbf{v}_{1:t}$ to denote the sequence $\mathbf{v}_1, \ldots, \mathbf{v}_t$. Taking expectation of Equation (14.2), we obtain

$$\mathop{\mathbb{E}}_{\mathbf{v}_{1:T}}[f(\bar{\mathbf{w}}) - f(\mathbf{w}^\star)] \le \mathop{\mathbb{E}}_{\mathbf{v}_{1:T}}\left[\tfrac{1}{T}\sum_{t=1}^{T}(f(\mathbf{w}^{(t)}) - f(\mathbf{w}^\star))\right].$$

Since Lemma 14.1 holds for any sequence $\mathbf{v}_1, \mathbf{v}_2, \ldots \mathbf{v}_T$, it applies to SGD as well. By taking expectation of the bound in the lemma we have

$$\mathop{\mathbb{E}}_{\mathbf{v}_{1:T}}\left[\frac{1}{T}\sum_{t=1}^{T}\langle \mathbf{w}^{(t)} - \mathbf{w}^\star, \mathbf{v}_t\rangle\right] \le \frac{B\rho}{\sqrt{T}}. \tag{14.9}$$

It is left to show that

$$\mathop{\mathbb{E}}_{\mathbf{v}_{1:T}}\left[\tfrac{1}{T}\sum_{t=1}^{T}(f(\mathbf{w}^{(t)}) - f(\mathbf{w}^\star))\right] \le \mathop{\mathbb{E}}_{\mathbf{v}_{1:T}}\left[\tfrac{1}{T}\sum_{t=1}^{T}\langle \mathbf{w}^{(t)} - \mathbf{w}^\star, \mathbf{v}_t\rangle\right], \tag{14.10}$$

which we will hereby prove.

Using the linearity of the expectation we have

$$\mathop{\mathbb{E}}_{\mathbf{v}_{1:T}}\left[\frac{1}{T}\sum_{t=1}^{T}\langle \mathbf{w}^{(t)} - \mathbf{w}^\star, \mathbf{v}_t\rangle\right] = \frac{1}{T}\sum_{t=1}^{T}\mathop{\mathbb{E}}_{\mathbf{v}_{1:T}}[\langle \mathbf{w}^{(t)} - \mathbf{w}^\star, \mathbf{v}_t\rangle].$$

Next, we recall the *law of total expectation*: For every two random variables α, β, and a function g, $\mathbb{E}_\alpha[g(\alpha)] = \mathbb{E}_\beta \mathbb{E}_\alpha[g(\alpha)|\beta]$. Setting $\alpha = \mathbf{v}_{1:t}$ and $\beta = \mathbf{v}_{1:t-1}$ we get that

$$\begin{aligned}\mathop{\mathbb{E}}_{\mathbf{v}_{1:T}}[\langle \mathbf{w}^{(t)} - \mathbf{w}^\star,\ \mathbf{v}_t\rangle] &= \mathop{\mathbb{E}}_{\mathbf{v}_{1:t}}[\langle \mathbf{w}^{(t)} - \mathbf{w}^\star,\ \mathbf{v}_t\rangle] \\ &= \mathop{\mathbb{E}}_{\mathbf{v}_{1:t-1}}\mathop{\mathbb{E}}_{\mathbf{v}_{1:t}}[\langle \mathbf{w}^{(t)} - \mathbf{w}^\star, \mathbf{v}_t\rangle \,|\, \mathbf{v}_{1:t-1}].\end{aligned}$$

Once we know $\mathbf{v}_{1:t-1}$, the value of $\mathbf{w}^{(t)}$ is not random any more and therefore

$$\mathop{\mathbb{E}}_{\mathbf{v}_{1:t-1}}\mathop{\mathbb{E}}_{\mathbf{v}_{1:t}}[\langle \mathbf{w}^{(t)} - \mathbf{w}^\star, \mathbf{v}_t\rangle \,|\, \mathbf{v}_{1:t-1}] = \mathop{\mathbb{E}}_{\mathbf{v}_{1:t-1}}\langle \mathbf{w}^{(t)} - \mathbf{w}^\star,\ \mathop{\mathbb{E}}_{\mathbf{v}_t}[\mathbf{v}_t \,|\, \mathbf{v}_{1:t-1}]\rangle.$$

Since $\mathbf{w}^{(t)}$ only depends on $\mathbf{v}_{1:t-1}$ and SGD requires that $\mathbb{E}_{\mathbf{v}_t}[\mathbf{v}_t \,|\, \mathbf{w}^{(t)}] \in \partial f(\mathbf{w}^{(t)})$ we obtain that $\mathbb{E}_{\mathbf{v}_t}[\mathbf{v}_t \,|\, \mathbf{v}_{1:t-1}] \in \partial f(\mathbf{w}^{(t)})$. Thus,

$$\mathop{\mathbb{E}}_{\mathbf{v}_{1:t-1}}\langle \mathbf{w}^{(t)} - \mathbf{w}^\star, \mathop{\mathbb{E}}_{\mathbf{v}_t}[\mathbf{v}_t \,|\, \mathbf{v}_{1:t-1}]\rangle \ge \mathop{\mathbb{E}}_{\mathbf{v}_{1:t-1}}[f(\mathbf{w}^{(t)}) - f(\mathbf{w}^\star)].$$

Overall, we have shown that

$$\begin{aligned}\mathop{\mathbb{E}}_{\mathbf{v}_{1:T}}[\langle \mathbf{w}^{(t)} - \mathbf{w}^\star, \mathbf{v}_t\rangle] &\ge \mathop{\mathbb{E}}_{\mathbf{v}_{1:t-1}}[f(\mathbf{w}^{(t)}) - f(\mathbf{w}^\star)] \\ &= \mathop{\mathbb{E}}_{\mathbf{v}_{1:T}}[f(\mathbf{w}^{(t)}) - f(\mathbf{w}^\star)].\end{aligned}$$

Summing over t, dividing by T, and using the linearity of expectation, we get that Equation (14.10) holds, which concludes our proof. □

14.4 VARIANTS

In this section we describe several variants of Stochastic Gradient Descent.

14.4.1 Adding a Projection Step

In the previous analyses of the GD and SGD algorithms, we required that the norm of $\mathbf{w}^\star$ will be at most B, which is equivalent to requiring that $\mathbf{w}^\star$ is in the set $\mathcal{H} = \{\mathbf{w} : \|\mathbf{w}\| \le B\}$. In terms of learning, this means restricting ourselves to a B-bounded hypothesis class. Yet any step we take in the opposite direction of the gradient (or its expected direction) might result in stepping out of this bound, and there is even no guarantee that $\bar{\mathbf{w}}$ satisfies it. We show in the following how to overcome this problem while maintaining the same convergence rate.

The basic idea is to add a *projection step*; namely, we will now have a two-step update rule, where we first subtract a subgradient from the current value of $\mathbf{w}$ and then project the resulting vector onto $\mathcal{H}$. Formally,

1. $\mathbf{w}^{(t+\frac{1}{2})} = \mathbf{w}^{(t)} - \eta \mathbf{v}_t$
2. $\mathbf{w}^{(t+1)} = \mathrm{argmin}_{\mathbf{w}\in\mathcal{H}} \|\mathbf{w} - \mathbf{w}^{(t+\frac{1}{2})}\|$

The projection step replaces the current value of $\mathbf{w}$ by the vector in $\mathcal{H}$ closest to it.

Clearly, the projection step guarantees that $\mathbf{w}^{(t)} \in \mathcal{H}$ for all t. Since $\mathcal{H}$ is convex this also implies that $\bar{\mathbf{w}} \in \mathcal{H}$ as required. We next show that the analysis of SGD with projections remains the same. This is based on the following lemma.

Lemma 14.9 (Projection Lemma). *Let $\mathcal{H}$ be a closed convex set and let $\mathbf{v}$ be the projection of $\mathbf{w}$ onto $\mathcal{H}$, namely,*

$$\mathbf{v} = \underset{\mathbf{x}\in\mathcal{H}}{\mathrm{argmin}} \|\mathbf{x} - \mathbf{w}\|^2.$$

Then, for every $\mathbf{u} \in \mathcal{H}$,

$$\|\mathbf{w} - \mathbf{u}\|^2 - \|\mathbf{v} - \mathbf{u}\|^2 \ge 0.$$

Proof. By the convexity of $\mathcal{H}$, for every $\alpha \in (0,1)$ we have that $\mathbf{v} + \alpha(\mathbf{u} - \mathbf{v}) \in \mathcal{H}$. Therefore, from the optimality of $\mathbf{v}$ we obtain

$$\begin{aligned} \|\mathbf{v} - \mathbf{w}\|^2 &\le \|\mathbf{v} + \alpha(\mathbf{u} - \mathbf{v}) - \mathbf{w}\|^2 \\ &= \|\mathbf{v} - \mathbf{w}\|^2 + 2\alpha\langle \mathbf{v} - \mathbf{w}, \mathbf{u} - \mathbf{v}\rangle + \alpha^2\|\mathbf{u} - \mathbf{v}\|^2. \end{aligned}$$

Rearranging, we obtain

$$2\langle \mathbf{v} - \mathbf{w}, \mathbf{u} - \mathbf{v}\rangle \ge -\alpha\,\|\mathbf{u} - \mathbf{v}\|^2.$$

Taking the limit $\alpha \to 0$ we get that

$$\langle \mathbf{v} - \mathbf{w}, \mathbf{u} - \mathbf{v}\rangle \ge 0.$$

Therefore,

$$\begin{aligned}\|\mathbf{w}-\mathbf{u}\|^2 &= \|\mathbf{w}-\mathbf{v}+\mathbf{v}-\mathbf{u}\|^2 \\ &= \|\mathbf{w}-\mathbf{v}\|^2+\|\mathbf{v}-\mathbf{u}\|^2+2\langle \mathbf{v}-\mathbf{w},\, \mathbf{u}-\mathbf{v}\rangle \\ &\geq \|\mathbf{v}-\mathbf{u}\|^2.\end{aligned}$$

□

Equipped with the preceding lemma, we can easily adapt the analysis of SGD to the case in which we add projection steps on a closed and convex set. Simply note that for every t,

$$\begin{aligned}&\|\mathbf{w}^{(t+1)}-\mathbf{w}^\star\|^2-\|\mathbf{w}^{(t)}-\mathbf{w}^\star\|^2 \\ &= \|\mathbf{w}^{(t+1)}-\mathbf{w}^\star\|^2-\|\mathbf{w}^{(t+\frac{1}{2})}-\mathbf{w}^\star\|^2+\|\mathbf{w}^{(t+\frac{1}{2})}-\mathbf{w}^\star\|^2-\|\mathbf{w}^{(t)}-\mathbf{w}^\star\|^2 \\ &\leq \|\mathbf{w}^{(t+\frac{1}{2})}-\mathbf{w}^\star\|^2-\|\mathbf{w}^{(t)}-\mathbf{w}^\star\|^2.\end{aligned}$$

Therefore, Lemma 14.1 holds when we add projection steps and hence the rest of the analysis follows directly.

14.4.2 Variable Step Size

Another variant of SGD is decreasing the step size as a function of t. That is, rather than updating with a constant η, we use η_t. For instance, we can set $\eta_t = \frac{B}{\rho\sqrt{t}}$ and achieve a bound similar to Theorem 14.8. The idea is that when we are closer to the minimum of the function, we take our steps more carefully, so as not to "overshoot" the minimum.

14.4.3 Other Averaging Techniques

We have set the output vector to be $\bar{\mathbf{w}} = \frac{1}{T}\sum_{t=1}^{T}\mathbf{w}^{(t)}$. There are alternative approaches such as outputting $\mathbf{w}^{(t)}$ for some random $t \in [t]$, or outputting the average of $\mathbf{w}^{(t)}$ over the last αT iterations, for some $\alpha \in (0,1)$. One can also take a weighted average of the last few iterates. These more sophisticated averaging schemes can improve the convergence speed in some situations, such as in the case of strongly convex functions defined in the following.

14.4.4 Strongly Convex Functions*

In this section we show a variant of SGD that enjoys a faster convergence rate for problems in which the objective function is strongly convex (see Definition 13.4 of strong convexity in the previous chapter). We rely on the following claim, which generalizes Lemma 13.5.

Claim 14.10. *If f is λ-strongly convex then for every $\mathbf{w},\mathbf{u}$ and $\mathbf{v} \in \partial f(\mathbf{w})$ we have*

$$\langle \mathbf{w}-\mathbf{u},\mathbf{v}\rangle \;\geq\; f(\mathbf{w})-f(\mathbf{u})+\tfrac{\lambda}{2}\|\mathbf{w}-\mathbf{u}\|^2.$$

The proof is similar to the proof of Lemma 13.5 and is left as an exercise.

SGD for minimizing a λ-strongly convex function

Goal: Solve $\min_{\mathbf{w}\in\mathcal{H}} f(\mathbf{w})$
parameter: T
initialize: $\mathbf{w}^{(1)} = \mathbf{0}$
for $t = 1, \ldots, T$
  Choose a random vector $\mathbf{v}_t$ s.t. $\mathbb{E}[\mathbf{v}_t|\mathbf{w}^{(t)}] \in \partial f(\mathbf{w}^{(t)})$
  Set $\eta_t = 1/(\lambda t)$
  Set $\mathbf{w}^{(t+\frac{1}{2})} = \mathbf{w}^{(t)} - \eta_t \mathbf{v}_t$
  Set $\mathbf{w}^{(t+1)} = \arg\min_{\mathbf{w}\in\mathcal{H}} \|\mathbf{w} - \mathbf{w}^{(t+\frac{1}{2})}\|^2$
output: $\bar{\mathbf{w}} = \frac{1}{T}\sum_{t=1}^{T} \mathbf{w}^{(t)}$

Theorem 14.11. *Assume that f is λ-strongly convex and that $\mathbb{E}[\|\mathbf{v}_t\|^2] \le \rho^2$. Let $\mathbf{w}^\star \in \operatorname{argmin}_{\mathbf{w}\in\mathcal{H}} f(\mathbf{w})$ be an optimal solution. Then,*

$$\mathbb{E}[f(\bar{\mathbf{w}})] - f(\mathbf{w}^\star) \le \frac{\rho^2}{2\lambda T}(1 + \log(T)).$$

Proof. Let $\nabla^{(t)} = \mathbb{E}[\mathbf{v}_t|\mathbf{w}^{(t)}]$. Since f is strongly convex and $\nabla^{(t)}$ is in the subgradient set of f at $\mathbf{w}^{(t)}$ we have that

$$\langle \mathbf{w}^{(t)} - \mathbf{w}^\star,\ \nabla^{(t)}\rangle \ \ge\ f(\mathbf{w}^{(t)}) - f(\mathbf{w}^\star) + \tfrac{\lambda}{2}\|\mathbf{w}^{(t)} - \mathbf{w}^\star\|^2. \tag{14.11}$$

Next, we show that

$$\langle \mathbf{w}^{(t)} - \mathbf{w}^\star,\ \nabla^{(t)}\rangle \ \le\ \frac{\mathbb{E}[\|\mathbf{w}^{(t)} - \mathbf{w}^\star\|^2 - \|\mathbf{w}^{(t+1)} - \mathbf{w}^\star\|^2]}{2\eta_t} + \frac{\eta_t}{2}\rho^2. \tag{14.12}$$

Since $\mathbf{w}^{(t+1)}$ is the projection of $\mathbf{w}^{(t+\frac{1}{2})}$ onto $\mathcal{H}$, and $\mathbf{w}^\star \in \mathcal{H}$ we have that $\|\mathbf{w}^{(t+\frac{1}{2})} - \mathbf{w}^\star\|^2 \ge \|\mathbf{w}^{(t+1)} - \mathbf{w}^\star\|^2$. Therefore,

$$\begin{aligned}\|\mathbf{w}^{(t)} - \mathbf{w}^\star\|^2 - \|\mathbf{w}^{(t+1)} - \mathbf{w}^\star\|^2 &\ge \|\mathbf{w}^{(t)} - \mathbf{w}^\star\|^2 - \|\mathbf{w}^{(t+\frac{1}{2})} - \mathbf{w}^\star\|^2 \\ &= 2\eta_t\langle \mathbf{w}^{(t)} - \mathbf{w}^\star,\ \mathbf{v}_t\rangle - \eta_t^2\|\mathbf{v}_t\|^2.\end{aligned}$$

Taking expectation of both sides, rearranging, and using the assumption $\mathbb{E}[\|\mathbf{v}_t\|^2] \le \rho^2$ yield Equation (14.12). Comparing Equation (14.11) and Equation (14.12) and summing over t we obtain

$$\begin{aligned}&\sum_{t=1}^{T}(\mathbb{E}[f(\mathbf{w}^{(t)})] - f(\mathbf{w}^\star)) \\ &\le \mathbb{E}\left[\sum_{t=1}^{T}\left(\frac{\|\mathbf{w}^{(t)} - \mathbf{w}^\star\|^2 - \|\mathbf{w}^{(t+1)} - \mathbf{w}^\star\|^2}{2\eta_t} - \tfrac{\lambda}{2}\|\mathbf{w}^{(t)} - \mathbf{w}^\star\|^2\right)\right] + \frac{\rho^2}{2}\sum_{t=1}^{T}\eta_t.\end{aligned}$$

Next, we use the definition $\eta_t = 1/(\lambda t)$ and note that the first sum on the right-hand side of the equation collapses to $-\lambda T\|\mathbf{w}^{(T+1)} - \mathbf{w}^\star\|^2 \le 0$. Thus,

$$\sum_{t=1}^{T}(\mathbb{E}[f(\mathbf{w}^{(t)})] - f(\mathbf{w}^\star)) \le \frac{\rho^2}{2\lambda}\sum_{t=1}^{T}\frac{1}{t} \le \frac{\rho^2}{2\lambda}(1 + \log(T)).$$

The theorem follows from the preceding by dividing by T and using Jensen's inequality. □

Remark 14.3. Rakhlin, Shamir, and Sridharan ((2012)) derived a convergence rate in which the $\log(T)$ term is eliminated for a variant of the algorithm in which we output the average of the last $T/2$ iterates, $\bar{\mathbf{w}} = \frac{2}{T}\sum_{t=T/2+1}^{T}\mathbf{w}^{(t)}$. Shamir and Zhang (2013) have shown that Theorem 14.11 holds even if we output $\bar{\mathbf{w}} = \mathbf{w}^{(T)}$.

14.5 LEARNING WITH SGD

We have so far introduced and analyzed the SGD algorithm for general convex functions. Now we shall consider its applicability to learning tasks.

14.5.1 SGD for Risk Minimization

Recall that in learning we face the problem of minimizing the risk function

$$L_{\mathcal{D}}(\mathbf{w}) = \mathop{\mathbb{E}}_{z\sim\mathcal{D}}[\ell(\mathbf{w}, z)].$$

We have seen the method of empirical risk minimization, where we minimize the empirical risk, $L_S(\mathbf{w})$, as an estimate to minimizing $L_{\mathcal{D}}(\mathbf{w})$. SGD allows us to take a different approach and minimize $L_{\mathcal{D}}(\mathbf{w})$ directly. Since we do not know $\mathcal{D}$, we cannot simply calculate $\nabla L_{\mathcal{D}}(\mathbf{w}^{(t)})$ and minimize it with the GD method. With SGD, however, all we need is to find an unbiased estimate of the gradient of $L_{\mathcal{D}}(\mathbf{w})$, that is, a random vector whose conditional expected value is $\nabla L_{\mathcal{D}}(\mathbf{w}^{(t)})$. We shall now see how such an estimate can be easily constructed.

For simplicity, let us first consider the case of differentiable loss functions. Hence the risk function $L_{\mathcal{D}}$ is also differentiable. The construction of the random vector $\mathbf{v}_t$ will be as follows: First, sample $z \sim \mathcal{D}$. Then, define $\mathbf{v}_t$ to be the gradient of the function $\ell(\mathbf{w}, z)$ with respect to $\mathbf{w}$, at the point $\mathbf{w}^{(t)}$. Then, by the linearity of the gradient we have

$$\mathbb{E}[\mathbf{v}_t|\mathbf{w}^{(t)}] = \mathop{\mathbb{E}}_{z\sim\mathcal{D}}[\nabla\ell(\mathbf{w}^{(t)}, z)] = \nabla \mathop{\mathbb{E}}_{z\sim\mathcal{D}}[\ell(\mathbf{w}^{(t)}, z)] = \nabla L_{\mathcal{D}}(\mathbf{w}^{(t)}). \tag{14.13}$$

The gradient of the loss function $\ell(\mathbf{w}, z)$ at $\mathbf{w}^{(t)}$ is therefore an unbiased estimate of the gradient of the risk function $L_{\mathcal{D}}(\mathbf{w}^{(t)})$ and is easily constructed by sampling a single fresh example $z \sim \mathcal{D}$ at each iteration t.

The same argument holds for nondifferentiable loss functions. We simply let $\mathbf{v}_t$ be a subgradient of $\ell(\mathbf{w}, z)$ at $\mathbf{w}^{(t)}$. Then, for every $\mathbf{u}$ we have

$$\ell(\mathbf{u}, z) - \ell(\mathbf{w}^{(t)}, z) \geq \langle \mathbf{u} - \mathbf{w}^{(t)}, \mathbf{v}_t \rangle.$$

Taking expectation on both sides with respect to $z \sim \mathcal{D}$ and conditioned on the value of $\mathbf{w}^{(t)}$ we obtain

$$\begin{aligned} L_{\mathcal{D}}(\mathbf{u}) - L_{\mathcal{D}}(\mathbf{w}^{(t)}) &= \mathbb{E}[\ell(\mathbf{u}, z) - \ell(\mathbf{w}^{(t)}, z)|\mathbf{w}^{(t)}] \\ &\geq \mathbb{E}[\langle \mathbf{u} - \mathbf{w}^{(t)}, \mathbf{v}_t\rangle|\mathbf{w}^{(t)}] \\ &= \langle \mathbf{u} - \mathbf{w}^{(t)}, \mathbb{E}[\mathbf{v}_t|\mathbf{w}^{(t)}]\rangle. \end{aligned}$$

It follows that $\mathbb{E}[\mathbf{v}_t|\mathbf{w}^{(t)}]$ is a subgradient of $L_{\mathcal{D}}(\mathbf{w})$ at $\mathbf{w}^{(t)}$.

To summarize, the stochastic gradient descent framework for minimizing the risk is as follows.

Stochastic Gradient Descent (SGD) for minimizing $L_{\mathcal{D}}(\mathbf{w})$

parameters: Scalar $\eta > 0$, integer $T > 0$
initialize: $\mathbf{w}^{(1)} = \mathbf{0}$
for $t = 1, 2, \ldots, T$
  sample $z \sim \mathcal{D}$
  pick $\mathbf{v}_t \in \partial \ell(\mathbf{w}^{(t)}, z)$
  update $\mathbf{w}^{(t+1)} = \mathbf{w}^{(t)} - \eta \mathbf{v}_t$
output $\bar{\mathbf{w}} = \frac{1}{T}\sum_{t=1}^{T} \mathbf{w}^{(t)}$

We shall now use our analysis of SGD to obtain a sample complexity analysis for learning convex-Lipschitz-bounded problems. Theorem 14.8 yields the following:

Corollary 14.12. *Consider a convex-Lipschitz-bounded learning problem with parameters ρ, B. Then, for every $\epsilon > 0$, if we run the SGD method for minimizing $L_{\mathcal{D}}(\mathbf{w})$ with a number of iterations (i.e., number of examples)*

$$T \geq \frac{B^2 \rho^2}{\epsilon^2}$$

and with $\eta = \sqrt{\frac{B^2}{\rho^2 T}}$, then the output of SGD satisfies

$$\mathbb{E}[L_{\mathcal{D}}(\bar{\mathbf{w}})] \leq \min_{\mathbf{w} \in \mathcal{H}} L_{\mathcal{D}}(\mathbf{w}) + \epsilon.$$

It is interesting to note that the required sample complexity is of the same order of magnitude as the sample complexity guarantee we derived for regularized loss minimization. In fact, the sample complexity of SGD is even better than what we have derived for regularized loss minimization by a factor of 8.

14.5.2 Analyzing SGD for Convex-Smooth Learning Problems

In the previous chapter we saw that the regularized loss minimization rule also learns the class of convex-smooth-bounded learning problems. We now show that the SGD algorithm can be also used for such problems.

Theorem 14.13. *Assume that for all z, the loss function $\ell(\cdot, z)$ is convex, β-smooth, and nonnegative. Then, if we run the SGD algorithm for minimizing $L_{\mathcal{D}}(\mathbf{w})$ we have that for every $\mathbf{w}^\star$,*

$$\mathbb{E}[L_{\mathcal{D}}(\bar{\mathbf{w}})] \leq \frac{1}{1 - \eta\beta}\left(L_{\mathcal{D}}(\mathbf{w}^\star) + \frac{\|\mathbf{w}^\star\|^2}{2\eta T}\right).$$

Proof. Recall that if a function is β-smooth and nonnegative then it is self-bounded:

$$\|\nabla f(\mathbf{w})\|^2 \leq 2\beta f(\mathbf{w}).$$

To analyze SGD for convex-smooth problems, let us define $z_1, \ldots, z_T$ the random samples of the SGD algorithm, let $f_t(\cdot) = \ell(\cdot, z_t)$, and note that $\mathbf{v}_t = \nabla f_t(\mathbf{w}^{(t)})$. For all t, f_t is a convex function and therefore $f_t(\mathbf{w}^{(t)}) - f_t(\mathbf{w}^\star) \le \langle \mathbf{v}_t, \mathbf{w}^{(t)} - \mathbf{w}^\star \rangle$. Summing over t and using Lemma 14.1 we obtain

$$\sum_{t=1}^{T} (f_t(\mathbf{w}^{(t)}) - f_t(\mathbf{w}^\star)) \le \sum_{t=1}^{T} \langle \mathbf{v}_t, \mathbf{w}^{(t)} - \mathbf{w}^\star \rangle \le \frac{\|\mathbf{w}^\star\|^2}{2\eta} + \frac{\eta}{2} \sum_{t=1}^{T} \|\mathbf{v}_t\|^2.$$

Combining the preceding with the self-boundedness of f_t yields

$$\sum_{t=1}^{T} (f_t(\mathbf{w}^{(t)}) - f_t(\mathbf{w}^\star)) \le \frac{\|\mathbf{w}^\star\|^2}{2\eta} + \eta\beta \sum_{t=1}^{T} f_t(\mathbf{w}^{(t)}).$$

Dividing by T and rearranging, we obtain

$$\frac{1}{T} \sum_{t=1}^{T} f_t(\mathbf{w}^{(t)}) \le \frac{1}{1 - \eta\beta} \left(\frac{1}{T} \sum_{t=1}^{T} f_t(\mathbf{w}^\star) + \frac{\|\mathbf{w}^\star\|^2}{2\eta T} \right).$$

Next, we take expectation of the two sides of the preceding equation with respect to $z_1, \ldots, z_T$. Clearly, $\mathbb{E}[f_t(\mathbf{w}^\star)] = L_\mathcal{D}(\mathbf{w}^\star)$. In addition, using the same argument as in the proof of Theorem 14.8 we have that

$$\mathbb{E}\left[\frac{1}{T} \sum_{t=1}^{T} f_t(\mathbf{w}^{(t)})\right] = \mathbb{E}\left[\frac{1}{T} \sum_{t=1}^{T} L_\mathcal{D}(\mathbf{w}^{(t)})\right] \ge \mathbb{E}[L_\mathcal{D}(\bar{\mathbf{w}})].$$

Combining all we conclude our proof. □

As a direct corollary we obtain:

Corollary 14.14. *Consider a convex-smooth-bounded learning problem with parameters β, B. Assume in addition that $\ell(\mathbf{0}, z) \le 1$ for all $z \in Z$. For every $\epsilon > 0$, set $\eta = \frac{1}{\beta(1+3/\epsilon)}$. Then, running SGD with $T \ge 12B^2\beta/\epsilon^2$ yields*

$$\mathbb{E}[L_\mathcal{D}(\bar{\mathbf{w}})] \le \min_{\mathbf{w} \in \mathcal{H}} L_\mathcal{D}(\mathbf{w}) + \epsilon.$$

14.5.3 SGD for Regularized Loss Minimization

We have shown that SGD enjoys the same worst-case sample complexity bound as regularized loss minimization. However, on some distributions, regularized loss minimization may yield a better solution. Therefore, in some cases we may want to solve the optimization problem associated with regularized loss minimization, namely,[1]

$$\min_{\mathbf{w}} \left(\frac{\lambda}{2} \|\mathbf{w}\|^2 + L_S(\mathbf{w}) \right). \tag{14.14}$$

Since we are dealing with convex learning problems in which the loss function is convex, the preceding problem is also a convex optimization problem that can be solved using SGD as well, as we shall see in this section.

[1] We divided λ by 2 for convenience.

Define $f(\mathbf{w}) = \frac{\lambda}{2}\|\mathbf{w}\|^2 + L_S(\mathbf{w})$. Note that f is a λ-strongly convex function; therefore, we can apply the SGD variant given in Section 14.4.4 (with $\mathcal{H} = \mathbb{R}^d$). To apply this algorithm, we only need to find a way to construct an unbiased estimate of a subgradient of f at $\mathbf{w}^{(t)}$. This is easily done by noting that if we pick z uniformly at random from S, and choose $\mathbf{v}_t \in \partial \ell(\mathbf{w}^{(t)}, z)$ then the expected value of $\lambda \mathbf{w}^{(t)} + \mathbf{v}_t$ is a subgradient of f at $\mathbf{w}^{(t)}$.

To analyze the resulting algorithm, we first rewrite the update rule (assuming that $\mathcal{H} = \mathbb{R}^d$ and therefore the projection step does not matter) as follows

$$
\begin{aligned}
\mathbf{w}^{(t+1)} &= \mathbf{w}^{(t)} - \frac{1}{\lambda t}\left(\lambda \mathbf{w}^{(t)} + \mathbf{v}_t\right) \\
&= \left(1 - \frac{1}{t}\right)\mathbf{w}^{(t)} - \frac{1}{\lambda t}\mathbf{v}_t \\
&= \frac{t-1}{t}\mathbf{w}^{(t)} - \frac{1}{\lambda t}\mathbf{v}_t \\
&= \frac{t-1}{t}\left(\frac{t-2}{t-1}\mathbf{w}^{(t-1)} - \frac{1}{\lambda(t-1)}\mathbf{v}_{t-1}\right) - \frac{1}{\lambda t}\mathbf{v}_t \\
&= -\frac{1}{\lambda t}\sum_{i=1}^{t}\mathbf{v}_i. \qquad (14.15)
\end{aligned}
$$

If we assume that the loss function is ρ-Lipschitz, it follows that for all t we have $\|\mathbf{v}_t\| \le \rho$ and therefore $\|\lambda \mathbf{w}^{(t)}\| \le \rho$, which yields

$$\|\lambda \mathbf{w}^{(t)} + \mathbf{v}_t\| \le 2\rho.$$

Theorem 14.11 therefore tells us that after performing T iterations we have that

$$\mathbb{E}[f(\bar{\mathbf{w}})] - f(\mathbf{w}^\star) \le \frac{4\rho^2}{\lambda T}(1 + \log(T)).$$

14.6 SUMMARY

We have introduced the Gradient Descent and Stochastic Gradient Descent algorithms, along with several of their variants. We have analyzed their convergence rate and calculated the number of iterations that would guarantee an expected objective of at most ϵ plus the optimal objective. Most importantly, we have shown that by using SGD we can directly minimize the risk function. We do so by sampling a point i.i.d from $\mathcal{D}$ and using a subgradient of the loss of the current hypothesis $\mathbf{w}^{(t)}$ at this point as an unbiased estimate of the gradient (or a subgradient) of the risk function. This implies that a bound on the number of iterations also yields a sample complexity bound. Finally, we have also shown how to apply the SGD method to the problem of regularized risk minimization. In future chapters we show how this yields extremely simple solvers to some optimization problems associated with regularized risk minimization.

14.7 BIBLIOGRAPHIC REMARKS

SGD dates back to Robbins and Monro (1951). It is especially effective in large scale machine learning problems. See, for example, (Murata 1998, Le Cun 2004, Zhang 2004, Bottou & Bousquet 2008, Shalev-Shwartz, Singer & Srebro 2007, Shalev-Shwartz & Srebro 2008). In the optimization community it was studied in the context of *stochastic optimization*. See, for example, (Nemirovski & Yudin 1978, Nesterov & Nesterov 2004, Nesterov 2005, Nemirovski, Juditsky, Lan & Shapiro 2009, Shapiro, Dentcheva & Ruszczyński 2009).

The bound we have derived for strongly convex function is due to Hazan, Agarwal, and Kale (2007). As mentioned previously, improved bounds have been obtained in Rakhlin, Shamir & Sridharan (2012).

14.8 EXERCISES

14.1 Prove Claim 14.10. *Hint:* Extend the proof of Lemma 13.5.

14.2 Prove Corollary 14.14.

14.3 **Perceptron as a subgradient descent algorithm:** Let $S = ((\mathbf{x}_1, y_1), \ldots, (\mathbf{x}_m, y_m)) \in (\mathbb{R}^d \times \{\pm 1\})^m$. Assume that there exists $\mathbf{w} \in \mathbb{R}^d$ such that for every $i \in [m]$ we have $y_i \langle \mathbf{w}, \mathbf{x}_i \rangle \geq 1$, and let $\mathbf{w}^\star$ be a vector that has the minimal norm among all vectors that satisfy the preceding requirement. Let $R = \max_i \|\mathbf{x}_i\|$. Define a function

$$f(\mathbf{w}) = \max_{i \in [m]} (1 - y_i \langle \mathbf{w}, \mathbf{x}_i \rangle).$$

- Show that $\min_{\mathbf{w}:\|\mathbf{w}\| \leq \|\mathbf{w}^\star\|} f(\mathbf{w}) = 0$ and show that any $\mathbf{w}$ for which $f(\mathbf{w}) < 1$ separates the examples in S.
- Show how to calculate a subgradient of f.
- Describe and analyze the subgradient descent algorithm for this case. Compare the algorithm and the analysis to the Batch Perceptron algorithm given in Section 9.1.2.

14.4 **Variable step size (*):** Prove an analog of Theorem 14.8 for SGD with a variable step size, $\eta_t = \frac{B}{\rho\sqrt{t}}$.

15

Support Vector Machines

In this chapter and the next we discuss a very useful machine learning tool: the support vector machine paradigm (SVM) for learning linear predictors in high dimensional feature spaces. The high dimensionality of the feature space raises both sample complexity and computational complexity challenges.

The SVM algorithmic paradigm tackles the sample complexity challenge by searching for "large margin" separators. Roughly speaking, a halfspace separates a training set with a large margin if all the examples are not only on the correct side of the separating hyperplane but also far away from it. Restricting the algorithm to output a large margin separator can yield a small sample complexity even if the dimensionality of the feature space is high (and even infinite). We introduce the concept of margin and relate it to the regularized loss minimization paradigm as well as to the convergence rate of the Perceptron algorithm.

In the next chapter we will tackle the computational complexity challenge using the idea of *kernels*.

15.1 MARGIN AND HARD-SVM

Let $S = (\mathbf{x}_1, y_1), \ldots, (\mathbf{x}_m, y_m)$ be a training set of examples, where each $\mathbf{x}_i \in \mathbb{R}^d$ and $y_i \in \{\pm 1\}$. We say that this training set is linearly separable, if there exists a halfspace, $(\mathbf{w}, b)$, such that $y_i = \mathrm{sign}(\langle \mathbf{w}, \mathbf{x}_i \rangle + b)$ for all i. Alternatively, this condition can be rewritten as

$$\forall i \in [m], \quad y_i(\langle \mathbf{w}, \mathbf{x}_i \rangle + b) > 0.$$

All halfspaces $(\mathbf{w}, b)$ that satisfy this condition are ERM hypotheses (their 0-1 error is zero, which is the minimum possible error). For any separable training sample, there are many ERM halfspaces. Which one of them should the learner pick?

Consider, for example, the training set described in the picture that follows.

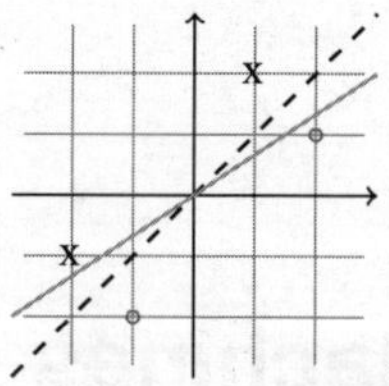

While both the dashed and solid hyperplanes separate the four examples, our intuition would probably lead us to prefer the dashed hyperplane over the solid one. One way to formalize this intuition is using the concept of *margin*.

The margin of a hyperplane with respect to a training set is defined to be the minimal distance between a point in the training set and the hyperplane. If a hyperplane has a large margin, then it will still separate the training set even if we slightly perturb each instance.

We will see later on that the true error of a halfspace can be bounded in terms of the margin it has over the training sample (the larger the margin, the smaller the error), regardless of the Euclidean dimension in which this halfspace resides.

Hard-SVM is the learning rule in which we return an ERM hyperplane that separates the training set with the largest possible margin. To define Hard-SVM formally, we first express the distance between a point $\mathbf{x}$ to a hyperplane using the parameters defining the halfspace.

Claim 15.1. *The distance between a point* $\mathbf{x}$ *and the hyperplane defined by* $(\mathbf{w}, b)$ *where* $\|\mathbf{w}\| = 1$ *is* $|\langle \mathbf{w}, \mathbf{x} \rangle + b|$.

Proof. The distance between a point $\mathbf{x}$ and the hyperplane is defined as

$$\min\{\|\mathbf{x} - \mathbf{v}\| : \langle \mathbf{w}, \mathbf{v} \rangle + b = 0\}.$$

Taking $\mathbf{v} = \mathbf{x} - (\langle \mathbf{w}, \mathbf{x} \rangle + b)\mathbf{w}$ we have that

$$\langle \mathbf{w}, \mathbf{v} \rangle + b = \langle \mathbf{w}, \mathbf{x} \rangle - (\langle \mathbf{w}, \mathbf{x} \rangle + b)\|\mathbf{w}\|^2 + b = 0,$$

and

$$\|\mathbf{x} - \mathbf{v}\| = |\langle \mathbf{w}, \mathbf{x} \rangle + b|\, \|\mathbf{w}\| = |\langle \mathbf{w}, \mathbf{x} \rangle + b|.$$

Hence, the distance is at most $|\langle \mathbf{w}, \mathbf{x} \rangle + b|$. Next, take any other point $\mathbf{u}$ on the hyperplane, thus $\langle \mathbf{w}, \mathbf{u} \rangle + b = 0$. We have

$$\begin{aligned}
\|\mathbf{x} - \mathbf{u}\|^2 &= \|\mathbf{x} - \mathbf{v} + \mathbf{v} - \mathbf{u}\|^2 \\
&= \|\mathbf{x} - \mathbf{v}\|^2 + \|\mathbf{v} - \mathbf{u}\|^2 + 2\langle \mathbf{x} - \mathbf{v}, \mathbf{v} - \mathbf{u} \rangle \\
&\geq \|\mathbf{x} - \mathbf{v}\|^2 + 2\langle \mathbf{x} - \mathbf{v}, \mathbf{v} - \mathbf{u} \rangle \\
&= \|\mathbf{x} - \mathbf{v}\|^2 + 2(\langle \mathbf{w}, \mathbf{x} \rangle + b)\langle \mathbf{w}, \mathbf{v} - \mathbf{u} \rangle \\
&= \|\mathbf{x} - \mathbf{v}\|^2,
\end{aligned}$$

where the last equality is because $\langle \mathbf{w}, \mathbf{v} \rangle = \langle \mathbf{w}, \mathbf{u} \rangle = -b$. Hence, the distance between $\mathbf{x}$ and $\mathbf{u}$ is at least the distance between $\mathbf{x}$ and $\mathbf{v}$, which concludes our proof. □

On the basis of the preceding claim, the closest point in the training set to the separating hyperplane is $\min_{i\in[m]} |\langle \mathbf{w}, \mathbf{x}_i\rangle + b|$. Therefore, the Hard-SVM rule is

$$\underset{(\mathbf{w},b):\|\mathbf{w}\|=1}{\operatorname{argmax}} \ \min_{i\in[m]} |\langle \mathbf{w}, \mathbf{x}_i\rangle + b| \quad \text{s.t.} \quad \forall i, \ y_i(\langle \mathbf{w}, \mathbf{x}_i\rangle + b) > 0.$$

Whenever there is a solution to the preceding problem (i.e., we are in the separable case), we can write an equivalent problem as follows (see Exercise 15.1):

$$\underset{(\mathbf{w},b):\|\mathbf{w}\|=1}{\operatorname{argmax}} \ \min_{i\in[m]} y_i(\langle \mathbf{w}, \mathbf{x}_i\rangle + b). \tag{15.1}$$

Next, we give another equivalent formulation of the Hard-SVM rule as a quadratic optimization problem.[1]

Hard-SVM

input: $(\mathbf{x}_1, y_1), \ldots, (\mathbf{x}_m, y_m)$
solve:

$$(\mathbf{w}_0, b_0) = \underset{(\mathbf{w},b)}{\operatorname{argmin}} \|\mathbf{w}\|^2 \ \text{s.t.} \ \forall i, \ y_i(\langle \mathbf{w}, \mathbf{x}_i\rangle + b) \geq 1 \tag{15.2}$$

output: $\hat{\mathbf{w}} = \frac{\mathbf{w}_0}{\|\mathbf{w}_0\|}, \ \hat{b} = \frac{b_0}{\|\mathbf{w}_0\|}$

The lemma that follows shows that the output of hard-SVM is indeed the separating hyperplane with the largest margin. Intuitively, hard-SVM searches for $\mathbf{w}$ of minimal norm among all the vectors that separate the data and for which $|\langle \mathbf{w}, \mathbf{x}_i\rangle + b| \geq 1$ for all i. In other words, we enforce the margin to be 1, but now the units in which we measure the margin scale with the norm of $\mathbf{w}$. Therefore, finding the largest margin halfspace boils down to finding $\mathbf{w}$ whose norm is minimal. Formally:

Lemma 15.2. *The output of Hard-SVM is a solution of Equation (15.1).*

Proof. Let $(\mathbf{w}^\star, b^\star)$ be a solution of Equation (15.1) and define the margin achieved by $(\mathbf{w}^\star, b^\star)$ to be $\gamma^\star = \min_{i\in[m]} y_i(\langle \mathbf{w}^\star, \mathbf{x}_i\rangle + b^\star)$. Therefore, for all i we have

$$y_i(\langle \mathbf{w}^\star, \mathbf{x}_i\rangle + b^\star) \geq \gamma^\star$$

or equivalently

$$y_i(\langle \tfrac{\mathbf{w}^\star}{\gamma^\star}, \mathbf{x}_i\rangle + \tfrac{b^\star}{\gamma^\star}) \geq 1.$$

Hence, the pair $(\frac{\mathbf{w}^\star}{\gamma^\star}, \frac{b^\star}{\gamma^\star})$ satisfies the conditions of the quadratic optimization problem given in Equation (15.2). Therefore, $\|\mathbf{w}_0\| \leq \|\frac{\mathbf{w}^\star}{\gamma^\star}\| = \frac{1}{\gamma^\star}$. It follows that for all i,

$$y_i(\langle \hat{\mathbf{w}}, \mathbf{x}_i\rangle + \hat{b}) = \frac{1}{\|\mathbf{w}_0\|} y_i(\langle \mathbf{w}_0, \mathbf{x}_i\rangle + b_0) \geq \frac{1}{\|\mathbf{w}_0\|} \geq \gamma^\star.$$

Since $\|\hat{\mathbf{w}}\| = 1$ we obtain that $(\hat{\mathbf{w}}, \hat{b})$ is an optimal solution of Equation (15.1). □

[1] A quadratic optimization problem is an optimization problem in which the objective is a convex quadratic function and the constraints are linear inequalities.

15.1.1 The Homogenous Case

It is often more convenient to consider homogenous halfspaces, namely, halfspaces that pass through the origin and are thus defined by $\text{sign}(\langle \mathbf{w}, \mathbf{x} \rangle)$, where the bias term b is set to be zero. Hard-SVM for homogenous halfspaces amounts to solving

$$\min_{\mathbf{w}} \|\mathbf{w}\|^2 \quad \text{s.t.} \quad \forall i, \; y_i \langle \mathbf{w}, \mathbf{x}_i \rangle \geq 1. \tag{15.3}$$

As we discussed in Chapter 9, we can reduce the problem of learning nonhomogenous halfspaces to the problem of learning homogenous halfspaces by adding one more feature to each instance of $\mathbf{x}_i$, thus increasing the dimension to $d+1$.

Note, however, that the optimization problem given in Equation (15.2) does not regularize the bias term b, while if we learn a homogenous halfspace in $\mathbb{R}^{d+1}$ using Equation (15.3) then we regularize the bias term (i.e., the $d+1$ component of the weight vector) as well. However, regularizing b usually does not make a significant difference to the sample complexity.

15.1.2 The Sample Complexity of Hard-SVM

Recall that the VC-dimension of halfspaces in $\mathbb{R}^d$ is $d+1$. It follows that the sample complexity of learning halfspaces grows with the dimensionality of the problem. Furthermore, the fundamental theorem of learning tells us that if the number of examples is significantly smaller than d/ϵ then no algorithm can learn an ϵ-accurate halfspace. This is problematic when d is very large.

To overcome this problem, we will make an additional assumption on the underlying data distribution. In particular, we will define a "separability with margin γ" assumption and will show that if the data is separable with margin γ then the sample complexity is bounded from above by a function of $1/\gamma^2$. It follows that even if the dimensionality is very large (or even infinite), as long as the data adheres to the separability with margin assumption we can still have a small sample complexity. There is no contradiction to the lower bound given in the fundamental theorem of learning because we are now making an additional assumption on the underlying data distribution.

Before we formally define the separability with margin assumption, there is a scaling issue we need to resolve. Suppose that a training set $S = (\mathbf{x}_1, y_1), \ldots, (\mathbf{x}_m, y_m)$ is separable with a margin γ; namely, the maximal objective value of Equation (15.1) is at least γ. Then, for any positive scalar $\alpha > 0$, the training set $S' = (\alpha\mathbf{x}_1, y_1), \ldots, (\alpha\mathbf{x}_m, y_m)$ is separable with a margin of $\alpha\gamma$. That is, a simple scaling of the data can make it separable with an arbitrarily large margin. It follows that in order to give a meaningful definition of margin we must take into account the scale of the examples as well. One way to formalize this is using the definition that follows.

Definition 15.3. Let $\mathcal{D}$ be a distribution over $\mathbb{R}^d \times \{\pm 1\}$. We say that $\mathcal{D}$ is separable with a (γ, ρ)-margin if there exists $(\mathbf{w}^\star, b^\star)$ such that $\|\mathbf{w}^\star\| = 1$ and such that with probability 1 over the choice of $(\mathbf{x}, y) \sim \mathcal{D}$ we have that $y(\langle \mathbf{w}^\star, \mathbf{x} \rangle + b^\star) \geq \gamma$ and $\|\mathbf{x}\| \leq \rho$. Similarly, we say that $\mathcal{D}$ is separable with a (γ, ρ)-margin using a homogenous halfspace if the preceding holds with a halfspace of the form $(\mathbf{w}^\star, 0)$.

In the advanced part of the book (Chapter 26), we will prove that the sample complexity of Hard-SVM depends on $(\rho/\gamma)^2$ and is independent of the dimension d. In particular, Theorem 26.13 in Section 26.3 states the following:

Theorem 15.4. *Let $\mathcal{D}$ be a distribution over $\mathbb{R}^d \times \{\pm 1\}$ that satisfies the (γ, ρ)-separability with margin assumption using a homogenous halfspace. Then, with probability of at least $1-\delta$ over the choice of a training set of size m, the 0-1 error of the output of Hard-SVM is at most*

$$\sqrt{\frac{4(\rho/\gamma)^2}{m}} + \sqrt{\frac{2\log(2/\delta)}{m}}.$$

Remark 15.1 (Margin and the Perceptron). In Section 9.1.2 we have described and analyzed the Perceptron algorithm for finding an ERM hypothesis with respect to the class of halfspaces. In particular, in Theorem 9.1 we upper bounded the number of updates the Perceptron might make on a given training set. It can be shown (see Exercise 15.2) that the upper bound is exactly $(\rho/\gamma)^2$, where ρ is the radius of examples and γ is the margin.

15.2 SOFT-SVM AND NORM REGULARIZATION

The Hard-SVM formulation assumes that the training set is linearly separable, which is a rather strong assumption. Soft-SVM can be viewed as a relaxation of the Hard-SVM rule that can be applied even if the training set is not linearly separable.

The optimization problem in Equation (15.2) enforces the hard constraints $y_i(\langle \mathbf{w}, \mathbf{x}_i\rangle + b) \geq 1$ for all i. A natural relaxation is to allow the constraint to be violated for some of the examples in the training set. This can be modeled by introducing nonnegative slack variables, $\xi_1, \ldots, \xi_m$, and replacing each constraint $y_i(\langle \mathbf{w}, \mathbf{x}_i\rangle + b) \geq 1$ by the constraint $y_i(\langle \mathbf{w}, \mathbf{x}_i\rangle + b) \geq 1 - \xi_i$. That is, ξ_i measures by how much the constraint $y_i(\langle \mathbf{w}, \mathbf{x}_i\rangle + b) \geq 1$ is being violated. Soft-SVM jointly minimizes the norm of $\mathbf{w}$ (corresponding to the margin) and the average of ξ_i (corresponding to the violations of the constraints). The tradeoff between the two terms is controlled by a parameter λ. This leads to the Soft-SVM optimization problem:

Soft-SVM

input: $(\mathbf{x}_1, y_1), \ldots, (\mathbf{x}_m, y_m)$
parameter: $\lambda > 0$
solve:

$$\min_{\mathbf{w},b,\xi} \left(\lambda \|\mathbf{w}\|^2 + \frac{1}{m}\sum_{i=1}^m \xi_i \right) \tag{15.4}$$
$$\text{s.t. } \forall i,\;\; y_i(\langle \mathbf{w}, \mathbf{x}_i\rangle + b) \geq 1 - \xi_i \;\text{ and }\; \xi_i \geq 0$$

output: $\mathbf{w}, b$

We can rewrite Equation (15.4) as a regularized loss minimization problem. Recall the definition of the hinge loss:

$$\ell^{\text{hinge}}((\mathbf{w},b),(\mathbf{x},y)) = \max\{0, 1 - y(\langle \mathbf{w},\mathbf{x}\rangle + b)\}.$$

Given $(\mathbf{w},b)$ and a training set S, the averaged hinge loss on S is denoted by $L_S^{\text{hinge}}((\mathbf{w},b))$. Now, consider the regularized loss minimization problem:

$$\min_{\mathbf{w},b} \left(\lambda\|\mathbf{w}\|^2 + L_S^{\text{hinge}}((\mathbf{w},b))\right). \tag{15.5}$$

Claim 15.5. *Equation (15.4) and Equation (15.5) are equivalent.*

Proof. Fix some $\mathbf{w}, b$ and consider the minimization over $\boldsymbol{\xi}$ in Equation (15.4). Fix some i. Since ξ_i must be nonnegative, the best assignment to ξ_i would be 0 if $y_i(\langle \mathbf{w},\mathbf{x}_i\rangle + b) \geq 1$ and would be $1 - y_i(\langle \mathbf{w},\mathbf{x}_i\rangle + b)$ otherwise. In other words, $\xi_i = \ell^{\text{hinge}}((\mathbf{w},b),(\mathbf{x}_i,y_i))$ for all i, and the claim follows. □

We therefore see that Soft-SVM falls into the paradigm of regularized loss minimization that we studied in the previous chapter. A Soft-SVM algorithm, that is, a solution for Equation (15.5), has a bias toward low norm separators. The objective function that we aim to minimize in Equation (15.5) penalizes not only for training errors but also for large norm.

It is often more convenient to consider Soft-SVM for learning a homogenous halfspace, where the bias term b is set to be zero, which yields the following optimization problem:

$$\min_{\mathbf{w}} \left(\lambda\|\mathbf{w}\|^2 + L_S^{\text{hinge}}(\mathbf{w})\right), \tag{15.6}$$

where

$$L_S^{\text{hinge}}(\mathbf{w}) = \frac{1}{m}\sum_{i=1}^{m} \max\{0, 1 - y\langle \mathbf{w},\mathbf{x}_i\rangle\}.$$

15.2.1 The Sample Complexity of Soft-SVM

We now analyze the sample complexity of Soft-SVM for the case of homogenous halfspaces (namely, the output of Equation (15.6)). In Corollary 13.8 we derived a generalization bound for the regularized loss minimization framework assuming that the loss function is convex and Lipschitz. We have already shown that the hinge loss is convex so it is only left to analyze the Lipschitzness of the hinge loss.

Claim 15.6. *Let $f(\mathbf{w}) = \max\{0, 1 - y\langle \mathbf{w},\mathbf{x}\rangle\}$. Then, f is $\|\mathbf{x}\|$-Lipschitz.*

Proof. It is easy to verify that any subgradient of f at $\mathbf{w}$ is of the form $\alpha\mathbf{x}$ where $|\alpha| \leq 1$. The claim now follows from Lemma 14.7. □

Corollary 13.8 therefore yields the following:

Corollary 15.7. *Let $\mathcal{D}$ be a distribution over $\mathcal{X} \times \{0,1\}$, where $\mathcal{X} = \{\mathbf{x} : \|\mathbf{x}\| \leq \rho\}$. Consider running Soft-SVM (Equation (15.6)) on a training set $S \sim \mathcal{D}^m$ and let $A(S)$ be the solution of Soft-SVM. Then, for every $\mathbf{u}$,*

$$\mathop{\mathbb{E}}_{S\sim\mathcal{D}^m}[L_{\mathcal{D}}^{\text{hinge}}(A(S))] \leq L_{\mathcal{D}}^{\text{hinge}}(\mathbf{u}) + \lambda\|\mathbf{u}\|^2 + \frac{2\rho^2}{\lambda m}.$$

Furthermore, since the hinge loss upper bounds the 0−1 *loss we also have*

$$\mathop{\mathbb{E}}_{S\sim\mathcal{D}^m}[L_{\mathcal{D}}^{0-1}(A(S))] \leq L_{\mathcal{D}}^{\text{hinge}}(\mathbf{u}) + \lambda\|\mathbf{u}\|^2 + \frac{2\rho^2}{\lambda m}.$$

Last, for every $B > 0$*, if we set* $\lambda = \sqrt{\frac{2\rho^2}{B^2 m}}$ *then*

$$\mathop{\mathbb{E}}_{S\sim\mathcal{D}^m}[L_{\mathcal{D}}^{0-1}(A(S))] \leq \mathop{\mathbb{E}}_{S\sim\mathcal{D}^m}[L_{\mathcal{D}}^{\text{hinge}}(A(S))] \leq \min_{\mathbf{w}:\|\mathbf{w}\|\leq B} L_{\mathcal{D}}^{\text{hinge}}(\mathbf{w}) + \sqrt{\frac{8\rho^2 B^2}{m}}.$$

We therefore see that we can control the sample complexity of learning a halfspace as a function of the norm of that halfspace, independently of the Euclidean dimension of the space over which the halfspace is defined. This becomes highly significant when we learn via embeddings into high dimensional feature spaces, as we will consider in the next chapter.

Remark 15.2. The condition that $\mathcal{X}$ will contain vectors with a bounded norm follows from the requirement that the loss function will be Lipschitz. This is not just a technicality. As we discussed before, separation with large margin is meaningless without imposing a restriction on the scale of the instances. Indeed, without a constraint on the scale, we can always enlarge the margin by multiplying all instances by a large scalar.

15.2.2 Margin and Norm-Based Bounds versus Dimension

The bounds we have derived for Hard-SVM and Soft-SVM do not depend on the dimension of the instance space. Instead, the bounds depend on the norm of the examples, ρ, the norm of the halfspace B (or equivalently the margin parameter γ) and, in the nonseparable case, the bounds also depend on the minimum hinge loss of all halfspaces of norm $\leq B$. In contrast, the VC-dimension of the class of homogenous halfspaces is d, which implies that the error of an ERM hypothesis decreases as $\sqrt{d/m}$ does. We now give an example in which $\rho^2 B^2 \ll d$; hence the bound given in Corollary 15.7 is much better than the VC bound.

Consider the problem of learning to classify a short text document according to its topic, say, whether the document is about sports or not. We first need to represent documents as vectors. One simple yet effective way is to use a *bag-of-words* representation. That is, we define a dictionary of words and set the dimension d to be the number of words in the dictionary. Given a document, we represent it as a vector $\mathbf{x} \in \{0,1\}^d$, where $x_i = 1$ if the i'th word in the dictionary appears in the document and $x_i = 0$ otherwise. Therefore, for this problem, the value of ρ^2 will be the maximal number of distinct words in a given document.

A halfspace for this problem assigns weights to words. It is natural to assume that by assigning positive and negative weights to a few dozen words we will be able to determine whether a given document is about sports or not with reasonable accuracy. Therefore, for this problem, the value of B^2 can be set to be less than 100. Overall, it is reasonable to say that the value of $B^2\rho^2$ is smaller than 10,000.

On the other hand, a typical size of a dictionary is much larger than 10,000. For example, there are more than 100,000 distinct words in English. We have therefore shown a problem in which there can be an order of magnitude difference between learning a halfspace with the SVM rule and learning a halfspace using the vanilla ERM rule.

Of course, it is possible to construct problems in which the SVM bound will be worse than the VC bound. When we use SVM, we in fact introduce another form of inductive bias – we prefer large margin halfspaces. While this inductive bias can significantly decrease our estimation error, it can also enlarge the approximation error.

15.2.3 The Ramp Loss*

The margin-based bounds we have derived in Corollary 15.7 rely on the fact that we minimize the hinge loss. As we have shown in the previous subsection, the term $\sqrt{\rho^2 B^2/m}$ can be much smaller than the corresponding term in the VC bound, $\sqrt{d/m}$. However, the approximation error in Corollary 15.7 is measured with respect to the hinge loss while the approximation error in VC bounds is measured with respect to the 0–1 loss. Since the hinge loss upper bounds the 0–1 loss, the approximation error with respect to the 0–1 loss will never exceed that of the hinge loss.

It is not possible to derive bounds that involve the estimation error term $\sqrt{\rho^2 B^2/m}$ for the 0–1 loss. This follows from the fact that the 0–1 loss is scale insensitive, and therefore there is no meaning to the norm of **w** or its margin when we measure error with the 0–1 loss. However, it is possible to define a loss function that on one hand it is scale sensitive and thus enjoys the estimation error $\sqrt{\rho^2 B^2/m}$ while on the other hand it is more similar to the 0–1 loss. One option is the *ramp loss*, defined as

$$\ell^{\text{ramp}}(\mathbf{w}, (\mathbf{x}, y)) = \min\{1, \ell^{\text{hinge}}(\mathbf{w}, (\mathbf{x}, y))\} = \min\{1\,,\, \max\{0, 1 - y\langle \mathbf{w}, \mathbf{x}\rangle\}\}.$$

The ramp loss penalizes mistakes in the same way as the 0–1 loss and does not penalize examples that are separated with margin. The difference between the ramp loss and the 0–1 loss is only with respect to examples that are correctly classified but not with a significant margin. Generalization bounds for the ramp loss are given in the advanced part of this book (see Appendix 26.3).

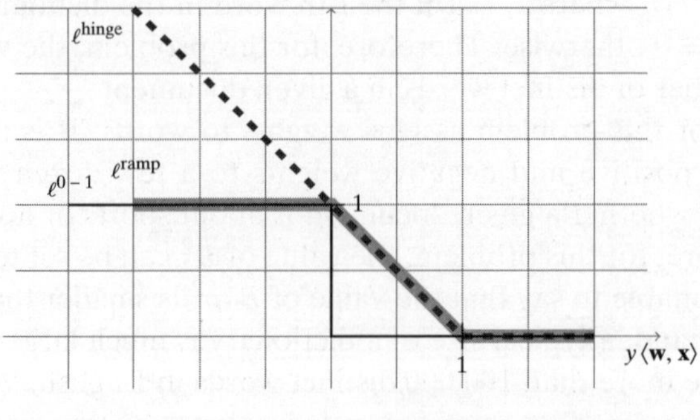

The reason SVM relies on the hinge loss and not on the ramp loss is that the hinge loss is convex and, therefore, from the *computational* point of view, minimizing the hinge loss can be performed efficiently. In contrast, the problem of minimizing the ramp loss is computationally intractable.

15.3 OPTIMALITY CONDITIONS AND "SUPPORT VECTORS"*

The name "Support Vector Machine" stems from the fact that the solution of hard-SVM, $\mathbf{w}_0$, is supported by (i.e., is in the linear span of) the examples that are exactly at distance $1/\|\mathbf{w}_0\|$ from the separating hyperplane. These vectors are therefore called *support vectors*. To see this, we rely on **Fritz John optimality conditions.**

Theorem 15.8. *Let $\mathbf{w}_0$ be as defined in Equation (15.3) and let $I = \{i : |\langle \mathbf{w}_0, \mathbf{x}_i\rangle| = 1\}$. Then, there exist coefficients $\alpha_1, \ldots, \alpha_m$ such that*

$$\mathbf{w}_0 = \sum_{i \in I} \alpha_i \mathbf{x}_i .$$

The examples $\{\mathbf{x}_i : i \in I\}$ are called *support vectors.*

The proof of this theorem follows by applying the following lemma to Equation (15.3).

Lemma 15.9 (Fritz John). *Suppose that*

$$\mathbf{w}^\star \in \operatorname*{argmin}_{\mathbf{w}} f(\mathbf{w}) \quad \text{s.t. } \forall i \in [m],\ g_i(\mathbf{w}) \le 0,$$

where $f, g_1, \ldots, g_m$ are differentiable. Then, there exists $\boldsymbol{\alpha} \in \mathbb{R}^m$ such that $\nabla f(\mathbf{w}^\star) + \sum_{i \in I} \alpha_i \nabla g_i(\mathbf{w}^\star) = \mathbf{0}$, where $I = \{i : g_i(\mathbf{w}^\star) = 0\}$.

15.4 DUALITY*

Historically, many of the properties of SVM have been obtained by considering the *dual* of Equation (15.3). Our presentation of SVM does not rely on duality. For completeness, we present in the following how to derive the dual of Equation (15.3).

We start by rewriting the problem in an equivalent form as follows. Consider the function

$$g(\mathbf{w}) = \max_{\boldsymbol{\alpha} \in \mathbb{R}^m : \boldsymbol{\alpha} \ge \mathbf{0}} \sum_{i=1}^{m} \alpha_i (1 - y_i \langle \mathbf{w}, \mathbf{x}_i \rangle) = \begin{cases} 0 & \text{if } \forall i,\ y_i \langle \mathbf{w}, \mathbf{x}_i \rangle \ge 1 \\ \infty & \text{otherwise} \end{cases} .$$

We can therefore rewrite Equation (15.3) as

$$\min_{\mathbf{w}} \left(\|\mathbf{w}\|^2 + g(\mathbf{w}) \right). \tag{15.7}$$

Rearranging the preceding we obtain that Equation (15.3) can be rewritten as the problem

$$\min_{\mathbf{w}} \max_{\boldsymbol{\alpha} \in \mathbb{R}^m : \boldsymbol{\alpha} \ge \mathbf{0}} \left(\frac{1}{2} \|\mathbf{w}\|^2 + \sum_{i=1}^{m} \alpha_i (1 - y_i \langle \mathbf{w}, \mathbf{x}_i \rangle) \right). \tag{15.8}$$

Now suppose that we flip the order of min and max in the equation. This can only decrease the objective value (see Exercise 15.4), and we have

$$\min_{\mathbf{w}} \max_{\boldsymbol{\alpha}\in\mathbb{R}^m:\boldsymbol{\alpha}\geq\mathbf{0}} \left(\frac{1}{2}\|\mathbf{w}\|^2 + \sum_{i=1}^m \alpha_i(1 - y_i\langle\mathbf{w},\mathbf{x}_i\rangle)\right)$$

$$\geq \max_{\boldsymbol{\alpha}\in\mathbb{R}^m:\boldsymbol{\alpha}\geq\mathbf{0}} \min_{\mathbf{w}} \left(\frac{1}{2}\|\mathbf{w}\|^2 + \sum_{i=1}^m \alpha_i(1 - y_i\langle\mathbf{w},\mathbf{x}_i\rangle)\right).$$

The preceding inequality is called *weak duality*. It turns out that in our case, *strong duality* also holds; namely, the inequality holds with equality. Therefore, the *dual* problem is

$$\max_{\boldsymbol{\alpha}\in\mathbb{R}^m:\boldsymbol{\alpha}\geq\mathbf{0}} \min_{\mathbf{w}} \left(\frac{1}{2}\|\mathbf{w}\|^2 + \sum_{i=1}^m \alpha_i(1 - y_i\langle\mathbf{w},\mathbf{x}_i\rangle)\right). \tag{15.9}$$

We can simplify the dual problem by noting that once $\boldsymbol{\alpha}$ is fixed, the optimization problem with respect to $\mathbf{w}$ is unconstrained and the objective is differentiable; thus, at the optimum, the gradient equals zero:

$$\mathbf{w} - \sum_{i=1}^m \alpha_i y_i \mathbf{x}_i = 0 \;\Rightarrow\; \mathbf{w} = \sum_{i=1}^m \alpha_i y_i \mathbf{x}_i.$$

This shows us that the solution must be in the linear span of the examples, a fact we will use later to derive SVM with kernels. Plugging the preceding into Equation (15.9) we obtain that the dual problem can be rewritten as

$$\max_{\boldsymbol{\alpha}\in\mathbb{R}^m:\boldsymbol{\alpha}\geq\mathbf{0}} \left(\frac{1}{2}\left\|\sum_{i=1}^m \alpha_i y_i \mathbf{x}_i\right\|^2 + \sum_{i=1}^m \alpha_i\left(1 - y_i\left\langle\sum_j \alpha_j y_j \mathbf{x}_j, \mathbf{x}_i\right\rangle\right)\right). \tag{15.10}$$

Rearranging yields the dual problem

$$\max_{\boldsymbol{\alpha}\in\mathbb{R}^m:\boldsymbol{\alpha}\geq\mathbf{0}} \left(\sum_{i=1}^m \alpha_i - \frac{1}{2}\sum_{i=1}^m\sum_{j=1}^m \alpha_i\alpha_j y_i y_j\langle\mathbf{x}_j,\mathbf{x}_i\rangle\right). \tag{15.11}$$

Note that the dual problem only involves inner products between instances and does not require direct access to specific elements within an instance. This property is important when implementing SVM with kernels, as we will discuss in the next chapter.

15.5 IMPLEMENTING SOFT-SVM USING SGD

In this section we describe a very simple algorithm for solving the optimization problem of Soft-SVM, namely,

$$\min_{\mathbf{w}} \left(\frac{\lambda}{2}\|\mathbf{w}\|^2 + \frac{1}{m}\sum_{i=1}^m \max\{0, 1 - y\langle\mathbf{w},\mathbf{x}_i\rangle\}\right). \tag{15.12}$$

We rely on the SGD framework for solving regularized loss minimization problems, as described in Section 14.5.3.

Recall that, on the basis of Equation (14.15), we can rewrite the update rule of SGD as

$$\mathbf{w}^{(t+1)} = -\frac{1}{\lambda t}\sum_{j=1}^{t} \mathbf{v}_j,$$

where $\mathbf{v}_j$ is a subgradient of the loss function at $\mathbf{w}^{(j)}$ on the random example chosen at iteration j. For the hinge loss, given an example $(\mathbf{x}, y)$, we can choose $\mathbf{v}_j$ to be $\mathbf{0}$ if $y\langle \mathbf{w}^{(j)}, \mathbf{x}\rangle \geq 1$ and $\mathbf{v}_j = -y\,\mathbf{x}$ otherwise (see Example 14.2). Denoting $\boldsymbol{\theta}^{(t)} = -\sum_{j<t} \mathbf{v}_j$ we obtain the following procedure.

SGD for Solving Soft-SVM

goal: Solve Equation (15.12)
parameter: T
initialize: $\boldsymbol{\theta}^{(1)} = \mathbf{0}$
for $t = 1, \ldots, T$
  Let $\mathbf{w}^{(t)} = \frac{1}{\lambda t}\boldsymbol{\theta}^{(t)}$
  Choose i uniformly at random from $[m]$
  If $(y_i \langle \mathbf{w}^{(t)}, \mathbf{x}_i\rangle < 1)$
    Set $\boldsymbol{\theta}^{(t+1)} = \boldsymbol{\theta}^{(t)} + y_i \mathbf{x}_i$
  Else
    Set $\boldsymbol{\theta}^{(t+1)} = \boldsymbol{\theta}^{(t)}$
output: $\bar{\mathbf{w}} = \frac{1}{T}\sum_{t=1}^{T} \mathbf{w}^{(t)}$

15.6 SUMMARY

SVM is an algorithm for learning halfspaces with a certain type of prior knowledge, namely, preference for large margin. Hard-SVM seeks the halfspace that separates the data perfectly with the largest margin, whereas soft-SVM does not assume separability of the data and allows the constraints to be violated to some extent. The sample complexity for both types of SVM is different from the sample complexity of straightforward halfspace learning, as it does not depend on the dimension of the domain but rather on parameters such as the maximal norms of $\mathbf{x}$ and $\mathbf{w}$.

The importance of dimension-independent sample complexity will be realized in the next chapter, where we will discuss the embedding of the given domain into some high dimensional feature space as means for enriching our hypothesis class. Such a procedure raises computational and sample complexity problems. The latter is solved by using SVM, whereas the former can be solved by using SVM with kernels, as we will see in the next chapter.

15.7 BIBLIOGRAPHIC REMARKS

SVMs have been introduced in (Cortes and Vapnik 1995, Boser, Guyon and Vapnik 1992). There are many good books on the theoretical and practical aspects of SVMs. For example, (Vapnik 1995, Cristianini & Shawe-Taylor 2000, Schölkopf & Smola 2002, Hsu et al. 2003, Steinwart and Christmann 2008). Using SGD for solving soft-SVM has been proposed in Shalev-Shwartz et al. (2007).

15.8 EXERCISES

15.1 Show that the hard-SVM rule, namely,

$$\underset{(\mathbf{w},b):\|\mathbf{w}\|=1}{\operatorname{argmax}} \ \min_{i\in[m]} |\langle \mathbf{w}, \mathbf{x}_i\rangle + b| \quad \text{s.t.} \quad \forall i, \ y_i(\langle \mathbf{w}, \mathbf{x}_i\rangle + b) > 0,$$

is equivalent to the following formulation:

$$\underset{(\mathbf{w},b):\|\mathbf{w}\|=1}{\operatorname{argmax}} \ \min_{i\in[m]} y_i(\langle \mathbf{w}, \mathbf{x}_i\rangle + b). \tag{15.13}$$

Hint: Define $\mathcal{G} = \{(\mathbf{w}, b) : \forall i, y_i(\langle \mathbf{w}, \mathbf{x}_i\rangle + b) > 0\}$.

1. Show that

$$\underset{(\mathbf{w},b):\|\mathbf{w}\|=1}{\operatorname{argmax}} \ \min_{i\in[m]} y_i(\langle \mathbf{w}, \mathbf{x}_i\rangle + b) \in \mathcal{G}$$

2. Show that $\forall (\mathbf{w}, b) \in \mathcal{G}$,

$$\min_{i\in[m]} y_i(\langle \mathbf{w}, \mathbf{x}_i\rangle + b) = \min_{i\in[m]} |\langle \mathbf{w}, \mathbf{x}_i\rangle + b|$$

15.2 **Margin and the Perceptron** Consider a training set that is linearly separable with a margin γ and such that all the instances are within a ball of radius ρ. Prove that the maximal number of updates the Batch Perceptron algorithm given in Section 9.1.2 will make when running on this training set is $(\rho/\gamma)^2$.

15.3 **Hard versus soft SVM:** Prove or refute the following claim:
There exists $\lambda > 0$ such that for every sample S of $m > 1$ examples, which is separable by the class of homogenous halfspaces, the hard-SVM and the soft-SVM (with parameter λ) learning rules return exactly the same weight vector.

15.4 **Weak duality:** Prove that for any function f of two vector variables $\mathbf{x} \in \mathcal{X}, \mathbf{y} \in \mathcal{Y}$, it holds that

$$\min_{\mathbf{x}\in\mathcal{X}} \max_{\mathbf{y}\in\mathcal{Y}} f(\mathbf{x}, \mathbf{y}) \geq \max_{\mathbf{y}\in\mathcal{Y}} \min_{\mathbf{x}\in\mathcal{X}} f(\mathbf{x}, \mathbf{y}).$$

16

Kernel Methods

In the previous chapter we described the SVM paradigm for learning halfspaces in high dimensional feature spaces. This enables us to enrich the expressive power of halfspaces by first mapping the data into a high dimensional feature space, and then learning a linear predictor in that space. This is similar to the AdaBoost algorithm, which learns a composition of a halfspace over base hypotheses. While this approach greatly extends the expressiveness of halfspace predictors, it raises both sample complexity and computational complexity challenges. In the previous chapter we tackled the sample complexity issue using the concept of margin. In this chapter we tackle the computational complexity challenge using the method of *kernels*.

We start the chapter by describing the idea of embedding the data into a high dimensional feature space. We then introduce the idea of kernels. A kernel is a type of a similarity measure between instances. The special property of kernel similarities is that they can be viewed as inner products in some Hilbert space (or Euclidean space of some high dimension) to which the instance space is virtually embedded. We introduce the "kernel trick" that enables computationally efficient implementation of learning, without explicitly handling the high dimensional representation of the domain instances. Kernel based learning algorithms, and in particular kernel-SVM, are very useful and popular machine learning tools. Their success may be attributed both to being flexible for accommodating domain specific prior knowledge and to having a well developed set of efficient implementation algorithms.

16.1 EMBEDDINGS INTO FEATURE SPACES

The expressive power of halfspaces is rather restricted – for example, the following training set is not separable by a halfspace.

Let the domain be the real line; consider the domain points $\{-10, -9, -8, \ldots, 0, 1, \ldots, 9, 10\}$ where the labels are $+1$ for all x such that $|x| > 2$ and -1 otherwise.

To make the class of halfspaces more expressive, we can first map the original instance space into another space (possibly of a higher dimension) and then learn a halfspace in that space. For example, consider the example mentioned previously.

Instead of learning a halfspace in the original representation let us first define a mapping $\psi : \mathbb{R} \to \mathbb{R}^2$ as follows:

$$\psi(x) = (x, x^2).$$

We use the term *feature space* to denote the range of ψ. After applying ψ the data can be easily explained using the halfspace $h(x) = \text{sign}(\langle \mathbf{w}, \psi(x)\rangle - b)$, where $\mathbf{w} = (0, 1)$ and $b = 5$.

The basic paradigm is as follows:

1. Given some domain set $\mathcal{X}$ and a learning task, choose a mapping $\psi : \mathcal{X} \to \mathcal{F}$, for some *feature space* $\mathcal{F}$, that will usually be $\mathbb{R}^n$ for some n (however, the range of such a mapping can be any *Hilbert space*, including such spaces of infinite dimension, as we will show later).
2. Given a sequence of labeled examples, $S = (\mathbf{x}_1, y_1), \ldots, (\mathbf{x}_m, y_m)$, create the image sequence $\hat{S} = (\psi(\mathbf{x}_1), y_1), \ldots, (\psi(\mathbf{x}_m), y_m)$.
3. Train a linear predictor h over $\hat{S}$.
4. Predict the label of a test point, $\mathbf{x}$, to be $h(\psi(\mathbf{x}))$.

Note that, for every probability distribution $\mathcal{D}$ over $\mathcal{X} \times \mathcal{Y}$, we can readily define its image probability distribution $\mathcal{D}^{\psi}$ over $\mathcal{F} \times \mathcal{Y}$ by setting, for every subset $A \subseteq \mathcal{F} \times \mathcal{Y}$, $\mathcal{D}^{\psi}(A) = \mathcal{D}(\psi^{-1}(A))$.[1] It follows that for every predictor h over the feature space, $L_{\mathcal{D}^{\psi}}(h) = L_{\mathcal{D}}(h \circ \psi)$, where $h \circ \psi$ is the composition of h onto ψ.

The success of this learning paradigm depends on choosing a good ψ for a given learning task: that is, a ψ that will make the image of the data distribution (close to being) linearly separable in the feature space, thus making the resulting algorithm a good learner for a given task. Picking such an embedding requires prior knowledge about that task. However, often some generic mappings that enable us to enrich the class of halfspaces and extend its expressiveness are used. One notable example is polynomial mappings, which are a generalization of the ψ we have seen in the previous example.

Recall that the prediction of a standard halfspace classifier on an instance $\mathbf{x}$ is based on the linear mapping $\mathbf{x} \mapsto \langle \mathbf{w}, \mathbf{x}\rangle$. We can generalize linear mappings to a polynomial mapping, $\mathbf{x} \mapsto p(\mathbf{x})$, where p is a multivariate polynomial of degree k. For simplicity, consider first the case in which $\mathbf{x}$ is 1 dimensional. In that case, $p(x) = \sum_{j=0}^{k} w_j x^j$, where $\mathbf{w} \in \mathbb{R}^{k+1}$ is the vector of coefficients of the polynomial we need to learn. We can rewrite $p(x) = \langle \mathbf{w}, \psi(x)\rangle$ where $\psi : \mathbb{R} \to \mathbb{R}^{k+1}$ is the mapping $x \mapsto (1, x, x^2, x^3, \ldots, x^k)$. It follows that learning a k degree polynomial over $\mathbb{R}$ can be done by learning a linear mapping in the $(k+1)$ dimensional feature space.

More generally, a degree k multivariate polynomial from $\mathbb{R}^n$ to $\mathbb{R}$ can be written as

$$p(\mathbf{x}) = \sum_{J \in [n]^r : r \le k} w_J \prod_{i=1}^{r} x_{J_i}. \tag{16.1}$$

As before, we can rewrite $p(\mathbf{x}) = \langle \mathbf{w}, \psi(\mathbf{x})\rangle$ where now $\psi : \mathbb{R}^n \to \mathbb{R}^d$ is such that for every $J \in [n]^r$, $r \le k$, the coordinate of $\psi(\mathbf{x})$ associated with J is the monomial $\prod_{i=1}^{r} x_{J_i}$.

[1] This is defined for every A such that $\psi^{-1}(A)$ is measurable with respect to $\mathcal{D}$.

Naturally, polynomial-based classifiers yield much richer hypothesis classes than halfspaces. We have seen at the beginning of this chapter an example in which the training set, in its original domain ($\mathcal{X} = \mathbb{R}$), cannot be separable by a halfspace, but after the embedding $x \mapsto (x, x^2)$ it is perfectly separable. So, while the classifier is always linear in the feature space, it can have highly nonlinear behavior on the original space from which instances were sampled.

In general, we can choose any feature mapping ψ that maps the original instances into some *Hilbert space*.[2] The Euclidean space $\mathbb{R}^d$ is a Hilbert space for any finite d. But there are also infinite dimensional Hilbert spaces (as we shall see later on in this chapter).

The bottom line of this discussion is that we can enrich the class of halfspaces by first applying a nonlinear mapping, ψ, that maps the instance space into some feature space, and then learning a halfspace in that feature space. However, if the range of ψ is a high dimensional space we face two problems. First, the VC-dimension of halfspaces in $\mathbb{R}^n$ is $n+1$, and therefore, if the range of ψ is very large, we need many more samples in order to learn a halfspace in the range of ψ. Second, from the computational point of view, performing calculations in the high dimensional space might be too costly. In fact, even the representation of the vector $\mathbf{w}$ in the feature space can be unrealistic. The first issue can be tackled using the paradigm of large margin (or low norm predictors), as we already discussed in the previous chapter in the context of the SVM algorithm. In the following section we address the computational issue.

16.2 THE KERNEL TRICK

We have seen that embedding the input space into some high dimensional feature space makes halfspace learning more expressive. However, the computational complexity of such learning may still pose a serious hurdle – computing linear separators over very high dimensional data may be computationally expensive. The common solution to this concern is kernel based learning. The term "kernels" is used in this context to describe inner products in the feature space. Given an embedding ψ of some domain space $\mathcal{X}$ into some Hilbert space, we define the kernel function $K(\mathbf{x}, \mathbf{x}') = \langle \psi(\mathbf{x}), \psi(\mathbf{x}') \rangle$. One can think of K as specifying similarity between instances and of the embedding ψ as mapping the domain set $\mathcal{X}$ into a space where these similarities are realized as inner products. It turns out that many learning algorithms for halfspaces can be carried out just on the basis of the values of the kernel function over pairs of domain points. The main advantage of such algorithms is that they implement linear separators in high dimensional feature spaces without having to specify points in that space or expressing the embedding ψ explicitly. The remainder of this section is devoted to constructing such algorithms.

[2] A Hilbert space is a vector space with an inner product, which is also complete. A space is complete if all Cauchy sequences in the space converge. In our case, the norm $\|\mathbf{w}\|$ is defined by the inner product $\sqrt{\langle \mathbf{w}, \mathbf{w} \rangle}$. The reason we require the range of ψ to be in a Hilbert space is that projections in a Hilbert space are well defined. In particular, if M is a linear subspace of a Hilbert space, then every $\mathbf{x}$ in the Hilbert space can be written as a sum $\mathbf{x} = \mathbf{u} + \mathbf{v}$ where $\mathbf{u} \in M$ and $\langle \mathbf{v}, \mathbf{w} \rangle = 0$ for all $\mathbf{w} \in M$. We use this fact in the proof of the representer theorem given in the next section.

In the previous chapter we saw that regularizing the norm of $\mathbf{w}$ yields a small sample complexity even if the dimensionality of the feature space is high. Interestingly, as we show later, regularizing the norm of $\mathbf{w}$ is also helpful in overcoming the computational problem. To do so, first note that all versions of the SVM optimization problem we have derived in the previous chapter are instances of the following general problem:

$$\min_{\mathbf{w}} \left(f\left(\langle \mathbf{w}, \psi(\mathbf{x}_1)\rangle, \ldots, \langle \mathbf{w}, \psi(\mathbf{x}_m)\rangle\right) + R(\|\mathbf{w}\|)\right), \tag{16.2}$$

where $f : \mathbb{R}^m \to \mathbb{R}$ is an arbitrary function and $R : \mathbb{R}_+ \to \mathbb{R}$ is a monotonically nondecreasing function. For example, Soft-SVM for homogenous halfspaces (Equation (15.6)) can be derived from Equation (16.2) by letting $R(a) = \lambda a^2$ and $f(a_1, \ldots, a_m) = \frac{1}{m}\sum_i \max\{0, 1 - y_i a_i\}$. Similarly, Hard-SVM for nonhomogenous halfspaces (Equation (15.2)) can be derived from Equation (16.2) by letting $R(a) = a^2$ and letting $f(a_1, \ldots, a_m)$ be 0 if there exists b such that $y_i(a_i + b) \geq 1$ for all i, and $f(a_1, \ldots, a_m) = \infty$ otherwise.

The following theorem shows that there exists an optimal solution of Equation (16.2) that lies in the span of $\{\psi(\mathbf{x}_1), \ldots, \psi(\mathbf{x}_m)\}$.

Theorem 16.1 (Representer Theorem). *Assume that ψ is a mapping from $\mathcal{X}$ to a Hilbert space. Then, there exists a vector $\boldsymbol{\alpha} \in \mathbb{R}^m$ such that $\mathbf{w} = \sum_{i=1}^m \alpha_i \psi(\mathbf{x}_i)$ is an optimal solution of Equation (16.2).*

Proof. Let $\mathbf{w}^\star$ be an optimal solution of Equation (16.2). Because $\mathbf{w}^\star$ is an element of a Hilbert space, we can rewrite $\mathbf{w}^\star$ as

$$\mathbf{w}^\star = \sum_{i=1}^m \alpha_i \psi(\mathbf{x}_i) + \mathbf{u},$$

where $\langle \mathbf{u}, \psi(\mathbf{x}_i)\rangle = 0$ for all i. Set $\mathbf{w} = \mathbf{w}^\star - \mathbf{u}$. Clearly, $\|\mathbf{w}^\star\|^2 = \|\mathbf{w}\|^2 + \|\mathbf{u}\|^2$, thus $\|\mathbf{w}\| \leq \|\mathbf{w}^\star\|$. Since R is nondecreasing we obtain that $R(\|\mathbf{w}\|) \leq R(\|\mathbf{w}^\star\|)$. Additionally, for all i we have that

$$y_i \langle \mathbf{w}, \psi(\mathbf{x}_i)\rangle = y_i \langle \mathbf{w}^\star - \mathbf{u}, \psi(\mathbf{x}_i)\rangle = y_i \langle \mathbf{w}^\star, \psi(\mathbf{x}_i)\rangle,$$

hence

$$f\left(y_1 \langle \mathbf{w}, \psi(\mathbf{x}_1)\rangle, \ldots, y_m \langle \mathbf{w}, \psi(\mathbf{x}_m)\rangle\right) = f\left(y_1 \langle \mathbf{w}^\star, \psi(\mathbf{x}_1)\rangle, \ldots, y_m \langle \mathbf{w}^\star, \psi(\mathbf{x}_m)\rangle\right).$$

We have shown that the objective of Equation (16.2) at $\mathbf{w}$ cannot be larger than the objective at $\mathbf{w}^\star$ and therefore $\mathbf{w}$ is also an optimal solution. Since $\mathbf{w} = \sum_{i=1}^m \alpha_i \psi(\mathbf{x}_i)$ we conclude our proof. □

On the basis of the representer theorem we can optimize Equation (16.2) with respect to the coefficients $\boldsymbol{\alpha}$ instead of the coefficients $\mathbf{w}$ as follows. Writing $\mathbf{w} = \sum_{j=1}^m \alpha_j \psi(\mathbf{x}_j)$ we have that for all i

$$\langle \mathbf{w}, \psi(\mathbf{x}_i)\rangle = \left\langle \sum_j \alpha_j \psi(\mathbf{x}_j), \psi(\mathbf{x}_i)\right\rangle = \sum_{j=1}^m \alpha_j \langle \psi(\mathbf{x}_j), \psi(\mathbf{x}_i)\rangle.$$

Similarly,

$$\|\mathbf{w}\|^2 = \left\langle \sum_j \alpha_j \psi(\mathbf{x}_j), \sum_j \alpha_j \psi(\mathbf{x}_j) \right\rangle = \sum_{i,j=1}^m \alpha_i \alpha_j \langle \psi(\mathbf{x}_i), \psi(\mathbf{x}_j) \rangle.$$

Let $K(\mathbf{x}, \mathbf{x}') = \langle \psi(\mathbf{x}), \psi(\mathbf{x}') \rangle$ be a function that implements the kernel function with respect to the embedding ψ. Instead of solving Equation (16.2) we can solve the equivalent problem

$$\min_{\boldsymbol{\alpha} \in \mathbb{R}^m} f\left(\sum_{j=1}^m \alpha_j K(\mathbf{x}_j, \mathbf{x}_1), \ldots, \sum_{j=1}^m \alpha_j K(\mathbf{x}_j, \mathbf{x}_m) \right) + R\left(\sqrt{\sum_{i,j=1}^m \alpha_i \alpha_j K(\mathbf{x}_j, \mathbf{x}_i)} \right). \tag{16.3}$$

To solve the optimization problem given in Equation (16.3), we do not need any direct access to elements in the feature space. The only thing we should know is how to calculate inner products in the feature space, or equivalently, to calculate the kernel function. In fact, to solve Equation (16.3) we solely need to know the value of the $m \times m$ matrix G s.t. $G_{i,j} = K(\mathbf{x}_i, \mathbf{x}_j)$, which is often called the *Gram* matrix.

In particular, specifying the preceding to the Soft-SVM problem given in Equation (15.6), we can rewrite the problem as

$$\min_{\boldsymbol{\alpha} \in \mathbb{R}^m} \left(\lambda \boldsymbol{\alpha}^T G \boldsymbol{\alpha} + \frac{1}{m} \sum_{i=1}^m \max\{0, 1 - y_i (G\boldsymbol{\alpha})_i\} \right), \tag{16.4}$$

where $(G\boldsymbol{\alpha})_i$ is the i'th element of the vector obtained by multiplying the Gram matrix G by the vector $\boldsymbol{\alpha}$. Note that Equation (16.4) can be written as quadratic programming and hence can be solved efficiently. In the next section we describe an even simpler algorithm for solving Soft-SVM with kernels.

Once we learn the coefficients $\boldsymbol{\alpha}$ we can calculate the prediction on a new instance by

$$\langle \mathbf{w}, \psi(\mathbf{x}) \rangle = \sum_{j=1}^m \alpha_j \langle \psi(\mathbf{x}_j), \psi(\mathbf{x}) \rangle = \sum_{j=1}^m \alpha_j K(\mathbf{x}_j, \mathbf{x}).$$

The advantage of working with kernels rather than directly optimizing $\mathbf{w}$ in the feature space is that in some situations the dimension of the feature space is extremely large while implementing the kernel function is very simple. A few examples are given in the following.

Example 16.1 (Polynomial Kernels). The k degree polynomial kernel is defined to be

$$K(\mathbf{x}, \mathbf{x}') = (1 + \langle \mathbf{x}, \mathbf{x}' \rangle)^k.$$

Now we will show that this is indeed a kernel function. That is, we will show that there exists a mapping ψ from the original space to some higher dimensional space for which $K(\mathbf{x},\mathbf{x}') = \langle \psi(\mathbf{x}), \psi(\mathbf{x}') \rangle$. For simplicity, denote $x_0 = x'_0 = 1$. Then, we have

$$\begin{aligned}
K(\mathbf{x},\mathbf{x}') &= (1+\langle \mathbf{x},\mathbf{x}'\rangle)^k = (1+\langle \mathbf{x},\mathbf{x}'\rangle)\cdot\cdots\cdot(1+\langle \mathbf{x},\mathbf{x}'\rangle) \\
&= \left(\sum_{j=0}^{n} x_j x'_j\right)\cdot\cdots\cdot\left(\sum_{j=0}^{n} x_j x'_j\right) \\
&= \sum_{J\in\{0,1,\ldots,n\}^k} \prod_{i=1}^{k} x_{J_i} x'_{J_i} \\
&= \sum_{J\in\{0,1,\ldots,n\}^k} \prod_{i=1}^{k} x_{J_i} \prod_{i=1}^{k} x'_{J_i}.
\end{aligned}$$

Now, if we define $\psi : \mathbb{R}^n \to \mathbb{R}^{(n+1)^k}$ such that for $J \in \{0, 1, \ldots, n\}^k$ there is an element of $\psi(\mathbf{x})$ that equals $\prod_{i=1}^{k} x_{J_i}$, we obtain that

$$K(\mathbf{x},\mathbf{x}') = \langle \psi(\mathbf{x}), \psi(\mathbf{x}') \rangle.$$

Since ψ contains all the monomials up to degree k, a halfspace over the range of ψ corresponds to a polynomial predictor of degree k over the original space. Hence, learning a halfspace with a k degree polynomial kernel enables us to learn polynomial predictors of degree k over the original space.

Note that here the complexity of implementing K is $O(n)$ while the dimension of the feature space is on the order of n^k.

Example 16.2 (Gaussian Kernel). Let the original instance space be $\mathbb{R}$ and consider the mapping ψ where for each nonnegative integer $n \geq 0$ there exists an element $\psi(x)_n$ that equals $\frac{1}{\sqrt{n!}} e^{-\frac{x^2}{2}} x^n$. Then,

$$\begin{aligned}
\langle \psi(x),\ \psi(x') \rangle &= \sum_{n=0}^{\infty} \left(\frac{1}{\sqrt{n!}} e^{-\frac{x^2}{2}} x^n\right)\left(\frac{1}{\sqrt{n!}} e^{-\frac{(x')^2}{2}} (x')^n\right) \\
&= e^{-\frac{x^2+(x')^2}{2}} \sum_{n=0}^{\infty} \left(\frac{(xx')^n}{n!}\right) \\
&= e^{-\frac{\|x-x'\|^2}{2}}.
\end{aligned}$$

Here the feature space is of infinite dimension while evaluating the kernel is very simple. More generally, given a scalar $\sigma > 0$, the Gaussian kernel is defined to be

$$K(\mathbf{x},\mathbf{x}') = e^{-\frac{\|\mathbf{x}-\mathbf{x}'\|^2}{2\sigma}}.$$

Intuitively, the Gaussian kernel sets the inner product in the feature space between $\mathbf{x}, \mathbf{x}'$ to be close to zero if the instances are far away from each other (in the original domain) and close to 1 if they are close. σ is a parameter that controls the scale determining what we mean by "close." It is easy to verify that K implements an inner product in a space in which for any n and any monomial of order k

there exists an element of $\psi(\mathbf{x})$ that equals $\frac{1}{\sqrt{n!}} e^{-\frac{\|\mathbf{x}\|^2}{2}} \prod_{i=1}^{n} x_{J_i}$. Hence, we can learn any polynomial predictor over the original space by using a Gaussian kernel.

Recall that the VC-dimension of the class of all polynomial predictors is infinite (see Exercise 16.12). There is no contradiction, because the sample complexity required to learn with Gaussian kernels depends on the margin in the feature space, which will be large if we are lucky, but can in general be arbitrarily small.

The Gaussian kernel is also called the RBF kernel, for "Radial Basis Functions."

16.2.1 Kernels as a Way to Express Prior Knowledge

As we discussed previously, a feature mapping, ψ, may be viewed as expanding the class of linear classifiers to a richer class (corresponding to linear classifiers over the feature space). However, as discussed in the book so far, the suitability of any hypothesis class to a given learning task depends on the nature of that task. One can therefore think of an embedding ψ as a way to express and utilize prior knowledge about the problem at hand. For example, if we believe that positive examples can be distinguished by some ellipse, we can define ψ to be all the monomials up to order 2, or use a degree 2 polynomial kernel.

As a more realistic example, consider the task of learning to find a sequence of characters ("signature") in a file that indicates whether it contains a virus or not. Formally, let $\mathcal{X}$ be the set of all finite strings over some alphabet set Σ, and let $\mathcal{X}_d$ be the set of all such strings of length at most d. The hypothesis class that one wishes to learn is $\mathcal{H} = \{h_v : v \in \mathcal{X}_d\}$, where, for a string $x \in \mathcal{X}$, $h_v(x)$ is 1 iff v is a substring of x (and $h_v(x) = -1$ otherwise). Let us show how using an appropriate embedding this class can be realized by linear classifiers over the resulting feature space. Consider a mapping ψ to a space $\mathbb{R}^s$ where $s = |\mathcal{X}_d|$, so that each coordinate of $\psi(x)$ corresponds to some string v and indicates whether v is a substring of x (that is, for every $x \in \mathcal{X}$, $\psi(x)$ is a vector in $\{0,1\}^{|\mathcal{X}_d|}$). Note that the dimension of this feature space is exponential in d. It is not hard to see that every member of the class $\mathcal{H}$ can be realized by composing a linear classifier over $\psi(x)$, and, moreover, by such a halfspace whose norm is 1 and that attains a margin of 1 (see Exercise 16.1). Furthermore, for every $x \in \mathcal{X}$, $\|\psi(x)\| = O(\sqrt{d})$. So, overall, it is learnable using SVM with a sample complexity that is polynomial in d. However, the dimension of the feature space is exponential in d so a direct implementation of SVM over the feature space is problematic. Luckily, it is easy to calculate the inner product in the feature space (i.e., the kernel function) without explicitly mapping instances into the feature space. Indeed, $K(x, x')$ is simply the number of common substrings of x and x', which can be easily calculated in time polynomial in d.

This example also demonstrates how feature mapping enables us to use halfspaces for nonvectorial domains.

16.2.2 Characterizing Kernel Functions*

As we have discussed in the previous section, we can think of the specification of the kernel matrix as a way to express prior knowledge. Consider a given similarity function of the form $K : \mathcal{X} \times \mathcal{X} \to \mathbb{R}$. Is it a valid kernel function? That is, does it represent an inner product between $\psi(\mathbf{x})$ and $\psi(\mathbf{x}')$ for some feature mapping ψ? The following lemma gives a sufficient and necessary condition.

Lemma 16.2. *A symmetric function $K : \mathcal{X} \times \mathcal{X} \to \mathbb{R}$ implements an inner product in some Hilbert space if and only if it is positive semidefinite; namely, for all $\mathbf{x}_1, \ldots, \mathbf{x}_m$, the Gram matrix, $G_{i,j} = K(\mathbf{x}_i, \mathbf{x}_j)$, is a positive semidefinite matrix.*

Proof. It is trivial to see that if K implements an inner product in some Hilbert space then the Gram matrix is positive semidefinite. For the other direction, define the space of functions over $\mathcal{X}$ as $\mathbb{R}^{\mathcal{X}} = \{f : \mathcal{X} \to \mathbb{R}\}$. For each $\mathbf{x} \in \mathcal{X}$ let $\psi(\mathbf{x})$ be the function $\mathbf{x} \mapsto K(\cdot, \mathbf{x})$. Define a vector space by taking all linear combinations of elements of the form $K(\cdot, \mathbf{x})$. Define an inner product on this vector space to be

$$\left\langle \sum_i \alpha_i K(\cdot, \mathbf{x}_i), \sum_j \beta_j K(\cdot, \mathbf{x}'_j) \right\rangle = \sum_{i,j} \alpha_i \beta_j K(\mathbf{x}_i, \mathbf{x}'_j).$$

This is a valid inner product since it is symmetric (because K is symmetric), it is linear (immediate), and it is positive definite (it is easy to see that $K(\mathbf{x}, \mathbf{x}) \geq 0$ with equality only for $\psi(\mathbf{x})$ being the zero function). Clearly,

$$\langle \psi(\mathbf{x}), \psi(\mathbf{x}') \rangle = \langle K(\cdot, \mathbf{x}), K(\cdot, \mathbf{x}) \rangle = K(\mathbf{x}, \mathbf{x}'),$$

which concludes our proof. □

16.3 IMPLEMENTING SOFT-SVM WITH KERNELS

Next, we turn to solving Soft-SVM with kernels. While we could have designed an algorithm for solving Equation (16.4), there is an even simpler approach that directly tackles the Soft-SVM optimization problem in the feature space,

$$\min_{\mathbf{w}} \left(\frac{\lambda}{2} \|\mathbf{w}\|^2 + \frac{1}{m} \sum_{i=1}^{m} \max\{0, 1 - y\langle \mathbf{w}, \psi(\mathbf{x}_i)\rangle\} \right), \tag{16.5}$$

while only using kernel evaluations. The basic observation is that the vector $\mathbf{w}^{(t)}$ maintained by the SGD procedure we have described in Section 15.5 is always in the linear span of $\{\psi(\mathbf{x}_1), \ldots, \psi(\mathbf{x}_m)\}$. Therefore, rather than maintaining $\mathbf{w}^{(t)}$ we can maintain the corresponding coefficients $\boldsymbol{\alpha}$.

Formally, let K be the kernel function, namely, for all $\mathbf{x}, \mathbf{x}'$, $K(\mathbf{x}, \mathbf{x}') = \langle \psi(\mathbf{x}), \psi(\mathbf{x}') \rangle$. We shall maintain two vectors in $\mathbb{R}^m$, corresponding to two vectors $\boldsymbol{\theta}^{(t)}$ and $\mathbf{w}^{(t)}$ defined in the SGD procedure of Section 15.5. That is, $\boldsymbol{\beta}^{(t)}$ will be a vector such that

$$\boldsymbol{\theta}^{(t)} = \sum_{j=1}^{m} \beta_j^{(t)} \psi(\mathbf{x}_j) \tag{16.6}$$

and $\boldsymbol{\alpha}^{(t)}$ be such that

$$\mathbf{w}^{(t)} = \sum_{j=1}^{m} \alpha_j^{(t)} \psi(\mathbf{x}_j). \tag{16.7}$$

The vectors $\boldsymbol{\beta}$ and $\boldsymbol{\alpha}$ are updated according to the following procedure.

SGD for Solving Soft-SVM with Kernels

Goal: Solve Equation (16.5)
parameter: T
Initialize: $\boldsymbol{\beta}^{(1)} = \mathbf{0}$
for $t = 1, \ldots, T$
  Let $\boldsymbol{\alpha}^{(t)} = \frac{1}{\lambda t} \boldsymbol{\beta}^{(t)}$
  Choose i uniformly at random from $[m]$
  For all $j \neq i$ set $\beta_j^{(t+1)} = \beta_j^{(t)}$
  If $(y_i \sum_{j=1}^m \alpha_j^{(t)} K(\mathbf{x}_j, \mathbf{x}_i) < 1)$
    Set $\beta_i^{(t+1)} = \beta_i^{(t)} + y_i$
  Else
    Set $\beta_i^{(t+1)} = \beta_i^{(t)}$
Output: $\bar{\mathbf{w}} = \sum_{j=1}^m \bar{\alpha}_j \psi(\mathbf{x}_j)$ where $\bar{\boldsymbol{\alpha}} = \frac{1}{T} \sum_{t=1}^T \boldsymbol{\alpha}^{(t)}$

The following lemma shows that the preceding implementation is equivalent to running the SGD procedure described in Section 15.5 on the feature space.

Lemma 16.3. *Let $\hat{\mathbf{w}}$ be the output of the SGD procedure described in Section 15.5, when applied on the feature space, and let $\bar{\mathbf{w}} = \sum_{j=1}^m \bar{\alpha}_j \psi(\mathbf{x}_j)$ be the output of applying SGD with kernels. Then $\bar{\mathbf{w}} = \hat{\mathbf{w}}$.*

Proof. We will show that for every t Equation (16.6) holds, where $\boldsymbol{\theta}^{(t)}$ is the result of running the SGD procedure described in Section 15.5 in the feature space. By the definition of $\boldsymbol{\alpha}^{(t)} = \frac{1}{\lambda t} \boldsymbol{\beta}^{(t)}$ and $\mathbf{w}^{(t)} = \frac{1}{\lambda t} \boldsymbol{\theta}^{(t)}$, this claim implies that Equation (16.7) also holds, and the proof of our lemma will follow. To prove that Equation (16.6) holds we use a simple inductive argument. For $t = 1$ the claim trivially holds. Assume it holds for $t \geq 1$. Then,

$$y_i \left\langle \mathbf{w}^{(t)}, \psi(\mathbf{x}_i) \right\rangle = y_i \left\langle \sum_j \alpha_j^{(t)} \psi(\mathbf{x}_j), \psi(\mathbf{x}_i) \right\rangle = y_i \sum_{j=1}^m \alpha_j^{(t)} K(\mathbf{x}_j, \mathbf{x}_i).$$

Hence, the condition in the two algorithms is equivalent and if we update $\boldsymbol{\theta}$ we have

$$\boldsymbol{\theta}^{(t+1)} = \boldsymbol{\theta}^{(t)} + y_i \psi(\mathbf{x}_i) = \sum_{j=1}^m \beta_j^{(t)} \psi(\mathbf{x}_j) + y_i \psi(\mathbf{x}_i) = \sum_{j=1}^m \beta_j^{(t+1)} \psi(\mathbf{x}_j),$$

which concludes our proof. □

16.4 SUMMARY

Mappings from the given domain to some higher dimensional space, on which a halfspace predictor is used, can be highly powerful. We benefit from a rich and complex hypothesis class, yet need to solve the problems of high sample and computational complexities. In Chapter 10, we discussed the AdaBoost algorithm, which faces these challenges by using a weak learner: Even though we're in a very high dimensional space, we have an "oracle" that bestows on us a single good coordinate to work with on each iteration. In this chapter we introduced a different approach, the kernel trick. The idea is that in order to find a halfspace predictor in the high dimensional space, we do not need to know the representation of instances in that space, but rather the values of inner products between the mapped instances. Calculating inner products between instances in the high dimensional space without using their representation in that space is done using kernel functions. We have also shown how the SGD algorithm can be implemented using kernels.

The ideas of feature mapping and the kernel trick allow us to use the framework of halfspaces and linear predictors for nonvectorial data. We demonstrated how kernels can be used to learn predictors over the domain of strings.

We presented the applicability of the kernel trick in SVM. However, the kernel trick can be applied in many other algorithms. A few examples are given as exercises.

This chapter ends the series of chapters on linear predictors and convex problems. The next two chapters deal with completely different types of hypothesis classes.

16.5 BIBLIOGRAPHIC REMARKS

In the context of SVM, the kernel-trick has been introduced in Boser et al. (1992). See also Aizerman et al. (1964). The observation that the kernel-trick can be applied whenever an algorithm only relies on inner products was first stated by Schölkopf et al. (1998). The proof of the representer theorem is given in (Schölkopf et al. 2000, Schölkopf et al. 2001). The conditions stated in Lemma 16.2 are a simplification of conditions due to Mercer. Many useful kernel functions have been introduced in the literature for various applications. We refer the reader to Schölkopf & Smola (2002).

16.6 EXERCISES

16.1 Consider the task of finding a sequence of characters in a file, as described in Section 16.2.1. Show that every member of the class $\mathcal{H}$ can be realized by composing a linear classifier over $\psi(x)$, whose norm is 1 and that attains a margin of 1.

16.2 **Kernelized Perceptron:** Show how to run the Perceptron algorithm while only accessing the instances via the kernel function. *Hint:* The derivation is similar to the derivation of implementing SGD with kernels.

16.3 **Kernel Ridge Regression:** The ridge regression problem, with a feature mapping ψ, is the problem of finding a vector $\mathbf{w}$ that minimizes the function

$$f(\mathbf{w}) = \lambda \|\mathbf{w}\|^2 + \frac{1}{2m}\sum_{i=1}^{m}(\langle \mathbf{w}, \psi(\mathbf{x}_i)\rangle - y_i)^2, \tag{16.8}$$

and then returning the predictor

$$h(\mathbf{x}) = \langle \mathbf{w}, \mathbf{x}\rangle.$$

Show how to implement the ridge regression algorithm with kernels.

Hint: The representer theorem tells us that there exists a vector $\boldsymbol{\alpha} \in \mathbb{R}^m$ such that $\sum_{i=1}^m \alpha_i \psi(\mathbf{x}_i)$ is a minimizer of Equation (16.8).

1. Let G be the Gram matrix with regard to S and K. That is, $G_{ij} = K(\mathbf{x}_i, \mathbf{x}_j)$. Define $g : \mathbb{R}^m \to \mathbb{R}$ by

$$g(\boldsymbol{\alpha}) = \lambda \cdot \boldsymbol{\alpha}^T G \boldsymbol{\alpha} + \frac{1}{2m} \sum_{i=1}^{m} (\langle \boldsymbol{\alpha}, G_{\cdot,i} \rangle - y_i)^2, \tag{16.9}$$

where $G_{\cdot,i}$ is the i'th column of G. Show that if $\boldsymbol{\alpha}^*$ minimizes Equation (16.9) then $\mathbf{w}^* = \sum_{i=1}^m \alpha_i^* \psi(\mathbf{x}_i)$ is a minimizer of f.
2. Find a closed form expression for $\boldsymbol{\alpha}^*$.

16.4 Let N be any positive integer. For every $x, x' \in \{1, \ldots, N\}$ define

$$K(x, x') = \min\{x, x'\}.$$

Prove that K is a valid kernel; namely, find a mapping $\psi : \{1, \ldots, N\} \to H$ where H is some Hilbert space, such that

$$\forall x, x' \in \{1, \ldots, N\},\ K(x, x') = \langle \psi(x), \psi(x') \rangle.$$

16.5 A supermarket manager would like to learn which of his customers have babies on the basis of their shopping carts. Specifically, he sampled i.i.d. customers, where for customer i, let $x_i \subset \{1, \ldots, d\}$ denote the subset of items the customer bought, and let $y_i \in \{\pm 1\}$ be the label indicating whether this customer has a baby. As prior knowledge, the manager knows that there are k items such that the label is determined to be 1 iff the customer bought at least one of these k items. Of course, the identity of these k items is not known (otherwise, there was nothing to learn). In addition, according to the store regulation, each customer can buy at most s items. Help the manager to design a learning algorithm such that both its time complexity and its sample complexity are polynomial in s, k, and $1/\epsilon$.

16.6 Let $\mathcal{X}$ be an instance set and let ψ be a feature mapping of $\mathcal{X}$ into some Hilbert feature space V. Let $K : \mathcal{X} \times \mathcal{X} \to \mathbb{R}$ be a kernel function that implements inner products in the feature space V.

Consider the binary classification algorithm that predicts the label of an unseen instance according to the class with the closest average. Formally, given a training sequence $S = (\mathbf{x}_1, y_1), \ldots, (\mathbf{x}_m, y_m)$, for every $y \in \{\pm 1\}$ we define

$$c_y = \frac{1}{m_y} \sum_{i: y_i = y} \psi(\mathbf{x}_i).$$

where $m_y = |\{i : y_i = y\}|$. We assume that m_+ and m_- are nonzero. Then, the algorithm outputs the following decision rule:

$$h(\mathbf{x}) = \begin{cases} 1 & \|\psi(\mathbf{x}) - c_+\| \le \|\psi(\mathbf{x}) - c_-\| \\ 0 & \text{otherwise.} \end{cases}$$

1. Let $\mathbf{w} = c_+ - c_-$ and let $b = \frac{1}{2}(\|c_-\|^2 - \|c_+\|^2)$. Show that

$$h(\mathbf{x}) = \mathrm{sign}(\langle \mathbf{w}, \psi(\mathbf{x}) \rangle + b).$$

2. Show how to express $h(\mathbf{x})$ on the basis of the kernel function, and without accessing individual entries of $\psi(\mathbf{x})$ or $\mathbf{w}$.

17

Multiclass, Ranking, and Complex Prediction Problems

Multiclass categorization is the problem of classifying instances into one of several possible target classes. That is, we are aiming at learning a predictor $h : \mathcal{X} \to \mathcal{Y}$, where $\mathcal{Y}$ is a finite set of categories. Applications include, for example, categorizing documents according to topic ($\mathcal{X}$ is the set of documents and $\mathcal{Y}$ is the set of possible topics) or determining which object appears in a given image ($\mathcal{X}$ is the set of images and $\mathcal{Y}$ is the set of possible objects).

The centrality of the multiclass learning problem has spurred the development of various approaches for tackling the task. Perhaps the most straightforward approach is a reduction from multiclass classification to binary classification. In Section 17.1 we discuss the most common two reductions as well as the main drawback of the reduction approach.

We then turn to describe a family of linear predictors for multiclass problems. Relying on the RLM and SGD frameworks from previous chapters, we describe several practical algorithms for multiclass prediction.

In Section 17.3 we show how to use the multiclass machinery for complex prediction problems in which $\mathcal{Y}$ can be extremely large but has some structure on it. This task is often called *structured output learning*. In particular, we demonstrate this approach for the task of recognizing handwritten words, in which $\mathcal{Y}$ is the set of all possible strings of some bounded length (hence, the size of $\mathcal{Y}$ is exponential in the maximal length of a word).

Finally, in Section 17.4 and Section 17.5 we discuss ranking problems in which the learner should order a set of instances according to their "relevance." A typical application is ordering results of a search engine according to their relevance to the query. We describe several performance measures that are adequate for assessing the performance of ranking predictors and describe how to learn linear predictors for ranking problems efficiently.

17.1 ONE-VERSUS-ALL AND ALL-PAIRS

The simplest approach to tackle multiclass prediction problems is by reduction to binary classification. Recall that in multiclass prediction we would like to learn a function $h : \mathcal{X} \to \mathcal{Y}$. Without loss of generality let us denote $\mathcal{Y} = \{1, \ldots, k\}$.

In the One-versus-All method (a.k.a. One-versus-Rest) we train k binary classifiers, each of which discriminates between one class and the rest of the classes. That is, given a training set $S = (\mathbf{x}_1, y_1), \ldots, (\mathbf{x}_m, y_m)$, where every y_i is in $\mathcal{Y}$, we construct k binary training sets, $S_1, \ldots, S_k$, where $S_i = (\mathbf{x}_1, (-1)^{\mathbb{1}_{[y_1 \neq i]}}), \ldots, (\mathbf{x}_m, (-1)^{\mathbb{1}_{[y_m \neq i]}})$. In words, S_i is the set of instances labeled 1 if their label in S was i, and -1 otherwise. For every $i \in [k]$ we train a binary predictor $h_i : \mathcal{X} \to \{\pm 1\}$ based on S_i, hoping that $h_i(\mathbf{x})$ should equal 1 if and only if $\mathbf{x}$ belongs to class i. Then, given $h_1, \ldots, h_k$, we construct a multiclass predictor using the rule

$$h(\mathbf{x}) \in \underset{i \in [k]}{\operatorname{argmax}}\, h_i(\mathbf{x}). \tag{17.1}$$

When more than one binary hypothesis predicts "1" we should somehow decide which class to predict (e.g., we can arbitrarily decide to break ties by taking the minimal index in $\operatorname{argmax}_i h_i(\mathbf{x})$). A better approach can be applied whenever each h_i hides additional information, which can be interpreted as the confidence in the prediction $y = i$. For example, this is the case in halfspaces, where the actual prediction is $\operatorname{sign}(\langle \mathbf{w}, \mathbf{x} \rangle)$, but we can interpret $\langle \mathbf{w}, \mathbf{x} \rangle$ as the confidence in the prediction. In such cases, we can apply the multiclass rule given in Equation (17.1) on the real valued predictions. A pseudocode of the One-versus-All approach is given in the following.

One-versus-All

input:
  training set $S = (\mathbf{x}_1, y_1), \ldots, (\mathbf{x}_m, y_m)$
  algorithm for binary classification A
foreach $i \in \mathcal{Y}$
  let $S_i = (\mathbf{x}_1,\ (-1)^{\mathbb{1}_{[y_1 \neq i]}}), \ldots, (\mathbf{x}_m,\ (-1)^{\mathbb{1}_{[y_m \neq i]}})$
  let $h_i = A(S_i)$
output:
  the multiclass hypothesis defined by $h(\mathbf{x}) \in \operatorname{argmax}_{i \in \mathcal{Y}} h_i(\mathbf{x})$

Another popular reduction is the *All-Pairs* approach, in which all pairs of classes are compared to each other. Formally, given a training set $S = (\mathbf{x}_1, y_1), \ldots, (\mathbf{x}_m, y_m)$, where every y_i is in $[k]$, for every $1 \le i < j \le k$ we construct a binary training sequence, $S_{i,j}$, containing all examples from S whose label is either i or j. For each such an example, we set the binary label in $S_{i,j}$ to be $+1$ if the multiclass label in S is i and -1 if the multiclass label in S is j. Next, we train a binary classification algorithm based on every $S_{i,j}$ to get $h_{i,j}$. Finally, we construct a multiclass classifier by predicting the class that had the highest number of "wins." A pseudocode of the All-Pairs approach is given in the following.

All-Pairs

input:
training set $S = (\mathbf{x}_1, y_1), \ldots, (\mathbf{x}_m, y_m)$
algorithm for binary classification A
foreach $i, j \in \mathcal{Y}$ s.t. $i < j$
initialize $S_{i,j}$ to be the empty sequence
for $t = 1, \ldots, m$
If $y_t = i$ add $(\mathbf{x}_t, 1)$ to $S_{i,j}$
If $y_t = j$ add $(\mathbf{x}_t, -1)$ to $S_{i,j}$
let $h_{i,j} = A(S_{i,j})$
output:
the multiclass hypothesis defined by
$h(\mathbf{x}) \in \operatorname{argmax}_{i \in \mathcal{Y}} \left(\sum_{j \in \mathcal{Y}} \operatorname{sign}(j - i) h_{i,j}(\mathbf{x}) \right)$

Although reduction methods such as the One-versus-All and All-Pairs are simple and easy to construct from existing algorithms, their simplicity has a price. The binary learner is not aware of the fact that we are going to use its output hypotheses for constructing a multiclass predictor, and this might lead to suboptimal results, as illustrated in the following example.

Example 17.1. Consider a multiclass categorization problem in which the instance space is $\mathcal{X} = \mathbb{R}^2$ and the label set is $\mathcal{Y} = \{1, 2, 3\}$. Suppose that instances of the different classes are located in nonintersecting balls as depicted in the following.

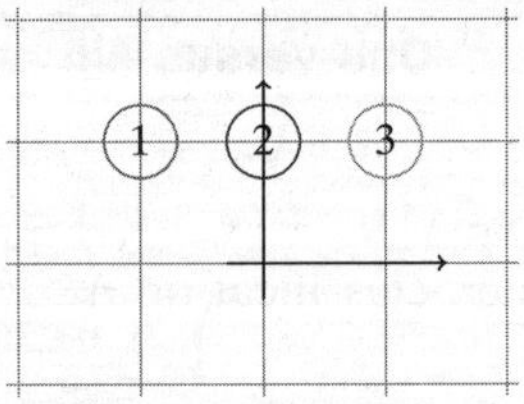

Suppose that the probability masses of classes 1, 2, 3 are 40%, 20%, and 40%, respectively. Consider the application of One-versus-All to this problem, and assume that the binary classification algorithm used by One-versus-All is ERM with respect to the hypothesis class of halfspaces. Observe that for the problem of discriminating between class 2 and the rest of the classes, the optimal halfspace would be the all negative classifier. Therefore, the multiclass predictor constructed by One-versus-All might err on all the examples from class 2 (this will be the case if the tie in the definition of $h(\mathbf{x})$ is broken by the numerical value of the class label). In contrast, if we choose $h_i(\mathbf{x}) = \langle \mathbf{w}_i, \mathbf{x} \rangle$, where $\mathbf{w}_1 = \left(-\frac{1}{\sqrt{2}}, \frac{1}{\sqrt{2}}\right)$, $\mathbf{w}_2 = (0, 1)$, and $\mathbf{w}_3 = \left(\frac{1}{\sqrt{2}}, \frac{1}{\sqrt{2}}\right)$, then the classifier defined by $h(\mathbf{x}) = \operatorname{argmax}_i h_i(\mathbf{x})$ perfectly predicts all the examples. We see that even though the approximation error of the class of predictors of the form $h(\mathbf{x}) = \operatorname{argmax}_i \langle \mathbf{w}_i, \mathbf{x} \rangle$ is zero, the One-versus-All approach might fail to find a good predictor from this class.

17.2 LINEAR MULTICLASS PREDICTORS

In light of the inadequacy of reduction methods, in this section we study a more direct approach for learning multiclass predictors. We describe the family of linear multiclass predictors. To motivate the construction of this family, recall that a linear predictor for binary classification (i.e., a halfspace) takes the form

$$h(\mathbf{x}) = \text{sign}(\langle \mathbf{w}, \mathbf{x} \rangle).$$

An equivalent way to express the prediction is as follows:

$$h(\mathbf{x}) = \underset{y \in \{\pm 1\}}{\text{argmax}} \langle \mathbf{w}, y\mathbf{x} \rangle,$$

where $y\mathbf{x}$ is the vector obtained by multiplying each element of $\mathbf{x}$ by y.

This representation leads to a natural generalization of halfspaces to multiclass problems as follows. Let $\Psi : \mathcal{X} \times \mathcal{Y} \to \mathbb{R}^d$ be a *class-sensitive feature mapping*. That is, Ψ takes as input a pair $(\mathbf{x}, y)$ and maps it into a d dimensional feature vector. Intuitively, we can think of the elements of $\Psi(\mathbf{x}, y)$ as score functions that assess how well the label y fits the instance $\mathbf{x}$. We will elaborate on Ψ later on. Given Ψ and a vector $\mathbf{w} \in \mathbb{R}^d$, we can define a multiclass predictor, $h : \mathcal{X} \to \mathcal{Y}$, as follows:

$$h(\mathbf{x}) = \underset{y \in \mathcal{Y}}{\text{argmax}} \langle \mathbf{w}, \Psi(\mathbf{x}, y) \rangle.$$

That is, the prediction of h for the input $\mathbf{x}$ is the label that achieves the highest weighted score, where weighting is according to the vector $\mathbf{w}$.

Let W be some set of vectors in $\mathbb{R}^d$, for example, $W = \{\mathbf{w} \in \mathbb{R}^d : \|\mathbf{w}\| \leq B\}$, for some scalar $B > 0$. Each pair (Ψ, W) defines a hypothesis class of multiclass predictors:

$$\mathcal{H}_{\Psi, W} = \{\mathbf{x} \mapsto \underset{y \in \mathcal{Y}}{\text{argmax}} \langle \mathbf{w}, \Psi(\mathbf{x}, y) \rangle \; : \; \mathbf{w} \in W\}.$$

Of course, the immediate question, which we discuss in the sequel, is how to construct a good Ψ. Note that if $\mathcal{Y} = \{\pm 1\}$ and we set $\Psi(\mathbf{x}, y) = y\mathbf{x}$ and $W = \mathbb{R}^d$, then $\mathcal{H}_{\Psi, W}$ becomes the hypothesis class of homogeneous halfspace predictors for binary classification.

17.2.1 How to Construct Ψ

As mentioned before, we can think of the elements of $\Psi(\mathbf{x}, y)$ as score functions that assess how well the label y fits the instance $\mathbf{x}$. Naturally, designing a good Ψ is similar to the problem of designing a good feature mapping (as we discussed in Chapter 16 and as we will discuss in more detail in Chapter 25). Two examples of useful constructions are given in the following.

The Multivector Construction:
Let $\mathcal{Y} = \{1, \ldots, k\}$ and let $\mathcal{X} = \mathbb{R}^n$. We define $\Psi : \mathcal{X} \times \mathcal{Y} \to \mathbb{R}^d$, where $d = nk$, as follows

$$\Psi(\mathbf{x}, \; y) = [\, \underbrace{0, \ldots, 0}_{\in \mathbb{R}^{(y-1)n}}, \underbrace{x_1, \ldots, x_n}_{\in \mathbb{R}^n}, \underbrace{0, \ldots, 0}_{\in \mathbb{R}^{(k-y)n}} \,]. \tag{17.2}$$

That is, $\Psi(\mathbf{x}, y)$ is composed of k vectors, each of which is of dimension n, where we set all the vectors to be the all zeros vector except the y'th vector, which is set to be $\mathbf{x}$. It follows that we can think of $\mathbf{w} \in \mathbb{R}^{nk}$ as being composed of k weight vectors in $\mathbb{R}^n$, that is, $\mathbf{w} = [\mathbf{w}_1; \ \ldots \ ; \mathbf{w}_k]$, hence the name *multivector construction*. By the construction we have that $\langle \mathbf{w}, \Psi(\mathbf{x}, y) \rangle = \langle \mathbf{w}_y, \mathbf{x} \rangle$, and therefore the multiclass prediction becomes

$$h(\mathbf{x}) = \underset{y \in \mathcal{Y}}{\operatorname{argmax}} \ \langle \mathbf{w}_y, \mathbf{x} \rangle.$$

A geometric illustration of the multiclass prediction over $\mathcal{X} = \mathbb{R}^2$ is given in the following.

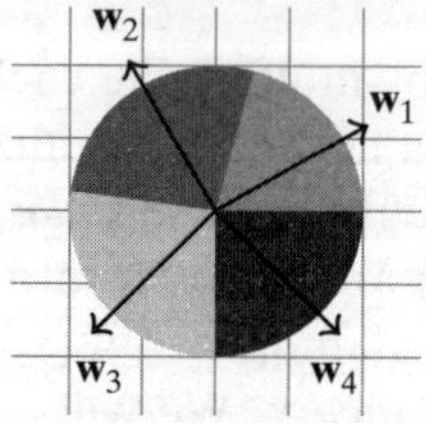

TF-IDF:

The previous definition of $\Psi(\mathbf{x}, \ y)$ does not incorporate any prior knowledge about the problem. We next describe an example of a feature function Ψ that does incorporate prior knowledge. Let $\mathcal{X}$ be a set of text documents and $\mathcal{Y}$ be a set of possible topics. Let d be a size of a dictionary of words. For each word in the dictionary, whose corresponding index is j, let $TF(j, \mathbf{x})$ be the number of times the word corresponding to j appears in the document $\mathbf{x}$. This quantity is called Term-Frequency. Additionally, let $DF(j, y)$ be the number of times the word corresponding to j appears in documents in our training set that are not about topic y. This quantity is called Document-Frequency and measures whether word j is frequent in other topics. Now, define $\Psi : \mathcal{X} \times \mathcal{Y} \to \mathbb{R}^d$ to be such that

$$\Psi_j(\mathbf{x}, \ y) = TF(j, \mathbf{x}) \log \left(\frac{m}{DF(j, y)} \right),$$

where m is the total number of documents in our training set. The preceding quantity is called term-frequency-inverse-document-frequency or TF-IDF for short. Intuitively, $\Psi_j(\mathbf{x}, \ y)$ should be large if the word corresponding to j appears a lot in the document $\mathbf{x}$ but does not appear at all in documents that are not on topic y. If this is the case, we tend to believe that the document $\mathbf{x}$ is on topic y. Note that unlike the multivector construction described previously, in the current construction the dimension of Ψ does not depend on the number of topics (i.e., the size of $\mathcal{Y}$).

17.2.2 Cost-Sensitive Classification

So far we used the zero-one loss as our performance measure of the quality of $h(\mathbf{x})$. That is, the loss of a hypothesis h on an example $(\mathbf{x}, y)$ is 1 if $h(\mathbf{x}) \neq y$ and 0 otherwise. In some situations it makes more sense to penalize different levels of loss for different mistakes. For example, in object recognition tasks, it is less severe to predict that an image of a tiger contains a cat than predicting that the image contains a whale. This can be modeled by specifying a loss function, $\Delta : \mathcal{Y} \times \mathcal{Y} \to \mathbb{R}_+$, where for every pair of labels, y', y, the loss of predicting the label y' when the correct label is y is defined to be $\Delta(y', y)$. We assume that $\Delta(y, y) = 0$. Note that the zero-one loss can be easily modeled by setting $\Delta(y', y) = \mathbb{1}_{[y' \neq y]}$.

17.2.3 ERM

We have defined the hypothesis class $\mathcal{H}_{\Psi,W}$ and specified a loss function Δ. To learn the class with respect to the loss function, we can apply the ERM rule with respect to this class. That is, we search for a multiclass hypothesis $h \in \mathcal{H}_{\Psi,W}$, parameterized by a vector $\mathbf{w}$, that minimizes the empirical risk with respect to Δ,

$$L_S(h) = \frac{1}{m} \sum_{i=1}^{m} \Delta(h(\mathbf{x}_i), y_i).$$

We now show that when $W = \mathbb{R}^d$ and we are in the realizable case, then it is possible to solve the ERM problem efficiently using linear programming. Indeed, in the realizable case, we need to find a vector $\mathbf{w} \in \mathbb{R}^d$ that satisfies

$$\forall i \in [m], \quad y_i = \operatorname*{argmax}_{y \in \mathcal{Y}} \langle \mathbf{w}, \Psi(\mathbf{x}_i, y) \rangle.$$

Equivalently, we need that $\mathbf{w}$ will satisfy the following set of linear inequalities

$$\forall i \in [m],\ \forall y \in \mathcal{Y} \setminus \{y_i\}, \quad \langle \mathbf{w}, \Psi(\mathbf{x}_i, y_i) \rangle > \langle \mathbf{w}, \Psi(\mathbf{x}_i, y) \rangle.$$

Finding $\mathbf{w}$ that satisfies the preceding set of linear equations amounts to solving a linear program.

As in the case of binary classification, it is also possible to use a generalization of the Perceptron algorithm for solving the ERM problem. See Exercise 17.2.

In the nonrealizable case, solving the ERM problem is in general computationally hard. We tackle this difficulty using the method of convex surrogate loss functions (see Section 12.3). In particular, we generalize the hinge loss to multiclass problems.

17.2.4 Generalized Hinge Loss

Recall that in binary classification, the hinge loss is defined to be $\max\{0, 1 - y\langle \mathbf{w}, \mathbf{x} \rangle\}$. We now generalize the hinge loss to multiclass predictors of the form

$$h_{\mathbf{w}}(\mathbf{x}) = \operatorname*{argmax}_{y' \in \mathcal{Y}} \langle \mathbf{w}, \Psi(\mathbf{x}, \mathbf{y}') \rangle.$$

Recall that a surrogate convex loss should upper bound the original nonconvex loss, which in our case is $\Delta(h_{\mathbf{w}}(\mathbf{x}), y)$. To derive an upper bound on $\Delta(h_{\mathbf{w}}(\mathbf{x}), y)$ we first note that the definition of $h_{\mathbf{w}}(\mathbf{x})$ implies that

$$\langle \mathbf{w}, \Psi(\mathbf{x}, y) \rangle \leq \langle \mathbf{w}, \Psi(\mathbf{x}, h_{\mathbf{w}}(\mathbf{x})) \rangle.$$

Therefore,

$$\Delta(h_{\mathbf{w}}(\mathbf{x}), y) \leq \Delta(h_{\mathbf{w}}(\mathbf{x}), y) + \langle \mathbf{w}, \Psi(\mathbf{x}, h_{\mathbf{w}}(\mathbf{x})) - \Psi(\mathbf{x}, y) \rangle.$$

Since $h_{\mathbf{w}}(\mathbf{x}) \in \mathcal{Y}$ we can upper bound the right-hand side of the preceding by

$$\max_{y' \in \mathcal{Y}} \left(\Delta(y', y) + \langle \mathbf{w}, \Psi(\mathbf{x}, y') - \Psi(\mathbf{x}, y) \rangle \right) \stackrel{\text{def}}{=} \ell(\mathbf{w}, (\mathbf{x}, y)). \tag{17.3}$$

We use the term "generalized hinge loss" to denote the preceding expression. As we have shown, $\ell(\mathbf{w}, (\mathbf{x}, y)) \geq \Delta(h_{\mathbf{w}}(\mathbf{x}), y)$. Furthermore, equality holds whenever the score of the correct label is larger than the score of any other label, y', by at least $\Delta(y', y)$, namely,

$$\forall y' \in \mathcal{Y} \setminus \{y\}, \quad \langle \mathbf{w}, \Psi(\mathbf{x}, \mathbf{y}) \rangle \geq \langle \mathbf{w}, \Psi(\mathbf{x}, \mathbf{y}') \rangle + \Delta(y', y).$$

It is also immediate to see that $\ell(\mathbf{w}, (\mathbf{x}, y))$ is a convex function with respect to $\mathbf{w}$ since it is a maximum over linear functions of $\mathbf{w}$ (see Claim 12.5 in Chapter 12), and that $\ell(\mathbf{w}, (\mathbf{x}, y))$ is ρ-Lipschitz with $\rho = \max_{y' \in \mathcal{Y}} \|\Psi(\mathbf{x}, y') - \Psi(\mathbf{x}, y)\|$.

Remark 17.2. We use the name "generalized hinge loss" since in the binary case, when $\mathcal{Y} = \{\pm 1\}$, if we set $\Psi(\mathbf{x}, y) = \frac{y\mathbf{x}}{2}$, then the generalized hinge loss becomes the vanilla hinge loss for binary classification,

$$\ell(\mathbf{w}, (\mathbf{x}, y)) = \max\{0, 1 - y\langle \mathbf{w}, \mathbf{x} \rangle\}.$$

Geometric Intuition:

The feature function $\Psi : \mathcal{X} \times \mathcal{Y} \to \mathbb{R}^d$ maps each $\mathbf{x}$ into $|\mathcal{Y}|$ vectors in $\mathbb{R}^d$. The value of $\ell(\mathbf{w}, (\mathbf{x}, y))$ will be zero if there exists a direction $\mathbf{w}$ such that when projecting the $|\mathcal{Y}|$ vectors onto this direction we obtain that each vector is represented by the scalar $\langle \mathbf{w}, \Psi(\mathbf{x}, y) \rangle$, and we can rank the different points on the basis of these scalars so that

- The point corresponding to the correct y is top-ranked
- For each $y' \neq y$, the difference between $\langle \mathbf{w}, \Psi(\mathbf{x}, y) \rangle$ and $\langle \mathbf{w}, \Psi(\mathbf{x}, y') \rangle$ is larger than the loss of predicting y' instead of y. The difference $\langle \mathbf{w}, \Psi(\mathbf{x}, y) \rangle - \langle \mathbf{w}, \Psi(\mathbf{x}, y') \rangle$ is also referred to as the "margin" (see Section 15.1).

This is illustrated in the following figure:

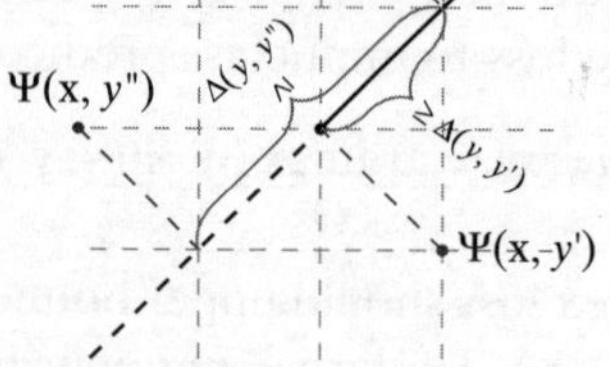

17.2.5 Multiclass SVM and SGD

Once we have defined the generalized hinge loss, we obtain a convex-Lipschitz learning problem and we can apply our general techniques for solving such problems. In particular, the RLM technique we have studied in Chapter 13 yields the multiclass SVM rule:

Multiclass SVM

input: $(\mathbf{x}_1, y_1), \ldots, (\mathbf{x}_m, y_m)$
parameters:
regularization parameter $\lambda > 0$
loss function $\Delta : \mathcal{Y} \times \mathcal{Y} \to \mathbb{R}_+$
class-sensitive feature mapping $\Psi : \mathcal{X} \times \mathcal{Y} \to \mathbb{R}^d$
solve:

$$\min_{\mathbf{w} \in \mathbb{R}^d} \left(\lambda \|\mathbf{w}\|^2 + \frac{1}{m} \sum_{i=1}^{m} \max_{y' \in \mathcal{Y}} \left(\Delta(y', y_i) + \langle \mathbf{w}, \Psi(\mathbf{x}_i, y') - \Psi(\mathbf{x}_i, y_i) \rangle \right) \right)$$

output the predictor $h_{\mathbf{w}}(\mathbf{x}) = \mathrm{argmax}_{y \in \mathcal{Y}} \langle \mathbf{w}, \Psi(\mathbf{x}, y) \rangle$

We can solve the optimization problem associated with multiclass SVM using generic convex optimization algorithms (or using the method described in Section 15.5). Let us analyze the risk of the resulting hypothesis. The analysis seamlessly follows from our general analysis for convex-Lipschitz problems given in Chapter 13. In particular, applying Corollary 13.8 and using the fact that the generalized hinge loss upper bounds the Δ loss, we immediately obtain an analog of Corollary 15.7:

Corollary 17.1. *Let $\mathcal{D}$ be a distribution over $\mathcal{X} \times \mathcal{Y}$, let $\Psi : \mathcal{X} \times \mathcal{Y} \to \mathbb{R}^d$, and assume that for all $\mathbf{x} \in \mathcal{X}$ and $y \in \mathcal{Y}$ we have $\|\Psi(\mathbf{x}, y)\| \le \rho/2$. Let $B > 0$. Consider running Multiclass SVM with $\lambda = \sqrt{\frac{2\rho^2}{B^2 m}}$ on a training set $S \sim \mathcal{D}^m$ and let $h_{\mathbf{w}}$ be the output of Multiclass SVM. Then,*

$$\mathop{\mathbb{E}}_{S \sim \mathcal{D}^m} [L_{\mathcal{D}}^{\Delta}(h_{\mathbf{w}})] \le \mathop{\mathbb{E}}_{S \sim \mathcal{D}^m} [L_{\mathcal{D}}^{\text{g-hinge}}(\mathbf{w})] \le \min_{\mathbf{u} : \|\mathbf{u}\| \le B} L_{\mathcal{D}}^{\text{g-hinge}}(\mathbf{u}) + \sqrt{\frac{8\rho^2 B^2}{m}},$$

where $L_{\mathcal{D}}^{\Delta}(h) = \mathbb{E}_{(\mathbf{x},y)\sim\mathcal{D}}[\Delta(h(\mathbf{x}), y)]$ and $L_{\mathcal{D}}^{\text{g-hinge}}(\mathbf{w}) = \mathbb{E}_{(\mathbf{x},y)\sim\mathcal{D}}[\ell(\mathbf{w}, (\mathbf{x}, y))]$ with ℓ being the generalized hinge-loss as defined in Equation (17.3).

We can also apply the SGD learning framework for minimizing $L_{\mathcal{D}}^{\text{g-hinge}}(\mathbf{w})$ as described in Chapter 14. Recall Claim 14.6, which dealt with subgradients of max functions. In light of this claim, in order to find a subgradient of the generalized hinge loss all we need to do is to find $y \in \mathcal{Y}$ that achieves the maximum in the definition of the generalized hinge loss. This yields the following algorithm:

SGD for Multiclass Learning

parameters:
Scalar $\eta > 0$, integer $T > 0$
loss function $\Delta : \mathcal{Y} \times \mathcal{Y} \to \mathbb{R}_+$
class-sensitive feature mapping $\Psi : \mathcal{X} \times \mathcal{Y} \to \mathbb{R}^d$
initialize: $\mathbf{w}^{(1)} = \mathbf{0} \in \mathbb{R}^d$
for $t = 1, 2, \ldots, T$
sample $(\mathbf{x}, y) \sim \mathcal{D}$
find $\hat{y} \in \operatorname{argmax}_{y' \in \mathcal{Y}} \left(\Delta(y', y) + \langle \mathbf{w}^{(t)}, \Psi(\mathbf{x}, y') - \Psi(\mathbf{x}, y) \rangle\right)$
set $\mathbf{v}_t = \Psi(\mathbf{x}, \hat{y}) - \Psi(\mathbf{x}, y)$
update $\mathbf{w}^{(t+1)} = \mathbf{w}^{(t)} - \eta \mathbf{v}_t$
output $\bar{\mathbf{w}} = \frac{1}{T} \sum_{t=1}^{T} \mathbf{w}^{(t)}$

Our general analysis of SGD given in Corollary 14.12 immediately implies:

Corollary 17.2. *Let $\mathcal{D}$ be a distribution over $\mathcal{X} \times \mathcal{Y}$, let $\Psi : \mathcal{X} \times \mathcal{Y} \to \mathbb{R}^d$, and assume that for all $\mathbf{x} \in \mathcal{X}$ and $y \in \mathcal{Y}$ we have $\|\Psi(\mathbf{x}, y)\| \le \rho/2$. Let $B > 0$. Then, for every $\epsilon > 0$, if we run SGD for multiclass learning with a number of iterations (i.e., number of examples)*

$$T \ge \frac{B^2 \rho^2}{\epsilon^2}$$

and with $\eta = \sqrt{\frac{B^2}{\rho^2 T}}$, then the output of SGD satisfies

$$\mathop{\mathbb{E}}_{S \sim \mathcal{D}^m}[L_{\mathcal{D}}^{\Delta}(h_{\bar{\mathbf{w}}})] \le \mathop{\mathbb{E}}_{S \sim \mathcal{D}^m}[L_{\mathcal{D}}^{\text{g-hinge}}(\bar{\mathbf{w}})] \le \min_{\mathbf{u} : \|\mathbf{u}\| \le B} L_{\mathcal{D}}^{\text{g-hinge}}(\mathbf{u}) + \epsilon.$$

Remark 17.3. It is interesting to note that the risk bounds given in Corollary 17.1 and Corollary 17.2 do not depend explicitly on the size of the label set $\mathcal{Y}$, a fact we will rely on in the next section. However, the bounds may depend implicitly on the size of $\mathcal{Y}$ via the norm of $\Psi(\mathbf{x}, y)$ and the fact that the bounds are meaningful only when there exists some vector $\mathbf{u}$, $\|\mathbf{u}\| \le B$, for which $L_{\mathcal{D}}^{\text{g-hinge}}(\mathbf{u})$ is not excessively large.

17.3 STRUCTURED OUTPUT PREDICTION

Structured output prediction problems are multiclass problems in which $\mathcal{Y}$ is very large but is endowed with a predefined structure. The structure plays a key role in constructing efficient algorithms. To motivate structured learning problems, consider the problem of optical character recognition (OCR). Suppose we receive an image of some handwritten word and would like to predict which word is written in the image. To simplify the setting, suppose we know how to segment the image into a sequence of images, each of which contains a patch of the image corresponding to a single letter. Therefore, $\mathcal{X}$ is the set of sequences of images and $\mathcal{Y}$ is the set of sequences of letters. Note that the size of $\mathcal{Y}$ grows exponentially with the maximal length of a word. An example of an image $\mathbf{x}$ corresponding to the label $\mathbf{y}=$ "workable" is given in the following.

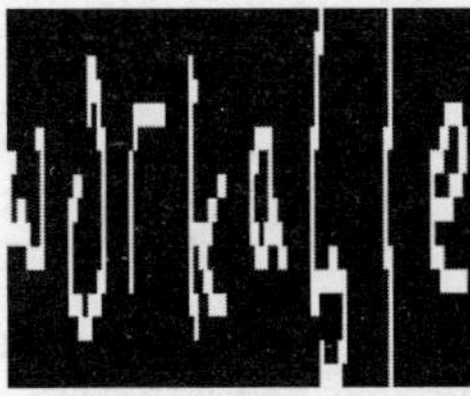

To tackle structure prediction we can rely on the family of linear predictors described in the previous section. In particular, we need to define a reasonable loss function for the problem, Δ, as well as a good class-sensitive feature mapping, Ψ. By "good" we mean a feature mapping that will lead to a low approximation error for the class of linear predictors with respect to Ψ and Δ. Once we do this, we can rely, for example, on the SGD learning algorithm defined in the previous section.

However, the huge size of $\mathcal{Y}$ poses several challenges:

1. To apply the multiclass prediction we need to solve a maximization problem over $\mathcal{Y}$. How can we predict efficiently when $\mathcal{Y}$ is so large?
2. How do we train $\mathbf{w}$ efficiently? In particular, to apply the SGD rule we again need to solve a maximization problem over $\mathcal{Y}$.
3. How can we avoid overfitting?

In the previous section we have already shown that the sample complexity of learning a linear multiclass predictor does not depend explicitly on the number of classes. We just need to make sure that the norm of the range of Ψ is not too large. This will take care of the overfitting problem. To tackle the computational challenges we rely on the structure of the problem, and define the functions Ψ and Δ so that calculating the maximization problems in the definition of $h_{\mathbf{w}}$ and in the SGD algorithm can be performed efficiently. In the following we demonstrate one way to achieve these goals for the OCR task mentioned previously.

To simplify the presentation, let us assume that all the words in $\mathcal{Y}$ are of length r and that the number of different letters in our alphabet is q. Let $\mathbf{y}$ and $\mathbf{y}'$ be two words (i.e., sequences of letters) in $\mathcal{Y}$. We define the function $\Delta(\mathbf{y}', \mathbf{y})$ to be the average number of letters that are different in y' and y, namely, $\frac{1}{r}\sum_{i=1}^{r} \mathbb{1}_{[y_i \neq y'_i]}$.

Next, let us define a class-sensitive feature mapping $\Psi(\mathbf{x}, \mathbf{y})$. It will be convenient to think about $\mathbf{x}$ as a matrix of size $n \times r$, where n is the number of pixels in each image, and r is the number of images in the sequence. The j'th column of $\mathbf{x}$ corresponds to the j'th image in the sequence (encoded as a vector of gray level values of pixels). The dimension of the range of Ψ is set to be $d = nq + q^2$.

The first nq feature functions are "type 1" features and take the form:

$$\Psi_{i,j,1}(\mathbf{x}, \mathbf{y}) = \frac{1}{r}\sum_{t=1}^{r} x_{i,t}\, \mathbb{1}_{[y_t = j]}.$$

That is, we sum the value of the i'th pixel only over the images for which $\mathbf{y}$ assigns the letter j. The triple index $(i, j, 1)$ indicates that we are dealing with feature (i, j) of type 1. Intuitively, such features can capture pixels in the image whose gray level values are indicative of a certain letter. The second type of features take the form

$$\Psi_{i,j,2}(\mathbf{x},\mathbf{y}) = \frac{1}{r}\sum_{t=2}^{r} \mathbb{1}_{[y_t=i]}\,\mathbb{1}_{[y_{t-1}=j]}.$$

That is, we sum the number of times the letter i follows the letter j. Intuitively, these features can capture rules like "It is likely to see the pair 'qu' in a word" or "It is unlikely to see the pair 'rz' in a word." Of course, some of these features will not be very useful, so the goal of the learning process is to assign weights to features by learning the vector $\mathbf{w}$, so that the weighted score will give us a good prediction via

$$h_{\mathbf{w}}(\mathbf{x}) = \underset{\mathbf{y}\in\mathcal{Y}}{\operatorname{argmax}}\ \langle \mathbf{w}, \Psi(\mathbf{x},\mathbf{y})\rangle.$$

It is left to show how to solve the optimization problem in the definition of $h_{\mathbf{w}}(\mathbf{x})$ efficiently, as well as how to solve the optimization problem in the definition of $\hat{y}$ in the SGD algorithm. We can do this by applying a dynamic programming procedure. We describe the procedure for solving the maximization in the definition of $h_{\mathbf{w}}$ and leave as an exercise the maximization problem in the definition of $\hat{y}$ in the SGD algorithm.

To derive the dynamic programming procedure, let us first observe that we can write

$$\Psi(\mathbf{x},\mathbf{y}) = \sum_{t=1}^{r} \boldsymbol{\phi}(\mathbf{x}, y_t, y_{t-1}),$$

for an appropriate $\boldsymbol{\phi} : \mathcal{X}\times[q]\times[q]\cup\{0\} \to \mathbb{R}^d$, and for simplicity we assume that y_0 is always equal to 0. Indeed, each feature function $\Psi_{i,j,1}$ can be written in terms of

$$\phi_{i,j,1}(\mathbf{x}, y_t, y_{t-1}) = x_{i,t}\,\mathbb{1}_{[y_t=j]},$$

while the feature function $\Psi_{i,j,2}$ can be written in terms of

$$\phi_{i,j,2}(\mathbf{x}, y_t, y_{t-1}) = \mathbb{1}_{[y_t=i]}\,\mathbb{1}_{[y_{t-1}=j]}.$$

Therefore, the prediction can be written as

$$h_{\mathbf{w}}(\mathbf{x}) = \underset{\mathbf{y}\in\mathcal{Y}}{\operatorname{argmax}} \sum_{t=1}^{r} \langle \mathbf{w}, \boldsymbol{\phi}(\mathbf{x}, y_t, y_{t-1})\rangle. \tag{17.4}$$

In the following we derive a dynamic programming procedure that solves every problem of the form given in Equation (17.4). The procedure will maintain a matrix $M \in \mathbb{R}^{q,r}$ such that

$$M_{s,\tau} = \max_{(y_1,\ldots,y_\tau): y_\tau = s} \sum_{t=1}^{\tau} \langle \mathbf{w}, \boldsymbol{\phi}(\mathbf{x}, y_t, y_{t-1})\rangle.$$

Clearly, the maximum of $\langle \mathbf{w}, \Psi(\mathbf{x},\mathbf{y})\rangle$ equals $\max_s M_{s,r}$. Furthermore, we can calculate M in a recursive manner:

$$M_{s,\tau} = \max_{s'} \left(M_{s',\tau-1} + \langle \mathbf{w}, \boldsymbol{\phi}(\mathbf{x}, s, s')\rangle \right). \tag{17.5}$$

This yields the following procedure:

Dynamic Programming for Calculating $h_{\mathbf{w}}(\mathbf{x})$ as Given in Equation (17.4)

input: a matrix $\mathbf{x} \in \mathbb{R}^{n,r}$ and a vector $\mathbf{w}$
initialize:
  foreach $s \in [q]$
    $M_{s,1} = \langle \mathbf{w}, \boldsymbol{\phi}(\mathbf{x}, s, -1) \rangle$
for $\tau = 2, \ldots, r$
  foreach $s \in [q]$
    set $M_{s,\tau}$ as in Equation (17.5)
    set $I_{s,\tau}$ to be the s' that maximizes Equation (17.5)
set $y_t = \text{argmax}_s M_{s,r}$
for $\tau = r, r-1, \ldots, 2$
  set $y_{\tau-1} = I_{y_\tau, \tau}$
output: $\mathbf{y} = (y_1, \ldots, y_r)$

17.4 RANKING

Ranking is the problem of ordering a set of instances according to their "relevance." A typical application is ordering results of a search engine according to their relevance to the query. Another example is a system that monitors electronic transactions and should alert for possible fraudulent transactions. Such a system should order transactions according to how suspicious they are.

Formally, let $\mathcal{X}^* = \bigcup_{n=1}^{\infty} \mathcal{X}^n$ be the set of all sequences of instances from $\mathcal{X}$ of arbitrary length. A ranking hypothesis, h, is a function that receives a sequence of instances $\bar{\mathbf{x}} = (\mathbf{x}_1, \ldots, \mathbf{x}_r) \in \mathcal{X}^*$, and returns a permutation of $[r]$. It is more convenient to let the output of h be a vector $\mathbf{y} \in \mathbb{R}^r$, where by sorting the elements of $\mathbf{y}$ we obtain the permutation over $[r]$. We denote by $\pi(\mathbf{y})$ the permutation over $[r]$ induced by $\mathbf{y}$. For example, for $r = 5$, the vector $\mathbf{y} = (2, 1, 6, -1, 0.5)$ induces the permutation $\pi(\mathbf{y}) = (4, 3, 5, 1, 2)$. That is, if we sort $\mathbf{y}$ in an ascending order, then we obtain the vector $(-1, 0.5, 1, 2, 6)$. Now, $\pi(\mathbf{y})_i$ is the position of y_i in the sorted vector $(-1, 0.5, 1, 2, 6)$. This notation reflects that the top-ranked instances are those that achieve the highest values in $\pi(\mathbf{y})$.

In the notation of our PAC learning model, the examples domain is $Z = \bigcup_{r=1}^{\infty} (\mathcal{X}^r \times \mathbb{R}^r)$, and the hypothesis class, $\mathcal{H}$, is some set of ranking hypotheses. We next turn to describe loss functions for ranking. There are many possible ways to define such loss functions, and here we list a few examples. In all the examples we define $\ell(h, (\bar{\mathbf{x}}, \mathbf{y})) = \Delta(h(\bar{\mathbf{x}}), \mathbf{y})$, for some function $\Delta : \bigcup_{r=1}^{\infty} (\mathbb{R}^r \times \mathbb{R}^r) \to \mathbb{R}_+$.

- **0–1 Ranking loss:** $\Delta(\mathbf{y}', \mathbf{y})$ is zero if $\mathbf{y}$ and $\mathbf{y}'$ induce exactly the same ranking and $\Delta(\mathbf{y}', \mathbf{y}) = 1$ otherwise. That is, $\Delta(\mathbf{y}', \mathbf{y}) = \mathbb{1}_{[\pi(\mathbf{y}') \neq \pi(\mathbf{y})]}$. Such a loss function is almost never used in practice as it does not distinguish between the case in which $\pi(\mathbf{y}')$ is almost equal to $\pi(\mathbf{y})$ and the case in which $\pi(\mathbf{y}')$ is completely different from $\pi(\mathbf{y})$.

- **Kendall-Tau Loss:** We count the number of pairs (i, j) that are in different order in the two permutations. This can be written as

$$\Delta(\mathbf{y}', \mathbf{y}) = \frac{2}{r(r-1)} \sum_{i=1}^{r-1} \sum_{j=i+1}^{r} \mathbb{1}_{[\mathrm{sign}(y'_i - y'_j) \neq \mathrm{sign}(y_i - y_j)]}.$$

This loss function is more useful than the 0–1 loss as it reflects the level of similarity between the two rankings.

- **Normalized Discounted Cumulative Gain (NDCG):** This measure emphasizes the correctness at the top of the list by using a monotonically nondecreasing discount function $D : \mathbb{N} \to \mathbb{R}_+$. We first define a discounted cumulative gain measure:

$$G(\mathbf{y}', \mathbf{y}) = \sum_{i=1}^{r} D(\pi(\mathbf{y}')_i)\, y_i.$$

In words, if we interpret y_i as a score of the "true relevance" of item i, then we take a weighted sum of the relevance of the elements, while the weight of y_i is determined on the basis of the position of i in $\pi(\mathbf{y}')$. Assuming that all elements of $\mathbf{y}$ are nonnegative, it is easy to verify that $0 \leq G(\mathbf{y}', \mathbf{y}) \leq G(\mathbf{y}, \mathbf{y})$. We can therefore define a normalized discounted cumulative gain by the ratio $G(\mathbf{y}', \mathbf{y})/G(\mathbf{y}, \mathbf{y})$, and the corresponding loss function would be

$$\Delta(\mathbf{y}', \mathbf{y}) = 1 - \frac{G(\mathbf{y}', \mathbf{y})}{G(\mathbf{y}, \mathbf{y})} = \frac{1}{G(\mathbf{y}, \mathbf{y})} \sum_{i=1}^{r} \left(D(\pi(\mathbf{y})_i) - D(\pi(\mathbf{y}')_i)\right) y_i.$$

We can easily see that $\Delta(\mathbf{y}', \mathbf{y}) \in [0, 1]$ and that $\Delta(\mathbf{y}', \mathbf{y}) = 0$ whenever $\pi(\mathbf{y}') = \pi(\mathbf{y})$.

A typical way to define the discount function is by

$$D(i) = \begin{cases} \frac{1}{\log_2(r-i+2)} & \text{if } i \in \{r-k+1, \ldots, r\} \\ 0 & \text{otherwise} \end{cases}$$

where $k < r$ is a parameter. This means that we care more about elements that are ranked higher, and we completely ignore elements that are not at the top-k ranked elements. The NDCG measure is often used to evaluate the performance of search engines since in such applications it makes sense completely to ignore elements that are not at the top of the ranking.

Once we have a hypothesis class and a ranking loss function, we can learn a ranking function using the ERM rule. However, from the computational point of view, the resulting optimization problem might be hard to solve. We next discuss how to learn linear predictors for ranking.

17.4.1 Linear Predictors for Ranking

A natural way to define a ranking function is by projecting the instances onto some vector $\mathbf{w}$ and then outputting the resulting scalars as our representation of the ranking function. That is, assuming that $\mathcal{X} \subset \mathbb{R}^d$, for every $\mathbf{w} \in \mathbb{R}^d$ we define a ranking function

$$h_{\mathbf{w}}((\mathbf{x}_1,\ldots,\mathbf{x}_r)) = (\langle \mathbf{w},\mathbf{x}_1\rangle,\ldots,\langle \mathbf{w},\mathbf{x}_r\rangle). \tag{17.6}$$

As we discussed in Chapter 16, we can also apply a feature mapping that maps instances into some feature space and then takes the inner products with $\mathbf{w}$ in the feature space. For simplicity, we focus on the simpler form as in Equation (17.6).

Given some $W \subset \mathbb{R}^d$, we can now define the hypothesis class $\mathcal{H}_W = \{h_{\mathbf{w}} : \mathbf{w} \in W\}$. Once we have defined this hypothesis class, and have chosen a ranking loss function, we can apply the ERM rule as follows: Given a training set, $S = (\bar{\mathbf{x}}_1,\mathbf{y}_1),\ldots,(\bar{\mathbf{x}}_m,\mathbf{y}_m)$, where each $(\bar{\mathbf{x}}_i,\mathbf{y}_i)$ is in $(\mathcal{X}\times\mathbb{R})^{r_i}$, for some $r_i \in \mathbb{N}$, we should search $\mathbf{w} \in W$ that minimizes the empirical loss, $\sum_{i=1}^m \Delta(h_{\mathbf{w}}(\bar{\mathbf{x}}_i),\mathbf{y}_i)$. As in the case of binary classification, for many loss functions this problem is computationally hard, and we therefore turn to describe convex surrogate loss functions. We describe the surrogates for the Kendall tau loss and for the NDCG loss.

A Hinge Loss for the Kendall Tau Loss Function:
We can think of the Kendall tau loss as an average of 0–1 losses for each pair. In particular, for every (i,j) we can rewrite

$$\mathbb{1}_{[\mathrm{sign}(y'_i - y'_j) \neq \mathrm{sign}(y_i - y_j)]} = \mathbb{1}_{[\mathrm{sign}(y_i - y_j)(y'_i - y'_j) \leq 0]}.$$

In our case, $y'_i - y'_j = \langle \mathbf{w}, \mathbf{x}_i - \mathbf{x}_j\rangle$. It follows that we can use the hinge loss upper bound as follows:

$$\mathbb{1}_{[\mathrm{sign}(y_i - y_j)(y'_i - y'_j) \leq 0]} \leq \max\left\{0, 1 - \mathrm{sign}\left(y_i - y_j\right)\left\langle \mathbf{w}, \mathbf{x}_i - \mathbf{x}_j\right\rangle\right\}.$$

Taking the average over the pairs we obtain the following surrogate convex loss for the Kendall tau loss function:

$$\Delta(h_{\mathbf{w}}(\bar{\mathbf{x}}),\mathbf{y}) \leq \frac{2}{r(r-1)}\sum_{i=1}^{r-1}\sum_{j=i+1}^{r} \max\left\{0, 1 - \mathrm{sign}(y_i - y_j)\left\langle \mathbf{w}, \mathbf{x}_i - \mathbf{x}_j\right\rangle\right\}.$$

The right-hand side is convex with respect to $\mathbf{w}$ and upper bounds the Kendall tau loss. It is also a ρ-Lipschitz function with parameter $\rho \leq \max_{i,j}\|\mathbf{x}_i - \mathbf{x}_j\|$.

A Hinge Loss for the NDCG Loss Function:
The NDCG loss function depends on the predicted ranking vector $\mathbf{y}' \in \mathbb{R}^r$ via the permutation it induces. To derive a surrogate loss function we first make the following observation. Let V be the set of all permutations of $[r]$ encoded as vectors; namely, each $\mathbf{v} \in V$ is a vector in $[r]^r$ such that for all $i \neq j$ we have $v_i \neq v_j$. Then (see Exercise 17.4),

$$\pi(\mathbf{y}') = \underset{\mathbf{v}\in V}{\mathrm{argmax}} \sum_{i=1}^{r} v_i\, y'_i. \tag{17.7}$$

Let us denote $\Psi(\bar{\mathbf{x}}, \mathbf{v}) = \sum_{i=1}^{r} v_i \mathbf{x}_i$; it follows that

$$\begin{aligned}\pi(h_{\mathbf{w}}(\bar{\mathbf{x}})) &= \operatorname*{argmax}_{\mathbf{v}\in V} \sum_{i=1}^{r} v_i \langle \mathbf{w}, \mathbf{x}_i \rangle \\ &= \operatorname*{argmax}_{\mathbf{v}\in V} \left\langle \mathbf{w}, \sum_{i=1}^{r} v_i \mathbf{x}_i \right\rangle \\ &= \operatorname*{argmax}_{\mathbf{v}\in V} \langle \mathbf{w}, \Psi(\bar{\mathbf{x}}, \mathbf{v}) \rangle.\end{aligned}$$

On the basis of this observation, we can use the generalized hinge loss for cost-sensitive multiclass classification as a surrogate loss function for the NDCG loss as follows:

$$\begin{aligned}\Delta(h_{\mathbf{w}}(\bar{\mathbf{x}}), \mathbf{y}) &\le \Delta(h_{\mathbf{w}}(\bar{\mathbf{x}}), \mathbf{y}) + \langle \mathbf{w}, \Psi(\bar{\mathbf{x}}, \pi(h_{\mathbf{w}}(\bar{\mathbf{x}}))) \rangle - \langle \mathbf{w}, \Psi(\bar{\mathbf{x}}, \pi(\mathbf{y})) \rangle \\ &\le \max_{\mathbf{v}\in V} \left[\Delta(\mathbf{v}, \mathbf{y}) + \langle \mathbf{w}, \Psi(\bar{\mathbf{x}}, \mathbf{v}) \rangle - \langle \mathbf{w}, \Psi(\bar{\mathbf{x}}, \pi(\mathbf{y})) \rangle \right] \\ &= \max_{\mathbf{v}\in V} \left[\Delta(\mathbf{v}, \mathbf{y}) + \sum_{i=1}^{r} (v_i - \pi(\mathbf{y})_i) \langle \mathbf{w}, \mathbf{x}_i \rangle \right]. \qquad (17.8)\end{aligned}$$

The right-hand side is a convex function with respect to $\mathbf{w}$.

We can now solve the learning problem using SGD as described in Section 17.2.5. The main computational bottleneck is calculating a subgradient of the loss function, which is equivalent to finding $\mathbf{v}$ that achieves the maximum in Equation (17.8) (see Claim 14.6). Using the definition of the NDCG loss, this is equivalent to solving the problem

$$\operatorname*{argmin}_{\mathbf{v}\in V} \sum_{i=1}^{r} (\alpha_i v_i + \beta_i D(v_i)),$$

where $\alpha_i = -\langle \mathbf{w}, \mathbf{x}_i \rangle$ and $\beta_i = y_i / G(\mathbf{y}, \mathbf{y})$. We can think of this problem a little bit differently by defining a matrix $A \in \mathbb{R}^{r,r}$ where

$$A_{i,j} = j\alpha_i + D(j)\beta_i.$$

Now, let us think about each j as a "worker," each i as a "task," and $A_{i,j}$ as the cost of assigning task i to worker j. With this view, the problem of finding $\mathbf{v}$ becomes the problem of finding an assignment of the tasks to workers of minimal cost. This problem is called "the assignment problem" and can be solved efficiently. One particular algorithm is the "Hungarian method" (Kuhn 1955). Another way to solve the assignment problem is using linear programming. To do so, let us first write the assignment problem as

$$\underset{B\in\mathbb{R}_+^{r,r}}{\operatorname{argmin}} \sum_{i,j=1}^{r} A_{i,j}B_{i,j} \tag{17.9}$$

$$\text{s.t. } \forall i \in [r],\ \sum_{j=1}^{r} B_{i,j} = 1$$

$$\forall j \in [r],\ \sum_{i=1}^{r} B_{i,j} = 1$$

$$\forall i,j,\ \ B_{i,j} \in \{0,1\}$$

A matrix B that satisfies the constraints in the preceding optimization problem is called a permutation matrix. This is because the constraints guarantee that there is at most a single entry of each row that equals 1 and a single entry of each column that equals 1. Therefore, the matrix B corresponds to the permutation $\mathbf{v} \in V$ defined by $v_i = j$ for the single index j that satisfies $B_{i,j} = 1$.

The preceding optimization is still not a linear program because of the combinatorial constraint $B_{i,j} \in \{0,1\}$. However, as it turns out, this constraint is redundant – if we solve the optimization problem while simply omitting the combinatorial constraint, then we are still guaranteed that there is an optimal solution that will satisfy this constraint. This is formalized later.

Denote $\langle A, B\rangle = \sum_{i,j} A_{i,j}B_{i,j}$. Then, Equation (17.9) is the problem of minimizing $\langle A, B\rangle$ such that B is a permutation matrix.

A matrix $B \in \mathbb{R}^{r,r}$ is called *doubly stochastic* if all elements of B are nonnegative, the sum of each row of B is 1, and the sum of each column of B is 1. Therefore, solving Equation (17.9) without the constraints $B_{i,j} \in \{0,1\}$ is the problem

$$\underset{B\in\mathbb{R}^{r,r}}{\operatorname{argmin}} \langle A, B\rangle \text{ s.t. } B \text{ is a doubly stochastic matrix.} \tag{17.10}$$

The following claim states that every doubly stochastic matrix is a convex combination of permutation matrices.

Claim 17.3 (Birkhoff 1946, Von Neumann 1953). *The set of doubly stochastic matrices in $\mathbb{R}^{r,r}$ is the convex hull of the set of permutation matrices in $\mathbb{R}^{r,r}$.*

On the basis of the claim, we easily obtain the following:

Lemma 17.4. *There exists an optimal solution of Equation (17.10) that is also an optimal solution of Equation (17.9).*

Proof. Let B be a solution of Equation (17.10). Then, by Claim 17.3, we can write $B = \sum_i \gamma_i C_i$, where each C_i is a permutation matrix, each $\gamma_i > 0$, and $\sum_i \gamma_i = 1$. Since all the C_i are also doubly stochastic, we clearly have that $\langle A,\ B\rangle \le \langle A,\ C_i\rangle$ for every i. We claim that there is some i for which $\langle A,\ B\rangle = \langle A,\ C_i\rangle$. This must be true since otherwise, if for every i $\langle A,\ B\rangle < \langle A,\ C_i\rangle$, we would have that

$$\langle A, B\rangle = \left\langle A, \sum_i \gamma_i C_i \right\rangle = \sum_i \gamma_i \langle A, C_i\rangle > \sum_i \gamma_i \langle A, B\rangle = \langle A, B\rangle,$$

which cannot hold. We have thus shown that some permutation matrix, C_i, satisfies $\langle A, B\rangle = \langle A, C_i\rangle$. But, since for every other permutation matrix C we have $\langle A, B\rangle \leq \langle A, C\rangle$ we conclude that C_i is an optimal solution of both Equation (17.9) and Equation (17.10). □

17.5 BIPARTITE RANKING AND MULTIVARIATE PERFORMANCE MEASURES

In the previous section we described the problem of ranking. We used a vector $\mathbf{y} \in \mathbb{R}^r$ for representing an order over the elements $\mathbf{x}_1, \ldots, \mathbf{x}_r$. If all elements in $\mathbf{y}$ are different from each other, then $\mathbf{y}$ specifies a full order over $[r]$. However, if two elements of $\mathbf{y}$ attain the same value, $y_i = y_j$ for $i \neq j$, then $\mathbf{y}$ can only specify a partial order over $[r]$. In such a case, we say that $\mathbf{x}_i$ and $\mathbf{x}_j$ are of equal relevance according to $\mathbf{y}$. In the extreme case, $\mathbf{y} \in \{\pm 1\}^r$, which means that each $\mathbf{x}_i$ is either relevant or nonrelevant. This setting is often called "bipartite ranking." For example, in the fraud detection application mentioned in the previous section, each transaction is labeled as either fraudulent ($y_i = 1$) or benign ($y_i = -1$).

Seemingly, we can solve the bipartite ranking problem by learning a binary classifier, applying it on each instance, and putting the positive ones at the top of the ranked list. However, this may lead to poor results as the goal of a binary learner is usually to minimize the zero-one loss (or some surrogate of it), while the goal of a ranker might be significantly different. To illustrate this, consider again the problem of fraud detection. Usually, most of the transactions are benign (say 99.9%). Therefore, a binary classifier that predicts "benign" on all transactions will have a zero-one error of 0.1%. While this is a very small number, the resulting predictor is meaningless for the fraud detection application. The crux of the problem stems from the inadequacy of the zero-one loss for what we are really interested in. A more adequate performance measure should take into account the predictions over the entire set of instances. For example, in the previous section we have defined the NDCG loss, which emphasizes the correctness of the top-ranked items. In this section we describe additional loss functions that are specifically adequate for bipartite ranking problems.

As in the previous section, we are given a sequence of instances, $\bar{\mathbf{x}} = (\mathbf{x}_1, \ldots, \mathbf{x}_r)$, and we predict a ranking vector $\mathbf{y}' \in \mathbb{R}^r$. The feedback vector is $\mathbf{y} \in \{\pm 1\}^r$. We define a loss that depends on $\mathbf{y}'$ and $\mathbf{y}$ and depends on a threshold $\theta \in \mathbb{R}$. This threshold transforms the vector $\mathbf{y}' \in \mathbb{R}^r$ into the vector $(\mathrm{sign}(y'_i - \theta), \ldots, \mathrm{sign}(y'_r - \theta)) \in \{\pm 1\}^r$. Usually, the value of θ is set to be 0. However, as we will see, we sometimes set θ while taking into account additional constraints on the problem.

The loss functions we define in the following depend on the following 4 numbers:

$$
\begin{aligned}
\text{True positives: } & a = |\{i : y_i = +1 \wedge \mathrm{sign}(y'_i - \theta) = +1\}| \\
\text{False positives: } & b = |\{i : y_i = -1 \wedge \mathrm{sign}(y'_i - \theta) = +1\}| \\
\text{False negatives: } & c = |\{i : y_i = +1 \wedge \mathrm{sign}(y'_i - \theta) = -1\}| \\
\text{True negatives: } & d = |\{i : y_i = -1 \wedge \mathrm{sign}(y'_i - \theta) = -1\}|
\end{aligned}
\tag{17.11}
$$

The **recall** (a.k.a. **sensitivity**) of a prediction vector is the fraction of true positives $\mathbf{y}'$ "catches," namely, $\frac{a}{a+c}$. The **precision** is the fraction of correct predictions among the positive labels we predict, namely, $\frac{a}{a+b}$. The **specificity** is the fraction of true negatives that our predictor "catches," namely, $\frac{d}{d+b}$.

Note that as we decrease θ the recall increases (attaining the value 1 when $\theta = -\infty$). On the other hand, the precision and the specificity usually decrease as we decrease θ. Therefore, there is a tradeoff between precision and recall, and we can control it by changing θ. The loss functions defined in the following use various techniques for combining both the precision and recall.

- **Averaging sensitivity and specificity**: This measure is the average of the sensitivity and specificity, namely, $\frac{1}{2}\left(\frac{a}{a+c}+\frac{d}{d+b}\right)$. This is also the accuracy on positive examples averaged with the accuracy on negative examples. Here, we set $\theta = 0$ and the corresponding loss function is $\Delta(\mathbf{y}',\mathbf{y}) = 1 - \frac{1}{2}\left(\frac{a}{a+c}+\frac{d}{d+b}\right)$.
- **F_1-score**: The F_1 score is the harmonic mean of the precision and recall: $\frac{2}{\frac{1}{\text{Precision}}+\frac{1}{\text{Recall}}}$. Its maximal value (of 1) is obtained when both precision and recall are 1, and its minimal value (of 0) is obtained whenever one of them is 0 (even if the other one is 1). The F_1 score can be written using the numbers a, b, c as follows; $F_1 = \frac{2a}{2a+b+c}$. Again, we set $\theta = 0$, and the loss function becomes $\Delta(\mathbf{y}', \mathbf{y}) = 1 - F_1$.
- **F_β-score**: It is like F_1 score, but we attach β^2 times more importance to recall than to precision, that is, $\frac{1+\beta^2}{\frac{1}{\text{Precision}}+\beta^2\frac{1}{\text{Recall}}}$. It can also be written as $F_\beta = \frac{(1+\beta^2)a}{(1+\beta^2)a+b+\beta^2 c}$. Again, we set $\theta = 0$, and the loss function becomes $\Delta(\mathbf{y}',\mathbf{y}) = 1 - F_\beta$.
- **Recall at k**: We measure the recall while the prediction must contain at most k positive labels. That is, we should set θ so that $a + b \leq k$. This is convenient, for example, in the application of a fraud detection system, where a bank employee can only handle a small number of suspicious transactions.
- **Precision at k**: We measure the precision while the prediction must contain at least k positive labels. That is, we should set θ so that $a + b \geq k$.

The measures defined previously are often referred to as *multivariate performance measures*. Note that these measures are highly different from the average zero-one loss, which in the preceding notation equals $\frac{b+d}{a+b+c+d}$. In the aforementioned example of fraud detection, when 99.9% of the examples are negatively labeled, the zero-one loss of predicting that all the examples are negatives is 0.1%. In contrast, the recall of such prediction is 0 and hence the F_1 score is also 0, which means that the corresponding loss will be 1.

17.5.1 Linear Predictors for Bipartite Ranking

We next describe how to train linear predictors for bipartite ranking. As in the previous section, a linear predictor for ranking is defined to be

$$h_{\mathbf{w}}(\bar{\mathbf{x}}) = (\langle \mathbf{w}, \mathbf{x}_1 \rangle, \ldots, \langle \mathbf{w}, \mathbf{x}_r \rangle).$$

The corresponding loss function is one of the multivariate performance measures described before. The loss function depends on $\mathbf{y}' = h_{\mathbf{w}}(\bar{\mathbf{x}})$ via the binary vector it induces, which we denote by

$$\mathbf{b}(\mathbf{y}') = (\text{sign}(y'_1 - \theta), \ldots, \text{sign}(y'_r - \theta)) \in \{\pm 1\}^r. \tag{17.12}$$

As in the previous section, to facilitate an efficient algorithm we derive a convex surrogate loss function on Δ. The derivation is similar to the derivation of the generalized hinge loss for the NDCG ranking loss, as described in the previous section.

Our first observation is that for all the values of θ defined before, there is some $V \subseteq \{\pm 1\}^r$ such that $\mathbf{b}(\mathbf{y}')$ can be rewritten as

$$\mathbf{b}(\mathbf{y}') = \underset{\mathbf{v} \in V}{\text{argmax}} \sum_{i=1}^{r} v_i y'_i. \tag{17.13}$$

This is clearly true for the case $\theta = 0$ if we choose $V = \{\pm 1\}^r$. The two measures for which θ is not taken to be 0 are precision at k and recall at k. For precision at k we can take V to be the set $V_{\geq k}$, containing all vectors in $\{\pm 1\}^r$ whose number of ones is at least k. For recall at k, we can take V to be $V_{\leq k}$, which is defined analogously. See Exercise 17.5.

Once we have defined $\mathbf{b}$ as in Equation (17.13), we can easily derive a convex surrogate loss as follows. Assuming that $\mathbf{y} \in V$, we have that

$$\begin{aligned}
\Delta(h_{\mathbf{w}}(\bar{\mathbf{x}}), \mathbf{y}) &= \Delta(\mathbf{b}(h_{\mathbf{w}}(\bar{\mathbf{x}})), \mathbf{y}) \\
&\leq \Delta(\mathbf{b}(h_{\mathbf{w}}(\bar{\mathbf{x}})), \mathbf{y}) + \sum_{i=1}^{r} (b_i(h_{\mathbf{w}}(\bar{\mathbf{x}})) - y_i)\langle \mathbf{w}, \mathbf{x}_i \rangle \\
&\leq \max_{\mathbf{v} \in V} \left[\Delta(\mathbf{v}, \mathbf{y}) + \sum_{i=1}^{r} (v_i - y_i) \langle \mathbf{w}, \mathbf{x}_i \rangle \right].
\end{aligned} \tag{17.14}$$

The right-hand side is a convex function with respect to $\mathbf{w}$.

We can now solve the learning problem using SGD as described in Section 17.2.5. The main computational bottleneck is calculating a subgradient of the loss function, which is equivalent to finding $\mathbf{v}$ that achieves the maximum in Equation (17.14) (see Claim 14.6).

In the following we describe how to find this maximizer efficiently for any performance measure that can be written as a function of the numbers a, b, c, d given in Equation (17.11), and for which the set V contains all elements in $\{\pm 1\}^r$ for which the values of a, b satisfy some constraints. For example, for "recall at k" the set V is all vectors for which $a + b \leq k$.

The idea is as follows. For any $a, b \in [r]$, let

$$\bar{\mathcal{Y}}_{a,b} = \{\mathbf{v} : |\{i : v_i = 1 \wedge y_i = 1\}| = a \wedge |\{i : v_i = 1 \wedge y_i = -1\}| = b\}.$$

Any vector $\mathbf{v} \in V$ falls into $\bar{\mathcal{Y}}_{a,b}$ for some $a, b \in [r]$. Furthermore, if $\bar{\mathcal{Y}}_{a,b} \cap V$ is not empty for some $a, b \in [r]$ then $\bar{\mathcal{Y}}_{a,b} \cap V = \bar{\mathcal{Y}}_{a,b}$. Therefore, we can search within each $\bar{\mathcal{Y}}_{a,b}$ that has a nonempty intersection with V separately, and then take the optimal value. The key observation is that once we are searching only within $\bar{\mathcal{Y}}_{a,b}$, the value of Δ is fixed so we only need to maximize the expression

$$\max_{\mathbf{v}\in\bar{\mathcal{Y}}_{a,b}} \sum_{i=1}^{r} v_i \langle \mathbf{w}, \mathbf{x}_i \rangle.$$

Suppose the examples are sorted so that $\langle \mathbf{w}, \mathbf{x}_1 \rangle \geq \cdots \geq \langle \mathbf{w}, \mathbf{x}_r \rangle$. Then, it is easy to verify that we would like to set v_i to be positive for the smallest indices i. Doing this, with the constraint on a, b, amounts to setting $v_i = 1$ for the a top ranked positive examples and for the b top-ranked negative examples. This yields the following procedure.

Solving Equation (17.14)

input:
  $(\mathbf{x}_1, \ldots, \mathbf{x}_r), (y_1, \ldots, y_r), \mathbf{w}, V, \Delta$
assumptions:
  Δ is a function of $a,\ b,\ c,\ d$
  V contains all vectors for which $f(a, b) = 1$ for some function f
initialize:
  $P = |\{i : y_i = 1\}|,\ N = |\{i : y_i = -1\}|$
  $\boldsymbol{\mu} = (\langle \mathbf{w}, \mathbf{x}_1 \rangle, \ldots, \langle \mathbf{w}, \mathbf{x}_r \rangle),\ \alpha^\star = -\infty$
  sort examples so that $\mu_1 \geq \mu_2 \geq \cdots \geq \mu_r$
  let $i_1, \ldots, i_P$ be the (sorted) indices of the positive examples
  let $j_1, \ldots, j_N$ be the (sorted) indices of the negative examples
for $a = 0, 1, \ldots, P$
  $c = P - a$
  for $b = 0, 1, \ldots, N$ such that $f(a, b) = 1$
    $d = N - b$
    calculate Δ using $a,\ b,\ c,\ d$
    set $v_1, \ldots, v_r$ s.t. $v_{i_1} = \cdots = v_{i_a} = v_{j_1} = \cdots = v_{j_b} = 1$
      and the rest of the elements of $\mathbf{v}$ equal -1
    set $\alpha = \Delta + \sum_{i=1}^{r} v_i \mu_i$
    if $\alpha \geq \alpha^\star$
      $\alpha^\star = \alpha,\ \mathbf{v}^\star = \mathbf{v}$
output $\mathbf{v}^\star$

17.6 SUMMARY

Many real world supervised learning problems can be cast as learning a multiclass predictor. We started the chapter by introducing reductions of multiclass learning to binary learning. We then described and analyzed the family of linear predictors for multiclass learning. We have shown how this family can be used even if the number of classes is extremely large, as long as we have an adequate structure on the problem. Finally, we have described ranking problems. In Chapter 29 we study the sample complexity of multiclass learning in more detail.

17.7 BIBLIOGRAPHIC REMARKS

The One-versus-All and All-Pairs approach reductions have been unified under the framework of Error Correction Output Codes (ECOC) (Dietterich & Bakiri 1995, Allwein, Schapire & Singer 2000). There are also other types of reductions such as tree-based classifiers (see, for example, Beygelzimer, Langford & Ravikumar (2007)). The limitations of reduction techniques have been studied in (Daniely et al. 2011, Daniely et al. 2012). See also Chapter 29, in which we analyze the sample complexity of multiclass learning.

Direct approaches to multiclass learning with linear predictors have been studied in (Vapnik 1998, Weston & Watkins 1999, Crammer & Singer 2001). In particular, the multivector construction is due to Crammer and Singer (2001).

Collins (2000) has shown how to apply the Perceptron algorithm for structured output problems. See also Collins (2002). A related approach is discriminative learning of conditional random fields; see Lafferty et al. (2001). Structured output SVM has been studied in (Weston et al. 2002, Collins 2002, Taskar et al. 2003, Tsochantaridis et al. 2004).

The dynamic procedure we have presented for calculating the prediction $h_{\mathbf{w}}(\mathbf{x})$ in the structured output section is similar to the forward-backward variables calculated by the Viterbi procedure in HMMs (see, for instance, (Rabiner & Juang 1986)). More generally, solving the maximization problem in structured output is closely related to the problem of inference in graphical models (see, for example, Koller & Friedman (2009*a*)).

Chapelle, Le, and Smola (2007) proposed to learn a ranking function with respect to the NDCG loss using ideas from structured output learning. They also observed that the maximization problem in the definition of the generalized hinge loss is equivalent to the assignment problem.

Agarwal and Roth (2005) analyzed the sample complexity of bipartite ranking. Joachims (2005) studied the applicability of structured output SVM to bipartite ranking with multivariate performance measures.

17.8 EXERCISES

17.1 Consider a set S of examples in $\mathbb{R}^n \times [k]$ for which there exist vectors $\boldsymbol{\mu}_1, \ldots, \boldsymbol{\mu}_k$ such that every example $(\mathbf{x}, y) \in S$ falls within a ball centered at $\boldsymbol{\mu}_y$ whose radius is $r \geq 1$. Assume also that for every $i \neq j$, $\|\boldsymbol{\mu}_i - \boldsymbol{\mu}_j\| \geq 4r$. Consider concatenating each instance by the constant 1 and then applying the multivector construction, namely,

$$\Psi(\mathbf{x}, y) = [\underbrace{0, \ldots, 0}_{\in \mathbb{R}^{(y-1)(n+1)}}, \underbrace{x_1, \ldots, x_n, 1}_{\in \mathbb{R}^{n+1}}, \underbrace{0, \ldots, 0}_{\in \mathbb{R}^{(k-y)(n+1)}}].$$

Show that there exists a vector $\mathbf{w} \in \mathbb{R}^{k(n+1)}$ such that $\ell(\mathbf{w}, (\mathbf{x}, y)) = 0$ for every $(\mathbf{x}, y) \in S$.

Hint: Observe that for every example $(\mathbf{x}, y) \in S$ we can write $\mathbf{x} = \boldsymbol{\mu}_y + \mathbf{v}$ for some $\|\mathbf{v}\| \leq r$. Now, take $\mathbf{w} = [\mathbf{w}_1, \ldots, \mathbf{w}_k]$, where $\mathbf{w}_i = [\boldsymbol{\mu}_i, -\|\boldsymbol{\mu}_i\|^2/2]$.

17.2 **Multiclass Perceptron:** Consider the following algorithm:

Multiclass Batch Perceptron

Input:
A training set $(\mathbf{x}_1, y_1), \ldots, (\mathbf{x}_m, y_m)$
A class-sensitive feature mapping $\Psi : \mathcal{X} \times \mathcal{Y} \to \mathbb{R}^d$
Initialize: $\mathbf{w}^{(1)} = (0, \ldots, 0) \in \mathbb{R}^d$
For $t = 1, 2, \ldots$
If $(\exists\, i$ and $y \neq y_i$ s.t. $\langle \mathbf{w}^{(t)}, \Psi(\mathbf{x}_i, y_i)\rangle \leq \langle \mathbf{w}^{(t)}, \Psi(\mathbf{x}_i, y)\rangle)$ then
$\mathbf{w}^{(t+1)} = \mathbf{w}^{(t)} + \Psi(\mathbf{x}_i, y_i) - \Psi(\mathbf{x}_i, y)$
else
output $\mathbf{w}^{(t)}$

Prove the following:

Theorem 17.5. *Assume that there exists* $\mathbf{w}^\star$ *such that for all* i *and for all* $y \neq y_i$ *it holds that* $\langle \mathbf{w}^\star, \Psi(\mathbf{x}_i, y_i)\rangle \geq \langle \mathbf{w}^\star, \Psi(\mathbf{x}_i, y)\rangle + 1$. *Let* $R = \max_{i,y} \|\Psi(\mathbf{x}_i, y_i) - \Psi(\mathbf{x}_i, y)\|$. *Then, the multiclass Perceptron algorithm stops after at most* $(R\|\mathbf{w}^\star\|)^2$ *iterations, and when it stops it holds that* $\forall i \in [m],\;\; y_i = \operatorname{argmax}_y \langle \mathbf{w}^{(t)}, \Psi(\mathbf{x}_i, y)\rangle$.

17.3 Generalize the dynamic programming procedure given in Section 17.3 for solving the maximization problem given in the definition of $\hat{h}$ in the SGD procedure for multiclass prediction. You can assume that $\Delta(\mathbf{y}', \mathbf{y}) = \sum_{t=1}^{r} \delta(y'_t, y_t)$ for some arbitrary function δ.

17.4 Prove that Equation (17.7) holds.

17.5 Show that the two definitions of π as defined in Equation (17.12) and Equation (17.13) are indeed equivalent for all the multivariate performance measures.

18

Decision Trees

A decision tree is a predictor, $h : \mathcal{X} \to \mathcal{Y}$, that predicts the label associated with an instance $\mathbf{x}$ by traveling from a root node of a tree to a leaf. For simplicity we focus on the binary classification setting, namely, $\mathcal{Y} = \{0, 1\}$, but decision trees can be applied for other prediction problems as well. At each node on the root-to-leaf path, the successor child is chosen on the basis of a splitting of the input space. Usually, the splitting is based on one of the features of $\mathbf{x}$ or on a predefined set of splitting rules. A leaf contains a specific label. An example of a decision tree for the papayas example (described in Chapter 2) is given in the following:

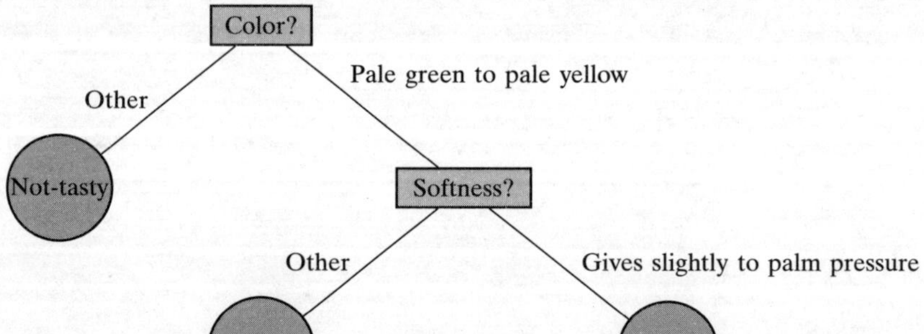

To check if a given papaya is tasty or not, the decision tree first examines the color of the Papaya. If this color is not in the range pale green to pale yellow, then the tree immediately predicts that the papaya is not tasty without additional tests. Otherwise, the tree turns to examine the softness of the papaya. If the softness level of the papaya is such that it gives slightly to palm pressure, the decision tree predicts that the papaya is tasty. Otherwise, the prediction is "not-tasty." The preceding example underscores one of the main advantages of decision trees – the resulting classifier is very simple to understand and interpret.

18.1 SAMPLE COMPLEXITY

A popular splitting rule at internal nodes of the tree is based on thresholding the value of a single feature. That is, we move to the right or left child of the node on the basis of $\mathbb{1}_{[x_i<\theta]}$, where $i \in [d]$ is the index of the relevant feature and $\theta \in \mathbb{R}$ is the threshold. In such cases, we can think of a decision tree as a splitting of the instance space, $\mathcal{X} = \mathbb{R}^d$, into cells, where each leaf of the tree corresponds to one cell. It follows that a tree with k leaves can shatter a set of k instances. Hence, if we allow decision trees of arbitrary size, we obtain a hypothesis class of infinite VC dimension. Such an approach can easily lead to overfitting.

To avoid overfitting, we can rely on the minimum description length (MDL) principle described in Chapter 7, and aim at learning a decision tree that on one hand fits the data well while on the other hand is not too large.

For simplicity, we will assume that $\mathcal{X} = \{0,1\}^d$. In other words, each instance is a vector of d bits. In that case, thresholding the value of a single feature corresponds to a splitting rule of the form $\mathbb{1}_{[x_i=1]}$ for some $i = [d]$. For instance, we can model the "papaya decision tree" earlier by assuming that a papaya is parameterized by a two-dimensional bit vector $\mathbf{x} \in \{0,1\}^2$, where the bit x_1 represents whether the color is pale green to pale yellow or not, and the bit x_2 represents whether the softness is gives slightly to palm pressure or not. With this representation, the node Color? can be replaced with $\mathbb{1}_{[x_1=1]}$, and the node Softness? can be replaced with $\mathbb{1}_{[x_2=1]}$. While this is a big simplification, the algorithms and analysis we provide in the following can be extended to more general cases.

With the aforementioned simplifying assumption, the hypothesis class becomes finite, but is still very large. In particular, any classifier from $\{0,1\}^d$ to $\{0,1\}$ can be represented by a decision tree with 2^d leaves and depth of $d+1$ (see Exercise 18.1). Therefore, the VC dimension of the class is 2^d, which means that the number of examples we need to PAC learn the hypothesis class grows with 2^d. Unless d is very small, this is a huge number of examples.

To overcome this obstacle, we rely on the MDL scheme described in Chapter 7. The underlying prior knowledge is that we should prefer smaller trees over larger trees. To formalize this intuition, we first need to define a description language for decision trees, which is prefix free and requires fewer bits for smaller decision trees. Here is one possible way: A tree with n nodes will be described in $n+1$ blocks, each of size $\log_2(d+3)$ bits. The first n blocks encode the nodes of the tree, in a depth-first order (preorder), and the last block marks the end of the code. Each block indicates whether the current node is:

- An internal node of the form $\mathbb{1}_{[x_i=1]}$ for some $i \in [d]$
- A leaf whose value is 1
- A leaf whose value is 0
- End of the code

Overall, there are $d+3$ options, hence we need $\log_2(d+3)$ bits to describe each block.

Assuming each internal node has two children,[1] it is not hard to show that this is a prefix-free encoding of the tree, and that the description length of a tree with n nodes is $(n+1)\log_2(d+3)$.

By Theorem 7.7 we have that with probability of at least $1-\delta$ over a sample of size m, for every n and every decision tree $h \in \mathcal{H}$ with n nodes it holds that

$$L_{\mathcal{D}}(h) \leq L_S(h) + \sqrt{\frac{(n+1)\log_2(d+3) + \log(2/\delta)}{2m}}. \tag{18.1}$$

This bound performs a tradeoff: on the one hand, we expect larger, more complex decision trees to have a smaller training risk, $L_S(h)$, but the respective value of n will be larger. On the other hand, smaller decision trees will have a smaller value of n, but $L_S(h)$ might be larger. Our hope (or prior knowledge) is that we can find a decision tree with both low empirical risk, $L_S(h)$, and a number of nodes n not too high. Our bound indicates that such a tree will have low true risk, $L_{\mathcal{D}}(h)$.

18.2 DECISION TREE ALGORITHMS

The bound on $L_{\mathcal{D}}(h)$ given in Equation (18.1) suggests a learning rule for decision trees – search for a tree that minimizes the right-hand side of Equation (18.1). Unfortunately, it turns out that solving this problem is computationally hard.[2] Consequently, practical decision tree learning algorithms are based on heuristics such as a greedy approach, where the tree is constructed gradually, and locally optimal decisions are made at the construction of each node. Such algorithms cannot guarantee to return the globally optimal decision tree but tend to work reasonably well in practice.

A general framework for growing a decision tree is as follows. We start with a tree with a single leaf (the root) and assign this leaf a label according to a majority vote among all labels over the training set. We now perform a series of iterations. On each iteration, we examine the effect of splitting a single leaf. We define some "gain" measure that quantifies the improvement due to this split. Then, among all possible splits, we either choose the one that maximizes the gain and perform it, or choose not to split the leaf at all.

In the following we provide a possible implementation. It is based on a popular decision tree algorithm known as "ID3" (short for "Iterative Dichotomizer 3"). We describe the algorithm for the case of binary features, namely, $\mathcal{X} = \{0,1\}^d$, and therefore all splitting rules are of the form $\mathbb{1}_{[x_i=1]}$ for some feature $i \in [d]$. We discuss the case of real valued features in Section 18.2.3.

The algorithm works by recursive calls, with the initial call being $\texttt{ID3}(S,[d])$, and returns a decision tree. In the pseudocode that follows, we use a call to a procedure $\texttt{Gain}(S,i)$, which receives a training set S and an index i and evaluates the gain of a split of the tree according to the ith feature. We describe several gain measures in Section 18.2.1.

[1] We may assume this without loss of generality, because if a decision node has only one child, we can replace the node by its child without affecting the predictions of the decision tree.

[2] More precisely, if NP≠P then no algorithm can solve Equation (18.1) in time polynomial in n, d, and m.

ID3(S, A)

INPUT: training set S, feature subset $A \subseteq [d]$
if all examples in S are labeled by 1, return a leaf 1
if all examples in S are labeled by 0, return a leaf 0
if $A = \emptyset$, return a leaf whose value = majority of labels in S
else :
  Let $j = \text{argmax}_{i \in A} \text{Gain}(S, i)$
  if all examples in S have the same label
    Return a leaf whose value = majority of labels in S
  else
    Let T_1 be the tree returned by ID3($\{(\mathbf{x}, y) \in S : x_j = 1\}, A \setminus \{j\}$).
    Let T_2 be the tree returned by ID3($\{(\mathbf{x}, y) \in S : x_j = 0\}, A \setminus \{j\}$).
    Return the tree:

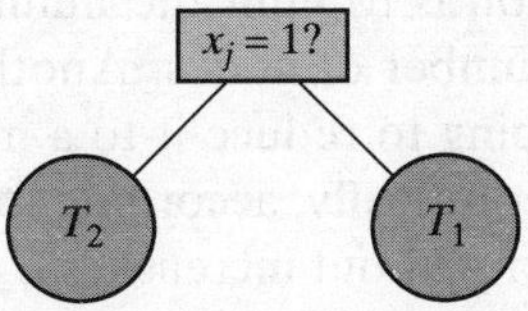

18.2.1 Implementations of the Gain Measure

Different algorithms use different implementations of $\text{Gain}(S, i)$. Here we present three. We use the notation $\mathbb{P}_S[F]$ to denote the probability that an event holds with respect to the uniform distribution over S.

Train Error: The simplest definition of gain is the decrease in training error. Formally, let $C(a) = \min\{a, 1 - a\}$. Note that the training error before splitting on feature i is $C(\mathbb{P}_S[y = 1])$, since we took a majority vote among labels. Similarly, the error after splitting on feature i is

$$\underset{S}{\mathbb{P}}[x_i = 1]\, C(\underset{S}{\mathbb{P}}[y = 1 | x_i = 1]) + \underset{S}{\mathbb{P}}[x_i = 0]\, C(\underset{S}{\mathbb{P}}[y = 1 | x_i = 0]).$$

Therefore, we can define Gain to be the difference between the two, namely,

$$\begin{aligned}\text{Gain}(S, i) &:= C(\underset{S}{\mathbb{P}}[y = 1]) \\ &\quad - \left(\underset{S}{\mathbb{P}}[x_i = 1]\, C(\underset{S}{\mathbb{P}}[y = 1 | x_i = 1]) + \underset{S}{\mathbb{P}}[x_i = 0]\, C(\underset{S}{\mathbb{P}}[y = 1 | x_i = 0]) \right).\end{aligned}$$

Information Gain: Another popular gain measure that is used in the ID3 and C4.5 algorithms of Quinlan (1993) is the information gain. The information gain is the difference between the entropy of the label before and after the split, and is achieved by replacing the function C in the previous expression by the entropy function,

$$C(a) = -a \log(a) - (1 - a) \log(1 - a).$$

Gini Index: Yet another definition of a gain, which is used by the CART algorithm of Breiman, Friedman, Olshen, and Stone (1984), is the Gini index,

$$C(a) = 2a(1-a).$$

Both the information gain and the Gini index are smooth and concave upper bounds of the train error. These properties can be advantageous in some situations (see, for example, Kearns & Mansour (1996)).

18.2.2 Pruning

The ID3 algorithm described previously still suffers from a big problem: The returned tree will usually be very large. Such trees may have low empirical risk, but their true risk will tend to be high – both according to our theoretical analysis, and in practice. One solution is to limit the number of iterations of ID3, leading to a tree with a bounded number of nodes. Another common solution is to *prune* the tree after it is built, hoping to reduce it to a much smaller tree, but still with a similar empirical error. Theoretically, according to the bound in Equation (18.1), if we can make n much smaller without increasing $L_S(h)$ by much, we are likely to get a decision tree with a smaller true risk.

Usually, the pruning is performed by a bottom-up walk on the tree. Each node might be replaced with one of its subtrees or with a leaf, based on some bound or estimate of $L_{\mathcal{D}}(h)$ (for example, the bound in Equation (18.1)). A pseudocode of a common template is given in the following.

Generic Tree Pruning Procedure

input:
function $f(T, m)$ (bound/estimate for the generalization error
of a decision tree T, based on a sample of size m),
tree T.
foreach node j in a bottom-up walk on T (from leaves to root):
find T' which minimizes $f(T', m)$, where T' is any of the following:
the current tree after replacing node j with a leaf 1.
the current tree after replacing node j with a leaf 0.
the current tree after replacing node j with its left subtree.
the current tree after replacing node j with its right subtree.
the current tree.
let $T := T'$.

18.2.3 Threshold-Based Splitting Rules for Real-Valued Features

In the previous section we have described an algorithm for growing a decision tree assuming that the features are binary and the splitting rules are of the form $\mathbb{1}_{[x_i=1]}$. We now extend this result to the case of real-valued features and threshold-based splitting rules, namely, $\mathbb{1}_{[x_i<\theta]}$. Such splitting rules yield decision stumps, and we have studied them in Chapter 10.

The basic idea is to reduce the problem to the case of binary features as follows. Let $\mathbf{x}_1, \ldots, \mathbf{x}_m$ be the instances of the training set. For each real-valued feature i, sort the instances so that $x_{1,i} \leq \cdots \leq x_{m,i}$. Define a set of thresholds $\theta_{0,i}, \ldots, \theta_{m+1,i}$ such that $\theta_{j,i} \in (x_{j,i}, x_{j+1,i})$ (where we use the convention $x_{0,i} = -\infty$ and $x_{m+1,i} = \infty$). Finally, for each i and j we define the binary feature $\mathbb{1}_{[x_i < \theta_{j,i}]}$. Once we have constructed these binary features, we can run the ID3 procedure described in the previous section. It is easy to verify that for any decision tree with threshold-based splitting rules over the original real-valued features there exists a decision tree over the constructed binary features with the same training error and the same number of nodes.

If the original number of real-valued features is d and the number of examples is m, then the number of constructed binary features becomes dm. Calculating the Gain of each feature might therefore take $O(dm^2)$ operations. However, using a more clever implementation, the runtime can be reduced to $O(dm \log(m))$. The idea is similar to the implementation of ERM for decision stumps as described in Section 10.1.1.

18.3 RANDOM FORESTS

As mentioned before, the class of decision trees of arbitrary size has infinite VC dimension. We therefore restricted the size of the decision tree. Another way to reduce the danger of overfitting is by constructing an ensemble of trees. In particular, in the following we describe the method of *random forests*, introduced by Breiman (2001).

A random forest is a classifier consisting of a collection of decision trees, where each tree is constructed by applying an algorithm A on the training set S and an additional random vector, θ, where θ is sampled i.i.d. from some distribution. The prediction of the random forest is obtained by a majority vote over the predictions of the individual trees.

To specify a particular random forest, we need to define the algorithm A and the distribution over θ. There are many ways to do this and here we describe one particular option. We generate θ as follows. First, we take a random subsample from S with replacements; namely, we sample a new training set S' of size m' using the uniform distribution over S. Second, we construct a sequence $I_1, I_2, \ldots$, where each I_t is a subset of $[d]$ of size k, which is generated by sampling uniformly at random elements from $[d]$. All these random variables form the vector θ. Then, the algorithm A grows a decision tree (e.g., using the ID3 algorithm) based on the sample S', where at each splitting stage of the algorithm, the algorithm is restricted to choosing a feature that maximizes Gain from the set I_t. Intuitively, if k is small, this restriction may prevent overfitting.

18.4 SUMMARY

Decision trees are very intuitive predictors. Typically, if a human programmer creates a predictor it will look like a decision tree. We have shown that the VC dimension of decision trees with k leaves is k and proposed the MDL paradigm for learning decision trees. The main problem with decision trees is that they are computationally hard to learn; therefore we described several heuristic procedures for training them.

18.5 BIBLIOGRAPHIC REMARKS

Many algorithms for learning decision trees (such as ID3 and C4.5) have been derived by Quinlan (1986). The CART algorithm is due to Breiman, Friedman, Olshen & Stone (1984). Random forests were introduced by Breiman (2001). For additional reading we refer the reader to (Hastie, Tibshirani & Friedman 2001, Rokach 2007).

The proof of the hardness of training decision trees is given in Hyafil and Rivest (1976).

18.6 EXERCISES

18.1 1. Show that any binary classifier $h:\{0,1\}^d \mapsto \{0,1\}$ can be implemented as a decision tree of height at most $d+1$, with internal nodes of the form $(x_i = 0?)$ for some $i \in \{1,\ldots,d\}$.
2. Conclude that the VC dimension of the class of decision trees over the domain $\{0,1\}^d$ is 2^d.

18.2 **(Suboptimality of ID3)**
Consider the following training set, where $\mathcal{X} = \{0,1\}^3$ and $\mathcal{Y} = \{0,1\}$:

$$((1,1,1),1)$$
$$((1,0,0),1)$$
$$((1,1,0),0)$$
$$((0,0,1),0)$$

Suppose we wish to use this training set in order to build a decision tree of depth 2 (i.e., for each input we are allowed to ask two questions of the form $(x_i = 0?)$ before deciding on the label).

1. Suppose we run the ID3 algorithm up to depth 2 (namely, we pick the root node and its children according to the algorithm, but instead of keeping on with the recursion, we stop and pick leaves according to the majority label in each subtree). Assume that the subroutine used to measure the quality of each feature is based on the entropy function (so we measure the *information gain*), and that if two features get the same score, one of them is picked arbitrarily. Show that the training error of the resulting decision tree is at least $1/4$.
2. Find a decision tree of depth 2 that attains zero training error.

19

Nearest Neighbor

Nearest Neighbor algorithms are among the simplest of all machine learning algorithms. The idea is to memorize the training set and then to predict the label of any new instance on the basis of the labels of its closest neighbors in the training set. The rationale behind such a method is based on the assumption that the features that are used to describe the domain points are relevant to their labelings in a way that makes close-by points likely to have the same label. Furthermore, in some situations, even when the training set is immense, finding a nearest neighbor can be done extremely fast (for example, when the training set is the entire Web and distances are based on links).

Note that, in contrast with the algorithmic paradigms that we have discussed so far, like ERM, SRM, MDL, or RLM, that are determined by some hypothesis class, $\mathcal{H}$, the Nearest Neighbor method figures out a label on any test point without searching for a predictor within some predefined class of functions.

In this chapter we describe Nearest Neighbor methods for classification and regression problems. We analyze their performance for the simple case of binary classification and discuss the efficiency of implementing these methods.

19.1 *k* NEAREST NEIGHBORS

Throughout the entire chapter we assume that our instance domain, $\mathcal{X}$, is endowed with a metric function ρ. That is, $\rho : \mathcal{X} \times \mathcal{X} \to \mathbb{R}$ is a function that returns the distance between any two elements of $\mathcal{X}$. For example, if $\mathcal{X} = \mathbb{R}^d$ then ρ can be the Euclidean distance, $\rho(\mathbf{x}, \mathbf{x}') = \|\mathbf{x} - \mathbf{x}'\| = \sqrt{\sum_{i=1}^{d} (x_i - x_i')^2}$.

Let $S = (\mathbf{x}_1, y_1), \ldots, (\mathbf{x}_m, y_m)$ be a sequence of training examples. For each $\mathbf{x} \in \mathcal{X}$, let $\pi_1(\mathbf{x}), \ldots, \pi_m(\mathbf{x})$ be a reordering of $\{1, \ldots, m\}$ according to their distance to $\mathbf{x}$, $\rho(\mathbf{x}, \mathbf{x}_i)$. That is, for all $i < m$,

$$\rho(\mathbf{x}, \mathbf{x}_{\pi_i(\mathbf{x})}) \leq \rho(\mathbf{x}, \mathbf{x}_{\pi_{i+1}(\mathbf{x})}).$$

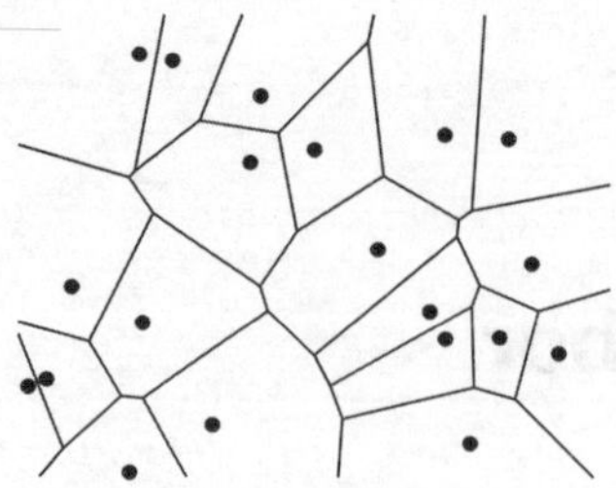

Figure 19.1. An illustration of the decision boundaries of the 1-NN rule. The points depicted are the sample points, and the predicted label of any new point will be the label of the sample point in the center of the cell it belongs to. These cells are called a Voronoi Tessellation of the space.

For a number k, the k-NN rule for binary classification is defined as follows:

k-NN

input: a training sample $S = (\mathbf{x}_1, y_1), \ldots, (\mathbf{x}_m, y_m)$
output: for every point $\mathbf{x} \in \mathcal{X}$,
return the majority label among $\{y_{\pi_i(\mathbf{x})} : i \le k\}$

When $k = 1$, we have the 1-NN rule:

$$h_S(\mathbf{x}) = y_{\pi_1(\mathbf{x})}.$$

A geometric illustration of the 1-NN rule is given in Figure 19.1.

For regression problems, namely, $\mathcal{Y} = \mathbb{R}$, one can define the prediction to be the average target of the k nearest neighbors. That is, $h_S(\mathbf{x}) = \frac{1}{k}\sum_{i=1}^{k} y_{\pi_i(\mathbf{x})}$. More generally, for some function $\phi : (\mathcal{X} \times \mathcal{Y})^k \to \mathcal{Y}$, the k-NN rule with respect to ϕ is:

$$h_S(\mathbf{x}) = \phi\left((\mathbf{x}_{\pi_1(\mathbf{x})}, y_{\pi_1(\mathbf{x})}), \ldots, (\mathbf{x}_{\pi_k(\mathbf{x})}, y_{\pi_k(\mathbf{x})})\right). \tag{19.1}$$

It is easy to verify that we can cast the prediction by majority of labels (for classification) or by the averaged target (for regression) as in Equation (19.1) by an appropriate choice of ϕ. The generality can lead to other rules; for example, if $\mathcal{Y} = \mathbb{R}$, we can take a weighted average of the targets according to the distance from $\mathbf{x}$:

$$h_S(\mathbf{x}) = \sum_{i=1}^{k} \frac{\rho(\mathbf{x}, \mathbf{x}_{\pi_i(\mathbf{x})})}{\sum_{j=1}^{k} \rho(\mathbf{x}, \mathbf{x}_{\pi_j(\mathbf{x})})} y_{\pi_i(\mathbf{x})}.$$

19.2 ANALYSIS

Since the NN rules are such natural learning methods, their generalization properties have been extensively studied. Most previous results are asymptotic consistency results, analyzing the performance of NN rules when the sample size, m, goes to infinity, and the rate of convergence depends on the underlying distribution. As we have argued in Section 7.4, this type of analysis is not satisfactory. One would like to learn from finite training samples and to understand the generalization performance as a function of the size of such finite training sets and clear prior assumptions on the data distribution. We therefore provide a finite-sample analysis of the 1-NN rule, showing how the error decreases as a function of m and how it depends on properties of the distribution. We will also explain how the analysis can be generalized to k-NN rules for arbitrary values of k. In particular, the analysis specifies the number of examples required to achieve a true error of $2L_{\mathcal{D}}(h^\star)+\epsilon$, where $h^\star$ is the Bayes optimal hypothesis, assuming that the labeling rule is "well behaved" (in a sense we will define later).

19.2.1 A Generalization Bound for the 1-NN Rule

We now analyze the true error of the 1-NN rule for binary classification with the 0-1 loss, namely, $\mathcal{Y}=\{0,1\}$ and $\ell(h,(\mathbf{x},y)) = \mathbb{1}_{[h(\mathbf{x})\neq y]}$. We also assume throughout the analysis that $\mathcal{X}=[0,1]^d$ and ρ is the Euclidean distance.

We start by introducing some notation. Let $\mathcal{D}$ be a distribution over $\mathcal{X}\times\mathcal{Y}$. Let $\mathcal{D}_{\mathcal{X}}$ denote the induced marginal distribution over $\mathcal{X}$ and let $\eta:\mathbb{R}^d\to\mathbb{R}$ be the conditional probability[1] over the labels, that is,

$$\eta(\mathbf{x}) = \mathbb{P}[y=1|\mathbf{x}].$$

Recall that the Bayes optimal rule (that is, the hypothesis that minimizes $L_{\mathcal{D}}(h)$ over all functions) is

$$h^\star(\mathbf{x}) = \mathbb{1}_{[\eta(\mathbf{x})>1/2]}.$$

We assume that the conditional probability function η is c-Lipschitz for some $c>0$: Namely, for all $\mathbf{x},\mathbf{x}'\in\mathcal{X}$, $|\eta(\mathbf{x})-\eta(\mathbf{x}')|\le c\,\|\mathbf{x}-\mathbf{x}'\|$. In other words, this assumption means that if two vectors are close to each other then their labels are likely to be the same.

The following lemma applies the Lipschitzness of the conditional probability function to upper bound the true error of the 1-NN rule as a function of the expected distance between each test instance and its nearest neighbor in the training set.

Lemma 19.1. *Let $\mathcal{X}=[0,1]^d$, $\mathcal{Y}=\{0,1\}$, and $\mathcal{D}$ be a distribution over $\mathcal{X}\times\mathcal{Y}$ for which the conditional probability function, η, is a c-Lipschitz function. Let $S=(\mathbf{x}_1,y_1),\ldots,(\mathbf{x}_m,y_m)$ be an i.i.d. sample and let h_S be its corresponding 1-NN hypothesis. Let $h^\star$ be the Bayes optimal rule for η. Then,*

$$\mathop{\mathbb{E}}_{S\sim\mathcal{D}^m}[L_{\mathcal{D}}(h_S)] \le 2\,L_{\mathcal{D}}(h^\star) + c \mathop{\mathbb{E}}_{S\sim\mathcal{D}^m,\mathbf{x}\sim\mathcal{D}}[\|\mathbf{x}-\mathbf{x}_{\pi_1(\mathbf{x})}\|].$$

Proof. Since $L_{\mathcal{D}}(h_S) = \mathbb{E}_{(\mathbf{x},y)\sim\mathcal{D}}[\mathbb{1}_{[h_S(\mathbf{x})\neq y]}]$, we obtain that $\mathbb{E}_S[L_{\mathcal{D}}(h_S)]$ is the probability to sample a training set S and an additional example $(\mathbf{x},y)$, such that the label of $\pi_1(\mathbf{x})$ is different from y. In other words, we can first sample m unlabeled examples, $S_x=(\mathbf{x}_1,\ldots,\mathbf{x}_m)$, according to $\mathcal{D}_{\mathcal{X}}$, and an additional unlabeled example, $\mathbf{x}\sim\mathcal{D}_{\mathcal{X}}$, then find $\pi_1(\mathbf{x})$ to be the nearest neighbor of $\mathbf{x}$ in S_x, and finally sample

[1] Formally, $\mathbb{P}[y=1|\mathbf{x}] = \lim_{\delta\to 0}\frac{\mathcal{D}(\{(\mathbf{x}',1):\mathbf{x}'\in B(\mathbf{x},\delta)\})}{\mathcal{D}(\{(\mathbf{x}',y):\mathbf{x}'\in B(\mathbf{x},\delta),y\in\mathcal{Y}\})}$, where $B(\mathbf{x},\delta)$ is a ball of radius δ centered around $\mathbf{x}$.

$y \sim \eta(\mathbf{x})$ and $y_{\pi_1(\mathbf{x})} \sim \eta(\pi_1(\mathbf{x}))$. It follows that

$$\begin{aligned}\mathbb{E}_S[L_{\mathcal{D}}(h_S)] &= \mathop{\mathbb{E}}_{S_x \sim \mathcal{D}_{\mathcal{X}}^m, \mathbf{x} \sim \mathcal{D}_{\mathcal{X}}, y \sim \eta(\mathbf{x}), y' \sim \eta(\pi_1(\mathbf{x}))} [\mathbb{1}_{[y \neq y']}] \\ &= \mathop{\mathbb{E}}_{S_x \sim \mathcal{D}_{\mathcal{X}}^m, \mathbf{x} \sim \mathcal{D}_{\mathcal{X}}} \left[\mathop{\mathbb{P}}_{y \sim \eta(\mathbf{x}), y' \sim \eta(\pi_1(\mathbf{x}))} [y \neq y'] \right]. \end{aligned} \tag{19.2}$$

We next upper bound $\mathbb{P}_{y \sim \eta(\mathbf{x}), y' \sim \eta(\mathbf{x}')}[y \neq y']$ for any two domain points $\mathbf{x}, \mathbf{x}'$:

$$\begin{aligned}\mathop{\mathbb{P}}_{y \sim \eta(\mathbf{x}), y' \sim \eta(\mathbf{x}')} [y \neq y'] &= \eta(\mathbf{x}')(1 - \eta(\mathbf{x})) + (1 - \eta(\mathbf{x}'))\eta(\mathbf{x}) \\ &= (\eta(\mathbf{x}) - \eta(\mathbf{x}) + \eta(\mathbf{x}'))(1 - \eta(\mathbf{x})) \\ &\quad + (1 - \eta(\mathbf{x}) + \eta(\mathbf{x}) - \eta(\mathbf{x}'))\eta(\mathbf{x}) \\ &= 2\eta(\mathbf{x})(1 - \eta(\mathbf{x})) + (\eta(\mathbf{x}) - \eta(\mathbf{x}'))(2\eta(\mathbf{x}) - 1). \end{aligned}$$

Using $|2\eta(\mathbf{x}) - 1| \leq 1$ and the assumption that η is c-Lipschitz, we obtain that the probability is at most:

$$\mathop{\mathbb{P}}_{y \sim \eta(\mathbf{x}), y' \sim \eta(\mathbf{x}')} [y \neq y'] \leq 2\eta(\mathbf{x})(1 - \eta(\mathbf{x})) + c\,\|\mathbf{x} - \mathbf{x}'\|.$$

Plugging this into Equation (19.2) we conclude that

$$\mathop{\mathbb{E}}_S[L_{\mathcal{D}}(h_S)] \leq \mathop{\mathbb{E}}_{\mathbf{x}}[2\eta(\mathbf{x})(1 - \eta(\mathbf{x}))] + c \mathop{\mathbb{E}}_{S,\mathbf{x}}[\|\mathbf{x} - \mathbf{x}_{\pi_1(\mathbf{x})}\|].$$

Finally, the error of the Bayes optimal classifier is

$$L_{\mathcal{D}}(h^\star) = \mathop{\mathbb{E}}_{\mathbf{x}}[\min\{\eta(\mathbf{x}), 1 - \eta(\mathbf{x})\}] \geq \mathop{\mathbb{E}}_{\mathbf{x}}[\eta(\mathbf{x})(1 - \eta(\mathbf{x}))].$$

Combining the preceding two inequalities concludes our proof. □

The next step is to bound the expected distance between a random $\mathbf{x}$ and its closest element in S. We first need the following general probability lemma. The lemma bounds the probability weight of subsets that are not hit by a random sample, as a function of the size of that sample.

Lemma 19.2. *Let $C_1, \ldots, C_r$ be a collection of subsets of some domain set, $\mathcal{X}$. Let S be a sequence of m points sampled i.i.d. according to some probability distribution, $\mathcal{D}$ over $\mathcal{X}$. Then,*

$$\mathop{\mathbb{E}}_{S \sim \mathcal{D}^m} \left[\sum_{i : C_i \cap S = \emptyset} \mathbb{P}[C_i] \right] \leq \frac{r}{m\,e}.$$

Proof. From the linearity of expectation, we can rewrite:

$$\mathop{\mathbb{E}}_S \left[\sum_{i : C_i \cap S = \emptyset} \mathbb{P}[C_i] \right] = \sum_{i=1}^{r} \mathbb{P}[C_i] \mathop{\mathbb{E}}_S \left[\mathbb{1}_{[C_i \cap S = \emptyset]} \right].$$

Next, for each i we have

$$\mathop{\mathbb{E}}_S \left[\mathbb{1}_{[C_i \cap S = \emptyset]} \right] = \mathop{\mathbb{P}}_S [C_i \cap S = \emptyset] = (1 - \mathbb{P}[C_i])^m \leq e^{-\mathbb{P}[C_i]\,m}.$$

Combining the preceding two equations we get

$$\mathbb{E}_S\left[\sum_{i:C_i\cap S=\emptyset} \mathbb{P}[C_i]\right] \le \sum_{i=1}^{r} \mathbb{P}[C_i]e^{-\mathbb{P}[C_i]m} \le r\max_i \mathbb{P}[C_i]e^{-\mathbb{P}[C_i]m}.$$

Finally, by a standard calculus, $\max_a ae^{-ma} \le \frac{1}{me}$ and this concludes the proof. □

Equipped with the preceding lemmas we are now ready to state and prove the main result of this section – an upper bound on the expected error of the 1-NN learning rule.

Theorem 19.3. *Let $\mathcal{X} = [0,1]^d, \mathcal{Y} = \{0,1\}$, and $\mathcal{D}$ be a distribution over $\mathcal{X}\times\mathcal{Y}$ for which the conditional probability function, η, is a c-Lipschitz function. Let h_S denote the result of applying the 1-NN rule to a sample $S \sim \mathcal{D}^m$. Then,*

$$\mathbb{E}_{S\sim\mathcal{D}^m}[L_{\mathcal{D}}(h_S)] \le 2L_{\mathcal{D}}(h^\star) + 4c\sqrt{d}\,m^{-\frac{1}{d+1}}.$$

Proof. Fix some $\epsilon = 1/T$, for some integer T, let $r = T^d$ and let $C_1,\ldots,C_r$ be the cover of the set $\mathcal{X}$ using boxes of length ϵ: Namely, for every $(\alpha_1,\ldots,\alpha_d) \in [T]^d$, there exists a set C_i of the form $\{\mathbf{x} : \forall j, x_j \in [(\alpha_j-1)/T, \alpha_j/T]\}$. An illustration for $d = 2$, $T = 5$ and the set corresponding to $\alpha = (2,4)$ is given in the following.

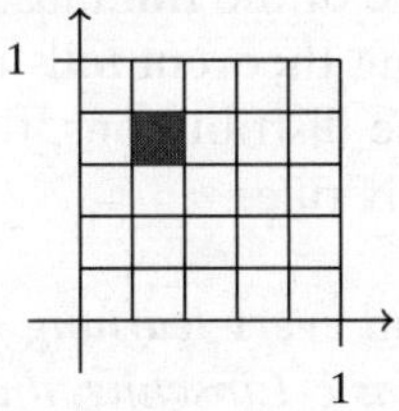

For each $\mathbf{x},\mathbf{x}'$ in the same box we have $\|\mathbf{x}-\mathbf{x}'\| \le \sqrt{d}\,\epsilon$. Otherwise, $\|\mathbf{x}-\mathbf{x}'\| \le \sqrt{d}$. Therefore,

$$\mathbb{E}_{\mathbf{x},S}[\|\mathbf{x}-\mathbf{x}_{\pi_1(\mathbf{x})}\|] \le \mathbb{E}_S\left[\mathbb{P}\left[\bigcup_{i:C_i\cap S=\emptyset} C_i\right]\sqrt{d} + \mathbb{P}\left[\bigcup_{i:C_i\cap S\ne\emptyset} C_i\right]\epsilon\sqrt{d}\right],$$

and by combining Lemma 19.2 with the trivial bound $\mathbb{P}[\bigcup_{i:C_i\cap S\ne\emptyset} C_i] \le 1$ we get that

$$\mathbb{E}_{\mathbf{x},S}[\|\mathbf{x}-\mathbf{x}_{\pi_1(\mathbf{x})}\|] \le \sqrt{d}\left(\tfrac{r}{me}+\epsilon\right).$$

Since the number of boxes is $r = (1/\epsilon)^d$ we get that

$$\mathbb{E}_{S,\mathbf{x}}[\|\mathbf{x}-\mathbf{x}_{\pi_1(\mathbf{x})}\|] \le \sqrt{d}\left(\frac{2^d\,\epsilon^{-d}}{m\,e}+\epsilon\right).$$

Combining the preceding with Lemma 19.1 we obtain that

$$\mathbb{E}_S[L_{\mathcal{D}}(h_S)] \le 2L_{\mathcal{D}}(h^\star) + c\sqrt{d}\left(\frac{2^d\,\epsilon^{-d}}{m\,e}+\epsilon\right).$$

Finally, setting $\epsilon = 2m^{-1/(d+1)}$ and noting that

$$\frac{2^d \epsilon^{-d}}{m\,e} + \epsilon = \frac{2^d 2^{-d} m^{d/(d+1)}}{m\,e} + 2m^{-1/(d+1)}$$
$$= m^{-1/(d+1)}(1/e + 2) \leq 4m^{-1/(d+1)}$$

we conclude our proof. □

The theorem implies that if we first fix the data-generating distribution and then let m go to infinity, then the error of the 1-NN rule converges to twice the Bayes error. The analysis can be generalized to larger values of k, showing that the expected error of the k-NN rule converges to $(1+\sqrt{8/k})$ times the error of the Bayes classifier. This is formalized in Theorem 19.5, whose proof is left as a guided exercise.

19.2.2 The "Curse of Dimensionality"

The upper bound given in Theorem 19.3 grows with c (the Lipschitz coefficient of η) and with d, the Euclidean dimension of the domain set $\mathcal{X}$. In fact, it is easy to see that a necessary condition for the last term in Theorem 19.3 to be smaller than ϵ is that $m \geq (4c\sqrt{d}/\epsilon)^{d+1}$. That is, the size of the training set should increase exponentially with the dimension. The following theorem tells us that this is not just an artifact of our upper bound, but, for some distributions, this amount of examples is indeed necessary for learning with the NN rule.

Theorem 19.4. *For any $c > 1$, and every learning rule, L, there exists a distribution over $[0,1]^d \times \{0,1\}$, such that $\eta(\mathbf{x})$ is c-Lipschitz, the Bayes error of the distribution is 0, but for sample sizes $m \leq (c+1)^d/2$, the true error of the rule L is greater than $1/4$.*

Proof. Fix any values of c and d. Let G_c^d be the grid on $[0,1]^d$ with distance of $1/c$ between points on the grid. That is, each point on the grid is of the form $(a_1/c, \ldots, a_d/c)$ where a_i is in $\{0, \ldots, c-1, c\}$. Note that, since any two distinct points on this grid are at least $1/c$ apart, any function $\eta : G_C^D \rightarrow [0,1]$ is a c-Lipschitz function. It follows that the set of all c-Lipschitz functions over G_c^d contains the set of *all* binary valued functions over that domain. We can therefore invoke the No-Free-Lunch result (Theorem 5.1) to obtain a lower bound on the needed sample sizes for learning that class. The number of points on the grid is $(c+1)^d$; hence, if $m < (c+1)^d/2$, Theorem 5.1 implies the lower bound we are after. □

The exponential dependence on the dimension is known as the *curse of dimensionality*. As we saw, the 1-NN rule might fail if the number of examples is smaller than $\Omega((c+1)^d)$. Therefore, while the 1-NN rule does not restrict itself to a predefined set of hypotheses, it still relies on some prior knowledge – its success depends on the assumption that the dimension and the Lipschitz constant of the underlying distribution, η, are not too high.

19.3 EFFICIENT IMPLEMENTATION*

Nearest Neighbor is a learning-by-memorization type of rule. It requires the entire training data set to be stored, and at test time, we need to scan the entire data set in order to find the neighbors. The time of applying the NN rule is therefore $\Theta(dm)$. This leads to expensive computation at test time.

When d is small, several results from the field of computational geometry have proposed data structures that enable to apply the NN rule in time $o(d^{O(1)} \log(m))$. However, the space required by these data structures is roughly $m^{O(d)}$, which makes these methods impractical for larger values of d.

To overcome this problem, it was suggested to improve the search method by allowing an *approximate* search. Formally, an r-approximate search procedure is guaranteed to retrieve a point within distance of at most r times the distance to the nearest neighbor. Three popular approximate algorithms for NN are the kd-tree, balltrees, and locality-sensitive hashing (LSH). We refer the reader, for example, to (Shakhnarovich, Darrell & Indyk 2006).

19.4 SUMMARY

The k-NN rule is a very simple learning algorithm that relies on the assumption that "things that look alike must be alike." We formalized this intuition using the Lipschitzness of the conditional probability. We have shown that with a sufficiently large training set, the risk of the 1-NN is upper bounded by twice the risk of the Bayes optimal rule. We have also derived a lower bound that shows the "curse of dimensionality" – the required sample size might increase exponentially with the dimension. As a result, NN is usually performed in practice after a dimensionality reduction preprocessing step. We discuss dimensionality reduction techniques later on in Chapter 23.

19.5 BIBLIOGRAPHIC REMARKS

Cover and Hart (1967) gave the first analysis of 1-NN, showing that its risk converges to twice the Bayes optimal error under mild conditions. Following a lemma due to Stone (1977), Devroye and Györfi (1985) have shown that the k-NN rule is consistent (with respect to the hypothesis class of all functions from $\mathbb{R}^d$ to $\{0,1\}$). A good presentation of the analysis is given in the book by Devroye et al. (1996). Here, we give a finite sample guarantee that explicitly underscores the prior assumption on the distribution. See Section 7.4 for a discussion on consistency results. Finally, Gottlieb, Kontorovich, and Krauthgamer (2010) derived another finite sample bound for NN that is more similar to VC bounds.

19.6 EXERCISES

In this exercise we will prove the following theorem for the **k-NN** rule.

Theorem 19.5. *Let $\mathcal{X} = [0,1]^d, \mathcal{Y} = \{0,1\}$, and $\mathcal{D}$ be a distribution over $\mathcal{X} \times \mathcal{Y}$ for which the conditional probability function, η, is a c-Lipschitz function. Let h_S denote* *the result of applying the k-NN rule to a sample $S \sim \mathcal{D}^m$, where $k \geq 10$. Let $h^\star$ be the Bayes optimal hypothesis. Then,*

$$\mathop{\mathbb{E}}_S[L_{\mathcal{D}}(h_S)] \leq \left(1+\sqrt{\frac{8}{k}}\right) L_{\mathcal{D}}(h^\star) + \left(6c\sqrt{d}+k\right) m^{-1/(d+1)}.$$

19.1 Prove the following lemma.

Lemma 19.6. *Let $C_1, \ldots, C_r$ be a collection of subsets of some domain set, $\mathcal{X}$. Let S be a sequence of m points sampled i.i.d. according to some probability distribution, $\mathcal{D}$ over $\mathcal{X}$. Then, for every $k \geq 2$,*

$$\mathop{\mathbb{E}}_{S \sim \mathcal{D}^m}\left[\sum_{i:|C_i \cap S|<k} \mathbb{P}[C_i]\right] \leq \frac{2rk}{m}.$$

Hints:

- Show that

$$\mathop{\mathbb{E}}_S\left[\sum_{i:|C_i \cap S|<k} \mathbb{P}[C_i]\right] = \sum_{i=1}^{r} \mathbb{P}[C_i] \mathop{\mathbb{P}}_S[|C_i \cap S| < k].$$

- Fix some i and suppose that $k < \mathbb{P}[C_i]m/2$. Use Chernoff's bound to show that

$$\mathop{\mathbb{P}}_S[|C_i \cap S| < k] \leq \mathop{\mathbb{P}}_S[|C_i \cap S| < \mathbb{P}[C_i]m/2] \leq e^{-\mathbb{P}[C_i]m/8}.$$

- Use the inequality $\max_a ae^{-ma} \leq \frac{1}{me}$ to show that for such i we have

$$\mathbb{P}[C_i] \mathop{\mathbb{P}}_S[|C_i \cap S| < k] \leq \mathbb{P}[C_i] e^{-\mathbb{P}[C_i]m/8} \leq \frac{8}{me}.$$

- Conclude the proof by using the fact that for the case $k \geq \mathbb{P}[C_i]m/2$ we clearly have:

$$\mathbb{P}[C_i] \mathop{\mathbb{P}}_S[|C_i \cap S| < k] \leq \mathbb{P}[C_i] \leq \frac{2k}{m}.$$

19.2 We use the notation $y \sim p$ as a shorthand for "y is a Bernoulli random variable with expected value p." Prove the following lemma:

Lemma 19.7. *Let $k \geq 10$ and let $Z_1, \ldots, Z_k$ be independent Bernoulli random variables with $\mathbb{P}[Z_i = 1] = p_i$. Denote $p = \frac{1}{k}\sum_i p_i$ and $p' = \frac{1}{k}\sum_{i=1}^k Z_i$. Show that*

$$\mathop{\mathbb{E}}_{Z_1,\ldots,Z_k} \mathop{\mathbb{P}}_{y \sim p}[y \neq \mathbb{1}_{[p'>1/2]}] \leq \left(1+\sqrt{\frac{8}{k}}\right) \mathop{\mathbb{P}}_{y \sim p}[y \neq \mathbb{1}_{[p>1/2]}].$$

Hints:

W.l.o.g. assume that $p \leq 1/2$. Then, $\mathbb{P}_{y \sim p}[y \neq \mathbb{1}_{[p>1/2]}] = p$. Let $y' = \mathbb{1}_{[p'>1/2]}$.

- Show that

$$\mathop{\mathbb{E}}_{Z_1,\ldots,Z_k} \mathop{\mathbb{P}}_{y \sim p}[y \neq y'] - p = \mathop{\mathbb{P}}_{Z_1,\ldots,Z_k}[p' > 1/2](1-2p).$$

- Use Chernoff's bound (Lemma B.3) to show that

$$\mathbb{P}[p' > 1/2] \leq e^{-kp\,h\left(\frac{1}{2p}-1\right)},$$

where

$$h(a) = (1+a)\log(1+a) - a.$$

- To conclude the proof of the lemma, you can rely on the following inequality (without proving it): For every $p \in [0, 1/2]$ and $k \geq 10$:

$$(1-2p)\, e^{-k\,p+\frac{k}{2}(\log(2p)+1)} \;\leq\; \sqrt{\frac{8}{k}}\, p.$$

19.3 Fix some $p, p' \in [0,1]$ and $y' \in \{0,1\}$. Show that

$$\underset{y\sim p}{\mathbb{P}}[y \neq y'] \leq \underset{y\sim p'}{\mathbb{P}}[y \neq y'] + |p - p'|.$$

19.4 Conclude the proof of the theorem according to the following steps:

- As in the proof of Theorem 19.3, six some $\epsilon > 0$ and let $C_1, \ldots, C_r$ be the cover of the set $\mathcal{X}$ using boxes of length ϵ. For each $\mathbf{x}, \mathbf{x}'$ in the same box we have $\|\mathbf{x} - \mathbf{x}'\| \leq \sqrt{d}\,\epsilon$. Otherwise, $\|\mathbf{x} - \mathbf{x}'\| \leq 2\sqrt{d}$. Show that

$$\begin{aligned} \underset{S}{\mathbb{E}}[L_{\mathcal{D}}(h_S)] \leq &\ \underset{S}{\mathbb{E}}\left[\sum_{i:|C_i \cap S| < k} \mathbb{P}[C_i]\right] \\ &+ \max_i \underset{S,(\mathbf{x},y)}{\mathbb{P}}\left[h_S(\mathbf{x}) \neq y \mid \forall j \in [k],\ \|\mathbf{x} - \mathbf{x}_{\pi_j(\mathbf{x})}\| \leq \epsilon\sqrt{d}\right]. \end{aligned} \tag{19.3}$$

- Bound the first summand using Lemma 19.6.
- To bound the second summand, let us fix $S|_x$ and $\mathbf{x}$ such that all the k neighbors of $\mathbf{x}$ in $S|_x$ are at distance of at most $\epsilon\sqrt{d}$ from $\mathbf{x}$. W.l.o.g assume that the k NN are $\mathbf{x}_1, \ldots, \mathbf{x}_k$. Denote $p_i = \eta(\mathbf{x}_i)$ and let $p = \frac{1}{k}\sum_i p_i$. Use Exercise 19.3 to show that

$$\underset{y_1,\ldots,y_j}{\mathbb{E}}\ \underset{y\sim\eta(\mathbf{x})}{\mathbb{P}}[h_S(\mathbf{x}) \neq y] \leq \underset{y_1,\ldots,y_j}{\mathbb{E}}\ \underset{y\sim p}{\mathbb{P}}[h_S(\mathbf{x}) \neq y] + |p - \eta(\mathbf{x})|.$$

W.l.o.g. assume that $p \leq 1/2$. Now use Lemma 19.7 to show that

$$\underset{y_1,\ldots,y_j}{\mathbb{P}}\ \underset{y\sim p}{\mathbb{P}}[h_S(\mathbf{x}) \neq y] \leq \left(1 + \sqrt{\frac{8}{k}}\right) \underset{y\sim p}{\mathbb{P}}[\mathbb{1}_{[p>1/2]} \neq y].$$

- Show that

$$\underset{y\sim p}{\mathbb{P}}[\mathbb{1}_{[p>1/2]} \neq y] = p = \min\{p, 1-p\} \leq \min\{\eta(\mathbf{x}), 1 - \eta(\mathbf{x})\} + |p - \eta(\mathbf{x})|.$$

- Combine all the preceding to obtain that the second summand in Equation (19.3) is bounded by

$$\left(1 + \sqrt{\frac{8}{k}}\right) L_{\mathcal{D}}(h^\star) + 3\,c\,\epsilon\sqrt{d}.$$

- Use $r = (2/\epsilon)^d$ to obtain that:

$$\underset{S}{\mathbb{E}}[L_{\mathcal{D}}(h_S)] \leq \left(1 + \sqrt{\frac{8}{k}}\right) L_{\mathcal{D}}(h^\star) + 3\,c\,\epsilon\sqrt{d} + \frac{2(2/\epsilon)^d\, k}{m}.$$

Set $\epsilon = 2m^{-1/(d+1)}$ and use

$$6\,c\,m^{-1/(d+1)}\sqrt{d} + \frac{2k}{e} m^{-1/(d+1)} \leq \left(6c\sqrt{d} + k\right) m^{-1/(d+1)}$$

to conclude the proof.

20 Neural Networks

An artificial neural network is a model of computation inspired by the structure of neural networks in the brain. In simplified models of the brain, it consists of a large number of basic computing devices (neurons) that are connected to each other in a complex communication network, through which the brain is able to carry out highly complex computations. Artificial neural networks are formal computation constructs that are modeled after this computation paradigm.

Learning with neural networks was proposed in the mid-20th century. It yields an effective learning paradigm and has recently been shown to achieve cutting-edge performance on several learning tasks.

A neural network can be described as a directed graph whose nodes correspond to neurons and edges correspond to links between them. Each neuron receives as input a weighted sum of the outputs of the neurons connected to its incoming edges. We focus on *feedforward* networks in which the underlying graph does not contain cycles.

In the context of learning, we can define a hypothesis class consisting of neural network predictors, where all the hypotheses share the underlying graph structure of the network and differ in the weights over edges. As we will show in Section 20.3, every predictor over n variables that can be implemented in time $T(n)$ can also be expressed as a neural network predictor of size $O(T(n)^2)$, where the size of the network is the number of nodes in it. It follows that the family of hypothesis classes of neural networks of polynomial size can suffice for all practical learning tasks, in which our goal is to learn predictors which can be implemented efficiently. Furthermore, in Section 20.4 we will show that the sample complexity of learning such hypothesis classes is also bounded in terms of the size of the network. Hence, it seems that this is the ultimate learning paradigm we would want to adapt, in the sense that it both has a polynomial sample complexity and has the minimal approximation error among all hypothesis classes consisting of efficiently implementable predictors.

The caveat is that the problem of training such hypothesis classes of neural network predictors is computationally hard. This will be formalized in Section 20.5.

A widely used heuristic for training neural networks relies on the SGD framework we studied in Chapter 14. There, we have shown that SGD is a successful learner if the loss function is convex. In neural networks, the loss function is highly nonconvex. Nevertheless, we can still implement the SGD algorithm and hope it will find a reasonable solution (as happens to be the case in several practical tasks). In Section 20.6 we describe how to implement SGD for neural networks. In particular, the most complicated operation is the calculation of the gradient of the loss function with respect to the parameters of the network. We present the *backpropagation* algorithm that efficiently calculates the gradient.

20.1 FEEDFORWARD NEURAL NETWORKS

The idea behind neural networks is that many neurons can be joined together by communication links to carry out complex computations. It is common to describe the structure of a neural network as a graph whose nodes are the neurons and each (directed) edge in the graph links the output of some neuron to the input of another neuron. We will restrict our attention to feedforward network structures in which the underlying graph does not contain cycles.

A feedforward neural network is described by a directed acyclic graph, $G = (V, E)$, and a weight function over the edges, $w : E \to \mathbb{R}$. Nodes of the graph correspond to neurons. Each single neuron is modeled as a simple scalar function, $\sigma : \mathbb{R} \to \mathbb{R}$. We will focus on three possible functions for σ: the sign function, $\sigma(a) = \mathrm{sign}(a)$, the threshold function, $\sigma(a) = \mathbb{1}_{[a>0]}$, and the sigmoid function, $\sigma(a) = 1/(1+\exp(-a))$, which is a smooth approximation to the threshold function. We call σ the "activation" function of the neuron. Each edge in the graph links the output of some neuron to the input of another neuron. The input of a neuron is obtained by taking a weighted sum of the outputs of all the neurons connected to it, where the weighting is according to w.

To simplify the description of the calculation performed by the network, we further assume that the network is organized in *layers*. That is, the set of nodes can be decomposed into a union of (nonempty) disjoint subsets, $V = \cup_{t=0}^{T} V_t$, such that every edge in E connects some node in V_{t-1} to some node in V_t, for some $t \in [T]$. The bottom layer, V_0, is called the input layer. It contains $n+1$ neurons, where n is the dimensionality of the input space. For every $i \in [n]$, the output of neuron i in V_0 is simply x_i. The last neuron in V_0 is the "constant" neuron, which always outputs 1. We denote by $v_{t,i}$ the ith neuron of the tth layer and by $o_{t,i}(\mathbf{x})$ the output of $v_{t,i}$ when the network is fed with the input vector $\mathbf{x}$. Therefore, for $i \in [n]$ we have $o_{0,i}(\mathbf{x}) = x_i$ and for $i = n+1$ we have $o_{0,i}(\mathbf{x}) = 1$. We now proceed with the calculation in a layer by layer manner. Suppose we have calculated the outputs of the neurons at layer t. Then, we can calculate the outputs of the neurons at layer $t+1$ as follows. Fix some $v_{t+1,j} \in V_{t+1}$. Let $a_{t+1,j}(\mathbf{x})$ denote the input to $v_{t+1,j}$ when the network is fed with the input vector $\mathbf{x}$. Then,

$$a_{t+1,j}(\mathbf{x}) = \sum_{r:\,(v_{t,r},v_{t+1,j})\in E} w((v_{t,r}, v_{t+1,j}))\, o_{t,r}(\mathbf{x}),$$

and

$$o_{t+1,j}(\mathbf{x}) = \sigma\left(a_{t+1,j}(\mathbf{x})\right).$$

That is, the input to $v_{t+1,j}$ is a weighted sum of the outputs of the neurons in V_t that are connected to $v_{t+1,j}$, where weighting is according to w, and the output of $v_{t+1,j}$ is simply the application of the activation function σ on its input.

Layers $V_1, \ldots, V_{T-1}$ are often called *hidden layers*. The top layer, V_T, is called the output layer. In simple prediction problems the output layer contains a single neuron whose output is the output of the network.

We refer to T as the number of layers in the network (excluding V_0), or the "depth" of the network. The size of the network is $|V|$. The "width" of the network is $\max_t |V_t|$. An illustration of a layered feedforward neural network of depth 2, size 10, and width 5, is given in the following. Note that there is a neuron in the hidden layer that has no incoming edges. This neuron will output the constant $\sigma(0)$.

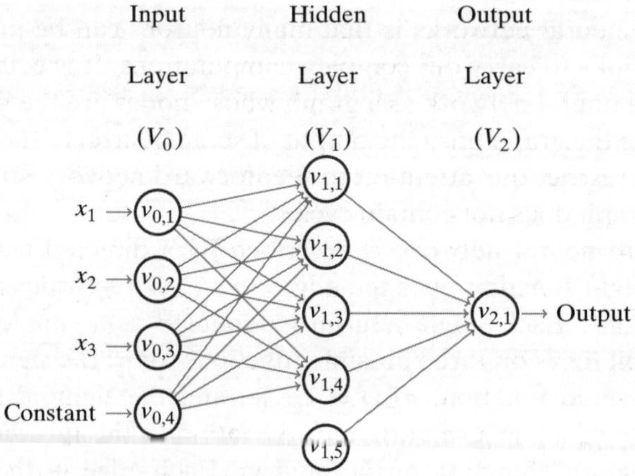

20.2 LEARNING NEURAL NETWORKS

Once we have specified a neural network by (V, E, σ, w), we obtain a function $h_{V,E,\sigma,w} : \mathbb{R}^{|V_0|-1} \to \mathbb{R}^{|V_T|}$. Any set of such functions can serve as a hypothesis class for learning. Usually, we define a hypothesis class of neural network predictors by fixing the graph (V, E) as well as the activation function σ and letting the hypothesis class be all functions of the form $h_{V,E,\sigma,w}$ for some $w : E \to \mathbb{R}$. The triplet (V, E, σ) is often called the *architecture* of the network. We denote the hypothesis class by

$$\mathcal{H}_{V,E,\sigma} = \{h_{V,E,\sigma,w} : w \text{ is a mapping from } E \text{ to } \mathbb{R}\}. \tag{20.1}$$

That is, the parameters specifying a hypothesis in the hypothesis class are the weights over the edges of the network.

We can now study the approximation error, estimation error, and optimization error of such hypothesis classes. In Section 20.3 we study the approximation error of $\mathcal{H}_{V,E,\sigma}$ by studying what type of functions hypotheses in $\mathcal{H}_{V,E,\sigma}$ can implement, in terms of the size of the underlying graph. In Section 20.4 we study the estimation error of $\mathcal{H}_{V,E,\sigma}$, for the case of binary classification (i.e., $V_T = 1$ and σ is the sign function), by analyzing its VC dimension. Finally, in Section 20.5 we show that it is computationally hard to learn the class $\mathcal{H}_{V,E,\sigma}$, even if the underlying graph is small, and in Section 20.6 we present the most commonly used heuristic for training $\mathcal{H}_{V,E,\sigma}$.

20.3 THE EXPRESSIVE POWER OF NEURAL NETWORKS

In this section we study the expressive power of neural networks, namely, what type of functions can be implemented using a neural network. More concretely, we will fix some architecture, V, E, σ, and will study what functions hypotheses in $\mathcal{H}_{V,E,\sigma}$ can implement, as a function of the size of V.

We start the discussion with studying which type of Boolean functions (i.e., functions from $\{\pm 1\}^n$ to $\{\pm 1\}$) can be implemented by $\mathcal{H}_{V,E,\text{sign}}$. Observe that for every computer in which real numbers are stored using b bits, whenever we calculate a function $f : \mathbb{R}^n \to \mathbb{R}$ on such a computer we in fact calculate a function $g : \{\pm 1\}^{nb} \to \{\pm 1\}^b$. Therefore, studying which Boolean functions can be implemented by $\mathcal{H}_{V,E,\text{sign}}$ can tell us which functions can be implemented on a computer that stores real numbers using b bits.

We begin with a simple claim, showing that without restricting the size of the network, every Boolean function can be implemented using a neural network of depth 2.

Claim 20.1. *For every n, there exists a graph (V, E) of depth 2, such that $\mathcal{H}_{V,E,sign}$ contains all functions from $\{\pm 1\}^n$ to $\{\pm 1\}$.*

Proof. We construct a graph with $|V_0| = n+1$, $|V_1| = 2^n + 1$, and $|V_2| = 1$. Let E be all possible edges between adjacent layers. Now, let $f : \{\pm 1\}^n \to \{\pm 1\}$ be some Boolean function. We need to show that we can adjust the weights so that the network will implement f. Let $\mathbf{u}_1, \ldots, \mathbf{u}_k$ be all vectors in $\{\pm 1\}^n$ on which f outputs 1. Observe that for every i and every $\mathbf{x} \in \{\pm 1\}^n$, if $\mathbf{x} \neq \mathbf{u}_i$ then $\langle \mathbf{x}, \mathbf{u}_i \rangle \leq n - 2$ and if $\mathbf{x} = \mathbf{u}_i$ then $\langle \mathbf{x}, u_i \rangle = n$. It follows that the function $g_i(\mathbf{x}) = \text{sign}(\langle \mathbf{x}, \mathbf{u}_i \rangle - n + 1)$ equals 1 if and only if $\mathbf{x} = \mathbf{u}_i$. It follows that we can adapt the weights between V_0 and V_1 so that for every $i \in [k]$, the neuron $v_{1,i}$ implements the function $g_i(\mathbf{x})$. Next, we observe that $f(\mathbf{x})$ is the disjunction of the functions $g_i(\mathbf{x})$, and therefore can be written as

$$f(\mathbf{x}) = \text{sign}\left(\sum_{i=1}^{k} g_i(\mathbf{x}) + k - 1 \right),$$

which concludes our proof. □

The preceding claim shows that neural networks can implement any Boolean function. However, this is a very weak property, as the size of the resulting network might be exponentially large. In the construction given at the proof of Claim 20.1, the number of nodes in the hidden layer is exponentially large. This is not an artifact of our proof, as stated in the following theorem.

Theorem 20.2. *For every n, let $s(n)$ be the minimal integer such that there exists a graph (V, E) with $|V| = s(n)$ such that the hypothesis class $\mathcal{H}_{V,E,sign}$ contains all the functions from $\{0,1\}^n$ to $\{0,1\}$. Then, $s(n)$ is exponential in n. Similar results hold for $\mathcal{H}_{V,E,\sigma}$ where σ is the sigmoid function.*

Proof. Suppose that for some (V, E) we have that $\mathcal{H}_{V,E,\text{sign}}$ contains all functions from $\{0,1\}^n$ to $\{0,1\}$. It follows that it can shatter the set of $m = 2^n$ vectors in $\{0,1\}^n$ and hence the VC dimension of $\mathcal{H}_{V,E,\text{sign}}$ is 2^n. On the other hand, the VC dimension of $\mathcal{H}_{V,E,\text{sign}}$ is bounded by $O(|E|\log(|E|)) \leq O(|V|^3)$, as we will show in the next section. This implies that $|V| \geq \Omega(2^{n/3})$, which concludes our proof for the case of networks with the sign activation function. The proof for the sigmoid case is analogous. $\square$

Remark 20.1. It is possible to derive a similar theorem for $\mathcal{H}_{V,E,\sigma}$ for any σ, as long as we restrict the weights so that it is possible to express every weight using a number of bits which is bounded by a universal constant. We can even consider hypothesis classes where different neurons can employ different activation functions, as long as the number of allowed activation functions is also finite.

Which functions can we express using a network of polynomial size? The preceding claim tells us that it is impossible to express all Boolean functions using a network of polynomial size. On the positive side, in the following we show that all Boolean functions that can be calculated in time $O(T(n))$ can also be expressed by a network of size $O(T(n)^2)$.

Theorem 20.3. *Let $T : \mathbb{N} \to \mathbb{N}$ and for every n, let $\mathcal{F}_n$ be the set of functions that can be implemented using a Turing machine using runtime of at most $T(n)$. Then, there exist constants $b, c \in \mathbb{R}_+$ such that for every n, there is a graph (V_n, E_n) of size at most $c\,T(n)^2 + b$ such that $\mathcal{H}_{V_n,E_n,sign}$ contains $\mathcal{F}_n$.*

The proof of this theorem relies on the relation between the time complexity of programs and their circuit complexity (see, for example, Sipser (2006)). In a nutshell, a Boolean circuit is a type of network in which the individual neurons implement conjunctions, disjunctions, and negation of their inputs. Circuit complexity measures the size of Boolean circuits required to calculate functions. The relation between time complexity and circuit complexity can be seen intuitively as follows. We can model each step of the execution of a computer program as a simple operation on its memory state. Therefore, the neurons at each layer of the network will reflect the memory state of the computer at the corresponding time, and the translation to the next layer of the network involves a simple calculation that can be carried out by the network. To relate Boolean circuits to networks with the sign activation function, we need to show that we can implement the operations of conjunction, disjunction, and negation, using the sign activation function. Clearly, we can implement the negation operator using the sign activation function. The following lemma shows that the sign activation function can also implement conjunctions and disjunctions of its inputs.

Lemma 20.4. *Suppose that a neuron v, that implements the sign activation function, has k incoming edges, connecting it to neurons whose outputs are in $\{\pm 1\}$. Then, by adding one more edge, linking a "constant" neuron to v, and by adjusting the weights on the edges to v, the output of v can implement the conjunction or the disjunction of its inputs.*

Proof. Simply observe that if $f : \{\pm 1\}^k \to \{\pm 1\}$ is the conjunction function, $f(\mathbf{x}) = \wedge_i x_i$, then it can be written as $f(\mathbf{x}) = \mathrm{sign}\left(1 - k + \sum_{i=1}^k x_i\right)$. Similarly, the disjunction function, $f(\mathbf{x}) = \vee_i x_i$, can be written as $f(\mathbf{x}) = \mathrm{sign}\left(k - 1 + \sum_{i=1}^k x_i\right)$. $\square$

So far we have discussed Boolean functions. In Exercise 20.1 we show that neural networks are *universal approximators*. That is, for every fixed precision parameter, $\epsilon > 0$, and every Lipschitz function $f : [-1,1]^n \to [-1,1]$, it is possible to construct a network such that for every input $\mathbf{x} \in [-1,1]^n$, the network outputs a number between $f(\mathbf{x}) - \epsilon$ and $f(\mathbf{x}) + \epsilon$. However, as in the case of Boolean functions, the size of the network here again cannot be polynomial in n. This is formalized in the following theorem, whose proof is a direct corollary of Theorem 20.2 and is left as an exercise.

Theorem 20.5. *Fix some $\epsilon \in (0,1)$. For every n, let $s(n)$ be the minimal integer such that there exists a graph (V,E) with $|V| = s(n)$ such that the hypothesis class $\mathcal{H}_{V,E,\sigma}$, with σ being the sigmoid function, can approximate, to within precision of ϵ, every 1-Lipschitz function $f : [-1,1]^n \to [-1,1]$. Then $s(n)$ is exponential in n.*

20.3.1 Geometric Intuition

We next provide several geometric illustrations of functions $f : \mathbb{R}^2 \to \{\pm 1\}$ and show how to express them using a neural network with the sign activation function.

Let us start with a depth 2 network, namely, a network with a single hidden layer. Each neuron in the hidden layer implements a halfspace predictor. Then, the single neuron at the output layer applies a halfspace on top of the binary outputs of the neurons in the hidden layer. As we have shown before, a halfspace can implement the conjunction function. Therefore, such networks contain all hypotheses which are an intersection of $k-1$ halfspaces, where k is the number of neurons in the hidden layer; namely, they can express all convex polytopes with $k-1$ faces. An example of an intersection of 5 halfspaces is given in the following.

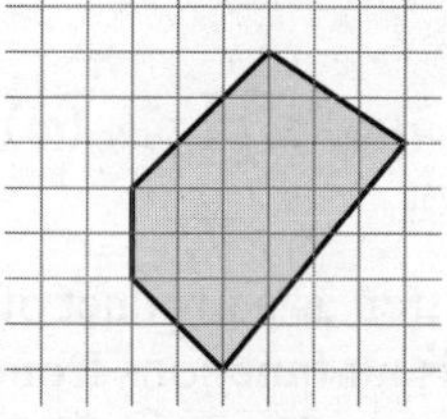

We have shown that a neuron in layer V_2 can implement a function that indicates whether $\mathbf{x}$ is in some convex polytope. By adding one more layer, and letting the neuron in the output layer implement the disjunction of its inputs, we get a network that computes the union of polytopes. An illustration of such a function is given in the following.

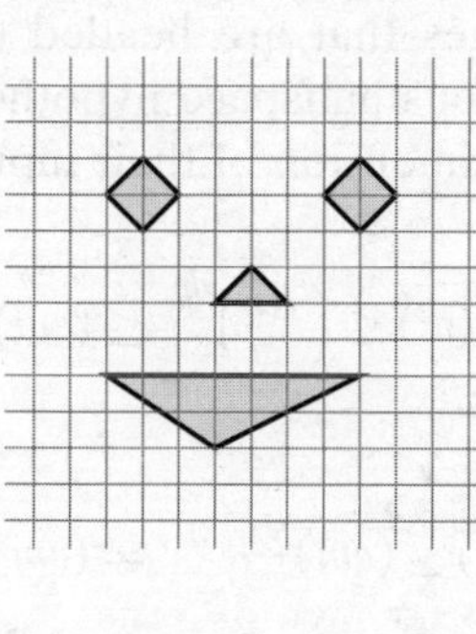

20.4 THE SAMPLE COMPLEXITY OF NEURAL NETWORKS

Next we discuss the sample complexity of learning the class $\mathcal{H}_{V,E,\sigma}$. Recall that the fundamental theorem of learning tells us that the sample complexity of learning a hypothesis class of binary classifiers depends on its VC dimension. Therefore, we focus on calculating the VC dimension of hypothesis classes of the form $\mathcal{H}_{V,E,\sigma}$, where the output layer of the graph contains a single neuron.

We start with the sign activation function, namely, with $\mathcal{H}_{V,E,\text{sign}}$. What is the VC dimension of this class? Intuitively, since we learn $|E|$ parameters, the VC dimension should be order of $|E|$. This is indeed the case, as formalized by the following theorem.

Theorem 20.6. *The VC dimension of $\mathcal{H}_{V,E,sign}$ is $O(|E|\log(|E|))$.*

Proof. To simplify the notation throughout the proof, let us denote the hypothesis class by $\mathcal{H}$. Recall the definition of the growth function, $\tau_{\mathcal{H}}(m)$, from Section 6.5.1. This function measures $\max_{C\subset\mathcal{X}:|C|=m}|\mathcal{H}_C|$, where $\mathcal{H}_C$ is the restriction of $\mathcal{H}$ to functions from C to $\{0,1\}$. We can naturally extend the definition for a set of functions from $\mathcal{X}$ to some finite set $\mathcal{Y}$, by letting $\mathcal{H}_C$ be the restriction of $\mathcal{H}$ to functions from C to $\mathcal{Y}$, and keeping the definition of $\tau_{\mathcal{H}}(m)$ intact.

Our neural network is defined by a layered graph. Let $V_0,\ldots,V_T$ be the layers of the graph. Fix some $t\in[T]$. By assigning different weights on the edges between V_{t-1} and V_t, we obtain different functions from $\mathbb{R}^{|V_{t-1}|}\to\{\pm1\}^{|V_t|}$. Let $\mathcal{H}^{(t)}$ be the class of all possible such mappings from $\mathbb{R}^{|V_{t-1}|}\to\{\pm1\}^{|V_t|}$. Then, $\mathcal{H}$ can be written as a composition, $\mathcal{H}=\mathcal{H}^{(T)}\circ\ldots\circ\mathcal{H}^{(1)}$. In Exercise 20.4 we show that the growth function of a composition of hypothesis classes is bounded by the products of the growth functions of the individual classes. Therefore,

$$\tau_{\mathcal{H}}(m)\le\prod_{t=1}^{T}\tau_{\mathcal{H}^{(t)}}(m).$$

In addition, each $\mathcal{H}^{(t)}$ can be written as a product of function classes, $\mathcal{H}^{(t)}=\mathcal{H}^{(t,1)}\times\cdots\times\mathcal{H}^{(t,|V_t|)}$, where each $\mathcal{H}^{(t,j)}$ is all functions from layer $t-1$ to $\{\pm1\}$ that the jth neuron of layer t can implement. In Exercise 20.3 we bound product classes, and this yields

$$\tau_{\mathcal{H}^{(t)}}(m)\le\prod_{i=1}^{|V_t|}\tau_{\mathcal{H}^{(t,i)}}(m).$$

Let $d_{t,i}$ be the number of edges that are headed to the ith neuron of layer t. Since the neuron is a homogenous halfspace hypothesis and the VC dimension of homogenous halfspaces is the dimension of their input, we have by Sauer's lemma that

$$\tau_{\mathcal{H}^{(t,i)}}(m)\le\left(\frac{em}{d_{t,i}}\right)^{d_{t,i}}\le(em)^{d_{t,i}}.$$

Overall, we obtained that

$$\tau_{\mathcal{H}}(m)\le(em)^{\sum_{t,i}d_{t,i}}=(em)^{|E|}.$$

Now, assume that there are m shattered points. Then, we must have $\tau_{\mathcal{H}}(m) = 2^m$, from which we obtain

$$2^m \leq (em)^{|E|} \;\Rightarrow\; m \leq |E|\log(em)/\log(2).$$

The claim follows by Lemma A.2. □

Next, we consider $\mathcal{H}_{V,E,\sigma}$, where σ is the sigmoid function. Surprisingly, it turns out that the VC dimension of $\mathcal{H}_{V,E,\sigma}$ is lower bounded by $\Omega(|E|^2)$ (see Exercise 20.5.) That is, the VC dimension is the number of tunable parameters squared. It is also possible to upper bound the VC dimension by $O(|V|^2\,|E|^2)$, but the proof is beyond the scope of this book. In any case, since in practice we only consider networks in which the weights have a short representation as floating point numbers with $O(1)$ bits, by using the discretization trick we easily obtain that such networks have a VC dimension of $O(|E|)$, even if we use the sigmoid activation function.

20.5 THE RUNTIME OF LEARNING NEURAL NETWORKS

In the previous sections we have shown that the class of neural networks with an underlying graph of polynomial size can express all functions that can be implemented efficiently, and that the sample complexity has a favorable dependence on the size of the network. In this section we turn to the analysis of the time complexity of training neural networks.

We first show that it is NP hard to implement the ERM rule with respect to $\mathcal{H}_{V,E,\text{sign}}$ even for networks with a single hidden layer that contain just 4 neurons in the hidden layer.

Theorem 20.7. *Let $k \geq 3$. For every n, let (V,E) be a layered graph with n input nodes, $k+1$ nodes at the (single) hidden layer, where one of them is the constant neuron, and a single output node. Then, it is NP hard to implement the ERM rule with respect to $\mathcal{H}_{V,E,sign}$.*

The proof relies on a reduction from the k-coloring problem and is left as Exercise 20.6.

One way around the preceding hardness result could be that for the purpose of learning, it may suffice to find a predictor $h \in \mathcal{H}$ with low empirical error, not necessarily an exact ERM. However, it turns out that even the task of finding weights that result in close-to-minimal empirical error is computationally infeasible (see (Bartlett & Ben-David 2002)).

One may also wonder whether it may be possible to change the architecture of the network so as to circumvent the hardness result. That is, maybe ERM with respect to the original network structure is computationally hard but ERM with respect to some other, larger, network may be implemented efficiently (see Chapter 8 for examples of such cases). Another possibility is to use other activation functions (such as sigmoids, or any other type of efficiently computable activation functions). There is a strong indication that all of such approaches are doomed to fail. Indeed, under some cryptographic assumption, the problem of learning intersections of halfspaces is known to be hard even in the representation independent model of learning (see Klivans & Sherstov (2006)). This implies that, under the same cryptographic assumption, any hypothesis class which contains intersections of halfspaces cannot be learned efficiently.

A widely used heuristic for training neural networks relies on the SGD framework we studied in Chapter 14. There, we have shown that SGD is a successful learner if the loss function is convex. In neural networks, the loss function is highly nonconvex. Nevertheless, we can still implement the SGD algorithm and hope it will find a reasonable solution (as happens to be the case in several practical tasks).

20.6 SGD AND BACKPROPAGATION

The problem of finding a hypothesis in $\mathcal{H}_{V,E,\sigma}$ with a low risk amounts to the problem of tuning the weights over the edges. In this section we show how to apply a heuristic search for good weights using the SGD algorithm. Throughout this section we assume that σ is the sigmoid function, $\sigma(a) = 1/(1+e^{-a})$, but the derivation holds for any differentiable scalar function.

Since E is a finite set, we can think of the weight function as a vector $\mathbf{w} \in \mathbb{R}^{|E|}$. Suppose the network has n input neurons and k output neurons, and denote by $h_{\mathbf{w}} : \mathbb{R}^n \to \mathbb{R}^k$ the function calculated by the network if the weight function is defined by $\mathbf{w}$. Let us denote by $\Delta(h_{\mathbf{w}}(\mathbf{x}), \mathbf{y})$ the loss of predicting $h_{\mathbf{w}}(\mathbf{x})$ when the target is $\mathbf{y} \in \mathcal{Y}$. For concreteness, we will take Δ to be the squared loss, $\Delta(h_{\mathbf{w}}(\mathbf{x}), y) = \frac{1}{2}\|h_{\mathbf{w}}(\mathbf{x}) - \mathbf{y}\|^2$; however, similar derivation can be obtained for every differentiable function. Finally, given a distribution $\mathcal{D}$ over the examples domain, $\mathbb{R}^n \times \mathbb{R}^k$, let $L_{\mathcal{D}}(\mathbf{w})$ be the risk of the network, namely,

$$L_{\mathcal{D}}(\mathbf{w}) = \mathop{\mathbb{E}}_{(\mathbf{x},\mathbf{y})\sim\mathcal{D}} [\Delta(h_{\mathbf{w}}(\mathbf{x}), \mathbf{y})].$$

Recall the SGD algorithm for minimizing the risk function $L_{\mathcal{D}}(\mathbf{w})$. We repeat the pseudocode from Chapter 14 with a few modifications, which are relevant to the neural network application because of the nonconvexity of the objective function. First, while in Chapter 14 we initialized $\mathbf{w}$ to be the zero vector, here we initialize $\mathbf{w}$ to be a randomly chosen vector with values close to zero. This is because an initialization with the zero vector will lead all hidden neurons to have the same weights (if the network is a full layered network). In addition, the hope is that if we repeat the SGD procedure several times, where each time we initialize the process with a new random vector, one of the runs will lead to a good local minimum. Second, while a fixed step size, η, is guaranteed to be good enough for convex problems, here we utilize a variable step size, η_t, as defined in Section 14.4.2. Because of the nonconvexity of the loss function, the choice of the sequence η_t is more significant, and it is tuned in practice by a trial and error manner. Third, we output the best performing vector on a validation set. In addition, it is sometimes helpful to add regularization on the weights, with parameter λ. That is, we try to minimize $L_{\mathcal{D}}(\mathbf{w}) + \frac{\lambda}{2}\|\mathbf{w}\|^2$. Finally, the gradient does not have a closed form solution. Instead, it is implemented using the backpropagation algorithm, which will be described in the sequel.

SGD for Neural Networks

parameters:
number of iterations τ
step size sequence $\eta_1, \eta_2, \dots, \eta_\tau$
regularization parameter $\lambda > 0$
input:
layered graph (V, E)
differentiable activation function $\sigma : \mathbb{R} \to \mathbb{R}$
initialize:
choose $\mathbf{w}^{(1)} \in \mathbb{R}^{|E|}$ at random
(from a distribution s.t. $\mathbf{w}^{(1)}$ is close enough to $\mathbf{0}$)
for $i = 1, 2, \dots, \tau$
sample $(\mathbf{x}, \mathbf{y}) \sim \mathcal{D}$
calculate gradient $\mathbf{v}_i = \text{backpropagation}(\mathbf{x}, \mathbf{y}, \mathbf{w}, (V, E), \sigma)$
update $\mathbf{w}^{(i+1)} = \mathbf{w}^{(i)} - \eta_i(\mathbf{v}_i + \lambda \mathbf{w}^{(i)})$
output:
$\bar{\mathbf{w}}$ is the best performing $\mathbf{w}^{(i)}$ on a validation set

Backpropagation

input:
example $(\mathbf{x}, \mathbf{y})$, weight vector $\mathbf{w}$, layered graph (V, E),
activation function $\sigma : \mathbb{R} \to \mathbb{R}$
initialize:
denote layers of the graph $V_0, \dots, V_T$ where $V_t = \{v_{t,1}, \dots, v_{t,k_t}\}$
define $W_{t,i,j}$ as the weight of $(v_{t,j}, v_{t+1,i})$
(where we set $W_{t,i,j} = 0$ if $(v_{t,j}, v_{t+1,i}) \notin E$)
forward:
set $\mathbf{o}_0 = \mathbf{x}$
for $t = 1, \dots, T$
for $i = 1, \dots, k_t$
set $a_{t,i} = \sum_{j=1}^{k_{t-1}} W_{t-1,i,j}\, o_{t-1,j}$
set $o_{t,i} = \sigma(a_{t,i})$
backward:
set $\boldsymbol{\delta}_T = \mathbf{o}_T - \mathbf{y}$
for $t = T-1, T-2, \dots, 1$
for $i = 1, \dots, k_t$
$\delta_{t,i} = \sum_{j=1}^{k_{t+1}} W_{t,j,i}\, \delta_{t+1,j}\, \sigma'(a_{t+1,j})$
output:
foreach edge $(v_{t-1,j}, v_{t,i}) \in E$
set the partial derivative to $\delta_{t,i}\, \sigma'(a_{t,i})\, o_{t-1,j}$

Explaining How Backpropagation Calculates the Gradient:
We next explain how the backpropagation algorithm calculates the gradient of the loss function on an example $(\mathbf{x}, \mathbf{y})$ with respect to the vector $\mathbf{w}$. Let us first recall

a few definitions from vector calculus. Each element of the gradient is the partial derivative with respect to the variable in $\mathbf{w}$ corresponding to one of the edges of the network. Recall the definition of a partial derivative. Given a function $f : \mathbb{R}^n \to \mathbb{R}$, the partial derivative with respect to the ith variable at $\mathbf{w}$ is obtained by fixing the values of $w_1, \ldots, w_{i-1}, w_{i+1}, w_n$, which yields the scalar function $g : \mathbb{R} \to \mathbb{R}$ defined by $g(a) = f((w_1, \ldots, w_{i-1}, w_i + a, w_{i+1}, \ldots, w_n))$, and then taking the derivative of g at 0. For a function with multiple outputs, $\mathbf{f} : \mathbb{R}^n \to \mathbb{R}^m$, the *Jacobian* of $\mathbf{f}$ at $\mathbf{w} \in \mathbb{R}^n$, denoted $J_{\mathbf{w}}(\mathbf{f})$, is the $m \times n$ matrix whose i, j element is the partial derivative of $f_i : \mathbb{R}^n \to \mathbb{R}$ w.r.t. its jth variable at $\mathbf{w}$. Note that if $m = 1$ then the Jacobian matrix is the gradient of the function (represented as a row vector). Two examples of Jacobian calculations, which we will later use, are as follows.

- Let $\mathbf{f}(\mathbf{w}) = A\mathbf{w}$ for $A \in \mathbb{R}^{m,n}$. Then $J_{\mathbf{w}}(\mathbf{f}) = A$.
- For every n, we use the notation $\boldsymbol{\sigma}$ to denote the function from $\mathbb{R}^n$ to $\mathbb{R}^n$ which applies the sigmoid function element-wise. That is, $\boldsymbol{\alpha} = \boldsymbol{\sigma}(\boldsymbol{\theta})$ means that for every i we have $\alpha_i = \sigma(\theta_i) = \frac{1}{1+\exp(-\theta_i)}$. It is easy to verify that $J_{\boldsymbol{\theta}}(\boldsymbol{\sigma})$ is a diagonal matrix whose (i,i) entry is $\sigma'(\theta_i)$, where σ' is the derivative function of the (scalar) sigmoid function, namely, $\sigma'(\theta_i) = \frac{1}{(1+\exp(\theta_i))(1+\exp(-\theta_i))}$. We also use the notation $\mathrm{diag}(\boldsymbol{\sigma}'(\boldsymbol{\theta}))$ to denote this matrix.

The *chain rule* for taking the derivative of a composition of functions can be written in terms of the Jacobian as follows. Given two functions $\mathbf{f} : \mathbb{R}^n \to \mathbb{R}^m$ and $\mathbf{g} : \mathbb{R}^k \to \mathbb{R}^n$, we have that the Jacobian of the composition function, $(\mathbf{f} \circ \mathbf{g}) : \mathbb{R}^k \to \mathbb{R}^m$, at $\mathbf{w}$, is

$$J_{\mathbf{w}}(\mathbf{f} \circ \mathbf{g}) = J_{g(\mathbf{w})}(\mathbf{f}) J_{\mathbf{w}}(\mathbf{g}).$$

For example, for $\mathbf{g}(\mathbf{w}) = A\mathbf{w}$, where $A \in \mathbb{R}^{n,k}$, we have that

$$J_{\mathbf{w}}(\boldsymbol{\sigma} \circ \mathbf{g}) = \mathrm{diag}(\boldsymbol{\sigma}'(A\mathbf{w}))\, A.$$

To describe the backpropagation algorithm, let us first decompose V into the layers of the graph, $V = \cup_{t=0}^T V_t$. For every t, let us write $V_t = \{v_{t,1}, \ldots, v_{t,k_t}\}$, where $k_t = |V_t|$. In addition, for every t denote $W_t \in \mathbb{R}^{k_{t+1},k_t}$ a matrix which gives a weight to every potential edge between V_t and V_{t+1}. If the edge exists in E then we set $W_{t,i,j}$ to be the weight, according to $\mathbf{w}$, of the edge $(v_{t,j}, v_{t+1,i})$. Otherwise, we add a "phantom" edge and set its weight to be zero, $W_{t,i,j} = 0$. Since when calculating the partial derivative with respect to the weight of some edge we fix all other weights, these additional "phantom" edges have no effect on the partial derivative with respect to existing edges. It follows that we can assume, without loss of generality, that all edges exist, that is, $E = \cup_t (V_t \times V_{t+1})$.

Next, we discuss how to calculate the partial derivatives with respect to the edges from V_{t-1} to V_t, namely, with respect to the elements in W_{t-1}. Since we fix all other weights of the network, it follows that the outputs of all the neurons in V_{t-1} are fixed numbers which do not depend on the weights in W_{t-1}. Denote the corresponding vector by $\mathbf{o}_{t-1}$. In addition, let us denote by $\ell_t : \mathbb{R}^{k_t} \to \mathbb{R}$ the loss function of the subnetwork defined by layers $V_t, \ldots, V_T$ as a function of the outputs of the neurons in V_t. The input to the neurons of V_t can be written as $\mathbf{a}_t = W_{t-1}\mathbf{o}_{t-1}$ and the output of the neurons of V_t is $\mathbf{o}_t = \boldsymbol{\sigma}(\mathbf{a}_t)$. That is, for every j we have $o_{t,j} = \sigma(a_{t,j})$. We obtain that the loss, as a function of W_{t-1}, can be written as

$$g_t(W_{t-1}) = \ell_t(\mathbf{o}_t) = \ell_t(\sigma(\mathbf{a}_t)) = \ell_t(\sigma(W_{t-1}\mathbf{o}_{t-1})).$$

It would be convenient to rewrite this as follows. Let $\mathbf{w}_{t-1} \in \mathbb{R}^{k_{t-1}k_t}$ be the column vector obtained by concatenating the rows of W_{t-1} and then taking the transpose of the resulting long vector. Define by O_{t-1} the $k_t \times (k_{t-1}k_t)$ matrix

$$O_{t-1} = \begin{pmatrix} \mathbf{o}_{t-1}^\top & 0 & \cdots & 0 \\ 0 & \mathbf{o}_{t-1}^\top & \cdots & 0 \\ \vdots & \vdots & \ddots & \vdots \\ 0 & 0 & \cdots & \mathbf{o}_{t-1}^\top \end{pmatrix}. \qquad (20.2)$$

Then, $W_{t-1}\mathbf{o}_{t-1} = O_{t-1}\mathbf{w}_{t-1}$, so we can also write

$$g_t(\mathbf{w}_{t-1}) = \ell_t(\sigma(O_{t-1}\mathbf{w}_{t-1})).$$

Therefore, applying the chain rule, we obtain that

$$J_{\mathbf{w}_{t-1}}(g_t) = J_{\sigma(O_{t-1}\mathbf{w}_{t-1})}(\ell_t)\,\mathrm{diag}(\sigma'(O_{t-1}\mathbf{w}_{t-1}))\,O_{t-1}.$$

Using our notation we have $\mathbf{o}_t = \sigma(O_{t-1}\mathbf{w}_{t-1})$ and $\mathbf{a}_t = O_{t-1}\mathbf{w}_{t-1}$, which yields

$$J_{\mathbf{w}_{t-1}}(g_t) = J_{\mathbf{o}_t}(\ell_t)\,\mathrm{diag}(\sigma'(\mathbf{a}_t))\,O_{t-1}.$$

Let us also denote $\boldsymbol{\delta}_t = J_{\mathbf{o}_t}(\ell_t)$. Then, we can further rewrite the preceding as

$$J_{\mathbf{w}_{t-1}}(g_t) = \left(\delta_{t,1}\,\sigma'(a_{t,1})\,\mathbf{o}_{t-1}^\top\,,\ \ldots\,,\ \delta_{t,k_t}\,\sigma'(a_{t,k_t})\,\mathbf{o}_{t-1}^\top\right). \qquad (20.3)$$

It is left to calculate the vector $\boldsymbol{\delta}_t = J_{\mathbf{o}_t}(\ell_t)$ for every t. This is the gradient of ℓ_t at $\mathbf{o}_t$. We calculate this in a recursive manner. First observe that for the last layer we have that $\ell_T(\mathbf{u}) = \Delta(\mathbf{u}, \mathbf{y})$, where Δ is the loss function. Since we assume that $\Delta(\mathbf{u}, \mathbf{y}) = \frac{1}{2}\|\mathbf{u} - \mathbf{y}\|^2$ we obtain that $J_{\mathbf{u}}(\ell_T) = (\mathbf{u} - \mathbf{y})$. In particular, $\boldsymbol{\delta}_T = J_{\mathbf{o}_T}(\ell_T) = (\mathbf{o}_T - \mathbf{y})$. Next, note that

$$\ell_t(\mathbf{u}) = \ell_{t+1}(\sigma(W_t\mathbf{u})).$$

Therefore, by the chain rule,

$$J_{\mathbf{u}}(\ell_t) = J_{\sigma(W_t\mathbf{u})}(\ell_{t+1})\,\mathrm{diag}(\sigma'(W_t\mathbf{u}))\,W_t.$$

In particular,

$$\begin{aligned} \boldsymbol{\delta}_t = J_{\mathbf{o}_t}(\ell_t) &= J_{\sigma(W_t\mathbf{o}_t)}(\ell_{t+1})\,\mathrm{diag}(\sigma'(W_t\mathbf{o}_t))\,W_t \\ &= J_{\mathbf{o}_{t+1}}(\ell_{t+1})\,\mathrm{diag}(\sigma'(\mathbf{a}_{t+1}))\,W_t \\ &= \boldsymbol{\delta}_{t+1}\,\mathrm{diag}(\sigma'(\mathbf{a}_{t+1}))\,W_t. \end{aligned}$$

In summary, we can first calculate the vectors $\{\mathbf{a}_t, \mathbf{o}_t\}$ from the bottom of the network to its top. Then, we calculate the vectors $\{\boldsymbol{\delta}_t\}$ from the top of the network back to its bottom. Once we have all of these vectors, the partial derivatives are easily obtained using Equation (20.3). We have thus shown that the pseudocode of backpropagation indeed calculates the gradient.

20.7 SUMMARY

Neural networks over graphs of size $s(n)$ can be used to describe hypothesis classes of all predictors that can be implemented in runtime of $O(\sqrt{s(n)})$. We have also shown that their sample complexity depends polynomially on $s(n)$ (specifically, it depends on the number of edges in the network). Therefore, classes of neural network hypotheses seem to be an excellent choice. Regrettably, the problem of training the network on the basis of training data is computationally hard. We have presented the SGD framework as a heuristic approach for training neural networks and described the backpropagation algorithm which efficiently calculates the gradient of the loss function with respect to the weights over the edges.

20.8 BIBLIOGRAPHIC REMARKS

Neural networks were extensively studied in the 1980s and early 1990s, but with mixed empirical success. In recent years, a combination of algorithmic advancements, as well as increasing computational power and data size, has led to a breakthrough in the effectiveness of neural networks. In particular, "deep networks" (i.e., networks of more than 2 layers) have shown very impressive practical performance on a variety of domains. A few examples include convolutional networks (LeCun & Bengio 1995), restricted Boltzmann machines (Hinton, Osindero & Teh 2006), auto-encoders (Ranzato et al. 2007, Bengio & LeCun 2007, Collobert & Weston 2008, Lee et al. 2009, Le et al. 2012), and sum-product networks (Livni, Shalev-Shwartz & Shamir 2013, Poon & Domingos 2011). See also (Bengio 2009) and the references therein.

The expressive power of neural networks and the relation to circuit complexity have been extensively studied in (Parberry 1994). For the analysis of the sample complexity of neural networks we refer the reader to (Anthony & Bartlet 1999). Our proof technique of Theorem 20.6 is due to Kakade and Tewari lecture notes.

Klivans and Sherstov (2006) have shown that for any $c > 0$, intersections of n^c halfspaces over $\{\pm 1\}^n$ are not efficiently PAC learnable, even if we allow representation independent learning. This hardness result relies on the cryptographic assumption that there is no polynomial time solution to the unique-shortest-vector problem. As we have argued, this implies that there cannot be an efficient algorithm for training neural networks, even if we allow larger networks or other activation functions that can be implemented efficiently.

The backpropagation algorithm has been introduced in Rumelhart, Hinton, and Williams (1986).

20.9 EXERCISES

20.1 **Neural Networks are universal approximators:** Let $f : [-1,1]^n \to [-1,1]$ be a ρ-Lipschitz function. Fix some $\epsilon > 0$. Construct a neural network $N : [-1,1]^n \to [-1,1]$, with the sigmoid activation function, such that for every $\mathbf{x} \in [-1,1]^n$ it holds that $|f(\mathbf{x}) - N(\mathbf{x})| \le \epsilon$.
Hint: Similarly to the proof of Theorem 19.3, partition $[-1,1]^n$ into small boxes. Use the Lipschitzness of f to show that it is approximately constant at each box.

Finally, show that a neural network can first decide which box the input vector belongs to, and then predict the averaged value of f at that box.

20.2 Prove Theorem 20.5.
Hint: For every $f : \{-1,1\}^n \to \{-1,1\}$ construct a 1-Lipschitz function $g : [-1,1]^n \to [-1,1]$ such that if you can approximate g then you can express f.

20.3 **Growth function of product:** For $i = 1,2$, let $\mathcal{F}_i$ be a set of functions from $\mathcal{X}$ to $\mathcal{Y}_i$. Define $\mathcal{H} = \mathcal{F}_1 \times \mathcal{F}_2$ to be the Cartesian product class. That is, for every $f_1 \in \mathcal{F}_1$ and $f_2 \in \mathcal{F}_2$, there exists $h \in \mathcal{H}$ such that $h(\mathbf{x}) = (f_1(\mathbf{x}), f_2(\mathbf{x}))$. Prove that $\tau_{\mathcal{H}}(m) \le \tau_{\mathcal{F}_1}(m)\,\tau_{\mathcal{F}_2}(m)$.

20.4 **Growth function of composition:** Let $\mathcal{F}_1$ be a set of functions from $\mathcal{X}$ to Z and let $\mathcal{F}_2$ be a set of functions from Z to $\mathcal{Y}$. Let $\mathcal{H} = \mathcal{F}_2 \circ \mathcal{F}_1$ be the composition class. That is, for every $f_1 \in \mathcal{F}_1$ and $f_2 \in \mathcal{F}_2$, there exists $h \in \mathcal{H}$ such that $h(\mathbf{x}) = f_2(f_1(\mathbf{x}))$. Prove that $\tau_{\mathcal{H}}(m) \le \tau_{\mathcal{F}_2}(m)\tau_{\mathcal{F}_1}(m)$.

20.5 **VC of sigmoidal networks:** In this exercise we show that there is a graph (V,E) such that the VC dimension of the class of neural networks over these graphs with the sigmoid activation function is $\Omega(|E|^2)$. Note that for every $\epsilon > 0$, the sigmoid activation function can approximate the threshold activation function, $\mathbb{1}_{[\sum_i x_i]}$, up to accuracy ϵ. To simplify the presentation, throughout the exercise we assume that we can exactly implement the activation function $\mathbb{1}_{[\sum_i x_i > 0]}$ using a sigmoid activation function.
Fix some n.

1. Construct a network, N_1, with $O(n)$ weights, which implements a function from $\mathbb{R}$ to $\{0,1\}^n$ and satisfies the following property. For every $\mathbf{x} \in \{0,1\}^n$, if we feed the network with the real number $0.x_1x_2\ldots x_n$, then the output of the network will be $\mathbf{x}$.
Hint: Denote $\alpha = 0.x_1x_2\ldots x_n$ and observe that $10^k\alpha - 0.5$ is at least 0.5 if $x_k = 1$ and is at most -0.3 if $x_k = -1$.
2. Construct a network, N_2, with $O(n)$ weights, which implements a function from $[n]$ to $\{0,1\}^n$ such that $N_2(i) = \mathbf{e}_i$ for all i. That is, upon receiving the input i, the network outputs the vector of all zeros except 1 at the i'th neuron.
3. Let $\alpha_1,\ldots,\alpha_n$ be n real numbers such that every α_i is of the form $0.a_1^{(i)}a_2^{(i)}\ldots a_n^{(i)}$, with $a_j^{(i)} \in \{0,1\}$. Construct a network, N_3, with $O(n)$ weights, which implements a function from $[n]$ to $\mathbb{R}$, and satisfies $N_2(i) = \alpha_i$ for every $i \in [n]$.
4. Combine N_1, N_3 to obtain a network that receives $i \in [n]$ and output $\mathbf{a}^{(i)}$.
5. Construct a network N_4 that receives $(i,j) \in [n] \times [n]$ and outputs $a_j^{(i)}$.
Hint: Observe that the AND function over $\{0,1\}^2$ can be calculated using $O(1)$ weights.
6. Conclude that there is a graph with $O(n)$ weights such that the VC dimension of the resulting hypothesis class is n^2.

20.6 Prove Theorem 20.7.
Hint: The proof is similar to the hardness of learning intersections of halfspaces – see Exercise 32 in Chapter 8.

PART 3

Additional Learning Models

21

Online Learning

In this chapter we describe a different model of learning, which is called *online* learning. Previously, we studied the PAC learning model, in which the learner first receives a batch of training examples, uses the training set to learn a hypothesis, and only when learning is completed uses the learned hypothesis for predicting the label of new examples. In our papayas learning problem, this means that we should first buy a bunch of papayas and taste them all. Then, we use all of this information to learn a prediction rule that determines the taste of new papayas. In contrast, in online learning there is no separation between a training phase and a prediction phase. Instead, each time we buy a papaya, it is first considered a *test* example since we should predict whether it is going to taste good. Then, after taking a bite from the papaya, we know the true label, and the same papaya can be used as a *training* example that can help us improve our prediction mechanism for future papayas.

Concretely, online learning takes place in a sequence of consecutive rounds. On each online round, the learner first receives an instance (the learner buys a papaya and knows its shape and color, which form the instance). Then, the learner is required to predict a label (is the papaya tasty?). At the end of the round, the learner obtains the correct label (he tastes the papaya and then knows whether it is tasty or not). Finally, the learner uses this information to improve his future predictions.

To analyze online learning, we follow a similar route to our study of PAC learning. We start with online binary classification problems. We consider both the realizable case, in which we assume, as prior knowledge, that all the labels are generated by some hypothesis from a given hypothesis class, and the unrealizable case, which corresponds to the agnostic PAC learning model. In particular, we present an important algorithm called *Weighted-Majority*. Next, we study online learning problems in which the loss function is convex. Finally, we present the *Perceptron* algorithm as an example of the use of surrogate convex loss functions in the online learning model.

21.1 ONLINE CLASSIFICATION IN THE REALIZABLE CASE

Online learning is performed in a sequence of consecutive rounds, where at round t the learner is given an instance, $\mathbf{x}_t$, taken from an instance domain $\mathcal{X}$, and is required to provide its label. We denote the predicted label by p_t. After predicting the label, the correct label, $y_t \in \{0,1\}$, is revealed to the learner. The learner's goal is to make as few prediction mistakes as possible during this process. The learner tries to deduce information from previous rounds so as to improve its predictions on future rounds.

Clearly, learning is hopeless if there is no correlation between past and present rounds. Previously in the book, we studied the PAC model in which we assume that past and present examples are sampled i.i.d. from the same distribution source. In the online learning model we make no statistical assumptions regarding the origin of the sequence of examples. The sequence is allowed to be deterministic, stochastic, or even adversarially adaptive to the learner's own behavior (as in the case of spam e-mail filtering). Naturally, an adversary can make the number of prediction mistakes of our online learning algorithm arbitrarily large. For example, the adversary can present the same instance on each online round, wait for the learner's prediction, and provide the opposite label as the correct label.

To make nontrivial statements we must further restrict the problem. The realizability assumption is one possible natural restriction. In the realizable case, we assume that all the labels are generated by some hypothesis, $h^\star : \mathcal{X} \to \mathcal{Y}$. Furthermore, $h^\star$ is taken from a hypothesis class $\mathcal{H}$, which is known to the learner. This is analogous to the PAC learning model we studied in Chapter 3. With this restriction on the sequence, the learner should make as few mistakes as possible, assuming that both $h^\star$ and the sequence of instances can be chosen by an adversary. For an online learning algorithm, A, we denote by $M_A(\mathcal{H})$ the maximal number of mistakes A might make on a sequence of examples which is labeled by some $h^\star \in \mathcal{H}$. We emphasize again that both $h^\star$ and the sequence of instances can be chosen by an adversary. A bound on $M_A(\mathcal{H})$ is called a *mistake-bound* and we will study how to design algorithms for which $M_A(\mathcal{H})$ is minimal. Formally:

Definition 21.1 (Mistake Bounds, Online Learnability). Let $\mathcal{H}$ be a hypothesis class and let A be an online learning algorithm. Given any sequence $S = (x_1, h^\star(y_1)), \ldots, (x_T, h^\star(y_T))$, where T is any integer and $h^\star \in \mathcal{H}$, let $M_A(S)$ be the number of mistakes A makes on the sequence S. We denote by $M_A(\mathcal{H})$ the supremum of $M_A(S)$ over all sequences of the preceding form. A bound of the form $M_A(\mathcal{H}) \leq B < \infty$ is called a *mistake bound*. We say that a hypothesis class $\mathcal{H}$ is online learnable if there exists an algorithm A for which $M_A(\mathcal{H}) \leq B < \infty$.

Our goal is to study which hypothesis classes are learnable in the online model, and in particular to find good learning algorithms for a given hypothesis class.

Remark 21.1. Throughout this section and the next, we ignore the computational aspect of learning, and do not restrict the algorithms to be efficient. In Section 21.3 and Section 21.4 we study efficient online learning algorithms.

To simplify the presentation, we start with the case of a finite hypothesis class, namely, $|\mathcal{H}| < \infty$.

In PAC learning, we identified ERM as a good learning algorithm, in the sense that if $\mathcal{H}$ is learnable then it is learnable by the rule $\text{ERM}_{\mathcal{H}}$. A natural learning rule for online learning is to use (at any online round) any ERM hypothesis, namely, any hypothesis which is consistent with all past examples.

Consistent

input: A finite hypothesis class $\mathcal{H}$
initialize: $V_1 = \mathcal{H}$
for $t = 1, 2, \ldots$
  receive $\mathbf{x}_t$
  choose any $h \in V_t$
  predict $p_t = h(\mathbf{x}_t)$
  receive true label $y_t = h^\star(\mathbf{x}_t)$
  update $V_{t+1} = \{h \in V_t : h(\mathbf{x}_t) = y_t\}$

The Consistent algorithm maintains a set, V_t, of all the hypotheses which are consistent with $(\mathbf{x}_1, y_1), \ldots, (\mathbf{x}_{t-1}, y_{t-1})$. This set is often called the version space. It then picks any hypothesis from V_t and predicts according to this hypothesis.

Obviously, whenever Consistent makes a prediction mistake, at least one hypothesis is removed from V_t. Therefore, after making M mistakes we have $|V_t| \le |\mathcal{H}| - M$. Since V_t is always nonempty (by the realizability assumption it contains $h^\star$) we have $1 \le |V_t| \le |\mathcal{H}| - M$. Rearranging, we obtain the following:

Corollary 21.2. *Let $\mathcal{H}$ be a finite hypothesis class. The Consistent algorithm enjoys the mistake bound $M_{\text{Consistent}}(\mathcal{H}) \le |\mathcal{H}| - 1$.*

It is rather easy to construct a hypothesis class and a sequence of examples on which Consistent will indeed make $|\mathcal{H}| - 1$ mistakes (see Exercise 21.1.) Therefore, we present a better algorithm in which we choose $h \in V_t$ in a smarter way. We shall see that this algorithm is guaranteed to make exponentially fewer mistakes.

Halving

input: A finite hypothesis class $\mathcal{H}$
initialize: $V_1 = \mathcal{H}$
for $t = 1, 2, \ldots$
  receive $\mathbf{x}_t$
  predict $p_t = \text{argmax}_{r \in \{0,1\}} |\{h \in V_t : h(\mathbf{x}_t) = r\}|$
   (in case of a tie predict $p_t = 1$)
  receive true label $y_t = h^\star(\mathbf{x}_t)$
  update $V_{t+1} = \{h \in V_t : h(\mathbf{x}_t) = y_t\}$

Theorem 21.3. *Let $\mathcal{H}$ be a finite hypothesis class. The Halving algorithm enjoys the mistake bound $M_{\text{Halving}}(\mathcal{H}) \le \log_2(|\mathcal{H}|)$.*

Proof. We simply note that whenever the algorithm errs we have $|V_{t+1}| \le |V_t|/2$, (hence the name Halving). Therefore, if M is the total number of mistakes, we have

$$1 \le |V_{T+1}| \le |\mathcal{H}| 2^{-M}.$$

Rearranging this inequality we conclude our proof. □

Of course, Halving's mistake bound is much better than Consistent's mistake bound. We already see that online learning is different from PAC learning—while in PAC, any ERM hypothesis is good, in online learning choosing an arbitrary ERM hypothesis is far from being optimal.

21.1.1 Online Learnability

We next take a more general approach, and aim at characterizing online learnability. In particular, we target the following question: What is the optimal online learning algorithm for a given hypothesis class $\mathcal{H}$?

We present a dimension of hypothesis classes that characterizes the best achievable mistake bound. This measure was proposed by Nick Littlestone and we therefore refer to it as Ldim($\mathcal{H}$).

To motivate the definition of Ldim it is convenient to view the online learning process as a game between two players: the learner versus the environment. On round t of the game, the environment picks an instance $\mathbf{x}_t$, the learner predicts a label $p_t \in \{0,1\}$, and finally the environment outputs the true label, $y_t \in \{0,1\}$. Suppose that the environment wants to make the learner err on the first T rounds of the game. Then, it must output $y_t = 1 - p_t$, and the only question is how it should choose the instances $\mathbf{x}_t$ in such a way that ensures that for some $h^\star \in \mathcal{H}$ we have $y_t = h^\star(\mathbf{x}_t)$ for all $t \in [T]$.

A strategy for an adversarial environment can be formally described as a binary tree, as follows. Each node of the tree is associated with an instance from $\mathcal{X}$. Initially, the environment presents to the learner the instance associated with the root of the tree. Then, if the learner predicts $p_t = 1$ the environment will declare that this is a wrong prediction (i.e., $y_t = 0$) and will traverse to the right child of the current node. If the learner predicts $p_t = 0$ then the environment will set $y_t = 1$ and will traverse to the left child. This process will continue and at each round, the environment will present the instance associated with the current node.

Formally, consider a complete binary tree of depth T (we define the depth of the tree as the number of edges in a path from the root to a leaf). We have $2^{T+1} - 1$ nodes in such a tree, and we attach an instance to each node. Let $\mathbf{v}_1, \ldots, \mathbf{v}_{2^{T+1}-1}$ be these instances. We start from the root of the tree, and set $\mathbf{x}_1 = \mathbf{v}_1$. At round t, we set $\mathbf{x}_t = \mathbf{v}_{i_t}$ where i_t is the current node. At the end of round t, we go to the left child of i_t if $y_t = 0$ or to the right child if $y_t = 1$. That is, $i_{t+1} = 2i_t + y_t$. Unraveling the recursion we obtain $i_t = 2^{t-1} + \sum_{j=1}^{t-1} y_j \, 2^{t-1-j}$.

The preceding strategy for the environment succeeds only if for every $(y_1, \ldots, y_T)$ there exists $h \in \mathcal{H}$ such that $y_t = h(\mathbf{x}_t)$ for all $t \in [T]$. This leads to the following definition.

Definition 21.4 ($\mathcal{H}$ Shattered Tree). A shattered tree of depth d is a sequence of instances $\mathbf{v}_1, \ldots, \mathbf{v}_{2^d-1}$ in $\mathcal{X}$ such that for every labeling $(y_1, \ldots, y_d) \in \{0,1\}^d$

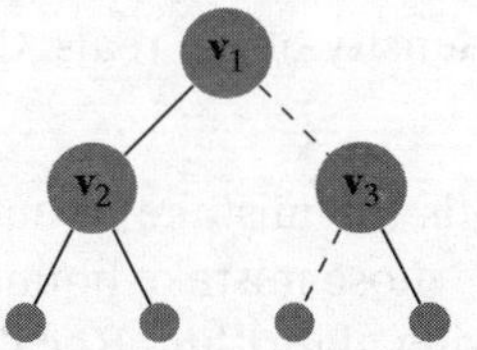

	h_1	h_2	h_3	h_4
$\mathbf{v}_1$	0	0	1	1
$\mathbf{v}_2$	0	1	*	*
$\mathbf{v}_3$	*	*	0	1

Figure 21.1. An illustration of a shattered tree of depth 2. The dashed path corresponds to the sequence of examples $((\mathbf{v}_1, 1), (\mathbf{v}_3, 0))$. The tree is shattered by $\mathcal{H} = \{h_1, h_2, h_3, h_4\}$, where the predictions of each hypothesis in $\mathcal{H}$ on the instances $\mathbf{v}_1, \mathbf{v}_2, \mathbf{v}_3$ is given in the table (the * mark means that $h_j(\mathbf{v}_i)$ can be either 1 or 0).

there exists $h \in \mathcal{H}$ such that for all $t \in [d]$ we have $h(\mathbf{v}_{i_t}) = y_t$ where $i_t = 2^{t-1} + \sum_{j=1}^{t-1} y_j 2^{t-1-j}$.

An illustration of a shattered tree of depth 2 is given in Figure 21.1.

Definition 21.5 (Littlestone's Dimension (Ldim)). Ldim($\mathcal{H}$) is the maximal integer T such that there exists a shattered tree of depth T, which is shattered by $\mathcal{H}$.

The definition of Ldim and the previous discussion immediately imply the following:

Lemma 21.6. *No algorithm can have a mistake bound strictly smaller than* Ldim($\mathcal{H}$)*; namely, for every algorithm, A, we have* $M_A(\mathcal{H}) \geq \text{Ldim}(\mathcal{H})$.

Proof. Let $T = \text{Ldim}(\mathcal{H})$ and let $\mathbf{v}_1, \ldots, \mathbf{v}_{2^T-1}$ be a sequence that satisfies the requirements in the definition of Ldim. If the environment sets $\mathbf{x}_t = \mathbf{v}_{i_t}$ and $y_t = 1 - p_t$ for all $t \in [T]$, then the learner makes T mistakes while the definition of Ldim implies that there exists a hypothesis $h \in \mathcal{H}$ such that $y_t = h(\mathbf{x}_t)$ for all t. □

Let us now give several examples.

Example 21.2. Let $\mathcal{H}$ be a finite hypothesis class. Clearly, any tree that is shattered by $\mathcal{H}$ has depth of at most $\log_2(|\mathcal{H}|)$. Therefore, $\text{Ldim}(\mathcal{H}) \leq \log_2(|\mathcal{H}|)$. Another way to conclude this inequality is by combining Lemma 21.6 with Theorem 21.3.

Example 21.3. Let $\mathcal{X} = \{1, \ldots, d\}$ and $\mathcal{H} = \{h_1, \ldots, h_d\}$ where $h_j(x) = 1$ iff $x = j$. Then, it is easy to show that $\text{Ldim}(\mathcal{H}) = 1$ while $|\mathcal{H}| = d$ can be arbitrarily large. Therefore, this example shows that $\text{Ldim}(\mathcal{H})$ can be significantly smaller than $\log_2(|\mathcal{H}|)$.

Example 21.4. Let $\mathcal{X} = [0,1]$ and $\mathcal{H} = \{x \mapsto \mathbb{1}_{[x<a]} : a \in [0,1]\}$; namely, $\mathcal{H}$ is the class of thresholds on the interval $[0,1]$. Then, $\text{Ldim}(\mathcal{H}) = \infty$. To see this, consider the tree

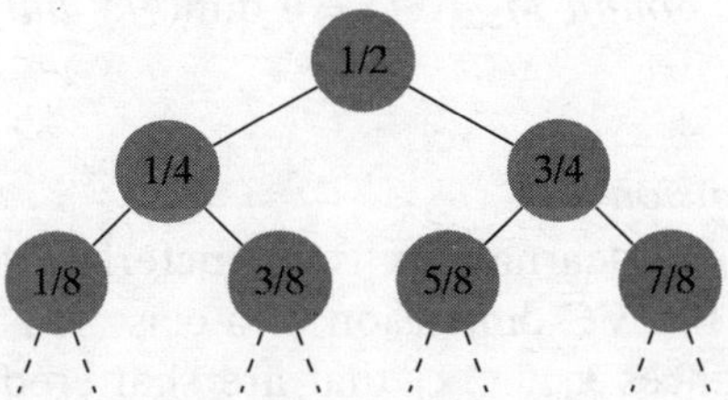

This tree is shattered by $\mathcal{H}$. And, because of the density of the reals, this tree can be made arbitrarily deep.

Lemma 21.6 states that $\text{Ldim}(\mathcal{H})$ lower bounds the mistake bound of any algorithm. Interestingly, there is a standard algorithm whose mistake bound matches this lower bound. The algorithm is similar to the Halving algorithm. Recall that the prediction of Halving is made according to a majority vote of the hypotheses which are consistent with previous examples. We denoted this set by V_t. Put another way, Halving partitions V_t into two sets: $V_t^+ = \{h \in V_t : h(\mathbf{x}_t) = 1\}$ and $V_t^- = \{h \in V_t : h(\mathbf{x}_t) = 0\}$. It then predicts according to the larger of the two groups. The rationale behind this prediction is that whenever Halving makes a mistake it ends up with $|V_{t+1}| \le 0.5\,|V_t|$.

The optimal algorithm we present in the following uses the same idea, but instead of predicting according to the larger class, it predicts according to the class with larger Ldim.

Standard Optimal Algorithm (SOA)

input: A hypothesis class $\mathcal{H}$
initialize: $V_1 = \mathcal{H}$
for $t = 1, 2, \ldots$
  receive $\mathbf{x}_t$
  for $r \in \{0,1\}$ let $V_t^{(r)} = \{h \in V_t : h(\mathbf{x}_t) = r\}$
  predict $p_t = \text{argmax}_{r \in \{0,1\}} \text{Ldim}(V_t^{(r)})$
   (in case of a tie predict $p_t = 1$)
  receive true label y_t
  update $V_{t+1} = \{h \in V_t : h(\mathbf{x}_t) = y_t\}$

The following lemma formally establishes the optimality of the preceding algorithm.

Lemma 21.7. *SOA enjoys the mistake bound* $M_{SOA}(\mathcal{H}) \le \text{Ldim}(\mathcal{H})$.

Proof. It suffices to prove that whenever the algorithm makes a prediction mistake we have $\text{Ldim}(V_{t+1}) \le \text{Ldim}(V_t) - 1$. We prove this claim by assuming the contrary, that is, $\text{Ldim}(V_{t+1}) = \text{Ldim}(V_t)$. If this holds true, then the definition of p_t implies that $\text{Ldim}(V_t^{(r)}) = \text{Ldim}(V_t)$ for both $r = 1$ and $r = 0$. But, then we can construct a shaterred tree of depth $\text{Ldim}(V_t) + 1$ for the class V_t, which leads to the desired contradiction. □

Combining Lemma 21.7 and Lemma 21.6 we obtain:

Corollary 21.8. *Let $\mathcal{H}$ be any hypothesis class. Then, the standard optimal algorithm enjoys the mistake bound $M_{SOA}(\mathcal{H}) = \text{Ldim}(\mathcal{H})$ and no other algorithm can have $M_A(\mathcal{H}) < \text{Ldim}(\mathcal{H})$.*

Comparison to VC Dimension

In the PAC learning model, learnability is characterized by the VC dimension of the class $\mathcal{H}$. Recall that the VC dimension of a class $\mathcal{H}$ is the maximal number d such that there are instances $\mathbf{x}_1, \ldots, \mathbf{x}_d$ that are shattered by $\mathcal{H}$. That is, for any sequence of labels $(y_1,\ldots,y_d) \in \{0,1\}^d$ there exists a hypothesis $h \in \mathcal{H}$ that gives exactly this sequence of labels. The following theorem relates the VC dimension to the Littlestone dimension.

Theorem 21.9. *For any class $\mathcal{H}$, $\mathrm{VCdim}(\mathcal{H}) \leq \mathrm{Ldim}(\mathcal{H})$, and there are classes for which strict inequality holds. Furthermore, the gap can be arbitrarily larger.*

Proof. We first prove that $\mathrm{VCdim}(\mathcal{H}) \leq \mathrm{Ldim}(\mathcal{H})$. Suppose $\mathrm{VCdim}(\mathcal{H}) = d$ and let $\mathbf{x}_1,\ldots,\mathbf{x}_d$ be a shattered set. We now construct a complete binary tree of instances $\mathbf{v}_1,\ldots,\mathbf{v}_{2^d-1}$, where all nodes at depth i are set to be $\mathbf{x}_i$ – see the following illustration:

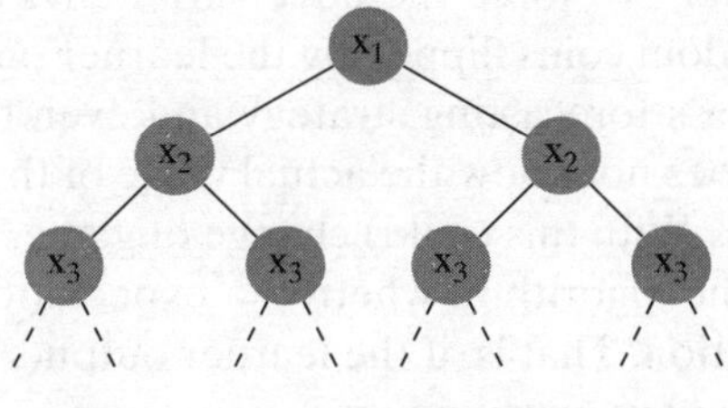

Now, the definition of a shattered set clearly implies that we got a valid shattered tree of depth d, and we conclude that $\mathrm{VCdim}(\mathcal{H}) \leq \mathrm{Ldim}(\mathcal{H})$. To show that the gap can be arbitrarily large simply note that the class given in Example 21.4 has VC dimension of 1 whereas its Littlestone dimension is infinite. □

21.2 ONLINE CLASSIFICATION IN THE UNREALIZABLE CASE

In the previous section we studied online learnability in the realizable case. We now consider the unrealizable case. Similarly to the agnostic PAC model, we no longer assume that all labels are generated by some $h^\star \in \mathcal{H}$, but we require the learner to be competitive with the best fixed predictor from $\mathcal{H}$. This is captured by the *regret* of the algorithm, which measures how "sorry" the learner is, in retrospect, not to have followed the predictions of some hypothesis $h \in \mathcal{H}$. Formally, the regret of an algorithm A relative to h when running on a sequence of T examples is defined as

$$\mathrm{Regret}_A(h,T) = \sup_{(x_1,y_1),\ldots,(x_T,y_T)} \left[\sum_{t=1}^{T} |p_t - y_t| - \sum_{t=1}^{T} |h(x_t) - y_t| \right], \tag{21.1}$$

and the regret of the algorithm relative to a hypothesis class $\mathcal{H}$ is

$$\mathrm{Regret}_A(\mathcal{H},T) = \sup_{h\in\mathcal{H}} \mathrm{Regret}_A(h,T). \tag{21.2}$$

We restate the learner's goal as having the lowest possible regret relative to $\mathcal{H}$. An interesting question is whether we can derive an algorithm with low regret, meaning that $\mathrm{Regret}_A(\mathcal{H},T)$ grows sublinearly with the number of rounds, T, which implies that the difference between the *error rate* of the learner and the best hypothesis in $\mathcal{H}$ tends to zero as T goes to infinity.

We first show that this is an impossible mission—no algorithm can obtain a sublinear regret bound even if $|\mathcal{H}| = 2$. Indeed, consider $\mathcal{H} = \{h_0, h_1\}$, where h_0 is the function that always returns 0 and h_1 is the function that always returns 1. An adversary can make the number of mistakes of any online algorithm be equal to T, by simply waiting for the learner's prediction and then providing the opposite label as the true label. In contrast, for any sequence of true labels, $y_1, \ldots, y_T$, let b be the majority of labels in $y_1, \ldots, y_T$, then the number of mistakes of h_b is at most $T/2$. Therefore, the regret of any online algorithm might be at least $T - T/2 = T/2$, which is not sublinear in T. This impossibility result is attributed to Cover (Cover 1965).

To sidestep Cover's impossibility result, we must further restrict the power of the adversarial environment. We do so by allowing the learner to randomize his predictions. Of course, this by itself does not circumvent Cover's impossibility result, since in deriving this result we assumed nothing about the learner's strategy. To make the randomization meaningful, we force the adversarial environment to decide on y_t without knowing the random coins flipped by the learner on round t. The adversary can still know the learner's forecasting strategy and even the random coin flips of previous rounds, but it does not know the actual value of the random coin flips used by the learner on round t. With this (mild) change of game, we analyze the *expected* number of mistakes of the algorithm, where the expectation is with respect to the learner's own randomization. That is, if the learner outputs $\hat{y}_t$ where $\mathbb{P}[\hat{y}_t = 1] = p_t$, then the expected loss he pays on round t is

$$\mathbb{P}[\hat{y}_t \neq y_t] = |p_t - y_t|.$$

Put another way, instead of having the predictions of the learner being in $\{0,1\}$ we allow them to be in $[0,1]$, and interpret $p_t \in [0,1]$ as the probability to predict the label 1 on round t.

With this assumption it is possible to derive a low regret algorithm. In particular, we will prove the following theorem.

Theorem 21.10. *For every hypothesis class $\mathcal{H}$, there exists an algorithm for online classification, whose predictions come from* $[0,1]$, *that enjoys the regret bound*

$$\forall h \in \mathcal{H}, \; \sum_{t=1}^{T} |p_t - y_t| - \sum_{t=1}^{T} |h(\mathbf{x}_t) - y_t| \leq \sqrt{2 \min\{\log(|\mathcal{H}|), \, \mathrm{Ldim}(\mathcal{H}) \log(eT)\}\, T}.$$

Furthermore, no algorithm can achieve an expected regret bound smaller than $\Omega\left(\sqrt{\mathrm{Ldim}(\mathcal{H})\, T}\right)$.

We will provide a constructive proof of the upper bound part of the preceding theorem. The proof of the lower bound part can be found in (Ben-David, Pal, & Shalev-Shwartz 2009).

The proof of Theorem 21.10 relies on the *Weighted-Majority* algorithm for learning with expert advice. This algorithm is important by itself and we dedicate the next subsection to it.

21.2.1 Weighted-Majority

Weighted-majority is an algorithm for the problem of *prediction with expert advice*. In this online learning problem, on round t the learner has to choose the advice of d given experts. We also allow the learner to randomize his choice by defining a distribution over the d experts, that is, picking a vector $\mathbf{w}^{(t)} \in [0,1]^d$, with

$\sum_i w_i^{(t)} = 1$, and choosing the ith expert with probability $w_i^{(t)}$. After the learner chooses an expert, it receives a vector of costs, $\mathbf{v}_t \in [0,1]^d$, where $v_{t,i}$ is the cost of following the advice of the ith expert. If the learner's predictions are randomized, then its loss is defined to be the averaged cost, namely, $\sum_i w_i^{(t)} v_{t,i} = \langle \mathbf{w}^{(t)}, \mathbf{v}_t \rangle$. The algorithm assumes that the number of rounds T is given. In Exercise 21.4 we show how to get rid of this dependence using the *doubling trick*.

Weighted-Majority

input: number of experts, d ; number of rounds, T
parameter: $\eta = \sqrt{2\log(d)/T}$
initialize: $\tilde{\mathbf{w}}^{(1)} = (1,\ldots,1)$
for $t = 1,2,\ldots$
  set $\mathbf{w}^{(t)} = \tilde{\mathbf{w}}^{(t)}/Z_t$ where $Z_t = \sum_i \tilde{w}_i^{(t)}$
  choose expert i at random according to $\mathbb{P}[i] = w_i^{(t)}$
  receive costs of all experts $\mathbf{v}_t \in [0,1]^d$
  pay cost $\langle \mathbf{w}^{(t)}, \mathbf{v}_t \rangle$
  update rule $\forall i,\ \tilde{w}_i^{(t+1)} = \tilde{w}_i^{(t)} e^{-\eta v_{t,i}}$

The following theorem is key for analyzing the regret bound of Weighted-Majority.

Theorem 21.11. *Assuming that $T > 2\log(d)$, the Weighted-Majority algorithm enjoys the bound*

$$\sum_{t=1}^{T} \langle \mathbf{w}^{(t)}, \mathbf{v}_t \rangle - \min_{i\in[d]} \sum_{t=1}^{T} v_{t,i} \ \le\ \sqrt{2\log(d)\,T}.$$

Proof. We have:

$$\log\frac{Z_{t+1}}{Z_t} = \log\sum_i \frac{\tilde{w}_i^{(t)}}{Z_t} e^{-\eta v_{t,i}} = \log\sum_i w_i^{(t)} e^{-\eta v_{t,i}}.$$

Using the inequality $e^{-a} \le 1 - a + a^2/2$, which holds for all $a \in (0,1)$, and the fact that $\sum_i w_i^{(t)} = 1$, we obtain

$$\begin{aligned}\log\frac{Z_{t+1}}{Z_t} &\le \log\sum_i w_i^{(t)}\left(1 - \eta v_{t,i} + \eta^2 v_{t,i}^2/2\right)\\ &= \log(1 - \underbrace{\sum_i w_i^{(t)}\left(\eta v_{t,i} - \eta^2 v_{t,i}^2/2\right)}_{\stackrel{\text{def}}{=} b}).\end{aligned}$$

Next, note that $b \in (0,1)$. Therefore, taking log of the two sides of the inequality $1 - b \le e^{-b}$ we obtain the inequality $\log(1-b) \le -b$, which holds for all $b \le 1$, and obtain

$$\begin{aligned}
\log \frac{Z_{t+1}}{Z_t} &\le -\sum_i w_i^{(t)} \left(\eta v_{t,i} - \eta^2 v_{t,i}^2/2\right) \\
&= -\eta \langle \mathbf{w}^{(t)}, \mathbf{v}_t \rangle + \eta^2 \sum_i w_i^{(t)} v_{t,i}^2/2 \\
&\le -\eta \langle \mathbf{w}^{(t)}, \mathbf{v}_t \rangle + \eta^2/2.
\end{aligned}$$

Summing this inequality over t we get

$$\log(Z_{T+1}) - \log(Z_1) = \sum_{t=1}^{T} \log \frac{Z_{t+1}}{Z_t} \le -\eta \sum_{t=1}^{T} \langle \mathbf{w}^{(t)}, \mathbf{v}_t \rangle + \frac{T\eta^2}{2}. \tag{21.3}$$

Next, we lower bound Z_{T+1}. For each i, we can rewrite $\tilde{w}_i^{(T+1)} = e^{-\eta \sum_t v_{t,i}}$ and we get that

$$\log Z_{T+1} = \log\left(\sum_i e^{-\eta \sum_t v_{t,i}}\right) \ge \log\left(\max_i e^{-\eta \sum_t v_{t,i}}\right) = -\eta \min_i \sum_t v_{t,i}.$$

Combining the preceding with Equation (21.3) and using the fact that $\log(Z_1) = \log(d)$ we get that

$$-\eta \min_i \sum_t v_{t,i} - \log(d) \le -\eta \sum_{t=1}^{T} \langle \mathbf{w}^{(t)}, \mathbf{v}_t \rangle + \frac{T\eta^2}{2},$$

which can be rearranged as follows:

$$\sum_{t=1}^{T} \langle \mathbf{w}^{(t)}, \mathbf{v}_t \rangle - \min_i \sum_t v_{t,i} \le \frac{\log(d)}{\eta} + \frac{\eta T}{2}.$$

Plugging the value of η into the equation concludes our proof. □

Proof of Theorem 21.10

Equipped with the Weighted-Majority algorithm and Theorem 21.11, we are ready to prove Theorem 21.10. We start with the simpler case, in which $\mathcal{H}$ is a finite class, and let us write $\mathcal{H} = \{h_1, \ldots, h_d\}$. In this case, we can refer to each hypothesis, h_i, as an expert, whose advice is to predict $h_i(\mathbf{x}_t)$, and whose cost is $v_{t,i} = |h_i(\mathbf{x}_t) - y_t|$. The prediction of the algorithm will therefore be $p_t = \sum_i w_i^{(t)} h_i(\mathbf{x}_t) \in [0,1]$, and the loss is

$$|p_t - y_t| = \left|\sum_{i=1}^{d} w_i^{(t)} h_i(\mathbf{x}_t) - y_t\right| = \left|\sum_{i=1}^{d} w_i^{(t)} (h_i(\mathbf{x}_t) - y_t)\right|.$$

Now, if $y_t = 1$, then for all i, $h_i(\mathbf{x}_t) - y_t \le 0$. Therefore, the above equals to $\sum_i w_i^{(t)} |h_i(\mathbf{x}_t) - y_t|$. If $y_t = 0$ then for all i, $h_i(\mathbf{x}_t) - y_t \ge 0$, and the above also equals

$\sum_i w_i^{(t)}|h_i(\mathbf{x}_t) - y_t|$. All in all, we have shown that

$$|p_t - y_t| = \sum_{i=1}^{d} w_i^{(t)}|h_i(\mathbf{x}_t) - y_t| = \langle \mathbf{w}^{(t)}, \mathbf{v}_t \rangle.$$

Furthermore, for each i, $\sum_t v_{t,i}$ is exactly the number of mistakes hypothesis h_i makes. Applying Theorem 21.11 we obtain

Corollary 21.12. *Let $\mathcal{H}$ be a finite hypothesis class. There exists an algorithm for online classification, whose predictions come from* $[0,1]$*, that enjoys the regret bound*

$$\sum_{t=1}^{T} |p_t - y_t| - \min_{h\in\mathcal{H}} \sum_{t=1}^{T} |h(\mathbf{x}_t) - y_t| \;\le\; \sqrt{2\log(|\mathcal{H}|)\,T}.$$

Next, we consider the case of a general hypothesis class. Previously, we constructed an expert for each individual hypothesis. However, if $\mathcal{H}$ is infinite this leads to a vacuous bound. The main idea is to construct a set of experts in a more sophisticated way. The challenge is how to define a set of experts that, on one hand, is not excessively large and, on the other hand, contains experts that give accurate predictions.

We construct the set of experts so that for each hypothesis $h \in \mathcal{H}$ and every sequence of instances, $\mathbf{x}_1, \mathbf{x}_2, \ldots, \mathbf{x}_T$, there exists at least one expert in the set which behaves exactly as h on these instances. For each $L \le \mathrm{Ldim}(\mathcal{H})$ and each sequence $1 \le i_1 < i_2 < \cdots < i_L \le T$ we define an expert. The expert simulates the game between SOA (presented in the previous section) and the environment on the sequence of instances $\mathbf{x}_1, \mathbf{x}_2, \ldots, \mathbf{x}_T$ assuming that SOA makes a mistake precisely in rounds $i_1, i_2, \ldots, i_L$. The expert is defined by the following algorithm.

Expert$(i_1, i_2, \ldots, i_L)$

input A hypothesis class $\mathcal{H}$; Indices $i_1 < i_2 < \cdots < i_L$
initialize: $V_1 = \mathcal{H}$
for $t = 1, 2, \ldots, T$
  receive $\mathbf{x}_t$
  for $r \in \{0,1\}$ let $V_t^{(r)} = \{h \in V_t : h(\mathbf{x}_t) = r\}$
  define $\tilde{y}_t = \mathrm{argmax}_r \, \mathrm{Ldim}\left(V_t^{(r)}\right)$
   (in case of a tie set $\tilde{y}_t = 0$)
  if $t \in \{i_1, i_2, \ldots, i_L\}$
    predict $\hat{y}_t = 1 - \tilde{y}_t$
  else
    predict $\hat{y}_t = \tilde{y}_t$
  update $V_{t+1} = V_t^{(\hat{y}_t)}$

Note that each such expert can give us predictions at every round t while only observing the instances $\mathbf{x}_1, \ldots, \mathbf{x}_t$. Our generic online learning algorithm is now an application of the Weighted-Majority algorithm with these experts.

To analyze the algorithm we first note that the number of experts is

$$d = \sum_{L=0}^{\mathrm{Ldim}(\mathcal{H})} \binom{T}{L}. \tag{21.4}$$

It can be shown that when $T \geq \mathrm{Ldim}(\mathcal{H}) + 2$, the right-hand side of the equation is bounded by $\left(eT/\mathrm{Ldim}(\mathcal{H})\right)^{\mathrm{Ldim}(\mathcal{H})}$ (the proof can be found in Lemma A.5).

Theorem 21.11 tells us that the expected number of mistakes of Weighted-Majority is at most the number of mistakes of the best expert plus $\sqrt{2\log(d)T}$. We will next show that the number of mistakes of the best expert is at most the number of mistakes of the best hypothesis in $\mathcal{H}$. The following key lemma shows that, on any sequence of instances, for each hypothesis $h \in \mathcal{H}$ there exists an expert with the same behavior.

Lemma 21.13. *Let $\mathcal{H}$ be any hypothesis class with* $\mathrm{Ldim}(\mathcal{H}) < \infty$. *Let $\mathbf{x}_1, \mathbf{x}_2, \ldots, \mathbf{x}_T$ be any sequence of instances. For any $h \in \mathcal{H}$, there exists $L \leq \mathrm{Ldim}(\mathcal{H})$ and indices $1 \leq i_1 < i_2 < \cdots < i_L \leq T$ such that when running* Expert$(i_1, i_2, \ldots, i_L)$ *on the sequence $\mathbf{x}_1, \mathbf{x}_2, \ldots, \mathbf{x}_T$, the expert predicts $h(\mathbf{x}_t)$ on each online round $t = 1, 2, \ldots, T$.*

Proof. Fix $h \in \mathcal{H}$ and the sequence $\mathbf{x}_1, \mathbf{x}_2, \ldots, \mathbf{x}_T$. We must construct L and the indices $i_1, i_2, \ldots, i_L$. Consider running SOA on the input $(\mathbf{x}_1, h(\mathbf{x}_1))$, $(\mathbf{x}_2, h(\mathbf{x}_2))$, ..., $(\mathbf{x}_T, h(\mathbf{x}_T))$. SOA makes at most $\mathrm{Ldim}(\mathcal{H})$ mistakes on such input. We define L to be the number of mistakes made by SOA and we define $\{i_1, i_2, \ldots, i_L\}$ to be the set of rounds in which SOA made the mistakes.

Now, consider the Expert$(i_1, i_2, \ldots, i_L)$ running on the sequence $\mathbf{x}_1, \mathbf{x}_2, \ldots, \mathbf{x}_T$. By construction, the set V_t maintained by Expert$(i_1, i_2, \ldots, i_L)$ equals the set V_t maintained by SOA when running on the sequence $(\mathbf{x}_1, h(\mathbf{x}_1)), \ldots, (\mathbf{x}_T, h(\mathbf{x}_T))$. The predictions of SOA differ from the predictions of h if and only if the round is in $\{i_1, i_2, \ldots, i_L\}$. Since Expert$(i_1, i_2, \ldots, i_L)$ predicts exactly like SOA if t is not in $\{i_1, i_2, \ldots, i_L\}$ and the opposite of SOAs' predictions if t is in $\{i_1, i_2, \ldots, i_L\}$, we conclude that the predictions of the expert are always the same as the predictions of h. □

The previous lemma holds in particular for the hypothesis in $\mathcal{H}$ that makes the least number of mistakes on the sequence of examples, and we therefore obtain the following:

Corollary 21.14. *Let $(\mathbf{x}_1, y_1), (\mathbf{x}_2, y_2), \ldots, (\mathbf{x}_T, y_T)$ be a sequence of examples and let $\mathcal{H}$ be a hypothesis class with* $\mathrm{Ldim}(\mathcal{H}) < \infty$. *There exists $L \leq \mathrm{Ldim}(\mathcal{H})$ and indices $1 \leq i_1 < i_2 < \cdots < i_L \leq T$, such that* Expert$(i_1, i_2, \ldots, i_L)$ *makes at most as many mistakes as the best $h \in \mathcal{H}$ does, namely,*

$$\min_{h \in \mathcal{H}} \sum_{t=1}^{T} |h(\mathbf{x}_t) - y_t|$$

mistakes on the sequence of examples.

Together with Theorem 21.11, the upper bound part of Theorem 21.10 is proven.

21.3 ONLINE CONVEX OPTIMIZATION

In Chapter 12 we studied convex learning problems and showed learnability results for these problems in the agnostic PAC learning framework. In this section we show that similar learnability results hold for convex problems in the online learning framework. In particular, we consider the following problem.

Online Convex Optimization

definitions:
hypothesis class $\mathcal{H}$; domain Z ; loss function $\ell : \mathcal{H} \times Z \to \mathbb{R}$
assumptions:
$\mathcal{H}$ is convex
$\forall z \in Z$, $\ell(\cdot, z)$ is a convex function
for $t = 1, 2, \ldots, T$
learner predicts a vector $\mathbf{w}^{(t)} \in \mathcal{H}$
environment responds with $z_t \in Z$
learner suffers loss $\ell(\mathbf{w}^{(t)}, z_t)$

As in the online classification problem, we analyze the *regret* of the algorithm. Recall that the regret of an online algorithm with respect to a competing hypothesis, which here will be some vector $\mathbf{w}^\star \in \mathcal{H}$, is defined as

$$\text{Regret}_A(\mathbf{w}^\star, T) = \sum_{t=1}^{T} \ell(\mathbf{w}^{(t)}, z_t) - \sum_{t=1}^{T} \ell(\mathbf{w}^\star, z_t). \tag{21.5}$$

As before, the regret of the algorithm relative to a set of competing vectors, $\mathcal{H}$, is defined as

$$\text{Regret}_A(\mathcal{H}, T) = \sup_{\mathbf{w}^\star \in \mathcal{H}} \text{Regret}_A(\mathbf{w}^\star, T).$$

In Chapter 14 we have shown that Stochastic Gradient Descent solves convex learning problems in the agnostic PAC model. We now show that a very similar algorithm, Online Gradient Descent, solves online convex learning problems.

Online Gradient Descent

parameter: $\eta > 0$
initialize: $\mathbf{w}^{(1)} = \mathbf{0}$
for $t = 1, 2, \ldots, T$
predict $\mathbf{w}^{(t)}$
receive z_t and let $f_t(\cdot) = \ell(\cdot, z_t)$
choose $\mathbf{v}_t \in \partial f_t(\mathbf{w}^{(t)})$
update:
1. $\mathbf{w}^{(t+\frac{1}{2})} = \mathbf{w}^{(t)} - \eta \mathbf{v}_t$
2. $\mathbf{w}^{(t+1)} = \text{argmin}_{\mathbf{w} \in \mathcal{H}} \|\mathbf{w} - \mathbf{w}^{(t+\frac{1}{2})}\|$

Theorem 21.15. *The Online Gradient Descent algorithm enjoys the following regret bound for every* $\mathbf{w}^\star \in \mathcal{H}$,

$$\text{Regret}_A(\mathbf{w}^\star, T) \le \frac{\|\mathbf{w}^\star\|^2}{2\eta} + \frac{\eta}{2}\sum_{t=1}^{T}\|\mathbf{v}_t\|^2.$$

If we further assume that f_t *is* ρ*-Lipschitz for all* t*, then setting* $\eta = 1/\sqrt{T}$ *yields*

$$\text{Regret}_A(\mathbf{w}^\star, T) \le \frac{1}{2}(\|\mathbf{w}^\star\|^2 + \rho^2)\sqrt{T}.$$

If we further assume that $\mathcal{H}$ *is* B*-bounded and we set* $\eta = \frac{B}{\rho\sqrt{T}}$ *then*

$$\text{Regret}_A(\mathcal{H}, T) \le B\,\rho\,\sqrt{T}.$$

Proof. The analysis is similar to the analysis of Stochastic Gradient Descent with projections. Using the projection lemma, the definition of $\mathbf{w}^{(t+\frac{1}{2})}$, and the definition of subgradients, we have that for every t,

$$\begin{aligned}
&\|\mathbf{w}^{(t+1)} - \mathbf{w}^\star\|^2 - \|\mathbf{w}^{(t)} - \mathbf{w}^\star\|^2 \\
&= \|\mathbf{w}^{(t+1)} - \mathbf{w}^\star\|^2 - \|\mathbf{w}^{(t+\frac{1}{2})} - \mathbf{w}^\star\|^2 + \|\mathbf{w}^{(t+\frac{1}{2})} - \mathbf{w}^\star\|^2 - \|\mathbf{w}^{(t)} - \mathbf{w}^\star\|^2 \\
&\le \|\mathbf{w}^{(t+\frac{1}{2})} - \mathbf{w}^\star\|^2 - \|\mathbf{w}^{(t)} - \mathbf{w}^\star\|^2 \\
&= \|\mathbf{w}^{(t)} - \eta\mathbf{v}_t - \mathbf{w}^\star\|^2 - \|\mathbf{w}^{(t)} - \mathbf{w}^\star\|^2 \\
&= -2\eta\langle \mathbf{w}^{(t)} - \mathbf{w}^\star, \mathbf{v}_t\rangle + \eta^2\|\mathbf{v}_t\|^2 \\
&\le -2\eta(f_t(\mathbf{w}^{(t)}) - f_t(\mathbf{w}^\star)) + \eta^2\|\mathbf{v}_t\|^2.
\end{aligned}$$

Summing over t and observing that the left-hand side is a telescopic sum we obtain that

$$\|\mathbf{w}^{(T+1)} - \mathbf{w}^\star\|^2 - \|\mathbf{w}^{(1)} - \mathbf{w}^\star\|^2 \le -2\eta\sum_{t=1}^{T}(f_t(\mathbf{w}^{(t)}) - f_t(\mathbf{w}^\star)) + \eta^2\sum_{t=1}^{T}\|\mathbf{v}_t\|^2.$$

Rearranging the inequality and using the fact that $\mathbf{w}^{(1)} = \mathbf{0}$, we get that

$$\begin{aligned}
\sum_{t=1}^{T}(f_t(\mathbf{w}^{(t)}) - f_t(\mathbf{w}^\star)) &\le \frac{\|\mathbf{w}^{(1)} - \mathbf{w}^\star\|^2 - \|\mathbf{w}^{(T+1)} - \mathbf{w}^\star\|^2}{2\eta} + \frac{\eta}{2}\sum_{t=1}^{T}\|\mathbf{v}_t\|^2 \\
&\le \frac{\|\mathbf{w}^\star\|^2}{2\eta} + \frac{\eta}{2}\sum_{t=1}^{T}\|\mathbf{v}_t\|^2.
\end{aligned}$$

This proves the first bound in the theorem. The second bound follows from the assumption that f_t is ρ-Lipschitz, which implies that $\|\mathbf{v}_t\| \le \rho$. □

21.4 THE ONLINE PERCEPTRON ALGORITHM

The Perceptron is a classic online learning algorithm for binary classification with the hypothesis class of homogenous halfspaces, namely, $\mathcal{H} = \{\mathbf{x} \mapsto \text{sign}(\langle \mathbf{w}, \mathbf{x}\rangle) :$

$\mathbf{w} \in \mathbb{R}^d\}$. In Section 9.1.2 we have presented the batch version of the Perceptron, which aims to solve the ERM problem with respect to $\mathcal{H}$. We now present an online version of the Perceptron algorithm.

Let $\mathcal{X} = \mathbb{R}^d$, $\mathcal{Y} = \{-1, 1\}$. On round t, the learner receives a vector $\mathbf{x}_t \in \mathbb{R}^d$. The learner maintains a weight vector $\mathbf{w}^{(t)} \in \mathbb{R}^d$ and predicts $p_t = \text{sign}(\langle \mathbf{w}^{(t)}, \mathbf{x}_t \rangle)$. Then, it receives $y_t \in \mathcal{Y}$ and pays 1 if $p_t \neq y_t$ and 0 otherwise.

The goal of the learner is to make as few prediction mistakes as possible. In Section 21.1 we characterized the optimal algorithm and showed that the best achievable mistake bound depends on the Littlestone dimension of the class. We show later that if $d \geq 2$ then $\text{Ldim}(\mathcal{H}) = \infty$, which implies that we have no hope of making few prediction mistakes. Indeed, consider the tree for which $\mathbf{v}_1 = (\frac{1}{2}, 1, 0, \ldots, 0)$, $\mathbf{v}_2 = (\frac{1}{4}, 1, 0, \ldots, 0)$, $\mathbf{v}_3 = (\frac{3}{4}, 1, 0, \ldots, 0)$, etc. Because of the density of the reals, this tree is shattered by the subset of $\mathcal{H}$ which contains all hypotheses that are parametrized by $\mathbf{w}$ of the form $\mathbf{w} = (-1, a, 0, \ldots, 0)$, for $a \in [0, 1]$. We conclude that indeed $\text{Ldim}(\mathcal{H}) = \infty$.

To sidestep this impossibility result, the Perceptron algorithm relies on the technique of *surrogate convex losses* (see Section 12.3). This is also closely related to the notion of *margin* we studied in Chapter 15.

A weight vector $\mathbf{w}$ makes a mistake on an example $(\mathbf{x}, y)$ whenever the sign of $\langle \mathbf{w}, \mathbf{x} \rangle$ does not equal y. Therefore, we can write the 0–1 loss function as follows

$$\ell(\mathbf{w}, (\mathbf{x}, y)) = \mathbb{1}_{[y\langle \mathbf{w}, \mathbf{x} \rangle \leq 0]}.$$

On rounds on which the algorithm makes a prediction mistake, we shall use the hinge-loss as a surrogate convex loss function

$$f_t(\mathbf{w}) = \max\{0, 1 - y_t \langle \mathbf{w}, \mathbf{x}_t \rangle\}.$$

The hinge-loss satisfies the two conditions:

- f_t is a convex function
- For all $\mathbf{w}$, $f_t(\mathbf{w}) \geq \ell(\mathbf{w}, (\mathbf{x}_t, y_t))$. In particular, this holds for $\mathbf{w}^{(t)}$.

On rounds on which the algorithm is correct, we shall define $f_t(\mathbf{w}) = 0$. Clearly, f_t is convex in this case as well. Furthermore, $f_t(\mathbf{w}^{(t)}) = \ell(\mathbf{w}^{(t)}, (\mathbf{x}_t, y_t)) = 0$.

Remark 21.5. In Section 12.3 we used the same surrogate loss function for all the examples. In the online model, we allow the surrogate to depend on the specific round. It can even depend on $\mathbf{w}^{(t)}$. Our ability to use a round specific surrogate stems from the worst-case type of analysis we employ in online learning.

Let us now run the Online Gradient Descent algorithm on the sequence of functions, $f_1, \ldots, f_T$, with the hypothesis class being all vectors in $\mathbb{R}^d$ (hence, the projection step is vacuous). Recall that the algorithm initializes $\mathbf{w}^{(1)} = \mathbf{0}$ and its update rule is

$$\mathbf{w}^{(t+1)} = \mathbf{w}^{(t)} - \eta \mathbf{v}_t$$

for some $\mathbf{v}_t \in \partial f_t(\mathbf{w}^{(t)})$. In our case, if $y_t \langle \mathbf{w}^{(t)}, \mathbf{x}_t \rangle > 0$ then f_t is the zero function and we can take $\mathbf{v}_t = \mathbf{0}$. Otherwise, it is easy to verify that $\mathbf{v}_t = -y_t \mathbf{x}_t$ is in $\partial f_t(\mathbf{w}^{(t)})$. We therefore obtain the update rule

$$\mathbf{w}^{(t+1)} = \begin{cases} \mathbf{w}^{(t)} & \text{if } y_t \langle \mathbf{w}^{(t)}, \mathbf{x}_t \rangle > 0 \\ \mathbf{w}^{(t)} + \eta y_t \mathbf{x}_t & \text{otherwise} \end{cases}$$

Denote by $\mathcal{M}$ the set of rounds in which $\text{sign}(\langle \mathbf{w}^{(t)}, \mathbf{x}_t \rangle) \neq y_t$. Note that on round t, the prediction of the Perceptron can be rewritten as

$$p_t = \text{sign}(\langle \mathbf{w}^{(t)}, \mathbf{x}_t \rangle) = \text{sign}\left(\eta \sum_{i \in \mathcal{M}: i < t} y_i \langle \mathbf{x}_i, \mathbf{x}_t \rangle \right).$$

This form implies that the predictions of the Perceptron algorithm and the set $\mathcal{M}$ do not depend on the actual value of η as long as $\eta > 0$. We have therefore obtained the Perceptron algorithm:

Perceptron

initialize: $\mathbf{w}_1 = \mathbf{0}$
for $t = 1, 2, \ldots, T$
  receive $\mathbf{x}_t$
  predict $p_t = \text{sign}(\langle \mathbf{w}^{(t)}, \mathbf{x}_t \rangle)$
  if $y_t \langle \mathbf{w}^{(t)}, \mathbf{x}_t \rangle \leq 0$
    $\mathbf{w}^{(t+1)} = \mathbf{w}^{(t)} + y_t \mathbf{x}_t$
  else
    $\mathbf{w}^{(t+1)} = \mathbf{w}^{(t)}$

To analyze the Perceptron, we rely on the analysis of Online Gradient Descent given in the previous section. In our case, the subgradient of f_t we use in the Perceptron is $\mathbf{v}_t = -\mathbb{1}_{[y_t \langle \mathbf{w}^{(t)}, \mathbf{x}_t \rangle \leq 0]} \, y_t \mathbf{x}_t$. Indeed, the Perceptron's update is $\mathbf{w}^{(t+1)} = \mathbf{w}^{(t)} - \mathbf{v}_t$, and as discussed before this is equivalent to $\mathbf{w}^{(t+1)} = \mathbf{w}^{(t)} - \eta \mathbf{v}_t$ for every $\eta > 0$. Therefore, Theorem 21.15 tells us that

$$\sum_{t=1}^{T} f_t(\mathbf{w}^{(t)}) - \sum_{t=1}^{T} f_t(\mathbf{w}^\star) \leq \frac{1}{2\eta} \|\mathbf{w}^\star\|_2^2 + \frac{\eta}{2} \sum_{t=1}^{T} \|\mathbf{v}_t\|_2^2.$$

Since $f_t(\mathbf{w}^{(t)})$ is a surrogate for the 0−1 loss we know that $\sum_{t=1}^{T} f_t(\mathbf{w}^{(t)}) \geq |\mathcal{M}|$. Denote $R = \max_t \|\mathbf{x}_t\|$; then we obtain

$$|\mathcal{M}| - \sum_{t=1}^{T} f_t(\mathbf{w}^\star) \leq \frac{1}{2\eta} \|\mathbf{w}^\star\|_2^2 + \frac{\eta}{2} |\mathcal{M}| \, R^2$$

Setting $\eta = \frac{\|\mathbf{w}^\star\|}{R\sqrt{|\mathcal{M}|}}$ and rearranging, we obtain

$$|\mathcal{M}| - R\|\mathbf{w}^\star\| \sqrt{|\mathcal{M}|} - \sum_{t=1}^{T} f_t(\mathbf{w}^\star) \leq 0. \tag{21.6}$$

This inequality implies

Theorem 21.16. *Suppose that the Perceptron algorithm runs on a sequence* $(\mathbf{x}_1, y_1), \ldots, (\mathbf{x}_T, y_T)$ *and let* $R = \max_t \|\mathbf{x}_t\|$*. Let* $\mathcal{M}$ *be the rounds on which the Perceptron errs and let* $f_t(\mathbf{w}) = \mathbb{1}_{[t \in \mathcal{M}]} \, [1 - y_t \langle \mathbf{w}, \mathbf{x}_t \rangle]_+$*. Then, for every* $\mathbf{w}^\star$

$$|\mathcal{M}| \leq \sum_t f_t(\mathbf{w}^\star) + R \, \|\mathbf{w}^\star\| \sqrt{\sum_t f_t(\mathbf{w}^\star) + R^2 \, \|\mathbf{w}^\star\|^2} \, .$$

In particular, if there exists $\mathbf{w}^\star$ *such that* $y_t \langle \mathbf{w}^\star, \mathbf{x}_t \rangle \geq 1$ *for all* t *then*

$$|\mathcal{M}| \leq R^2 \, \|\mathbf{w}^\star\|^2 .$$

Proof. The theorem follows from Equation (21.6) and the following claim: Given $x, b, c \in \mathbb{R}_+$, the inequality $x - b\sqrt{x} - c \leq 0$ implies that $x \leq c + b^2 + b\sqrt{c}$. The last claim can be easily derived by analyzing the roots of the convex parabola $Q(y) = y^2 - by - c$. □

The last assumption of Theorem 21.16 is called *separability with large margin* (see Chapter 15). That is, there exists $\mathbf{w}^\star$ that not only satisfies that the point $\mathbf{x}_t$ lies on the correct side of the halfspace, it also guarantees that $\mathbf{x}_t$ is not too close to the decision boundary. More specifically, the distance from $\mathbf{x}_t$ to the decision boundary is at least $\gamma = 1/\|\mathbf{w}^\star\|$ and the bound becomes $(R/\gamma)^2$.

When the separability assumption does not hold, the bound involves the term $[1 - y_t \langle \mathbf{w}^\star, \mathbf{x}_t \rangle]_+$ which measures how much the separability with margin requirement is violated.

As a last remark we note that there can be cases in which there exists some $\mathbf{w}^\star$ that makes zero errors on the sequence but the Perceptron will make many errors. Indeed, this is a direct consequence of the fact that $\text{Ldim}(\mathcal{H}) = \infty$. The way we sidestep this impossibility result is by assuming more on the sequence of examples – the bound in Theorem 21.16 will be meaningful only if the cumulative surrogate loss, $\sum_t f_t(\mathbf{w}^\star)$ is not excessively large.

21.5 SUMMARY

In this chapter we have studied the online learning model. Many of the results we derived for the PAC learning model have an analog in the online model. First, we have shown that a combinatorial dimension, the Littlestone dimension, characterizes online learnability. To show this, we introduced the SOA algorithm (for the realizable case) and the Weighted-Majority algorithm (for the unrealizable case). We have also studied online convex optimization and have shown that online gradient descent is a successful online learner whenever the loss function is convex and Lipschitz. Finally, we presented the online Perceptron algorithm as a combination of online gradient descent and the concept of surrogate convex loss functions.

21.6 BIBLIOGRAPHIC REMARKS

The Standard Optimal Algorithm was derived by the seminal work of Littlestone (1988). A generalization to the nonrealizable case, as well as other variants like margin-based Littlestone's dimension, were derived in (Ben-David et al. 2009). Characterizations of online learnability beyond classification have been obtained in (Abernethy, Bartlett, Rakhlin & Tewari 2008, Rakhlin, Sridharan & Tewari 2010, Daniely et al. 2011). The Weighted-Majority algorithm is due to (Littlestone & Warmuth 1994) and (Vovk 1990).

The term "online convex programming" was introduced by Zinkevich (2003) but this setting was introduced some years earlier by Gordon (1999). The Perceptron dates back to Rosenblatt (Rosenblatt 1958). An analysis for the realizable case (with margin assumptions) appears in (Agmon 1954, Minsky & Papert 1969). Freund and Schapire (Freund & Schapire 1999) presented an analysis for the unrealizable case with a squared-hinge-loss based on a reduction to the realizable case. A direct analysis for the unrealizable case with the hinge-loss was given by Gentile (Gentile 2003).

For additional information we refer the reader to Cesa-Bianchi and Lugosi (2006) and Shalev-Shwartz (2011).

21.7 EXERCISES

21.1 Find a hypothesis class $\mathcal{H}$ and a sequence of examples on which Consistent makes $|\mathcal{H}|-1$ mistakes.

21.2 Find a hypothesis class $\mathcal{H}$ and a sequence of examples on which the mistake bound of the *Halving* algorithm is tight.

21.3 Let $d \geq 2$, $\mathcal{X} = \{1,\ldots,d\}$ and let $\mathcal{H} = \{h_j : j \in [d]\}$, where $h_j(x) = \mathbb{1}_{[x=j]}$. Calculate $M_{\text{Halving}}(\mathcal{H})$ (i.e., derive lower and upper bounds on $M_{\text{Halving}}(\mathcal{H})$, and prove that they are equal).

21.4 **The Doubling Trick:**
In Theorem 21.15, the parameter η depends on the time horizon T. In this exercise we show how to get rid of this dependence by a simple trick.

Consider an algorithm that enjoys a regret bound of the form $\alpha\sqrt{T}$, but its parameters require the knowledge of T. The doubling trick, described in the following, enables us to convert such an algorithm into an algorithm that does not need to know the time horizon. The idea is to divide the time into periods of increasing size and run the original algorithm on each period.

The Doubling Trick

input: algorithm A whose parameters depend on the time horizon
for $m = 0, 1, 2, \ldots$
  run A on the 2^m rounds $t = 2^m, \ldots, 2^{m+1}-1$

Show that if the regret of A on each period of 2^m rounds is at most $\alpha\sqrt{2^m}$, then the total regret is at most

$$\frac{\sqrt{2}}{\sqrt{2}-1}\alpha\sqrt{T}.$$

21.5 **Online-to-batch Conversions:** In this exercise we demonstrate how a successful online learning algorithm can be used to derive a successful PAC learner as well.

Consider a PAC learning problem for binary classification parameterized by an instance domain, $\mathcal{X}$, and a hypothesis class, $\mathcal{H}$. Suppose that there exists an online learning algorithm, A, which enjoys a mistake bound $M_A(\mathcal{H}) < \infty$. Consider running this algorithm on a sequence of T examples which are sampled i.i.d. from a distribution $\mathcal{D}$ over the instance space $\mathcal{X}$, and are labeled by some $h^\star \in \mathcal{H}$. Suppose that for every round t, the prediction of the algorithm is based on a hypothesis $h_t : \mathcal{X} \to \{0,1\}$. Show that

$$\mathbb{E}[L_{\mathcal{D}}(h_r)] \leq \frac{M_A(\mathcal{H})}{T},$$

where the expectation is over the random choice of the instances as well as a random choice of r according to the uniform distribution over $[T]$.
Hint: Use similar arguments to the ones appearing in the proof of Theorem 14.8.

22

Clustering

Clustering is one of the most widely used techniques for exploratory data analysis. Across all disciplines, from social sciences to biology to computer science, people try to get a first intuition about their data by identifying meaningful groups among the data points. For example, computational biologists cluster genes on the basis of similarities in their expression in different experiments; retailers cluster customers, on the basis of their customer profiles, for the purpose of targeted marketing; and astronomers cluster stars on the basis of their spacial proximity.

The first point that one should clarify is, naturally, what is clustering? Intuitively, clustering is the task of grouping a set of objects such that similar objects end up in the same group and dissimilar objects are separated into different groups. Clearly, this description is quite imprecise and possibly ambiguous. Quite surprisingly, it is not at all clear how to come up with a more rigorous definition.

There are several sources for this difficulty. One basic problem is that the two objectives mentioned in the earlier statement may in many cases contradict each other. Mathematically speaking, similarity (or proximity) is not a transitive relation, while cluster sharing is an equivalence relation and, in particular, it is a transitive relation. More concretely, it may be the case that there is a long sequence of objects, $x_1, \ldots, x_m$ such that each x_i is very similar to its two neighbors, x_{i-1} and x_{i+1}, but x_1 and x_m are very dissimilar. If we wish to make sure that whenever two elements are similar they share the same cluster, then we must put all of the elements of the sequence in the same cluster. However, in that case, we end up with dissimilar elements (x_1 and x_m) sharing a cluster, thus violating the second requirement.

To illustrate this point further, suppose that we would like to cluster the points in the following picture into two clusters.

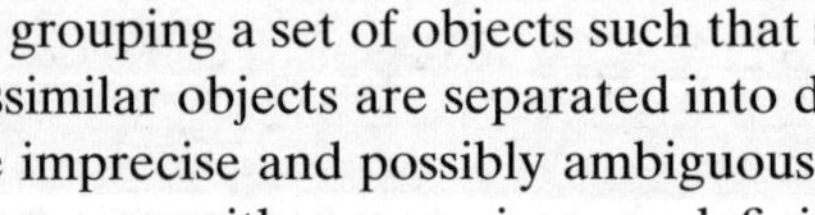

A clustering algorithm that emphasizes not separating close-by points (e.g., the Single Linkage algorithm that will be described in Section 22.1) will cluster this input by separating it horizontally according to the two lines:

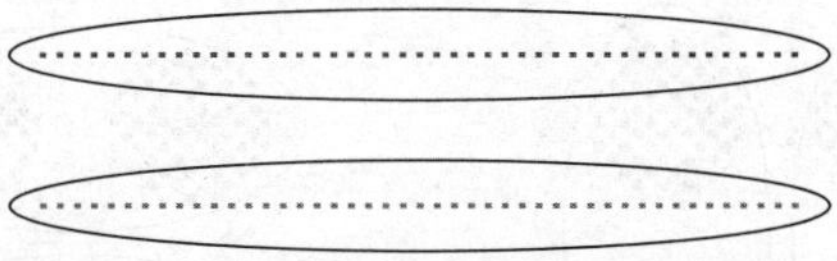

In contrast, a clustering method that emphasizes not having far-away points share the same cluster (e.g., the 2-means algorithm that will be described in Section 22.1) will cluster the same input by dividing it vertically into the right-hand half and the left-hand half:

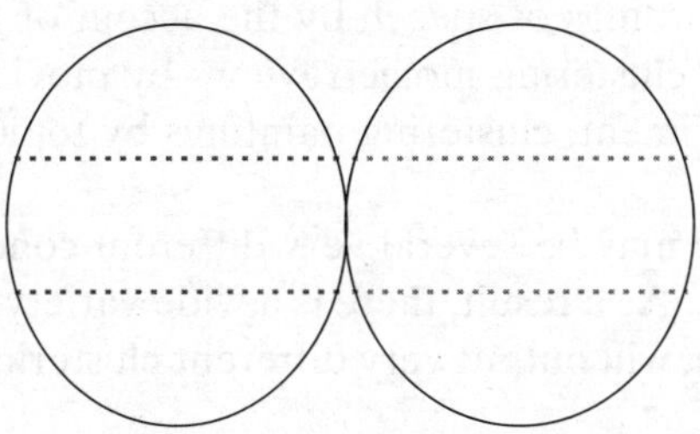

Another basic problem is the lack of "ground truth" for clustering, which is a common problem in *unsupervised learning*. So far in the book, we have mainly dealt with *supervised* learning (e.g., the problem of learning a classifier from labeled training data). The goal of supervised learning is clear – we wish to learn a classifier which will predict the labels of future examples as accurately as possible. Furthermore, a supervised learner can estimate the success, or the risk, of its hypotheses using the labeled training data by computing the empirical loss. In contrast, clustering is an *unsupervised learning* problem; namely, there are no labels that we try to predict. Instead, we wish to organize the data in some meaningful way. As a result, there is no clear success evaluation procedure for clustering. In fact, even on the basis of full knowledge of the underlying data distribution, it is not clear what is the "correct" clustering for that data or how to evaluate a proposed clustering.

Consider, for example, the following set of points in $\mathbb{R}^2$:

and suppose we are required to cluster them into two clusters. We have two highly justifiable solutions:

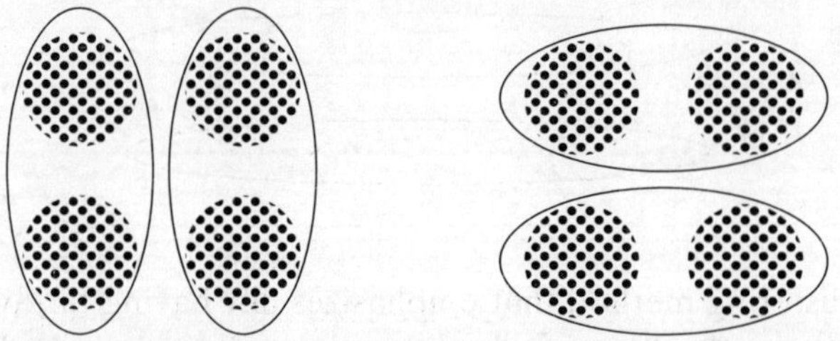

This phenomenon is not just artificial but occurs in real applications. A given set of objects can be clustered in various different meaningful ways. This may be due to having different implicit notions of distance (or similarity) between objects, for example, clustering recordings of speech by the accent of the speaker versus clustering them by content, clustering movie reviews by movie topic versus clustering them by the review sentiment, clustering paintings by topic versus clustering them by style, and so on.

To summarize, there may be several very different conceivable clustering solutions for a given data set. As a result, there is a wide variety of clustering algorithms that, on some input data, will output very different clusterings.

A Clustering Model:
Clustering tasks can vary in terms of both the type of input they have and the type of outcome they are expected to compute. For concreteness, we shall focus on the following common setup:

Input – a set of elements, $\mathcal{X}$, and a distance function over it. That is, a function $d : \mathcal{X} \times \mathcal{X} \to \mathbb{R}_+$ that is symmetric, satisfies $d(x,x) = 0$ for all $x \in \mathcal{X}$, and often also satisfies the triangle inequality. Alternatively, the function could be a similarity function $s : \mathcal{X} \times \mathcal{X} \to [0,1]$ that is symmetric and satisfies $s(x,x) = 1$ for all $x \in \mathcal{X}$. Additionally, some clustering algorithms also require an input parameter k (determining the number of required clusters).

Output – a partition of the domain set $\mathcal{X}$ into subsets. That is, $C = (C_1, \ldots C_k)$ where $\bigcup_{i=1}^{k} C_i = \mathcal{X}$ and for all $i \neq j$, $C_i \cap C_j = \emptyset$. In some situations the clustering is "soft," namely, the partition of $\mathcal{X}$ into the different clusters is probabilistic where the output is a function assigning to each domain point, $x \in \mathcal{X}$, a vector $(p_1(x), \ldots, p_k(x))$, where $p_i(x) = \mathbb{P}[\mathbf{x} \in C_i]$ is the probability that $\mathbf{x}$ belongs to cluster C_i. Another possible output is a clustering *dendrogram* (from Greek dendron = tree, gramma = drawing), which is a hierarchical tree of domain subsets, having the singleton sets in its leaves, and the full domain as its root. We shall discuss this formulation in more detail in the following.

In the following we survey some of the most popular clustering methods. In the last section of this chapter we return to the high level discussion of what is clustering.

22.1 LINKAGE-BASED CLUSTERING ALGORITHMS

Linkage-based clustering is probably the simplest and most straightforward paradigm of clustering. These algorithms proceed in a sequence of rounds. They start from the trivial clustering that has each data point as a single-point cluster. Then, repeatedly, these algorithms merge the "closest" clusters of the previous clustering. Consequently, the number of clusters decreases with each such round. If kept going, such algorithms would eventually result in the trivial clustering in which all of the domain points share one large cluster. Two parameters, then, need to be determined to define such an algorithm clearly. First, we have to decide how to measure (or define) the distance between clusters, and, second, we have to determine when to stop merging. Recall that the input to a clustering algorithm is a between-points distance function, d. There are many ways of extending d to a measure of distance between domain subsets (or clusters). The most common ways are

1. Single Linkage clustering, in which the between-clusters distance is defined by the minimum distance between members of the two clusters, namely,
$$D(A,B) \stackrel{\text{def}}{=} \min\{d(x,y) : x \in A,\ y \in B\}$$
2. Average Linkage clustering, in which the distance between two clusters is defined to be the average distance between a point in one of the clusters and a point in the other, namely,
$$D(A,B) \stackrel{\text{def}}{=} \frac{1}{|A||B|} \sum_{x \in A,\ y \in B} d(x,y)$$
3. Max Linkage clustering, in which the distance between two clusters is defined as the maximum distance between their elements, namely,
$$D(A,B) \stackrel{\text{def}}{=} \max\{d(x,y) : x \in A,\ y \in B\}.$$

The linkage-based clustering algorithms are *agglomerative* in the sense that they start from data that is completely fragmented and keep building larger and larger clusters as they proceed. Without employing a stopping rule, the outcome of such an algorithm can be described by a clustering *dendrogram*: that is, a tree of domain subsets, having the singleton sets in its leaves, and the full domain as its root. For example, if the input is the elements $\mathcal{X} = \{a,b,c,d,e\} \subset \mathbb{R}^2$ with the Euclidean distance as depicted on the left, then the resulting dendrogram is the one depicted on the right:

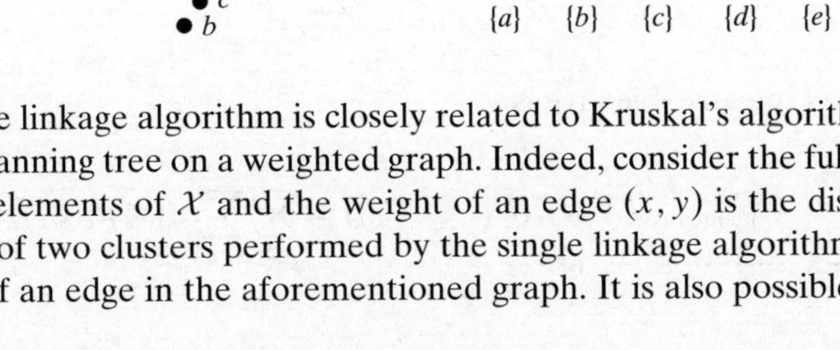

The single linkage algorithm is closely related to Kruskal's algorithm for finding a minimal spanning tree on a weighted graph. Indeed, consider the full graph whose vertices are elements of $\mathcal{X}$ and the weight of an edge (x, y) is the distance $d(x, y)$. Each merge of two clusters performed by the single linkage algorithm corresponds to a choice of an edge in the aforementioned graph. It is also possible to show that the set of edges the single linkage algorithm chooses along its run forms a minimal spanning tree.

If one wishes to turn a dendrogram into a partition of the space (a clustering), one needs to employ a *stopping criterion*. Common stopping criteria include

- Fixed number of clusters – fix some parameter, k, and stop merging clusters as soon as the number of clusters is k.
- Distance upper bound – fix some $r \in \mathbb{R}_+$. Stop merging as soon as all the between-clusters distances are larger than r. We can also set r to be $\alpha \max\{d(x,y) : x, y \in \mathcal{X}\}$ for some $\alpha < 1$. In that case the stopping criterion is called "scaled distance upper bound."

22.2 k-MEANS AND OTHER COST MINIMIZATION CLUSTERINGS

Another popular approach to clustering starts by defining a cost function over a parameterized set of possible clusterings and the goal of the clustering algorithm is to find a partitioning (clustering) of minimal cost. Under this paradigm, the clustering task is turned into an optimization problem. The objective function is a function from pairs of an input, $(\mathcal{X}, d)$, and a proposed clustering solution $C = (C_1, \ldots, C_k)$, to positive real numbers. Given such an objective function, which we denote by G, the *goal* of a clustering algorithm is defined as finding, for a given input $(\mathcal{X}, d)$, a clustering C so that $G((\mathcal{X}, d), C)$ is minimized. In order to reach that goal, one has to apply some appropriate search algorithm.

As it turns out, most of the resulting optimization problems are NP-hard, and some are even NP-hard to approximate. Consequently, when people talk about, say, k-means clustering, they often refer to some particular common approximation algorithm rather than the cost function or the corresponding exact solution of the minimization problem.

Many common objective functions require the number of clusters, k, as a parameter. In practice, it is often up to the user of the clustering algorithm to choose the parameter k that is most suitable for the given clustering problem.

In the following we describe some of the most common objective functions.

The k-means objective function is one of the most popular clustering objectives. In k-means the data is partitioned into disjoint sets $C_1, \ldots, C_k$ where each C_i is represented by a centroid μ_i. It is assumed that the input set $\mathcal{X}$ is embedded in some larger metric space $(\mathcal{X}', d)$ (so that $\mathcal{X} \subseteq \mathcal{X}'$) and centroids are members of $\mathcal{X}'$. The k-means objective function measures the squared distance between each point in $\mathcal{X}$ to the centroid of its cluster. The centroid of C_i is defined to be

$$\mu_i(C_i) = \operatorname*{argmin}_{\mu \in \mathcal{X}'} \sum_{x \in C_i} d(x, \mu)^2.$$

Then, the k-means objective is

$$G_{k\text{-means}}((\mathcal{X}, d), (C_1, \ldots, C_k)) = \sum_{i=1}^{k} \sum_{x \in C_i} d(x, \mu_i(C_i))^2.$$

This can also be rewritten as

$$G_{\text{k-means}}((\mathcal{X},d),(C_1,\ldots,C_k)) = \min_{\mu_1,\ldots\mu_k\in\mathcal{X}'} \sum_{i=1}^{k}\sum_{x\in C_i} d(x,\mu_i)^2. \tag{22.1}$$

The k-means objective function is relevant, for example, in digital communication tasks, where the members of $\mathcal{X}$ may be viewed as a collection of signals that have to be transmitted. While $\mathcal{X}$ may be a very large set of real valued vectors, digital transmission allows transmitting of only a finite number of bits for each signal. One way to achieve good transmission under such constraints is to represent each member of $\mathcal{X}$ by a "close" member of some finite set $\mu_1,\ldots\mu_k$, and replace the transmission of any $x \in \mathcal{X}$ by transmitting the index of the closest μ_i. The k-means objective can be viewed as a measure of the distortion created by such a transmission representation scheme.

The k-medoids objective function is similar to the k-means objective, except that it requires the cluster centroids to be members of the input set. The objective function is defined by

$$G_{\text{K-medoid}}((\mathcal{X},d),(C_1,\ldots,C_k)) = \min_{\mu_1,\ldots\mu_k\in\mathcal{X}} \sum_{i=1}^{k}\sum_{x\in C_i} d(x,\mu_i)^2.$$

The k-median objective function is quite similar to the k-medoids objective, except that the "distortion" between a data point and the centroid of its cluster is measured by distance, rather than by the square of the distance:

$$G_{\text{K-median}}((\mathcal{X},d),(C_1,\ldots,C_k)) = \min_{\mu_1,\ldots\mu_k\in\mathcal{X}} \sum_{i=1}^{k}\sum_{x\in C_i} d(x,\mu_i).$$

An example where such an objective makes sense is the *facility location* problem. Consider the task of locating k fire stations in a city. One can model houses as data points and aim to place the stations so as to minimize the average distance between a house and its closest fire station.

The previous examples can all be viewed as *center-based* objectives. The solution to such a clustering problem is determined by a set of cluster centers, and the clustering assigns each instance to the center closest to it. More generally, center-based objective is determined by choosing some monotonic function $f : \mathbb{R}_+ \to \mathbb{R}_+$ and then defining

$$G_f((\mathcal{X},d),(C_1,\ldots C_k)) = \min_{\mu_1,\ldots\mu_k\in\mathcal{X}'} \sum_{i=1}^{k}\sum_{x\in C_i} f(d(x,\mu_i)),$$

where $\mathcal{X}'$ is either $\mathcal{X}$ or some superset of $\mathcal{X}$.

Some objective functions are not center based. For example, the *sum of in-cluster distances (SOD)*

$$G_{\text{SOD}}((\mathcal{X},d),(C_1,\ldots C_k)) = \sum_{i=1}^{k}\sum_{x,y\in C_i} d(x,y)$$

and the MinCut objective that we shall discuss in Section 22.3 are not center-based objectives.

22.2.1 The k-Means Algorithm

The k-means objective function is quite popular in practical applications of clustering. However, it turns out that finding the optimal k-means solution is often computationally infeasible (the problem is NP-hard, and even NP-hard to approximate to within some constant). As an alternative, the following simple iterative algorithm is often used, so often that, in many cases, the term k-means Clustering refers to the outcome of this algorithm rather than to the clustering that minimizes the k-means objective cost. We describe the algorithm with respect to the Euclidean distance function $d(\mathbf{x},\mathbf{y}) = \|\mathbf{x}-\mathbf{y}\|$.

k-Means

input: $\mathcal{X} \subset \mathbb{R}^n$; Number of clusters k
initialize: Randomly choose initial centroids $\boldsymbol{\mu}_1,\ldots,\boldsymbol{\mu}_k$
repeat until convergence
$\forall i \in [k]$ set $C_i = \{\mathbf{x} \in \mathcal{X} : i = \text{argmin}_j \|\mathbf{x}-\boldsymbol{\mu}_j\|\}$
(break ties in some arbitrary manner)
$\forall i \in [k]$ update $\boldsymbol{\mu}_i = \frac{1}{|C_i|}\sum_{\mathbf{x}\in C_i}\mathbf{x}$

Lemma 22.1. *Each iteration of the k-means algorithm does not increase the k-means objective function (as given in Equation (22.1)).*

Proof. To simplify the notation, let us use the shorthand $G(C_1,\ldots,C_k)$ for the k-means objective, namely,

$$G(C_1,\ldots,C_k) = \min_{\boldsymbol{\mu}_1,\ldots,\boldsymbol{\mu}_k\in\mathbb{R}^n} \sum_{i=1}^{k}\sum_{\mathbf{x}\in C_i}\|\mathbf{x}-\boldsymbol{\mu}_i\|^2. \tag{22.2}$$

It is convenient to define $\boldsymbol{\mu}(C_i) = \frac{1}{|C_i|}\sum_{\mathbf{x}\in C_i}\mathbf{x}$ and note that $\boldsymbol{\mu}(C_i) = \text{argmin}_{\boldsymbol{\mu}\in\mathbb{R}^n}\sum_{\mathbf{x}\in C_i}\|\mathbf{x}-\boldsymbol{\mu}\|^2$. Therefore, we can rewrite the k-means objective as

$$G(C_1,\ldots,C_k) = \sum_{i=1}^{k}\sum_{\mathbf{x}\in C_i}\|\mathbf{x}-\boldsymbol{\mu}(C_i)\|^2. \tag{22.3}$$

Consider the update at iteration t of the k-means algorithm. Let $C_1^{(t-1)},\ldots,C_k^{(t-1)}$ be the previous partition, let $\boldsymbol{\mu}_i^{(t-1)} = \boldsymbol{\mu}(C_i^{(t-1)})$, and let $C_1^{(t)},\ldots,C_k^{(t)}$ be the new partition assigned at iteration t. Using the definition of the objective as given in Equation (22.2) we clearly have that

$$G(C_1^{(t)},\ldots,C_k^{(t)}) \le \sum_{i=1}^{k}\sum_{\mathbf{x}\in C_i^{(t)}}\|\mathbf{x}-\boldsymbol{\mu}_i^{(t-1)}\|^2. \tag{22.4}$$

In addition, the definition of the new partition $(C_1^{(t)},\ldots,C_k^{(t)})$ implies that it minimizes the expression $\sum_{i=1}^{k}\sum_{\mathbf{x}\in C_i}\|\mathbf{x}-\boldsymbol{\mu}_i^{(t-1)}\|^2$ over all possible partitions

$(C_1,\ldots,C_k)$. Hence,

$$\sum_{i=1}^{k}\sum_{\mathbf{x}\in C_i^{(t)}}\|\mathbf{x}-\boldsymbol{\mu}_i^{(t-1)}\|^2 \le \sum_{i=1}^{k}\sum_{\mathbf{x}\in C_i^{(t-1)}}\|\mathbf{x}-\boldsymbol{\mu}_i^{(t-1)}\|^2. \tag{22.5}$$

Using Equation (22.3) we have that the right-hand side of Equation (22.5) equals $G(C_1^{(t-1)},\ldots,C_k^{(t-1)})$. Combining this with Equation (22.4) and Equation (22.5), we obtain that $G(C_1^{(t)},\ldots,C_k^{(t)}) \le G(C_1^{(t-1)},\ldots,C_k^{(t-1)})$, which concludes our proof. □

While the preceding lemma tells us that the k-means objective is monotonically nonincreasing, there is no guarantee on the number of iterations the k-means algorithm needs in order to reach convergence. Furthermore, there is no nontrivial lower bound on the gap between the value of the k-means objective of the algorithm's output and the minimum possible value of that objective function. In fact, k-means might converge to a point which is not even a local minimum (see Exercise 22.2). To improve the results of k-means it is often recommended to repeat the procedure several times with different randomly chosen initial centroids (e.g., we can choose the initial centroids to be random points from the data).

22.3 SPECTRAL CLUSTERING

Often, a convenient way to represent the relationships between points in a data set $\mathcal{X}=\{x_1,\ldots,x_m\}$ is by a *similarity graph*; each vertex represents a data point x_i, and every two vertices are connected by an edge whose weight is their similarity, $W_{i,j} = s(x_i,x_j)$, where $W\in\mathbb{R}^{m,m}$. For example, we can set $W_{i,j}=\exp(-d(x_i,x_j)^2/\sigma^2)$, where $d(\cdot,\cdot)$ is a distance function and σ is a parameter. The clustering problem can now be formulated as follows: We want to find a partition of the graph such that the edges between different groups have low weights and the edges within a group have high weights.

In the clustering objectives described previously, the focus was on one side of our intuitive definition of clustering – making sure that points in the same cluster are similar. We now present objectives that focus on the other requirement – points separated into different clusters should be nonsimilar.

22.3.1 Graph Cut

Given a graph represented by a similarity matrix W, the simplest and most direct way to construct a partition of the graph is to solve the mincut problem, which chooses a partition $C_1,\ldots,C_k$ that minimizes the objective

$$\operatorname{cut}(C_1,\ldots,C_k)=\sum_{i=1}^{k}\sum_{r\in C_i,s\notin C_i} W_{r,s}.$$

For $k=2$, the mincut problem can be solved efficiently. However, in practice it often does not lead to satisfactory partitions. The problem is that in many cases, the solution of mincut simply separates one individual vertex from the rest of the graph.

Of course, this is not what we want to achieve in clustering, as clusters should be reasonably large groups of points.

Several solutions to this problem have been suggested. The simplest solution is to normalize the cut and define the normalized mincut objective as follows:

$$\text{RatioCut}(C_1,\ldots,C_k) = \sum_{i=1}^{k} \frac{1}{|C_i|} \sum_{r\in C_i, s\notin C_i} W_{r,s}.$$

The preceding objective assumes smaller values if the clusters are not too small. Unfortunately, introducing this balancing makes the problem computationally hard to solve. Spectral clustering is a way to relax the problem of minimizing RatioCut.

22.3.2 Graph Laplacian and Relaxed Graph Cuts

The main mathematical object for spectral clustering is the graph Laplacian matrix. There are several different definitions of graph Laplacian in the literature, and in the following we describe one particular definition.

Definition 22.2 (Unnormalized Graph Laplacian). The *unnormalized graph Laplacian* is the $m \times m$ matrix $L = D - W$ where D is a diagonal matrix with $D_{i,i} = \sum_{j=1}^{m} W_{i,j}$. The matrix D is called the *degree matrix*.

The following lemma underscores the relation between RatioCut and the Laplacian matrix.

Lemma 22.3. *Let $C_1,\ldots,C_k$ be a clustering and let $H \in \mathbb{R}^{m,k}$ be the matrix such that*

$$H_{i,j} = \frac{1}{\sqrt{|C_j|}} \mathbb{1}_{[i\in C_j]}.$$

Then, the columns of H are orthonormal to each other and

$$\mathit{RatioCut}(C_1,\ldots,C_k) = \text{trace}(H^\top L H).$$

Proof. Let $\mathbf{h}_1,\ldots,\mathbf{h}_k$ be the columns of H. The fact that these vectors are orthonormal is immediate from the definition. Next, by standard algebraic manipulations, it can be shown that $\text{trace}(H^\top L H) = \sum_{i=1}^{k} \mathbf{h}_i^\top L \mathbf{h}_i$ and that for any vector $\mathbf{v}$ we have

$$\mathbf{v}^\top L \mathbf{v} = \frac{1}{2}\left(\sum_r D_{r,r} v_r^2 - 2\sum_{r,s} v_r v_s W_{r,s} + \sum_s D_{s,s} v_s^2\right) = \frac{1}{2}\sum_{r,s} W_{r,s}(v_r - v_s)^2.$$

Applying this with $\mathbf{v} = \mathbf{h}_i$ and noting that $(h_{i,r} - h_{i,s})^2$ is nonzero only if $r \in C_i, s \notin C_i$ or the other way around, we obtain that

$$\mathbf{h}_i^\top L \mathbf{h}_i = \frac{1}{|C_i|} \sum_{r\in C_i, s\notin C_i} W_{r,s}.$$

□

Therefore, to minimize RatioCut we can search for a matrix H whose columns are orthonormal and such that each $H_{i,j}$ is either 0 or $1/\sqrt{|C_j|}$. Unfortunately, this is an integer programming problem which we cannot solve efficiently. Instead, we relax the latter requirement and simply search an orthonormal matrix $H \in \mathbb{R}^{m,k}$ that minimizes trace($H^\top L H$). As we will see in the next chapter about PCA (particularly, the proof of Theorem 23.2), the solution to this problem is to set U to be the matrix whose columns are the eigenvectors corresponding to the k minimal eigenvalues of L. The resulting algorithm is called Unnormalized Spectral Clustering.

22.3.3 Unnormalized Spectral Clustering

Unnormalized Spectral Clustering

Input: $W \in \mathbb{R}^{m,m}$; Number of clusters k
Initialize: Compute the unnormalized graph Laplacian L
Let $U \in \mathbb{R}^{m,k}$ be the matrix whose columns are the eigenvectors of L corresponding to the k smallest eigenvalues
Let $\mathbf{v}_1, \ldots, \mathbf{v}_m$ be the rows of U
Cluster the points $\mathbf{v}_1, \ldots, \mathbf{v}_m$ using k-means
Output: Clusters $C_1, \ldots, C_K$ of the k-means algorithm

The spectral clustering algorithm starts with finding the matrix H of the k eigenvectors corresponding to the smallest eigenvalues of the graph Laplacian matrix. It then represents points according to the rows of H. It is due to the properties of the graph Laplacians that this change of representation is useful. In many situations, this change of representation enables the simple k-means algorithm to detect the clusters seamlessly. Intuitively, if H is as defined in Lemma 22.3 then each point in the new representation is an indicator vector whose value is nonzero only on the element corresponding to the cluster it belongs to.

22.4 INFORMATION BOTTLENECK*

The information bottleneck method is a clustering technique introduced by Tishby, Pereira, and Bialek. It relies on notions from *information theory*. To illustrate the method, consider the problem of clustering text documents where each document is represented as a bag-of-words; namely, each document is a vector $\mathbf{x} = \{0,1\}^n$, where n is the size of the dictionary and $x_i = 1$ iff the word corresponding to index i appears in the document. Given a set of m documents, we can interpret the bag-of-words representation of the m documents as a joint probability over a random variable x, indicating the identity of a document (thus taking values in $[m]$), and a random variable y, indicating the identity of a word in the dictionary (thus taking values in $[n]$).

With this interpretation, the information bottleneck refers to the identity of a clustering as another random variable, denoted C, that takes values in $[k]$ (where k will be set by the method as well). Once we have formulated x, y, C as random variables, we can use tools from information theory to express a clustering objective. In particular, the information bottleneck objective is

$$\min_{p(C|x)} I(x;C) - \beta I(C;y),$$

where $I(\cdot;\cdot)$ is the mutual information between two random variables,[1] β is a parameter, and the minimization is over all possible probabilistic assignments of points to clusters. Intuitively, we would like to achieve two contradictory goals. On one hand, we would like the mutual information between the identity of the document and the identity of the cluster to be as small as possible. This reflects the fact that we would like a strong compression of the original data. On the other hand, we would like high mutual information between the clustering variable and the identity of the words, which reflects the goal that the "relevant" information about the document (as reflected by the words that appear in the document) is retained. This generalizes the classical notion of minimal sufficient statistics[2] used in parametric statistics to arbitrary distributions.

Solving the optimization problem associated with the information bottleneck principle is hard in the general case. Some of the proposed methods are similar to the EM principle, which we will discuss in Chapter 24.

22.5 A HIGH-LEVEL VIEW OF CLUSTERING

So far, we have mainly listed various useful clustering tools. However, some fundamental questions remain unaddressed. First and foremost, what is clustering? What is it that distinguishes a *clustering* algorithm from any arbitrary function that takes an input space and outputs a partition of that space? Are there any basic properties of clustering that are independent of any specific algorithm or task?

One method for addressing such questions is via an axiomatic approach. There have been several attempts to provide an axiomatic definition of clustering. Let us demonstrate this approach by presenting the attempt made by Kleinberg (2003).

Consider a clustering function, F, that takes as input any finite domain $\mathcal{X}$ with a dissimilarity function d over its pairs and returns a partition of $\mathcal{X}$.

Consider the following three properties of such a function:

Scale Invariance (SI) For any domain set $\mathcal{X}$, dissimilarity function d, and any $\alpha > 0$, the following should hold: $F(\mathcal{X}, d) = F(\mathcal{X}, \alpha d)$ (where $(\alpha d)(x, y) \stackrel{\text{def}}{=} \alpha\, d(x, y)$).

Richness (Ri) For any finite $\mathcal{X}$ and every partition $C = (C_1, \ldots C_k)$ of X (into nonempty subsets) there exists some dissimilarity function d over $\mathcal{X}$ such that $F(\mathcal{X}, d) = C$.

Consistency (Co) If d and d' are dissimilarity functions over $\mathcal{X}$, such that for every $x, y \in \mathcal{X}$, if x, y belong to the same cluster in $F(\mathcal{X}, d)$ then $d'(x, y) \le d(x, y)$ and if x, y belong to different clusters in $F(\mathcal{X}, d)$ then $d'(x, y) \ge d(x, y)$, then $F(\mathcal{X}, d) = F(\mathcal{X}, d')$.

[1] That is, given a probability function, p over the pairs (x, C), $I(x; C) = \sum_a \sum_b p(a, b) \log\left(\frac{p(a,b)}{p(a)p(b)}\right)$, where the sum is over all values x can take and all values C can take.

[2] A sufficient statistic is a function of the data which has the property of sufficiency with respect to a statistical model and its associated unknown parameter, meaning that "no other statistic which can be calculated from the same sample provides any additional information as to the value of the parameter." For example, if we assume that a variable is distributed normally with a unit variance and an unknown expectation, then the average function is a sufficient statistic.

A moment of reflection reveals that the Scale Invariance is a very natural requirement – it would be odd to have the result of a clustering function depend on the units used to measure between-point distances. The Richness requirement basically states that the outcome of the clustering function is fully controlled by the function d, which is also a very intuitive feature. The third requirement, Consistency, is the only requirement that refers to the basic (informal) definition of clustering – we wish that similar points will be clustered together and that dissimilar points will be separated to different clusters, and therefore, if points that already share a cluster become more similar, and points that are already separated become even less similar to each other, the clustering function should have even stronger "support" of its previous clustering decisions.

However, Kleinberg (2003) has shown the following "impossibility" result:

Theorem 22.4. *There exists no function, F, that satisfies all the three properties: Scale Invariance, Richness, and Consistency.*

Proof. Assume, by way of contradiction, that some F does satisfy all three properties. Pick some domain set $\mathcal{X}$ with at least three points. By Richness, there must be some d_1 such that $F(\mathcal{X}, d_1) = \{\{x\} : x \in \mathcal{X}\}$ and there also exists some d_2 such that $F(\mathcal{X}, d_2) \neq F(\mathcal{X}, d_1)$.

Let $\alpha \in \mathbb{R}_+$ be such that for every $x, y \in \mathcal{X}$, $\alpha d_2(x, y) \geq d_1(x, y)$. Let $d_3 = \alpha d_2$. Consider $F(\mathcal{X}, d_3)$. By the Scale Invariance property of F, we should have $F(\mathcal{X}, d_3) = F(\mathcal{X}, d_2)$. On the other hand, since all distinct $x, y \in \mathcal{X}$ reside in different clusters w.r.t. $F(\mathcal{X}, d_1)$, and $d_3(x, y) \geq d_1(x, y)$, the Consistency of F implies that $F(\mathcal{X}, d_3) = F(\mathcal{X}, d_1)$. This is a contradiction, since we chose d_1, d_2 so that $F(\mathcal{X}, d_2) \neq F(\mathcal{X}, d_1)$. □

It is important to note that there is no single "bad property" among the three properties. For every pair of the three axioms, there exist natural clustering functions that satisfy the two properties in that pair (one can even construct such examples just by varying the stopping criteria for the Single Linkage clustering function). On the other hand, Kleinberg shows that any clustering algorithm that minimizes any center-based objective function inevitably fails the consistency property (yet, the k-sum-of-in-cluster-distances minimization clustering does satisfy Consistency).

The Kleinberg impossibility result can be easily circumvented by varying the properties. For example, if one wishes to discuss clustering functions that have a fixed number-of-clusters parameter, then it is natural to replace Richness by k-Richness (namely, the requirement that every partition of the domain into k subsets is attainable by the clustering function). k-Richness, Scale Invariance and Consistency all hold for the k-means clustering and are therefore consistent. Alternatively, one can relax the Consistency property. For example, say that two clusterings $C = (C_1, \ldots C_k)$ and $C' = (C'_1, \ldots C'_l)$ are *compatible* if for every clusters $C_i \in C$ and $C'_j \in C'$, either $C_i \subseteq C'_j$ or $C'_j \subseteq C_i$ or $C_i \cap C'_j = \emptyset$ (it is worthwhile noting that for every dendrogram, every two clusterings that are obtained by trimming that dendrogram are compatible). "Refinement Consistency" is the requirement that, under the assumptions of the Consistency property, the new clustering $F(\mathcal{X}, d')$ is compatible with the old clustering $F(\mathcal{X}, d)$. Many common clustering functions satisfy this requirement as well as Scale Invariance and Richness. Furthermore, one can come up with many other, different, properties of clustering functions that sound intuitive and desirable and are satisfied by some common clustering functions.

There are many ways to interpret these results. We suggest to view it as indicating that there is no "ideal" clustering function. Every clustering function will inevitably have some "undesirable" properties. The choice of a clustering function for any given task must therefore take into account the specific properties of that task. There is no generic clustering solution, just as there is no classification algorithm that will learn every learnable task (as the No-Free-Lunch theorem shows). Clustering, just like classification prediction, must take into account some prior knowledge about the specific task at hand.

22.6 SUMMARY

Clustering is an unsupervised learning problem, in which we wish to partition a set of points into "meaningful" subsets. We presented several clustering approaches including linkage-based algorithms, the k-means family, spectral clustering, and the information bottleneck. We discussed the difficulty of formalizing the intuitive meaning of clustering.

22.7 BIBLIOGRAPHIC REMARKS

The k-means algorithm is sometimes named Lloyd's algorithm, after Stuart Lloyd, who proposed the method in 1957. For a more complete overview of spectral clustering we refer the reader to the excellent tutorial by Von Luxburg (2007). The information bottleneck method was introduced by Tishby, Pereira, and Bialek (1999). For an additional discussion on the axiomatic approach see Ackerman and Ben-David (2008).

22.8 EXERCISES

22.1 **Suboptimality of k-Means:** For every parameter $t > 1$, show that there exists an instance of the k-means problem for which the k-means algorithm (might) find a solution whose k-means objective is at least $t \cdot \text{OPT}$, where OPT is the minimum k-means objective.

22.2 **k-Means Might Not Necessarily Converge to a Local Minimum:** Show that the k-means algorithm might converge to a point which is not a local minimum. *Hint*: Suppose that $k = 2$ and the sample points are $\{1, 2, 3, 4\} \subset \mathbb{R}$ suppose we initialize the k-means with the centers $\{2, 4\}$; and suppose we break ties in the definition of C_i by assigning i to be the smallest value in $\text{argmin}_j \|\mathbf{x} - \boldsymbol{\mu}_j\|$.

22.3 Given a metric space $(\mathcal{X}, d)$, where $|\mathcal{X}| < \infty$, and $k \in \mathbb{N}$, we would like to find a partition of $\mathcal{X}$ into $C_1, \ldots, C_k$ which minimizes the expression

$$G_{\text{k-diam}}((\mathcal{X}, d), (C_1, \ldots, C_k)) = \max_{j \in [d]} \text{diam}(C_j),$$

where $\text{diam}(C_j) = \max_{x, x' \in C_j} d(x, x')$ (we use the convention $\text{diam}(C_j) = 0$ if $|C_j| < 2$).

Similarly to the k-means objective, it is NP-hard to minimize the *k-diam* objective. Fortunately, we have a very simple approximation algorithm: Initially, we pick some $x \in \mathcal{X}$ and set $\mu_1 = x$. Then, the algorithm iteratively sets

$$\forall j \in \{2,\ldots,k\},\ \mu_j = \underset{x\in X}{\operatorname{argmax}} \min_{i\in[j-1]} d(x,\mu_i).$$

Finally, we set

$$\forall i \in [k],\ C_i = \{x \in X : i = \underset{j\in[k]}{\operatorname{argmin}}\, d(x,\mu_j)\}.$$

Prove that the algorithm described is a 2-approximation algorithm. That is, if we denote its output by $\hat{C}_1,\ldots,\hat{C}_k$, and denote the optimal solution by $C_1^*,\ldots,C_k^*$, then,

$$G_{\text{k-diam}}((\mathcal{X},d),(\hat{C}_1,\ldots,\hat{C}_k)) \le 2\cdot G_{\text{k-diam}}((\mathcal{X},d),(C_1^*,\ldots,C_k^*)).$$

Hint: Consider the point μ_{k+1} (in other words, the next center we would have chosen, if we wanted $k+1$ clusters). Let $r = \min_{j\in[k]} d(\mu_j,\mu_{k+1})$. Prove the following inequalities

$$G_{\text{k-diam}}((\mathcal{X},d),(\hat{C}_1,\ldots,\hat{C}_k)) \le 2r$$
$$G_{\text{k-diam}}((X,d),(C_1^*,\ldots,C_k^*)) \ge r.$$

22.4 Recall that a clustering function, F, is called Center-Based Clustering if, for some monotonic function $f : \mathbb{R}_+ \to \mathbb{R}_+$, on every given input $(\mathcal{X},d)$, $F(\mathcal{X},d)$ is a clustering that minimizes the objective

$$G_f((\mathcal{X},d),(C_1,\ldots C_k)) = \min_{\mu_1,\ldots\mu_k\in\mathcal{X}'} \sum_{i=1}^{k}\sum_{x\in C_i} f(d(x,\mu_i)),$$

where $\mathcal{X}'$ is either $\mathcal{X}$ or some superset of $\mathcal{X}$.

Prove that for every $k > 1$ the k-diam clustering function defined in the previous exercise is not a center-based clustering function.

Hint: Given a clustering input $(\mathcal{X},d)$, with $|\mathcal{X}| > 2$, consider the effect of adding many close-by points to some (but not all) of the members of $\mathcal{X}$, on either the k-diam clustering or any given center-based clustering.

22.5 Recall that we discussed three clustering "properties": Scale Invariance, Richness, and Consistency. Consider the Single Linkage clustering algorithm.
1. Find which of the three properties is satisfied by Single Linkage with the Fixed Number of Clusters (any fixed nonzero number) stopping rule.
2. Find which of the three properties is satisfied by Single Linkage with the Distance Upper Bound (any fixed nonzero upper bound) stopping rule.
3. Show that for any pair of these properties there exists a stopping criterion for Single Linkage clustering, under which these two axioms are satisfied.

22.6 Given some number k, let k-Richness be the following requirement:
For any finite $\mathcal{X}$ and every partition $C = (C_1,\ldots C_k)$ of $\mathcal{X}$ (into nonempty subsets) there exists some dissimilarity function d over $\mathcal{X}$ such that $F(\mathcal{X},d) = C$.

Prove that, for every number k, there exists a clustering function that satisfies the three properties: Scale Invariance, k-Richness, and Consistency.

23

Dimensionality Reduction

Dimensionality reduction is the process of taking data in a high dimensional space and mapping it into a new space whose dimensionality is much smaller. This process is closely related to the concept of (lossy) compression in information theory. There are several reasons to reduce the dimensionality of the data. First, high dimensional data impose computational challenges. Moreover, in some situations high dimensionality might lead to poor generalization abilities of the learning algorithm (for example, in Nearest Neighbor classifiers the sample complexity increases exponentially with the dimension—see Chapter 19). Finally, dimensionality reduction can be used for interpretability of the data, for finding meaningful structure of the data, and for illustration purposes.

In this chapter we describe popular methods for dimensionality reduction. In those methods, the reduction is performed by applying a linear transformation to the original data. That is, if the original data is in $\mathbb{R}^d$ and we want to embed it into $\mathbb{R}^n$ ($n < d$) then we would like to find a matrix $W \in \mathbb{R}^{n,d}$ that induces the mapping $\mathbf{x} \mapsto W\mathbf{x}$. A natural criterion for choosing W is in a way that will enable a reasonable recovery of the original $\mathbf{x}$. It is not hard to show that in general, exact recovery of $\mathbf{x}$ from $W\mathbf{x}$ is impossible (see Exercise 23.1).

The first method we describe is called Principal Component Analysis (PCA). In PCA, both the compression and the recovery are performed by linear transformations and the method finds the linear transformations for which the differences between the recovered vectors and the original vectors are minimal in the least squared sense.

Next, we describe dimensionality reduction using random matrices W. We derive an important lemma, often called the "Johnson-Lindenstrauss lemma," which analyzes the distortion caused by such a random dimensionality reduction technique.

Last, we show how one can reduce the dimension of all *sparse* vectors using again a random matrix. This process is known as Compressed Sensing. In this case, the recovery process is nonlinear but can still be implemented efficiently using linear programming.

We conclude by underscoring the underlying "prior assumptions" behind PCA and compressed sensing, which can help us understand the merits and pitfalls of the two methods.

23.1 PRINCIPAL COMPONENT ANALYSIS (PCA)

Let $\mathbf{x}_1, \ldots, \mathbf{x}_m$ be m vectors in $\mathbb{R}^d$. We would like to reduce the dimensionality of these vectors using a linear transformation. A matrix $W \in \mathbb{R}^{n,d}$, where $n < d$, induces a mapping $\mathbf{x} \mapsto W\mathbf{x}$, where $W\mathbf{x} \in \mathbb{R}^n$ is the lower dimensionality representation of $\mathbf{x}$. Then, a second matrix $U \in \mathbb{R}^{d,n}$ can be used to (approximately) recover each original vector $\mathbf{x}$ from its compressed version. That is, for a compressed vector $\mathbf{y} = W\mathbf{x}$, where $\mathbf{y}$ is in the low dimensional space $\mathbb{R}^n$, we can construct $\tilde{\mathbf{x}} = U\mathbf{y}$, so that $\tilde{\mathbf{x}}$ is the recovered version of $\mathbf{x}$ and resides in the original high dimensional space $\mathbb{R}^d$.

In PCA, we find the compression matrix W and the recovering matrix U so that the total squared distance between the original and recovered vectors is minimal; namely, we aim at solving the problem

$$\underset{W \in \mathbb{R}^{n,d}, U \in \mathbb{R}^{d,n}}{\operatorname{argmin}} \sum_{i=1}^{m} \|\mathbf{x}_i - UW\mathbf{x}_i\|_2^2. \tag{23.1}$$

To solve this problem we first show that the optimal solution takes a specific form.

Lemma 23.1. *Let (U, W) be a solution to Equation (23.1). Then the columns of U are orthonormal (namely, $U^\top U$ is the identity matrix of $\mathbb{R}^n$) and $W = U^\top$.*

Proof. Fix any U, W and consider the mapping $\mathbf{x} \mapsto UW\mathbf{x}$. The range of this mapping, $R = \{UW\mathbf{x} : \mathbf{x} \in \mathbb{R}^d\}$, is an n dimensional linear subspace of $\mathbb{R}^d$. Let $V \in \mathbb{R}^{d,n}$ be a matrix whose columns form an orthonormal basis of this subspace, namely, the range of V is R and $V^\top V = I$. Therefore, each vector in R can be written as $V\mathbf{y}$ where $\mathbf{y} \in \mathbb{R}^n$. For every $\mathbf{x} \in \mathbb{R}^d$ and $\mathbf{y} \in \mathbb{R}^n$ we have

$$\|\mathbf{x} - V\mathbf{y}\|_2^2 = \|\mathbf{x}\|^2 + \mathbf{y}^\top V^\top V\mathbf{y} - 2\mathbf{y}^\top V^\top \mathbf{x} = \|\mathbf{x}\|^2 + \|\mathbf{y}\|^2 - 2\mathbf{y}^\top (V^\top \mathbf{x}),$$

where we used the fact that $V^\top V$ is the identity matrix of $\mathbb{R}^n$. Minimizing the preceding expression with respect to $\mathbf{y}$ by comparing the gradient with respect to $\mathbf{y}$ to zero gives that $\mathbf{y} = V^\top \mathbf{x}$. Therefore, for each $\mathbf{x}$ we have that

$$VV^\top \mathbf{x} = \underset{\tilde{\mathbf{x}} \in R}{\operatorname{argmin}} \|\mathbf{x} - \tilde{\mathbf{x}}\|_2^2.$$

In particular this holds for $\mathbf{x}_1, \ldots, \mathbf{x}_m$ and therefore we can replace U, W by $V, V^\top$ and by that do not increase the objective

$$\sum_{i=1}^{m} \|\mathbf{x}_i - UW\mathbf{x}_i\|_2^2 \geq \sum_{i=1}^{m} \|\mathbf{x}_i - VV^\top \mathbf{x}_i\|_2^2.$$

Since this holds for every U, W the proof of the lemma follows. □

On the basis of the preceding lemma, we can rewrite the optimization problem given in Equation (23.1) as follows:

$$\underset{U\in\mathbb{R}^{d,n}:U^\top U=I}{\operatorname{argmin}} \sum_{i=1}^{m} \|\mathbf{x}_i - UU^\top \mathbf{x}_i\|_2^2. \tag{23.2}$$

We further simplify the optimization problem by using the following elementary algebraic manipulations. For every $\mathbf{x}\in\mathbb{R}^d$ and a matrix $U\in\mathbb{R}^{d,n}$ such that $U^\top U = I$ we have

$$\begin{aligned}\|\mathbf{x} - UU^\top\mathbf{x}\|^2 &= \|\mathbf{x}\|^2 - 2\mathbf{x}^\top UU^\top \mathbf{x} + \mathbf{x}^\top UU^\top UU^\top \mathbf{x}\\ &= \|\mathbf{x}\|^2 - \mathbf{x}^\top UU^\top \mathbf{x}\\ &= \|\mathbf{x}\|^2 - \operatorname{trace}(U^\top \mathbf{x}\mathbf{x}^\top U),\end{aligned} \tag{23.3}$$

where the trace of a matrix is the sum of its diagonal entries. Since the trace is a linear operator, this allows us to rewrite Equation (23.2) as follows:

$$\underset{U\in\mathbb{R}^{d,n}:U^\top U=I}{\operatorname{argmax}} \operatorname{trace}\left(U^\top \sum_{i=1}^{m} \mathbf{x}_i\mathbf{x}_i^\top U\right). \tag{23.4}$$

Let $A = \sum_{i=1}^{m} \mathbf{x}_i\mathbf{x}_i^\top$. The matrix A is symmetric and therefore it can be written using its spectral decomposition as $A = VDV^\top$, where D is diagonal and $V^\top V = VV^\top = I$. Here, the elements on the diagonal of D are the eigenvalues of A and the columns of V are the corresponding eigenvectors. We assume without loss of generality that $D_{1,1} \ge D_{2,2} \ge \cdots \ge D_{d,d}$. Since A is positive semidefinite it also holds that $D_{d,d} \ge 0$. We claim that the solution to Equation (23.4) is the matrix U whose columns are the n eigenvectors of A corresponding to the largest n eigenvalues.

Theorem 23.2. *Let $\mathbf{x}_1,\ldots,\mathbf{x}_m$ be arbitrary vectors in $\mathbb{R}^d$, let $A = \sum_{i=1}^{m}\mathbf{x}_i\mathbf{x}_i^\top$, and let $\mathbf{u}_1,\ldots,\mathbf{u}_n$ be n eigenvectors of the matrix A corresponding to the largest n eigenvalues of A. Then, the solution to the PCA optimization problem given in Equation (23.1) is to set U to be the matrix whose columns are $\mathbf{u}_1,\ldots,\mathbf{u}_n$ and to set $W = U^\top$.*

Proof. Let $VDV^\top$ be the spectral decomposition of A. Fix some matrix $U\in\mathbb{R}^{d,n}$ with orthonormal columns and let $B = V^\top U$. Then, $VB = VV^\top U = U$. It follows that

$$U^\top AU = B^\top V^\top VDV^\top VB = B^\top DB,$$

and therefore

$$\operatorname{trace}(U^\top AU) = \sum_{j=1}^{d} D_{j,j}\sum_{i=1}^{n} B_{j,i}^2.$$

Note that $B^\top B = U^\top VV^\top U = U^\top U = I$. Therefore, the columns of B are also orthonormal, which implies that $\sum_{j=1}^{d}\sum_{i=1}^{n} B_{j,i}^2 = n$. In addition, let $\tilde{B}\in\mathbb{R}^{d,d}$ be a matrix such that its first n columns are the columns of B and in addition $\tilde{B}^\top\tilde{B} = I$. Then, for every j we have $\sum_{i=1}^{d}\tilde{B}_{j,i}^2 = 1$, which implies that $\sum_{i=1}^{n} B_{j,i}^2 \le 1$. It follows that

$$\text{trace}(U^\top AU) \le \max_{\beta \in [0,1]^d : \|\beta\|_1 \le n} \sum_{j=1}^{d} D_{j,j}\beta_j.$$

It is not hard to verify (see 23.2) that the right-hand side equals $\sum_{j=1}^{n} D_{j,j}$. We have therefore shown that for every matrix $U \in \mathbb{R}^{d,n}$ with orthonormal columns it holds that $\text{trace}(U^\top AU) \le \sum_{j=1}^{n} D_{j,j}$. On the other hand, if we set U to be the matrix whose columns are the n leading eigenvectors of A we obtain that $\text{trace}(U^\top AU) = \sum_{j=1}^{n} D_{j,j}$, and this concludes our proof. □

Remark 23.1. The proof of Theorem 23.2 also tells us that the value of the objective of Equation (23.4) is $\sum_{i=1}^{n} D_{i,i}$. Combining this with Equation (23.3) and noting that $\sum_{i=1}^{m} \|\mathbf{x}_i\|^2 = \text{trace}(A) = \sum_{i=1}^{d} D_{i,i}$ we obtain that the optimal objective value of Equation (23.1) is $\sum_{i=n+1}^{d} D_{i,i}$.

Remark 23.2. It is a common practice to "center" the examples before applying PCA. That is, we first calculate $\boldsymbol{\mu} = \frac{1}{m}\sum_{i=1}^{m} \mathbf{x}_i$ and then apply PCA on the vectors $(\mathbf{x}_1 - \boldsymbol{\mu}), \ldots, (\mathbf{x}_m - \boldsymbol{\mu})$. This is also related to the interpretation of PCA as variance maximization (see Exercise 23.4).

23.1.1 A More Efficient Solution for the Case $d \gg m$

In some situations the original dimensionality of the data is much larger than the number of examples m. The computational complexity of calculating the PCA solution as described previously is $O(d^3)$ (for calculating eigenvalues of A) plus $O(md^2)$ (for constructing the matrix A). We now show a simple trick that enables us to calculate the PCA solution more efficiently when $d \gg m$.

Recall that the matrix A is defined to be $\sum_{i=1}^{m} \mathbf{x}_i\mathbf{x}_i^\top$. It is convenient to rewrite $A = X^\top X$ where $X \in \mathbb{R}^{m,d}$ is a matrix whose ith row is $\mathbf{x}_i^\top$. Consider the matrix $B = XX^\top$. That is, $B \in \mathbb{R}^{m,m}$ is the matrix whose i,j element equals $\langle \mathbf{x}_i, \mathbf{x}_j \rangle$. Suppose that $\mathbf{u}$ is an eigenvector of B: That is, $B\mathbf{u} = \lambda\mathbf{u}$ for some $\lambda \in \mathbb{R}$. Multiplying the equality by $X^\top$ and using the definition of B we obtain $X^\top XX^\top\mathbf{u} = \lambda X^\top\mathbf{u}$. But, using the definition of A, we get that $A(X^\top\mathbf{u}) = \lambda(X^\top\mathbf{u})$. Thus, $\frac{X^\top\mathbf{u}}{\|X^\top\mathbf{u}\|}$ is an eigenvector of A with eigenvalue of λ.

We can therefore calculate the PCA solution by calculating the eigenvalues of B instead of A. The complexity is $O(m^3)$ (for calculating eigenvalues of B) and m^2d (for constructing the matrix B).

Remark 23.3. The previous discussion also implies that to calculate the PCA solution we only need to know how to calculate inner products between vectors. This enables us to calculate PCA implicitly even when d is very large (or even infinite) using kernels, which yields the *kernel PCA* algorithm.

23.1.2 Implementation and Demonstration

A pseudocode of PCA is given in the following.

PCA

input
A matrix of m examples $X \in \mathbb{R}^{m,d}$
number of components n
if $(m > d)$
$A = X^\top X$
Let $\mathbf{u}_1, \ldots, \mathbf{u}_n$ be the eigenvectors of A with largest eigenvalues
else
$B = XX^\top$
Let $\mathbf{v}_1, \ldots, \mathbf{v}_n$ be the eigenvectors of B with largest eigenvalues
for $i = 1, \ldots, n$ set $\mathbf{u}_i = \frac{1}{\|X^\top \mathbf{v}_i\|} X^\top \mathbf{v}_i$
output: $\mathbf{u}_1, \ldots, \mathbf{u}_n$

To illustrate how PCA works, let us generate vectors in $\mathbb{R}^2$ that approximately reside on a line, namely, on a one dimensional subspace of $\mathbb{R}^2$. For example, suppose that each example is of the form $(x, x+y)$ where x is chosen uniformly at random from $[-1, 1]$ and y is sampled from a Gaussian distribution with mean 0 and standard deviation of 0.1. Suppose we apply PCA on this data. Then, the eigenvector corresponding to the largest eigenvalue will be close to the vector $(1/\sqrt{2}, 1/\sqrt{2})$. When projecting a point $(x, x+y)$ on this principal component we will obtain the scalar $\frac{2x+y}{\sqrt{2}}$. The reconstruction of the original vector will be $((x+y/2), (x+y/2))$. In Figure 23.1 we depict the original versus reconstructed data.

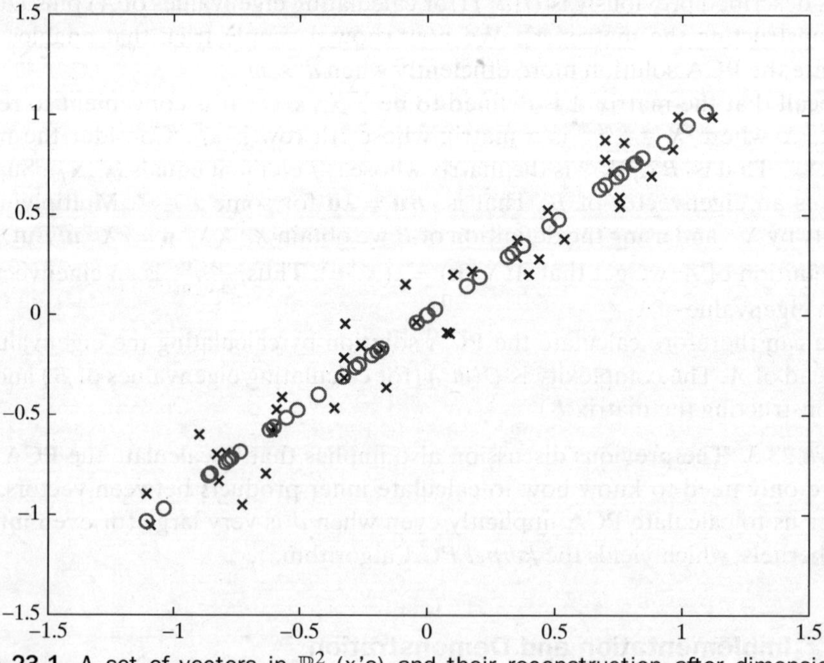

Figure 23.1. A set of vectors in $\mathbb{R}^2$ (x's) and their reconstruction after dimensionality reduction to $\mathbb{R}^1$ using PCA (circles).

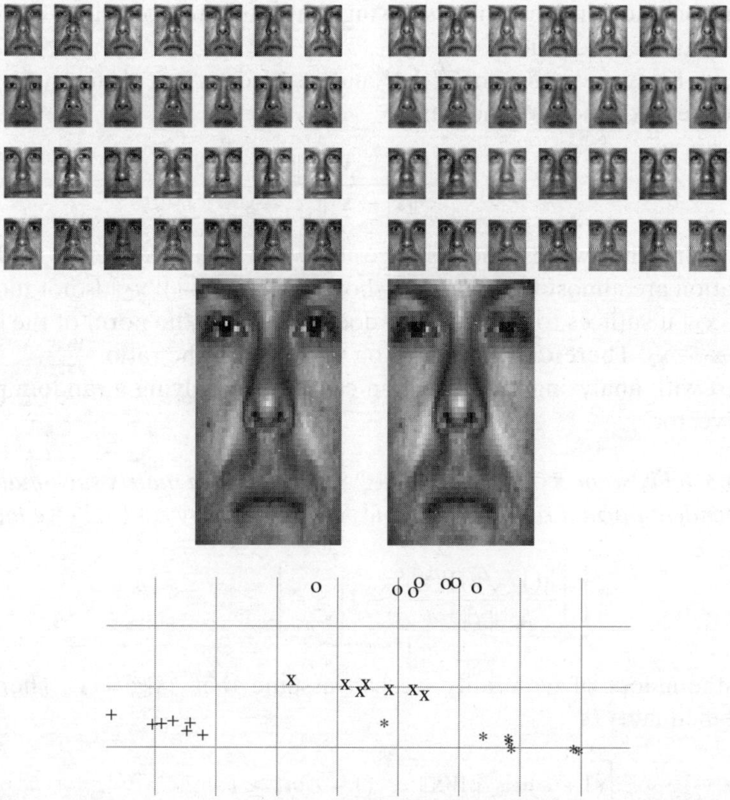

Figure 23.2. Images of faces extracted from the Yale data set. Top-left: the original images in $\mathbb{R}^{50x50}$. Top-right: the images after dimensionality reduction to $\mathbb{R}^{10}$ and reconstruction. Middle row: an enlarged version of one of the images before and after PCA. Bottom: the images after dimensionality reduction to $\mathbb{R}^2$. The different marks indicate different individuals.

Next, we demonstrate the effectiveness of PCA on a data set of faces. We extracted images of faces from the Yale data set (Georghiades, Belhumeur & Kriegman 2001). Each image contains $50 \times 50 = 2500$ pixels; therefore the original dimensionality is very high.

Some images of faces are depicted on the top-left side of Figure 23.2. Using PCA, we reduced the dimensionality to $\mathbb{R}^{10}$ and reconstructed back to the original dimension, which is 50^2. The resulting reconstructed images are depicted on the top-right side of Figure 23.2. Finally, on the bottom of Figure 23.2 we depict a 2 dimensional representation of the images. As can be seen, even from a 2 dimensional representation of the images we can still roughly separate different individuals.

23.2 RANDOM PROJECTIONS

In this section we show that reducing the dimension by using a random linear transformation leads to a simple compression scheme with a surprisingly low distortion. The transformation $\mathbf{x} \mapsto W\mathbf{x}$, when W is a random matrix, is often referred to as a random projection. In particular, we provide a variant of a famous lemma due to Johnson and Lindenstrauss, showing that random projections do not distort Euclidean distances too much.

Let $\mathbf{x}_1, \mathbf{x}_2$ be two vectors in $\mathbb{R}^d$. A matrix W does not distort too much the distance between $\mathbf{x}_1$ and $\mathbf{x}_2$ if the ratio

$$\frac{\|W\mathbf{x}_1 - W\mathbf{x}_2\|}{\|\mathbf{x}_1 - \mathbf{x}_2\|}$$

is close to 1. In other words, the distances between $\mathbf{x}_1$ and $\mathbf{x}_2$ before and after the transformation are almost the same. To show that $\|W\mathbf{x}_1 - W\mathbf{x}_2\|$ is not too far away from $\|\mathbf{x}_1 - \mathbf{x}_2\|$ it suffices to show that W does not distort the norm of the difference vector $\mathbf{x} = \mathbf{x}_1 - \mathbf{x}_2$. Therefore, from now on we focus on the ratio $\frac{\|W\mathbf{x}\|}{\|\mathbf{x}\|}$.

We start with analyzing the distortion caused by applying a random projection to a single vector.

Lemma 23.3. *Fix some $\mathbf{x} \in \mathbb{R}^d$. Let $W \in \mathbb{R}^{n,d}$ be a random matrix such that each $W_{i,j}$ is an independent normal random variable. Then, for every $\epsilon \in (0,3)$ we have*

$$\mathbb{P}\left[\left|\frac{\|(1/\sqrt{n})W\mathbf{x}\|^2}{\|\mathbf{x}\|^2} - 1\right| > \epsilon\right] \le 2e^{-\epsilon^2 n/6}.$$

Proof. Without loss of generality we can assume that $\|\mathbf{x}\|^2 = 1$. Therefore, an equivalent inequality is

$$\mathbb{P}\left[(1-\epsilon)n \le \|W\mathbf{x}\|^2 \le (1+\epsilon)n\right] \ge 1 - 2e^{-\epsilon^2 n/6}.$$

Let $\mathbf{w}_i$ be the ith row of W. The random variable $\langle \mathbf{w}_i, \mathbf{x}\rangle$ is a weighted sum of d independent normal random variables and therefore it is normally distributed with zero mean and variance $\sum_j x_j^2 = \|\mathbf{x}\|^2 = 1$. Therefore, the random variable $\|W\mathbf{x}\|^2 = \sum_{i=1}^n (\langle \mathbf{w}_i, \mathbf{x}\rangle)^2$ has a χ_n^2 distribution. The claim now follows directly from a measure concentration property of χ^2 random variables stated in Lemma B.12 given in Section B.7. □

The Johnson-Lindenstrauss lemma follows from this using a simple union bound argument.

Lemma 23.4 (Johnson-Lindenstrauss Lemma). *Let Q be a finite set of vectors in $\mathbb{R}^d$. Let $\delta \in (0,1)$ and n be an integer such that*

$$\epsilon = \sqrt{\frac{6\log(2|Q|/\delta)}{n}} \le 3.$$

Then, with probability of at least $1-\delta$ over a choice of a random matrix $W \in \mathbb{R}^{n,d}$ such that each element of W is distributed normally with zero mean and variance of $1/n$ we have

$$\sup_{\mathbf{x}\in Q}\left|\frac{\|W\mathbf{x}\|^2}{\|\mathbf{x}\|^2} - 1\right| < \epsilon.$$

Proof. Combining Lemma 23.3 and the union bound we have that for every $\epsilon \in (0,3)$:

$$\mathbb{P}\left[\sup_{\mathbf{x}\in Q}\left|\frac{\|W\mathbf{x}\|^2}{\|\mathbf{x}\|^2}-1\right|>\epsilon\right]\leq 2|Q|e^{-\epsilon^2 n/6}.$$

Let δ denote the right-hand side of the inequality; thus we obtain that

$$\epsilon=\sqrt{\frac{6\log(2|Q|/\delta)}{n}}.$$

□

Interestingly, the bound given in Lemma 23.4 does not depend on the original dimension of $\mathbf{x}$. In fact, the bound holds even if $\mathbf{x}$ is in an infinite dimensional Hilbert space.

23.3 COMPRESSED SENSING

Compressed sensing is a dimensionality reduction technique which utilizes a prior assumption that the original vector is sparse in some basis. To motivate compressed sensing, consider a vector $\mathbf{x} \in \mathbb{R}^d$ that has at most s nonzero elements. That is,

$$\|\mathbf{x}\|_0 \stackrel{\text{def}}{=} |\{i : x_i \neq 0\}| \leq s.$$

Clearly, we can compress $\mathbf{x}$ by representing it using s (index,value) pairs. Furthermore, this compression is lossless – we can reconstruct $\mathbf{x}$ exactly from the s (index,value) pairs. Now, lets take one step forward and assume that $\mathbf{x} = U\boldsymbol{\alpha}$, where $\boldsymbol{\alpha}$ is a sparse vector, $\|\boldsymbol{\alpha}\|_0 \leq s$, and U is a fixed orthonormal matrix. That is, $\mathbf{x}$ has a sparse representation in another basis. It turns out that many natural vectors are (at least approximately) sparse in some representation. In fact, this assumption underlies many modern compression schemes. For example, the JPEG-2000 format for image compression relies on the fact that natural images are approximately sparse in a wavelet basis.

Can we still compress $\mathbf{x}$ into roughly s numbers? Well, one simple way to do this is to multiply $\mathbf{x}$ by $U^\top$, which yields the sparse vector $\boldsymbol{\alpha}$, and then represent $\boldsymbol{\alpha}$ by its s (index,value) pairs. However, this requires us first to "sense" $\mathbf{x}$, to store it, and then to multiply it by $U^\top$. This raises a very natural question: Why go to so much effort to acquire all the data when most of what we get will be thrown away? Cannot we just directly measure the part that will not end up being thrown away?

Compressed sensing is a technique that simultaneously acquires and compresses the data. The key result is that a random linear transformation can compress $\mathbf{x}$ without losing information. The number of measurements needed is order of $s\log(d)$. That is, we roughly acquire only the important information about the signal. As we will see later, the price we pay is a slower reconstruction phase. In some situations, it makes sense to save time in compression even at the price of a slower reconstruction. For example, a security camera should sense and compress a large amount of images while most of the time we do not need to decode the compressed data at all. Furthermore, in many practical applications, compression by a linear transformation is advantageous because it can be performed efficiently in hardware. For example, a team led by Baraniuk and Kelly has proposed a camera architecture that employs a digital micromirror array to perform optical calculations of a linear transformation of an image. In this case, obtaining each compressed measurement is as easy as obtaining a single raw measurement. Another important application of compressed sensing is medical imaging, in which requiring fewer measurements translates to less radiation for the patient.

Informally, the main premise of compressed sensing is the following three "surprising" results:

1. It is possible to reconstruct any sparse signal fully if it was compressed by $\mathbf{x} \mapsto W\mathbf{x}$, where W is a matrix which satisfies a condition called the Restricted Isoperimetric Property (RIP). A matrix that satisfies this property is guaranteed to have a low distortion of the norm of any sparse representable vector.
2. The reconstruction can be calculated in polynomial time by solving a linear program.
3. A random $n \times d$ matrix is likely to satisfy the RIP condition provided that n is greater than an order of $s \log(d)$.

Formally,

Definition 23.5 (RIP). A matrix $W \in \mathbb{R}^{n,d}$ is (ϵ, s)-RIP if for all $\mathbf{x} \neq 0$ s.t. $\|\mathbf{x}\|_0 \leq s$ we have

$$\left| \frac{\|W\mathbf{x}\|_2^2}{\|\mathbf{x}\|_2^2} - 1 \right| \leq \epsilon.$$

The first theorem establishes that RIP matrices yield a lossless compression scheme for sparse vectors. It also provides a (nonefficient) reconstruction scheme.

Theorem 23.6. *Let $\epsilon < 1$ and let W be a $(\epsilon, 2s)$-RIP matrix. Let $\mathbf{x}$ be a vector s.t. $\|\mathbf{x}\|_0 \leq s$, let $\mathbf{y} = W\mathbf{x}$ be the compression of $\mathbf{x}$, and let*

$$\tilde{\mathbf{x}} \in \underset{\mathbf{v}: W\mathbf{v} = \mathbf{y}}{\operatorname{argmin}} \|\mathbf{v}\|_0$$

be a reconstructed vector. Then, $\tilde{\mathbf{x}} = \mathbf{x}$.

Proof. We assume, by way of contradiction, that $\tilde{\mathbf{x}} \neq \mathbf{x}$. Since $\mathbf{x}$ satisfies the constraints in the optimization problem that defines $\tilde{\mathbf{x}}$ we clearly have that $\|\tilde{\mathbf{x}}\|_0 \leq \|\mathbf{x}\|_0 \leq s$. Therefore, $\|\mathbf{x} - \tilde{\mathbf{x}}\|_0 \leq 2s$ and we can apply the RIP inequality on the vector $\mathbf{x} - \tilde{\mathbf{x}}$. But, since $W(\mathbf{x} - \tilde{\mathbf{x}}) = \mathbf{0}$ we get that $|0 - 1| \leq \epsilon$, which leads to a contradiction. □

The reconstruction scheme given in Theorem 23.6 seems to be nonefficient because we need to minimize a combinatorial objective (the sparsity of $\mathbf{v}$). Quite surprisingly, it turns out that we can replace the combinatorial objective, $\|\mathbf{v}\|_0$, with a convex objective, $\|\mathbf{v}\|_1$, which leads to a linear programming problem that can be solved efficiently. This is stated formally in the following theorem.

Theorem 23.7. *Assume that the conditions of Theorem 23.6 holds and that $\epsilon < \frac{1}{1+\sqrt{2}}$. Then,*

$$\mathbf{x} = \underset{\mathbf{v}: W\mathbf{v} = \mathbf{y}}{\operatorname{argmin}} \|\mathbf{v}\|_0 = \underset{\mathbf{v}: W\mathbf{v} = \mathbf{y}}{\operatorname{argmin}} \|\mathbf{v}\|_1.$$

In fact, we will prove a stronger result, which holds even if $\mathbf{x}$ is not a sparse vector.

Theorem 23.8. *Let $\epsilon < \frac{1}{1+\sqrt{2}}$ and let W be a $(\epsilon, 2s)$-RIP matrix. Let $\mathbf{x}$ be an arbitrary vector and denote*

$$\mathbf{x}_s \in \operatorname*{argmin}_{\mathbf{v}:\|\mathbf{v}\|_0 \le s} \|\mathbf{x}-\mathbf{v}\|_1.$$

That is, $\mathbf{x}_s$ is the vector which equals $\mathbf{x}$ on the s largest elements of $\mathbf{x}$ and equals 0 elsewhere. Let $\mathbf{y} = W\mathbf{x}$ be the compression of $\mathbf{x}$ and let

$$\mathbf{x}^\star \in \operatorname*{argmin}_{\mathbf{v}:W\mathbf{v}=\mathbf{y}} \|\mathbf{v}\|_1$$

be the reconstructed vector. Then,

$$\|\mathbf{x}^\star - \mathbf{x}\|_2 \le 2\frac{1+\rho}{1-\rho} s^{-1/2}\|\mathbf{x}-\mathbf{x}_s\|_1,$$

where $\rho = \sqrt{2}\epsilon/(1-\epsilon)$.

Note that in the special case that $\mathbf{x} = \mathbf{x}_s$ we get an exact recovery, $\mathbf{x}^\star = \mathbf{x}$, so Theorem 23.7 is a special case of Theorem 23.8. The proof of Theorem 23.8 is given in Section 23.3.1.

Finally, the third result tells us that random matrices with $n \ge \Omega(s\log(d))$ are likely to be RIP. In fact, the theorem shows that multiplying a random matrix by an orthonormal matrix also provides an RIP matrix. This is important for compressing signals of the form $\mathbf{x} = U\boldsymbol{\alpha}$ where $\mathbf{x}$ is not sparse but $\boldsymbol{\alpha}$ is sparse. In that case, if W is a random matrix and we compress using $\mathbf{y} = W\mathbf{x}$ then this is the same as compressing $\boldsymbol{\alpha}$ by $\mathbf{y} = (WU)\boldsymbol{\alpha}$ and since WU is also RIP we can reconstruct $\boldsymbol{\alpha}$ (and thus also $\mathbf{x}$) from $\mathbf{y}$.

Theorem 23.9. *Let U be an arbitrary fixed $d \times d$ orthonormal matrix, let ϵ, δ be scalars in $(0,1)$, let s be an integer in $[d]$, and let n be an integer that satisfies*

$$n \ge 100\frac{s\log(40d/(\delta\,\epsilon))}{\epsilon^2}.$$

Let $W \in \mathbb{R}^{n,d}$ be a matrix s.t. each element of W is distributed normally with zero mean and variance of $1/n$. Then, with proabability of at least $1-\delta$ over the choice of W, the matrix WU is (ϵ, s)-RIP.

23.3.1 Proofs*

Proof of Theorem 23.8

We follow a proof due to Candès (2008).

Let $\mathbf{h} = \mathbf{x}^\star - \mathbf{x}$. Given a vector $\mathbf{v}$ and a set of indices I we denote by $\mathbf{v}_I$ the vector whose ith element is v_i if $i \in I$ and 0 otherwise.

The first trick we use is to partition the set of indices $[d] = \{1,\ldots,d\}$ into disjoint sets of size s. That is, we will write $[d] = T_0 \cup T_1 \cup T_2 \ldots T_{d/s-1}$ where for all i, $|T_i| = s$, and we assume for simplicity that d/s is an integer. We define the partition as follows. In T_0 we put the s indices corresponding to the s largest elements in absolute values of $\mathbf{x}$ (ties are broken arbitrarily). Let $T_0^c = [d] \setminus T_0$. Next, T_1 will be the s indices corresponding to the s largest elements in absolute value of $\mathbf{h}_{T_0^c}$. Let $T_{0,1} = T_0 \cup T_1$ and $T_{0,1}^c = [d] \setminus T_{0,1}$. Next, T_2 will correspond to the s largest elements in absolute value of $\mathbf{h}_{T_{0,1}^c}$. And, we will construct $T_3, T_4, \ldots$ in the same way.

To prove the theorem we first need the following lemma, which shows that RIP also implies approximate orthogonality.

Lemma 23.10 *Let W be an $(\epsilon, 2s)$-RIP matrix. Then, for any two disjoint sets I, J, both of size at most s, and for any vector $\mathbf{u}$ we have that $\langle W\mathbf{u}_I, W\mathbf{u}_J \rangle \le \epsilon \|\mathbf{u}_I\|_2 \|\mathbf{u}_J\|_2$.*

Proof. W.l.o.g. assume $\|\mathbf{u}_I\|_2 = \|\mathbf{u}_J\|_2 = 1$.

$$\langle W\mathbf{u}_I, W\mathbf{u}_J \rangle = \frac{\|W\mathbf{u}_I + W\mathbf{u}_J\|_2^2 - \|W\mathbf{u}_I - W\mathbf{u}_J\|_2^2}{4}.$$

But, since $|J \cup I| \le 2s$ we get from the RIP condition that $\|W\mathbf{u}_I + W\mathbf{u}_J\|_2^2 \le (1+\epsilon)(\|\mathbf{u}_I\|_2^2 + \|\mathbf{u}_J\|_2^2) = 2(1+\epsilon)$ and that $-\|W\mathbf{u}_I - W\mathbf{u}_J\|_2^2 \le -(1-\epsilon)(\|\mathbf{u}_I\|_2^2 + \|\mathbf{u}_J\|_2^2) = -2(1-\epsilon)$, which concludes our proof. □

We are now ready to prove the theorem. Clearly,

$$\|\mathbf{h}\|_2 = \|\mathbf{h}_{T_{0,1}} + \mathbf{h}_{T_{0,1}^c}\|_2 \le \|\mathbf{h}_{T_{0,1}}\|_2 + \|\mathbf{h}_{T_{0,1}^c}\|_2. \tag{23.5}$$

To prove the theorem we will show the following two claims:

Claim 1: $\|\mathbf{h}_{T_{0,1}^c}\|_2 \le \|\mathbf{h}_{T_0}\|_2 + 2s^{-1/2}\|\mathbf{x} - \mathbf{x}_s\|_1$.

Claim 2: $\|\mathbf{h}_{T_{0,1}}\|_2 \le \frac{2\rho}{1-\rho} s^{-1/2}\|\mathbf{x} - \mathbf{x}_s\|_1$.

Combining these two claims with Equation (23.5) we get that

$$\begin{aligned}
\|\mathbf{h}\|_2 &\le \|\mathbf{h}_{T_{0,1}}\|_2 + \|\mathbf{h}_{T_{0,1}^c}\|_2 \le 2\|\mathbf{h}_{T_{0,1}}\|_2 + 2s^{-1/2}\|\mathbf{x} - \mathbf{x}_s\|_1 \\
&\le 2\left(\tfrac{2\rho}{1-\rho} + 1\right) s^{-1/2}\|\mathbf{x} - \mathbf{x}_s\|_1 \\
&= 2\frac{1+\rho}{1-\rho} s^{-1/2}\|\mathbf{x} - \mathbf{x}_s\|_1,
\end{aligned}$$

and this will conclude our proof.

Proving Claim 1:
To prove this claim we do not use the RIP condition at all but only use the fact that $\mathbf{x}^\star$ minimizes the ℓ_1 norm. Take $j > 1$. For each $i \in T_j$ and $i' \in T_{j-1}$ we have that $|h_i| \le |h_{i'}|$. Therefore, $\|\mathbf{h}_{T_j}\|_\infty \le \|\mathbf{h}_{T_{j-1}}\|_1 / s$. Thus,

$$\|\mathbf{h}_{T_j}\|_2 \le s^{1/2}\|\mathbf{h}_{T_j}\|_\infty \le s^{-1/2}\|\mathbf{h}_{T_{j-1}}\|_1.$$

Summing this over $j = 2, 3, \ldots$ and using the triangle inequality we obtain that

$$\|\mathbf{h}_{T_{0,1}^c}\|_2 \le \sum_{j \ge 2} \|\mathbf{h}_{T_j}\|_2 \le s^{-1/2}\|\mathbf{h}_{T_0^c}\|_1 \tag{23.6}$$

Next, we show that $\|\mathbf{h}_{T_0^c}\|_1$ cannot be large. Indeed, from the definition of $\mathbf{x}^\star$ we have that $\|\mathbf{x}\|_1 \geq \|\mathbf{x}^\star\|_1 = \|\mathbf{x}+\mathbf{h}\|_1$. Thus, using the triangle inequality we obtain that

$$\|\mathbf{x}\|_1 \geq \|\mathbf{x}+\mathbf{h}\|_1 = \sum_{i\in T_0} |x_i + h_i| + \sum_{i \in T_0^c} |x_i + h_i| \geq \|\mathbf{x}_{T_0}\|_1 - \|\mathbf{h}_{T_0}\|_1 + \|\mathbf{h}_{T_0^c}\|_1 - \|\mathbf{x}_{T_0^c}\|_1 \tag{23.7}$$

and since $\|\mathbf{x}_{T_0^c}\|_1 = \|\mathbf{x} - \mathbf{x}_s\|_1 = \|\mathbf{x}\|_1 - \|\mathbf{x}_{T_0}\|_1$ we get that

$$\|\mathbf{h}_{T_0^c}\|_1 \leq \|\mathbf{h}_{T_0}\|_1 + 2\|\mathbf{x}_{T_0^c}\|_1. \tag{23.8}$$

Combining this with Equation (23.6) we get that

$$\|\mathbf{h}_{T_{0,1}^c}\|_2 \leq s^{-1/2}\left(\|\mathbf{h}_{T_0}\|_1 + 2\|\mathbf{x}_{T_0^c}\|_1\right) \leq \|\mathbf{h}_{T_0}\|_2 + 2s^{-1/2}\|\mathbf{x}_{T_0^c}\|_1,$$

which concludes the proof of claim 1.

Proving Claim 2:
For the second claim we use the RIP condition to get that

$$(1-\epsilon)\|\mathbf{h}_{T_{0,1}}\|_2^2 \leq \|W\mathbf{h}_{T_{0,1}}\|_2^2. \tag{23.9}$$

Since $W\mathbf{h}_{T_{0,1}} = W\mathbf{h} - \sum_{j\geq 2} W\mathbf{h}_{T_j} = -\sum_{j\geq 2} W\mathbf{h}_{T_j}$ we have that

$$\|W\mathbf{h}_{T_{0,1}}\|_2^2 = -\sum_{j\geq 2}\langle W\mathbf{h}_{T_{0,1}}, W\mathbf{h}_{T_j}\rangle = -\sum_{j\geq 2}\langle W\mathbf{h}_{T_0} + W\mathbf{h}_{T_1}, W\mathbf{h}_{T_j}\rangle.$$

From the RIP condition on inner products we obtain that for all $i \in \{1,2\}$ and $j \geq 2$ we have

$$|\langle W\mathbf{h}_{T_i}, W\mathbf{h}_{T_j}\rangle| \leq \epsilon\|\mathbf{h}_{T_i}\|_2\|\mathbf{h}_{T_j}\|_2.$$

Since $\|\mathbf{h}_{T_0}\|_2 + \|\mathbf{h}_{T_1}\|_2 \leq \sqrt{2}\|\mathbf{h}_{T_{0,1}}\|_2$ we therefore get that

$$\|W\mathbf{h}_{T_{0,1}}\|_2^2 \;\leq\; \sqrt{2}\epsilon\|\mathbf{h}_{T_{0,1}}\|_2 \sum_{j\geq 2}\|\mathbf{h}_{T_j}\|_2.$$

Combining this with Equation (23.6) and Equation (23.9) we obtain

$$(1-\epsilon)\|\mathbf{h}_{T_{0,1}}\|_2^2 \leq \sqrt{2}\epsilon\|\mathbf{h}_{T_{0,1}}\|_2 s^{-1/2}\|\mathbf{h}_{T_0^c}\|_1.$$

Rearranging the inequality gives

$$\|\mathbf{h}_{T_{0,1}}\|_2 \leq \frac{\sqrt{2}\epsilon}{1-\epsilon}s^{-1/2}\|\mathbf{h}_{T_0^c}\|_1.$$

Finally, using Equation (23.8) we get that

$$\|\mathbf{h}_{T_{0,1}}\|_2 \leq \rho s^{-1/2}(\|\mathbf{h}_{T_0}\|_1 + 2\|\mathbf{x}_{T_0^c}\|_1) \leq \rho\|\mathbf{h}_{T_0}\|_2 + 2\rho s^{-1/2}\|\mathbf{x}_{T_0^c}\|_1,$$

but since $\|\mathbf{h}_{T_0}\|_2 \leq \|\mathbf{h}_{T_{0,1}}\|_2$ this implies

$$\|\mathbf{h}_{T_{0,1}}\|_2 \leq \frac{2\rho}{1-\rho}s^{-1/2}\|\mathbf{x}_{T_0^c}\|_1,$$

which concludes the proof of the second claim.

Proof of Theorem 23.9

To prove the theorem we follow an approach due to (Baraniuk, Davenport, DeVore & Wakin 2008). The idea is to combine the Johnson-Lindenstrauss (JL) lemma with a simple covering argument.

We start with a covering property of the unit ball.

Lemma 23.11 *Let $\epsilon \in (0,1)$. There exists a finite set $Q \subset \mathbb{R}^d$ of size $|Q| \le \left(\frac{3}{\epsilon}\right)^d$ such that*

$$\sup_{\mathbf{x}:\|\mathbf{x}\|\le 1} \min_{\mathbf{v}\in Q} \|\mathbf{x}-\mathbf{v}\| \le \epsilon.$$

Proof. Let k be an integer and let

$$Q' = \{\mathbf{x} \in \mathbb{R}^d : \forall j \in [d], \exists i \in \{-k, -k+1, \ldots, k\} \text{ s.t. } x_j = \tfrac{i}{k}\}.$$

Clearly, $|Q'| = (2k+1)^d$. We shall set $Q = Q' \cap B_2(1)$, where $B_2(1)$ is the unit ℓ_2 ball of $\mathbb{R}^d$. Since the points in Q' are distributed evenly on the unit ℓ_∞ ball, the size of Q is the size of Q' times the ratio between the volumes of the unit ℓ_2 and ℓ_∞ balls. The volume of the ℓ_∞ ball is 2^d and the volume of $B_2(1)$ is

$$\frac{\pi^{d/2}}{\Gamma(1+d/2)}.$$

For simplicity, assume that d is even and therefore

$$\Gamma(1+d/2) = (d/2)! \ge \left(\frac{d/2}{e}\right)^{d/2},$$

where in the last inequality we used Stirling's approximation. Overall we obtained that

$$|Q| \le (2k+1)^d\,(\pi/e)^{d/2}\,(d/2)^{-d/2}\,2^{-d}. \tag{23.10}$$

Now let us specify k. For each $\mathbf{x} \in B_2(1)$ let $\mathbf{v} \in Q$ be the vector whose ith element is $\text{sign}(x_i)\,\lfloor |x_i|\,k \rfloor / k$. Then, for each element we have that $|x_i - v_i| \le 1/k$ and thus

$$\|\mathbf{x}-\mathbf{v}\| \le \frac{\sqrt{d}}{k}.$$

To ensure that the right-hand side will be at most ϵ we shall set $k = \lceil \sqrt{d}/\epsilon \rceil$. Plugging this value into Equation (23.10) we conclude that

$$|Q| \le (3\sqrt{d}/(2\epsilon))^d\,(\pi/e)^{d/2}\,(d/2)^{-d/2} = \left(\frac{3}{\epsilon}\sqrt{\frac{\pi}{2e}}\right)^d \le \left(\frac{3}{\epsilon}\right)^d.$$

□

Let $\mathbf{x}$ be a vector that can be written as $\mathbf{x} = U\boldsymbol{\alpha}$ with U being some orthonormal matrix and $\|\boldsymbol{\alpha}\|_0 \le s$. Combining the earlier covering property and the JL lemma (Lemma 23.4) enables us to show that a random W will not distort any such $\mathbf{x}$.

Lemma 23.12 *Let U be an orthonormal $d \times d$ matrix and let $I \subset [d]$ be a set of indices of size $|I| = s$. Let S be the span of $\{U_i : i \in I\}$, where U_i is the ith column of U. Let $\delta \in (0,1)$, $\epsilon \in (0,1)$, and $n \in \mathbb{N}$ such that*

$$n \ge 24\,\frac{\log(2/\delta) + s\,\log(12/\epsilon)}{\epsilon^2}.$$

Then, with probability of at least $1-\delta$ over a choice of a random matrix $W \in \mathbb{R}^{n,d}$ such that each element of W is independently distributed according to $N(0,1/n)$, we have

$$\sup_{\mathbf{x}\in S}\left|\frac{\|W\mathbf{x}\|}{\|\mathbf{x}\|}-1\right| < \epsilon.$$

Proof. It suffices to prove the lemma for all $\mathbf{x}\in S$ with $\|\mathbf{x}\|=1$. We can write $\mathbf{x}=U_I\boldsymbol{\alpha}$ where $\boldsymbol{\alpha}\in\mathbb{R}^s$, $\|\boldsymbol{\alpha}\|_2=1$, and U_I is the matrix whose columns are $\{U_i : i\in I\}$. Using Lemma 23.11 we know that there exists a set Q of size $|Q|\le(12/\epsilon)^s$ such that

$$\sup_{\alpha:\|\alpha\|=1}\min_{\mathbf{v}\in Q}\|\boldsymbol{\alpha}-\mathbf{v}\|\le(\epsilon/4).$$

But since U is orthogonal we also have that

$$\sup_{\alpha:\|\alpha\|=1}\min_{\mathbf{v}\in Q}\|U_I\boldsymbol{\alpha}-U_I\mathbf{v}\|\le(\epsilon/4).$$

Applying Lemma 23.4 on the set $\{U_I\mathbf{v}:\mathbf{v}\in Q\}$ we obtain that for n satisfying the condition given in the lemma, the following holds with probability of at least $1-\delta$:

$$\sup_{\mathbf{v}\in Q}\left|\frac{\|WU_I\mathbf{v}\|^2}{\|U_I\mathbf{v}\|^2}-1\right|\le\epsilon/2,$$

This also implies that

$$\sup_{\mathbf{v}\in Q}\left|\frac{\|WU_I\mathbf{v}\|}{\|U_I\mathbf{v}\|}-1\right|\le\epsilon/2.$$

Let a be the smallest number such that

$$\forall\mathbf{x}\in S,\quad\frac{\|W\mathbf{x}\|}{\|\mathbf{x}\|}\le 1+a.$$

Clearly $a<\infty$. Our goal is to show that $a\le\epsilon$. This follows from the fact that for any $\mathbf{x}\in S$ of unit norm there exists $\mathbf{v}\in Q$ such that $\|\mathbf{x}-U_I\mathbf{v}\|\le\epsilon/4$ and therefore

$$\|W\mathbf{x}\|\le\|WU_I\mathbf{v}\|+\|W(\mathbf{x}-U_I\mathbf{v})\|\le 1+\epsilon/2+(1+a)\epsilon/4.$$

Thus,

$$\forall\mathbf{x}\in S,\quad\frac{\|W\mathbf{x}\|}{\|\mathbf{x}\|}\le 1+\left(\epsilon/2+(1+a)\epsilon/4\right).$$

But the definition of a implies that

$$a\le\epsilon/2+(1+a)\epsilon/4\ \Rightarrow\ a\le\frac{\epsilon/2+\epsilon/4}{1-\epsilon/4}\le\epsilon.$$

This proves that for all $\mathbf{x}\in S$ we have $\frac{\|W\mathbf{x}\|}{\|\mathbf{x}\|}-1\le\epsilon$. The other side follows from this as well since

$$\|W\mathbf{x}\|\ge\|WU_I\mathbf{v}\|-\|W(\mathbf{x}-U_I\mathbf{v})\|\ge 1-\epsilon/2-(1+\epsilon)\epsilon/4\ge 1-\epsilon.$$

□

The preceding lemma tells us that for $\mathbf{x}\in S$ of unit norm we have

$$(1-\epsilon)\le\|W\mathbf{x}\|\le(1+\epsilon),$$

which implies that

$$(1-2\epsilon) \leq \|W\mathbf{x}\|^2 \leq (1+3\epsilon).$$

The proof of Theorem 23.9 follows from this by a union bound over all choices of I.

23.4 PCA OR COMPRESSED SENSING?

Suppose we would like to apply a dimensionality reduction technique to a given set of examples. Which method should we use, PCA or compressed sensing? In this section we tackle this question, by underscoring the underlying assumptions behind the two methods.

It is helpful first to understand when each of the methods can guarantee perfect recovery. PCA guarantees perfect recovery whenever the set of examples is contained in an n dimensional subspace of $\mathbb{R}^d$. Compressed sensing guarantees perfect recovery whenever the set of examples is sparse (in some basis). On the basis of these observations, we can describe cases in which PCA will be better than compressed sensing and vice versa.

As a first example, suppose that the examples are the vectors of the standard basis of $\mathbb{R}^d$, namely, $\mathbf{e}_1,\ldots,\mathbf{e}_d$, where each $\mathbf{e}_i$ is the all zeros vector except 1 in the ith coordinate. In this case, the examples are 1-sparse. Hence, compressed sensing will yield a perfect recovery whenever $n \geq \Omega(\log(d))$. On the other hand, PCA will lead to poor performance, since the data is far from being in an n dimensional subspace, as long as $n < d$. Indeed, it is easy ro verify that in such a case, the averaged recovery error of PCA (i.e., the objective of Equation (23.1) divided by m) will be $(d-n)/d$, which is larger than $1/2$ whenever $n \leq d/2$.

We next show a case where PCA is better than compressed sensing. Consider m examples that are exactly on an n dimensional subspace. Clearly, in such a case, PCA will lead to perfect recovery. As to compressed sensing, note that the examples are n-sparse in any orthonormal basis whose first n vectors span the subspace. Therefore, compressed sensing would also work if we will reduce the dimension to $\Omega(n\log(d))$. However, with exactly n dimensions, compressed sensing might fail. PCA has also better resilience to certain types of noise. See (Chang, Weiss & Freeman 2009) for a discussion.

23.5 SUMMARY

We introduced two methods for dimensionality reduction using linear transformations: PCA and random projections. We have shown that PCA is optimal in the sense of averaged squared reconstruction error, if we restrict the reconstruction procedure to be linear as well. However, if we allow nonlinear reconstruction, PCA is not necessarily the optimal procedure. In particular, for sparse data, random projections can significantly outperform PCA. This fact is at the heart of the compressed sensing method.

23.6 BIBLIOGRAPHIC REMARKS

PCA is equivalent to best subspace approximation using singular value decomposition (SVD). The SVD method is described in Appendix C. SVD dates back to

Eugenio Beltrami (1873) and Camille Jordan (1874). It has been rediscovered many times. In the statistical literature, it was introduced by Pearson (1901). Besides PCA and SVD, there are additional names that refer to the same idea and are being used in different scientific communities. A few examples are the Eckart-Young theorem (after Carl Eckart and Gale Young who analyzed the method in 1936), the Schmidt-Mirsky theorem, factor analysis, and the Hotelling transform.

Compressed sensing was introduced in Donoho (2006) and in (Candes & Tao 2005). See also Candes (2006).

23.7 EXERCISES

23.1 In this exercise we show that in the general case, exact recovery of a linear compression scheme is impossible.

1. let $A \in \mathbb{R}^{n,d}$ be an arbitrary compression matrix where $n \le d-1$. Show that there exists $\mathbf{u}, \mathbf{v} \in \mathbb{R}^n$, $\mathbf{u} \neq \mathbf{v}$ such that $A\mathbf{u} = A\mathbf{v}$.
2. Conclude that exact recovery of a linear compression scheme is impossible.

23.2 Let $\boldsymbol{\alpha} \in \mathbb{R}^d$ such that $\alpha_1 \ge \alpha_2 \ge \cdots \ge \alpha_d \ge 0$. Show that

$$\max_{\boldsymbol{\beta} \in [0,1]^d : \|\boldsymbol{\beta}\|_1 \le n} \sum_{j=1}^{d} \alpha_j \beta_j = \sum_{j=1}^{n} \alpha_j .$$

Hint: Take every vector $\boldsymbol{\beta} \in [0,1]^d$ such that $\|\boldsymbol{\beta}\|_1 \le n$. Let i be the minimal index for which $\beta_i < 1$. If $i = n+1$ we are done. Otherwise, show that we can increase β_i, while possibly decreasing β_j for some $j > i$, and obtain a better solution. This will imply that the optimal solution is to set $\beta_i = 1$ for $i \le n$ and $\beta_i = 0$ for $i > n$.

23.3 **Kernel PCA:** In this exercise we show how PCA can be used for constructing nonlinear dimensionality reduction on the basis of the kernel trick (see Chapter 16).

Let $\mathcal{X}$ be some instance space and let $S = \{\mathbf{x}_1, \ldots, \mathbf{x}_m\}$ be a set of points in $\mathcal{X}$. Consider a feature mapping $\psi : \mathcal{X} \to V$, where V is some Hilbert space (possibly of infinite dimension). Let $K : \mathcal{X} \times \mathcal{X}$ be a kernel function, that is, $k(\mathbf{x}, \mathbf{x}') = \langle \psi(\mathbf{x}), \psi(\mathbf{x}') \rangle$. Kernel PCA is the process of mapping the elements in S into V using ψ, and then applying PCA over $\{\psi(\mathbf{x}_1), \ldots, \psi(\mathbf{x}_m)\}$ into $\mathbb{R}^n$. The output of this process is the set of reduced elements.

Show how this process can be done in polynomial time in terms of m and n, assuming that each evaluation of $K(\cdot,\cdot)$ can be calculated in a constant time. In particular, if your implementation requires multiplication of two matrices A and B, verify that their product can be computed. Similarly, if an eigenvalue decomposition of some matrix C is required, verify that this decomposition can be computed.

23.4 **An Interpretation of PCA as Variance Maximization:**

Let $\mathbf{x}_1, \ldots, \mathbf{x}_m$ be m vectors in $\mathbb{R}^d$, and let $\mathbf{x}$ be a random vector distributed according to the uniform distribution over $\mathbf{x}_1, \ldots, \mathbf{x}_m$. Assume that $\mathbb{E}[\mathbf{x}] = \mathbf{0}$.

1. Consider the problem of finding a unit vector, $\mathbf{w} \in \mathbb{R}^d$, such that the random variable $\langle \mathbf{w}, \mathbf{x} \rangle$ has maximal variance. That is, we would like to solve the problem

$$\underset{\mathbf{w}:\|\mathbf{w}\|=1}{\operatorname{argmax}} \operatorname{Var}[\langle \mathbf{w}, \mathbf{x} \rangle] = \underset{\mathbf{w}:\|\mathbf{w}\|=1}{\operatorname{argmax}} \frac{1}{m} \sum_{i=1}^{m} (\langle \mathbf{w}, \mathbf{x}_i \rangle)^2 .$$

Show that the solution of the problem is to set $\mathbf{w}$ to be the first principle vector of $\mathbf{x}_1, \ldots, \mathbf{x}_m$.

2. Let $\mathbf{w}_1$ be the first principal component as in the previous question. Now, suppose we would like to find a second unit vector, $\mathbf{w}_2 \in \mathbb{R}^d$, that maximizes the variance of $\langle \mathbf{w}_2, \mathbf{x} \rangle$, but is also uncorrelated to $\langle \mathbf{w}_1, \mathbf{x} \rangle$. That is, we would like to solve

$$\underset{\mathbf{w}:\|\mathbf{w}\|=1,\ \mathbb{E}[(\langle \mathbf{w}_1,\mathbf{x}\rangle)(\langle \mathbf{w},\mathbf{x}\rangle)]=0}{\operatorname{argmax}} \quad \operatorname{Var}[\langle \mathbf{w}, \mathbf{x} \rangle].$$

Show that the solution to this problem is to set $\mathbf{w}$ to be the second principal component of $\mathbf{x}_1, \ldots, \mathbf{x}_m$.
Hint: Note that

$$\mathbb{E}[(\langle \mathbf{w}_1, \mathbf{x} \rangle)(\langle \mathbf{w}, \mathbf{x} \rangle)] = \mathbf{w}_1^\top \mathbb{E}[\mathbf{x}\mathbf{x}^\top]\mathbf{w} = m\mathbf{w}_1^\top A\mathbf{w},$$

where $A = \sum_i \mathbf{x}_i \mathbf{x}_i^\top$. Since $\mathbf{w}$ is an eigenvector of A we have that the constraint $\mathbb{E}[(\langle \mathbf{w}_1, \mathbf{x} \rangle)(\langle \mathbf{w}, \mathbf{x} \rangle)] = 0$ is equivalent to the constraint

$$\langle \mathbf{w}_1, \mathbf{w} \rangle = 0.$$

23.5 **The Relation between SVD and PCA:** Use the SVD theorem (Corollary C.6) for providing an alternative proof of Theorem 23.2.

23.6 **Random Projections Preserve Inner Products:** The Johnson-Lindenstrauss lemma tells us that a random projection preserves distances between a finite set of vectors. In this exercise you need to prove that if the set of vectors are within the unit ball, then not only are the distances between any two vectors preserved, but the inner product is also preserved.

Let Q be a finite set of vectors in $\mathbb{R}^d$ and assume that for every $\mathbf{x} \in Q$ we have $\|\mathbf{x}\| \le 1$.

1. Let $\delta \in (0,1)$ and n be an integer such that

$$\epsilon = \sqrt{\frac{6\log(|Q|^2/\delta)}{n}} \le 3.$$

Prove that with probability of at least $1 - \delta$ over a choice of a random matrix $W \in \mathbb{R}^{n,d}$, where each element of W is independently distributed according to $\mathcal{N}(0, 1/n)$, we have

$$|\langle W\mathbf{u}, W\mathbf{v} \rangle - \langle \mathbf{u}, \mathbf{v} \rangle| \le \epsilon$$

for every $\mathbf{u}, \mathbf{v} \in Q$.
Hint: Use JL to bound both $\frac{\|W(\mathbf{u}+\mathbf{v})\|}{\|\mathbf{u}+\mathbf{v}\|}$ and $\frac{\|W(\mathbf{u}-\mathbf{v})\|}{\|\mathbf{u}-\mathbf{v}\|}$.

2. **(*)** Let $\mathbf{x}_1, \ldots, \mathbf{x}_m$ be a set of vectors in $\mathbb{R}^d$ of norm at most 1, and assume that these vectors are linearly separable with margin of γ. Assume that $d \gg 1/\gamma^2$. Show that there exists a constant $c > 0$ such that if we randomly project these vectors into $\mathbb{R}^n$, for $n = c/\gamma^2$, then with probability of at least 99% it holds that the projected vectors are linearly separable with margin $\gamma/2$.

24

Generative Models

We started this book with a *distribution free* learning framework; namely, we did not impose any assumptions on the underlying distribution over the data. Furthermore, we followed a *discriminative* approach in which our goal is not to learn the underlying distribution but rather to learn an accurate predictor. In this chapter we describe a *generative* approach, in which it is assumed that the underlying distribution over the data has a specific parametric form and our goal is to estimate the parameters of the model. This task is called *parametric density estimation*.

The discriminative approach has the advantage of directly optimizing the quantity of interest (the prediction accuracy) instead of learning the underlying distribution. This was phrased as follows by Vladimir Vapnik in his principle for solving problems using a restricted amount of information:

When solving a given problem, try to avoid a more general problem as an intermediate step.

Of course, if we succeed in learning the underlying distribution accurately, we are considered to be "experts" in the sense that we can predict by using the Bayes optimal classifier. The problem is that it is usually more difficult to learn the underlying distribution than to learn an accurate predictor. However, in some situations, it is reasonable to adopt the generative learning approach. For example, sometimes it is easier (computationally) to estimate the parameters of the model than to learn a discriminative predictor. Additionally, in some cases we do not have a specific task at hand but rather would like to model the data either for making predictions at a later time without having to retrain a predictor or for the sake of interpretability of the data.

We start with a popular statistical method for estimating the parameters of the data, which is called the maximum likelihood principle. Next, we describe two generative assumptions which greatly simplify the learning process. We also describe the EM algorithm for calculating the maximum likelihood in the presence of latent variables. We conclude with a brief description of Bayesian reasoning.

24.1 MAXIMUM LIKELIHOOD ESTIMATOR

Let us start with a simple example. A drug company developed a new drug to treat some deadly disease. We would like to estimate the probability of survival when using the drug. To do so, the drug company sampled a training set of m people and gave them the drug. Let $S = (x_1, \ldots, x_m)$ denote the training set, where for each i, $x_i = 1$ if the ith person survived and $x_i = 0$ otherwise. We can model the underlying distribution using a single parameter, $\theta \in [0,1]$, indicating the probability of survival.

We now would like to estimate the parameter θ on the basis of the training set S. A natural idea is to use the average number of 1's in S as an estimator. That is,

$$\hat{\theta} = \frac{1}{m} \sum_{i=1}^{m} x_i. \tag{24.1}$$

Clearly, $\mathbb{E}_S[\hat{\theta}] = \theta$. That is, $\hat{\theta}$ is an *unbiased estimator* of θ. Furthermore, since $\hat{\theta}$ is the average of m i.i.d. binary random variables we can use Hoeffding's inequality to get that with probability of at least $1 - \delta$ over the choice of S we have that

$$|\hat{\theta} - \theta| \le \sqrt{\frac{\log(2/\delta)}{2m}}. \tag{24.2}$$

Another interpretation of $\hat{\theta}$ is as the *Maximum Likelihood Estimator*, as we formally explain now. We first write the probability of generating the sample S:

$$\mathbb{P}[S = (x_1, \ldots, x_m)] = \prod_{i=1}^{m} \theta^{x_i} (1-\theta)^{1-x_i} = \theta^{\sum_i x_i} (1-\theta)^{\sum_i (1-x_i)}.$$

We define the *log likelihood* of S, given the parameter θ, as the log of the preceding expression:

$$L(S;\theta) = \log\left(\mathbb{P}[S = (x_1, \ldots, x_m)]\right) = \log(\theta) \sum_i x_i + \log(1-\theta) \sum_i (1 - x_i).$$

The maximum likelihood estimator is the parameter that maximizes the likelihood

$$\hat{\theta} \in \operatorname*{argmax}_{\theta} L(S;\theta). \tag{24.3}$$

Next, we show that in our case, Equation (24.1) is a maximum likelihood estimator. To see this, we take the derivative of $L(S;\theta)$ with respect to θ and equate it to zero:

$$\frac{\sum_i x_i}{\theta} - \frac{\sum_i (1 - x_i)}{1 - \theta} = 0.$$

Solving the equation for θ we obtain the estimator given in Equation (24.1).

24.1.1 Maximum Likelihood Estimation for Continuous Random Variables

Let X be a continuous random variable. Then, for most $x \in \mathbb{R}$ we have $\mathbb{P}[X = x] = 0$ and therefore the definition of likelihood as given before is trivialized. To overcome this technical problem we define the likelihood as log of the *density* of the probability of X at x. That is, given an i.i.d. training set $S = (x_1, \ldots, x_m)$ sampled according to a density distribution $\mathcal{P}_\theta$ we define the likelihood of S given θ as

$$L(S;\theta) = \log\left(\prod_{i=1}^{m} \mathcal{P}_\theta(x_i)\right) = \sum_{i=1}^{m} \log(\mathcal{P}_\theta(x_i)).$$

As before, the maximum likelihood estimator is a maximizer of $L(S;\theta)$ with respect to θ.

As an example, consider a Gaussian random variable, for which the density function of X is parameterized by $\theta = (\mu, \sigma)$ and is defined as follows:

$$\mathcal{P}_\theta(x) = \frac{1}{\sigma\sqrt{2\pi}} \exp\left(-\frac{(x-\mu)^2}{2\sigma^2}\right).$$

We can rewrite the likelihood as

$$L(S;\theta) = -\frac{1}{2\sigma^2}\sum_{i=1}^{m}(x_i-\mu)^2 - m\log(\sigma\sqrt{2\pi}).$$

To find a parameter $\theta = (\mu, \sigma)$ that optimizes this we take the derivative of the likelihood w.r.t. μ and w.r.t. σ and compare it to 0. We obtain the following two equations:

$$\frac{d}{d\mu}L(S;\theta) = \frac{1}{\sigma^2}\sum_{i=1}^{m}(x_i-\mu) = 0$$

$$\frac{d}{d\sigma}L(S;\theta) = \frac{1}{\sigma^3}\sum_{i=1}^{m}(x_i-\mu)^2 - \frac{m}{\sigma} = 0$$

Solving the preceding equations we obtain the maximum likelihood estimates:

$$\hat{\mu} = \frac{1}{m}\sum_{i=1}^{m}x_i \quad \text{and} \quad \hat{\sigma} = \sqrt{\frac{1}{m}\sum_{i=1}^{m}(x_i-\hat{\mu})^2}$$

Note that the maximum likelihood estimate is not always an unbiased estimator. For example, while $\hat{\mu}$ is unbiased, it is possible to show that the estimate $\hat{\sigma}$ of the variance is biased (Exercise 24.1).

Simplifying Notation

To simplify our notation, we use $\mathcal{P}[X = x]$ in this chapter to describe both the probability that $X = x$ (for discrete random variables) and the density of the distribution at x (for continuous variables).

24.1.2 Maximum Likelihood and Empirical Risk Minimization

The maximum likelihood estimator shares some similarity with the Empirical Risk Minimization (ERM) principle, which we studied extensively in previous chapters. Recall that in the ERM principle we have a hypothesis class $\mathcal{H}$ and we use the training set for choosing a hypothesis $h \in \mathcal{H}$ that minimizes the empirical risk. We now show that the maximum likelihood estimator is an ERM for a particular loss function.

Given a parameter θ and an observation x, we define the loss of θ on x as

$$\ell(\theta, x) = -\log(\mathcal{P}_\theta[x]). \tag{24.4}$$

That is, $\ell(\theta, x)$ is the negation of the log-likelihood of the observation x, assuming the data is distributed according to $\mathcal{P}_\theta$. This loss function is often referred to as the log-loss. On the basis of this definition it is immediate that the maximum likelihood principle is equivalent to minimizing the empirical risk with respect to the loss function given in Equation (24.4). That is,

$$\underset{\theta}{\operatorname{argmin}} \sum_{i=1}^{m} (-\log(\mathcal{P}_\theta[x_i])) = \underset{\theta}{\operatorname{argmax}} \sum_{i=1}^{m} \log(\mathcal{P}_\theta[x_i]).$$

Assuming that the data is distributed according to a distribution $\mathcal{P}$ (not necessarily of the parametric form we employ), the true risk of a parameter θ becomes

$$\begin{aligned} \mathop{\mathbb{E}}_x[\ell(\theta, x)] &= -\sum_x \mathcal{P}[x] \log(\mathcal{P}_\theta[x]) \\ &= \underbrace{\sum_x \mathcal{P}[x] \log\left(\frac{\mathcal{P}[x]}{\mathcal{P}_\theta[x]}\right)}_{D_{\mathrm{RE}}[\mathcal{P}||\mathcal{P}_\theta]} + \underbrace{\sum_x \mathcal{P}[x] \log\left(\frac{1}{\mathcal{P}[x]}\right)}_{H(\mathcal{P})}, \end{aligned} \tag{24.5}$$

where D_{RE} is called the *relative entropy*, and H is called the *entropy function*. The relative entropy is a divergence measure between two probabilities. For discrete variables, it is always nonnegative and is equal to 0 only if the two distributions are the same. It follows that the true risk is minimal when $\mathcal{P}_\theta = \mathcal{P}$.

The expression given in Equation (24.5) underscores how our generative assumption affects our density estimation, even in the limit of infinite data. It shows that if the underlying distribution is indeed of a parametric form, then by choosing the correct parameter we can make the risk be the entropy of the distribution. However, if the distribution is not of the assumed parametric form, even the best parameter leads to an inferior model and the suboptimality is measured by the relative entropy divergence.

24.1.3 Generalization Analysis

How good is the maximum likelihood estimator when we learn from a finite training set?

To answer this question we need to define how we assess the quality of an approximated solution of the density estimation problem. Unlike discriminative learning, where there is a clear notion of "loss," in generative learning there are various ways to define the loss of a model. On the basis of the previous subsection, one natural candidate is the expected log-loss as given in Equation (24.5).

In some situations, it is easy to prove that the maximum likelihood principle guarantees low true risk as well. For example, consider the problem of estimating the mean of a Gaussian variable of unit variance. We saw previously that the maximum likelihood estimator is the average: $\hat{\mu} = \frac{1}{m}\sum_i x_i$. Let $\mu^\star$ be the optimal parameter. Then,

$$\begin{aligned}
\mathop{\mathbb{E}}_{x\sim N(\mu^\star,1)}[\ell(\hat{\mu},x)-\ell(\mu^\star,x)] &= \mathop{\mathbb{E}}_{x\sim N(\mu^\star,1)} \log\left(\frac{\mathcal{P}_{\mu^\star}[x]}{\mathcal{P}_{\hat{\mu}}[x]}\right)\\
&= \mathop{\mathbb{E}}_{x\sim N(\mu^\star,1)}\left(-\frac{1}{2}(x-\mu^\star)^2+\frac{1}{2}(x-\hat{\mu})^2\right)\\
&= \frac{\hat{\mu}^2}{2}-\frac{(\mu^\star)^2}{2}+(\mu^\star-\hat{\mu})\mathop{\mathbb{E}}_{x\sim N(\mu^\star,1)}[x]\\
&= \frac{\hat{\mu}^2}{2}-\frac{(\mu^\star)^2}{2}+(\mu^\star-\hat{\mu})\mu^\star\\
&= \frac{1}{2}(\hat{\mu}-\mu^\star)^2. \qquad (24.6)
\end{aligned}$$

Next, we note that $\hat{\mu}$ is the average of m Gaussian variables and therefore it is also distributed normally with mean $\mu^\star$ and variance $\sigma^\star/m$. From this fact we can derive bounds of the form: with probability of at least $1-\delta$ we have that $|\hat{\mu}-\mu^\star|\leq\epsilon$ where ϵ depends on $\sigma^\star/m$ and on δ.

In some situations, the maximum likelihood estimator clearly overfits. For example, consider a Bernoulli random variable X and let $\mathcal{P}[X=1]=\theta^\star$. As we saw previously, using Hoeffding's inequality we can easily derive a guarantee on $|\theta^\star-\hat{\theta}|$ that holds with high probability (see Equation (24.2)). However, if our goal is to obtain a small value of the expected log-loss function as defined in Equation (24.5) we might fail. For example, assume that $\theta^\star$ is nonzero but very small. Then, the probability that no element of a sample of size m will be 1 is $(1-\theta^\star)^m$, which is greater than $e^{-2\theta^\star m}$. It follows that whenever $m\leq\frac{\log(2)}{2\theta^\star}$, the probability that the sample is all zeros is at least 50%, and in that case, the maximum likelihood rule will set $\hat{\theta}=0$. But the true risk of the estimate $\hat{\theta}=0$ is

$$\begin{aligned}
\mathop{\mathbb{E}}_{x\sim\theta^\star}[\ell(\hat{\theta},x)] &= \theta^\star\ell(\hat{\theta},1)+(1-\theta^\star)\ell(\hat{\theta},0)\\
&= \theta^\star\log(1/\hat{\theta})+(1-\theta^\star)\log(1/(1-\hat{\theta}))\\
&= \theta^\star\log(1/0)=\infty.
\end{aligned}$$

This simple example shows that we should be careful in applying the maximum likelihood principle.

To overcome overfitting, we can use the variety of tools we encountered previously in the book. A simple regularization technique is outlined in Exercise 24.2.

24.2 NAIVE BAYES

The Naive Bayes classifier is a classical demonstration of how generative assumptions and parameter estimations simplify the learning process. Consider the problem of predicting a label $y\in\{0,1\}$ on the basis of a vector of features $\mathbf{x}=(x_1,\ldots,x_d)$, where we assume that each x_i is in $\{0,1\}$. Recall that the Bayes optimal classifier is

$$h_{\text{Bayes}}(\mathbf{x})=\mathop{\text{argmax}}_{y\in\{0,1\}}\mathcal{P}[Y=y|X=\mathbf{x}].$$

To describe the probability function $\mathcal{P}[Y=y|X=\mathbf{x}]$ we need 2^d parameters, each of which corresponds to $\mathcal{P}[Y=1|X=\mathbf{x}]$ for a certain value of $\mathbf{x} \in \{0,1\}^d$. This implies that the number of examples we need grows exponentially with the number of features.

In the Naive Bayes approach we make the (rather naive) generative assumption that given the label, the features are independent of each other. That is,

$$\mathcal{P}[X=\mathbf{x}|Y=y] = \prod_{i=1}^{d} \mathcal{P}[X_i = x_i|Y=y].$$

With this assumption and using Bayes' rule, the Bayes optimal classifier can be further simplified:

$$\begin{aligned} h_{\text{Bayes}}(\mathbf{x}) &= \underset{y\in\{0,1\}}{\operatorname{argmax}} \mathcal{P}[Y=y|X=\mathbf{x}] \\ &= \underset{y\in\{0,1\}}{\operatorname{argmax}} \mathcal{P}[Y=y]\mathcal{P}[X=\mathbf{x}|Y=y] \\ &= \underset{y\in\{0,1\}}{\operatorname{argmax}} \mathcal{P}[Y=y]\prod_{i=1}^{d}\mathcal{P}[X_i=x_i|Y=y]. \end{aligned} \tag{24.7}$$

That is, now the number of parameters we need to estimate is only $2d+1$. Here, the generative assumption we made reduced significantly the number of parameters we need to learn.

When we also estimate the parameters using the maximum likelihood principle, the resulting classifier is called the *Naive Bayes* classifier.

24.3 LINEAR DISCRIMINANT ANALYSIS

Linear discriminant analysis (LDA) is another demonstration of how generative assumptions simplify the learning process. As in the Naive Bayes classifier we consider again the problem of predicting a label $y \in \{0,1\}$ on the basis of a vector of features $\mathbf{x} = (x_1,\ldots,x_d)$. But now the generative assumption is as follows. First, we assume that $\mathcal{P}[Y=1] = \mathcal{P}[Y=0] = 1/2$. Second, we assume that the conditional probability of X given Y is a Gaussian distribution. Finally, the covariance matrix of the Gaussian distribution is the same for both values of the label. Formally, let $\boldsymbol{\mu}_0, \boldsymbol{\mu}_1 \in \mathbb{R}^d$ and let Σ be a covariance matrix. Then, the density distribution is given by

$$\mathcal{P}[X=\mathbf{x}|Y=y] = \frac{1}{(2\pi)^{d/2}|\Sigma|^{1/2}} \exp\left(-\frac{1}{2}(\mathbf{x}-\boldsymbol{\mu}_y)^T\Sigma^{-1}(\mathbf{x}-\boldsymbol{\mu}_y)\right).$$

As we have shown in the previous section, using Bayes' rule we can write

$$h_{\text{Bayes}}(\mathbf{x}) = \underset{y\in\{0,1\}}{\operatorname{argmax}} \mathcal{P}[Y=y]\mathcal{P}[X=\mathbf{x}|Y=y].$$

This means that we will predict $h_{\text{Bayes}}(\mathbf{x}) = 1$ iff

$$\log\left(\frac{\mathcal{P}[Y=1]\mathcal{P}[X=\mathbf{x}|Y=1]}{\mathcal{P}[Y=0]\mathcal{P}[X=\mathbf{x}|Y=0]}\right) > 0.$$

This ratio is often called the *log-likelihood ratio*.

In our case, the log-likelihood ratio becomes

$$\tfrac{1}{2}(\mathbf{x}-\boldsymbol{\mu}_0)^T\Sigma^{-1}(\mathbf{x}-\boldsymbol{\mu}_0)-\tfrac{1}{2}(\mathbf{x}-\boldsymbol{\mu}_1)^T\Sigma^{-1}(\mathbf{x}-\boldsymbol{\mu}_1)$$

We can rewrite this as $\langle \mathbf{w},\mathbf{x}\rangle + b$ where

$$\mathbf{w}=(\boldsymbol{\mu}_1-\boldsymbol{\mu}_0)^T\Sigma^{-1} \quad \text{and} \quad b=\tfrac{1}{2}\left(\boldsymbol{\mu}_0^T\Sigma^{-1}\boldsymbol{\mu}_0-\boldsymbol{\mu}_1^T\Sigma^{-1}\boldsymbol{\mu}_1\right). \tag{24.8}$$

As a result of the preceding derivation we obtain that under the aforementioned generative assumptions, the Bayes optimal classifier is a linear classifier. Additionally, one may train the classifier by estimating the parameter $\boldsymbol{\mu}_0, \boldsymbol{\mu}_1$ and Σ from the data, using, for example, the maximum likelihood estimator. With those estimators at hand, the values of $\mathbf{w}$ and b can be calculated as in Equation (24.8).

24.4 LATENT VARIABLES AND THE EM ALGORITHM

In generative models we assume that the data is generated by sampling from a specific parametric distribution over our instance space $\mathcal{X}$. Sometimes, it is convenient to express this distribution using latent random variables. A natural example is a mixture of k Gaussian distributions. That is, $\mathcal{X}=\mathbb{R}^d$ and we assume that each $\mathbf{x}$ is generated as follows. First, we choose a random number in $\{1,\ldots,k\}$. Let Y be a random variable corresponding to this choice, and denote $\mathcal{P}[Y=y]=c_y$. Second, we choose $\mathbf{x}$ on the basis of the value of Y according to a Gaussian distribution

$$\mathcal{P}[X=\mathbf{x}|Y=y]=\frac{1}{(2\pi)^{d/2}|\Sigma_y|^{1/2}}\exp\left(-\frac{1}{2}(\mathbf{x}-\boldsymbol{\mu}_y)^T\Sigma_y^{-1}(\mathbf{x}-\boldsymbol{\mu}_y)\right). \tag{24.9}$$

Therefore, the density of X can be written as:

$$\begin{aligned}\mathcal{P}[X=\mathbf{x}] &= \sum_{y=1}^{k}\mathcal{P}[Y=y]\mathcal{P}[X=\mathbf{x}|Y=y]\\ &= \sum_{y=1}^{k}c_y\frac{1}{(2\pi)^{d/2}|\Sigma_y|^{1/2}}\exp\left(-\frac{1}{2}(\mathbf{x}-\boldsymbol{\mu}_y)^T\Sigma_y^{-1}(\mathbf{x}-\boldsymbol{\mu}_y)\right).\end{aligned}$$

Note that Y is a hidden variable that we do not observe in our data. Nevertheless, we introduce Y since it helps us describe a simple parametric form of the probability of X.

More generally, let $\boldsymbol{\theta}$ be the parameters of the joint distribution of X and Y (e.g., in the preceding example, $\boldsymbol{\theta}$ consists of c_y, $\boldsymbol{\mu}_y$, and Σ_y, for all $y=1,\ldots,k$). Then, the log-likelihood of an observation $\mathbf{x}$ can be written as

$$\log\left(\mathcal{P}_{\boldsymbol{\theta}}[X=\mathbf{x}]\right)=\log\left(\sum_{y=1}^{k}\mathcal{P}_{\boldsymbol{\theta}}[X=\mathbf{x},Y=y]\right).$$

Given an i.i.d. sample, $S = (\mathbf{x}_1, \ldots, \mathbf{x}_m)$, we would like to find $\boldsymbol{\theta}$ that maximizes the log-likelihood of S,

$$\begin{aligned} L(\boldsymbol{\theta}) &= \log \prod_{i=1}^{m} \mathcal{P}_{\boldsymbol{\theta}}[X = \mathbf{x}_i] \\ &= \sum_{i=1}^{m} \log \mathcal{P}_{\boldsymbol{\theta}}[X = \mathbf{x}_i] \\ &= \sum_{i=1}^{m} \log \left(\sum_{y=1}^{k} \mathcal{P}_{\boldsymbol{\theta}}[X = \mathbf{x}_i, Y = y] \right). \end{aligned}$$

The maximum-likelihood estimator is therefore the solution of the maximization problem

$$\underset{\boldsymbol{\theta}}{\operatorname{argmax}}\, L(\boldsymbol{\theta}) = \underset{\boldsymbol{\theta}}{\operatorname{argmax}} \sum_{i=1}^{m} \log \left(\sum_{y=1}^{k} \mathcal{P}_{\boldsymbol{\theta}}[X = \mathbf{x}_i, Y = y] \right).$$

In many situations, the summation inside the log makes the preceding optimization problem computationally hard. The *Expectation-Maximization* (EM) algorithm, due to Dempster, Laird, and Rubin, is an iterative procedure for searching a (local) maximum of $L(\boldsymbol{\theta})$. While EM is not guaranteed to find the global maximum, it often works reasonably well in practice.

EM is designed for those cases in which, had we known the values of the latent variables Y, then the maximum likelihood optimization problem would have been tractable. More precisely, define the following function over $m \times k$ matrices and the set of parameters $\boldsymbol{\theta}$:

$$F(Q, \boldsymbol{\theta}) = \sum_{i=1}^{m} \sum_{y=1}^{k} Q_{i,y} \log \left(\mathcal{P}_{\boldsymbol{\theta}}[X = \mathbf{x}_i, Y = y] \right).$$

If each row of Q defines a probability over the ith latent variable given $X = \mathbf{x}_i$, then we can interpret $F(Q, \boldsymbol{\theta})$ as the expected log-likelihood of a training set $(\mathbf{x}_1, y_1), \ldots, (\mathbf{x}_m, y_m)$, where the expectation is with respect to the choice of each y_i on the basis of the ith row of Q. In the definition of F, the summation is outside the log, and we assume that this makes the optimization problem with respect to $\boldsymbol{\theta}$ tractable:

Assumption 24.1. For any matrix $Q \in [0,1]^{m,k}$, such that each row of Q sums to 1, the optimization problem

$$\underset{\boldsymbol{\theta}}{\operatorname{argmax}}\, F(Q, \boldsymbol{\theta})$$

is tractable.

The intuitive idea of EM is that we have a "chicken and egg" problem. On one hand, had we known Q, then by our assumption, the optimization problem of finding the best $\boldsymbol{\theta}$ is tractable. On the other hand, had we known the parameters $\boldsymbol{\theta}$ we could have set $Q_{i,y}$ to be the probability of $Y = y$ given that $X = \mathbf{x}_i$. The EM algorithm therefore alternates between finding $\boldsymbol{\theta}$ given Q and finding Q given $\boldsymbol{\theta}$. Formally, EM finds a sequence of solutions $(Q^{(1)}, \boldsymbol{\theta}^{(1)}), (Q^{(2)}, \boldsymbol{\theta}^{(2)}), \ldots$ where at iteration t, we construct $(Q^{(t+1)}, \boldsymbol{\theta}^{(t+1)})$ by performing two steps.

- Expectation Step: Set

$$Q_{i,y}^{(t+1)} = \mathcal{P}_{\boldsymbol{\theta}^{(t)}}[Y = y | X = \mathbf{x}_i]. \tag{24.10}$$

  This step is called the Expectation step, because it yields a new probability over the latent variables, which defines a new *expected* log-likelihood function over $\boldsymbol{\theta}$.
- Maximization Step: Set $\boldsymbol{\theta}^{(t+1)}$ to be the maximizer of the expected log-likelihood, where the expectation is according to $Q^{(t+1)}$:

$$\boldsymbol{\theta}^{(t+1)} = \underset{\boldsymbol{\theta}}{\operatorname{argmax}}\, F(Q^{(t+1)}, \boldsymbol{\theta}). \tag{24.11}$$

  By our assumption, it is possible to solve this optimization problem efficiently.

The initial values of $\boldsymbol{\theta}^{(1)}$ and $Q^{(1)}$ are usually chosen at random and the procedure terminates after the improvement in the likelihood value stops being significant.

24.4.1 EM as an Alternate Maximization Algorithm

To analyze the EM algorithm, we first view it as an alternate maximization algorithm. Define the following objective function

$$G(Q, \boldsymbol{\theta}) = F(Q, \boldsymbol{\theta}) - \sum_{i=1}^{m} \sum_{y=1}^{k} Q_{i,y} \log(Q_{i,y}).$$

The second term is the sum of the *entropies* of the rows of Q. Let

$$\mathbb{Q} = \left\{ Q \in [0,1]^{m,k} : \forall i, \sum_{y=1}^{k} Q_{i,y} = 1 \right\}$$

be the set of matrices whose rows define probabilities over $[k]$. The following lemma shows that EM performs alternate maximization iterations for maximizing G.

Lemma 24.2. *The EM procedure can be rewritten as*

$$Q^{(t+1)} = \underset{Q \in \mathbb{Q}}{\operatorname{argmax}}\, G(Q, \boldsymbol{\theta}^{(t)})$$

$$\boldsymbol{\theta}^{(t+1)} = \underset{\boldsymbol{\theta}}{\operatorname{argmax}}\, G(Q^{(t+1)}, \boldsymbol{\theta}).$$

Furthermore, $G(Q^{(t+1)}, \boldsymbol{\theta}^{(t)}) = L(\boldsymbol{\theta}^{(t)})$.

Proof. Given $Q^{(t+1)}$ we clearly have that

$$\underset{\boldsymbol{\theta}}{\operatorname{argmax}}\, G(Q^{(t+1)}, \boldsymbol{\theta}) = \underset{\boldsymbol{\theta}}{\operatorname{argmax}}\, F(Q^{(t+1)}, \boldsymbol{\theta}).$$

Therefore, we only need to show that for any $\boldsymbol{\theta}$, the solution of $\text{argmax}_{Q\in\mathbb{Q}} G(Q,\boldsymbol{\theta})$ is to set $Q_{i,y} = \mathcal{P}_{\boldsymbol{\theta}}[Y = y|X = \mathbf{x}_i]$. Indeed, by Jensen's inequality, for any $Q \in \mathbb{Q}$ we have that

$$G(Q,\boldsymbol{\theta}) = \sum_{i=1}^{m}\left(\sum_{y=1}^{k} Q_{i,y}\log\left(\frac{\mathcal{P}_{\boldsymbol{\theta}}[X=\mathbf{x}_i, Y=y]}{Q_{i,y}}\right)\right)$$

$$\leq \sum_{i=1}^{m}\left(\log\left(\sum_{y=1}^{k} Q_{i,y}\frac{\mathcal{P}_{\boldsymbol{\theta}}[X=\mathbf{x}_i, Y=y]}{Q_{i,y}}\right)\right)$$

$$= \sum_{i=1}^{m}\log\left(\sum_{y=1}^{k}\mathcal{P}_{\boldsymbol{\theta}}[X=\mathbf{x}_i, Y=y]\right)$$

$$= \sum_{i=1}^{m}\log\left(\mathcal{P}_{\boldsymbol{\theta}}[X=\mathbf{x}_i]\right) = L(\boldsymbol{\theta}),$$

while for $Q_{i,y} = \mathcal{P}_{\boldsymbol{\theta}}[Y = y|X = \mathbf{x}_i]$ we have

$$G(Q,\boldsymbol{\theta}) = \sum_{i=1}^{m}\left(\sum_{y=1}^{k}\mathcal{P}_{\boldsymbol{\theta}}[Y=y|X=\mathbf{x}_i]\log\left(\frac{\mathcal{P}_{\boldsymbol{\theta}}[X=\mathbf{x}_i, Y=y]}{\mathcal{P}_{\boldsymbol{\theta}}[Y=y|X=\mathbf{x}_i]}\right)\right)$$

$$= \sum_{i=1}^{m}\sum_{y=1}^{k}\mathcal{P}_{\boldsymbol{\theta}}[Y=y|X=\mathbf{x}_i]\log\left(\mathcal{P}_{\boldsymbol{\theta}}[X=\mathbf{x}_i]\right)$$

$$= \sum_{i=1}^{m}\log\left(\mathcal{P}_{\boldsymbol{\theta}}[X=\mathbf{x}_i]\right)\sum_{y=1}^{k}\mathcal{P}_{\boldsymbol{\theta}}[Y=y|X=\mathbf{x}_i]$$

$$= \sum_{i=1}^{m}\log\left(\mathcal{P}_{\boldsymbol{\theta}}[X=\mathbf{x}_i]\right) = L(\boldsymbol{\theta}).$$

This shows that setting $Q_{i,y} = \mathcal{P}_{\boldsymbol{\theta}}[Y = y|X = \mathbf{x}_i]$ maximizes $G(Q,\boldsymbol{\theta})$ over $Q \in \mathbb{Q}$ and shows that $G(Q^{(t+1)},\boldsymbol{\theta}^{(t)}) = L(\boldsymbol{\theta}^{(t)})$. □

The preceding lemma immediately implies:

Theorem 24.3. *The EM procedure never decreases the log-likelihood; namely, for all t,*

$$L(\boldsymbol{\theta}^{(t+1)}) \geq L(\boldsymbol{\theta}^{(t)}).$$

Proof. By the lemma we have

$$L(\boldsymbol{\theta}^{(t+1)}) = G(Q^{(t+2)},\boldsymbol{\theta}^{(t+1)}) \geq G(Q^{(t+1)},\boldsymbol{\theta}^{(t)}) = L(\boldsymbol{\theta}^{(t)}).$$

□

24.4.2 EM for Mixture of Gaussians (Soft k-Means)

Consider the case of a mixture of k Gaussians in which $\boldsymbol{\theta}$ is a triplet $(\mathbf{c},\{\boldsymbol{\mu}_1,\ldots,\boldsymbol{\mu}_k\},\{\Sigma_1,\ldots,\Sigma_k\})$ where $\mathcal{P}_{\boldsymbol{\theta}}[Y = y] = c_y$ and $\mathcal{P}_{\boldsymbol{\theta}}[X = \mathbf{x}|Y = y]$ is as given in Equation (24.9). For simplicity, we assume that $\Sigma_1 = \Sigma_2 = \cdots = \Sigma_k = I$, where I is the identity matrix. Specifying the EM algorithm for this case we obtain the following:

- Expectation step: For each $i \in [m]$ and $y \in [k]$ we have that

$$\begin{aligned}\mathcal{P}_{\boldsymbol{\theta}^{(t)}}[Y=y|X=\mathbf{x}_i] &= \frac{1}{Z_i}\mathcal{P}_{\boldsymbol{\theta}^{(t)}}[Y=y]\mathcal{P}_{\boldsymbol{\theta}^{(t)}}[X=\mathbf{x}_i|Y=y] \\ &= \frac{1}{Z_i}c_y^{(t)}\exp\left(-\frac{1}{2}\|\mathbf{x}_i-\boldsymbol{\mu}_y^{(t)}\|^2\right),\end{aligned} \tag{24.12}$$

  where Z_i is a normalization factor which ensures that $\sum_y \mathcal{P}_{\boldsymbol{\theta}^{(t)}}[Y=y|X=\mathbf{x}_i]$ sums to 1.
- Maximization step: We need to set $\boldsymbol{\theta}^{t+1}$ to be a maximizer of Equation (24.11), which in our case amounts to maximizing the following expression w.r.t. $\mathbf{c}$ and $\boldsymbol{\mu}$:

$$\sum_{i=1}^{m}\sum_{y=1}^{k}\mathcal{P}_{\boldsymbol{\theta}^{(t)}}[Y=y|X=\mathbf{x}_i]\left(\log(c_y)-\frac{1}{2}\|\mathbf{x}_i-\boldsymbol{\mu}_y\|^2\right). \tag{24.13}$$

  Comparing the derivative of Equation (24.13) w.r.t. $\boldsymbol{\mu}_y$ to zero and rearranging terms we obtain:

$$\boldsymbol{\mu}_y = \sum_{i=1}^{m}\mathcal{P}_{\boldsymbol{\theta}^{(t)}}[Y=y|X=\mathbf{x}_i]\mathbf{x}_i.$$

  That is, $\boldsymbol{\mu}_y$ is a weighted average of the $\mathbf{x}_i$ where the weights are according to the probabilities calculated in the E step. To find the optimal $\mathbf{c}$ we need to be more careful since we must ensure that $\mathbf{c}$ is a probability vector. In Exercise 24.3 we show that the solution is

$$c_y = \frac{\sum_{i=1}^{m}\mathcal{P}_{\boldsymbol{\theta}^{(t)}}[Y=y|X=\mathbf{x}_i]}{\sum_{y'=1}^{k}\sum_{i=1}^{m}\mathcal{P}_{\boldsymbol{\theta}^{(t)}}[Y=y'|X=\mathbf{x}_i]}. \tag{24.14}$$

It is interesting to compare the preceding algorithm to the k-means algorithm described in Chapter 22. In the k-means algorithm, we first assign each example to a cluster according to the distance $\|\mathbf{x}_i-\boldsymbol{\mu}_y\|$. Then, we update each center $\boldsymbol{\mu}_y$ according to the average of the examples assigned to this cluster. In the EM approach, however, we determine the probability that each example belongs to each cluster. Then, we update the centers on the basis of a weighted sum over the entire sample. For this reason, the EM approach for k-means is sometimes called "soft k-means."

24.5 BAYESIAN REASONING

The maximum likelihood estimator follows a frequentist approach. This means that we refer to the parameter θ as a fixed parameter and the only problem is that we do not know its value. A different approach to parameter estimation is called Bayesian reasoning. In the Bayesian approach, our uncertainty about θ is also modeled using probability theory. That is, we think of θ as a random variable as well and refer to the distribution $\mathcal{P}[\theta]$ as a *prior distribution*. As its name indicates, the prior distribution should be defined by the learner prior to observing the data.

As an example, let us consider again the drug company which developed a new drug. On the basis of past experience, the statisticians at the drug company believe that whenever a drug has reached the level of clinic experiments on people, it is likely to be effective. They model this prior belief by defining a density distribution on θ such that

$$\mathcal{P}[\theta] = \begin{cases} 0.8 & \text{if } \theta > 0.5 \\ 0.2 & \text{if } \theta \leq 0.5 \end{cases} \tag{24.15}$$

As before, given a specific value of θ, it is assumed that the conditional probability, $\mathcal{P}[X = x|\theta]$, is known. In the drug company example, X takes values in $\{0,1\}$ and $\mathcal{P}[X = x|\theta] = \theta^x(1-\theta)^{1-x}$.

Once the prior distribution over θ and the conditional distribution over X given θ are defined, we again have complete knowledge of the distribution over X. This is because we can write the probability over X as a marginal probability

$$\mathcal{P}[X = x] = \sum_\theta \mathcal{P}[X = x, \theta] = \sum_\theta \mathcal{P}[\theta]\mathcal{P}[X = x|\theta],$$

where the last equality follows from the definition of conditional probability. If θ is continuous we replace $\mathcal{P}[\theta]$ with the density function and the sum becomes an integral:

$$\mathcal{P}[X = x] = \int_\theta \mathcal{P}[\theta]\mathcal{P}[X = x|\theta]\,d\theta.$$

Seemingly, once we know $\mathcal{P}[X = x]$, a training set $S = (x_1, \ldots, x_m)$ tells us nothing as we are already experts who know the distribution over a new point X. However, the Bayesian view introduces dependency between S and X. This is because we now refer to θ as a random variable. A new point X and the previous points in S are independent *only* conditioned on θ. This is different from the frequentist philosophy in which θ is a parameter that we might not know, but since it is just a parameter of the distribution, a new point X and previous points S are always independent.

In the Bayesian framework, since X and S are not independent anymore, what we would like to calculate is the probability of X given S, which by the chain rule can be written as follows:

$$\mathcal{P}[X = x|S] = \sum_\theta \mathcal{P}[X = x|\theta, S]\,\mathcal{P}[\theta|S] = \sum_\theta \mathcal{P}[X = x|\theta]\,\mathcal{P}[\theta|S].$$

The second inequality follows from the assumption that X and S are independent when we condition on θ. Using *Bayes' rule* we have

$$\mathcal{P}[\theta|S] = \frac{\mathcal{P}[S|\theta]\,\mathcal{P}[\theta]}{\mathcal{P}[S]},$$

and together with the assumption that points are independent conditioned on θ, we can write

$$\mathcal{P}[\theta|S] = \frac{\mathcal{P}[S|\theta]\,\mathcal{P}[\theta]}{\mathcal{P}[S]} = \frac{1}{\mathcal{P}[S]} \prod_{i=1}^{m} \mathcal{P}[X = x_i|\theta]\,\mathcal{P}[\theta].$$

We therefore obtain the following expression for Bayesian prediction:

$$\mathcal{P}[X = x|S] = \frac{1}{\mathcal{P}[S]} \sum_{\theta} \mathcal{P}[X = x|\theta] \prod_{i=1}^{m} \mathcal{P}[X = x_i|\theta] \mathcal{P}[\theta]. \tag{24.16}$$

Getting back to our drug company example, we can rewrite $\mathcal{P}[X = x|S]$ as

$$\mathcal{P}[X = x|S] = \frac{1}{\mathcal{P}[S]} \int \theta^{x+\sum_i x_i} (1-\theta)^{1-x+\sum_i (1-x_i)} \mathcal{P}[\theta] \, d\theta.$$

It is interesting to note that when $\mathcal{P}[\theta]$ is uniform we obtain that

$$\mathcal{P}[X = x|S] \propto \int \theta^{x+\sum_i x_i} (1-\theta)^{1-x+\sum_i (1-x_i)} \, d\theta.$$

Solving the preceding integral (using integration by parts) we obtain

$$\mathcal{P}[X = 1|S] = \frac{(\sum_i x_i) + 1}{m+2}.$$

Recall that the prediction according to the maximum likelihood principle in this case is $\mathcal{P}[X = 1|\hat{\theta}] = \frac{\sum_i x_i}{m}$. The Bayesian prediction with uniform prior is rather similar to the maximum likelihood prediction, except it adds "pseudoexamples" to the training set, thus biasing the prediction toward the uniform prior.

Maximum A Posteriori

In many situations, it is difficult to find a closed form solution to the integral given in Equation (24.16). Several numerical methods can be used to approximate this integral. Another popular solution is to find a single θ which maximizes $\mathcal{P}[\theta|S]$. The value of θ which maximizes $\mathcal{P}[\theta|S]$ is called the *Maximum A Posteriori* estimator. Once this value is found, we can calculate the probability that $X = x$ given the maximum *a posteriori* estimator and independently on S.

24.6 SUMMARY

In the generative approach to machine learning we aim at modeling the distribution over the data. In particular, in parametric density estimation we further assume that the underlying distribution over the data has a specific parametric form and our goal is to estimate the parameters of the model. We have described several principles for parameter estimation, including maximum likelihood, Bayesian estimation, and maximum *a posteriori*. We have also described several specific algorithms for implementing the maximum likelihood under different assumptions on the underlying data distribution, in particular, Naive Bayes, LDA, and EM.

24.7 BIBLIOGRAPHIC REMARKS

The maximum likelihood principle was studied by Ronald Fisher in the beginning of the 20th century. Bayesian statistics follow Bayes' rule, which is named after the 18th century English mathematician Thomas Bayes.

There are many excellent books on the generative and Bayesian approaches to machine learning. See, for example, (Bishop 2006, Koller & Friedman 2009*a*, MacKay 2003, Murphy 2012, Barber 2012).

24.8 EXERCISES

24.1 Prove that the maximum likelihood estimator of the variance of a Gaussian variable is biased.

24.2 Regularization for Maximum Likelihood: Consider the following regularized loss minimization:

$$\frac{1}{m}\sum_{i=1}^{m}\log(1/\mathcal{P}_\theta[x_i]) + \frac{1}{m}\left(\log(1/\theta)+\log(1/(1-\theta))\right).$$

- Show that the preceding objective is equivalent to the usual empirical error had we added two pseudoexamples to the training set. Conclude that the regularized maximum likelihood estimator would be

$$\hat{\theta} = \frac{1}{m+2}\left(1+\sum_{i=1}^{m}x_i\right).$$

- Derive a high probability bound on $|\hat{\theta}-\theta^\star|$. *Hint*: Rewrite this as $|\hat{\theta}-\mathbb{E}[\hat{\theta}]+\mathbb{E}[\hat{\theta}]-\theta^\star|$ and then use the triangle inequality and Hoeffding inequality.
- Use this to bound the true risk. Hint: Use the fact that now $\hat{\theta}\geq\frac{1}{m+2}$ to relate $|\hat{\theta}-\theta^\star|$ to the relative entropy.

24.3 Consider a general optimization problem of the form

$$\max_{\mathbf{c}}\sum_{y=1}^{k}\nu_y\log(c_y) \quad \text{s.t.} \quad c_y>0, \sum_y c_y=1,$$

where $\boldsymbol{\nu}\in\mathbb{R}_+^k$ is a vector of nonnegative weights.

Verify that the M step of soft k-means involves solving such an optimization problem.

- Let $\mathbf{c}^\star=\frac{1}{\sum_y \nu_y}\boldsymbol{\nu}$. Show that $\mathbf{c}^\star$ is a probability vector.
- Show that the optimization problem is equivalent to the problem

$$\min_{\mathbf{c}} D_{\mathrm{RE}}(\mathbf{c}^\star||\mathbf{c}) \quad \text{s.t.} \quad c_y>0, \sum_y c_y=1.$$

- Using properties of the relative entropy, conclude that $\mathbf{c}^\star$ is the solution to the optimization problem.

25

Feature Selection and Generation

In the beginning of the book, we discussed the abstract model of learning, in which the prior knowledge utilized by the learner is fully encoded by the choice of the hypothesis class. However, there is another modeling choice, which we have so far ignored: How do we represent the instance space $\mathcal{X}$? For example, in the papayas learning problem, we proposed the hypothesis class of rectangles in the softness-color two dimensional plane. That is, our first modeling choice was to represent a papaya as a two dimensional point corresponding to its softness and color. Only after that did we choose the hypothesis class of rectangles as a class of mappings from the plane into the label set. The transformation from the real world object "papaya" into the scalar representing its softness or its color is called a *feature function* or a feature for short; namely, any measurement of the real world object can be regarded as a feature. If $\mathcal{X}$ is a subset of a vector space, each $x \in \mathcal{X}$ is sometimes referred to as a *feature vector*. It is important to understand that the way we encode real world objects as an instance space $\mathcal{X}$ is by itself prior knowledge about the problem.

Furthermore, even when we already have an instance space $\mathcal{X}$ which is represented as a subset of a vector space, we might still want to change it into a different representation and apply a hypothesis class on top of it. That is, we may define a hypothesis class on $\mathcal{X}$ by composing some class $\mathcal{H}$ on top of a feature function which maps $\mathcal{X}$ into some other vector space $\mathcal{X}'$. We have already encountered examples of such compositions – in Chapter 15 we saw that kernel-based SVM learns a composition of the class of halfspaces over a feature mapping ψ that maps each original instance in $\mathcal{X}$ into some Hilbert space. And, indeed, the choice of ψ is another form of prior knowledge we impose on the problem.

In this chapter we study several methods for constructing a good feature set. We start with the problem of *feature selection*, in which we have a large pool of features and our goal is to select a small number of features that will be used by our predictor. Next, we discuss *feature manipulations and normalization*. These include simple transformations that we apply on our original features. Such transformations may decrease the sample complexity of our learning algorithm, its bias, or its computational complexity. Last, we discuss several approaches for *feature learning*. In these methods, we try to automate the process of feature construction.

We emphasize that while there are some common techniques for feature learning one may want to try, the No-Free-Lunch theorem implies that there is no ultimate feature learner. Any feature learning algorithm might fail on some problem. In other words, the success of each feature learner relies (sometimes implicitly) on some form of prior assumption on the data distribution. Furthermore, the relative quality of features highly depends on the learning algorithm we are later going to apply using these features. This is illustrated in the following example.

Example 25.1. Consider a regression problem in which $\mathcal{X} = \mathbb{R}^2$, $\mathcal{Y} = \mathbb{R}$, and the loss function is the squared loss. Suppose that the underlying distribution is such that an example $(\mathbf{x}, y)$ is generated as follows: First, we sample x_1 from the uniform distribution over $[-1, 1]$. Then, we deterministically set $y = x_1{}^2$. Finally, the second feature is set to be $x_2 = y + z$, where z is sampled from the uniform distribution over $[-0.01, 0.01]$. Suppose we would like to choose a single feature. Intuitively, the first feature should be preferred over the second feature as the target can be perfectly predicted based on the first feature alone, while it cannot be perfectly predicted based on the second feature. Indeed, choosing the first feature would be the right choice if we are later going to apply polynomial regression of degree at least 2. However, if the learner is going to be a linear regressor, then we should prefer the *second* feature over the first one, since the optimal linear predictor based on the first feature will have a larger risk than the optimal linear predictor based on the second feature.

25.1 FEATURE SELECTION

Throughout this section we assume that $\mathcal{X} = \mathbb{R}^d$. That is, each instance is represented as a vector of d features. Our goal is to learn a predictor that only relies on $k \ll d$ features. Predictors that use only a small subset of features require a smaller memory footprint and can be applied faster. Furthermore, in applications such as medical diagnostics, obtaining each possible "feature" (e.g., test result) can be costly; therefore, a predictor that uses only a small number of features is desirable even at the cost of a small degradation in performance, relative to a predictor that uses more features. Finally, constraining the hypothesis class to use a small subset of features can reduce its estimation error and thus prevent overfitting.

Ideally, we could have tried all subsets of k out of d features and choose the subset which leads to the best performing predictor. However, such an exhaustive search is usually computationally intractable. In the following we describe three computationally feasible approaches for feature selection. While these methods cannot guarantee finding the optimal subset, they often work reasonably well in practice. Some of the methods come with formal guarantees on the quality of the selected subsets under certain assumptions. We do not discuss these guarantees here.

25.1.1 Filters

Maybe the simplest approach for feature selection is the filter method, in which we assess individual features, independently of other features, according to some quality measure. We can then select the k features that achieve the highest score (alternatively, decide also on the number of features to select according to the value of their scores).

Many quality measures for features have been proposed in the literature. Maybe the most straightforward approach is to set the score of a feature according to the error rate of a predictor that is trained solely by that feature.

To illustrate this, consider a linear regression problem with the squared loss. Let $\mathbf{v} = (x_{1,j}, \ldots, x_{m,j}) \in \mathbb{R}^m$ be a vector designating the values of the jth feature on a training set of m examples and let $\mathbf{y} = (y_1, \ldots, y_m) \in \mathbb{R}^m$ be the values of the target on the same m examples. The empirical squared loss of an ERM linear predictor that uses only the jth feature would be

$$\min_{a,b \in \mathbb{R}} \frac{1}{m} \|a\mathbf{v} + b - \mathbf{y}\|^2,$$

where the meaning of adding a scalar b to a vector $\mathbf{v}$ is adding b to all coordinates of $\mathbf{v}$. To solve this problem, let $\bar{v} = \frac{1}{m}\sum_{i=1}^m v_i$ be the averaged value of the feature and let $\bar{y} = \frac{1}{m}\sum_{i=1}^m y_i$ be the averaged value of the target. Clearly (see Exercise 25.1),

$$\min_{a,b \in \mathbb{R}} \frac{1}{m} \|a\mathbf{v} + b - \mathbf{y}\|^2 = \min_{a,b \in \mathbb{R}} \frac{1}{m} \|a(\mathbf{v} - \bar{v}) + b - (\mathbf{y} - \bar{y})\|^2. \tag{25.1}$$

Taking the derivative of the right-hand side objective with respect to b and comparing it to zero we obtain that $b = 0$. Similarly, solving for a (once we know that $b = 0$) yields $a = \langle \mathbf{v} - \bar{v}, \mathbf{y} - \bar{y} \rangle / \|\mathbf{v} - \bar{v}\|^2$. Plugging this value back into the objective we obtain the value

$$\|\mathbf{y} - \bar{y}\|^2 - \frac{(\langle \mathbf{v} - \bar{v}, \mathbf{y} - \bar{y} \rangle)^2}{\|\mathbf{v} - \bar{v}\|^2}.$$

Ranking the features according to the minimal loss they achieve is equivalent to ranking them according to the absolute value of the following score (where now a higher score yields a better feature):

$$\frac{\langle \mathbf{v} - \bar{v}, \mathbf{y} - \bar{y} \rangle}{\|\mathbf{v} - \bar{v}\| \, \|\mathbf{y} - \bar{y}\|} = \frac{\frac{1}{m}\langle \mathbf{v} - \bar{v}, \mathbf{y} - \bar{y} \rangle}{\sqrt{\frac{1}{m}\|\mathbf{v} - \bar{v}\|^2} \sqrt{\frac{1}{m}\|\mathbf{y} - \bar{y}\|^2}}. \tag{25.2}$$

The preceding expression is known as *Pearson's correlation coefficient*. The numerator is the empirical estimate of the *covariance* of the jth feature and the target value, $\mathbb{E}[(v - \mathbb{E}v)(y - \mathbb{E}y)]$, while the denominator is the squared root of the empirical estimate for the *variance* of the jth feature, $\mathbb{E}[(v - \mathbb{E}v)^2]$, times the variance of the target. Pearson's coefficient ranges from -1 to 1, where if the Pearson's coefficient is either 1 or -1, there is a linear mapping from $\mathbf{v}$ to $\mathbf{y}$ with zero empirical risk.

If Pearson's coefficient equals zero it means that the optimal linear function from $\mathbf{v}$ to $\mathbf{y}$ is the all-zeros function, which means that $\mathbf{v}$ *alone* is useless for predicting $\mathbf{y}$. However, this does not mean that $\mathbf{v}$ is a bad feature, as it might be the case that together with other features $\mathbf{v}$ can perfectly predict $\mathbf{y}$. Indeed, consider a simple example in which the target is generated by the function $y = x_1 + 2x_2$. Assume also that x_1 is generated from the uniform distribution over $\{\pm 1\}$, and $x_2 = -\frac{1}{2}x_1 + \frac{1}{2}z$, where z is also generated i.i.d. from the uniform distribution over $\{\pm 1\}$. Then, $\mathbb{E}[x_1] = \mathbb{E}[x_2] = \mathbb{E}[y] = 0$, and we also have

$$\mathbb{E}[yx_1] = \mathbb{E}[x_1^2] + 2\mathbb{E}[x_2x_1] = \mathbb{E}[x_1^2] - \mathbb{E}[x_1^2] + \mathbb{E}[zx_1] = 0.$$

Therefore, for a large enough training set, the first feature is likely to have a Pearson's correlation coefficient that is close to zero, and hence it will most probably not be selected. However, no function can predict the target value well without knowing the first feature.

There are many other score functions that can be used by a filter method. Notable examples are estimators of the mutual information or the area under the receiver operating characteristic (ROC) curve. All of these score functions suffer from similar problems to the one illustrated previously. We refer the reader to Guyon and Elisseeff (2003).

25.1.2 Greedy Selection Approaches

Greedy selection is another popular approach for feature selection. Unlike filter methods, greedy selection approaches are coupled with the underlying learning algorithm. The simplest instance of greedy selection is forward greedy selection. We start with an empty set of features, and then we gradually add one feature at a time to the set of selected features. Given that our current set of selected features is I, we go over all $i \notin I$, and apply the learning algorithm on the set of features $I \cup \{i\}$. Each such application yields a different predictor, and we choose to add the feature that yields the predictor with the smallest risk (on the training set or on a validation set). This process continues until we either select k features, where k is a predefined budget of allowed features, or achieve an accurate enough predictor.

Example 25.2 (Orthogonal Matching Pursuit). To illustrate the forward greedy selection approach, we specify it to the problem of linear regression with the squared loss. Let $X \in \mathbb{R}^{m,d}$ be a matrix whose rows are the m training instances. Let $\mathbf{y} \in \mathbb{R}^m$ be the vector of the m labels. For every $i \in [d]$, let X_i be the ith column of X. Given a set $I \subset [d]$ we denote by X_I the matrix whose columns are $\{X_i : i \in I\}$.

The forward greedy selection method starts with $I_0 = \emptyset$. At iteration t, we look for the feature index j_t, which is in

$$\underset{j}{\operatorname{argmin}} \min_{\mathbf{w} \in \mathbb{R}^t} \|X_{I_{t-1} \cup \{j\}} \mathbf{w} - \mathbf{y}\|^2.$$

Then, we update $I_t = I_{t-1} \cup \{j_t\}$.

We now describe a more efficient implementation of the forward greedy selection approach for linear regression which is called *Orthogonal Matching Pursuit (OMP)*. The idea is to keep an orthogonal basis of the features aggregated so far. Let V_t be a matrix whose columns form an orthonormal basis of the columns of X_{I_t}.

Clearly,

$$\min_{\mathbf{w}} \|X_{I_t}\mathbf{w} - \mathbf{y}\|^2 = \min_{\boldsymbol{\theta} \in \mathbb{R}^t} \|V_t\boldsymbol{\theta} - \mathbf{y}\|^2.$$

We will maintain a vector $\boldsymbol{\theta}_t$ which minimizes the right-hand side of the equation.

Initially, we set $I_0 = \emptyset$, $V_0 = \emptyset$, and $\boldsymbol{\theta}_1$ to be the empty vector. At round t, for every j, we decompose $X_j = \mathbf{v}_j + \mathbf{u}_j$ where $\mathbf{v}_j = V_{t-1}V_{t-1}^\top X_j$ is the projection of X_j

onto the subspace spanned by V_{t-1} and $\mathbf{u}_j$ is the part of X_j orthogonal to V_{t-1} (see Appendix C). Then,

$$\begin{aligned}
&\min_{\boldsymbol{\theta},\alpha} \|V_{t-1}\boldsymbol{\theta} + \alpha \mathbf{u}_j - \mathbf{y}\|^2 \\
&= \min_{\boldsymbol{\theta},\alpha} \left[\|V_{t-1}\boldsymbol{\theta} - \mathbf{y}\|^2 + \alpha^2 \|\mathbf{u}_j\|^2 + 2\alpha \langle \mathbf{u}_j, V_{t-1}\boldsymbol{\theta} - \mathbf{y}\rangle \right] \\
&= \min_{\boldsymbol{\theta},\alpha} \left[\|V_{t-1}\boldsymbol{\theta} - \mathbf{y}\|^2 + \alpha^2 \|\mathbf{u}_j\|^2 + 2\alpha \langle \mathbf{u}_j, -\mathbf{y}\rangle \right] \\
&= \min_{\boldsymbol{\theta}} \left[\|V_{t-1}\boldsymbol{\theta} - \mathbf{y}\|^2 \right] + \min_{\alpha} \left[\alpha^2 \|\mathbf{u}_j\|^2 - 2\alpha \langle \mathbf{u}_j, \mathbf{y}\rangle \right] \\
&= \left[\|V_{t-1}\boldsymbol{\theta}_{t-1} - \mathbf{y}\|^2 \right] + \min_{\alpha} \left[\alpha^2 \|\mathbf{u}_j\|^2 - 2\alpha \langle \mathbf{u}_j, \mathbf{y}\rangle \right] \\
&= \|V_{t-1}\boldsymbol{\theta}_{t-1} - \mathbf{y}\|^2 - \frac{(\langle \mathbf{u}_j, \mathbf{y}\rangle)^2}{\|\mathbf{u}_j\|^2}.
\end{aligned}$$

It follows that we should select the feature

$$j_t = \operatorname*{argmax}_j \frac{(\langle \mathbf{u}_j, \mathbf{y}\rangle)^2}{\|\mathbf{u}_j\|^2}.$$

The rest of the update is to set

$$V_t = \left[V_{t-1}, \frac{\mathbf{u}_{j_t}}{\|\mathbf{u}_{j_t}\|^2} \right], \qquad \boldsymbol{\theta}_t = \left[\boldsymbol{\theta}_{t-1}; \frac{\langle \mathbf{u}_{j_t}, \mathbf{y}\rangle}{\|\mathbf{u}_{j_t}\|^2} \right].$$

The OMP procedure maintains an orthonormal basis of the selected features, where in the preceding description, the orthonormalization property is obtained by a procedure similar to Gram-Schmidt orthonormalization. In practice, the Gram-Schmidt procedure is often numerically unstable. In the pseudocode that follows we use SVD (see Section C.4) at the end of each round to obtain an orthonormal basis in a numerically stable manner.

Orthogonal Matching Pursuit (OMP)

input:
  data matrix $X \in \mathbb{R}^{m,d}$, labels vector $\mathbf{y} \in \mathbb{R}^m$,
  budget of features T
initialize: $I_1 = \emptyset$
for $t = 1, \ldots, T$
  use SVD to find an orthonormal basis $V \in \mathbb{R}^{m,t-1}$ of X_{I_t}
   (for $t = 1$ set V to be the all zeros matrix)
  foreach $j \in [d] \setminus I_t$ let $\mathbf{u}_j = X_j - VV^\top X_j$
  let $j_t = \operatorname{argmax}_{j \notin I_t : \|\mathbf{u}_j\| > 0} \frac{(\langle \mathbf{u}_j, \mathbf{y}\rangle)^2}{\|\mathbf{u}_j\|^2}$
  update $I_{t+1} = I_t \cup \{j_t\}$
output I_{T+1}

More Efficient Greedy Selection Criteria

Let $R(\mathbf{w})$ be the empirical risk of a vector $\mathbf{w}$. At each round of the forward greedy selection method, and for every possible j, we should minimize $R(\mathbf{w})$ over the vectors $\mathbf{w}$ whose support is $I_{t-1} \cup \{j\}$. This might be time consuming.

A simpler approach is to choose j_t that minimizes

$$\operatorname*{argmin}_j \min_{\eta \in \mathbb{R}} R(\mathbf{w}_{t-1} + \eta \mathbf{e}_j),$$

where $\mathbf{e}_j$ is the all zeros vector except 1 in the jth element. That is, we keep the weights of the previously chosen coordinates intact and only optimize over the new variable. Therefore, for each j we need to solve an optimization problem over a single variable, which is a much easier task than optimizing over t.

An even simpler approach is to upper bound $R(\mathbf{w})$ using a "simple" function and then choose the feature which leads to the largest decrease in this upper bound. For example, if R is a β-smooth function (see Equation (12.5) in Chapter 12), then

$$R(\mathbf{w} + \eta \mathbf{e}_j) \le R(\mathbf{w}) + \eta \frac{\partial R(\mathbf{w})}{\partial w_j} + \beta \eta^2 / 2.$$

Minimizing the right-hand side over η yields $\eta = -\frac{\partial R(\mathbf{w})}{\partial w_j} \cdot \frac{1}{\beta}$ and plugging this value into the inequality yields

$$R(\mathbf{w} + \eta \mathbf{e}_j) \le R(\mathbf{w}) - \frac{1}{2\beta} \left(\frac{\partial R(\mathbf{w})}{\partial w_j} \right)^2 .$$

This value is minimized if the partial derivative of $R(\mathbf{w})$ with respect to w_j is maximal. We can therefore choose j_t to be the index of the largest coordinate of the gradient of $R(\mathbf{w})$ at $\mathbf{w}$.

Remark 25.3 (AdaBoost as a Forward Greedy Selection Procedure). It is possible to interpret the AdaBoost algorithm from Chapter 10 as a forward greedy selection procedure with respect to the function

$$R(\mathbf{w}) = \log \left(\sum_{i=1}^{m} \exp \left(-y_i \sum_{j=1}^{d} w_j h_j(\mathbf{x}_j) \right) \right) . \tag{25.3}$$

See Exercise 25.3.

Backward Elimination

Another popular greedy selection approach is *backward elimination*. Here, we start with the full set of features, and then we gradually remove one feature at a time from the set of features. Given that our current set of selected features is I, we go over all $i \in I$, and apply the learning algorithm on the set of features $I \setminus \{i\}$. Each such application yields a different predictor, and we choose to remove the feature i for which the predictor obtained from $I \setminus \{i\}$ has the smallest risk (on the training set or on a validation set).

Naturally, there are many possible variants of the backward elimination idea. It is also possible to combine forward and backward greedy steps.

25.1.3 Sparsity-Inducing Norms

The problem of minimizing the empirical risk subject to a budget of k features can be written as

$$\min_{\mathbf{w}} L_S(\mathbf{w}) \quad \text{s.t.} \quad \|\mathbf{w}\|_0 \le k,$$

where[1]

$$\|\mathbf{w}\|_0 = |\{i : w_i \neq 0\}|.$$

In other words, we want $\mathbf{w}$ to be sparse, which implies that we only need to measure the features corresponding to nonzero elements of $\mathbf{w}$.

Solving this optimization problem is computationally hard (Natarajan 1995, Davis, Mallat & Avellaneda 1997). A possible relaxation is to replace the nonconvex function $\|\mathbf{w}\|_0$ with the ℓ_1 norm, $\|\mathbf{w}\|_1 = \sum_{i=1}^{d} |w_i|$, and to solve the problem

$$\min_{\mathbf{w}} L_S(\mathbf{w}) \quad \text{s.t.} \quad \|\mathbf{w}\|_1 \le k_1, \tag{25.4}$$

where k_1 is a parameter. Since the ℓ_1 norm is a convex function, this problem can be solved efficiently as long as the loss function is convex. A related problem is minimizing the sum of $L_S(\mathbf{w})$ plus an ℓ_1 norm regularization term,

$$\min_{\mathbf{w}} \left(L_S(\mathbf{w}) + \lambda \|\mathbf{w}\|_1 \right), \tag{25.5}$$

where λ is a regularization parameter. Since for any k_1 there exists a λ such that Equation (25.4) and Equation (25.5) lead to the same solution, the two problems are in some sense equivalent.

The ℓ_1 regularization often induces sparse solutions. To illustrate this, let us start with the simple optimization problem

$$\min_{w \in \mathbb{R}} \left(\tfrac{1}{2} w^2 - x w + \lambda |w| \right). \tag{25.6}$$

It is easy to verify (see Exercise 25.2) that the solution to this problem is the "soft thresholding" operator

$$w = \text{sign}(x) \left[|x| - \lambda \right]_+, \tag{25.7}$$

where $[a]_+ \stackrel{\text{def}}{=} \max\{a, 0\}$. That is, as long as the absolute value of x is smaller than λ, the optimal solution will be zero.

Next, consider a one dimensional regression problem with respect to the squared loss:

$$\underset{w \in \mathbb{R}^m}{\text{argmin}} \left(\frac{1}{2m} \sum_{i=1}^{m} (x_i w - y_i)^2 + \lambda |w| \right).$$

We can rewrite the problem as

$$\underset{w \in \mathbb{R}^m}{\text{argmin}} \left(\frac{1}{2} \left(\frac{1}{m} \sum_i x_i^2 \right) w^2 - \left(\frac{1}{m} \sum_{i=1}^{m} x_i y_i \right) w + \lambda |w| \right).$$

[1] The function $\|\cdot\|_0$ is often referred to as the ℓ_0 norm. Despite the use of the "norm" notation, $\|\cdot\|_0$ is not really a norm; for example, it does not satisfy the positive homogeneity property of norms, $\|a\mathbf{w}\|_0 \neq |a| \, \|\mathbf{w}\|_0$.

For simplicity let us assume that $\frac{1}{m}\sum_i x_i^2 = 1$, and denote $\langle \mathbf{x}, \mathbf{y} \rangle = \sum_{i=1}^m x_i y_i$; then the optimal solution is

$$w = \operatorname{sign}(\langle \mathbf{x}, \mathbf{y} \rangle)\,[|\langle \mathbf{x}, \mathbf{y} \rangle|/m - \lambda]_+ .$$

That is, the solution will be zero unless the correlation between the feature $\mathbf{x}$ and the labels vector $\mathbf{y}$ is larger than λ.

Remark 25.4. Unlike the ℓ_1 norm, the ℓ_2 norm does not induce sparse solutions. Indeed, consider the aforementioned problem with an ℓ_2 regularization, namely,

$$\underset{w \in \mathbb{R}^m}{\operatorname{argmin}} \left(\frac{1}{2m} \sum_{i=1}^m (x_i w - y_i)^2 + \lambda w^2 \right).$$

Then, the optimal solution is

$$w = \frac{\langle \mathbf{x}, \mathbf{y} \rangle / m}{\|\mathbf{x}\|^2/m + 2\lambda}.$$

This solution will be nonzero even if the correlation between $\mathbf{x}$ and $\mathbf{y}$ is very small. In contrast, as we have shown before, when using ℓ_1 regularization, w will be nonzero only if the correlation between $\mathbf{x}$ and $\mathbf{y}$ is larger than the regularization parameter λ.

Adding ℓ_1 regularization to a linear regression problem with the squared loss yields the LASSO algorithm, defined as

$$\underset{\mathbf{w}}{\operatorname{argmin}} \left(\frac{1}{2m} \|X\mathbf{w} - \mathbf{y}\|^2 + \lambda \|\mathbf{w}\|_1 \right). \tag{25.8}$$

Under some assumptions on the distribution and the regularization parameter λ, the LASSO will find sparse solutions (see, for example, (Zhao & Yu 2006) and the references therein). Another advantage of the ℓ_1 norm is that a vector with low ℓ_1 norm can be "sparsified" (see, for example, (Shalev-Shwartz, Zhang, and Srebro 2010) and the references therein).

25.2 FEATURE MANIPULATION AND NORMALIZATION

Feature manipulations or normalization include simple transformations that we apply on each of our original features. Such transformations may decrease the approximation or estimation errors of our hypothesis class or can yield a faster algorithm. Similarly to the problem of feature selection, here again there are no absolute "good" and "bad" transformations, but rather each transformation that we apply should be related to the learning algorithm we are going to apply on the resulting feature vector as well as to our prior assumptions on the problem.

To motivate *normalization*, consider a linear regression problem with the squared loss. Let $X \in \mathbb{R}^{m,d}$ be a matrix whose rows are the instance vectors and let $\mathbf{y} \in \mathbb{R}^m$ be a vector of target values. Recall that ridge regression returns the vector

$$\underset{\mathbf{w}}{\operatorname{argmin}} \left[\frac{1}{m} \|X\mathbf{w} - \mathbf{y}\|^2 + \lambda \|\mathbf{w}\|^2 \right] = (2\lambda m I + X^\top X)^{-1} X^\top \mathbf{y}.$$

Suppose that $d = 2$ and the underlying data distribution is as follows. First we sample y uniformly at random from $\{\pm 1\}$. Then, we set x_1 to be $y + 0.5\alpha$, where α is sampled uniformly at random from $\{\pm 1\}$, and we set x_2 to be $0.0001y$. Note that the optimal weight vector is $\mathbf{w}^\star = [0;10000]$, and $L_\mathcal{D}(\mathbf{w}^\star) = 0$. However, the objective of ridge regression at $\mathbf{w}^\star$ is $\lambda 10^8$. In contrast, the objective of ridge regression at $\mathbf{w} = [1;0]$ is likely to be close to $0.25 + \lambda$. It follows that whenever $\lambda > \frac{0.25}{10^8 - 1} \approx 0.25 \times 10^{-8}$, the objective of ridge regression is smaller at the suboptimal solution $\mathbf{w} = [1;0]$. Since λ typically should be at least $1/m$ (see the analysis in Chapter 13), it follows that in the aforementioned example, if the number of examples is smaller than 10^8 then we are likely to output a suboptimal solution.

The crux of the preceding example is that the two features have completely different scales. Feature normalization can overcome this problem. There are many ways to perform feature normalization, and one of the simplest approaches is simply to make sure that each feature receives values between -1 and 1. In the preceding example, if we divide each feature by the maximal value it attains we will obtain that $x_1 = \frac{y+0.5\alpha}{1.5}$ and $x_2 = y$. Then, for $\lambda \leq 10^{-3}$ the solution of ridge regression is quite close to $\mathbf{w}^\star$.

Moreover, the generalization bounds we have derived in Chapter 13 for regularized loss minimization depend on the norm of the optimal vector $\mathbf{w}^\star$ and on the maximal norm of the instance vectors.[2] Therefore, in the aforementioned example, before we normalize the features we have that $\|\mathbf{w}^\star\|^2 = 10^8$, while after we normalize the features we have that $\|\mathbf{w}^\star\|^2 = 1$. The maximal norm of the instance vector remains roughly the same; hence the normalization greatly improves the estimation error.

Feature normalization can also improve the runtime of the learning algorithm. For example, in Section 14.5.3 we have shown how to use the Stochastic Gradient Descent (SGD) optimization algorithm for solving the regularized loss minimization problem. The number of iterations required by SGD to converge also depends on the norm of $\mathbf{w}^\star$ and on the maximal norm of $\|\mathbf{x}\|$. Therefore, as before, using normalization can greatly decrease the runtime of SGD.

Next, we demonstrate in the following how a simple transformation on features, such as *clipping*, can sometime decrease the approximation error of our hypothesis class. Consider again linear regression with the squared loss. Let $a > 1$ be a large number, suppose that the target y is chosen uniformly at random from $\{\pm 1\}$, and then the single feature x is set to be y with probability $(1 - 1/a)$ and set to be ay with probability $1/a$. That is, most of the time our feature is bounded but with a very small probability it gets a very high value. Then, for any w, the expected squared loss of w is

$$\begin{aligned} L_\mathcal{D}(w) &= \mathbb{E}\,\frac{1}{2}(wx - y)^2 \\ &= \left(1 - \frac{1}{a}\right)\frac{1}{2}(wy - y)^2 + \frac{1}{a}\frac{1}{2}(awy - y)^2. \end{aligned}$$

[2] More precisely, the bounds we derived in Chapter 13 for regularized loss minimization depend on $\|\mathbf{w}^\star\|^2$ and on either the Lipschitzness or the smoothness of the loss function. For linear predictors and loss functions of the form $\ell(\mathbf{w},(\mathbf{x},y)) = \phi(\langle \mathbf{w},\mathbf{x}\rangle, y)$, where ϕ is convex and either 1-Lipschitz or 1-smooth with respect to its first argument, we have that ℓ is either $\|\mathbf{x}\|$-Lipschitz or $\|\mathbf{x}\|^2$-smooth. For example, for the squared loss, $\phi(a,y) = \frac{1}{2}(a-y)^2$, and $\ell(\mathbf{w},(\mathbf{x},y)) = \frac{1}{2}(\langle \mathbf{w},\mathbf{x}\rangle - y)^2$ is $\|\mathbf{x}\|^2$-smooth with respect to its first argument.

Solving for w we obtain that $w^\star = \frac{2a-1}{a^2+a-1}$, which goes to zero as a goes to infinity. Therefore, the objective at $w^\star$ goes to 0.5 as a goes to infinity. For example, for $a = 100$ we will obtain $L_{\mathcal{D}}(w^\star) \geq 0.48$. Next, suppose we apply a "clipping" transformation; that is, we use the transformation $x \mapsto \text{sign}(x)\min\{1, |x|\}$. Then, following this transformation, $w^\star$ becomes 1 and $L_{\mathcal{D}}(w^\star) = 0$. This simple example shows that a simple transformation can have a significant influence on the approximation error.

Of course, it is not hard to think of examples in which the same feature transformation actually hurts performance and increases the approximation error. This is not surprising, as we have already argued that feature transformations should rely on our prior assumptions on the problem. In the aforementioned example, a prior assumption that may lead us to use the "clipping" transformation is that features that get values larger than a predefined threshold value give us no additional useful information, and therefore we can clip them to the predefined threshold.

25.2.1 Examples of Feature Transformations

We now list several common techniques for feature transformations. Usually, it is helpful to combine some of these transformations (e.g., centering + scaling). In the following, we denote by $\mathbf{f} = (f_1, \ldots, f_m) \in \mathbb{R}^m$ the value of the feature f over the m training examples. Also, we denote by $\bar{f} = \frac{1}{m}\sum_{i=1}^m f_i$ the empirical mean of the feature over all examples.

Centering:
This transformation makes the feature have zero mean, by setting $f_i \leftarrow f_i - \bar{f}$.

Unit Range:
This transformation makes the range of each feature be $[0,1]$. Formally, let $f_{\max} = \max_i f_i$ and $f_{\min} = \min_i f_i$. Then, we set $f_i \leftarrow \frac{f_i - f_{\min}}{f_{\max} - f_{\min}}$. Similarly, we can make the range of each feature be $[-1,1]$ by the transformation $f_i \leftarrow 2\frac{f_i - f_{\min}}{f_{\max} - f_{\min}} - 1$. Of course, it is easy to make the range $[0,b]$ or $[-b,b]$, where b is a user-specified parameter.

Standardization:
This transformation makes all features have a zero mean and unit variance. Formally, let $\nu = \frac{1}{m}\sum_{i=1}^m (f_i - \bar{f})^2$ be the empirical variance of the feature. Then, we set $f_i \leftarrow \frac{f_i - \bar{f}}{\sqrt{\nu}}$.

Clipping:
This transformation clips high or low values of the feature. For example, $f_i \leftarrow \text{sign}(f_i)\max\{b, |f_i|\}$, where b is a user-specified parameter.

Sigmoidal Transformation:
As its name indicates, this transformation applies a sigmoid function on the feature. For example, $f_i \leftarrow \frac{1}{1+\exp(b\, f_i)}$, where b is a user-specified parameter. This transformation can be thought of as a "soft" version of clipping: It has a small effect

on values close to zero and behaves similarly to clipping on values far away from zero.

Logarithmic Transformation:
The transformation is $f_i \leftarrow \log(b + f_i)$, where b is a user-specified parameter. This is widely used when the feature is a "counting" feature. For example, suppose that the feature represents the number of appearances of a certain word in a text document. Then, the difference between zero occurrences of the word and a single occurrence is much more important than the difference between 1000 occurrences and 1001 occurrences.

Remark 25.5. In the aforementioned transformations, each feature is transformed on the basis of the values it obtains on the training set, independently of other features' values. In some situations we would like to set the parameter of the transformation on the basis of other features as well. A notable example is a transformation in which one applies a scaling to the features so that the empirical average of some norm of the instances becomes 1.

25.3 FEATURE LEARNING

So far we have discussed feature selection and manipulations. In these cases, we start with a predefined vector space $\mathbb{R}^d$, representing our features. Then, we select a subset of features (feature selection) or transform individual features (feature transformation). In this section we describe *feature learning*, in which we start with some instance space, $\mathcal{X}$, and would like to learn a function, $\psi : \mathcal{X} \to \mathbb{R}^d$, which maps instances in $\mathcal{X}$ into a representation as d-dimensional feature vectors.

The idea of feature learning is to automate the process of finding a good representation of the input space. As mentioned before, the No-Free-Lunch theorem tells us that we must incorporate some prior knowledge on the data distribution in order to build a good feature representation. In this section we present a few feature learning approaches and demonstrate conditions on the underlying data distribution in which these methods can be useful.

Throughout the book we have already seen several useful feature constructions. For example, in the context of polynomial regression, we have mapped the original instances into the vector space of all their monomials (see Section 9.2.2 in Chapter 9). After performing this mapping, we trained a *linear* predictor on top of the constructed features. Automation of this process would be to learn a transformation $\psi : \mathcal{X} \to \mathbb{R}^d$, such that the composition of the class of linear predictors on top of ψ yields a good hypothesis class for the task at hand.

In the following we describe a technique of feature construction called *dictionary learning*.

25.3.1 Dictionary Learning Using Auto-Encoders

The motivation of dictionary learning stems from a commonly used representation of documents as a "bag-of-words": Given a dictionary of words $D = \{w_1, \ldots, w_k\}$, where each w_i is a string representing a word in the dictionary, and given a document, $(p_1,\ldots,p_d)$, where each p_i is a word in the document, we represent the document as a vector $\mathbf{x} \in \{0,1\}^k$, where x_i is 1 if $w_i = p_j$ for some $j \in [d]$, and $x_i = 0$ otherwise. It was empirically observed in many text processing tasks that linear predictors are quite powerful when applied on this representation. Intuitively, we can think of each word as a feature that measures some aspect of the document. Given labeled examples (e.g., topics of the documents), a learning algorithm searches for a linear predictor that weights these features so that a right combination of appearances of words is indicative of the label.

While in text processing there is a natural meaning to words and to the dictionary, in other applications we do not have such an intuitive representation of an instance. For example, consider the computer vision application of object recognition. Here, the instance is an image and the goal is to recognize which object appears in the image. Applying a linear predictor on the pixel-based representation of the image does not yield a good classifier. What we would like to have is a mapping ψ that would take the pixel-based representation of the image and would output a bag of "visual words," representing the content of the image. For example, a "visual word" can be "there is an eye in the image." If we had such representation, we could have applied a linear predictor on top of this representation to train a classifier for, say, face recognition. Our question is, therefore, how can we learn a dictionary of "visual words" such that a bag-of-words representation of an image would be helpful for predicting which object appears in the image?

A first naive approach for dictionary learning relies on a *clustering* algorithm (see Chapter 22). Suppose that we learn a function $c : \mathcal{X} \to \{1,\ldots,k\}$, where $c(\mathbf{x})$ is the cluster to which $\mathbf{x}$ belongs. Then, we can think of the clusters as "words," and of instances as "documents," where a document $\mathbf{x}$ is mapped to the vector $\psi(\mathbf{x}) \in \{0,1\}^k$, where $\psi(\mathbf{x})_i$ is 1 if and only if $\mathbf{x}$ belongs to the ith cluster. Now, it is straightforward to see that applying a linear predictor on $\psi(\mathbf{x})$ is equivalent to assigning the same target value to all instances that belong to the same cluster. Furthermore, if the clustering is based on distances from a class center (e.g., k-means), then a linear predictor on $\psi(\mathbf{x})$ yields a piece-wise constant predictor on $\mathbf{x}$.

Both the k-means and PCA approaches can be regarded as special cases of a more general approach for dictionary learning which is called *auto-encoders*. In an auto-encoder we learn a pair of functions: an "encoder" function, $\psi : \mathbb{R}^d \to \mathbb{R}^k$, and a "decoder" function, $\phi : \mathbb{R}^k \to \mathbb{R}^d$. The goal of the learning process is to find a pair of functions such that the reconstruction error, $\sum_i \|\mathbf{x}_i - \phi(\psi(\mathbf{x}_i))\|^2$, is small. Of course, we can trivially set $k = d$ and both ψ, ϕ to be the identity mapping, which yields a perfect reconstruction. We therefore must restrict ψ and ϕ in some way. In PCA, we constrain $k < d$ and further restrict ψ and ϕ to be linear functions. In k-means, k is not restricted to be smaller than d, but now ψ and ϕ rely on k centroids, $\boldsymbol{\mu}_1,\ldots,\boldsymbol{\mu}_k$, and $\psi(\mathbf{x})$ returns an indicator vector in $\{0,1\}^k$ that indicates the closest centroid to $\mathbf{x}$, while ϕ takes as input an indicator vector and returns the centroid representing this vector.

An important property of the k-means construction, which is key in allowing k to be larger than d, is that ψ maps instances into *sparse* vectors. In fact, in k-means only a single coordinate of $\psi(\mathbf{x})$ is nonzero. An immediate extension of the k-means construction is therefore to restrict the range of ψ to be vectors with at most s nonzero elements, where s is a small integer. In particular, let ψ and ϕ be functions that depend on $\boldsymbol{\mu}_1,\ldots,\boldsymbol{\mu}_k$. The function ψ maps an instance vector $\mathbf{x}$ to a vector $\psi(\mathbf{x}) \in \mathbb{R}^k$, where $\psi(\mathbf{x})$ should have at most s nonzero elements. The function $\phi(\mathbf{v})$ is defined to be $\sum_{i=1}^k v_i \boldsymbol{\mu}_i$. As before, our goal is to have a small reconstruction error, and therefore we can define

$$\psi(\mathbf{x}) = \operatorname*{argmin}_{\mathbf{v}} \|\mathbf{x} - \phi(\mathbf{v})\|^2 \ \text{ s.t. } \ \|\mathbf{v}\|_0 \le s,$$

where $\|\mathbf{v}\|_0 = |\{j : v_j \neq 0\}|$. Note that when $s = 1$ and we further restrict $\|\mathbf{v}\|_1 = 1$ then we obtain the k-means encoding function; that is, $\psi(\mathbf{x})$ is the indicator vector of the centroid closest to $\mathbf{x}$. For larger values of s, the optimization problem in the preceding definition of ψ becomes computationally difficult. Therefore, in practice, we sometime use ℓ_1 regularization instead of the sparsity constraint and define ψ to be

$$\psi(\mathbf{x}) = \operatorname*{argmin}_{\mathbf{v}} \left[\|\mathbf{x} - \phi(\mathbf{v})\|^2 + \lambda \|\mathbf{v}\|_1 \right],$$

where $\lambda > 0$ is a regularization parameter. Anyway, the dictionary learning problem is now to find the vectors $\boldsymbol{\mu}_1,\ldots,\boldsymbol{\mu}_k$ such that the reconstruction error, $\sum_{i=1}^m \|\mathbf{x}_i - \phi(\psi(\mathbf{x}))\|^2$, is as small as possible. Even if ψ is defined using the ℓ_1 regularization, this is still a computationally hard problem (similar to the k-means problem). However, several heuristic search algorithms may give reasonably good solutions. These algorithms are beyond the scope of this book.

25.4 SUMMARY

Many machine learning algorithms take the feature representation of instances for granted. Yet the choice of representation requires careful attention. We discussed approaches for feature selection, introducing filters, greedy selection algorithms, and sparsity-inducing norms. Next we presented several examples for feature transformations and demonstrated their usefulness. Last, we discussed feature learning, and in particular dictionary learning. We have shown that feature selection, manipulation, and learning all depend on some prior knowledge on the data.

25.5 BIBLIOGRAPHIC REMARKS

Guyon and Elisseeff (2003) surveyed several feature selection procedures, including many types of filters.

Forward greedy selection procedures for minimizing a convex objective subject to a polyhedron constraint date back to the Frank-Wolfe algorithm (Frank & Wolfe 1956). The relation to boosting has been studied by several authors, including, (Warmuth, Liao & Ratsch 2006, Warmuth, Glocer & Vishwanathan 2008, Shalev-Shwartz & Singer 2008). Matching pursuit has been studied in the signal processing community (Mallat & Zhang 1993). Several papers analyzed greedy selection methods under various conditions. See, for example, Shalev-Shwartz, Zhang, and Srebro (2010) and the references therein.

The use of the ℓ_1-norm as a surrogate for sparsity has a long history (e.g., Tibshirani (1996) and the references therein), and much work has been done on understanding the relationship between the ℓ_1-norm and sparsity. It is also closely related to compressed sensing (see Chapter 23). The ability to sparsify low ℓ_1 norm predictors dates back to Maurey (Pisier 1980–1981). In Section 26.4 we also show that low ℓ_1 norm can be used to bound the estimation error of our predictor.

Feature learning and dictionary learning have been extensively studied recently in the context of deep neural networks. See, for example, (LeCun & Bengio 1995, Hinton et al. 2006, Ranzato et al. 2007, Collobert & Weston 2008, Lee et al. 2009, Le et al. 2012, Bengio 2009) and the references therein.

25.6 EXERCISES

25.1 Prove the equality given in Equation (25.1). *Hint*: Let a^*, b^* be minimizers of the left-hand side. Find a, b such that the objective value of the right-hand side is smaller than that of the left-hand side. Do the same for the other direction.

25.2 Show that Equation (25.7) is the solution of Equation (25.6).

25.3 **AdaBoost as a Forward Greedy Selection Algorithm:** Recall the AdaBoost algorithm from Chapter 10. In this section we give another interpretation of AdaBoost as a forward greedy selection algorithm.

- Given a set of m instances $\mathbf{x}_1, \ldots, \mathbf{x}_m$, and a hypothesis class $\mathcal{H}$ of finite VC dimension, show that there exist d and $h_1, \ldots, h_d$ such that for every $h \in \mathcal{H}$ there exists $i \in [d]$ with $h_i(\mathbf{x}_j) = h(\mathbf{x}_j)$ for every $j \in [m]$.
- Let $R(\mathbf{w})$ be as defined in Equation (25.3). Given some $\mathbf{w}$, define $f_{\mathbf{w}}$ to be the function

$$f_{\mathbf{w}}(\cdot) = \sum_{i=1}^{d} w_i h_i(\cdot).$$

Let $\mathbf{D}$ be the distribution over $[m]$ defined by

$$D_i = \frac{\exp(-y_i f_{\mathbf{w}}(\mathbf{x}_i))}{Z},$$

where Z is a normalization factor that ensures that $\mathbf{D}$ is a probability vector. Show that

$$\frac{\partial R(\mathbf{w})}{w_j} = -\sum_{i=1}^{m} D_i y_i h_j(\mathbf{x}_i).$$

Furthermore, denoting $\epsilon_j = \sum_{i=1}^{m} D_i \mathbb{1}_{[h_j(\mathbf{x}_i) \neq y_i]}$, show that

$$\frac{\partial R(\mathbf{w})}{w_j} = 2\epsilon_j - 1.$$

Conclude that if $\epsilon_j \leq 1/2 - \gamma$ then $\left|\frac{\partial R(\mathbf{w})}{w_j}\right| \geq \gamma/2$.

- Show that the update of AdaBoost guarantees $R(\mathbf{w}^{(t+1)}) - R(\mathbf{w}^{(t)}) \leq \log(\sqrt{1-4\gamma^2})$. *Hint*: Use the proof of Theorem 10.2.

PART 4

Advanced Theory

26

Rademacher Complexities

In Chapter 4 we have shown that uniform convergence is a sufficient condition for learnability. In this chapter we study the Rademacher complexity, which measures the rate of uniform convergence. We will provide generalization bounds based on this measure.

26.1 THE RADEMACHER COMPLEXITY

Recall the definition of an ϵ-representative sample from Chapter 4, repeated here for convenience.

Definition 26.1 (ϵ-Representative Sample). A training set S is called ϵ-representative (w.r.t. domain Z, hypothesis class $\mathcal{H}$, loss function ℓ, and distribution $\mathcal{D}$) if

$$\sup_{h\in\mathcal{H}} |L_{\mathcal{D}}(h) - L_S(h)| \le \epsilon.$$

We have shown that if S is an $\epsilon/2$ representative sample then the ERM rule is ϵ-consistent, namely, $L_{\mathcal{D}}(\mathrm{ERM}_{\mathcal{H}}(S)) \le \min_{h\in\mathcal{H}} L_{\mathcal{D}}(h) + \epsilon$.

To simplify our notation, let us denote

$$\mathcal{F} \stackrel{\text{def}}{=} \ell \circ \mathcal{H} \stackrel{\text{def}}{=} \{z \mapsto \ell(h,z) : h \in \mathcal{H}\},$$

and given $f \in \mathcal{F}$, we define

$$L_{\mathcal{D}}(f) = \mathop{\mathbb{E}}_{z\sim\mathcal{D}}[f(z)], \quad L_S(f) = \frac{1}{m}\sum_{i=1}^{m} f(z_i).$$

We define the *representativeness* of S with respect to $\mathcal{F}$ as the largest gap between the true error of a function f and its empirical error, namely,

$$\mathrm{Rep}_{\mathcal{D}}(\mathcal{F}, S) \stackrel{\text{def}}{=} \sup_{f\in\mathcal{F}} \left(L_{\mathcal{D}}(f) - L_S(f)\right). \tag{26.1}$$

Now, suppose we would like to estimate the representativeness of S using the sample S only. One simple idea is to split S into two disjoint sets, $S = S_1 \cup S_2$;

refer to S_1 as a validation set and to S_2 as a training set. We can then estimate the representativeness of S by

$$\sup_{f\in\mathcal{F}} (L_{S_1}(f) - L_{S_2}(f)). \tag{26.2}$$

This can be written more compactly by defining $\boldsymbol{\sigma} = (\sigma_1,\ldots,\sigma_m) \in \{\pm 1\}^m$ to be a vector such that $S_1 = \{z_i : \sigma_i = 1\}$ and $S_2 = \{z_i : \sigma_i = -1\}$. Then, if we further assume that $|S_1| = |S_2|$ then Equation (26.2) can be rewritten as

$$\frac{2}{m} \sup_{f\in\mathcal{F}} \sum_{i=1}^{m} \sigma_i f(z_i). \tag{26.3}$$

The Rademacher complexity measure captures this idea by considering the expectation of the term appearing in Equation 26.3 with respect to a random choice of $\boldsymbol{\sigma}$. Formally, let $\mathcal{F}\circ S$ be the set of all possible evaluations a function $f \in \mathcal{F}$ can achieve on a sample S, namely,

$$\mathcal{F}\circ S = \{(f(z_1),\ldots,f(z_m)) : f \in \mathcal{F}\}.$$

Let the variables in $\boldsymbol{\sigma}$ be distributed i.i.d. according to $\mathbb{P}[\sigma_i = 1] = \mathbb{P}[\sigma_i = -1] = \frac{1}{2}$. Then, the Rademacher complexity of $\mathcal{F}$ with respect to S is defined as follows:

$$R(\mathcal{F}\circ S) \stackrel{\text{def}}{=} \frac{1}{m} \mathop{\mathbb{E}}_{\boldsymbol{\sigma}\sim\{\pm1\}^m}\left[\sup_{f\in\mathcal{F}} \sum_{i=1}^{m} \sigma_i f(z_i)\right]. \tag{26.4}$$

More generally, given a set of vectors, $A \subset \mathbb{R}^m$, we define

$$R(A) \stackrel{\text{def}}{=} \frac{1}{m} \mathop{\mathbb{E}}_{\boldsymbol{\sigma}}\left[\sup_{\mathbf{a}\in A} \sum_{i=1}^{m} \sigma_i a_i\right]. \tag{26.5}$$

The following lemma bounds the expected value of the representativeness of S by twice the expected Rademacher complexity.

Lemma 26.2.

$$\mathop{\mathbb{E}}_{S\sim\mathcal{D}^m} [\mathrm{Rep}_{\mathcal{D}}(\mathcal{F}, S)] \le 2 \mathop{\mathbb{E}}_{S\sim\mathcal{D}^m} R(\mathcal{F}\circ S).$$

Proof. Let $S' = \{z'_1,\ldots,z'_m\}$ be another i.i.d. sample. Clearly, for all $f \in \mathcal{F}$, $L_{\mathcal{D}}(f) = \mathbb{E}_{S'}[L_{S'}(f)]$. Therefore, for every $f \in \mathcal{F}$ we have

$$L_{\mathcal{D}}(f) - L_S(f) = \mathop{\mathbb{E}}_{S'}[L_{S'}(f)] - L_S(f) = \mathop{\mathbb{E}}_{S'}[L_{S'}(f) - L_S(f)].$$

Taking supremum over $f \in \mathcal{F}$ of both sides, and using the fact that the supremum of expectation is smaller than expectation of the supremum we obtain

$$\begin{aligned}\sup_{f\in\mathcal{F}} (L_{\mathcal{D}}(f) - L_S(f)) &= \sup_{f\in\mathcal{F}} \mathop{\mathbb{E}}_{S'}[L_{S'}(f) - L_S(f)] \\ &\le \mathop{\mathbb{E}}_{S'}\left[\sup_{f\in\mathcal{F}} (L_{S'}(f) - L_S(f))\right].\end{aligned}$$

Taking expectation over S on both sides we obtain

$$\mathbb{E}_S\left[\sup_{f\in\mathcal{F}} (L_{\mathcal{D}}(f)-L_S(f))\right] \le \mathbb{E}_{S,S'}\left[\sup_{f\in\mathcal{F}} (L_{S'}(f)-L_S(f))\right]$$
$$= \frac{1}{m}\mathbb{E}_{S,S'}\left[\sup_{f\in\mathcal{F}}\sum_{i=1}^m (f(z_i')-f(z_i))\right]. \quad (26.6)$$

Next, we note that for each j, z_j and z_j' are i.i.d. variables. Therefore, we can replace them without affecting the expectation:

$$\mathbb{E}_{S,S'}\left[\sup_{f\in\mathcal{F}}\left((f(z_j')-f(z_j))+\sum_{i\neq j}(f(z_i')-f(z_i))\right)\right]$$
$$= \mathbb{E}_{S,S'}\left[\sup_{f\in\mathcal{F}}\left((f(z_j)-f(z_j'))+\sum_{i\neq j}(f(z_i')-f(z_i))\right)\right]. \quad (26.7)$$

Let σ_j be a random variable such that $\mathbb{P}[\sigma_j=1]=\mathbb{P}[\sigma_j=-1]=1/2$. From Equation (26.7) we obtain that

$$\mathbb{E}_{S,S',\sigma_j}\left[\sup_{f\in\mathcal{F}}\left(\sigma_j(f(z_j')-f(z_j))+\sum_{i\neq j}(f(z_i')-f(z_i))\right)\right]$$
$$= \frac{1}{2}(\text{l.h.s. of Equation (26.7)})+\frac{1}{2}(\text{r.h.s. of Equation (26.7)})$$
$$= \mathbb{E}_{S,S'}\left[\sup_{f\in\mathcal{F}}\left((f(z_j')-f(z_j))+\sum_{i\neq j}(f(z_i')-f(z_i))\right)\right]. \quad (26.8)$$

Repeating this for all j we obtain that

$$\mathbb{E}_{S,S'}\left[\sup_{f\in\mathcal{F}}\sum_{i=1}^m(f(z_i')-f(z_i))\right] = \mathbb{E}_{S,S',\sigma}\left[\sup_{f\in\mathcal{F}}\sum_{i=1}^m\sigma_i(f(z_i')-f(z_i))\right]. \quad (26.9)$$

Finally,

$$\sup_{f\in\mathcal{F}}\sum_i\sigma_i(f(z_i')-f(z_i)) \le \sup_{f\in\mathcal{F}}\sum_i\sigma_i f(z_i')+\sup_{f\in\mathcal{F}}\sum_i -\sigma_i f(z_i)$$

and since the probability of $\boldsymbol{\sigma}$ is the same as the probability of $-\boldsymbol{\sigma}$, the right-hand side of Equation (26.9) can be bounded by

$$\mathbb{E}_{S,S',\sigma}\left[\sup_{f\in\mathcal{F}}\sum_i\sigma_i f(z_i')+\sup_{f\in\mathcal{F}}\sum_i\sigma_i f(z_i)\right]$$
$$= m\,\mathbb{E}_{S'}[R(\mathcal{F}\circ S')]+m\,\mathbb{E}_S[R(\mathcal{F}\circ S)] = 2m\,\mathbb{E}_S[R(\mathcal{F}\circ S)].$$

□

The lemma immediately yields that, in expectation, the ERM rule finds a hypothesis which is close to the optimal hypothesis in $\mathcal{H}$.

Theorem 26.3. *We have*

$$\mathop{\mathbb{E}}_{S\sim\mathcal{D}^m}[L_\mathcal{D}(\mathrm{ERM}_\mathcal{H}(S)) - L_S(\mathrm{ERM}_\mathcal{H}(S))] \le 2 \mathop{\mathbb{E}}_{S\sim\mathcal{D}^m} R(\ell\circ\mathcal{H}\circ S).$$

Furthermore, for any $h^\star \in \mathcal{H}$

$$\mathop{\mathbb{E}}_{S\sim\mathcal{D}^m}[L_\mathcal{D}(\mathrm{ERM}_\mathcal{H}(S)) - L_\mathcal{D}(h^\star)] \le 2 \mathop{\mathbb{E}}_{S\sim\mathcal{D}^m} R(\ell\circ\mathcal{H}\circ S).$$

Furthermore, if $h^\star = \mathrm{argmin}_h L_\mathcal{D}(h)$ *then for each* $\delta\in(0,1)$ *with probability of at least* $1-\delta$ *over the choice of* S *we have*

$$L_\mathcal{D}(\mathrm{ERM}_\mathcal{H}(S)) - L_\mathcal{D}(h^\star) \le \frac{2\,\mathbb{E}_{S'\sim\mathcal{D}^m} R(\ell\circ\mathcal{H}\circ S')}{\delta}.$$

Proof. The first inequality follows directly from Lemma 26.2. The second inequality follows because for any fixed $h^\star$,

$$L_\mathcal{D}(h^\star) = \mathop{\mathbb{E}}_S[L_S(h^\star)] \ge \mathop{\mathbb{E}}_S[L_S(\mathrm{ERM}_\mathcal{H}(S))].$$

The third inequality follows from the previous inequality by relying on Markov's inequality (note that the random variable $L_\mathcal{D}(\mathrm{ERM}_\mathcal{H}(S)) - L_\mathcal{D}(h^\star)$ is nonnegative). □

Next, we derive bounds similar to the bounds in Theorem 26.3 with a better dependence on the confidence parameter δ. To do so, we first introduce the following bounded differences concentration inequality.

Lemma 26.4 **(McDiarmid's Inequality).** *Let* V *be some set and let* $f: V^m \to \mathbb{R}$ *be a function of* m *variables such that for some* $c>0$, *for all* $i\in[m]$ *and for all* $x_1,\ldots,x_m,x_i'\in V$ *we have*

$$|f(x_1,\ldots,x_m) - f(x_1,\ldots,x_{i-1},x_i',x_{i+1},\ldots,x_m)| \le c.$$

Let $X_1,\ldots,X_m$ *be* m *independent random variables taking values in* V. *Then, with probability of at least* $1-\delta$ *we have*

$$|f(X_1,\ldots,X_m) - \mathbb{E}[f(X_1,\ldots,X_m)]| \le c\sqrt{\ln\left(\tfrac{2}{\delta}\right) m/2}.$$

On the basis of the McDiarmid inequality we can derive generalization bounds with a better dependence on the confidence parameter.

Theorem 26.5. *Assume that for all* z *and* $h\in\mathcal{H}$ *we have that* $|\ell(h,z)|\le c$. *Then,*

1. *With probability of at least* $1-\delta$, *for all* $h\in\mathcal{H}$,

$$L_\mathcal{D}(h) - L_S(h) \le 2 \mathop{\mathbb{E}}_{S'\sim\mathcal{D}^m} R(\ell\circ\mathcal{H}\circ S') + c\sqrt{\frac{2\ln(2/\delta)}{m}}.$$

In particular, this holds for $h = \mathrm{ERM}_\mathcal{H}(S)$.

2. *With probability of at least* $1-\delta$, *for all* $h\in\mathcal{H}$,

$$L_\mathcal{D}(h) - L_S(h) \le 2R(\ell\circ\mathcal{H}\circ S) + 4c\sqrt{\frac{2\ln(4/\delta)}{m}}.$$

In particular, this holds for $h = \mathrm{ERM}_\mathcal{H}(S)$.

3. *For any $h^\star$, with probability of at least* $1-\delta$,

$$L_{\mathcal{D}}(\mathrm{ERM}_{\mathcal{H}}(S)) - L_{\mathcal{D}}(h^\star) \;\le\; 2\,R(\ell\circ\mathcal{H}\circ S) + 5\,c\,\sqrt{\frac{2\ln(8/\delta)}{m}}.$$

Proof. First note that the random variable $\mathrm{Rep}_{\mathcal{D}}(\mathcal{F},S) = \sup_{h\in\mathcal{H}}\left(L_{\mathcal{D}}(h) - L_S(h)\right)$ satisfies the bounded differences condition of Lemma 26.4 with a constant $2c/m$. Combining the bounds in Lemma 26.4 with Lemma 26.2 we obtain that with probability of at least $1-\delta$,

$$\mathrm{Rep}_{\mathcal{D}}(\mathcal{F},S) \le \mathbb{E}\,\mathrm{Rep}_{\mathcal{D}}(\mathcal{F},S) + c\sqrt{\frac{2\ln(2/\delta)}{m}} \le 2\mathop{\mathbb{E}}_{S'} R(\ell\circ\mathcal{H}\circ S') + c\sqrt{\frac{2\ln(2/\delta)}{m}}.$$

The first inequality of the theorem follows from the definition of $\mathrm{Rep}_{\mathcal{D}}(\mathcal{F},S)$. For the second inequality we note that the random variable $R(\ell\circ\mathcal{H}\circ S)$ also satisfies the bounded differences condition of Lemma 26.4 with a constant $2c/m$. Therefore, the second inequality follows from the first inequality, Lemma 26.4, and the union bound. Finally, for the last inequality, denote $h_S = \mathrm{ERM}_{\mathcal{H}}(S)$ and note that

$$\begin{aligned} & L_{\mathcal{D}}(h_S) - L_{\mathcal{D}}(h^\star) \\ & \quad = L_{\mathcal{D}}(h_S) - L_S(h_S) + L_S(h_S) - L_S(h^\star) + L_S(h^\star) - L_{\mathcal{D}}(h^\star) \\ & \quad \le \left(L_{\mathcal{D}}(h_S) - L_S(h_S)\right) + \left(L_S(h^\star) - L_{\mathcal{D}}(h^\star)\right). \end{aligned} \tag{26.10}$$

The first summand on the right-hand side is bounded by the second inequality of the theorem. For the second summand, we use the fact that $h^\star$ does not depend on S; hence by using Hoeffding's inequality we obtain that with probaility of at least $1-\delta/2$,

$$L_S(h^\star) - L_{\mathcal{D}}(h^\star) \;\le\; c\sqrt{\frac{\ln(4/\delta)}{2m}}. \tag{26.11}$$

Combining this with the union bound we conclude our proof. □

The preceding theorem tells us that if the quantity $R(\ell\circ\mathcal{H}\circ S)$ is small then it is possible to learn the class $\mathcal{H}$ using the ERM rule. It is important to emphasize that the last two bounds given in the theorem depend on the specific training set S. That is, we use S both for learning a hypothesis from $\mathcal{H}$ as well as for estimating the quality of it. This type of bound is called a *data-dependent bound.*

26.1.1 Rademacher Calculus

Let us now discuss some properties of the Rademacher complexity measure. These properties will help us in deriving some simple bounds on $R(\ell\circ\mathcal{H}\circ S)$ for specific cases of interest.

The following lemma is immediate from the definition.

Lemma 26.6. *For any $A\subset\mathbb{R}^m$, scalar $c\in\mathbb{R}$, and vector $\mathbf{a}_0\in\mathbb{R}^m$, we have*

$$R(\{c\,\mathbf{a}+\mathbf{a}_0 : \mathbf{a}\in A\}) \le |c|\,R(A).$$

The following lemma tells us that the convex hull of A has the same complexity as A.

Lemma 26.7. *Let A be a subset of $\mathbb{R}^m$ and let $A' = \{\sum_{j=1}^N \alpha_j \mathbf{a}^{(j)} : N \in \mathbb{N}, \forall j, \mathbf{a}^{(j)} \in A, \alpha_j \geq 0, \|\boldsymbol{\alpha}\|_1 = 1\}$. Then, $R(A') = R(A)$.*

Proof. The main idea follows from the fact that for any vector $\mathbf{v}$ we have

$$\sup_{\boldsymbol{\alpha}\geq \mathbf{0}:\|\boldsymbol{\alpha}\|_1=1} \sum_{j=1}^{N} \alpha_j v_j = \max_j v_j .$$

Therefore,

$$\begin{aligned}
m\,R(A') &= \mathbb{E}_{\boldsymbol{\sigma}} \sup_{\boldsymbol{\alpha}\geq \mathbf{0}:\|\boldsymbol{\alpha}\|_1=1} \ \sup_{\mathbf{a}^{(1)},\ldots,\mathbf{a}^{(N)}} \sum_{i=1}^{m} \sigma_i \sum_{j=1}^{N} \alpha_j a_i^{(j)} \\
&= \mathbb{E}_{\boldsymbol{\sigma}} \sup_{\boldsymbol{\alpha}\geq \mathbf{0}:\|\boldsymbol{\alpha}\|_1=1} \sum_{j=1}^{N} \alpha_j \sup_{\mathbf{a}^{(j)}} \sum_{i=1}^{m} \sigma_i a_i^{(j)} \\
&= \mathbb{E}_{\boldsymbol{\sigma}} \sup_{\mathbf{a}\in A} \sum_{i=1}^{m} \sigma_i a_i \\
&= m\,R(A),
\end{aligned}$$

and we conclude our proof. □

The next lemma, due to Massart, states that the Rademacher complexity of a finite set grows logarithmically with the size of the set.

Lemma 26.8 (Massart Lemma). *Let $A = \{\mathbf{a}_1, \ldots, \mathbf{a}_N\}$ be a finite set of vectors in $\mathbb{R}^m$. Define $\bar{\mathbf{a}} = \frac{1}{N}\sum_{i=1}^N \mathbf{a}_i$. Then,*

$$R(A) \leq \max_{\mathbf{a}\in A} \|\mathbf{a} - \bar{\mathbf{a}}\| \frac{\sqrt{2\log(N)}}{m}.$$

Proof. On the basis of Lemma 26.6, we can assume without loss of generality that $\bar{\mathbf{a}} = \mathbf{0}$. Let $\lambda > 0$ and let $A' = \{\lambda \mathbf{a}_1, \ldots, \lambda \mathbf{a}_N\}$. We upper bound the Rademacher complexity as follows:

$$\begin{aligned}
mR(A') &= \mathbb{E}_{\boldsymbol{\sigma}}\left[\max_{\mathbf{a}\in A'} \langle \boldsymbol{\sigma}, \mathbf{a}\rangle\right] = \mathbb{E}_{\boldsymbol{\sigma}}\left[\log\left(\max_{\mathbf{a}\in A'} e^{\langle \boldsymbol{\sigma}, \mathbf{a}\rangle}\right)\right] \\
&\leq \mathbb{E}_{\boldsymbol{\sigma}}\left[\log\left(\sum_{\mathbf{a}\in A'} e^{\langle \boldsymbol{\sigma}, \mathbf{a}\rangle}\right)\right] \\
&\leq \log\left(\mathbb{E}_{\boldsymbol{\sigma}}\left[\sum_{\mathbf{a}\in A'} e^{\langle \boldsymbol{\sigma}, \mathbf{a}\rangle}\right]\right) \qquad \text{// Jensen's inequality} \\
&= \log\left(\sum_{\mathbf{a}\in A'} \prod_{i=1}^{m} \mathbb{E}_{\sigma_i}[e^{\sigma_i a_i}]\right),
\end{aligned}$$

where the last equality occurs because the Rademacher variables are independent. Next, using Lemma A.6 we have that for all $a_i \in \mathbb{R}$,

$$\mathbb{E}_{\sigma_i} e^{\sigma_i a_i} = \frac{\exp(a_i) + \exp(-a_i)}{2} \leq \exp(a_i^2/2),$$

and therefore

$$m R(A') \le \log\left(\sum_{\mathbf{a}\in A'}\prod_{i=1}^{m}\exp\left(\frac{a_i^2}{2}\right)\right) = \log\left(\sum_{\mathbf{a}\in A'}\exp\left(\|\mathbf{a}\|^2/2\right)\right)$$
$$\le \log\left(|A'|\max_{\mathbf{a}\in A'}\exp\left(\|\mathbf{a}\|^2/2\right)\right) = \log(|A'|) + \max_{\mathbf{a}\in A'}(\|\mathbf{a}\|^2/2).$$

Since $R(A) = \frac{1}{\lambda}R(A')$ we obtain from the equation that

$$R(A) \le \frac{\log(|A|) + \lambda^2 \max_{\mathbf{a}\in A}(\|\mathbf{a}\|^2/2)}{\lambda m}.$$

Setting $\lambda = \sqrt{2\log(|A|)/\max_{\mathbf{a}\in A}\|\mathbf{a}\|^2}$ and rearranging terms we conclude our proof. □

The following lemma shows that composing A with a Lipschitz function does not blow up the Rademacher complexity. The proof is due to Kakade and Tewari.

Lemma 26.9 (Contraction Lemma). *For each $i \in [m]$, let $\phi_i : \mathbb{R} \to \mathbb{R}$ be a ρ-Lipschitz function; namely, for all $\alpha, \beta \in \mathbb{R}$ we have $|\phi_i(\alpha) - \phi_i(\beta)| \le \rho\,|\alpha - \beta|$. For $\mathbf{a} \in \mathbb{R}^m$ let $\boldsymbol{\phi}(\mathbf{a})$ denote the vector $(\phi_1(a_1), \ldots, \phi_m(y_m))$. Let $\boldsymbol{\phi} \circ A = \{\boldsymbol{\phi}(\mathbf{a}) : a \in A\}$. Then,*

$$R(\boldsymbol{\phi} \circ A) \le \rho\, R(A).$$

Proof. For simplicity, we prove the lemma for the case $\rho = 1$. The case $\rho \ne 1$ will follow by defining $\phi' = \frac{1}{\rho}\phi$ and then using Lemma 26.6. Let $A_i = \{(a_1, \ldots, a_{i-1}, \phi_i(a_i), a_{i+1}, \ldots, a_m) : \mathbf{a} \in A\}$. Clearly, it suffices to prove that for any set A and all i we have $R(A_i) \le R(A)$. Without loss of generality we will prove the latter claim for $i = 1$ and to simplify notation we omit the subscript from ϕ_1. We have

$$m R(A_1) = \mathbb{E}_{\sigma}\left[\sup_{\mathbf{a}\in A_1}\sum_{i=1}^{m}\sigma_i a_i\right]$$
$$= \mathbb{E}_{\sigma}\left[\sup_{\mathbf{a}\in A}\sigma_1\phi(a_1) + \sum_{i=2}^{m}\sigma_i a_i\right]$$
$$= \frac{1}{2}\mathbb{E}_{\sigma_2,\ldots,\sigma_m}\left[\sup_{\mathbf{a}\in A}\left(\phi(a_1) + \sum_{i=2}^{m}\sigma_i a_i\right) + \sup_{\mathbf{a}\in A}\left(-\phi(a_1) + \sum_{i=2}^{m}\sigma_i a_i\right)\right]$$
$$= \frac{1}{2}\mathbb{E}_{\sigma_2,\ldots,\sigma_m}\left[\sup_{\mathbf{a},\mathbf{a}'\in A}\left(\phi(a_1) - \phi(a_1') + \sum_{i=2}^{m}\sigma_i a_i + \sum_{i=2}^{m}\sigma_i a_i'\right)\right]$$
$$\le \frac{1}{2}\mathbb{E}_{\sigma_2,\ldots,\sigma_m}\left[\sup_{\mathbf{a},\mathbf{a}'\in A}\left(|a_1 - a_1'| + \sum_{i=2}^{m}\sigma_i a_i + \sum_{i=2}^{m}\sigma_i a_i'\right)\right], \tag{26.12}$$

where in the last inequality we used the assumption that ϕ is Lipschitz. Next, we note that the absolute value on $|a_1 - a_1'|$ in the preceding expression can be omitted since both $\mathbf{a}$ and $\mathbf{a}'$ are from the same set A and the rest of the expression in the supremum is not affected by replacing $\mathbf{a}$ and $\mathbf{a}'$. Therefore,

$$mR(A_1) \le \frac{1}{2} \mathop{\mathbb{E}}_{\sigma_2,\ldots,\sigma_m} \left[\sup_{\mathbf{a},\mathbf{a}' \in A} \left(a_1 - a_1' + \sum_{i=2}^m \sigma_i a_i + \sum_{i=2}^m \sigma_i a_i' \right) \right]. \tag{26.13}$$

But, using the same equalities as in Equation (26.12), it is easy to see that the right-hand side of Equation (26.13) exactly equals $m\,R(A)$, which concludes our proof. □

26.2 RADEMACHER COMPLEXITY OF LINEAR CLASSES

In this section we analyze the Rademacher complexity of linear classes. To simplify the derivation we first define the following two classes:

$$\mathcal{H}_1 = \{\mathbf{x} \mapsto \langle \mathbf{w}, \mathbf{x} \rangle : \|\mathbf{w}\|_1 \le 1\}, \quad \mathcal{H}_2 = \{\mathbf{x} \mapsto \langle \mathbf{w}, \mathbf{x} \rangle : \|\mathbf{w}\|_2 \le 1\}. \tag{26.14}$$

The following lemma bounds the Rademacher complexity of $\mathcal{H}_2$. We allow the $\mathbf{x}_i$ to be vectors in any Hilbert space (even infinite dimensional), and the bound does not depend on the dimensionality of the Hilbert space. This property becomes useful when analyzing kernel methods.

Lemma 26.10. *Let $S = (\mathbf{x}_1, \ldots, \mathbf{x}_m)$ be vectors in a Hilbert space. Define: $\mathcal{H}_2 \circ S = \{(\langle \mathbf{w}, \mathbf{x}_1 \rangle, \ldots, \langle \mathbf{w}, \mathbf{x}_m \rangle) : \|\mathbf{w}\|_2 \le 1\}$. Then,*

$$R(\mathcal{H}_2 \circ S) \le \frac{\max_i \|\mathbf{x}_i\|_2}{\sqrt{m}}.$$

Proof. Using Cauchy-Schwartz inequality we know that for any vectors $\mathbf{w}, \mathbf{v}$ we have $\langle \mathbf{w}, \mathbf{v} \rangle \le \|\mathbf{w}\| \, \|\mathbf{v}\|$. Therefore,

$$\begin{aligned} mR(\mathcal{H}_2 \circ S) &= \mathop{\mathbb{E}}_{\sigma} \left[\sup_{\mathbf{a} \in \mathcal{H}_2 \circ S} \sum_{i=1}^m \sigma_i a_i \right] \\ &= \mathop{\mathbb{E}}_{\sigma} \left[\sup_{\mathbf{w}: \|\mathbf{w}\| \le 1} \sum_{i=1}^m \sigma_i \langle \mathbf{w}, \mathbf{x}_i \rangle \right] \\ &= \mathop{\mathbb{E}}_{\sigma} \left[\sup_{\mathbf{w}: \|\mathbf{w}\| \le 1} \langle \mathbf{w}, \sum_{i=1}^m \sigma_i \mathbf{x}_i \rangle \right] \\ &\le \mathop{\mathbb{E}}_{\sigma} \left[\| \sum_{i=1}^m \sigma_i \mathbf{x}_i \|_2 \right]. \end{aligned} \tag{26.15}$$

Next, using Jensen's inequality we have that

$$\mathop{\mathbb{E}}_{\sigma} \left[\left\| \sum_{i=1}^m \sigma_i \mathbf{x}_i \right\|_2 \right] = \mathop{\mathbb{E}}_{\sigma} \left[\left(\left\| \sum_{i=1}^m \sigma_i \mathbf{x}_i \right\|_2^2 \right)^{1/2} \right] \le \left(\mathop{\mathbb{E}}_{\sigma} \left[\left\| \sum_{i=1}^m \sigma_i \mathbf{x}_i \right\|_2^2 \right] \right)^{1/2}. \tag{26.16}$$

Finally, since the variables $\sigma_1,\ldots,\sigma_m$ are independent we have

$$\begin{aligned}\mathbb{E}_{\sigma}\left[\|\sum_{i=1}^m \sigma_i \mathbf{x}_i\|_2^2\right] &= \mathbb{E}_{\sigma}\left[\sum_{i,j} \sigma_i\sigma_j \langle \mathbf{x}_i,\mathbf{x}_j\rangle\right] \\ &= \sum_{i\neq j}\langle \mathbf{x}_i,\mathbf{x}_j\rangle \mathbb{E}_{\sigma}[\sigma_i\sigma_j] + \sum_{i=1}^m \langle \mathbf{x}_i,\mathbf{x}_i\rangle \mathbb{E}_{\sigma}\left[\sigma_i^2\right] \\ &= \sum_{i=1}^m \|\mathbf{x}_i\|_2^2 \le m \max_i \|\mathbf{x}_i\|_2^2.\end{aligned}$$

Combining this with Equation (26.15) and Equation (26.16) we conclude our proof. □

Next we bound the Rademacher complexity of $\mathcal{H}_1\circ S$.

Lemma 26.11. *Let $S=(\mathbf{x}_1,\ldots,\mathbf{x}_m)$ be vectors in $\mathbb{R}^n$. Then,*

$$R(\mathcal{H}_1\circ S) \le \max_i \|\mathbf{x}_i\|_\infty \sqrt{\frac{2\log(2n)}{m}}.$$

Proof. Using Holder's inequality we know that for any vectors $\mathbf{w},\mathbf{v}$ we have $\langle \mathbf{w},\mathbf{v}\rangle \le \|\mathbf{w}\|_1\,\|\mathbf{v}\|_\infty$. Therefore,

$$\begin{aligned}mR(\mathcal{H}_1\circ S) &= \mathbb{E}_{\sigma}\left[\sup_{\mathbf{a}\in H_1\circ S}\sum_{i=1}^m \sigma_i a_i\right] \\ &= \mathbb{E}_{\sigma}\left[\sup_{\mathbf{w}:\|\mathbf{w}\|_1\le 1}\sum_{i=1}^m \sigma_i\langle \mathbf{w},\mathbf{x}_i\rangle\right] \\ &= \mathbb{E}_{\sigma}\left[\sup_{\mathbf{w}:\|\mathbf{w}\|_1\le 1}\langle \mathbf{w},\sum_{i=1}^m \sigma_i\mathbf{x}_i\rangle\right] \\ &\le \mathbb{E}_{\sigma}\left[\|\sum_{i=1}^m \sigma_i\mathbf{x}_i\|_\infty\right]. \qquad (26.17)\end{aligned}$$

For each $j\in[n]$, let $\mathbf{v}_j=(x_{1,j},\ldots,x_{m,j})\in\mathbb{R}^m$. Note that $\|\mathbf{v}_j\|_2\le\sqrt{m}\max_i\|\mathbf{x}_i\|_\infty$. Let $V=\{\mathbf{v}_1,\ldots,\mathbf{v}_n,-\mathbf{v}_1,\ldots,-\mathbf{v}_n\}$. The right-hand side of Equation (26.17) is $m\,R(V)$. Using Massart lemma (Lemma 26.8) we have that

$$R(V)\le \max_i \|\mathbf{x}_i\|_\infty \sqrt{2\log(2n)/m},$$

which concludes our proof. □

26.3 GENERALIZATION BOUNDS FOR SVM

In this section we use Rademacher complexity to derive generalization bounds for generalized linear predictors with Euclidean norm constraint. We will show how this leads to generalization bounds for hard-SVM and soft-SVM.

We shall consider the following general constraint-based formulation. Let $\mathcal{H} = \{\mathbf{w} : \|\mathbf{w}\|_2 \le B\}$ be our hypothesis class, and let $Z = \mathcal{X} \times \mathcal{Y}$ be the examples domain. Assume that the loss function $\ell : \mathcal{H} \times Z \to \mathbb{R}$ is of the form

$$\ell(\mathbf{w}, (\mathbf{x}, y)) = \phi(\langle \mathbf{w}, \mathbf{x} \rangle, y), \tag{26.18}$$

where $\phi : \mathbb{R} \times \mathcal{Y} \to \mathbb{R}$ is such that for all $y \in \mathcal{Y}$, the scalar function $a \mapsto \phi(a, y)$ is ρ-Lipschitz. For example, the hinge-loss function, $\ell(\mathbf{w}, (\mathbf{x}, y)) = \max\{0, 1 - y\langle \mathbf{w}, \mathbf{x} \rangle\}$, can be written as in Equation (26.18) using $\phi(a, y) = \max\{0, 1 - ya\}$, and note that ϕ is 1-Lipschitz for all $y \in \{\pm 1\}$. Another example is the absolute loss function, $\ell(\mathbf{w}, (\mathbf{x}, y)) = |\langle \mathbf{w}, \mathbf{x} \rangle - y|$, which can be written as in Equation (26.18) using $\phi(a, y) = |a - y|$, which is also 1-Lipschitz for all $y \in \mathbb{R}$.

The following theorem bounds the generalization error of all predictors in $\mathcal{H}$ using their empirical error.

Theorem 26.12. *Suppose that $\mathcal{D}$ is a distribution over $\mathcal{X} \times \mathcal{Y}$ such that with probability 1 we have that $\|\mathbf{x}\|_2 \le R$. Let $\mathcal{H} = \{\mathbf{w} : \|\mathbf{w}\|_2 \le B\}$ and let $\ell : \mathcal{H} \times Z \to \mathbb{R}$ be a loss function of the form given in Equation (26.18) such that for all $y \in \mathcal{Y}$, $a \mapsto \phi(a, y)$ is a ρ-Lipschitz function and such that $\max_{a \in [-BR, BR]} |\phi(a, y)| \le c$. Then, for any $\delta \in (0, 1)$, with probability of at least $1 - \delta$ over the choice of an i.i.d. sample of size m,*

$$\forall \mathbf{w} \in \mathcal{H}, \quad L_{\mathcal{D}}(\mathbf{w}) \le L_S(\mathbf{w}) + \frac{2\rho B R}{\sqrt{m}} + c\sqrt{\frac{2\ln(2/\delta)}{m}}.$$

Proof. Let $F = \{(\mathbf{x}, y) \mapsto \phi(\langle \mathbf{w}, \mathbf{x} \rangle, y) : \mathbf{w} \in \mathcal{H}\}$. We will show that with probability 1, $R(F \circ S) \le \rho B R/\sqrt{m}$ and then the theorem will follow from Theorem 26.5. Indeed, the set $F \circ S$ can be written as

$$F \circ S = \{(\phi(\langle \mathbf{w}, \mathbf{x}_1 \rangle, y_1), \ldots, \phi(\langle \mathbf{w}, \mathbf{x}_m \rangle, y_m)) : \mathbf{w} \in \mathcal{H}\},$$

and the bound on $R(F \circ S)$ follows directly by combining Lemma 26.9, Lemma 26.10, and the assumption that $\|\mathbf{x}\|_2 \le R$ with probability 1. □

We next derive a generalization bound for hard-SVM based on the previous theorem. For simplicity, we do not allow a bias term and consider the hard-SVM problem:

$$\operatorname*{argmin}_{\mathbf{w}} \|\mathbf{w}\|^2 \quad \text{s.t.} \quad \forall i, \; y_i \langle \mathbf{w}, \mathbf{x}_i \rangle \ge 1 \tag{26.19}$$

Theorem 26.13. *Consider a distribution $\mathcal{D}$ over $\mathcal{X} \times \{\pm 1\}$ such that there exists some vector $\mathbf{w}^\star$ with $\mathbb{P}_{(\mathbf{x}, y) \sim \mathcal{D}}[y\langle \mathbf{w}^\star, \mathbf{x} \rangle \ge 1] = 1$ and such that $\|\mathbf{x}\|_2 \le R$ with probability 1. Let $\mathbf{w}_S$ be the output of Equation (26.19). Then, with probability of at least $1 - \delta$ over the choice of $S \sim \mathcal{D}^m$, we have that*

$$\mathop{\mathbb{P}}_{(\mathbf{x}, y) \sim \mathcal{D}} [y \ne sign(\langle \mathbf{w}_S, \mathbf{x} \rangle)] \le \frac{2\, R\, \|\mathbf{w}^\star\|}{\sqrt{m}} + (1 + R\, \|\mathbf{w}^\star\|)\sqrt{\frac{2\ln(2/\delta)}{m}}.$$

Proof. Throughout the proof, let the loss function be the ramp loss (see Section 15.2.3). Note that the range of the ramp loss is $[0, 1]$ and that it is a 1-Lipschitz function. Since the ramp loss upper bounds the zero-one loss, we have that

$$\mathop{\mathbb{P}}_{(\mathbf{x}, y) \sim \mathcal{D}} [y \ne \operatorname{sign}(\langle \mathbf{w}_S, \mathbf{x} \rangle)] \le L_{\mathcal{D}}(\mathbf{w}_S).$$

Let $B = \|\mathbf{w}^\star\|_2$ and consider the set $\mathcal{H} = \{\mathbf{w} : \|\mathbf{w}\|_2 \le B\}$. By the definition of hard-SVM and our assumption on the distribution, we have that $\mathbf{w}_S \in \mathcal{H}$ with probability 1 and that $L_S(\mathbf{w}_S) = 0$. Therefore, using Theorem 26.12 we have that

$$L_{\mathcal{D}}(\mathbf{w}_S) \le L_S(\mathbf{w}_S) + \frac{2BR}{\sqrt{m}} + \sqrt{\frac{2\ln(2/\delta)}{m}}.$$

□

Remark 26.1. Theorem 26.13 implies that the sample complexity of hard-SVM grows like $\frac{R^2\|\mathbf{w}^\star\|^2}{\epsilon^2}$. Using a more delicate analysis and the separability assumption, it is possible to improve the bound to an order of $\frac{R^2\|\mathbf{w}^\star\|^2}{\epsilon}$.

The bound in the preceding theorem depends on $\|\mathbf{w}^\star\|$, which is unknown. In the following we derive a bound that depends on the norm of the output of SVM; hence it can be calculated from the training set itself. The proof is similar to the derivation of bounds for structure risk minimization (SRM).

Theorem 26.14. *Assume that the conditions of Theorem 26.13 hold. Then, with probability of at least $1-\delta$ over the choice of $S \sim \mathcal{D}^m$, we have that*

$$\underset{(\mathbf{x},y)\sim\mathcal{D}}{\mathbb{P}}[y \ne \mathit{sign}(\langle \mathbf{w}_S, \mathbf{x}\rangle)] \le \frac{4R\|\mathbf{w}_S\|}{\sqrt{m}} + \sqrt{\frac{\ln\left(\frac{4\log_2(\|\mathbf{w}_S\|)}{\delta}\right)}{m}}.$$

Proof. For any integer i, let $B_i = 2^i$, $\mathcal{H}_i = \{\mathbf{w} : \|\mathbf{w}\| \le B_i\}$, and let $\delta_i = \frac{\delta}{2i^2}$. Fix i, then using Theorem 26.12 we have that with probability of at least $1-\delta_i$

$$\forall \mathbf{w} \in \mathcal{H}_i, \;\; L_{\mathcal{D}}(\mathbf{w}) \le L_S(\mathbf{w}) + \frac{2B_iR}{\sqrt{m}} + \sqrt{\frac{2\ln(2/\delta_i)}{m}}$$

Applying the union bound and using $\sum_{i=1}^{\infty}\delta_i \le \delta$ we obtain that with probability of at least $1-\delta$ this holds for all i. Therefore, for all $\mathbf{w}$, if we let $i = \lceil \log_2(\|\mathbf{w}\|)\rceil$ then $\mathbf{w} \in \mathcal{H}_i$, $B_i \le 2\|\mathbf{w}\|$, and $\frac{2}{\delta_i} = \frac{(2i)^2}{\delta} \le \frac{(4\log_2(\|\mathbf{w}\|))^2}{\delta}$. Therefore,

$$\begin{aligned} L_{\mathcal{D}}(\mathbf{w}) &\le L_S(\mathbf{w}) + \frac{2B_iR}{\sqrt{m}} + \sqrt{\frac{2\ln(2/\delta_i)}{m}} \\ &\le L_S(\mathbf{w}) + \frac{4\|\mathbf{w}\|R}{\sqrt{m}} + \sqrt{\frac{4(\ln(4\log_2(\|\mathbf{w}\|)) + \ln(1/\delta))}{m}}. \end{aligned}$$

In particular, it holds for $\mathbf{w}_S$, which concludes our proof. □

Remark 26.2. Note that all the bounds we have derived do not depend on the dimension of $\mathbf{w}$. This property is utilized when learning SVM with kernels, where the dimension of $\mathbf{w}$ can be extremely large.

26.4 GENERALIZATION BOUNDS FOR PREDICTORS WITH LOW ℓ_1 NORM

In the previous section we derived generalization bounds for linear predictors with an ℓ_2-norm constraint. In this section we consider the following general ℓ_1-norm constraint formulation. Let $\mathcal{H} = \{\mathbf{w} : \|\mathbf{w}\|_1 \le B\}$ be our hypothesis class, and let

$Z = \mathcal{X} \times \mathcal{Y}$ be the examples domain. Assume that the loss function, $\ell : \mathcal{H} \times Z \to \mathbb{R}$, is of the same form as in Equation (26.18), with $\phi : \mathbb{R} \times \mathcal{Y} \to \mathbb{R}$ being ρ-Lipschitz w.r.t. its first argument. The following theorem bounds the generalization error of all predictors in $\mathcal{H}$ using their empirical error.

Theorem 26.15. *Suppose that $\mathcal{D}$ is a distribution over $\mathcal{X} \times \mathcal{Y}$ such that with probability 1 we have that $\|\mathbf{x}\|_\infty \le R$. Let $\mathcal{H} = \{\mathbf{w} \in \mathbb{R}^d : \|\mathbf{w}\|_1 \le B\}$ and let $\ell : \mathcal{H} \times Z \to \mathbb{R}$ be a loss function of the form given in Equation (26.18) such that for all $y \in \mathcal{Y}$, $a \mapsto \phi(a, y)$ is an ρ-Lipschitz function and such that $\max_{a \in [-BR, BR]} |\phi(a, y)| \le c$. Then, for any $\delta \in (0, 1)$, with probability of at least $1 - \delta$ over the choice of an i.i.d. sample of size m,*

$$\forall \mathbf{w} \in \mathcal{H}, \quad L_{\mathcal{D}}(\mathbf{w}) \le L_S(\mathbf{w}) + 2\rho B R \sqrt{\frac{2 \log(2d)}{m}} + c \sqrt{\frac{2 \ln(2/\delta)}{m}}.$$

Proof. The proof is identical to the proof of Theorem 26.12, while relying on Lemma 26.11 instead of relying on Lemma 26.10. □

It is interesting to compare the two bounds given in Theorem 26.12 and Theorem 26.15. Apart from the extra $\log(d)$ factor that appears in Theorem 26.15, both bounds look similar. However, the parameters B, R have different meanings in the two bounds. In Theorem 26.12, the parameter B imposes an ℓ_2 constraint on $\mathbf{w}$ and the parameter R captures a low ℓ_2-norm assumption on the instances. In contrast, in Theorem 26.15 the parameter B imposes an ℓ_1 constraint on $\mathbf{w}$ (which is stronger than an ℓ_2 constraint) while the parameter R captures a low ℓ_∞-norm assumption on the instance (which is weaker than a low ℓ_2-norm assumption). Therefore, the choice of the constraint should depend on our prior knowledge of the set of instances and on prior assumptions on good predictors.

26.5 BIBLIOGRAPHIC REMARKS

The use of Rademacher complexity for bounding the uniform convergence is due to (Koltchinskii & Panchenko 2000, Bartlett & Mendelson 2001, Bartlett & Mendelson 2002). For additional reading see, for example, (Bousquet 2002, Boucheron, Bousquet & Lugosi 2005, Bartlett, Bousquet & Mendelson 2005). Our proof of the concentration lemma is due to Kakade and Tewari lecture notes. Kakade, Sridharan, and Tewari (2008) gave a unified framework for deriving bounds on the Rademacher complexity of linear classes with respect to different assumptions on the norms.

27

Covering Numbers

In this chapter we describe another way to measure the complexity of sets, which is called covering numbers.

27.1 COVERING

Definition 27.1 (Covering). Let $A \subset \mathbb{R}^m$ be a set of vectors. We say that A is r-covered by a set A', with respect to the Euclidean metric, if for all $\mathbf{a} \in A$ there exists $\mathbf{a}' \in A'$ with $\|\mathbf{a} - \mathbf{a}'\| \le r$. We define by $N(r, A)$ the cardinality of the smallest A' that r-covers A.

Example 27.1 (Subspace). Suppose that $A \subset \mathbb{R}^m$, let $c = \max_{\mathbf{a} \in A} \|\mathbf{a}\|$, and assume that A lies in a d-dimensional subspace of $\mathbb{R}^m$. Then, $N(r, A) \le (2c\sqrt{d}/r)^d$. To see this, let $\mathbf{v}_1, \ldots, \mathbf{v}_d$ be an orthonormal basis of the subspace. Then, any $\mathbf{a} \in A$ can be written as $\mathbf{a} = \sum_{i=1}^d \alpha_i \mathbf{v}_i$ with $\|\boldsymbol{\alpha}\|_\infty \le \|\boldsymbol{\alpha}\|_2 = \|\mathbf{a}\|_2 \le c$. Let $\epsilon \in \mathbb{R}$ and consider the set

$$A' = \left\{ \sum_{i=1}^d \alpha_i' \mathbf{v}_i : \forall i, \alpha_i' \in \{-c, -c+\epsilon, -c+2\epsilon, \ldots, c\} \right\}.$$

Given $\mathbf{a} \in A$ s.t. $\mathbf{a} = \sum_{i=1}^d \alpha_i \mathbf{v}_i$ with $\|\boldsymbol{\alpha}\|_\infty \le c$, there exists $\mathbf{a}' \in A'$ such that

$$\|\mathbf{a} - \mathbf{a}'\|^2 = \|\sum_i (\alpha_i' - \alpha_i)\mathbf{v}_i\|^2 \le \epsilon^2 \sum_i \|\mathbf{v}_i\|^2 \le \epsilon^2 d.$$

Choose $\epsilon = r/\sqrt{d}$; then $\|\mathbf{a} - \mathbf{a}'\| \le r$ and therefore A' is an r-cover of A. Hence,

$$N(r, A) \le |A'| = \left(\frac{2c}{\epsilon}\right)^d = \left(\frac{2c\sqrt{d}}{r}\right)^d.$$

27.1.1 Properties

The following lemma is immediate from the definition.

Lemma 27.2. *For any $A \subset \mathbb{R}^m$, scalar $c > 0$, and vector $\mathbf{a}_0 \in \mathbb{R}^m$, we have*

$$\forall r > 0, \quad N(r, \{c\,\mathbf{a} + \mathbf{a}_0 : \mathbf{a} \in A\}) \le N(cr, A).$$

Next, we derive a contraction principle.

Lemma 27.3. *For each $i \in [m]$, let $\phi_i : \mathbb{R} \to \mathbb{R}$ be a ρ-Lipschitz function; namely, for all $\alpha, \beta \in \mathbb{R}$ we have $|\phi_i(\alpha) - \phi_i(\beta)| \le \rho\,|\alpha - \beta|$. For $\mathbf{a} \in \mathbb{R}^m$ let $\boldsymbol{\phi}(\mathbf{a})$ denote the vector $(\phi_1(a_1), \ldots, \phi_m(a_m))$. Let $\boldsymbol{\phi} \circ A = \{\boldsymbol{\phi}(\mathbf{a}) : a \in A\}$. Then,*

$$N(\rho\, r, \boldsymbol{\phi} \circ A) \le N(r, A).$$

Proof. Define $B = \boldsymbol{\phi} \circ A$. Let A' be an r-cover of A and define $B' = \boldsymbol{\phi} \circ A'$. Then, for all $\mathbf{a} \in A$ there exists $\mathbf{a}' \in A'$ with $\|\mathbf{a} - \mathbf{a}'\| \le r$. So,

$$\|\boldsymbol{\phi}(\mathbf{a}) - \boldsymbol{\phi}(\mathbf{a}')\|^2 = \sum_i (\phi_i(a_i) - \phi_i(a_i'))^2 \le \rho^2 \sum_i (a_i - a_i')^2 \le (\rho r)^2.$$

Hence, B' is an $(\rho\, r)$-cover of B. □

27.2 FROM COVERING TO RADEMACHER COMPLEXITY VIA CHAINING

The following lemma bounds the Rademacher complexity of A based on the covering numbers $N(r, A)$. This technique is called *Chaining* and is attributed to Dudley.

Lemma 27.4. *Let $c = \min_{\bar{\mathbf{a}}} \max_{\mathbf{a} \in A} \|\mathbf{a} - \bar{\mathbf{a}}\|$. Then, for any integer $M > 0$,*

$$R(A) \le \frac{c\,2^{-M}}{\sqrt{m}} + \frac{6c}{m} \sum_{k=1}^{M} 2^{-k} \sqrt{\log(N(c\,2^{-k}, A))}.$$

Proof. Let $\bar{\mathbf{a}}$ be a minimizer of the objective function given in the definition of c. On the basis of Lemma 26.6, we can analyze the Rademacher complexity assuming that $\bar{\mathbf{a}} = \mathbf{0}$.

Consider the set $B_0 = \{\mathbf{0}\}$ and note that it is a c-cover of A. Let $B_1, \ldots, B_M$ be sets such that each B_k corresponds to a minimal $(c2^{-k})$-cover of A. Let $\mathbf{a}^* = \operatorname{argmax}_{\mathbf{a} \in A} \langle \boldsymbol{\sigma}, \mathbf{a} \rangle$ (where if there is more than one maximizer, choose one in an arbitrary way, and if a maximizer does not exist, choose $\mathbf{a}^*$ such that $\langle \boldsymbol{\sigma}, \mathbf{a}^* \rangle$ is close enough to the supremum). Note that $\mathbf{a}^*$ is a function of $\boldsymbol{\sigma}$. For each k, let $\mathbf{b}^{(k)}$ be the nearest neighbor of $\mathbf{a}^*$ in B_k (hence $\mathbf{b}^{(k)}$ is also a function of $\boldsymbol{\sigma}$). Using the triangle inequality,

$$\|\mathbf{b}^{(k)} - \mathbf{b}^{(k-1)}\| \le \|\mathbf{b}^{(k)} - \mathbf{a}^*\| + \|\mathbf{a}^* - \mathbf{b}^{(k-1)}\| \le c\,(2^{-k} + 2^{-(k-1)}) = 3c\,2^{-k}.$$

For each k define the set

$$\hat{B}_k = \{(\mathbf{a} - \mathbf{a}') : \mathbf{a} \in B_k, \mathbf{a}' \in B_{k-1}, \|\mathbf{a} - \mathbf{a}'\| \le 3c\,2^{-k}\}.$$

We can now write

$$
\begin{aligned}
R(A) &= \frac{1}{m}\,\mathbb{E}\langle \boldsymbol{\sigma}, \mathbf{a}^*\rangle \\
&= \frac{1}{m}\,\mathbb{E}\left[\langle \boldsymbol{\sigma}, \mathbf{a}^* - \mathbf{b}^{(M)}\rangle + \sum_{k=1}^{M}\langle \boldsymbol{\sigma}, \mathbf{b}^{(k)} - \mathbf{b}^{(k-1)}\rangle\right] \\
&\le \frac{1}{m}\,\mathbb{E}\left[\|\sigma\|\,\|\mathbf{a}^* - \mathbf{b}^{(M)}\|\right] + \sum_{k=1}^{M}\frac{1}{m}\,\mathbb{E}\left[\sup_{\mathbf{a}\in\hat{B}_k}\langle \boldsymbol{\sigma}, \mathbf{a}\rangle\right].
\end{aligned}
$$

Since $\|\boldsymbol{\sigma}\| = \sqrt{m}$ and $\|\mathbf{a}^* - \mathbf{b}^{(M)}\| \le c\,2^{-M}$, the first summand is at most $\frac{c}{\sqrt{m}}2^{-M}$. Additionally, by Massart lemma,

$$
\frac{1}{m}\,\mathbb{E}\sup_{\mathbf{a}\in\hat{B}_k}\langle \boldsymbol{\sigma}, \mathbf{a}\rangle \le 3c\,2^{-k}\frac{\sqrt{2\log(N(c\,2^{-k},A)^2)}}{m} = 6c\,2^{-k}\frac{\sqrt{\log(N(c\,2^{-k},A))}}{m}.
$$

Therefore,

$$
R(A) \le \frac{c\,2^{-M}}{\sqrt{m}} + \frac{6c}{m}\sum_{k=1}^{M}2^{-k}\sqrt{\log(N(c2^{-k},A))}.
$$

□

As a corollary we obtain the following:

Lemma 27.5. *Assume that there are $\alpha, \beta > 0$ such that for any $k \ge 1$ we have*

$$
\sqrt{\log(N(c2^{-k},A))} \le \alpha + \beta k.
$$

Then,

$$
R(A) \le \frac{6c}{m}\,(\alpha + 2\beta).
$$

Proof. The bound follows from Lemma 27.4 by taking $M \to \infty$ and noting that $\sum_{k=1}^{\infty} 2^{-k} = 1$ and $\sum_{k=1}^{\infty} k2^{-k} = 2$. □

Example 27.2. Consider a set A which lies in a d dimensional subspace of $\mathbb{R}^m$ and such that $c = \max_{\mathbf{a}\in A}\|\mathbf{a}\|$. We have shown that $N(r,A) \le \left(\frac{2c\sqrt{d}}{r}\right)^d$. Therefore, for any k,

$$
\begin{aligned}
\sqrt{\log(N(c2^{-k},A))} &\le \sqrt{d\log\left(2^{k+1}\sqrt{d}\right)} \\
&\le \sqrt{d\log(2\sqrt{d})} + \sqrt{k\,d} \\
&\le \sqrt{d\log(2\sqrt{d})} + \sqrt{d}\,k.
\end{aligned}
$$

Hence Lemma 27.5 yields

$$
R(A) \;\le\; \frac{6c}{m}\left(\sqrt{d\log(2\sqrt{d})} + 2\sqrt{d}\right) \;=\; O\left(\frac{c\sqrt{d\log(d)}}{m}\right).
$$

27.3 BIBLIOGRAPHIC REMARKS

The chaining technique is due to Dudley (1987). For an extensive study of covering numbers as well as other complexity measures that can be used to bound the rate of uniform convergence we refer the reader to (Anthony & Bartlet 1999).

28

Proof of the Fundamental Theorem of Learning Theory

In this chapter we prove Theorem 6.8 from Chapter 6. We remind the reader the conditions of the theorem, which will hold throughout this chapter: $\mathcal{H}$ is a hypothesis class of functions from a domain $\mathcal{X}$ to $\{0,1\}$, the loss function is the $0-1$ loss, and $\text{VCdim}(\mathcal{H}) = d < \infty$.

We shall prove the upper bound for both the realizable and agnostic cases and shall prove the lower bound for the agnostic case. The lower bound for the realizable case is left as an exercise.

28.1 THE UPPER BOUND FOR THE AGNOSTIC CASE

For the upper bound we need to prove that there exists C such that $\mathcal{H}$ is agnostic PAC learnable with sample complexity

$$m_{\mathcal{H}}(\epsilon,\delta) \le C\frac{d+\ln(1/\delta)}{\epsilon^2}.$$

We will prove the slightly looser bound:

$$m_{\mathcal{H}}(\epsilon,\delta) \le C\frac{d\log(d/\epsilon)+\ln(1/\delta)}{\epsilon^2}. \tag{28.1}$$

The tighter bound in the theorem statement requires a more involved proof, in which a more careful analysis of the Rademacher complexity using a technique called "chaining" should be used. This is beyond the scope of this book.

To prove Equation (28.1), it suffices to show that applying the ERM with a sample size

$$m \ge 4\frac{32d}{\epsilon^2}\cdot\log\left(\frac{64d}{\epsilon^2}\right)+\frac{8}{\epsilon^2}\cdot(8d\log(e/d)+2\log(4/\delta))$$

yields an ϵ,δ-learner for $\mathcal{H}$. We prove this result on the basis of Theorem 26.5.

Let $(\mathbf{x}_1,y_1),\ldots,(\mathbf{x}_m,y_m)$ be a classification training set. Recall that the Sauer-Shelah lemma tells us that if $\text{VCdim}(\mathcal{H}) = d$ then

$$\left|\{(h(\mathbf{x}_1),\ldots,h(\mathbf{x}_m)) : h\in\mathcal{H}\}\right| \le \left(\frac{em}{d}\right)^d.$$

Denote $A = \{(\mathbb{1}_{[h(\mathbf{x}_1)\neq y_1]}, \ldots, \mathbb{1}_{[h(\mathbf{x}_m)\neq y_m]}) : h \in \mathcal{H}\}$. This clearly implies that

$$|A| \leq \left(\frac{em}{d}\right)^d.$$

Combining this with Lemma 26.8 we obtain the following bound on the Rademacher complexity:

$$R(A) \leq \sqrt{\frac{2d\log(em/d)}{m}}.$$

Using Theorem 26.5 we obtain that with probability of at least $1-\delta$, for every $h \in \mathcal{H}$ we have that

$$L_{\mathcal{D}}(h) - L_S(h) \leq \sqrt{\frac{8d\log(em/d)}{m}} + \sqrt{\frac{2\log(2/\delta)}{m}}.$$

Repeating the previous argument for minus the zero-one loss and applying the union bound we obtain that with probability of at least $1-\delta$, for every $h \in \mathcal{H}$ it holds that

$$|L_{\mathcal{D}}(h) - L_S(h)| \leq \sqrt{\frac{8d\log(em/d)}{m}} + \sqrt{\frac{2\log(4/\delta)}{m}}$$
$$\leq 2\sqrt{\frac{8d\log(em/d) + 2\log(4/\delta)}{m}}.$$

To ensure that this is smaller than ϵ we need

$$m \geq \frac{4}{\epsilon^2} \cdot (8d\log(m) + 8d\log(e/d) + 2\log(4/\delta)).$$

Using Lemma A.2, a sufficient condition for the inequality to hold is that

$$m \geq 4\frac{32d}{\epsilon^2} \cdot \log\left(\frac{64d}{\epsilon^2}\right) + \frac{8}{\epsilon^2} \cdot (8d\log(e/d) + 2\log(4/\delta)).$$

28.2 THE LOWER BOUND FOR THE AGNOSTIC CASE

Here, we prove that there exists C such that $\mathcal{H}$ is agnostic PAC learnable with sample complexity

$$m_{\mathcal{H}}(\epsilon,\delta) \geq C\frac{d + \ln(1/\delta)}{\epsilon^2}.$$

We will prove the lower bound in two parts. First, we will show that $m(\epsilon,\delta) \geq 0.5\log(1/(4\delta))/\epsilon^2$, and second we will show that for every $\delta \leq 1/8$ we have that $m(\epsilon,\delta) \geq 8d/\epsilon^2$. These two bounds will conclude the proof.

28.2.1 Showing That $m(\epsilon,\delta) \geq 0.5\log(1/(4\delta))/\epsilon^2$

We first show that for any $\epsilon < 1/\sqrt{2}$ and any $\delta \in (0,1)$, we have that $m(\epsilon,\delta) \geq 0.5\log(1/(4\delta))/\epsilon^2$. To do so, we show that for $m \leq 0.5\log(1/(4\delta))/\epsilon^2$, $\mathcal{H}$ is not learnable.

Choose one example that is shattered by $\mathcal{H}$. That is, let c be an example such that there are $h_+, h_- \in \mathcal{H}$ for which $h_+(c) = 1$ and $h_-(c) = -1$. Define two distributions,

$\mathcal{D}_+$ and $\mathcal{D}_-$, such that for $b \in \{\pm 1\}$ we have

$$\mathcal{D}_b(\{(x,y)\}) = \begin{cases} \frac{1+yb\epsilon}{2} & \text{if } x = c \\ 0 & \text{otherwise.} \end{cases}$$

That is, all the distribution mass is concentrated on two examples $(c,1)$ and $(c,-1)$, where the probability of (c,b) is $\frac{1+b\epsilon}{2}$ and the probability of $(c,-b)$ is $\frac{1-b\epsilon}{2}$.

Let A be an arbitrary algorithm. Any training set sampled from $\mathcal{D}_b$ has the form $S = (c,y_1),\ldots,(c,y_m)$. Therefore, it is fully characterized by the vector $\mathbf{y} = (y_1,\ldots,y_m) \in \{\pm 1\}^m$. Upon receiving a training set S, the algorithm A returns a hypothesis $h : \mathcal{X} \to \{\pm 1\}$. Since the error of A w.r.t. $\mathcal{D}_b$ only depends on $h(c)$, we can think of A as a mapping from $\{\pm 1\}^m$ into $\{\pm 1\}$. Therefore, we denote by $A(\mathbf{y})$ the value in $\{\pm 1\}$ corresponding to the prediction of $h(c)$, where h is the hypothesis that A outputs upon receiving the training set $S = (c,y_1),\ldots,(c,y_m)$.

Note that for any hypothesis h we have

$$L_{\mathcal{D}_b}(h) = \frac{1 - h(c)b\epsilon}{2}.$$

In particular, the Bayes optimal hypothesis is h_b and

$$L_{\mathcal{D}_b}(A(\mathbf{y})) - L_{\mathcal{D}_b}(h_b) = \frac{1 - A(\mathbf{y})b\epsilon}{2} - \frac{1-\epsilon}{2} = \begin{cases} \epsilon & \text{if } A(\mathbf{y}) \neq b \\ 0 & \text{otherwise.} \end{cases}$$

Fix A. For $b \in \{\pm 1\}$, let $Y^b = \{\mathbf{y} \in \{0,1\}^m : A(\mathbf{y}) \neq b\}$. The distribution $\mathcal{D}_b$ induces a probability P_b over $\{\pm 1\}^m$. Hence,

$$\mathbb{P}[L_{\mathcal{D}_b}(A(\mathbf{y})) - L_{\mathcal{D}_b}(h_b) = \epsilon] = \mathcal{D}_b(Y^b) = \sum_{\mathbf{y}} P_b[\mathbf{y}]\mathbb{1}_{[A(\mathbf{y}) \neq b]}.$$

Denote $N^+ = \{\mathbf{y} : |\{i : y_i = 1\}| \geq m/2\}$ and $N^- = \{\pm 1\}^m \setminus N^+$. Note that for any $\mathbf{y} \in N^+$ we have $P_+[\mathbf{y}] \geq P_-[\mathbf{y}]$ and for any $\mathbf{y} \in N^-$ we have $P_-[\mathbf{y}] \geq P_+[\mathbf{y}]$. Therefore,

$$\begin{aligned}
&\max_{b \in \{\pm 1\}} \mathbb{P}[L_{\mathcal{D}_b}(A(\mathbf{y})) - L_{\mathcal{D}_b}(h_b) = \epsilon] \\
&= \max_{b \in \{\pm 1\}} \sum_{\mathbf{y}} P_b[\mathbf{y}]\mathbb{1}_{[A(\mathbf{y}) \neq b]} \\
&\geq \frac{1}{2}\sum_{\mathbf{y}} P_+[\mathbf{y}]\mathbb{1}_{[A(\mathbf{y}) \neq +]} + \frac{1}{2}\sum_{\mathbf{y}} P_-[\mathbf{y}]\mathbb{1}_{[A(\mathbf{y}) \neq -]} \\
&= \frac{1}{2}\sum_{\mathbf{y} \in N^+} (P_+[\mathbf{y}]\mathbb{1}_{[A(\mathbf{y}) \neq +]} + P_-[\mathbf{y}]\mathbb{1}_{[A(\mathbf{y}) \neq -]}) \\
&\quad + \frac{1}{2}\sum_{\mathbf{y} \in N^-} (P_+[\mathbf{y}]\mathbb{1}_{[A(\mathbf{y}) \neq +]} + P_-[\mathbf{y}]\mathbb{1}_{[A(\mathbf{y}) \neq -]})
\end{aligned}$$

$$\geq \frac{1}{2}\sum_{\mathbf{y}\in N^+}\left(P_-[\mathbf{y}]\mathbb{1}_{[A(\mathbf{y})\neq +]} + P_-[\mathbf{y}]\mathbb{1}_{[A(\mathbf{y})\neq -]}\right)$$

$$+\frac{1}{2}\sum_{\mathbf{y}\in N^-}\left(P_+[\mathbf{y}]\mathbb{1}_{[A(\mathbf{y})\neq +]} + P_+[\mathbf{y}]\mathbb{1}_{[A(\mathbf{y})\neq -]}\right)$$

$$= \frac{1}{2}\sum_{\mathbf{y}\in N^+} P_-[\mathbf{y}] + \frac{1}{2}\sum_{\mathbf{y}\in N^-} P_+[\mathbf{y}].$$

Next note that $\sum_{\mathbf{y}\in N^+} P_-[\mathbf{y}] = \sum_{\mathbf{y}\in N^-} P_+[\mathbf{y}]$, and both values are the probability that a Binomial $(m,(1-\epsilon)/2)$ random variable will have value greater than $m/2$. Using Lemma B.11, this probability is lower bounded by

$$\frac{1}{2}\left(1-\sqrt{1-\exp(-m\epsilon^2/(1-\epsilon^2))}\right) \geq \frac{1}{2}\left(1-\sqrt{1-\exp(-2m\epsilon^2)}\right),$$

where we used the assumption that $\epsilon^2 \leq 1/2$. It follows that if $m \leq 0.5\log(1/(4\delta))/\epsilon^2$ then there exists b such that

$$\mathbb{P}[L_{\mathcal{D}_b}(A(\mathbf{y})) - L_{\mathcal{D}_b}(h_b) = \epsilon]$$
$$\geq \frac{1}{2}\left(1-\sqrt{1-\sqrt{4\delta}}\right) \geq \delta,$$

where the last inequality follows by standard algebraic manipulations. This concludes our proof.

28.2.2 Showing That $m(\epsilon, 1/8) \geq 8d/\epsilon^2$

We shall now prove that for every $\epsilon < 1/(8\sqrt{2})$ we have that $m(\epsilon,\delta) \geq \frac{8d}{\epsilon^2}$.

Let $\rho = 8\epsilon$ and note that $\rho \in (0, 1/\sqrt{2})$. We will construct a family of distributions as follows. First, let $C = \{c_1,\ldots,c_d\}$ be a set of d instances which are shattered by $\mathcal{H}$. Second, for each vector $(b_1,\ldots,b_d) \in \{\pm 1\}^d$, define a distribution $\mathcal{D}_b$ such that

$$\mathcal{D}_b(\{(x,y)\}) = \begin{cases} \frac{1}{d}\cdot\frac{1+yb_i\rho}{2} & \text{if } \exists i: x = c_i \\ 0 & \text{otherwise.}\end{cases}$$

That is, to sample an example according to $\mathcal{D}_b$, we first sample an element $c_i \in C$ uniformly at random, and then set the label to be b_i with probability $(1+\rho)/2$ or $-b_i$ with probability $(1-\rho)/2$.

It is easy to verify that the Bayes optimal predictor for $\mathcal{D}_b$ is the hypothesis $h \in \mathcal{H}$ such that $h(c_i) = b_i$ for all $i \in [d]$, and its error is $\frac{1-\rho}{2}$. In addition, for any other function $f: \mathcal{X} \to \{\pm 1\}$, it is easy to verify that

$$L_{\mathcal{D}_b}(f) = \frac{1+\rho}{2}\cdot\frac{|\{i\in[d]: f(c_i)\neq b_i\}|}{d} + \frac{1-\rho}{2}\cdot\frac{|\{i\in[d]: f(c_i)= b_i\}|}{d}.$$

Therefore,

$$L_{\mathcal{D}_b}(f) - \min_{h\in\mathcal{H}} L_{\mathcal{D}_b}(h) = \rho\cdot\frac{|\{i\in[d]: f(c_i)\neq b_i\}|}{d}. \qquad (28.2)$$

Next, fix some learning algorithm A. As in the proof of the No-Free-Lunch theorem, we have that

$$\max_{\mathcal{D}_b : b \in \{\pm 1\}^d} \mathbb{E}_{S \sim \mathcal{D}_b^m} \left[L_{\mathcal{D}_b}(A(S)) - \min_{h \in \mathcal{H}} L_{\mathcal{D}_b}(h) \right] \tag{28.3}$$

$$\geq \mathbb{E}_{\mathcal{D}_b : b \sim U(\{\pm 1\}^d)} \mathbb{E}_{S \sim \mathcal{D}_b^m} \left[L_{\mathcal{D}_b}(A(S)) - \min_{h \in \mathcal{H}} L_{\mathcal{D}_b}(h) \right] \tag{28.4}$$

$$= \mathbb{E}_{\mathcal{D}_b : b \sim U(\{\pm 1\}^d)} \mathbb{E}_{S \sim \mathcal{D}_b^m} \left[\rho \cdot \frac{|\{i \in [d] : A(S)(c_i) \neq b_i|}{d} \right] \tag{28.5}$$

$$= \frac{\rho}{d} \sum_{i=1}^{d} \mathbb{E}_{\mathcal{D}_b : b \sim U(\{\pm 1\}^d)} \mathbb{E}_{S \sim \mathcal{D}_b^m} \mathbb{1}_{[A(S)(c_i) \neq b_i]}, \tag{28.6}$$

where the first equality follows from Equation (28.2). In addition, using the definition of $\mathcal{D}_b$, to sample $S \sim \mathcal{D}_b$ we can first sample $(j_1, \ldots, j_m) \sim U([d])^m$, set $x_r = c_{j_i}$, and finally sample y_r such that $\mathbb{P}[y_r = b_{j_i}] = (1+\rho)/2$. Let us simplify the notation and use $y \sim b$ to denote sampling according to $\mathbb{P}[y = b] = (1+\rho)/2$. Therefore, the right-hand side of Equation (28.6) equals

$$\frac{\rho}{d} \sum_{i=1}^{d} \mathbb{E}_{j \sim U([d])^m} \mathbb{E}_{b \sim U(\{\pm 1\}^d)} \mathbb{E}_{\forall r, y_r \sim b_{j_r}} \mathbb{1}_{[A(S)(c_i) \neq b_i]}. \tag{28.7}$$

We now proceed in two steps. First, we show that among all learning algorithms, A, the one which minimizes Equation (28.7) (and hence also Equation (28.4)) is the Maximum-Likelihood learning rule, denoted A_{ML}. Formally, for each i, $A_{ML}(S)(c_i)$ is the majority vote among the set $\{y_r : r \in [m], x_r = c_i\}$. Second, we lower bound Equation (28.7) for A_{ML}.

Lemma 28.1. *Among all algorithms, Equation (28.4) is minimized for A being the Maximum-Likelihood algorithm, A_{ML}, defined as*

$$\forall i, \;\; A_{ML}(S)(c_i) = sign\left(\sum_{r : x_r = c_i} y_r \right).$$

Proof. Fix some $j \in [d]^m$. Note that given j and $y \in \{\pm 1\}^m$, the training set S is fully determined. Therefore, we can write $A(j, y)$ instead of $A(S)$. Let us also fix $i \in [d]$. Denote $b^{\neg i}$ the sequence $(b_1, \ldots, b_{i-1}, b_{i+1}, \ldots, b_m)$. Also, for any $y \in \{\pm 1\}^m$, let y^I denote the elements of y corresponding to indices for which $j_r = i$ and let $y^{\neg I}$ be the rest of the elements of y. We have

$$\mathbb{E}_{b \sim U(\{\pm 1\}^d)} \mathbb{E}_{\forall r, y_r \sim b_{j_r}} \mathbb{1}_{[A(S)(c_i) \neq b_i]}$$

$$= \frac{1}{2} \sum_{b_i \in \{\pm 1\}} \mathbb{E}_{b^{\neg i} \sim U(\{\pm 1\}^{d-1})} \sum_{y} P[y | b^{\neg i}, b_i] \mathbb{1}_{[A(j,y)(c_i) \neq b_i]}$$

$$= \mathbb{E}_{b^{\neg i} \sim U(\{\pm 1\}^{d-1})} \sum_{y^{\neg I}} P[y^{\neg I} | b^{\neg i}] \frac{1}{2} \sum_{y^I} \left(\sum_{b_i \in \{\pm 1\}} P[y^I | b_i] \mathbb{1}_{[A(j,y)(c_i) \neq b_i]} \right).$$

The sum within the parentheses is minimized when $A(j,y)(c_i)$ is the maximizer of $P[y^I|b_i]$ over $b_i \in \{\pm 1\}$, which is exactly the Maximum-Likelihood rule. Repeating the same argument for all i we conclude our proof. □

Fix i. For every j, let $n_i(j) = \{|t : j_t = i|\}$ be the number of instances in which the instance is c_i. For the Maximum-Likelihood rule, we have that the quantity

$$\mathop{\mathbb{E}}_{b \sim U(\{\pm 1\}^d)} \mathop{\mathbb{E}}_{\forall r, y_r \sim b_{j_r}} \mathbb{1}_{[A_{ML}(S)(c_i) \neq b_i]}$$

is exactly the probability that a binomial $(n_i(j), (1-\rho)/2)$ random variable will be larger than $n_i(j)/2$. Using Lemma B.11, and the assumption $\rho^2 \leq 1/2$, we have that

$$P[B \geq n_i(j)/2] \geq \frac{1}{2}\left(1 - \sqrt{1 - e^{-2 n_i(j) \rho^2}}\right).$$

We have thus shown that

$$\begin{aligned}
&\frac{\rho}{d}\sum_{i=1}^{d} \mathop{\mathbb{E}}_{j \sim U([d])^m} \mathop{\mathbb{E}}_{b \sim U(\{\pm 1\}^d)} \mathop{\mathbb{E}}_{\forall r, y_r \sim b_{j_r}} \mathbb{1}_{[A(S)(c_i) \neq b_i]} \\
&\geq \frac{\rho}{2d}\sum_{i=1}^{d} \mathop{\mathbb{E}}_{j \sim U([d])^m}\left(1 - \sqrt{1 - e^{-2\rho^2 n_i(j)}}\right) \\
&\geq \frac{\rho}{2d}\sum_{i=1}^{d} \mathop{\mathbb{E}}_{j \sim U([d])^m}\left(1 - \sqrt{2\rho^2 n_i(j)}\right),
\end{aligned}$$

where in the last inequality we used the inequality $1 - e^{-a} \leq a$.

Since the square root function is concave, we can apply Jensen's inequality to obtain that the above is lower bounded by

$$\begin{aligned}
&\geq \frac{\rho}{2d}\sum_{i=1}^{d}\left(1 - \sqrt{2\rho^2 \mathop{\mathbb{E}}_{j \sim U([d])^m} n_i(j)}\right) \\
&= \frac{\rho}{2d}\sum_{i=1}^{d}\left(1 - \sqrt{2\rho^2 m/d}\right) \\
&= \frac{\rho}{2}\left(1 - \sqrt{2\rho^2 m/d}\right).
\end{aligned}$$

As long as $m < \frac{d}{8\rho^2}$, this term would be larger than $\rho/4$.

In summary, we have shown that if $m < \frac{d}{8\rho^2}$ then for any algorithm there exists a distribution such that

$$\mathop{\mathbb{E}}_{S \sim \mathcal{D}^m}\left[L_{\mathcal{D}}(A(S)) - \min_{h \in \mathcal{H}} L_{\mathcal{D}}(h)\right] \geq \rho/4.$$

Finally, Let $\Delta = \frac{1}{\rho}(L_{\mathcal{D}}(A(S)) - \min_{h\in\mathcal{H}} L_{\mathcal{D}}(h))$ and note that $\Delta \in [0,1]$ (see Equation (28.5)). Therefore, using Lemma B.1, we get that

$$\mathbb{P}[L_{\mathcal{D}}(A(S)) - \min_{h\in\mathcal{H}} L_{\mathcal{D}}(h) > \epsilon] = \mathbb{P}\left[\Delta > \frac{\epsilon}{\rho}\right] \geq \mathbb{E}[\Delta] - \frac{\epsilon}{\rho}$$
$$\geq \frac{1}{4} - \frac{\epsilon}{\rho}.$$

Choosing $\rho = 8\epsilon$ we conclude that if $m < \frac{8d}{\epsilon^2}$, then with probability of at least 1/8 we will have $L_{\mathcal{D}}(A(S)) - \min_{h\in\mathcal{H}} L_{\mathcal{D}}(h) \geq \epsilon$.

28.3 THE UPPER BOUND FOR THE REALIZABLE CASE

Here we prove that there exists C such that $\mathcal{H}$ is PAC learnable with sample complexity

$$m_{\mathcal{H}}(\epsilon,\delta) \leq C\frac{d\ln(1/\epsilon) + \ln(1/\delta)}{\epsilon}.$$

We do so by showing that for $m \geq C\frac{d\ln(1/\epsilon)+\ln(1/\delta)}{\epsilon}$, $\mathcal{H}$ is learnable using the ERM rule. We prove this claim on the basis of the notion of ϵ-nets.

Definition 28.2 (ϵ-net). Let $\mathcal{X}$ be a domain. $S \subset \mathcal{X}$ is an ϵ-net for $\mathcal{H} \subset 2^{\mathcal{X}}$ with respect to a distribution $\mathcal{D}$ over $\mathcal{X}$ if

$$\forall h \in \mathcal{H}: \ \mathcal{D}(h) \geq \epsilon \ \Rightarrow \ h \cap S \neq \emptyset.$$

Theorem 28.3. *Let $\mathcal{H} \subset 2^{\mathcal{X}}$ with* VCdim$(\mathcal{H}) = d$. *Fix $\epsilon \in (0,1)$, $\delta \in (0,1/4)$ and let*

$$m \geq \frac{8}{\epsilon}\left(2d\log\left(\frac{16e}{\epsilon}\right) + \log\left(\frac{2}{\delta}\right)\right).$$

Then, with probability of at least $1-\delta$ over a choice of $S \sim \mathcal{D}^m$ we have that S is an ϵ-net for $\mathcal{H}$.

Proof. Let

$$B = \{S \subset \mathcal{X} : |S| = m, \ \exists h \in \mathcal{H}, \mathcal{D}(h) \geq \epsilon, h \cap S = \emptyset\}$$

be the set of sets which are not ϵ-nets. We need to bound $\mathbb{P}[S \in B]$. Define

$$B' = \{(S,T) \subset \mathcal{X} : |S| = |T| = m, \ \exists h \in \mathcal{H}, \mathcal{D}(h) \geq \epsilon, h \cap S = \emptyset, \ |T \cap h| > \tfrac{\epsilon m}{2}\}.$$

Claim 1
$\mathbb{P}[S \in B] \leq 2\,\mathbb{P}[(S,T) \in B']$.
Proof of Claim 1: Since S and T are chosen independently we can write

$$\mathbb{P}[(S,T) \in B'] = \mathop{\mathbb{E}}_{(S,T)\sim\mathcal{D}^{2m}}\left[\mathbb{1}_{[(S,T)\in B']}\right] = \mathop{\mathbb{E}}_{S\sim\mathcal{D}^m}\left[\mathop{\mathbb{E}}_{T\sim\mathcal{D}^m}\left[\mathbb{1}_{[(S,T)\in B']}\right]\right].$$

Note that $(S,T) \in B'$ implies $S \in B$ and therefore $\mathbb{1}_{[(S,T)\in B']} = \mathbb{1}_{[(S,T)\in B']} \mathbb{1}_{[S\in B]}$, which gives

$$\begin{aligned}\mathbb{P}[(S,T) \in B'] &= \mathop{\mathbb{E}}_{S\sim\mathcal{D}^m} \mathop{\mathbb{E}}_{T\sim\mathcal{D}^m} \mathbb{1}_{[(S,T)\in B']} \mathbb{1}_{[S\in B]} \\ &= \mathop{\mathbb{E}}_{S\sim\mathcal{D}^m} \mathbb{1}_{[S\in B]} \mathop{\mathbb{E}}_{T\sim\mathcal{D}^m} \mathbb{1}_{[(S,T)\in B']}.\end{aligned}$$

Fix some S. Then, either $\mathbb{1}_{[S\in B]} = 0$ or $S \in B$ and then $\exists h_S$ such that $\mathcal{D}(h_S) \geq \epsilon$ and $|h_S \cap S| = 0$. It follows that a sufficient condition for $(S,T) \in B'$ is that $|T \cap h_S| > \frac{\epsilon m}{2}$. Therefore, whenever $S \in B$ we have

$$\mathop{\mathbb{E}}_{T\sim\mathcal{D}^m} \mathbb{1}_{[(S,T)\in B']} \geq \mathop{\mathbb{P}}_{T\sim\mathcal{D}^m} [|T \cap h_S| > \tfrac{\epsilon m}{2}].$$

But, since we now assume $S \in B$ we know that $\mathcal{D}(h_S) = \rho \geq \epsilon$. Therefore, $|T \cap h_S|$ is a binomial random variable with parameters ρ (probability of success for a single try) and m (number of tries). Chernoff's inequality implies

$$\mathbb{P}[|T \cap h_S| \leq \tfrac{\rho m}{2}] \leq e^{-\frac{2}{m\rho}(m\rho - m\rho/2)^2} = e^{-m\rho/2} \leq e^{-m\epsilon/2} \leq e^{-d\log(1/\delta)/2} = \delta^{d/2} \leq 1/2.$$

Thus,

$$\mathbb{P}[|T \cap h_S| > \tfrac{\epsilon m}{2}] = 1 - \mathbb{P}[|T \cap h_S| \leq \tfrac{\epsilon m}{2}] \geq 1 - \mathbb{P}[|T \cap h_S| \leq \tfrac{\rho m}{2}] \geq 1/2.$$

Combining all the preceding we *conclude the proof of Claim 1.*

Claim 2 (Symmetrization):
$\mathbb{P}[(S,T) \in B'] \leq e^{-\epsilon m/4}\, \tau_{\mathcal{H}}(2m)$.
Proof of Claim 2: To simplify notation, let $\alpha = m\epsilon/2$ and for a sequence $A = (x_1,\ldots,x_{2m})$ let $A_0 = (x_1,\ldots,x_m)$. Using the definition of B' we get that

$$\begin{aligned}\mathbb{P}[A \in B'] &= \mathop{\mathbb{E}}_{A\sim\mathcal{D}^{2m}} \max_{h\in\mathcal{H}} \mathbb{1}_{[\mathcal{D}(h)\geq\epsilon]} \mathbb{1}_{[|h\cap A_0|=0]} \mathbb{1}_{[|h\cap A|\geq\alpha]} \\ &\leq \mathop{\mathbb{E}}_{A\sim\mathcal{D}^{2m}} \max_{h\in\mathcal{H}} \mathbb{1}_{[|h\cap A_0|=0]} \mathbb{1}_{[|h\cap A|\geq\alpha]}.\end{aligned}$$

Now, let us define by $\mathcal{H}_A$ the effective number of different hypotheses on A, namely, $\mathcal{H}_A = \{h \cap A : h \in \mathcal{H}\}$. It follows that

$$\begin{aligned}\mathbb{P}[A \in B'] &\leq \mathop{\mathbb{E}}_{A\sim\mathcal{D}^{2m}} \max_{h\in\mathcal{H}_A} \mathbb{1}_{[|h\cap A_0|=0]} \mathbb{1}_{[|h\cap A|\geq\alpha]} \\ &\leq \mathop{\mathbb{E}}_{A\sim\mathcal{D}^{2m}} \sum_{h\in\mathcal{H}_A} \mathbb{1}_{[|h\cap A_0|=0]} \mathbb{1}_{[|h\cap A|\geq\alpha]}.\end{aligned}$$

Let $J = \{\mathbf{j} \subset [2m] : |\mathbf{j}| = m\}$. For any $\mathbf{j} \in J$ and $A = (x_1,\ldots,x_{2m})$ define $A_{\mathbf{j}} = (x_{j_1},\ldots,x_{j_m})$. Since the elements of A are chosen i.i.d., we have that for any $\mathbf{j} \in J$ and any function $f(A, A_0)$ it holds that $\mathbb{E}_{A\sim\mathcal{D}^{2m}}[f(A,A_0)] = \mathbb{E}_{A\sim\mathcal{D}^{2m}}[f(A,A_{\mathbf{j}})]$. Since this holds for any $\mathbf{j}$ it also holds for the expectation of $\mathbf{j}$ chosen at random from J. In particular, it holds for the function $f(A,A_0) = \sum_{h\in\mathcal{H}_A} \mathbb{1}_{[|h\cap A_0|=0]} \mathbb{1}_{[|h\cap A|\geq\alpha]}$. We therefore obtain that

$$\mathbb{P}[A \in B'] \leq \mathop{\mathbb{E}}_{A \sim \mathcal{D}^{2m}} \mathop{\mathbb{E}}_{j \sim J} \sum_{h \in \mathcal{H}_A} \mathbb{1}_{[|h \cap A_j| = 0]} \mathbb{1}_{[|h \cap A| \geq \alpha]}$$

$$= \mathop{\mathbb{E}}_{A \sim \mathcal{D}^{2m}} \sum_{h \in \mathcal{H}_A} \mathbb{1}_{[|h \cap A| \geq \alpha]} \mathop{\mathbb{E}}_{j \sim J} \mathbb{1}_{[|h \cap A_j| = 0]}.$$

Now, fix some A s.t. $|h \cap A| \geq \alpha$. Then, $\mathbb{E}_j \mathbb{1}_{[|h \cap A_j| = 0]}$ is the probability that when choosing m balls from a bag with at least α red balls, we will never choose a red ball. This probability is at most

$$(1 - \alpha/(2m))^m = (1 - \epsilon/4)^m \leq e^{-\epsilon m/4}.$$

We therefore get that

$$\mathbb{P}[A \in B'] \leq \mathop{\mathbb{E}}_{A \sim \mathcal{D}^{2m}} \sum_{h \in \mathcal{H}_A} e^{-\epsilon m/4} \leq e^{-\epsilon m/4} \mathop{\mathbb{E}}_{A \sim \mathcal{D}^{2m}} |\mathcal{H}_A|.$$

Using the definition of the growth function we *conclude the proof of Claim 2.*

Completing the Proof: By Sauer's lemma we know that $\tau_{\mathcal{H}}(2m) \leq (2em/d)^d$. Combining this with the two claims we obtain that

$$\mathbb{P}[S \in B] \leq 2(2em/d)^d e^{-\epsilon m/4}.$$

We would like the right-hand side of the inequality to be at most δ; that is,

$$2(2em/d)^d e^{-\epsilon m/4} \leq \delta.$$

Rearranging, we obtain the requirement

$$m \geq \frac{4}{\epsilon}\left(d \log(2em/d) + \log(2/\delta)\right) = \frac{4d}{\epsilon} \log(m) + \frac{4}{\epsilon}(d \log(2e/d) + \log(2/\delta).$$

Using Lemma A.2, a sufficient condition for the preceding to hold is that

$$m \geq \frac{16d}{\epsilon} \log\left(\frac{8d}{\epsilon}\right) + \frac{8}{\epsilon}(d \log(2e/d) + \log(2/\delta).$$

A sufficient condition for this is that

$$\begin{aligned} m &\geq \frac{16d}{\epsilon} \log\left(\frac{8d}{\epsilon}\right) + \frac{16}{\epsilon}(d \log(2e/d) + \tfrac{1}{2} \log(2/\delta) \\ &= \frac{16d}{\epsilon}\left(\log\left(\frac{8d\,2e}{d\epsilon}\right)\right) + \frac{8}{\epsilon} \log(2/\delta) \\ &= \frac{8}{\epsilon}\left(2d \log\left(\frac{16e}{\epsilon}\right) + \log\left(\frac{2}{\delta}\right)\right). \end{aligned}$$

and this concludes our proof. □

28.3.1 From ϵ-Nets to PAC Learnability

Theorem 28.4. *Let $\mathcal{H}$ be a hypothesis class over $\mathcal{X}$ with* VCdim$(\mathcal{H}) = d$. *Let $\mathcal{D}$ be a distribution over $\mathcal{X}$ and let $c \in \mathcal{H}$ be a target hypothesis. Fix $\epsilon, \delta \in (0,1)$ and let m be as defined in Theorem 28.3. Then, with probability of at least* $1 - \delta$ *over a choice of m*

i.i.d. instances from $\mathcal{X}$ with labels according to c we have that any ERM hypothesis has a true error of at most ϵ.

Proof. Define the class $\mathcal{H}^c = \{c \triangle h : h \in \mathcal{H}\}$, where $c \triangle h = (h \setminus c) \cup (c \setminus h)$. It is easy to verify that if some $A \subset \mathcal{X}$ is shattered by $\mathcal{H}$ then it is also shattered by $\mathcal{H}^c$ and vice versa. Hence, $\text{VCdim}(\mathcal{H}) = \text{VCdim}(\mathcal{H}^c)$. Therefore, using Theorem 28.3 we know that with probability of at least $1 - \delta$, the sample S is an ϵ-net for $\mathcal{H}^c$. Note that $L_{\mathcal{D}}(h) = \mathcal{D}(h \triangle c)$. Therefore, for any $h \in \mathcal{H}$ with $L_{\mathcal{D}}(h) \geq \epsilon$ we have that $|(h \triangle c) \cap S| > 0$, which implies that h cannot be an ERM hypothesis, which concludes our proof. □

29

Multiclass Learnability

In Chapter 17 we have introduced the problem of multiclass categorization, in which the goal is to learn a predictor $h : \mathcal{X} \to [k]$. In this chapter we address PAC learnability of multiclass predictors with respect to the 0-1 loss. As in Chapter 6, the main goal of this chapter is to:

- Characterize which classes of multiclass hypotheses are learnable in the (multiclass) PAC model.
- Quantify the sample complexity of such hypothesis classes.

In view of the fundamental theorem of learning theory (Theorem 6.8), it is natural to seek a generalization of the VC dimension to multiclass hypothesis classes. In Section 29.1 we show such a generalization, called the *Natarajan dimension*, and state a generalization of the fundamental theorem based on the Natarajan dimension. Then, we demonstrate how to calculate the Natarajan dimension of several important hypothesis classes.

Recall that the main message of the fundamental theorem of learning theory is that a hypothesis class of binary classifiers is learnable (with respect to the 0-1 loss) if and only if it has the uniform convergence property, and then it is learnable by any ERM learner. In Chapter 13, Exercise 29.2, we have shown that this equivalence breaks down for a certain convex learning problem. The last section of this chapter is devoted to showing that the equivalence between learnability and uniform convergence breaks down even in multiclass problems with the 0-1 loss, which are very similar to binary classification. Indeed, we construct a hypothesis class which is learnable by a specific ERM learner, but for which other ERM learners might fail and the uniform convergence property does not hold.

29.1 THE NATARAJAN DIMENSION

In this section we define the Natarajan dimension, which is a generalization of the VC dimension to classes of multiclass predictors. Throughout this section, let $\mathcal{H}$ be a hypothesis class of multiclass predictors; namely, each $h \in \mathcal{H}$ is a function from $\mathcal{X}$ to $[k]$.

To define the Natarajan dimension, we first generalize the definition of shattering.

Definition 29.1 (Shattering (Multiclass Version)). We say that a set $C \subset \mathcal{X}$ is shattered by $\mathcal{H}$ if there exist two functions $f_0, f_1 : C \to [k]$ such that

- For every $x \in C$, $f_0(x) \neq f_1(x)$.
- For every $B \subset C$, there exists a function $h \in \mathcal{H}$ such that

$$\forall x \in B, h(x) = f_0(x) \text{ and } \forall x \in C \setminus B, h(x) = f_1(x).$$

Definition 29.2 (Natarajan Dimension). The Natarajan dimension of $\mathcal{H}$, denoted $\mathrm{Ndim}(\mathcal{H})$, is the maximal size of a shattered set $C \subset \mathcal{X}$.

It is not hard to see that in the case that there are exactly two classes, $\mathrm{Ndim}(\mathcal{H}) = \mathrm{VCdim}(\mathcal{H})$. Therefore, the Natarajan dimension generalizes the VC dimension. We next show that the Natarajan dimension allows us to generalize the fundamental theorem of statistical learning from binary classification to multiclass classification.

29.2 THE MULTICLASS FUNDAMENTAL THEOREM

Theorem 29.3 (The Multiclass Fundamental Theorem). *There exist absolute constants $C_1, C_2 > 0$ such that the following holds. For every hypothesis class $\mathcal{H}$ of functions from $\mathcal{X}$ to $[k]$, such that the Natarajan dimension of $\mathcal{H}$ is d, we have*

1. *$\mathcal{H}$ has the uniform convergence property with sample complexity*

$$C_1 \frac{d + \log(1/\delta)}{\epsilon^2} \leq m_{\mathcal{H}}^{\mathrm{UC}}(\epsilon, \delta) \leq C_2 \frac{d \log(k) + \log(1/\delta)}{\epsilon^2}.$$

2. *$\mathcal{H}$ is agnostic PAC learnable with sample complexity*

$$C_1 \frac{d + \log(1/\delta)}{\epsilon^2} \leq m_{\mathcal{H}}(\epsilon, \delta) \leq C_2 \frac{d \log(k) + \log(1/\delta)}{\epsilon^2}.$$

3. *$\mathcal{H}$ is PAC learnable (assuming realizability) with sample complexity*

$$C_1 \frac{d + \log(1/\delta)}{\epsilon} \leq m_{\mathcal{H}}(\epsilon, \delta) \leq C_2 \frac{d \log\left(\frac{kd}{\epsilon}\right) + \log(1/\delta)}{\epsilon}.$$

29.2.1 On the Proof of Theorem 29.3

The lower bounds in Theorem 29.3 can be deduced by a reduction from the binary fundamental theorem (see Exercise 29.5).

The upper bounds in Theorem 29.3 can be proved along the same lines of the proof of the fundamental theorem for binary classification, given in Chapter 28 (see Exercise 29.4). The sole ingredient of that proof that should be modified in a nonstraightforward manner is Sauer's lemma. It applies only to binary classes and therefore must be replaced. An appropriate substitute is Natarajan's lemma:

Lemma 29.4 (Natarajan). $|\mathcal{H}| \leq |\mathcal{X}|^{\mathrm{Ndim}(\mathcal{H})} \cdot k^{2\mathrm{Ndim}(\mathcal{H})}$.

The proof of Natarajan's lemma shares the same spirit of the proof of Sauer's lemma and is left as an exercise (see Exercise 29.3).

29.3 CALCULATING THE NATARAJAN DIMENSION

In this section we show how to calculate (or estimate) the Natarajan dimension of several popular classes, some of which were studied in Chapter 17. As these calculations indicate, the Natarajan dimension is often proportional to the number of parameters required to define a hypothesis.

29.3.1 One-versus-All Based Classes

In Chapter 17 we have seen two reductions of multiclass categorization to binary classification: One-versus-All and All-Pairs. In this section we calculate the Natarajan dimension of the One-versus-All method.

Recall that in One-versus-All we train, for each label, a binary classifier that distinguishes between that label and the rest of the labels. This naturally suggests considering multiclass hypothesis classes of the following form. Let $\mathcal{H}_{\text{bin}} \subset \{0,1\}^{\mathcal{X}}$ be a binary hypothesis class. For every $\bar{h} = (h_1, \ldots, h_k) \in (\mathcal{H}_{\text{bin}})^k$ define $T(\bar{h}) : \mathcal{X} \to [k]$ by

$$T(\bar{h})(x) = \underset{i \in [k]}{\operatorname{argmax}}\, h_i(x).$$

If there are two labels that maximize $h_i(x)$, we choose the smaller one. Also, let

$$\mathcal{H}_{\text{bin}}^{\text{OvA,k}} = \{T(\bar{h}) \, : \, \bar{h} \in (\mathcal{H}_{\text{bin}})^k\}.$$

What "should" be the Natarajan dimension of $\mathcal{H}_{\text{bin}}^{\text{OvA,k}}$? Intuitively, to specify a hypothesis in $\mathcal{H}_{\text{bin}}$ we need $d = \text{VCdim}(\mathcal{H}_{\text{bin}})$ parameters. To specify a hypothesis in $\mathcal{H}_{\text{bin}}^{\text{OvA,k}}$, we need to specify k hypotheses in $\mathcal{H}_{\text{bin}}$. Therefore, kd parameters should suffice. The following lemma establishes this intuition.

Lemma 29.5. *If $d = \text{VCdim}(\mathcal{H}_{\text{bin}})$ then*

$$\text{Ndim}(\mathcal{H}_{\text{bin}}^{\text{OvA,k}}) \le 3kd \log(kd).$$

Proof. Let $C \subset \mathcal{X}$ be a shattered set. By the definition of shattering (for multiclass hypotheses)

$$\left| \left(\mathcal{H}_{\text{bin}}^{\text{OvA,k}} \right)_C \right| \ge 2^{|C|}.$$

On the other hand, each hypothesis in $\mathcal{H}_{\text{bin}}^{\text{OvA,k}}$ is determined by using k hypotheses from $\mathcal{H}_{\text{bin}}$. Therefore,

$$\left| \left(\mathcal{H}_{\text{bin}}^{\text{OvA,k}} \right)_C \right| \le |(\mathcal{H}_{\text{bin}})_C|^k.$$

By Sauer's lemma, $|(\mathcal{H}_{\text{bin}})_C| \le |C|^d$. We conclude that

$$2^{|C|} \le \left| \left(\mathcal{H}_{\text{bin}}^{\text{OvA,k}} \right)_C \right| \le |C|^{dk}.$$

The proof follows by taking the logarithm and applying Lemma A.1. □

How tight is Lemma 29.5? It is not hard to see that for some classes, $\text{Ndim}(\mathcal{H}_{\text{bin}}^{\text{OvA,k}})$ can be much smaller than dk (see Exercise 29.1). However, there are several natural binary classes, $\mathcal{H}_{\text{bin}}$ (e.g., halfspaces), for which $\text{Ndim}(\mathcal{H}_{\text{bin}}^{\text{OvA,k}}) = \Omega(dk)$ (see Exercise 29.6).

29.3.2 General Multiclass-to-Binary Reductions

The same reasoning used to establish Lemma 29.5 can be used to upper bound the Natarajan dimension of more general multiclass-to-binary reductions. These reductions train several binary classifiers on the data. Then, given a new instance, they predict its label by using some rule that takes into account the labels predicted by the binary classifiers. These reductions include One-versus-All and All-Pairs.

Suppose that such a method trains l binary classifiers from a binary class $\mathcal{H}_{\text{bin}}$, and $r : \{0,1\}^l \to [k]$ is the rule that determines the (multiclass) label according to the predictions of the binary classifiers. The hypothesis class corresponding to this method can be defined as follows. For every $\bar{h} = (h_1, \ldots, h_l) \in (\mathcal{H}_{\text{bin}})^l$ define $R(\bar{h}) : \mathcal{X} \to [k]$ by

$$R(\bar{h})(x) = r(h_1(x), \ldots, h_l(x)).$$

Finally, let

$$\mathcal{H}_{\text{bin}}^r = \{R(\bar{h}) \ : \ \bar{h} \in (\mathcal{H}_{\text{bin}})^l\}.$$

Similarly to Lemma 29.5 it can be proven that:

Lemma 29.6. *If $d = \text{VCdim}(\mathcal{H}_{\text{bin}})$ then*

$$\text{Ndim}(\mathcal{H}_{\text{bin}}^r) \le 3 l d \log(l d).$$

The proof is left as Exercise 29.2.

29.3.3 Linear Multiclass Predictors

Next, we consider the class of linear multiclass predictors (see Section 17.2). Let $\Psi : \mathcal{X} \times [k] \to \mathbb{R}^d$ be some class-sensitive feature mapping and let

$$\mathcal{H}_\Psi = \left\{ x \mapsto \underset{i \in [k]}{\text{argmax}} \langle \mathbf{w}, \Psi(x,i) \rangle \ : \ \mathbf{w} \in \mathbb{R}^d \right\}. \tag{29.1}$$

Each hypothesis in $\mathcal{H}_\Psi$ is determined by d parameters, namely, a vector $\mathbf{w} \in \mathbb{R}^d$. Therefore, we would expect that the Natarajan dimension would be upper bounded by d. Indeed:

Theorem 29.7. $\text{Ndim}(\mathcal{H}_\Psi) \le d$.

Proof. Let $C \subset \mathcal{X}$ be a shattered set, and let $f_0, f_1 : C \to [k]$ be the two functions that witness the shattering. We need to show that $|C| \le d$. For every $x \in C$ let $\rho(x) = \Psi(x, f_0(x)) - \Psi(x, f_1(x))$. We claim that the set $\rho(C) \stackrel{\text{def}}{=} \{\rho(x) \ : \ x \in C\}$ consists of $|C|$ elements (i.e., ρ is one to one) and is shattered by the binary hypothesis class of homogeneous linear separators on $\mathbb{R}^d$,

$$\mathcal{H} = \{\mathbf{x} \mapsto \text{sign}(\langle \mathbf{w}, \mathbf{x} \rangle) \ : \ \mathbf{w} \in \mathbb{R}^d\}.$$

Since $\text{VCdim}(\mathcal{H}) = d$, it will follow that $|C| = |\rho(C)| \le d$, as required.

To establish our claim it is enough to show that $|\mathcal{H}_{\rho(C)}| = 2^{|C|}$. Indeed, given a subset $B \subset C$, by the definition of shattering, there exists $h_B \in \mathcal{H}_\Psi$ for which

$$\forall x \in B, h_B(x) = f_0(x) \quad \text{and} \quad \forall x \in C \setminus B, h_B(x) = f_1(x).$$

Let $\mathbf{w}_B \in \mathbb{R}^d$ be a vector that defines h_B. We have that, for every $x \in B$,

$$\langle \mathbf{w}, \Psi(x, f_0(x)) \rangle > \langle \mathbf{w}, \Psi(x, f_1(x)) \rangle \;\Rightarrow\; \langle \mathbf{w}, \rho(x) \rangle > 0.$$

Similarly, for every $x \in C \setminus B$,

$$\langle \mathbf{w}, \rho(x) \rangle < 0.$$

It follows that the hypothesis $g_B \in \mathcal{H}$ defined by the same $\mathbf{w} \in \mathbb{R}^d$ label the points in $\rho(B)$ by 1 and the points in $\rho(C \setminus B)$ by 0. Since this holds for every $B \subseteq C$ we obtain that $|C| = |\rho(C)|$ and $|\mathcal{H}_{\rho(C)}| = 2^{|C|}$, which concludes our proof. □

The theorem is tight in the sense that there are mappings Ψ for which $\text{Ndim}(\mathcal{H}_\Psi) = \Omega(d)$. For example, this is true for the multivector construction (see Section 17.2 and the Bibliographic Remarks at the end of this chapter). We therefore conclude:

Corollary 29.8. *Let $\mathcal{X} = \mathbb{R}^n$ and let $\Psi : \mathcal{X} \times [k] \to \mathbb{R}^{nk}$ be the class sensitive feature mapping for the multi-vector construction:*

$$\Psi(\mathbf{x}, y) = [\, \underbrace{0, \ldots, 0}_{\in \mathbb{R}^{(y-1)n}}, \underbrace{x_1, \ldots, x_n}_{\in \mathbb{R}^n}, \underbrace{0, \ldots, 0}_{\in \mathbb{R}^{(k-y)n}} \,].$$

Let $\mathcal{H}_\Psi$ be as defined in Equation (29.1). Then, the Natarajan dimension of $\mathcal{H}_\Psi$ satisfies

$$(k-1)(n-1) \le \text{Ndim}(\mathcal{H}_\Psi) \le kn.$$

29.4 ON GOOD AND BAD ERMS

In this section we present an example of a hypothesis class with the property that not all ERMs for the class are equally successful. Furthermore, if we allow an infinite number of labels, we will also obtain an example of a class that is learnable by some ERM, but other ERMs will fail to learn it. Clearly, this also implies that the class is learnable but it does not have the uniform convergence property. For simplicity, we consider only the realizable case.

The class we consider is defined as follows. The instance space $\mathcal{X}$ will be any finite or countable set. Let $P_f(\mathcal{X})$ be the collection of all finite and cofinite subsets of $\mathcal{X}$ (that is, for each $A \in P_f(\mathcal{X})$, either A or $\mathcal{X} \setminus A$ must be finite). Instead of $[k]$, the label set is $\mathcal{Y} = P_f(\mathcal{X}) \cup \{*\}$, where $*$ is some special label. For every $A \in P_f(\mathcal{X})$ define $h_A : \mathcal{X} \to \mathcal{Y}$ by

$$h_A(x) = \begin{cases} A & x \in A \\ * & x \notin A \end{cases}$$

Finally, the hypothesis class we take is

$$\mathcal{H} = \{h_A : A \in P_f(\mathcal{X})\}.$$

Let $\mathcal{A}$ be some ERM algorithm for $\mathcal{H}$. Assume that $\mathcal{A}$ operates on a sample labeled by $h_A \in \mathcal{H}$. Since h_A is the *only* hypothesis in $\mathcal{H}$ that might return the label A, if $\mathcal{A}$ observes the label A, it "knows" that the learned hypothesis is h_A, and, as an ERM, must return it (note that in this case the error of the returned hypothesis is 0). Therefore, to specify an ERM, we should only specify the hypothesis it returns upon receiving a sample of the form

$$S = \{(x_1, *), \ldots, (x_m, *)\}.$$

We consider two ERMs: The first, $\mathcal{A}_{good}$, is defined by

$$\mathcal{A}_{good}(S) = h_\emptyset;$$

that is, it outputs the hypothesis which predicts '*' for every $x \in \mathcal{X}$. The second ERM, $\mathcal{A}_{bad}$, is defined by

$$\mathcal{A}_{bad}(S) = h_{\{x_1,\ldots,x_m\}^c}.$$

The following claim shows that the sample complexity of $\mathcal{A}_{bad}$ is about $|\mathcal{X}|$-times larger than the sample complexity of $\mathcal{A}_{good}$. This establishes a gap between different ERMs. If $\mathcal{X}$ is infinite, we even obtain a learnable class that is not learnable by every ERM.

Claim 29.9.

1. *Let $\epsilon, \delta > 0$, $\mathcal{D}$ a distribution over $\mathcal{X}$ and $h_A \in \mathcal{H}$. Let S be an i.i.d. sample consisting of $m \geq \frac{1}{\epsilon}\log\left(\frac{1}{\delta}\right)$ examples, sampled according to $\mathcal{D}$ and labeled by h_A. Then, with probability of at least $1-\delta$, the hypothesis returned by $\mathcal{A}_{good}$ will have an error of at most ϵ.*
2. *There exists a constant $a > 0$ such that for every $0 < \epsilon < a$ there exists a distribution $\mathcal{D}$ over $\mathcal{X}$ and $h_A \in \mathcal{H}$ such that the following holds. The hypothesis returned by $\mathcal{A}_{bad}$ upon receiving a sample of size $m \leq \frac{|\mathcal{X}|-1}{6\epsilon}$, sampled according to $\mathcal{D}$ and labeled by h_A, will have error $\geq \epsilon$ with probability $\geq e^{-\frac{1}{6}}$.*

Proof. Let $\mathcal{D}$ be a distribution over $\mathcal{X}$ and suppose that the correct labeling is h_A. For any sample, $\mathcal{A}_{good}$ returns either $h_\emptyset$ or h_A. If it returns h_A then its true error is zero. Thus, it returns a hypothesis with error $\geq \epsilon$ only if all the m examples in the sample are from $\mathcal{X} \setminus A$ while the error of $h_\emptyset$, $L_\mathcal{D}(h_\emptyset) = \mathbb{P}_\mathcal{D}[A]$, is $\geq \epsilon$. Assume $m \geq \frac{1}{\epsilon}\log(\frac{1}{\delta})$; then the probability of the latter event is no more than $(1-\epsilon)^m \leq e^{-\epsilon m} \leq \delta$. This establishes item 1.

Next we prove item 2. We restrict the proof to the case that $|\mathcal{X}| = d < \infty$. The proof for infinite $\mathcal{X}$ is similar. Suppose that $\mathcal{X} = \{x_0, \ldots, x_{d-1}\}$.

Let $a > 0$ be small enough such that $1 - 2\epsilon \geq e^{-4\epsilon}$ for every $\epsilon < a$ and fix some $\epsilon < a$. Define a distribution on $\mathcal{X}$ by setting $\mathbb{P}[x_0] = 1 - 2\epsilon$ and for all $1 \leq i \leq d-1$, $\mathbb{P}[x_i] = \frac{2\epsilon}{d-1}$. Suppose that the correct hypothesis is $h_\emptyset$ and let the sample size be m. Clearly, the hypothesis returned by $\mathcal{A}_{bad}$ will err on all the examples from $\mathcal{X}$ which are not in the sample. By Chernoff's bound, if $m \leq \frac{d-1}{6\epsilon}$, then with probability $\geq e^{-\frac{1}{6}}$, the sample will include no more than $\frac{d-1}{2}$ examples from $\mathcal{X}$. Thus the returned hypothesis will have error $\geq \epsilon$. □

The conclusion of the example presented is that in multiclass classification, the sample complexity of different ERMs may differ. Are there "good" ERMs for *every* hypothesis class? The following conjecture asserts that the answer is yes.

Conjecture 29.10. *The realizable sample complexity of every hypothesis class* $\mathcal{H} \subset [k]^{\mathcal{X}}$ *is*

$$m_{\mathcal{H}}(\epsilon,\delta) = \tilde{O}\left(\frac{\mathrm{Ndim}(\mathcal{H})}{\epsilon}\right).$$

We emphasize that the $\tilde{O}$ *notation may hide only poly-log factors of* ϵ, δ, *and* $\mathrm{Ndim}(\mathcal{H})$, *but no factor of* k.

29.5 BIBLIOGRAPHIC REMARKS

The Natarajan dimension is due to Natarajan (1989). That paper also established the Natarajan lemma and the generalization of the fundamental theorem. Generalizations and sharper versions of the Natarajan lemma are studied in Haussler and Long (1995). Ben-David, Cesa-Bianchi, Haussler, and Long (1995) defined a large family of notions of dimensions, all of which generalize the VC dimension and may be used to estimate the sample complexity of multiclass classification.

The calculation of the Natarajan dimension, presented here, together with calculation of other classes, can be found in Daniely et al. (2012). The example of good and bad ERMs, as well as conjecture 29.10, are from Daniely et al. (2011).

29.6 EXERCISES

29.1 Let $d, k > 0$. Show that there exists a binary hypothesis $\mathcal{H}_{\mathrm{bin}}$ of VC dimension d such that $\mathrm{Ndim}(\mathcal{H}_{\mathrm{bin}}^{\mathrm{OvA,k}}) = d$.

29.2 Prove Lemma 29.6.

29.3 Prove Natarajan's lemma.
Hint: Fix some $x_0 \in \mathcal{X}$. For $i, j \in [k]$, denote by $\mathcal{H}_{ij}$ all the functions $f : \mathcal{X} \setminus \{x_0\} \to [k]$ that can be extended to a function in $\mathcal{H}$ both by defining $f(x_0) = i$ and by defining $f(x_0) = j$. Show that $|\mathcal{H}| \le |\mathcal{H}_{\mathcal{X}\setminus\{x_0\}}| + \sum_{i \ne j} |\mathcal{H}_{ij}|$ and use induction.

29.4 Adapt the proof of the binary fundamental theorem and Natarajan's lemma to prove that, for some universal constant $C > 0$ and for every hypothesis class of Natarajan dimension d, the agnostic sample complexity of $\mathcal{H}$ is

$$m_{\mathcal{H}}(\epsilon,\delta) \le C \frac{d \log\left(\frac{kd}{\epsilon}\right) + \log(1/\delta)}{\epsilon^2}.$$

29.5 Prove that, for some universal constant $C > 0$ and for every hypothesis class of Natarajan dimension d, the agnostic sample complexity of $\mathcal{H}$ is

$$m_{\mathcal{H}}(\epsilon,\delta) \ge C \frac{d + \log(1/\delta)}{\epsilon^2}.$$

Hint: Deduce it from the binary fundamental theorem.

29.6 Let $\mathcal{H}$ be the binary hypothesis class of (nonhomogenous) halfspaces in $\mathbb{R}^d$. The goal of this exercise is to prove that $\mathrm{Ndim}(\mathcal{H}^{\mathrm{OvA,k}}) \ge (d-1)\cdot(k-1)$.

1. Let $\mathcal{H}_{\text{discrete}}$ be the class of all functions $f : [k-1] \times [d-1] \to \{0,1\}$ for which there exists some i_0 such that, for every $j \in [d-1]$

$$\forall i < i_0, f(i,j) = 1 \text{ while } \forall i > i_0, f(i,j) = 0.$$

Show that $\text{Ndim}(\mathcal{H}^{\text{OvA,k}}_{\text{discrete}}) = (d-1)\cdot(k-1)$.

2. Show that $\mathcal{H}_{\text{discrete}}$ can be realized by $\mathcal{H}$. That is, show that there exists a mapping $\psi : [k-1] \times [d-1] \to \mathbb{R}^d$ such that

$$\mathcal{H}_{\text{discrete}} \subset \{h \circ \psi \,:\, h \in \mathcal{H}\}.$$

Hint: You can take $\psi(i,j)$ to be the vector whose jth coordinate is 1, whose last coordinate is i, and the rest are zeros.

3. Conclude that $\text{Ndim}(\mathcal{H}^{\text{OvA,k}}) \geq (d-1)\cdot(k-1)$.

30

Compression Bounds

Throughout the book, we have tried to characterize the notion of learnability using different approaches. At first we have shown that the uniform convergence property of a hypothesis class guarantees successful learning. Later on we introduced the notion of stability and have shown that stable algorithms are guaranteed to be good learners. Yet there are other properties which may be sufficient for learning, and in this chapter and its sequel we will introduce two approaches to this issue: compression bounds and the PAC-Bayes approach.

In this chapter we study compression bounds. Roughly speaking, we shall see that if a learning algorithm can express the output hypothesis using a small subset of the training set, then the error of the hypothesis on the rest of the examples estimates its true error. In other words, an algorithm that can "compress" its output is a good learner.

30.1 COMPRESSION BOUNDS

To motivate the results, let us first consider the following learning protocol. First, we sample a sequence of k examples denoted T. On the basis of these examples, we construct a hypothesis denoted h_T. Now we would like to estimate the performance of h_T so we sample a fresh sequence of $m-k$ examples, denoted V, and calculate the error of h_T on V. Since V and T are independent, we immediately get the following from Bernstein's inequality (see Lemma B.10).

Lemma 30.1. *Assume that the range of the loss function is* $[0,1]$. *Then,*

$$\mathbb{P}\left[L_{\mathcal{D}}(h_T) - L_V(h_T) \geq \sqrt{\frac{2L_V(h_T)\log(1/\delta)}{|V|}} + \frac{4\log(1/\delta)}{|V|}\right] \leq \delta.$$

To derive this bound, all we needed was independence between T and V. Therefore, we can redefine the protocol as follows. First, we agree on a sequence of k indices $I = (i_1,\ldots,i_k) \in [m]^k$. Then, we sample a sequence of m examples $S = (z_1,\ldots,z_m)$. Now, define $T = S_I = (z_{i_1},\ldots,z_{i_k})$ and define V to be the rest of the examples in S. Note that this protocol is equivalent to the protocol we defined before – hence Lemma 30.1 still holds.

Applying a union bound over the choice of the sequence of indices we obtain the following theorem.

Theorem 30.2. *Let k be an integer and let $B : Z^k \to \mathcal{H}$ be a mapping from sequences of k examples to the hypothesis class. Let $m \geq 2k$ be a training set size and let $A : Z^m \to \mathcal{H}$ be a learning rule that receives a training sequence S of size m and returns a hypothesis such that $A(S) = B(z_{i_1}, \ldots, z_{i_k})$ for some $(i_1, \ldots, i_k) \in [m]^k$. Let $V = \{z_j : j \notin (i_1, \ldots, i_k)\}$ be the set of examples which were not selected for defining $A(S)$. Then, with probability of at least $1 - \delta$ over the choice of S we have*

$$L_{\mathcal{D}}(A(S)) \leq L_V(A(S)) + \sqrt{L_V(A(S))\frac{4k\log(m/\delta)}{m}} + \frac{8k\log(m/\delta)}{m}.$$

Proof. For any $I \in [m]^k$ let $h_I = B(z_{i_1}, \ldots, z_{i_k})$. Let $n = m - k$. Combining Lemma 30.1 with the union bound we have

$$\begin{aligned}
&\mathbb{P}\left[\exists I \in [m]^k \text{ s.t. } L_{\mathcal{D}}(h_I) - L_V(h_I) \geq \sqrt{\frac{2L_V(h_I)\log(1/\delta)}{n}} + \frac{4\log(1/\delta)}{n}\right] \\
&\leq \sum_{I \in [m]^k} \mathbb{P}\left[L_{\mathcal{D}}(h_I) - L_V(h_I) \geq \sqrt{\frac{2L_V(h_I)\log(1/\delta)}{n}} + \frac{4\log(1/\delta)}{n}\right] \\
&\leq m^k \delta.
\end{aligned}$$

Denote $\delta' = m^k \delta$. Using the assumption $k \leq m/2$, which implies that $n = m - k \geq m/2$, the above implies that with probability of at least $1 - \delta'$ we have that

$$L_{\mathcal{D}}(A(S)) \leq L_V(A(S)) + \sqrt{L_V(A(S))\frac{4k\log(m/\delta')}{m}} + \frac{8k\log(m/\delta')}{m},$$

which concludes our proof. □

As a direct corollary we obtain:

Corollary 30.3. *Assuming the conditions of Theorem 30.2, and further assuming that $L_V(A(S)) = 0$, then, with probability of at least $1 - \delta$ over the choice of S we have*

$$L_{\mathcal{D}}(A(S)) \leq \frac{8k\log(m/\delta)}{m}.$$

These results motivate the following definition:

Definition 30.4. (Compression Scheme) Let $\mathcal{H}$ be a hypothesis class of functions from $\mathcal{X}$ to $\mathcal{Y}$ and let k be an integer. We say that $\mathcal{H}$ has a compression scheme of size k if the following holds:

For all m there exists $A : Z^m \to [m]^k$ and $B : Z^k \to \mathcal{H}$ such that for all $h \in \mathcal{H}$, if we feed any training set of the form $(x_1, h(x_1)), \ldots, (x_m, h(x_m))$ into A and then feed $(x_{i_1}, h(x_{i_1})), \ldots, (x_{i_k}, h(x_{i_k}))$ into B, where $(i_1, \ldots, i_k)$ is the output of A, then the output of B, denoted h', satisfies $L_S(h') = 0$.

It is possible to generalize the definition for unrealizable sequences as follows.

Definition 30.5. (Compression Scheme for Unrealizable Sequences) Let $\mathcal{H}$ be a hypothesis class of functions from $\mathcal{X}$ to $\mathcal{Y}$ and let k be an integer. We say that $\mathcal{H}$ has a compression scheme of size k if the following holds:
For all m there exists $A : Z^m \to [m]^k$ and $B : Z^k \to \mathcal{H}$ such that for all $h \in \mathcal{H}$, if we feed any training set of the form $(x_1, y_1), \ldots, (x_m, y_m)$ into A and then feed $(x_{i_1}, y_{i_1}), \ldots, (x_{i_k}, y_{i_k})$ into B, where $(i_1, \ldots, i_k)$ is the output of A, then the output of B, denoted h', satisfies $L_S(h') \le L_S(h)$.

The following lemma shows that the existence of a compression scheme for the realizable case also implies the existence of a compression scheme for the unrealizable case.

Lemma 30.6. *Let $\mathcal{H}$ be a hypothesis class for binary classification, and assume it has a compression scheme of size k in the realizable case. Then, it has a compression scheme of size k for the unrealizable case as well.*

Proof. Consider the following scheme: First, find an ERM hypothesis and denote it by h. Then, discard all the examples on which h errs. Now, apply the realizable compression scheme on the examples that have not been removed. The output of the realizable compression scheme, denoted h', must be correct on the examples that have not been removed. Since h errs on the removed examples it follows that the error of h' cannot be larger than the error of h; hence h' is also an ERM hypothesis. □

30.2 EXAMPLES

In the examples that follows, we present compression schemes for several hypothesis classes for binary classification. In light of Lemma 30.6 we focus on the realizable case. Therefore, to show that a certain hypothesis class has a compression scheme, it is necessary to show that there exist A, B, and k for which $L_S(h') = 0$.

30.2.1 Axis Aligned Rectangles

Note that this is an uncountable infinite class. We show that there is a simple compression scheme. Consider the algorithm A that works as follows: For each dimension, choose the two positive examples with extremal values at this dimension. Define B to be the function that returns the minimal enclosing rectangle. Then, for $k = 2d$, we have that in the realizable case, $L_S(B(A(S))) = 0$.

30.2.2 Halfspaces

Let $\mathcal{X} = \mathbb{R}^d$ and consider the class of homogenous halfspaces, $\{\mathbf{x} \mapsto \text{sign}(\langle \mathbf{w}, \mathbf{x} \rangle) : \mathbf{w} \in \mathbb{R}^d\}$.

A Compression Scheme:

W.l.o.g. assume all labels are positive (otherwise, replace $\mathbf{x}_i$ by $y_i \mathbf{x}_i$). The compression scheme we propose is as follows. First, A finds the vector $\mathbf{w}$ which is in the convex hull of $\{\mathbf{x}_1, \ldots, \mathbf{x}_m\}$ and has minimal norm. Then, it represents it as a convex combination of d points in the sample (it will be shown later that this is always possible). The output of A are these d points. The algorithm B receives these d points and set $\mathbf{w}$ to be the point in their convex hull of minimal norm.

Next we prove that this indeed is a compression sceme. Since the data is linearly separable, the convex hull of $\{\mathbf{x}_1, \ldots, \mathbf{x}_m\}$ does not contain the origin. Consider the point $\mathbf{w}$ in this convex hull closest to the origin. (This is a unique point which is the Euclidean projection of the origin onto this convex hull.) We claim that $\mathbf{w}$ separates the data.[1] To see this, assume by contradiction that $\langle \mathbf{w}, \mathbf{x}_i \rangle \le 0$ for some i. Take $\mathbf{w}' = (1-\alpha)\mathbf{w} + \alpha \mathbf{x}_i$ for $\alpha = \frac{\|\mathbf{w}\|^2}{\|\mathbf{x}_i\|^2 + \|\mathbf{w}\|^2} \in (0,1)$. Then $\mathbf{w}'$ is also in the convex hull and

$$\begin{aligned}
\|\mathbf{w}'\|^2 &= (1-\alpha)^2 \|\mathbf{w}\|^2 + \alpha^2 \|\mathbf{x}_i\|^2 + 2\alpha(1-\alpha)\langle \mathbf{w}, \mathbf{x}_i \rangle \\
&\le (1-\alpha)^2 \|\mathbf{w}\|^2 + \alpha^2 \|\mathbf{x}_i\|^2 \\
&= \frac{\|\mathbf{x}_i\|^4 \|\mathbf{w}\|^2 + \|\mathbf{x}_i\|^2 \|\mathbf{w}\|^4}{(\|\mathbf{w}\|^2 + \|\mathbf{x}_i\|^2)^2} \\
&= \frac{\|\mathbf{x}_i\|^2 \|\mathbf{w}\|^2}{\|\mathbf{w}\|^2 + \|\mathbf{x}_i\|^2} \\
&= \|\mathbf{w}\|^2 \cdot \frac{1}{\|\mathbf{w}\|^2 / \|\mathbf{x}_i\|^2 + 1} \\
&< \|\mathbf{w}\|^2,
\end{aligned}$$

which leads to a contradiction.

We have thus shown that $\mathbf{w}$ is also an ERM. Finally, since $\mathbf{w}$ is in the convex hull of the examples, we can apply Caratheodory's theorem to obtain that $\mathbf{w}$ is also in the convex hull of a subset of $d+1$ points of the polygon. Furthermore, the minimality of $\mathbf{w}$ implies that $\mathbf{w}$ must be on a face of the polygon and this implies it can be represented as a convex combination of d points.

It remains to show that $\mathbf{w}$ is also the projection onto the polygon defined by the d points. But this must be true: On one hand, the smaller polygon is a subset of the larger one; hence the projection onto the smaller cannot be smaller in norm. On the other hand, $\mathbf{w}$ itself is a valid solution. The uniqueness of projection concludes our proof.

30.2.3 Separating Polynomials

Let $\mathcal{X} = \mathbb{R}^d$ and consider the class $\mathbf{x} \mapsto \mathrm{sign}(p(x))$ where p is a degree r polynomial.

Note that $p(x)$ can be rewritten as $\langle \mathbf{w}, \psi(\mathbf{x}) \rangle$ where the elements of $\psi(x)$ are all the monomials of $\mathbf{x}$ up to degree r. Therefore, the problem of constructing a compression scheme for $p(\mathbf{x})$ reduces to the problem of constructing a compression scheme for halfspaces in $\mathbb{R}^{d'}$ where $d' = O(d^r)$.

[1] It can be shown that $\mathbf{w}$ is the direction of the max-margin solution.

30.2.4 Separation with Margin

Suppose that a training set is separated with margin γ. The Perceptron algorithm guarantees to make at most $1/\gamma^2$ updates before converging to a solution that makes no mistakes on the entire training set. Hence, we have a compression scheme of size $k \leq 1/\gamma^2$.

30.3 BIBLIOGRAPHIC REMARKS

Compression schemes and their relation to learning were introduced by Littlestone and Warmuth (1986). As we have shown, if a class has a compression scheme then it is learnable. For binary classification problems, it follows from the fundamental theorem of learning that the class has a finite VC dimension. The other direction, namely, whether every hypothesis class of finite VC dimension has a compression scheme of finite size, is an open problem posed by Manfred Warmuth and is still open (see also (Floyd 1989, Floyd & Warmuth 1995, Ben-David & Litman 1998, Livni & Simon 2013).

31

PAC-Bayes

The Minimum Description Length (MDL) and Occam's razor principles allow a potentially very large hypothesis class but define a hierarchy over hypotheses and prefer to choose hypotheses that appear higher in the hierarchy. In this chapter we describe the PAC-Bayesian approach that further generalizes this idea. In the PAC-Bayesian approach, one expresses the prior knowledge by defining prior distribution over the hypothesis class.

31.1 PAC-BAYES BOUNDS

As in the MDL paradigm, we define a hierarchy over hypotheses in our class $\mathcal{H}$. Now, the hierarchy takes the form of a prior distribution over $\mathcal{H}$. That is, we assign a probability (or density if $\mathcal{H}$ is continuous) $P(h) \geq 0$ for each $h \in \mathcal{H}$ and refer to $P(h)$ as the prior score of h. Following the Bayesian reasoning approach, the output of the learning algorithm is not necessarily a single hypothesis. Instead, the learning process defines a posterior probability over $\mathcal{H}$, which we denote by Q. In the context of a supervised learning problem, where $\mathcal{H}$ contains functions from $\mathcal{X}$ to $\mathcal{Y}$, one can think of Q as defining a randomized prediction rule as follows. Whenever we get a new instance $\mathbf{x}$, we randomly pick a hypothesis $h \in \mathcal{H}$ according to Q and predict $h(\mathbf{x})$. We define the loss of Q on an example z to be

$$\ell(Q, z) \stackrel{\text{def}}{=} \underset{h \sim Q}{\mathbb{E}}[\ell(h, z)].$$

By the linearity of expectation, the generalization loss and training loss of Q can be written as

$$L_{\mathcal{D}}(Q) \stackrel{\text{def}}{=} \underset{h \sim Q}{\mathbb{E}}[L_{\mathcal{D}}(h)] \quad \text{and} \quad L_S(Q) \stackrel{\text{def}}{=} \underset{h \sim Q}{\mathbb{E}}[L_S(h)].$$

The following theorem tells us that the difference between the generalization loss and the empirical loss of a posterior Q is bounded by an expression that depends on the Kullback-Leibler divergence between Q and the prior distribution P. The Kullback-Leibler is a natural measure of the distance between two distributions. The theorem suggests that if we would like to minimize the generalization loss of Q, we should jointly minimize both the empirical loss of Q and the Kullback-Leibler distance between Q and the prior distribution. We will later show how in some cases this idea leads to the regularized risk minimization principle.

Theorem 31.1. *Let $\mathcal{D}$ be an arbitrary distribution over an example domain Z. Let $\mathcal{H}$ be a hypothesis class and let $\ell : \mathcal{H} \times Z \to [0,1]$ be a loss function. Let P be a prior distribution over $\mathcal{H}$ and let $\delta \in (0,1)$. Then, with probability of at least $1-\delta$ over the choice of an i.i.d. training set $S = \{z_1, \ldots, z_m\}$ sampled according to $\mathcal{D}$, for all distributions Q over $\mathcal{H}$ (even such that depend on S), we have*

$$L_{\mathcal{D}}(Q) \le L_S(Q) + \sqrt{\frac{D(Q||P) + \ln m/\delta}{2(m-1)}},$$

where

$$D(Q||P) \stackrel{\text{def}}{=} \mathop{\mathbb{E}}_{h\sim Q}[\ln(Q(h)/P(h))]$$

is the Kullback-Leibler divergence.

Proof. For any function $f(S)$, using Markov's inequality:

$$\mathop{\mathbb{P}}_S[f(S) \ge \epsilon] = \mathop{\mathbb{P}}_S[e^{f(S)} \ge e^{\epsilon}] \le \frac{\mathbb{E}_S[e^{f(S)}]}{e^{\epsilon}}. \tag{31.1}$$

Let $\Delta(h) = L_{\mathcal{D}}(h) - L_S(h)$. We will apply Equation (31.1) with the function

$$f(S) = \sup_Q \left(2(m-1)\mathop{\mathbb{E}}_{h\sim Q}(\Delta(h))^2 - D(Q||P)\right).$$

We now turn to bound $\mathbb{E}_S[e^{f(S)}]$. The main trick is to upper bound $f(S)$ by using an expression that does not depend on Q but rather depends on the prior probability P. To do so, fix some S and note that from the definition of $D(Q||P)$ we get that for all Q,

$$\begin{aligned}2(m-1)\mathop{\mathbb{E}}_{h\sim Q}(\Delta(h))^2 - D(Q||P) &= \mathop{\mathbb{E}}_{h\sim Q}[\ln(e^{2(m-1)\Delta(h)^2}P(h)/Q(h))]\\ &\le \ln \mathop{\mathbb{E}}_{h\sim Q}[e^{2(m-1)\Delta(h)^2}P(h)/Q(h)]\\ &= \ln \mathop{\mathbb{E}}_{h\sim P}[e^{2(m-1)\Delta(h)^2}],\end{aligned} \tag{31.2}$$

where the inequality follows from Jensen's inequality and the concavity of the log function. Therefore,

$$\mathop{\mathbb{E}}_S[e^{f(S)}] \le \mathop{\mathbb{E}}_S \mathop{\mathbb{E}}_{h\sim P}[e^{2(m-1)\Delta(h)^2}]. \tag{31.3}$$

The advantage of the expression on the right-hand side stems from the fact that we can switch the order of expectations (because P is a prior that does not depend on S), which yields

$$\mathbb{E}_S[e^{f(S)}] \leq \mathop{\mathbb{E}}_{h\sim P}\mathop{\mathbb{E}}_S[e^{2(m-1)\Delta(h)^2}]. \tag{31.4}$$

Next, we claim that for all h we have $\mathbb{E}_S[e^{2(m-1)\Delta(h)^2}] \leq m$. To do so, recall that Hoeffding's inequality tells us that

$$\mathop{\mathbb{P}}_S[\Delta(h) \geq \epsilon] \leq e^{-2m\epsilon^2}.$$

This implies that $\mathbb{E}_S[e^{2(m-1)\Delta(h)^2}] \leq m$ (see Exercise 31.1). Combining this with Equation (31.4) and plugging into Equation (31.1) we get

$$\mathop{\mathbb{P}}_S[f(S) \geq \epsilon] \leq \frac{m}{e^\epsilon}. \tag{31.5}$$

Denote the right-hand side of the above δ, thus $\epsilon = \ln(m/\delta)$, and we therefore obtain that with probability of at least $1-\delta$ we have that for all Q

$$2(m-1)\mathop{\mathbb{E}}_{h\sim Q}(\Delta(h))^2 - D(Q||P) \leq \epsilon = \ln(m/\delta).$$

Rearranging the inequality and using Jensen's inequality again (the function x^2 is convex) we conclude that

$$\left(\mathop{\mathbb{E}}_{h\sim Q}\Delta(h)\right)^2 \leq \mathop{\mathbb{E}}_{h\sim Q}(\Delta(h))^2 \leq \frac{\ln(m/\delta) + D(Q||P)}{2(m-1)}. \tag{31.6}$$

□

Remark 31.1 (Regularization). The PAC-Bayes bound leads to the following learning rule:

Given a prior P, return a posterior Q that minimizes the function

$$L_S(Q) + \sqrt{\frac{D(Q||P) + \ln m/\delta}{2(m-1)}}. \tag{31.7}$$

This rule is similar to the *regularized risk minimization* principle. That is, we jointly minimize the empirical loss of Q on the sample and the Kullback-Leibler "distance" between Q and P.

31.2 BIBLIOGRAPHIC REMARKS

PAC-Bayes bounds were first introduced by McAllester (1998). See also (McAllester 1999, McAllester 2003, Seeger 2003, Langford & Shawe-Taylor 2003, Langford 2006).

31.3 EXERCISES

31.1 Let X be a random variable that satisfies $\mathbb{P}[X \geq \epsilon] \leq e^{-2m\epsilon^2}$. Prove that $\mathbb{E}[e^{2(m-1)X^2}] \leq m$.

31.2 ■ Suppose that $\mathcal{H}$ is a finite hypothesis class, set the prior to be uniform over $\mathcal{H}$, and set the posterior to be $Q(h_S) = 1$ for some h_S and $Q(h) = 0$ for all other $h \in \mathcal{H}$. Show that

$$L_{\mathcal{D}}(h_S) \leq L_S(h) + \sqrt{\frac{\ln(|\mathcal{H}|) + \ln(m/\delta)}{2(m-1)}}.$$

Compare to the bounds we derived using uniform convergence.

■ Derive a bound similar to the Occam bound given in Chapter 7 using the PAC-Bayes bound

Appendix A

Technical Lemmas

Lemma A.1. *Let $a > 0$. Then: $x \geq 2a\log(a) \Rightarrow x \geq a\log(x)$. It follows that a necessary condition for the inequality $x < a\log(x)$ to hold is that $x < 2a\log(a)$.*

Proof. First note that for $a \in (0, \sqrt{e}]$ the inequality $x \geq a\log(x)$ holds unconditionally and therefore the claim is trivial. From now on, assume that $a > \sqrt{e}$. Consider the function $f(x) = x - a\log(x)$. The derivative is $f'(x) = 1 - a/x$. Thus, for $x > a$ the derivative is positive and the function increases. In addition,

$$\begin{aligned} f(2a\log(a)) &= 2a\log(a) - a\log(2a\log(a)) \\ &= 2a\log(a) - a\log(a) - a\log(2\log(a)) \\ &= a\log(a) - a\log(2\log(a)). \end{aligned}$$

Since $a - 2\log(a) > 0$ for all $a > 0$, the proof follows. □

Lemma A.2. *Let $a \geq 1$ and $b > 0$. Then: $x \geq 4a\log(2a) + 2b \Rightarrow x \geq a\log(x) + b$.*

Proof. It suffices to prove that $x \geq 4a\log(2a) + 2b$ implies that both $x \geq 2a\log(x)$ and $x \geq 2b$. Since we assume $a \geq 1$ we clearly have that $x \geq 2b$. In addition, since $b > 0$ we have that $x \geq 4a\log(2a)$ which using Lemma A.1 implies that $x \geq 2a\log(x)$. This concludes our proof. □

Lemma A.3. *Let X be a random variable and $x' \in \mathbb{R}$ be a scalar and assume that there exists $a > 0$ such that for all $t \geq 0$ we have $\mathbb{P}[|X - x'| > t] \leq 2e^{-t^2/a^2}$. Then, $\mathbb{E}[|X - x'|] \leq 4a$.*

Proof. For all $i = 0, 1, 2, \ldots$ denote $t_i = a\,i$. Since t_i is monotonically increasing we have that $\mathbb{E}[|X - x'|]$ is at most $\sum_{i=1}^{\infty} t_i\, \mathbb{P}[|X - x'| > t_{i-1}]$. Combining this with the assumption in the lemma we get that $\mathbb{E}[|X - x'|] \leq 2a\sum_{i=1}^{\infty} i e^{-(i-1)^2}$. The proof now follows from the inequalities

$$\sum_{i=1}^{\infty} i e^{-(i-1)^2} \leq \sum_{i=1}^{5} i e^{-(i-1)^2} + \int_5^{\infty} x e^{-(x-1)^2} dx < 1.8 + 10^{-7} < 2\,.$$

□

Lemma A.4. *Let X be a random variable and $x' \in \mathbb{R}$ be a scalar and assume that there exists $a > 0$ and $b \geq e$ such that for all $t \geq 0$ we have $\mathbb{P}[|X - x'| > t] \leq 2b\,e^{-t^2/a^2}$. Then, $\mathbb{E}[|X - x'|] \leq a(2 + \sqrt{\log(b)})$.*

Proof. For all $i = 0, 1, 2, \ldots$ denote $t_i = a\,(i + \sqrt{\log(b)})$. Since t_i is monotonically increasing we have that

$$\mathbb{E}[|X - x'|] \leq a\sqrt{\log(b)} + \sum_{i=1}^{\infty} t_i\,\mathbb{P}[|X - x'| > t_{i-1}].$$

Using the assumption in the lemma we have

$$\begin{aligned}
\sum_{i=1}^{\infty} t_i\,\mathbb{P}[|X - x'| > t_{i-1}] &\leq 2\,a\,b \sum_{i=1}^{\infty} (i + \sqrt{\log(b)})e^{-(i-1+\sqrt{\log(b)})^2} \\
&\leq 2\,a\,b \int_{1+\sqrt{\log(b)}}^{\infty} x e^{-(x-1)^2} dx \\
&= 2\,a\,b \int_{\sqrt{\log(b)}}^{\infty} (y+1)e^{-y^2} dy \\
&\leq 4\,a\,b \int_{\sqrt{\log(b)}}^{\infty} y e^{-y^2} dy \\
&= 2\,a\,b \left[-e^{-y^2}\right]_{\sqrt{\log(b)}}^{\infty} \\
&= 2\,a\,b/b = 2\,a.
\end{aligned}$$

Combining the preceding inequalities we conclude our proof. □

Lemma A.5. *Let m, d be two positive integers such that $d \leq m - 2$. Then,*

$$\sum_{k=0}^{d} \binom{m}{k} \leq \left(\frac{e\,m}{d}\right)^d.$$

Proof. We prove the claim by induction. For $d = 1$ the left-hand side equals $1 + m$ while the right-hand side equals em; hence the claim is true. Assume that the claim holds for d and let us prove it for $d + 1$. By the induction assumption we have

$$\begin{aligned}
\sum_{k=0}^{d+1} \binom{m}{k} &\leq \left(\frac{e\,m}{d}\right)^d + \binom{m}{d+1} \\
&= \left(\frac{e\,m}{d}\right)^d \left(1 + \left(\frac{d}{e\,m}\right)^d \frac{m(m-1)(m-2)\cdots(m-d)}{(d+1)d!}\right) \\
&\leq \left(\frac{em}{d}\right)^d \left(1 + \left(\frac{d}{e}\right)^d \frac{(m-d)}{(d+1)d!}\right).
\end{aligned}$$

Using Stirling's approximation we further have that

$$\begin{aligned}
&\le \left(\frac{em}{d}\right)^d \left(1+\left(\frac{d}{e}\right)^d \frac{(m-d)}{(d+1)\sqrt{2\pi d}(d/e)^d}\right) \\
&= \left(\frac{em}{d}\right)^d \left(1+\frac{m-d}{\sqrt{2\pi d}(d+1)}\right) \\
&= \left(\frac{em}{d}\right)^d \cdot \frac{d+1+(m-d)/\sqrt{2\pi d}}{d+1} \\
&\le \left(\frac{em}{d}\right)^d \cdot \frac{d+1+(m-d)/2}{d+1} \\
&= \left(\frac{em}{d}\right)^d \cdot \frac{d/2+1+m/2}{d+1} \\
&\le \left(\frac{em}{d}\right)^d \cdot \frac{m}{d+1},
\end{aligned}$$

where in the last inequality we used the assumption that $d \le m-2$. On the other hand,

$$\begin{aligned}
\left(\frac{em}{d+1}\right)^{d+1} &= \left(\frac{em}{d}\right)^d \cdot \frac{em}{d+1} \cdot \left(\frac{d}{d+1}\right)^d \\
&= \left(\frac{em}{d}\right)^d \cdot \frac{em}{d+1} \cdot \frac{1}{(1+1/d)^d} \\
&\ge \left(\frac{em}{d}\right)^d \cdot \frac{em}{d+1} \cdot \frac{1}{e} \\
&= \left(\frac{em}{d}\right)^d \cdot \frac{m}{d+1},
\end{aligned}$$

which proves our inductive argument. □

Lemma A.6. *For all $a \in \mathbb{R}$ we have*

$$\frac{e^a+e^{-a}}{2} \le e^{a^2/2}.$$

Proof. Observe that

$$e^a = \sum_{n=0}^{\infty} \frac{a^n}{n!}.$$

Therefore,

$$\frac{e^a+e^{-a}}{2} = \sum_{n=0}^{\infty} \frac{a^{2n}}{(2n)!},$$

and

$$e^{a^2/2} = \sum_{n=0}^{\infty} \frac{a^{2n}}{2^n\, n!}.$$

Observing that $(2n)! \ge 2^n\, n!$ for every $n \ge 0$ we conclude our proof. □

Appendix B

Measure Concentration

Let $Z_1, \ldots, Z_m$ be an i.i.d. sequence of random variables and let μ be their mean. The strong law of large numbers states that when m tends to infinity, the empirical average, $\frac{1}{m}\sum_{i=1}^{m} Z_i$, converges to the expected value μ, with probability 1. Measure concentration inequalities quantify the deviation of the empirical average from the expectation when m is finite.

B.1 MARKOV'S INEQUALITY

We start with an inequality which is called Markov's inequality. Let Z be a nonnegative random variable. The expectation of Z can be written as follows:

$$\mathbb{E}[Z] = \int_{x=0}^{\infty} \mathbb{P}[Z \geq x]dx. \tag{B.1}$$

Since $\mathbb{P}[Z \geq x]$ is monotonically nonincreasing we obtain

$$\forall a \geq 0, \;\; \mathbb{E}[Z] \geq \int_{x=0}^{a} \mathbb{P}[Z \geq x]dx \geq \int_{x=0}^{a} \mathbb{P}[Z \geq a]dx = a\,\mathbb{P}[Z \geq a]. \tag{B.2}$$

Rearranging the inequality yields Markov's inequality:

$$\forall a \geq 0, \;\; \mathbb{P}[Z \geq a] \leq \frac{\mathbb{E}[Z]}{a}. \tag{B.3}$$

For random variables that take value in $[0,1]$, we can derive from Markov's inequality the following.

Lemma B.1. *Let Z be a random variable that takes values in $[0,1]$. Assume that $\mathbb{E}[Z] = \mu$. Then, for any $a \in (0,1)$,*

$$\mathbb{P}[Z > 1 - a] \geq \frac{\mu - (1-a)}{a}.$$

This also implies that for every $a \in (0,1)$,

$$\mathbb{P}[Z > a] \geq \frac{\mu - a}{1 - a} \geq \mu - a.$$

Proof. Let $Y = 1 - Z$. Then Y is a nonnegative random variable with $\mathbb{E}[Y] = 1 - \mathbb{E}[Z] = 1 - \mu$. Applying Markov's inequality on Y we obtain

$$\mathbb{P}[Z \le 1 - a] = \mathbb{P}[1 - Z \ge a] = \mathbb{P}[Y \ge a] \le \frac{\mathbb{E}[Y]}{a} = \frac{1-\mu}{a}.$$

Therefore,

$$\mathbb{P}[Z > 1 - a] \ge 1 - \frac{1-\mu}{a} = \frac{a+\mu-1}{a}.$$

□

B.2 CHEBYSHEV'S INEQUALITY

Applying Markov's inequality on the random variable $(Z - \mathbb{E}[Z])^2$ we obtain Chebyshev's inequality:

$$\forall a > 0, \quad \mathbb{P}[|Z - \mathbb{E}[Z]| \ge a] = \mathbb{P}[(Z - \mathbb{E}[Z])^2 \ge a^2] \le \frac{\mathrm{Var}[Z]}{a^2}, \tag{B.4}$$

where $\mathrm{Var}[Z] = \mathbb{E}[(Z - \mathbb{E}[Z])^2]$ is the variance of Z.

Consider the random variable $\frac{1}{m}\sum_{i=1}^m Z_i$. Since $Z_1, \ldots, Z_m$ are i.i.d. it is easy to verify that

$$\mathrm{Var}\left[\frac{1}{m}\sum_{i=1}^m Z_i\right] = \frac{\mathrm{Var}[Z_1]}{m}.$$

Applying Chebyshev's inequality, we obtain the following:

Lemma B.2. *Let $Z_1, \ldots, Z_m$ be a sequence of i.i.d. random variables and assume that $\mathbb{E}[Z_1] = \mu$ and $\mathrm{Var}[Z_1] \le 1$. Then, for any $\delta \in (0,1)$, with probability of at least $1 - \delta$ we have*

$$\left|\frac{1}{m}\sum_{i=1}^m Z_i - \mu\right| \le \sqrt{\frac{1}{\delta\, m}}.$$

Proof. Applying Chebyshev's inequality we obtain that for all $a > 0$

$$\mathbb{P}\left[\left|\frac{1}{m}\sum_{i=1}^m Z_i - \mu\right| > a\right] \le \frac{\mathrm{Var}[Z_1]}{m\, a^2} \le \frac{1}{m\, a^2}.$$

The proof follows by denoting the right-hand side δ and solving for a. □

The deviation between the empirical average and the mean given previously decreases polynomially with m. It is possible to obtain a significantly faster decrease. In the sections that follow we derive bounds that decrease exponentially fast.

B.3 CHERNOFF'S BOUNDS

Let $Z_1, \ldots, Z_m$ be independent Bernoulli variables where for every i, $\mathbb{P}[Z_i = 1] = p_i$ and $\mathbb{P}[Z_i = 0] = 1 - p_i$. Let $p = \sum_{i=1}^m p_i$ and let $Z = \sum_{i=1}^m Z_i$. Using the monotonicity of the exponent function and Markov's inequality, we have that for every $t > 0$

$$\mathbb{P}[Z > (1+\delta)p] = \mathbb{P}[e^{tZ} > e^{t(1+\delta)p}] \le \frac{\mathbb{E}[e^{tZ}]}{e^{(1+\delta)tp}}. \tag{B.5}$$

Next,

$$\begin{aligned}
\mathbb{E}[e^{tZ}] &= \mathbb{E}[e^{t\sum_i Z_i}] = \mathbb{E}\left[\prod_i e^{tZ_i}\right] \\
&= \prod_i \mathbb{E}[e^{tZ_i}] && \text{by independence} \\
&= \prod_i \left(p_i e^t + (1-p_i)e^0\right) \\
&= \prod_i (1 + p_i(e^t - 1)) \\
&\le \prod_i e^{p_i(e^t-1)} && \text{using } 1+x \le e^x \\
&= e^{\sum_i p_i(e^t-1)} \\
&= e^{(e^t-1)p}.
\end{aligned}$$

Combining the equation with Equation (B.5) and choosing $t = \log(1+\delta)$ we obtain

Lemma B.3. *Let $Z_1, \ldots, Z_m$ be independent Bernoulli variables where for every i, $\mathbb{P}[Z_i = 1] = p_i$ and $\mathbb{P}[Z_i = 0] = 1 - p_i$. Let $p = \sum_{i=1}^m p_i$ and let $Z = \sum_{i=1}^m Z_i$. Then, for any $\delta > 0$,*

$$\mathbb{P}[Z > (1+\delta)p] \le e^{-h(\delta)\,p},$$

where

$$h(\delta) = (1+\delta)\log(1+\delta) - \delta.$$

Using the inequality $h(a) \ge a^2/(2+2a/3)$ we obtain

Lemma B.4. *Using the notation of Lemma B.3 we also have*

$$\mathbb{P}[Z > (1+\delta)p] \le e^{-p\frac{\delta^2}{2+2\delta/3}}.$$

For the other direction, we apply similar calculations:

$$\mathbb{P}[Z < (1-\delta)p] = \mathbb{P}[-Z > -(1-\delta)p] = \mathbb{P}[e^{-tZ} > e^{-t(1-\delta)p}] \le \frac{\mathbb{E}[e^{-tZ}]}{e^{-(1-\delta)tp}}, \tag{B.6}$$

and

$$\mathbb{E}[e^{-tZ}] = \mathbb{E}[e^{-t\sum_i Z_i}] = \mathbb{E}\left[\prod_i e^{-tZ_i}\right]$$
$$= \prod_i \mathbb{E}[e^{-tZ_i}] \qquad \text{by independence}$$
$$= \prod_i (1 + p_i(e^{-t} - 1))$$
$$\leq \prod_i e^{p_i(e^{-t}-1)} \qquad \text{using } 1 + a \leq e^x$$
$$= e^{(e^{-t}-1)p}.$$

Setting $t = -\log(1-\delta)$ yields

$$\mathbb{P}[Z < (1-\delta)p] \leq \frac{e^{-\delta p}}{e^{(1-\delta)\log(1-\delta)p}} = e^{-ph(-\delta)}.$$

It is easy to verify that $h(-\delta) \geq h(\delta)$ and hence

Lemma B.5. *Using the notation of Lemma B.3 we also have*

$$\mathbb{P}[Z < (1-\delta)p] \leq e^{-ph(-\delta)} \leq e^{-ph(\delta)} \leq e^{-p\frac{\delta^2}{2+2\delta/3}}.$$

B.4 HOEFFDING'S INEQUALITY

Lemma B.6 (Hoeffding's Inequality). *Let $Z_1, \ldots, Z_m$ be a sequence of i.i.d. random variables and let $\bar{Z} = \frac{1}{m}\sum_{i=1}^m Z_i$. Assume that $\mathbb{E}[\bar{Z}] = \mu$ and $\mathbb{P}[a \leq Z_i \leq b] = 1$ for every i. Then, for any $\epsilon > 0$*

$$\mathbb{P}\left[\left|\frac{1}{m}\sum_{i=1}^m Z_i - \mu\right| > \epsilon\right] \leq 2\exp\left(-2m\epsilon^2/(b-a)^2\right).$$

Proof. Denote $X_i = Z_i - \mathbb{E}[Z_i]$ and $\bar{X} = \frac{1}{m}\sum_i X_i$. Using the monotonicity of the exponent function and Markov's inequality, we have that for every $\lambda > 0$ and $\epsilon > 0$,

$$\mathbb{P}[\bar{X} \geq \epsilon] = \mathbb{P}[e^{\lambda\bar{X}} \geq e^{\lambda\epsilon}] \leq e^{-\lambda\epsilon}\,\mathbb{E}[e^{\lambda\bar{X}}].$$

Using the independence assumption we also have

$$\mathbb{E}[e^{\lambda\bar{X}}] = \mathbb{E}\left[\prod_i e^{\lambda X_i/m}\right] = \prod_i \mathbb{E}[e^{\lambda X_i/m}].$$

By Hoeffding's lemma (Lemma B.7 later), for every i we have

$$\mathbb{E}[e^{\lambda X_i/m}] \leq e^{\frac{\lambda^2(b-a)^2}{8m^2}}.$$

Therefore,

$$\mathbb{P}[\bar{X} \geq \epsilon] \leq e^{-\lambda\epsilon}\prod_i e^{\frac{\lambda^2(b-a)^2}{8m^2}} = e^{-\lambda\epsilon + \frac{\lambda^2(b-a)^2}{8m}}.$$

Setting $\lambda = 4m\epsilon/(b-a)^2$ we obtain

$$\mathbb{P}[\bar{X} \geq \epsilon] \leq e^{-\frac{2m\epsilon^2}{(b-a)^2}}.$$

Applying the same arguments on the variable $-\bar{X}$ we obtain that $\mathbb{P}[\bar{X} \leq -\epsilon] \leq e^{-\frac{2m\epsilon^2}{(b-a)^2}}$. The theorem follows by applying the union bound on the two cases. □

Lemma B.7 (Hoeffding's Lemma). *Let X be a random variable that takes values in the interval $[a,b]$ and such that $\mathbb{E}[X] = 0$. Then, for every $\lambda > 0$,*

$$\mathbb{E}[e^{\lambda X}] \leq e^{\frac{\lambda^2(b-a)^2}{8}}.$$

Proof. Since $f(x) = e^{\lambda x}$ is a convex function, we have that for every $\alpha \in (0,1)$, and $x \in [a,b]$,

$$f(x) \leq \alpha f(a) + (1-\alpha) f(b).$$

Setting $\alpha = \frac{b-x}{b-a} \in [0,1]$ yields

$$e^{\lambda x} \leq \frac{b-x}{b-a} e^{\lambda a} + \frac{x-a}{b-a} e^{\lambda b}.$$

Taking the expectation, we obtain that

$$\mathbb{E}[e^{\lambda X}] \leq \frac{b - \mathbb{E}[X]}{b-a} e^{\lambda a} + \frac{\mathbb{E}[x] - a}{b-a} e^{\lambda b} = \frac{b}{b-a} e^{\lambda a} - \frac{a}{b-a} e^{\lambda b},$$

where we used the fact that $\mathbb{E}[X] = 0$. Denote $h = \lambda(b-a)$, $p = \frac{-a}{b-a}$, and $L(h) = -hp + \log(1 - p + pe^h)$. Then, the expression on the right-hand side of the equation can be rewritten as $e^{L(h)}$. Therefore, to conclude our proof it suffices to show that $L(h) \leq \frac{h^2}{8}$. This follows from Taylor's theorem using the facts $L(0) = L'(0) = 0$ and $L''(h) \leq 1/4$ for all h. □

B.5 BENNET'S AND BERNSTEIN'S INEQUALITIES

Bennet's and Bernsein's inequalities are similar to Chernoff's bounds, but they hold for any sequence of independent random variables. We state the inequalities without proof, which can be found, for example, in Cesa-Bianchi and Lugosi (2006).

Lemma B.8 (Bennet's Inequality). *Let $Z_1, \ldots, Z_m$ be independent random variables with zero mean, and assume that $Z_i \leq 1$ with probability 1. Let*

$$\sigma^2 \geq \frac{1}{m} \sum_{i=1}^{m} \mathbb{E}[Z_i^2].$$

Then for all $\epsilon > 0$,

$$\mathbb{P}\left[\sum_{i=1}^{m} Z_i > \epsilon\right] \leq e^{-m\sigma^2 h\left(\frac{\epsilon}{m\sigma^2}\right)}.$$

where

$$h(a) = (1+a)\log(1+a) - a.$$

By using the inequality $h(a) \geq a^2/(2+2a/3)$ it is possible to derive the following:

Lemma B.9 (Bernstein's Inequality). *Let $Z_1, \ldots, Z_m$ be i.i.d. random variables with a zero mean. If for all i, $\mathbb{P}(|Z_i| < M) = 1$, then for all $t > 0$:*

$$\mathbb{P}\left[\sum_{i=1}^{m} Z_i > t\right] \leq \exp\left(-\frac{t^2/2}{\sum \mathbb{E} Z_j^2 + Mt/3}\right).$$

B.5.1 Application

Bernstein's inequality can be used to interpolate between the rate $1/\epsilon$ we derived for PAC learning in the realizable case (in Chapter 2) and the rate $1/\epsilon^2$ we derived for the unrealizable case (in Chapter 4).

Lemma B.10. *Let $\ell : \mathcal{H} \times Z \to [0,1]$ be a loss function. Let $\mathcal{D}$ be an arbitrary distribution over Z. Fix some h. Then, for any $\delta \in (0,1)$ we have*

1. $\underset{S \sim \mathcal{D}^m}{\mathbb{P}}\left[L_S(h) \geq L_{\mathcal{D}}(h) + \sqrt{\frac{2L_{\mathcal{D}}(h)\log(1/\delta)}{3m}} + \frac{2\log(1/\delta)}{m}\right] \leq \delta$
2. $\underset{S \sim \mathcal{D}^m}{\mathbb{P}}\left[L_{\mathcal{D}}(h) \geq L_S(h) + \sqrt{\frac{2L_S(h)\log(1/\delta)}{m}} + \frac{4\log(1/\delta)}{m}\right] \leq \delta$

Proof. Define random variables $\alpha_1, \ldots, \alpha_m$ s.t. $\alpha_i = \ell(h, z_i) - L_{\mathcal{D}}(h)$. Note that $\mathbb{E}[\alpha_i] = 0$ and that

$$\begin{aligned}
\mathbb{E}[\alpha_i^2] &= \mathbb{E}[\ell(h,z_i)^2] - 2L_{\mathcal{D}}(h)\mathbb{E}[\ell(h,z_i)] + L_{\mathcal{D}}(h)^2 \\
&= \mathbb{E}[\ell(h,z_i)^2] - L_{\mathcal{D}}(h)^2 \\
&\leq \mathbb{E}[\ell(h,z_i)^2] \\
&\leq \mathbb{E}[\ell(h,z_i)] = L_{\mathcal{D}}(h),
\end{aligned}$$

where in the last inequality we used the fact that $\ell(h,z_i) \in [0,1]$ and thus $\ell(h,z_i)^2 \leq \ell(h,z_i)$. Applying Bernsein's inequality over the α_i's yields

$$\begin{aligned}
\mathbb{P}\left[\sum_{i=1}^{m} \alpha_i > t\right] &\leq \exp\left(-\frac{t^2/2}{\sum \mathbb{E}\alpha_j^2 + t/3}\right) \\
&\leq \exp\left(-\frac{t^2/2}{m\, L_{\mathcal{D}}(h) + t/3}\right) \stackrel{\text{def}}{=} \delta.
\end{aligned}$$

Solving for t yields

$$\frac{t^2/2}{m\,L_{\mathcal{D}}(h)+t/3} = \log(1/\delta)$$

$$\Rightarrow\ t^2/2 - \frac{\log(1/\delta)}{3}t - \log(1/\delta)m\,L_{\mathcal{D}}(h) = 0$$

$$\Rightarrow\ t = \frac{\log(1/\delta)}{3} + \sqrt{\frac{\log^2(1/\delta)}{3^2} + 2\log(1/\delta)m\,L_{\mathcal{D}}(h)}$$

$$\leq 2\frac{\log(1/\delta)}{3} + \sqrt{2\log(1/\delta)m\,L_{\mathcal{D}}(h)}$$

Since $\frac{1}{m}\sum_i \alpha_i = L_S(h) - L_{\mathcal{D}}(h)$, it follows that with probability of at least $1-\delta$,

$$L_S(h) - L_{\mathcal{D}}(h) \leq 2\frac{\log(1/\delta)}{3m} + \sqrt{\frac{2\log(1/\delta)L_{\mathcal{D}}(h)}{m}},$$

which proves the first inequality. The second part of the lemma follows in a similar way. □

B.6 SLUD'S INEQUALITY

Let X be a (m,p) binomial variable. That is, $X=\sum_{i=1}^m Z_i$, where each Z_i is 1 with probability p and 0 with probability $1-p$. Assume that $p=(1-\epsilon)/2$. Slud's inequality (Slud 1977) tells us that $\mathbb{P}[X \geq m/2]$ is lower bounded by the probability that a normal variable will be greater than or equal to $\sqrt{m\epsilon^2/(1-\epsilon^2)}$. The following lemma follows by standard tail bounds for the normal distribution.

Lemma B.11. *Let X be a (m,p) binomial variable and assume that $p=(1-\epsilon)/2$. Then,*

$$\mathbb{P}[X \geq m/2] \geq \frac{1}{2}\left(1-\sqrt{1-\exp(-m\epsilon^2/(1-\epsilon^2))}\right).$$

B.7 CONCENTRATION OF χ^2 VARIABLES

Let $X_1,\ldots,X_k$ be k independent normally distributed random variables. That is, for all i, $X_i \sim N(0,1)$. The distribution of the random variable X_i^2 is called χ^2 (chi square) and the distribution of the random variable $Z=X_1^2+\cdots+X_k^2$ is called χ_k^2 (chi square with k degrees of freedom). Clearly, $\mathbb{E}[X_i^2]=1$ and $\mathbb{E}[Z]=k$. The following lemma states that X_k^2 is concentrated around its mean.

Lemma B.12. *Let $Z \sim \chi_k^2$. Then, for all $\epsilon>0$ we have*

$$\mathbb{P}[Z \leq (1-\epsilon)k] \leq e^{-\epsilon^2 k/6},$$

and for all $\epsilon \in (0,3)$ we have

$$\mathbb{P}[Z \geq (1+\epsilon)k] \leq e^{-\epsilon^2 k/6}.$$

Finally, for all $\epsilon \in (0,3)$,

$$\mathbb{P}[(1-\epsilon)k \leq Z \leq (1+\epsilon)k] \geq 1-2e^{-\epsilon^2 k/6}.$$

Proof. Let us write $Z = \sum_{i=1}^k X_i^2$ where $X_i \sim N(0,1)$. To prove both bounds we use Chernoff's bounding method. For the first inequality, we first bound $\mathbb{E}[e^{-\lambda X_1^2}]$, where $\lambda > 0$ will be specified later. Since $e^{-a} \leq 1 - a + \frac{a^2}{2}$ for all $a \geq 0$ we have that

$$\mathbb{E}[e^{-\lambda X_1^2}] \leq 1 - \lambda \mathbb{E}[X_1^2] + \frac{\lambda^2}{2} \mathbb{E}[X_1^4].$$

Using the well known equalities, $\mathbb{E}[X_1^2] = 1$ and $\mathbb{E}[X_1^4] = 3$, and the fact that $1 - a \leq e^{-a}$ we obtain that

$$\mathbb{E}[e^{-\lambda X_1^2}] \leq 1 - \lambda + \tfrac{3}{2}\lambda^2 \leq e^{-\lambda + \frac{3}{2}\lambda^2}.$$

Now, applying Chernoff's bounding method we get that

$$\begin{aligned}
\mathbb{P}[-Z \geq -(1-\epsilon)k] &= \mathbb{P}\left[e^{-\lambda Z} \geq e^{-(1-\epsilon)k\lambda}\right] \\
&\leq e^{(1-\epsilon)k\lambda}\, \mathbb{E}\left[e^{-\lambda Z}\right] \\
&= e^{(1-\epsilon)k\lambda} \left(\mathbb{E}\left[e^{-\lambda X_1^2}\right]\right)^k \\
&\leq e^{(1-\epsilon)k\lambda}\, e^{-\lambda k + \frac{3}{2}\lambda^2 k} \\
&= e^{-\epsilon k \lambda + \frac{3}{2} k \lambda^2}.
\end{aligned}$$

Choose $\lambda = \epsilon/3$ we obtain the first inequality stated in the lemma.

For the second inequality, we use a known closed form expression for the moment generating function of a χ_k^2 distributed random variable:

$$\forall \lambda < \tfrac{1}{2}, \quad \mathbb{E}\left[e^{\lambda Z^2}\right] = (1 - 2\lambda)^{-k/2}. \tag{B.7}$$

On the basis of the equation and using Chernoff's bounding method we have

$$\begin{aligned}
\mathbb{P}[Z \geq (1+\epsilon)k)] &= \mathbb{P}\left[e^{\lambda Z} \geq e^{(1+\epsilon)k\lambda}\right] \\
&\leq e^{-(1+\epsilon)k\lambda}\, \mathbb{E}\left[e^{\lambda Z}\right] \\
&= e^{-(1+\epsilon)k\lambda}\, (1 - 2\lambda)^{-k/2} \\
&\leq e^{-(1+\epsilon)k\lambda}\, e^{k\lambda} = e^{-\epsilon k \lambda},
\end{aligned}$$

where the last inequality occurs because $(1 - a) \leq e^{-a}$. Setting $\lambda = \epsilon/6$ (which is in $(0, 1/2)$ by our assumption) we obtain the second inequality stated in the lemma.

Finally, the last inequality follows from the first two inequalities and the union bound. □

Appendix C

Linear Algebra

C.1 BASIC DEFINITIONS

In this chapter we only deal with linear algebra over finite dimensional Euclidean spaces. We refer to vectors as column vectors.

Given two d dimensional vectors $\mathbf{u}, \mathbf{v} \in \mathbb{R}^d$, their inner product is

$$\langle \mathbf{u}, \mathbf{v} \rangle = \sum_{i=1}^{d} u_i v_i.$$

The Euclidean norm (a.k.a. the ℓ_2 norm) is $\|\mathbf{u}\| = \sqrt{\langle \mathbf{u}, \mathbf{u} \rangle}$. We also use the ℓ_1 norm, $\|\mathbf{u}\|_1 = \sum_{i=1}^{d} |u_i|$ and the ℓ_∞ norm $\|\mathbf{u}\|_\infty = \max_i |u_i|$.

A subspace of $\mathbb{R}^d$ is a subset of $\mathbb{R}^d$ which is closed under addition and scalar multiplication. The span of a set of vectors $\mathbf{u}_1, \ldots, \mathbf{u}_k$ is the subspace containing all vectors of the form

$$\sum_{i=1}^{k} \alpha_i \mathbf{u}_i$$

where for all i, $\alpha_i \in \mathbb{R}$.

A set of vectors $U = \{\mathbf{u}_1, \ldots, \mathbf{u}_k\}$ is independent if for every i, $\mathbf{u}_i$ is not in the span of $\mathbf{u}_1, \ldots, \mathbf{u}_{i-1}, \mathbf{u}_{i+1}, \ldots, \mathbf{u}_k$. We say that U spans a subspace V if V is the span of the vectors in U. We say that U is a *basis* of V if it is both independent and spans V. The dimension of V is the size of a basis of V (and it can be verified that all bases of V have the same size). We say that U is an orthogonal set if for all $i \neq j$, $\langle \mathbf{u}_i, \mathbf{u}_j \rangle = 0$. We say that U is an orthonormal set if it is orthogonal and if for every i, $\|\mathbf{u}_i\| = 1$.

Given a matrix $A \in \mathbb{R}^{n,d}$, the range of A is the span of its columns and the null space of A is the subspace of all vectors that satisfy $A\mathbf{u} = \mathbf{0}$. The rank of A is the dimension of its range.

The transpose of a matrix A, denoted $A^\top$, is the matrix whose (i, j) entry equals the (j, i) entry of A. We say that A is symmetric if $A = A^\top$.

C.2 EIGENVALUES AND EIGENVECTORS

Let $A \in \mathbb{R}^{d,d}$ be a matrix. A nonzero vector $\mathbf{u}$ is an eigenvector of A with a corresponding eigenvalue λ if

$$A\mathbf{u} = \lambda\mathbf{u}.$$

Theorem C.1 (Spectral Decomposition). *If $A \in \mathbb{R}^{d,d}$ is a symmetric matrix of rank k, then there exists an orthonormal basis of $\mathbb{R}^d$, $\mathbf{u}_1, \ldots, \mathbf{u}_d$, such that each $\mathbf{u}_i$ is an eigenvector of A. Furthermore, A can be written as $A = \sum_{i=1}^{d} \lambda_i \mathbf{u}_i \mathbf{u}_i^\top$, where each λ_i is the eigenvalue corresponding to the eigenvector $\mathbf{u}_i$. This can be written equivalently as $A = UDU^\top$, where the columns of U are the vectors $\mathbf{u}_1, \ldots, \mathbf{u}_d$, and D is a diagonal matrix with $D_{i,i} = \lambda_i$ and for $i \neq j$, $D_{i,j} = 0$. Finally, the number of λ_i which are nonzero is the rank of the matrix, the eigenvectors which correspond to the nonzero eigenvalues span the range of A, and the eigenvectors which correspond to zero eigenvalues span the null space of A.*

C.3 POSITIVE DEFINITE MATRICES

A symmetric matrix $A \in \mathbb{R}^{d,d}$ is positive definite if all its eigenvalues are positive. A is positive semidefinite if all its eigenvalues are nonnegative.

Theorem C.2. *Let $A \in \mathbb{R}^{d,d}$ be a symmetric matrix. Then, the following are equivalent definitions of positive semidefiniteness of A:*

- *All the eigenvalues of A are nonnegative.*
- *For every vector $\mathbf{u}$, $\langle \mathbf{u}, A\mathbf{u} \rangle \geq 0$.*
- *There exists a matrix B such that $A = BB^\top$.*

C.4 SINGULAR VALUE DECOMPOSITION (SVD)

Let $A \in \mathbb{R}^{m,n}$ be a matrix of rank r. When $m \neq n$, the eigenvalue decomposition given in Theorem C.1 cannot be applied. We will describe another decomposition of A, which is called Singular Value Decomposition, or SVD for short.

Unit vectors $\mathbf{v} \in \mathbb{R}^n$ and $\mathbf{u} \in \mathbb{R}^m$ are called right and left *singular vectors* of A with corresponding *singular value* $\sigma > 0$ if

$$A\mathbf{v} = \sigma\mathbf{u} \quad \text{and} \quad A^\top\mathbf{u} = \sigma\mathbf{v}.$$

We first show that if we can find r orthonormal singular vectors with positive singular values, then we can decompose $A = UDV^\top$, with the columns of U and V containing the left and right singular vectors, and D being a diagonal $r \times r$ matrix with the singular values on its diagonal.

Lemma C.3. *Let $A \in \mathbb{R}^{m,n}$ be a matrix of rank r. Assume that $\mathbf{v}_1, \ldots, \mathbf{v}_r$ is an orthonormal set of right singular vectors of A, $\mathbf{u}_1, \ldots, \mathbf{u}_r$ is an orthonormal set of corresponding left singular vectors of A, and $\sigma_1, \ldots, \sigma_r$ are the corresponding singular* *values. Then,*

$$A = \sum_{i=1}^{r} \sigma_i \mathbf{u}_i \mathbf{v}_i^\top .$$

It follows that if U is a matrix whose columns are the $\mathbf{u}_i$'s, V is a matrix whose columns are the $\mathbf{v}_i$'s, and D is a diagonal matrix with $D_{i,i} = \sigma_i$, then

$$A = UDV^\top .$$

Proof. Any right singular vector of A must be in the range of $A^\top$ (otherwise, the singular value will have to be zero). Therefore, $\mathbf{v}_1, \ldots, \mathbf{v}_r$ is an orthonormal basis of the range of A. Let us complete it to an orthonormal basis of $\mathbb{R}^n$ by adding the vectors $\mathbf{v}_{r+1}, \ldots, \mathbf{v}_n$. Define $B = \sum_{i=1}^{r} \sigma_i \mathbf{u}_i \mathbf{v}_i^\top$. It suffices to prove that for all i, $A\mathbf{v}_i = B\mathbf{v}_i$. Clearly, if $i > r$ then $A\mathbf{v}_i = 0$ and $B\mathbf{v}_i = 0$ as well. For $i \le r$ we have

$$B\mathbf{v}_i = \sum_{j=1}^{r} \sigma_j \mathbf{u}_j \mathbf{v}_j^\top \mathbf{v}_i = \sigma_i \mathbf{u}_i = A\mathbf{v}_i,$$

where the last equality follows from the definition. □

The next lemma relates the singular values of A to the eigenvalues of $A^\top A$ and $AA^\top$.

Lemma C.4. *$\mathbf{v}, \mathbf{u}$ are right and left singular vectors of A with singular value σ iff $\mathbf{v}$ is an eigenvector of $A^\top A$ with corresponding eigenvalue σ^2 and $\mathbf{u} = \sigma^{-1} A\mathbf{v}$ is an eigenvector of $AA^\top$ with corresponding eigenvalue σ^2.*

Proof. Suppose that σ is a singular value of A with $\mathbf{v} \in \mathbb{R}^n$ being the corresponding right singular vector. Then,

$$A^\top A\mathbf{v} = \sigma A^\top \mathbf{u} = \sigma^2 \mathbf{v}.$$

Similarly,

$$AA^\top u = \sigma A\mathbf{v} = \sigma^2 \mathbf{u}.$$

For the other direction, if $\lambda \neq 0$ is an eigenvalue of $A^\top A$, with $\mathbf{v}$ being the corresponding eigenvector, then $\lambda > 0$ because $A^\top A$ is positive semidefinite. Let $\sigma = \sqrt{\lambda}, \mathbf{u} = \sigma^{-1} A\mathbf{v}$. Then,

$$\sigma \mathbf{u} = \sqrt{\lambda} \frac{A\mathbf{v}}{\sqrt{\lambda}} = A\mathbf{v},$$

and

$$A^\top \mathbf{u} = \frac{1}{\sigma} A^\top A\mathbf{v} = \frac{\lambda}{\sigma} \mathbf{v} = \sigma \mathbf{v}.$$

□

Finally, we show that if A has rank r then it has r orthonormal singular vectors.

Lemma C.5. *Let $A \in \mathbb{R}^{m,n}$ with rank r. Define the following vectors:*

$$\mathbf{v}_1 = \underset{\mathbf{v}\in\mathbb{R}^n:\|\mathbf{v}\|=1}{\operatorname{argmax}} \|A\mathbf{v}\|$$

$$\mathbf{v}_2 = \underset{\substack{\mathbf{v}\in\mathbb{R}^n:\|\mathbf{v}\|=1\\ \langle \mathbf{v},\mathbf{v}_1\rangle=0}}{\operatorname{argmax}} \|A\mathbf{v}\|$$

$$\vdots$$

$$\mathbf{v}_r = \underset{\substack{\mathbf{v}\in\mathbb{R}^n:\|\mathbf{v}\|=1\\ \forall i<r,\ \langle \mathbf{v},\mathbf{v}_i\rangle=0}}{\operatorname{argmax}} \|A\mathbf{v}\|$$

Then, $\mathbf{v}_1,\ldots,\mathbf{v}_r$ is an orthonormal set of right singular vectors of A.

Proof. First note that since the rank of A is r, the range of A is a subspace of dimension r, and therefore it is easy to verify that for all $i = 1,\ldots,r$, $\|A\mathbf{v}_i\| > 0$. Let $W \in \mathbb{R}^{n,n}$ be an orthonormal matrix obtained by the eigenvalue decomposition of $A^\top A$, namely, $A^\top A = WDW^\top$, with D being a diagonal matrix with $D_{1,1} \geq D_{2,2} \geq \cdots \geq 0$. We will show that $\mathbf{v}_1,\ldots,\mathbf{v}_r$ are eigenvectors of $A^\top A$ that correspond to nonzero eigenvalues, and, hence, using Lemma C.4 it follows that these are also right singular vectors of A. The proof is by induction. For the basis of the induction, note that any unit vector $\mathbf{v}$ can be written as $\mathbf{v} = W\mathbf{x}$, for $\mathbf{x} = W^\top\mathbf{v}$, and note that $\|\mathbf{x}\| = 1$. Therefore,

$$\|A\mathbf{v}\|^2 = \|AW\mathbf{x}\|^2 = \|WDW^\top W\mathbf{x}\|^2 = \|WD\mathbf{x}\|^2 = \|D\mathbf{x}\|^2 = \sum_{i=1}^n D_{i,i}^2 x_i{}^2.$$

Therefore,

$$\max_{\mathbf{v}:\|\mathbf{v}\|=1} \|A\mathbf{v}\|^2 = \max_{\mathbf{x}:\|\mathbf{x}\|=1} \sum_{i=1}^n D_{i,i}^2 x_i{}^2.$$

The solution of the right-hand side is to set $\mathbf{x} = (1,0,\ldots,0)$, which implies that $\mathbf{v}_1$ is the first eigenvector of $A^\top A$. Since $\|A\mathbf{v}_1\| > 0$ it follows that $D_{1,1} > 0$ as required. For the induction step, assume that the claim holds for some $1 \leq t \leq r-1$. Then, any $\mathbf{v}$ which is orthogonal to $\mathbf{v}_1,\ldots,\mathbf{v}_t$ can be written as $\mathbf{v} = W\mathbf{x}$ with all the first t elements of $\mathbf{x}$ being zero. It follows that

$$\max_{\mathbf{v}:\|\mathbf{v}\|=1,\forall i\leq t,\mathbf{v}^\top\mathbf{v}_i=0} \|A\mathbf{v}\|^2 = \max_{\mathbf{x}:\|\mathbf{x}\|=1} \sum_{i=t+1}^n D_{i,i}^2 x_i{}^2.$$

The solution of the right-hand side is the all zeros vector except $x_{t+1} = 1$. This implies that $\mathbf{v}_{t+1}$ is the $(t+1)$th column of W. Finally, since $\|A\mathbf{v}_{t+1}\| > 0$ it follows that $D_{t+1,t+1} > 0$ as required. This concludes our proof. □

Corollary C.6 (The SVD Theorem). *Let $A \in \mathbb{R}^{m,n}$ with rank r. Then $A = UDV^\top$ where D is an $r \times r$ matrix with nonzero singular values of A and the columns of U, V are orthonormal left and right singular vectors of A. Furthermore, for all i, $D_{i,i}^2$ is an eigenvalue of $A^\top A$, the ith column of V is the corresponding eigenvector of $A^\top A$ and the ith column of U is the corresponding eigenvector of $AA^\top$.*

References

Abernethy, J., Bartlett, P. L., Rakhlin, A. & Tewari, A. (2008), "Optimal strategies and minimax lower bounds for online convex games," in *Proceedings of the nineteenth annual conference on computational learning theory*.

Ackerman, M. & Ben-David, S. (2008), "Measures of clustering quality: A working set of axioms for clustering," in *Proceedings of Neural Information Processing Systems* (NIPS), pp. 121–128.

Agarwal, S. & Roth, D. (2005), "Learnability of bipartite ranking functions," in *Proceedings of the 18th annual conference on learning theory*, pp. 16–31.

Agmon, S. (1954), "The relaxation method for linear inequalities," *Canadian Journal of Mathematics* **6**(3), 382–392.

Aizerman, M. A., Braverman, E. M. & Rozonoer, L. I. (1964), "Theoretical foundations of the potential function method in pattern recognition learning," *Automation and Remote Control* **25**, 821–837.

Allwein, E. L., Schapire, R. & Singer, Y. (2000), "Reducing multiclass to binary: A unifying approach for margin classifiers," *Journal of Machine Learning Research* **1**, 113–141.

Alon, N., Ben-David, S., Cesa-Bianchi, N. & Haussler, D. (1997), "Scale-sensitive dimensions, uniform convergence, and learnability," *Journal of the ACM* **44**(4), 615–631.

Anthony, M. & Bartlet, P. (1999), *Neural Network Learning: Theoretical Foundations*, Cambridge University Press.

Baraniuk, R., Davenport, M., DeVore, R. & Wakin, M. (2008), "A simple proof of the restricted isometry property for random matrices," *Constructive Approximation* **28**(3), 253–263.

Barber, D. (2012), *Bayesian reasoning and machine learning*, Cambridge University Press.

Bartlett, P., Bousquet, O. & Mendelson, S. (2005), "Local rademacher complexities," *Annals of Statistics* **33**(4), 1497–1537.

Bartlett, P. L. & Ben-David, S. (2002), "Hardness results for neural network approximation problems," *Theor. Comput. Sci.* **284**(1), 53–66.

Bartlett, P. L., Long, P. M. & Williamson, R. C. (1994), "Fat-shattering and the learnability of real-valued functions," in *Proceedings of the seventh annual conference on computational learning theory*, (ACM), pp. 299–310.

Bartlett, P. L. & Mendelson, S. (2001), "Rademacher and Gaussian complexities: Risk bounds and structural results," in *14th Annual Conference on Computational Learning Theory* (COLT) *2001*, Vol. 2111, Springer, Berlin, pp. 224–240.

Bartlett, P. L. & Mendelson, S. (2002), "Rademacher and Gaussian complexities: Risk bounds and structural results," *Journal of Machine Learning Research* **3**, 463–482.

Ben-David, S., Cesa-Bianchi, N., Haussler, D. & Long, P. (1995), "Characterizations of learnability for classes of $\{0, \ldots, n\}$-valued functions," *Journal of Computer and System Sciences* **50**, 74–86.

Ben-David, S., Eiron, N. & Long, P. (2003), "On the difficulty of approximately maximizing agreements," *Journal of Computer and System Sciences* **66**(3), 496–514.

Ben-David, S. & Litman, A. (1998), "Combinatorial variability of vapnik-chervonenkis classes with applications to sample compression schemes," *Discrete Applied Mathematics* **86**(1), 3–25.

Ben-David, S., Pal, D., & Shalev-Shwartz, S. (2009), "Agnostic online learning," in Conference on Learning Theory (COLT).

Ben-David, S. & Simon, H. (2001), "Efficient learning of linear perceptrons," *Advances in Neural Information Processing Systems*, pp. 189–195.

Bengio, Y. (2009), "Learning deep architectures for AI," *Foundations and Trends in Machine Learning* **2**(1), 1–127.

Bengio, Y. & LeCun, Y. (2007), "Scaling learning algorithms towards AI," *Large-Scale Kernel Machines* **34**.

Bertsekas, D. (1999), *Nonlinear programming*, Athena Scientific.

Beygelzimer, A., Langford, J. & Ravikumar, P. (2007), "Multiclass classification with filter trees," *Preprint, June* .

Birkhoff, G. (1946), "Three observations on linear algebra," *Revi. Univ. Nac. Tucuman, ser. A* **5**, 147–151.

Bishop, C. M. (2006), *Pattern recognition and machine learning*, Vol. 1, Springer: New York.

Blum, L., Shub, M. & Smale, S. (1989), "On a theory of computation and complexity over the real numbers: Np-completeness, recursive functions and universal machines," *Am. Math. Soc.* **21**(1), 1–46.

Blumer, A., Ehrenfeucht, A., Haussler, D. & Warmuth, M. K. (1987), "Occam's razor," *Information Processing Letters* **24**(6), 377–380.

Blumer, A., Ehrenfeucht, A., Haussler, D. & Warmuth, M. K. (1989), "Learnability and the Vapnik-Chervonenkis dimension," *Journal of the Association for Computing Machinery* **36**(4), 929–965.

Borwein, J. & Lewis, A. (2006), *Convex analysis and nonlinear optimization*, Springer.

Boser, B. E., Guyon, I. M. & Vapnik, V. N. (1992), "A training algorithm for optimal margin classifiers," in COLT, pp. 144–152.

Bottou, L. & Bousquet, O. (2008), "The tradeoffs of large scale learning," in NIPS, pp. 161–168.

Boucheron, S., Bousquet, O. & Lugosi, G. (2005), "Theory of classification: A survey of recent advances," *ESAIM: Probability and Statistics* **9**, 323–375.

Bousquet, O. (2002), Concentration Inequalities and Empirical Processes Theory Applied to the Analysis of Learning Algorithms, PhD thesis, Ecole Polytechnique.

Bousquet, O. & Elisseeff, A. (2002), "Stability and generalization," *Journal of Machine Learning Research* **2**, 499–526.

Boyd, S. & Vandenberghe, L. (2004), *Convex optimization*, Cambridge University Press.

Breiman, L. (1996), Bias, variance, and arcing classifiers, Technical Report 460, Statistics Department, University of California at Berkeley.

Breiman, L. (2001), "Random forests," *Machine Learning* **45**(1), 5–32.

Breiman, L., Friedman, J. H., Olshen, R. A. & Stone, C. J. (1984), *Classification and regression trees*, Wadsworth & Brooks.

Candès, E. (2008), "The restricted isometry property and its implications for compressed sensing," *Comptes Rendus Mathematique* **346**(9), 589–592.

Candes, E. J. (2006), "Compressive sampling," in *Proc. of the int. congress of math.*, Madrid, Spain.

Candes, E. & Tao, T. (2005), "Decoding by linear programming," *IEEE Trans. on Information Theory* **51**, 4203–4215.

Cesa-Bianchi, N. & Lugosi, G. (2006), *Prediction, learning, and games*, Cambridge University Press.

Chang, H. S., Weiss, Y. & Freeman, W. T. (2009), "Informative sensing," *arXiv preprint arXiv:0901.4275*.

Chapelle, O., Le, Q. & Smola, A. (2007), "Large margin optimization of ranking measures," in *NIPS workshop: Machine learning for Web search* (Machine Learning).

Collins, M. (2000), "Discriminative reranking for natural language parsing," in Machine Learning.

Collins, M. (2002), "Discriminative training methods for hidden Markov models: Theory and experiments with perceptron algorithms," in *Conference on Empirical Methods in Natural Language Processing*.

Collobert, R. & Weston, J. (2008), "A unified architecture for natural language processing: deep neural networks with multitask learning," in International Conference on Machine Learning (ICML).

Cortes, C. & Vapnik, V. (1995), "Support-vector networks," *Machine Learning* **20**(3), 273–297.

Cover, T. (1965), "Behavior of sequential predictors of binary sequences," *Trans. 4th Prague conf. information theory statistical decision functions, random processes*, pp. 263–272.

Cover, T. & Hart, P. (1967), "Nearest neighbor pattern classification," *Information Theory, IEEE Transactions on* **13**(1), 21–27.

Crammer, K. & Singer, Y. (2001), "On the algorithmic implementation of multiclass kernel-based vector machines," *Journal of Machine Learning Research* **2**, 265–292.

Cristianini, N. & Shawe-Taylor, J. (2000), *An introduction to support vector machines*, Cambridge University Press.

Daniely, A., Sabato, S., Ben-David, S. & Shalev-Shwartz, S. (2011), "Multiclass learnability and the erm principle," in COLT.

Daniely, A., Sabato, S. & Shwartz, S. S. (2012), "Multiclass learning approaches: A theoretical comparison with implications," in NIPS.

Davis, G., Mallat, S. & Avellaneda, M. (1997), "Greedy adaptive approximation," *Journal of Constructive Approximation* **13**, 57–98.

Devroye, L. & Györfi, L. (1985), *Nonparametric density estimation: The L B1 S view*, Wiley.

Devroye, L., Györfi, L. & Lugosi, G. (1996), *A probabilistic theory of pattern recognition*, Springer.

Dietterich, T. G. & Bakiri, G. (1995), "Solving multiclass learning problems via error-correcting output codes," *Journal of Artificial Intelligence Research* **2**, 263–286.

Donoho, D. L. (2006), "Compressed sensing," *Information Theory, IEEE Transactions* **52**(4), 1289–1306.

Dudley, R., Gine, E. & Zinn, J. (1991), "Uniform and universal glivenko-cantelli classes," *Journal of Theoretical Probability* **4**(3), 485–510.

Dudley, R. M. (1987), "Universal Donsker classes and metric entropy," *Annals of Probability* **15**(4), 1306–1326.

Fisher, R. A. (1922), "On the mathematical foundations of theoretical statistics," *Philosophical Transactions of the Royal Society of London. Series A, Containing Papers of a Mathematical or Physical Character* **222**, 309–368.

Floyd, S. (1989), "Space-bounded learning and the Vapnik-Chervonenkis dimension," in COLT, pp. 349–364.

Floyd, S. & Warmuth, M. (1995), "Sample compression, learnability, and the Vapnik-Chervonenkis dimension," *Machine Learning* **21**(3), 269–304.

Frank, M. & Wolfe, P. (1956), "An algorithm for quadratic programming," *Naval Res. Logist. Quart.* **3**, 95–110.

Freund, Y. & Schapire, R. (1995), "A decision-theoretic generalization of on-line learning and an application to boosting," in European Conference on Computational Learning Theory (EuroCOLT), Springer-Verlag, pp. 23–37.

Freund, Y. & Schapire, R. E. (1999), "Large margin classification using the perceptron algorithm," *Machine Learning* **37**(3), 277–296.

Garcia, J. & Koelling, R. (1996), "Relation of cue to consequence in avoidance learning," *Foundations of animal behavior: classic papers with commentaries* **4**, 374.

Gentile, C. (2003), "The robustness of the p-norm algorithms," *Machine Learning* **53**(3), 265–299.

Georghiades, A., Belhumeur, P. & Kriegman, D. (2001), "From few to many: Illumination cone models for face recognition under variable lighting and pose," *IEEE Trans. Pattern Anal. Mach. Intelligence* **23**(6), 643–660.

Gordon, G. (1999), "Regret bounds for prediction problems," in Conference on Learning Theory (COLT).

Gottlieb, L.-A., Kontorovich, L. & Krauthgamer, R. (2010), "Efficient classification for metric data," in *23rd conference on learning theory*, pp. 433–440.

Guyon, I. & Elisseeff, A. (2003), "An introduction to variable and feature selection," *Journal of Machine Learning Research, Special Issue on Variable and Feature Selection* **3**, 1157–1182.

Hadamard, J. (1902), "Sur les problèmes aux dérivées partielles et leur signification physique," *Princeton University Bulletin* **13**, 49–52.

Hastie, T., Tibshirani, R. & Friedman, J. (2001), *The elements of statistical learning*, Springer.

Haussler, D. (1992), "Decision theoretic generalizations of the PAC model for neural net and other learning applications," *Information and Computation* **100**(1), 78–150.

Haussler, D. & Long, P. M. (1995), "A generalization of sauer's lemma," *Journal of Combinatorial Theory, Series A* **71**(2), 219–240.

Hazan, E., Agarwal, A. & Kale, S. (2007), "Logarithmic regret algorithms for online convex optimization," *Machine Learning* **69**(2–3), 169–192.

Hinton, G. E., Osindero, S. & Teh, Y.-W. (2006), "A fast learning algorithm for deep belief nets," *Neural Computation* **18**(7), 1527–1554.

Hiriart-Urruty, J.-B. & Lemaréchal, C. (1993), *Convex analysis and minimization algorithms*, Springer.

Hsu, C.-W., Chang, C.-C., & Lin, C.-J. (2003), "A practical guide to support vector classification."

Hyafil, L. & Rivest, R. L. (1976), "Constructing optimal binary decision trees is NP-complete," *Information Processing Letters* **5**(1), 15–17.

Joachims, T. (2005), "A support vector method for multivariate performance measures," in *Proceedings of the international conference on machine learning* (ICML).

Kakade, S., Sridharan, K. & Tewari, A. (2008), "On the complexity of linear prediction: Risk bounds, margin bounds, and regularization," in NIPS.

Karp, R. M. (1972), *Reducibility among combinatorial problems*, Springer.

Kearns, M. & Mansour, Y. (1996), "On the boosting ability of top-down decision tree learning algorithms," in ACM Symposium on the Theory of Computing (STOC).

Kearns, M. & Ron, D. (1999), "Algorithmic stability and sanity-check bounds for leave-one-out cross-validation," *Neural Computation* **11**(6), 1427–1453.

Kearns, M. & Valiant, L. G. (1988), "Learning Boolean formulae or finite automata is as hard as factoring, Technical Report TR-14-88, Harvard University, Aiken Computation Laboratory.

Kearns, M. & Vazirani, U. (1994), *An Introduction to Computational Learning Theory*, MIT Press.

Kearns, M. J., Schapire, R. E. & Sellie, L. M. (1994), "Toward efficient agnostic learning," *Machine Learning* **17**, 115–141.

Kleinberg, J. (2003), "An impossibility theorem for clustering," NIPS, pp. 463–470.

Klivans, A. R. & Sherstov, A. A. (2006), Cryptographic hardness for learning intersections of halfspaces, in FOCS.

Koller, D. & Friedman, N. (2009), *Probabilistic graphical models: Principles and techniques*, MIT Press.

Koltchinskii, V. & Panchenko, D. (2000), "Rademacher processes and bounding the risk of function learning," in *High Dimensional Probability II*, Springer, pp. 443–457.

Kuhn, H. W. (1955), "The hungarian method for the assignment problem," *Naval Research Logistics Quarterly* **2**(1–2), 83–97.

Kutin, S. & Niyogi, P. (2002), "Almost-everywhere algorithmic stability and generalization error," in *Proceedings of the 18th conference in uncertainty in artificial intelligence*, pp. 275–282.

Lafferty, J., McCallum, A. & Pereira, F. (2001), "Conditional random fields: Probabilistic models for segmenting and labeling sequence data," in *International conference on machine learning*, pp. 282–289.

Langford, J. (2006), "Tutorial on practical prediction theory for classification," *Journal of machine learning research* **6**(1), 273.

Langford, J. & Shawe-Taylor, J. (2003), "PAC-Bayes & margins," in NIPS, pp. 423–430.

Le, Q. V., Ranzato, M.-A., Monga, R., Devin, M., Corrado, G., Chen, K., Dean, J. & Ng, A. Y. (2012), "Building high-level features using large scale unsupervised learning," in ICML.

Le Cun, L. (2004), "Large scale online learning," in *Advances in neural information processing systems 16: Proceedings of the 2003 conference*, Vol. 16, MIT Press, p. 217.

LeCun, Y. & Bengio, Y. (1995), "Convolutional networks for images, speech, and time series," in *The handbook of brain theory and neural networks*, The MIT Press.

Lee, H., Grosse, R., Ranganath, R. & Ng, A. (2009), "Convolutional deep belief networks for scalable unsupervised learning of hierarchical representations," in ICML.

Littlestone, N. (1988), "Learning quickly when irrelevant attributes abound: A new linear-threshold algorithm," *Machine Learning* **2**, 285–318.

Littlestone, N. & Warmuth, M. (1986), Relating data compression and learnability. Unpublished manuscript.

Littlestone, N. & Warmuth, M. K. (1994), "The weighted majority algorithm," *Information and Computation* **108**, 212–261.

Livni, R., Shalev-Shwartz, S. & Shamir, O. (2013), "A provably efficient algorithm for training deep networks," *arXiv preprint arXiv:1304.7045* .

Livni, R. & Simon, P. (2013), "Honest compressions and their application to compression schemes," in COLT.

MacKay, D. J. (2003), *Information theory, inference and learning algorithms*, Cambridge University Press.

Mallat, S. & Zhang, Z. (1993), "Matching pursuits with time-frequency dictionaries," *IEEE Transactions on Signal Processing* **41**, 3397–3415.

McAllester, D. A. (1998), "Some PAC-Bayesian theorems," in COLT.

McAllester, D. A. (1999), "PAC-Bayesian model averaging," in COLT, pp. 164–170.

McAllester, D. A. (2003), "Simplified PAC-Bayesian margin bounds," in COLT, pp. 203–215.

Minsky, M. & Papert, S. (1969), *Perceptrons: An introduction to computational geometry*, The MIT Press.

Mukherjee, S., Niyogi, P., Poggio, T. & Rifkin, R. (2006), "Learning theory: stability is sufficient for generalization and necessary and sufficient for consistency of empirical risk minimization," *Advances in Computational Mathematics* **25**(1–3), 161–193.

Murata, N. (1998), "A statistical study of on-line learning," *Online Learning and Neural Networks, Cambridge University Press*.

Murphy, K. P. (2012), *Machine learning: a probabilistic perspective*, The MIT Press.

Natarajan, B. (1995), "Sparse approximate solutions to linear systems," *SIAM J. Computing* **25**(2), 227–234.

Natarajan, B. K. (1989), "On learning sets and functions," *Mach. Learn.* **4**, 67–97.

Nemirovski, A., Juditsky, A., Lan, G. & Shapiro, A. (2009), "Robust stochastic approximation approach to stochastic programming," *SIAM Journal on Optimization* **19**(4), 1574–1609.

Nemirovski, A. & Yudin, D. (1978), *Problem complexity and method efficiency in optimization*, Nauka, Moscow.

Nesterov, Y. (2005), Primal-dual subgradient methods for convex problems, Technical report, Center for Operations Research and Econometrics (CORE), Catholic University of Louvain (UCL).

Nesterov, Y. & Nesterov, I. (2004), *Introductory lectures on convex optimization: A basic course*, Vol. 87, Springer, Netherlands.

Novikoff, A. B. J. (1962), "On convergence proofs on perceptrons," in *Proceedings of the symposium on the mathematical theory of automata*, Vol. XII, pp. 615–622.

Parberry, I. (1994), *Circuit complexity and neural networks*, The MIT press.

Pearson, K. (1901), "On lines and planes of closest fit to systems of points in space," *The London, Edinburgh, and Dublin Philosophical Magazine and Journal of Science* **2**(11), 559–572.

Phillips, D. L. (1962), "A technique for the numerical solution of certain integral equations of the first kind," *Journal of the ACM* **9**(1), 84–97.

Pisier, G. (1980–1981), "Remarques sur un résultat non publié de B. maurey."

Pitt, L. & Valiant, L. (1988), "Computational limitations on learning from examples," *Journal of the Association for Computing Machinery* **35**(4), 965–984.

Poon, H. & Domingos, P. (2011), "Sum-product networks: A new deep architecture," in Conference on Uncertainty in Artificial Intelligence (UAI).

Quinlan, J. R. (1986), "Induction of decision trees," *Machine Learning* **1**, 81–106.

Quinlan, J. R. (1993), *C4.5: Programs for machine learning*, Morgan Kaufmann.

Rabiner, L. & Juang, B. (1986), "An introduction to hidden markov models," *IEEE ASSP Magazine* **3**(1), 4–16.

Rakhlin, A., Shamir, O. & Sridharan, K. (2012), "Making gradient descent optimal for strongly convex stochastic optimization," in ICML.

Rakhlin, A., Sridharan, K. & Tewari, A. (2010), "Online learning: Random averages, combinatorial parameters, and learnability," in NIPS.

Rakhlin, S., Mukherjee, S. & Poggio, T. (2005), "Stability results in learning theory," *Analysis and Applications* **3**(4), 397–419.

Ranzato, M., Huang, F., Boureau, Y. & Lecun, Y. (2007), "Unsupervised learning of invariant feature hierarchies with applications to object recognition," in Computer Vision and Pattern Recognition, 2007. CVPR'07. IEEE Conference on, IEEE, pp. 1–8.

Rissanen, J. (1978), "Modeling by shortest data description," *Automatica* **14**, 465–471.

Rissanen, J. (1983), "A universal prior for integers and estimation by minimum description length," *The Annals of Statistics* **11**(2), 416–431.

Robbins, H. & Monro, S. (1951), "A stochastic approximation method," *The Annals of Mathematical Statistics*, pp. 400–407.

Rogers, W. & Wagner, T. (1978), "A finite sample distribution-free performance bound for local discrimination rules," *The Annals of Statistics* **6**(3), 506–514.

Rokach, L. (2007), *Data mining with decision trees: Theory and applications*, Vol. 69, World Scientific.

Rosenblatt, F. (1958), "The perceptron: A probabilistic model for information storage and organization in the brain," *Psychological Review* **65**, 386–407. (Reprinted in *Neurocomputing*, MIT Press, 1988).

Rumelhart, D. E., Hinton, G. E. & Williams, R. J. (1986), "Learning internal representations by error propagation," in D. E. Rumelhart & J. L. McClelland, eds, *Parallel distributed processing – explorations in the microstructure of cognition*, MIT Press, chapter 8, pp. 318–362.

Sankaran, J. K. (1993), "A note on resolving infeasibility in linear programs by constraint relaxation," *Operations Research Letters* **13**(1), 19–20.

Sauer, N. (1972), "On the density of families of sets," *Journal of Combinatorial Theory Series A* **13**, 145–147.

Schapire, R. (1990), "The strength of weak learnability," *Machine Learning* **5**(2), 197–227.

Schapire, R. E. & Freund, Y. (2012), *Boosting: Foundations and algorithms*, MIT Press.

Schölkopf, B. & Smola, A. J. (2002), *Learning with kernels: Support vector machines, regularization, optimization and beyond*, MIT Press.

Schölkopf, B., Herbrich, R. & Smola, A. (2001), "A generalized representer theorem," in *Computational learning theory*, pp. 416–426.

Schölkopf, B., Herbrich, R., Smola, A. & Williamson, R. (2000), "A generalized representer theorem," in *NeuroCOLT*.

Schölkopf, B., Smola, A. & Müller, K.-R. (1998), 'Nonlinear component analysis as a kernel eigenvalue problem', *Neural computation* **10**(5), 1299–1319.

Seeger, M. (2003), "Pac-bayesian generalisation error bounds for gaussian process classification," *The Journal of Machine Learning Research* **3**, 233–269.

Shakhnarovich, G., Darrell, T. & Indyk, P. (2006), *Nearest-neighbor methods in learning and vision: Theory and practice*, MIT Press.

Shalev-Shwartz, S. (2007), Online Learning: Theory, Algorithms, and Applications, PhD thesis, The Hebrew University.

Shalev-Shwartz, S. (2011), "Online learning and online convex optimization," *Foundations and Trends® in Machine Learning* **4**(2), 107–194.

Shalev-Shwartz, S., Shamir, O., Srebro, N. & Sridharan, K. (2010), "Learnability, stability and uniform convergence," *The Journal of Machine Learning Research* **9999**, 2635–2670.

Shalev-Shwartz, S., Shamir, O. & Sridharan, K. (2010), "Learning kernel-based halfspaces with the zero-one loss," in COLT.

Shalev-Shwartz, S., Shamir, O., Sridharan, K. & Srebro, N. (2009), "Stochastic convex optimization," in COLT.

Shalev-Shwartz, S. & Singer, Y. (2008), "On the equivalence of weak learnability and linear separability: New relaxations and efficient boosting algorithms," in *Proceedings of the nineteenth annual conference on computational learning theory*.

Shalev-Shwartz, S., Singer, Y. & Srebro, N. (2007), "Pegasos: Primal Estimated sub-GrAdient SOlver for SVM," in *International conference on machine learning*, pp. 807–814.

Shalev-Shwartz, S. & Srebro, N. (2008), "SVM optimization: Inverse dependence on training set size," in *International conference on machine learning* ICML, pp. 928–935.

Shalev-Shwartz, S., Zhang, T. & Srebro, N. (2010), "Trading accuracy for sparsity in optimization problems with sparsity constraints," *Siam Journal on Optimization* **20**, 2807–2832.

Shamir, O. & Zhang, T. (2013), "Stochastic gradient descent for non-smooth optimization: Convergence results and optimal averaging schemes," in ICML.

Shapiro, A., Dentcheva, D. & Ruszczyński, A. (2009), *Lectures on stochastic programming: modeling and theory*, Vol. 9, Society for Industrial and Applied Mathematics.

Shelah, S. (1972), "A combinatorial problem; stability and order for models and theories in infinitary languages," *Pac. J. Math* **4**, 247–261.

Sipser, M. (2006), *Introduction to the Theory of Computation*, Thomson Course Technology.

Slud, E. V. (1977), "Distribution inequalities for the binomial law," *The Annals of Probability* **5**(3), 404–412.

Steinwart, I. & Christmann, A. (2008), *Support vector machines*, Springerverlag, New York.

Stone, C. (1977), "Consistent nonparametric regression," *The Annals of Statistics* **5**(4), 595–620.

Taskar, B., Guestrin, C. & Koller, D. (2003), "Max-margin markov networks," in NIPS.

Tibshirani, R. (1996), "Regression shrinkage and selection via the lasso," *J. Royal. Statist. Soc B.* **58**(1), 267–288.

Tikhonov, A. N. (1943), "On the stability of inverse problems," *Dolk. Akad. Nauk SSSR* **39**(5), 195–198.

Tishby, N., Pereira, F. & Bialek, W. (1999), "The information bottleneck method," in *The 37'th Allerton conference on communication, control, and computing.*

Tsochantaridis, I., Hofmann, T., Joachims, T. & Altun, Y. (2004), "Support vector machine learning for interdependent and structured output spaces," in *Proceedings of the twenty-first international conference on machine learning.*

Valiant, L. G. (1984), "A theory of the learnable," *Communications of the ACM* **27**(11), 1134–1142.

Vapnik, V. (1992), "Principles of risk minimization for learning theory," in J. E. Moody, S. J. Hanson & R. P. Lippmann, eds., *Advances in Neural Information Processing Systems 4*, Morgan Kaufmann, pp. 831–838.

Vapnik, V. (1995), *The Nature of Statistical Learning Theory*, Springer.

Vapnik, V. N. (1982), *Estimation of Dependences Based on Empirical Data*, Springer-Verlag.

Vapnik, V. N. (1998), *Statistical Learning Theory*, Wiley.

Vapnik, V. N. & Chervonenkis, A. Y. (1971), "On the uniform convergence of relative frequencies of events to their probabilities," *Theory of Probability and Its Applications* **XVI**(2), 264–280.

Vapnik, V. N. & Chervonenkis, A. Y. (1974), *Theory of pattern recognition*, Nauka, Moscow (In Russian).

Von Luxburg, U. (2007), "A tutorial on spectral clustering," *Statistics and Computing* **17**(4), 395–416.

von Neumann, J. (1928), "Zur theorie der gesellschaftsspiele (on the theory of parlor games)," *Math. Ann.* **100**, 295—320.

Von Neumann, J. (1953), "A certain zero-sum two-person game equivalent to the optimal assignment problem," *Contributions to the Theory of Games* **2**, 5–12.

Vovk, V. G. (1990), "Aggregating strategies," in COLT, pp. 371–383.

Warmuth, M., Glocer, K. & Vishwanathan, S. (2008), "Entropy regularized lpboost," in *Algorithmic Learning Theory* (ALT).

Warmuth, M., Liao, J. & Ratsch, G. (2006), "Totally corrective boosting algorithms that maximize the margin," in *Proceedings of the 23rd international conference on machine learning.*

Weston, J., Chapelle, O., Vapnik, V., Elisseeff, A. & Schölkopf, B. (2002), "Kernel dependency estimation," in Advances in neural information processing systems, pp. 873–880.

Weston, J. & Watkins, C. (1999), "Support vector machines for multi-class pattern recognition," in *Proceedings of the seventh european symposium on artificial neural networks*.

Wolpert, D. H. & Macready, W. G. (1997), "No free lunch theorems for optimization," *Evolutionary Computation, IEEE Transactions on* **1**(1), 67–82.

Zhang, T. (2004), "Solving large scale linear prediction problems using stochastic gradient descent algorithms," in *Proceedings of the twenty-first international conference on machine learning*.

Zhao, P. & Yu, B. (2006), "On model selection consistency of Lasso," *Journal of Machine Learning Research* **7**, 2541–2567.

Zinkevich, M. (2003), "Online convex programming and generalized infinitesimal gradient ascent," in *International conference on machine learning*.

Index